ALLIANCE OF ENEMIES

ALLIANCE OF ENEMIES

THE UNTOLD STORY OF THE SECRET AMERICAN AND GERMAN COLLABORATION TO END WORLD WAR II

AGOSTINO von HASSELL
AND SIGRID MacRAE,
WITH SIMONE AMESKAMP

THOMAS DUNNE BOOKS
ST. MARTINS PRESS NEW YORK

THOMAS DUNNE BOOKS.
An imprint of St. Martin's Press.

www.thomasdunnebooks.com

www.stmartins.com

Library of Congress Cataloging-in-Publication Data

Von Hassell, Agostino.
    Alliance of enemies : the untold story of the secret American and German collabo-
ration to end World War II / Agostino von Hassell and Sigrid McRae, with Simone
Ameskamp.
        p. cm.
    Includes bibliographical reference and index.

    ISBN-13: 978-0-312-32369-1
    ISBN-10: 0-312-32369-7
    1. United States. Office of Strategic Services. 2. World War, 1939–1945—Secret
service—United States. 3. World War, 1939–1945—Military intelligence—United
States. 4. World War, 1939–1945—Secret Service—Germany. 5. Anti--Nazi movement. 6. World War, 1939–1945—Collaborationists——Germany. I. Sigrid McRae.
II. Simone Ameskamp. III. Title.

D810.S7 V67 2006
940.54'85—dc22

                                                                    2006048291

First Edition: November 2006

1 3 5 7 9 10 8 6 4 2

To Ulrich von Hassell
Executed September 8, 1944
One of the few Germans who dared to oppose Hitler

&

To Elizabeth von Hassell
For her dedication and what she has done to inspire the new
generation with a sense of courage against evil: Christian Ulrich von
Hassell and William Thassilo von Hassel
—Agostino von Hassell

To the memory of those who gave their lives for their convictions.
—Sigrid MacRae

CONTENTS

ACKNOWLEDGMENTS:
ALLIANCE OF FRIENDS

Researching and writing this book required long hours, dedication, and the ability to handle disappointment when sources proved difficult to find or promised leads disappeared in the mist of long-ago events or dusty files. It was a monumental task.

Apart from the enormous contribution of Simone Ameskamp, two other coworkers were essential. Lisa M. Pellegrino researched many OSS documents, talked with a number of those OSS veterans still alive, and provided constant and cheerful support. Equally essential was the work done in Lisbon—one of several spy capitals of World War II Europe—by Teresa Caiado Ramirez, who dug up long-forgotten files in various ministries in Lisbon and succeeded in obtaining the assistance of key people in that beautiful city.

Many in the United States and Europe provided assistance in unlocking the treasure troves of historical evidence. Much credit is due to the invaluable Larry McDonald, National Archives and Records Administration at College Park, Maryland, and to the knowledgeable Nick Scheetz, Special Collections, Georgetown University Library in Washington, D.C. In Germany, Carina Notzke, Bundesarchiv-Militärarchiv Freiburg, and Giles Bennett, Institut für Zeitgeschichte, Munich, never tired of following up on yet another request.

In Portugal, Dr. Cláudia Mesquita of the Lisbon Airport Administration provided data on flights in and out of Portugal during the war. Dr. Olga

Bettencourt and Margarida Leitão at "Espaços Exílios" (an exhibition on the Estoril Coast, the setting for exiles during WWII) were always ready to dig and volunteer more information. Dr. Maria de Lurdes Henriques, Vice Director of the Archives Department, helped access key documents at the Torre Do Tombo National Archive, Portugal's central archives. Dr. José António Barreiro, noted lawyer and expert on WWII espionage, offered invaluable advice and counsel. Ana Videira was a crucial source of information and enthusiasm.

Armin Mruck and Peter Sichel, are expert contemporary witnesses whose deep knowledge of the history of intelligence and the German resistance proved invaluable. Thomas Boghardt, Gevinon Freifrau von dem Bussche-Kessel, Paul Brown, Helga Fritsche, Christa von Hassell, Eugen Solf, and Jo Wolters helped identify and resolve conundrums of both past and present. David Alvarez, John Brunner, Christof Mauch, and Sid Shapiro deserve special thanks for their help in explaining what the authors describe as the "black hole" in Washington, into which significant intelligence disappeared during the Roosevelt administration. Without the permission of James D. Mooney, Jr., to access his father's papers *ad libitum,* several of Mooney's peace missions could not have been uncovered.

Charles Pinck, president of the Office of Strategic Services Society, and especially OSS Society members Julia Cuniberti, Edwin J. Putzell, Cordelia Dodson Hood, Albert Materazzi, Barbara L. Powdowski, Betty Lussier, Elizabeth McIntosh, James W. Hudson, Fisher Howe, James Donavan, Pat and Wanda Dailey, Richard Kranstover, and Robert E. Carter are owed a debt of gratitude for sharing their personal memories and knowledge of resources.

Michael Warner of the Central Intelligence Agency assisted in locating primary research materials. Michael Bradley was very helpful with the early research at the National Archives, and Yelena Yaeger, herself of Russian origin, worked to locate some of the long-lost files in formerly Soviet Archives. Professor Patrick Kelly, Adelphi University, drawing on his intimate knowledge of Grand Admiral Alfred von Tripitz and the Hassell family, provided significant advice. Captain Gregory Starace, U.S. Marine Corps, helped to clarify some of the more complex moral issues arising from disobedience within the military. Members of the U.S. intelligence community were also invaluable, but typically for this shadow world, while their silent help is greatly appreciated, they remain unnamed. In Virginia Ms. Diele Fleishman assisted with her personal knowledge of the period. Ambassador Richard N. Viets read parts of the manuscript and offered valuable advice and insights based on his long years of diplomatic service and interface with the intelligence community. Thanks also to Andre Takhteyez of Milberg Weiss, for his help with the forced labor lawsuit against Ford.

Finally—deep thanks to our intrepid agent, Alexander Hoyt, who did the necessary pushing and prodding with great tact, and to the superb team at Thomas Dunne Books, Peter Wolverton and John Parsley, who coaxed the manuscript to fruition.

—AGOSTINO VON HASSELL
—SIGRID MACRAE

CHRONOLOGY

30 January 1933 Nazis seize power; Hitler is appointed chancellor

2 August 1934 General Werner von Blomberg orders Reichswehr to swear loyalty to Hitler after the death of President von Hindenburg

2 January 1935 Wilhelm Canaris takes over as chief of the Amt Ausland/Abwehr, the German military intelligence service

12 March 1938 Anschluss: Austria is annexed

18 August 1938 Chief of General Staff Ludwig Beck resigns in protest against Hitler's aggressive policies

Summer 1938 Conspiracy of civilian and military resistance groups launched; Hans Bernd Gisevius, Franz Halder, Hans Oster, Hjalmar Schacht, and Erwin von Witzleben are the main participants

29 September 1938 Munich Conference grants the Sudetenland to Germany

23 August 1939 Molotov-Ribbentrop Pact on German-Soviet nonaggression divides Eastern Europe into spheres of interest

1 September 1939 Germany invades Poland

September 1939–May 1940 "Phony war" on the western front

October–November 1939 Erich Kordt and Oster prepare to assassinate Hitler

8 November 1939 Georg Elser attempts to kill Hitler in Munich's Bürgerbräukeller

9 November 1939 SD, pretending to represent anti-Hitler German conspirators, captures two MI-6 officers at Venlo near the Dutch-German border

9 April 1940 German invasion of Denmark and Norway

10 May 1940 Hitler launches campaign in the West (Netherlands, Belgium, Luxembourg)

10 May 1940 Winston Churchill takes office as prime minister

22 June 1940 Fall of France

August–October 1940 Battle of Britain

5 November 1940 FDR is reelected for a third term as president of the United States

20 January 1941 Churchill orders "absolute silence" in response to German peace feelers

11 March 1941 Lend-Lease Act is passed

22 June 1941 Germany attack the Soviet Union (Operation Barbarossa)

11 July 1941 William J. Donovan is appointed as Coordinator of Information

14 August 1941 Roosevelt and Churchill announce the Atlantic Charter

7–11 December 1941 Japanese attack Pearl Harbor; Hitler declares war on the United States

1 January 1942 Washington Pact following First Washington Conference (Arcadia)

13 June 1942 The OSS is established

November 1942 Allen Dulles sets up shop in Bern, Switzerland

24 January 1943 Franklin D. Roosevelt and Winston Churchill announce their demand for "unconditional surrender" at Casablanca

2 February 1943 Battle of Stalingrad ends in annihilation of the German Sixth Army

13 March 1943 Army Group Center conspirators under Tresckow attempt to blow up Hitler's plane

19–29 April 1943 British and American delegates at the Bermuda Conference fail to develop a plan for the rescue of European Jews and the relaxation of immigration policies

5 April 1943 Hans von Dohnanyi, Dietrich Bonhoeffer, Josef Müller, and other members of resistance group within the Abwehr are arrested

April 1943 Mass grave of Polish officers at Katyn is discovered

12 July 1943 National Committee for a Free Germany is formed in Krasnogorsk, near Moscow

28 November–12 December 1943 Roosevelt, Churchill, and Stalin agree on the division of Germany at Teheran Conference

19 January 1944 Helmuth James von Moltke and members of the Solf Circle are arrested

January–March 1944 Abortive assassination attempts by Axel von dem Bussche and Ewald Heinrich von Kleist-Schmenzin

4–11 February 1944 Yalta Conference

12 February 1944 Canaris is relieved of his duties; Hitler orders the creation of a unified German information service

25 May 1944 Churchill and Roosevelt rule out any negotiations with Germans

6 June 1944 D-Day, Allied armies land in Normandy

Early Summer 1944 Abwehr abolished and incorporated into RSHA as Amt Mil or Amt VIII (SD-Ausland)

20 July 1944 Claus Count Schenk von Stauffenberg's third assassination attempt on Hitler and plan for coup d'état fails

8 May 1945 V-E Day, Germany surrenders

15 September 1945 OSS is dissolved by Truman; SI and X-2 branches form core of peacetime successor SSU

26 July 1947 National Security Act turns Central Intelligence Group into the Central Intelligence Agency

PREFACE

In the early 1980s, co-author Agostino von Hassell accompanied a marine brigadier general on a visit to various German bases, including the Graf-Stauffenberg-Kaserne in Sigmaringen in southern Germany, near the ancestral castle of the Hohenzollern family. At one point, the German general who was their host told them, at once joking and serious: "You know, this garrison is named after a traitor." He was referring to the failed 1944 Stauffenberg coup attempt against Hitler, which in his view was treason.

It took all Hassell's discipline not to deck their host. His grandfather, Ulrich von Hassell, worked for years to rid Germany of Hitler's tyranny and had been hanged for it. While he was growing up, he knew those of his fellow conspirators who survived as family friends and came to the family's house often. No doubt this fellow would have classified his grandfather and his coconspirators as traitors, too. Later, the American marine general apologized to him and expressed his appreciation that an "international incident was avoided" because of Hassell's restraint.

This little anecdote points to several issues at the core of this book: attitudes toward, and ignorance of, the German resistance to Hitler. In Germany today, more than sixty years after the end of Hitler's Reich, the resistance is embraced and commemorated officially, yet "for most Germans of that generation, who had succumbed in various ways and in varying degrees to the temptations of Nazism, the heritage of the resistance remained deeply problematic. It gave rise to a general unease and even outright hostility among some who regarded the resistance as traitors for plotting against their nation's rulers in time of war."[1] So, privately, the resistance is often viewed with distrust, in part because its leaders, "all those little nobles," as one SPD— German Socialist Party—politician put it, had been of the wrong class.

Those in the world outside of Germany who are not entirely ignorant of the resistance, have always suspected that what resistance there was consisted of a fistful of ambitious aristocrats, probably Prussian, a designation many regard as synonymous with unbending, caricaturish militarism. This assumption coincides neatly with Hitler's characterization of the plotters, whom he described in a radio address on the evening of July 20, 1944, as a "a very small clique of ambitious, wicked, and stupid criminal officers."

To some extent, Hitler was right. He had smashed the communist and socialist opposition early, and driven the remainder underground. Of the notable churchmen such as Galen, Preysing, and Niemöller, who spoke out against the Nazis early, at least some were afforded a bit of protection by their positions. But the later, active resistance was limited. Among the final plotters were Prussians, and officers, and yes, aristocrats, a class Hitler had always loathed and feared.

As early as September 1938, Hassell wrote: "Hitler's speeches are all demagogic and spiced with sharp attacks on the entire upper class. . . . There is a growing aversion to all independent people. Whoever does not crawl in the dust is regarded as stuck-up."[2] And a year later: "There is every evidence that the hatred of the Party for the nobility and the so-called intelligentsia is growing ever stronger."[3] This attitude is also reflected in Hitler's 1940 prohibition against military roles for any princes of the former ruling houses of Germany, and his 1942 refusal of military honors for the burial of the son of Wilhem II.

A roll call of the names of many members of the resistance are like a last curtain call for three hundred years of Prussian history: Kleist, Moltke, Yorck von Wartenburg, Treskow, Schulenburg, Hammerstein, von dem Bussche. Many of these names resonated deeply in Germany; some were iconic. To the military historian, they recall famous battles—Fehrbellin, St. Privat and Sedan, the Battle of Jutland, of Königgrätz, and the Masurian Lakes, and of Waterloo, where Field Marshal Blücher came to the aid of Wellington.

While it may be surprising to many, resistance and disobedience were firmly embedded in Prussia's military values. One telling anecdote has a Prussian major being rebuked by his commanding officer for following orders to the letter: "The King of Prussia made you a staff officer so that you would know when you ought *not* to carry out his orders." Another, more famous example was Tauroggen, where, in December 1812, future Field Marshal Yorck von Wartenburg's troops were fighting with Napoleon's Grande Armée against Russia. Yorck decided, on his own authority, to declare his troops neutral, a step that hastened the ultimate defeat of Napoleon.

Yorck's initiative, revered as "The Spirit of Tauroggen," was celebrated in Germany in the period between the wars as *"Auftragstaktik"*—roughly, mission tactics.[4] A more recent example is that of General Dietrich von Choltitz, the German military governor of Paris in August 1944, who had clear orders from Hitler: "Paris must only fall into enemy hands as a heap of rubble." Choltitz refused the order and surrendered Paris to U.S. forces. Scant weeks earlier, one of Yorck's descendants died on the gallows for having opposed Hitler.

The tradition of independent initiative was also strong in the civil service, and Prussia came to represent tolerance and a social philosophy ahead of the times. The modern cultural historian, Hans Joachim Schoeps, a Prussian and a Jew, in praising the true Prussian spirit, quoted Madame de Staël, who described Prussia as *"la patrie de la pensée"*—the home of thought.[5] Both these strands of Prussian life are interwoven in Helmuth Karl von Moltke, whose brilliant military career, counterbalanced by a thoroughgoing humanism, helped shape Bismarck's Germany. His loose, innovative strategy devolved authority down through the ranks, and its success depended on the initiative of highly educated field commanders who shared a common philosophy and a worldview. "An order shall contain everything that a commander cannot do by himself, but nothing else," Moltke said. He also spoke out against military belligerence, warning: "Woe to him who sets fire to Europe." A half century later, after Hitler had set Europe afire, he executed another bearer of the Moltke name, for having thought independently, outside of Nazi ideology.

Virtually all of the key participants in the resistance to Hitler and those who collaborated with the OSS were deeply rooted in this spirit of independence. They resisted the *Kadavergehorsam*—the obedience of a cadaver—that Hitler demanded. Understanding this resistance is essential to understanding what motivated the opposition and the collaboration, leading them along secret and dangerous paths, which in the view of some Germans, led to treason and "betrayal," before and during World War II. The opposition felt a responsibility that superseded any one particular regime or tyrant. Catholic and Protestant alike, they struggled with their oath of allegiance to Hitler, and with their consciences. Many—Moltke and Yorck among them—were convinced that "they had to grapple with the guilt that lay upon the nation their ancestors had built."[6] For many, the religious issue was central. They might be willing to "render to Caesar the things that are Caesar's," but insisted on rendering "to God the things that are God's."[7]

QUESTIONS OF CONSCIENCE AND CULPABILITY, OF GUILT AND BLAME SELDOM FIND SIMple answers. Nor is assassination as simple as it may look to the armchair assassin. Are resistance, espionage, and collaboration with the "enemy" always treasonous, or are they justified in the name of a law higher than national interest? Are they the only morally acceptable choices when the regime one serves is essentially criminal?

Some members of the opposition made that moral choice quickly, protesting early and emphatically. The strong anti-Hitler stance of many members of the Abwehr—Canaris and Oster were only the tip of the iceberg—coincided with the military and civil service opposition related to July 20, 1944, putsch. In the end, they were all collaborators with the enemy for what they deemed a greater good. Critics argue, with some justification, that while many recognized the brutality of the Nazi regime from its very beginning—some even before—they waited too long to act. Perhaps so, but the earlier attempts, though unsuccessful, must not be discounted. They also never had the slightest bit of encouragement or support from the Allies, except from a few who were powerless to affect policy.

Why was dealing with the German opposition to Hitler so unthinkable? Was that why the opposition failed? After World War II, William Casey, later of the CIA, said that during his time with the OSS he had learned of the importance of reaching out to "opposition forces," to further the goals of the United States. He argued for reaching out (often with no effect on policy makers). Yet in fact, the post war history of the United States is littered with instances of collaboration—collaboration with terrorists, dictators, opposition groups. The Kennedy administration's support of Cuban expatriates (many of them from highly questionable backgrounds) is just one example. A more extreme example was the Iran-Contra scandal, which reached out to very questionable groups that might have helped the United States, and the willingness to reach out to opposition groups—no matter how distasteful—continues. The U.S. Department of State officially lists the Iranian resistance operating from Iraq, known as the Mujahedin-e Khalq Organization (MEK or MKO), as a terrorist organization, yet Congress is pushing for funding for the MEK, and senior officers in the Pentagon voice support for the MEK as a solid source of intelligence.

Is it morally acceptable to collaborate with or use official members of a criminal regime in the hope of overturning it? What *is* a moral war? What ensures the morality of the troops—from the lowest ranks all the way to general? In the days of Prussia the rules were clear, and the United States did and does subscribe to the same basic principles. Yet reliance on morality has often failed, as for example in Douglas MacArthur's brutal crackdown on World War I veterans.[8] In the days and weeks before the fatal bombing of the marine barracks in Beirut in October 1983, the behavior of some officers was similarly questionable. The officers in Beirut had been flooded with increasingly detailed intelligence warning of an impending attack, yet the single guard at the gate leading to the barracks was not allowed to have a round chambered in his weapon. Should they have ignored orders to avoid an offensive military posture dictated by an exceedingly complex chain of command? Would disobedience have been the better course? Marine Corps history has multiple examples of direct disobedience of orders for the greater good of Corps, country, and God.

These questions can be and are debated to this day, as they should be. Yet they often meet with too much animosity and prejudice to allow for reasonable discussion. With such issues facing the highest levels of governments in the United States and abroad, it is now crucial to look back at one of the most valiant and sadly frustrated efforts to end warfare and terror: the true alliance of enemies behind the enemy lines during World War II.

ALLIANCE OF ENEMIES

PROLOGUE

Discussions between the German resistance and the Allies remained to the
end a dialogue of the deaf.

WILLEM VISSER'T HOOFT[1]

Disentangling war is a thorny business. The strands of motive and hostility
that go into making it are brought together slowly. Only over the years
does ancient animus join with ambitions, slights—real or imagined—to at-
tain an easily ignited critical mass. World War II was no exception,

World War I left a bitter legacy. When the victors met at Versailles in
1919, President Woodrow Wilson's good intentions and Fourteen Points
notwithstanding, France's representative, Georges Clemenceau, managed
to exact Carthaginian terms. They were terms the German representative
characterized as "the death of many millions of German men, women and
children."[2] British economist John Maynard Keynes was present at Versailles and offered a more eloquent and apocalyptic vision:

> If we aim deliberately at the impoverishment of Central Europe, vengeance, I
> dare predict, will not limp. Nothing can then delay for very long that final
> civil war between the forces of Reaction and the despairing convulsions of
> Revolution, before which the horrors of the late German war will fade into
> nothing, and which will destroy, whoever is victor, the civilization and the
> progress of our generation.[3]

. . .

INDEED. THE MISERY AND HUMILIATION IN THE WAKE OF VERSAILLES SERVED HITLER WELL. He used them as a springboard to power, and just twenty years later, Keynes's dire prophecy was realized.

Yet in World War II there were some on both sides whose thinking transcended the knee-jerk nationalism that war so quickly fans into flame. They understood that the outcome of this war would shape the future more profoundly than previous wars, and they worked to break the boundaries and proscriptions of conventional wartime behavior. They worked first to avert the war, and then to stop it, hoping to find an early, equitable peace and thereby create a stable Europe. On the German side, the initial motivation was to avoid a war no one but Hitler wanted and for which no one felt prepared. Gradually the concern driving the anti-Hitler resistance shifted to preserving Germany's Western orientation. Ultimately it was simply a desperate statement, a cry of conscience and moral imperative. On the American side, the thinking grew out of in a larger, less parochial worldview. On both sides, the Germans and the Allies were well traveled, well connected, and often had longstanding family ties on both sides of the water. They were better informed, more sophisticated, less susceptible to jingoistic headlines and able to find the truth behind the propaganda. They knew that the world had become smaller, dominated by fewer but more powerful forces, and that any future, even more fearsome, war should be guarded against with all possible means. Perhaps not surprisingly, they operated at the top levels of the German and American intelligence services, the Abwehr and the OSS respectively. Both sides discovered the terrible truth behind Visser't Hooft's dictum.

SCHOOLBOOK HISTORIES SUGGEST THAT WARS ARE FOUGHT BETWEEN ANTAGONISTS united behind their respective causes. This is a myth; the truth is quite different. Beneath the ostensibly common cause—winning the war and vanquishing the enemy—lie innumerable differences: of opinion, interests, politics, prejudices, rivalries, jealousies, and goals. There are so many, in fact, that, looked at closely, the presumed unity of purpose dissolves quickly.

And so it was in the war. Many factions did not align themselves along the anticipated lines. America did not want to join another European war; the suffering and disillusion of the first was still a vivid memory. President Franklin D. Roosevelt faced a deeply divided populace. Aviator-idol Charles Lindbergh was a popular spokesman for a potent isolationist contingent, the America First Committee, whose large and vocal membership held to strict nonintervention.[4] Lindbergh charged that Roosevelt would renege on his election-year promise to America's mothers and fathers that their boys would not be sent to any foreign wars.

In early 1941, when FDR announced that the United States should become the "arsenal of democracy" and supply $7 billion worth of armaments to the British in the lend-lease program, the antiwar rhetoric only escalated. Lend-lease was described as a way of "waging an undeclared war." Some worried that America was committing suicide.[5] As it happened, Roosevelt did break his promise, but only after he had been elected to a third term, and Pearl Harbor had provided a horrific rationale. With Hitler's declaration of war on America four days later, the isolationist voices were silenced.

Yet several American corporate giants continued prewar business alliances that had helped Germany rearm. Some of them deliberately evaded U.S. laws and war objectives, flouting proscriptions against trading with the enemy in pursuit of profits and continued business alliances during the war. Roosevelt was well aware of the massive business involvement of major American corporations with Germany and its rearmament program, but he was willing to tolerate it, and even support it to a degree. The world was climbing out of a depression, and the reasoning was that a wartime economy brought prosperity; making money was good for the country and good for morale.

But the war deepened. Rifts developed between U.S. policy makers and the OSS intelligence operation that was feeding them information. The rifts gradually widened until much of the intelligence went either unheard, or unheeded, a situation that has parallels to the recent rift between policy makers and the CIA. The State Department was itself divided and increasingly at loggerheads with the Department of the Treasury. There were deep divisions between Roosevelt, his cabinet, senior military, and intelligence on the issue of unconditional surrender. The OSS's Allen Dulles and William Donovan anticipated future conflict with the Soviets and saw Germany as a crucial ally and stabilizing force in a postwar Europe. They advocated a "go easy on Germany" policy that was in direct conflict with Roosevelt and Treasury Secretary Henry Morgenthau.

Depleted and traumatized by the Great War, Britain was militarily and economically unequal to another war in 1938, but her political leaders were sharply divided on how to avoid it. Chamberlain had vivid memories of the horrors of the Great War and hoped to spare England another. Principal British policy makers, preoccupied with a crumbling empire, saw little to gain from establishing contacts with Germans. Senior officials in the British Foreign Office gave little weight or credence to German diplomats and private citizens urging a tough stand against Hitler. They chose to ignore even their own intelligence that confirmed what they were hearing from the Germans about Hitler's war plans. In their opinion, if there were troubles in Germany, they should stay in Germany. The messengers of German opposition to Hitler were seen as insufficiently democratic in any recognizably Anglo-American sense and traitorous to boot—reason enough to avoid contact with them. Though they were unaware of it at the time, the British had their own traitor working within their intelligence establishment, another instance of disunity.[6]

The Anglo-American relationship involved considerable hedging and deceit on both sides, and was complicated further by differing aims particularly in terms of empire. Before the United States entered the war, it was a relationship conducted between Roosevelt and Churchill, then First Lord of the Admiralty, largely without Chamberlain's participation. Nor were later British-American relations necessarily harmonious. Churchill agreed to unconditional surrender only grudgingly and not without qualms, and postwar policy toward Germany became another deeply divisive issue.

The notion that the United States, Britain, the Soviet Union, and France threw themselves wholeheartedly into defeating Germany with no aims but the common goal is as much a myth as is the idea of unity of purpose among the Axis powers. The so-called Grand Alliance—Britain, the United States, and the Soviet Union—was a paragon of instability. Both Roosevelt and Churchill played a complex game with Stalin, cajoling one day, promising support the next, only to then conspire against him. Stalin, meanwhile, kept his "allies" in a state of constant anxiety, relentlessly playing them against one another for his ultimate aim: vast territorial hegemony that would allow him to stretch his communism as far as his armies could reach. Though the Free French Forces operated in concert with the United States and Britain and participated in the Allied campaigns in North Africa, southern France, Normandy, and the liberation of Paris, their relationship with the British was marked by resentment, even rancor. Churchill referred to the Cross of Lorraine—the symbol chosen by General Charles de Gaulle for the Free French—as the heaviest of the crosses he had to bear.

As for the neutrals, neutrality was often more professed than observed. The Spanish, while technically neutral, had battalions fighting with Germany in Russia. The vaunted neutrality of Switzerland, Sweden, and Portugal did not extend to interrupting trading with Germany, shipping raw materials, and accepting gold known to be looted from occupied countries for huge profits. Neutrality did, however, provide a meeting ground where the opposition could try to establish contact, as the numerous trips of Adam von Trott zu Solz and Helmuth von Moltke to Turkey, Switzerland, Sweden, and Norway attest. It was through the neutrals, too, that an ongoing ecumenical dialogue played out.

Equally important, yet largely unknown in the United States and Britain, was—and still is—the internal debate and dissension within the Third Reich. Hitler's Germany, so often depicted as a fearsome, monolithic empire of evil, was anything but unified behind his drive to war. The enthusiasm of the army that had initially welcomed Hitler had waned; its generals warned of precipitating a war certain to become a long and unsustainable one. The people of Germany did not want a war; they were tired and destitute after the last one and the onerous peace that followed. The German Foreign Office was divided between the Nazi Joachim von Ribbentrop contingent and a significant number of diplomats under Ernst von Weizsäcker opposed to Hitler, playing a risky double game. Religious leaders stood up against the regime. Hitler's intelligence services were divided; domestic espionage, run by Nazi loyalists, fought ongoing turf wars with the Abwehr, but there was dissention even within the ranks of the SS, and several high-level defections to the opposition. The leadership of the Abwehr, the German military intelligence network, turned against Hitler early. Under the protection of Admiral Canaris, its upper echelon became home to many who opposed the Nazis and collaborated actively with Allied intelligence and the Office of Strategic Services, the OSS.

Even in 1939, before the war began, Germans opposed to Hitler struggled with differing political orientations and territorial claims. The older generation adhered to conservative, sometimes imperial traditions. The younger Kreisau group was striving for complete renewal and a pan-European future. As the war moved Germany closer to total destruction, these differences began to lose significance.

Alienated from their own nation, the German opposition to Hitler desperately wanted to maintain what one of its leaders referred to as ties to the "greater world."[7] They turned outward to inform, to find support in engineering conditions for a coup, and to keep alive the hope for a future that transcended the totalitarian, nationalist nightmare in which they felt trapped. The "unofficial opposition diplomacy," directed principally at Britain but also at the United States by Carl Goerdeler, Adam von Trott, and many others in the late 1930s, failed.[8] The hope for a coup to eliminate Hitler and bring down his regime to avert war collided with predictable prejudices and suspicions. Yet the hope survived, long after the war was truly begun. Well into 1944, the opposition still hoped to soften unconditional surrender and ameliorate the catastrophe for Germany and Europe that they were convinced would result from it.

Relatively early, the main oppositional impetus moved from the diplomatic front into the military and intelligence arenas. Diplomacy had not found an ear, but German military intelligence, the Abwehr, made significant contact with their new American counterpart, the OSS, and here at least, the opposition message found a more receptive audience. Yet once the intelligence gathered was sent to policy-making circles, their message fell on deaf ears and the same silence descended. If the pleas from OSS's Allen Dulles that Roosevelt offer support to the resistance were heard at all, they were not heeded. Whatever urgent, repeated entreaties came from diplomats, from intelligence, from the military, churchmen, industrialists, and civil servants, the official Allied stance remained intransigent. There seemed to be no interest in an early peace, and there was neither recognition nor support for the resistance to Hitler. All approaches were met with silence.

Given the many voices and the ample intelligence warnings the Allies received from German emmisaries of Hitler's intentions, it is surprising that so little notice was paid to the internal divisions within the Third Reich. Repeatedly, the German opposition to Hitler, desperate to bring about a change, engaged in treasonous contacts with the enemy, in the hope of finding allies. It cost most of them their lives. From today's perspective, the picture is one of greater unity of purpose between the upper levels of the Abwehr and the top tier of the OSS, who were "enemies," than between some of the proclaimed allies in the war.

THE WARTIME COROLLARY OF SOPHOCLES' FIRM IMPERATIVE "KNOW THYSELF" IS "KNOW your enemy." This is what has shaped intelligence over the centuries. Yet as Walter Laqueur wrote in *The World of Secrets:* "In intelligence the opportunities for mistakes are almost unlimited."[9] There are too many gaps in what is known, too many ways to be deceived. Prejudices are difficult to put aside; mistaken assumptions and misplaced suspicions can easily lead the analyst astray. Complacency, overconfidence, and misguided hopes are equally dangerous. The irrelevant and confusing "noise" of intelligence may not translate into comprehensible information. Even if the myriad variables are sorted and arranged into a reasonable theory, the theory is at risk of becoming enshrined. If contradictory evidence is discounted to save the cherished theory, the theory is a danger. All things considered, it might be as reasonable to consult Nostradamus or the stars as to rely on intelligence.

There are also instances where intelligence is impeccable, and is completely ignored. That is what this book is about—not the failure of intelligence but the failure to use good intelligence sensibly, or at all. This was true of the information that gradually revealed Hitler's policy of exterminating European Jewry, a dark veil that hung over the war—a known fact that was not acted upon.

It was also true of the German dissent, resistance, opposition—however it is styled—that was known but went unrecognized and unsupported by the Allies. Theirs is a complicated story, and difficult to present without obscuring passions or prejudices or both. It is also a sad story, because, for the most part, the voices of the German opposition fell on deaf ears, and a peace that might have been saved, or at least restored more quickly, was lost at a cost of millions of lives.

The subject is vast, and while this book makes no claim to comprehensiveness, it traces several of these people and their thinking in the midst of wartime politics and policies. It records their efforts to avert the war and, when that failed, to shorten it. It also tries to explain some of the reasons for their failure.

Part of the failure was certainly due to the split between intelligence and policy that surfaces so often in OSS files, specifically between Allen Dulles, William Donovan, and the Washington policy makers who felt that intelligence should have no part in shaping policy. What comes between intelligence and policy are the knee-jerk prejudices, old war wounds, and all the usual suspects that interfere with real communication and trust. James Mooney, an executive sent by Roosevelt to explore a negotiated peace with Germany before the war, was disheartened by what he called "an invisible barrier to understanding."[10] Mooney's motivations have been questioned, but he did see that just before the war, with so much at risk, men in corresponding positions in their respective governments were still unfamiliar with each other's ideas. There seemed to him to be little interest in any genuine exchange of thought, or a sincere effort to understand each other.

In the books and personal recollections of the relations between Britain and Germany in the years leading up to World War II, there are frequent references to two particular senses: sight and hearing. Actually, the references are to the lack of those senses. Visser't Hooft, whose observation opens this book, and Philip Conwell-Evans's *None So Blind* were only two of many contemporary witnesses to the sensory failings of the time.[11] What was missing both before and during the war was an ability to hear, to imagine, and, above all, to heed. In the preface to *The Secret War against Hitler,* William Casey, later director of the CIA, enumerates four critical lessons gleaned from the OSS's experience: close observation and analysis of the miscellany of intelligence; the danger of deception; the need for scrutiny and evaluation of new technology and weapons systems. Finally, he notes the *importance of remaining alert and receptive to assistance from forces within the ranks of our enemies.*[12]

It was here that the Allies failed, not in intelligence, but in putting intelligence to use. For those in the German resistance to Hitler, as for those on the Allied side most closely involved with them, it was a story of frustration, desperation, and ultimately tragedy. As Allen Dulles pointed out, at no time did the German resistance to Hitler benefit from any support, material or otherwise, such as the Allies offered the French Resistance. Was it a failure of communication, or a much larger failure—a failure of imagination?

In the eyes of the British, the German opposition inhabited what has been called "the landscape of treason."[13] They faced a hidebound unwillingness to think beyond the familiar, literal definitions of loyalty and patriotism, to transcend national interest for the sake of a larger responsibility.

It is an attitude neatly expressed by Anthony Eden, who remarked that any response to the opposition was "not in the national interest."

An exception to this thinking found a voice—a familiar voice—that provides appropriate and resonant book ends to this story. Speaking on the radio in 1938, Winston Churchill told an American audience just after Munich that "if the risks of war . . . had been boldly faced in good time, and bold declarations made and meant . . . [had Hitler been faced with] a formidable array of peace-defending powers . . . [it] would have been an opportunity for all peace loving and moderate forces in Germany . . . to make a great effort to reestablish . . . sane and civilized conditions in their country."[14]

Seven years later, after a brutal and devastating war, he revisited this theme: "If the Allies had resisted Hitler strongly in his early stages . . . the chance would have been given the sane elements in German life, which were very powerful . . . to free Germany from the maniacal system into the grip of which she was falling."[15]

In the meantime, those who had hoped to counteract the recognizable evil, and had moved bravely into the "landscape of treason" had not had a hearing. Their attempts to move the world beyond "national interest" and the comfortable prejudices that dictate national policies had had no perceptible impact on a war which ultimately ground them, and many millions of others, into dust.

CHAPTER 1

1918~1936

OVERTURES TO WAR

Mention of the Abwehr—the German military intelligence service—is likely to be met with a blank or questioning look. Mention Canaris, its enigmatic head from 1935 through the Hitler years until 1944, and eyes are likely to snap into focus. His veiled, secretive nature eluded definition; he was the perfect spy and his name stands for mystery and for the Abwehr itself. Of course, there was an Abwehr before Canaris. Germany's military intelligence service dates back to the imperial armed forces, but even now, largely because of Canaris, a fog of mystery hovers over it. In 1935, when an integrated U.S. intelligence service and what was to evolve into the OSS was at most a twinkle in Bill Donovan's eye, in one incarnation or another, Germany had already had such an entity for twenty-two years.

Understanding both the Abwehr and Canaris is crucial to understanding the role they played in attempting to bring down Hitler and his regime, for which it worked. The Abwehr had a history that set it apart from military operations. In this it found parallels with the American intelligence service begun by William Donovan in 1941 that soon became the OSS and later, the CIA. Independence from the military and in staffing had created an organization that sometimes found more agreement at the top levels of its American counterpart—the OSS—than with the regime for which it worked.

In the buildup to war, and even after, significant American businesses were involved in helping Germany rearm. Many top-level people from both sides knew one another, shared business and personal relationships. Over the course of the war, there was often more agreement among them about

what should be done and how, than between the military and policy-making
arms of their respective opposing governments. Were they enemies or allies?
The relationship was certainly not a partnership in any conventional sense,
but it was an odd and fascinating collaboration.

INTELLIGENCE: A VEHICLE OF WAR

World War I had disastrous aftereffects for Germany and left the nation on its knees. The Treaty of Versailles called for reparations that Germany, not surprisingly, was unable to meet.[1] Also, the peace terms, intending to emasculate the German military, stipulated permanent disarmament of Germany and limited the size of the Reichswehr to 100,000 men on long-term service.[2] To preempt future aggression, Germany's fleet was reduced to a coastal defense force. Warplanes, submarines, tanks, heavy artillery, and poison gas were forbidden, and there was to be neither a general staff nor a military intelligence service. German delegates had been excluded from the peace conference and complained that the treaty had not been negotiated, but dictated. The treaty's onerous territorial and financial demands were perceived as a national humiliation and created a great reservoir of wounded national pride, not to mention poverty and hunger.

The new republican government installed in Germany, named after the city in which its constitution had been drawn up, the so-called Weimar Republic was the unhappy child of war and defeat. Countless political parties struggled to control the new postwar, postimperial government, and it was battered by crushing circumstances. Emerging from the deprivations of a long war, Germany was hit by inflation, mass unemployment, and depression so powerful that all hope was effectively erased for many. Always a fragile vessel, the Weimar Republic veered from crisis to crisis in its short life, from 1919 to 1933. The people's dream of a popular democracy remained unfulfilled.

The turmoil and distress of the 1920s and early 1930s soon began knitting together the strands of a new war that—Allied intentions notwithstanding—found its origins in Germany. In attempting to disentangle at least some of those strands, the offices of the Abwehr, situated along Berlin's Tirpitzufer, overlooking the Landwehr Canal, are a reasonable a place to begin this book.

After Versailles, the Allied presumption was that Germany would remain powerless, yet during the Weimar Republic the intelligence service evolved from a handful of officers into a sizable foreign and counterintelligence operation. After Hitler came to power in early 1933, he began a conspicuous rearmament program—with no clear protest from the Allies—from which the military intelligence service benefited enormously. But the Abwehr still stood—as indeed it had always stood—at a significant remove from the

German military. The top rungs of the Abwehr were able to function independently in World War II, to the point of becoming a locus of resistance to the Nazi power they ostensibly served.

Field Marshal Paul von Hindenburg, in charge of the imperial German high command gearing up for first world war, set little store by intelligence; in his view it "did not win wars" and was only an annoyance.[3] But in 1913 Colonel Erich Ludendorff, soon to be Hindenburg's chief of staff, asked Prussian Army Lieutenant Colonel Walter Nicolai to direct the counterintelligence of the Kaiser's troops. Nicolai's outfit functioned as section III B of the Prussian general staff until the beginning of World War I.[4] Its focus on reconnaissance of the French and Russian armies and the British fleet was complemented by an outstanding German naval intelligence service that worked in support of submarine operations during that war.

When Hindenburg and Ludendorff usurped the civilian government of the German Reich in 1916, the intelligence service was given unprecedented powers, unmatched even by the much bigger Amt Ausland/Abwehr—the Office of Foreign Intelligence—of later years. As chief of III B, with Ludendorff's support, Nicolai had authority for secret intelligence and counterespionage, press censorship, and propaganda, and his aggressive expansion of powers into internal policing and the political arena foreshadowed the later tactics of some of Hitler's inner circle.[5] Leftists were not the only ones who referred to him as "the father of the lie."[6] With Germany's defeat and the dismissal of Ludendorff, Nicolai's intelligence career ended, and in the postwar turbulence of a new postimperial Germany his empire collapsed quickly.

In contravention of the terms of Versailles, a German general staff rose from the ashes of World War I in the guise of a *Truppenamt,* or Troop Department. An organ of the Ministry of War, its main mission was to prepare young officers for military service.[7] The army command also established a counterintelligence department, officially designated the Department of Army Statistics of the Truppenamt, or T3. In the summer of 1920 the agency moved into what were to become its permanent quarters on Berlin's Bendlerblock, and was renamed Abwehr—meaning literally "warding off" or "defense"—to differentiate it from its previous, aggressive character.[8] However, it, too, violated the Versailles Treaty and so operated inconspicuously. It consisted of only two or three general staff officers, five to seven officers, and a few secretaries and professed a modest goal: protection of Germany's troops from espionage, sabotage, and putschists, and the extremes of both left- and right-wing forces.

After the war, only 4,000 of the 34,000 officers serving in the Imperial Armies were able to transfer to the far smaller new Reichswehr. Of those, half the generals were monarchist aristocrats with conservative worldviews.[9] Army General Hans von Seekt was determined to keep the Reichswehr out of the reach of the government and turn it into an autonomous "state within a state," insulated from political forces. Soldiers and officers were not to be bogged down in the quagmire of domestic politics, but were to remain apolitical to the point of renouncing voting rights. To that end, the Defense Law of 1921 prohibited all political activity, including membership in political groups.[10] The resulting army was distanced from the political system and from Germany's first republic—a distance that had an enormous and lasting impact on the thinking of its officers.

Under the watchful eyes of the war's victors, the leaders of the Weimar Republic began to emerge from international isolation and to rebuild the military. In 1922, foreign minister Walther Rathenau signed the Treaty of Rapallo, an agreement with the Soviet Union that opened the door to the resumption of diplomatic relations, extensive commercial exchange, and the renunciation of reparations.[11] Western powers were suspicious and feared a German-Russian rapprochement, but with the exception of a few right-wing politicians and army leaders like Seekt, the German government had no intention of collaborating with Communist Russia. Seekt was certainly no communist either, but under this pact, he initiated cooperation between the Reichswehr and the Red Army. In contravention of Versailles, German soldiers began training in Russian tanks and airplanes and testing new weapons.[12]

The Rapallo Treaty created opportunities within a strict culture of secrecy and concealment: German officers trained in the Soviet Union in airplanes (forbidden to Germany under the terms of Versailles), and the young Heinz Guderian practiced tank tactics that would lay the groundwork for the blitzkrieg victories in Poland.[13]

In 1932 the Reichswehr counted just over 4,500 officers in all branches of the forces—a figure in compliance with the Versailles Treaty. Most came from the aristocratic and upper-bourgeois elites of German society and would share a visceral loathing of Hitler and Nazi organizations, such as the paramilitary SA—*Sturmabteilung*—Storm Troops, and the SS—*Schutzstaffel*—Protective Squadron. Although a small group of officers contemplated military intervention to keep Hitler from taking power as early as 1932 and 1933, the Reichswehr's political isolation was a serious impediment to action. Their plans failed.[14]

General von Seekt's prohibition against political involvement by the military endured. Not only was it still in effect in the spring of 1935, but it was extended to preclude membership in Nazi organizations while on active duty.[15] Predictably, this had a substantial effect on the thinking of the leading officers of the German army during Hitler's rearmament program. The army, and with it the Abwehr, was still effectively distanced from the political system.

As active Nazis entered the service after 1933, things began to change. The number of officers rose to more than 36,000, and the composition of the officer corps was altered significantly. The expansion created deep divisions between the older army officer corps and the waves of Nazis joining the ranks. The disdain of officers representative of the old Reichswehr toward the Nazi newcomers exacerbated tensions and street clashes erupted with members of the SA and the SS.

The Abwehr, too, was affected by this expansion, and its name and status changed several times. Before 1933, France's massive fortifications along the Maginot Line still seemed an impregnable obstacle to an Abwehr hampered by a lack of manpower and resources, so it turned its eyes and ears east to Poland. Then, as it evolved from a small national defense unit into a well-funded modern intelligence service, it concentrated on the military strength of Germany's European neighbors and their reactions to Hitler's politics of rearmament and expansion.

Secret intelligence had always been dominated by the army, and the June 1932 appointment of naval Captain Conrad Patzig as new head of the Abwehr in June 1932 caused a sensation. A naval officer, no matter how qualified, was greeted with distrust—a distrust that was heightened by the still vivid memory of a scandal involving the navy's Captain Walter Lohmann, who had defrauded the German Treasury of millions in an attempt to build up his own naval intelligence operation, leaving the Treasury 26 million Reichsmarks in debt and the navy's reputation in tatters. Yet even as Patzig was greeted with suspicion, he was expected to extend his trust and confidence to Abwehr section heads who had always been granted considerable independence and responsibility in the decentralized structure of the organization.

Previously the Abwehr had served as an organ of the Ministry of War on the domestic front, but Patzig's tenure marked an important shift. The Abwehr now began to develop into a military intelligence service with an expanded role in foreign policy. This was especially true after Hitler became Reich Chancellor on January 30, 1933. His shameless flouting of the terms of Versailles met with only feeble protestations from the Allied powers that did little to impede his drive to restore the luster to German military prowess, of which augmented intelligence operations were a feature. For the Abwehr, the Nazi seizure of power meant a dramatic budget increase and an expanding role. But like the army, it still stood at a critical remove from the political system, a factor that played a significant role in Hitler's seizing and maintaining power.

Patzig quickly recognized the threat posed by Nazi paramilitary organizations—the SS and SD—*Sicherheitsdienst* (Security Service of the SS)—operating independently of the Wehrmacht. He, like many others, awoke to the SS's insatiable quest for power with the murders of Ernst Röhm and many brown-shirted Storm Troopers on June 30, 1934. Patzig's Abwehr predecessor, General Kurt von Bredow, was among the victims on the "Night of the Long Knives," an operation meticulously planned by Hitler and Heinrich Himmler, and Bredow's assassination hit many Abwehr officers hard.

After the SS's eradication of the SA, its main political rivals, simmering tensions between Patzig and the Nazi Party organizations escalated. Reinhard Heydrich, head of the SD, the SS intelligence branch, had been pressing Patzig for matters that were not his business, such as a list of secret weapons plants in Germany. There was no list, Patzig replied. Were such a document to fall into the wrong hands it would be far too dangerous. Heydrich complained to Field Marshal Werner von Blomberg, Hitler's minister of war, and continued to press Patzig, who later recalled that "with Heydrich there was always 'trouble' "—and here he used the English.[16] Patzig tried to fend off the Nazis by welding the Abwehr and the Foreign Ministry into a united front, but relations deteriorated to the point where he no longer found any points of agreement with Blomberg.

On December 31, 1934, Patzig asked to be relieved as head of the Abwehr. He preferred to return to active duty in the navy, to take command of the armored cruiser *Graf Spee*. In a final interview with Blomberg, called the "Rubber Lion" behind his back for the tough demeanor that was intended, but failed, to mask his obvious political malleability, Patzig spoke his mind about recent political developments.

He told Blomberg that, after the death of Hindenburg, "the German people look to you, as the senior officer of the Wehrmacht, in the hope that you can protect them from the encroachment of the SS.[17] Today you still command the necessary authority to save the Wehrmacht and the people from these good-for-nothings; in six months, it may be too late." Blomberg was only in touch with the higher echelons, Patzig said, and had no idea what was really happening in the streets. As head of the Abwehr, he had come to understand that the SS was a catch basin for rootless lives and criminals who would stop at nothing that might enhance their power—not even murder. He could easily have made a deal with the SD or the Gestapo, he said, but doing so would have made him a "traitor to the Wehrmacht" and compromised its independence.[18]

"I won't have such remarks, Captain Patzig!" Blomberg shouted. "The SS is an organization of the Führer."

"Then I regret that the Führer doesn't know what a bunch of rogues he is in charge of," Patzig replied.

Asserting his authority, Blomberg insisted curtly that he alone had "political responsibility for the Wehrmacht, and my assessment of the situation is very different from yours. The future will prove who is right."[19]

Patzig's attempt to ward off the Nazis had failed. The Abwehr would need a new and astute leader, and Patzig said he could think of no one better suited than Captain Wilhelm Canaris. There were solid reasons behind his choice.

THE ADVENTURES OF "KIKA": A LIFE IN BRIEF[20]

Though Wilhelm Canaris was commonly referred to as "the little Greek" and liked to claim descent from the Greek freedom fighter and eventual prime minister Konstantin Canaris, his family had actually come to Germany from northern Italy about three hundred years before his birth. He joined the navy at eighteen, in 1905. In 1908, young Lieutenant Canaris was serving on the light cruiser *Bremen* along the east coast of Latin America, and was captivated by the lands and culture. He used his free time to learn Spanish, a skill that later proved to be extremely useful, and he revealed an extraordinary ability in dealing with all manner of people. A second stay in the region aboard the *Dresden* in 1913–14 expanded his contacts. Canaris's first encounters with the world of information gathering and spying were aboard the *Bremen,* and they now became his true métier.

The outbreak of World War I found the little *Dresden* thousands of miles from home, under orders to intercept and interfere however possible with the enemy—the British—the world's most powerful navy. For eight months, the *Dresden* played hide-and-seek with the British navy through bays and inlets along the Atlantic and Pacific coasts of South America. At last, in need of repairs and unable to acquire essential coal, the *Dresden* threw herself on the mercy of neutral Chile. To keep her out of British hands, the ship was blown up, and her crew was interned on a desolate island. Barren and uninhabited Quinriquina held no charms for Canaris. He decamped, and under the unlikely alias of "Reed Rosa," he escaped over the Andes and through the wilds of South America, largely on horseback. Two hard months later he reached Amsterdam, and finally home. Exhausted, physically racked, he reported immediately to the naval authorities on the last voyage of the *Dresden.*

Word of his talents in information gathering reached the upper echelons, and Canaris was soon in Spain, active as secret agent "Kika." He set about establishing a network of informants and was said to have done excellent work in what was then called "black armament"—the forbidden buildup of arms and provisioning of U-boats in the western Mediterranean—and distinguished himself further as a submarine commander, sinking three enemy ships, and severely damaging a fourth.[21]

In May 1934, Canaris was serving as commander of the liner *Schlesien* when the new Nazi leadership came from Berlin to see a demonstration of naval war games off Wilhelmshaven on the North Sea. On an unseasonably stormy day, Canaris played host to Reichsminister Hermann Göring, who got so seasick that he was forced to make what the seamen referred to as an "offering to Neptune" over the side of the ship.[22] Later, in the officers' mess, an earnest seaman came to inform the waxen Göring that a radio signal recently received from Neptune had declared him the official provider of fish food. Of the Nazi higher-ups, Göring was known to have a sense of humor, but he was not amused. Canaris had not endeared himself to the Nazi powers. It did not bode well.

No evidence ever surfaced to support the rumors that linked Canaris to the Lohmann scandal of the late 1920s, yet some of the tar and perhaps even a few feathers that had attached to the navy as a result of it seemed to have stuck to Canaris as well. In spite of his diligence, his obvious abilities, and his superior officer's passionate defense in regard to the Lohmann affair, Canaris's career seemed becalmed.[23] Struggling to restart it after the Lohmann taint, neither effort nor ability had any effect. For several years he had been waiting in vain for a call to Berlin and higher duties, and now he had offended Göring. In September 1934, he was assigned as commandant to the naval base at Swinemünde, a dead-end appointment, tantamount to retirement. His career was apparently over.

Yet barely had he withdrawn to his bleak, provincial exile when an extraordinary opportunity presented itself: The Abwehr needed a new head, and Patzig insisted that he knew of no officer better suited than Canaris. Canaris recognized his chance; he would not let it escape him. He would extricate himself from a ruined career and approach the seat of power. The invisible ink that had delighted the boy thrilled with espionage paled in comparison with the possibilities now within reach of the man. He presented himself in Berlin immediately.

When Patzig detailed his own difficulties with the SS and the Nazi hierarchy, Canaris reproached his predecessor for not getting on better with the Party. Speaking from experience, Patzig offered some advice: "You, too, will experience everything I've told you. If you succumb to the wishes of the SS, you'll do fine. They will bring you a gift horse, or anything else you want. But if you follow my course, Canaris, today is the beginning of your end."[24]

Canaris assured him that he would be "able to handle these fellows."[25] After his thirty-year navy career had turned to dust, he was being miraculously resuscitated. He was looking forward to his new post. But in spite of his cocky reply to Patzig's warning, Canaris must have wondered if he would fare any better. Initially, certainly, Canaris had welcomed the National Socialist revival of the military and its firm anticommunist stance, for though it was out of all proportion to the actual threat, he shared the vivid fear of Bolshevism then prevalent in Germany. He had had no great enthusiasm for the Weimar Republic; he was a patriot and an ardent supporter of rearmament.[26] And while many, including Patzig, thought him an fervid Nazi, his first contact with his new masters—specifically Göring—just a few months earlier, had been inauspicious at best.

THE BUSINESS OF AMERICA: FUELING THE BEAST

German military and intelligence operations were certainly aware of Hitler's ambitions and the push toward war, but so were others. American businesses, particularly such businesses as might be critical to a war effort, were also attuned to the temper of the Nazi regime's intentions and programs. Against a backdrop of many long-term interlocking interests and relationships, some major corporations held a finger to the wind and played a curious game: helping Germany to rebuild and—War Department objections or no—to rearm.

Since the earliest years of the century delegations of German business leaders had made extensive tours of the United States, seeing what there was to see of the latest American technology, meeting government dignitaries, exchanging visiting cards and ideas. One such visitor was Grand Admiral Alfred von Tirpitz. He came in 1902 in the company of Kaiser Wilhelm II's brother, Prince Heinrich of Prussia, and other notables to meet with American political dignitaries and was shown the latest in American industrial development.

These august visitors were a bit early to see Bethlehem Steel's Grey rolling mill, which produced the wide-flanged structural sections that made skyscrapers possible and soon revolutionized the building industry, but they surely saw enough to impress them with American technological innovation. Bethlehem Steel was already a behemoth. By the onset of the Great War, 1914, it employed nearly 16,000 workers and was producing 1.1 millions tons of steel a year for ships, armor, munitions, and ordnance that went to work in the European war. As a memento of their travels, the German visitors were given heavy silver spoons decorated with enamel scenes of Albany, New York; Mount Vernon, Virginia; and Bethlehem, Pennsylvania.

These spoons were not the lightweight souvenirs available today at any airport gift shop, but heavy sterling pieces, passed from Tirpitz to his daughter, and later used to serve jams and jellies at the family breakfast table of his son-in-law, Ulrich von Hassell. Their meaning was not lost on Hassell; he was active in several important German embassies in Europe of the 1920s and 1930s as consul, envoy, or ambassador, and in a position to pass on the perception of American might the spoons represented to his compatriots.

Hassell knew exactly what kind of power this new nation had. In 1905, he had met Jacob Schiff at a reception at Tokyo's Imperial Hotel. Schiff, a native German, had emigrated and married into the banking family of Solomon Loeb. At the time, Schiff was a very important man in Japan;

almost single-handedly, he had floated a $200 million bond issue to finance Japan's war against Czarist Russia—a significant sum in 1904–1905 dollars.

Germany's military also knew what a power the United States was, and Germany's business empire certainly knew. In 1912, a delegation of high-ranking German industrialists spent several weeks in the Eastern United States, inspecting, reviewing, and reporting every detail of what they saw at Pittsburgh Steel, Pierce-Arrow Motor Car Company, and General Electric, among other companies. Top managers and engineers from Friedr. Bayer & Co. (the future Bayer), key people from the Badische Anilin-u.Sodafabrik, Ludwigshafen (the future BASF)), and representatives from Blohm & Voss (still a major shipbuilder of both civilian and military ships), and Krupp were all greeted in Philadelphia by the German-born mayor, Rudolph Blankenburg.[27] This was only one of many such visits, and with each visit, the German captains of industry were more and more impressed by the enormous power of the United States.

The German business presence in the United States before the war had brought familiarity, technology, and comfort back to Germany. There was a significant network, an international confraternity, of bankers, lawyers, and business people who had known each other and had done business over the years. Just one example of many of these relationships involves Paul Leverkühn, a lawyer who came to the United States in the early 1920s on a special mission through friends in the German Foreign Office, as the German embassy was negotiating with the American alien property board for the return of German property in the United States.[28] According to the report on Leverkühn:

He then continued to remain in the United States and secured employment with the Warburg firm in New York, becoming manager of the company. Altogether this stay lasted eight years, and he made a great number of friends during his travels throughout the country. Among others, he became ecquainted [sic] with Mr. Bill DONOVAN (later Maj. Gen. DONOVAN of the OSS), and this friendship continued until war broke out.

In 1930 he finally returned to Germany and settled in Berlin as a lawyer. He was very successful in his practice, and his knowledge of America gained him many prominent German clients for their claims and law-suits in America. In like manner, his American friends entrusted him with their power of attorney to follow up their legal interests in Germany. LEVERKUEHN collaborated with the DONOVAN law firm in the United States by handling all of its German interests, and the American firm reciprocated by handling all business that the LEVERKUEHN firm had in the States.

After his return to Berlin, LEVERKUEHN made many trips to the States and frequently was a DONOVAN guest. His many friends included diplomats, newspapermen, artists, and business men [*sic*]. In Berlin banking and business circles he was appointed to the board of directors of various companies.

During the present war LEVERKUEHN again joined the army, but his age and rather weak physique did not permit combat service . . . [so] he performed special work provided by friends who knew of his capabilities. . . . In June or July of 1941 he was sent to Istanbul, Turkey. . . . [29]

Business and industrial contacts ran wide, deep, and strong. In this case they also led to an understanding between ostensible enemy factions in the Abwehr and the OSS. It is almost a surprise that the report makes no mention of Allen Dulles.

These contacts brought with them an almost inescapable side effect: trading with what was to become the enemy. American big business was deeply invested in Germany, and if a war was brewing, it would not stand in the way of opportunities. When Germany was unable to meet the crushing reparations payments set at Versailles, the mark collapsed, and delegations from J. P. Morgan, Germany's Reichsbank, and others met to arrange massive loans through Wall Street and big international banks. Two plans emerged from these meetings: the Dawes Plan of 1924, by which foreign loans to Germany would be paid off in German goods, and the Young Plan of 1928, structured much like a mortgage; German real assets were to be pledged, and American capital was to be repaid monetarily. Under the Young Plan, reparations were to continue for fifty-nine years, and Hitler could claim, with some justification, that young Germans who knew nothing about World War I would be paying the bill for their lifetimes.[30]

The plans and their loans did help Germany back on her feet, and for the lenders, the potential long-term profits were enormous. But given Germany's shaky financial condition and colossal unemployment, the potential for disaster was also great. Many German companies with American affiliates put themselves out of reach by being "sold" into foreign holding companies. While American investors reaped significant profits, there were unintended consequences. The plans intended to help German reconstruction resulted in the establishment of cartels of enormous power that eventually provided much of the materiel for World War II.

I. G. Farben's dominant role as Germany's industrial behemoth dated back to 1925, when Wall Street financing and some American technical know-how set it up as an imposing and influential cartel. By 1928, American holdings in I. G. Farben included Bayer, General Aniline, Agfa, and others, under German I.G. control, and subsequently reorganized into American I.G. Eventually, through a web of more than 200 domestic and nearly 250 foreign partners, I.G. was involved in almost every conceivable aspect of research, production, and sales of oil, gas, rubber, dyes, chemicals, and explosives. Legal support came from the venerable Wall Street law firm Sullivan and Cromwell, where John Foster Dulles and his brother Allen were both active. But the critical funding and technical expertise came from elsewhere.

In April 1929, the *New York Times* announced that Standard Oil of New Jersey had "for some years past enjoyed a very close relationship with certain branches of the research work of the I. G. Farbenindustrie, which bears closely on the oil industry."[31] Standard saw I. G. Farben as a way of protecting its commercial interests in Germany, and, fortunately for Germany, in 1926 their close relationship gave birth to American I.G. As a holding company for I.G. assets in the United States under Standard Oil management, Standard invested in American I.G., and vice versa. Among its board members were Edsel Ford; Walter C. Teagle, president of Standard Oil; Paul M. Warburg, chairman of the Federal Reserve; and his brother, Max Warburg, a director of American I.G. who ultimately helped to finance the war effort.[32]

In the buildup to Hitler's war, Germany faced one problem of particular importance: a shortage of certain essential raw materials and natural resources. Finding an alternative to her scarce crude petroleum reserves was critical. Modern war cannot be waged without sufficient oil and gas, and much of I.G.'s energy and capital had been going toward the development of the coal-to-oil conversion process. Then a solution was found with help from an unexpected quarter: Standard Oil.

Standard Oil's immense resources provided real hope for alleviating Germany's oil shortage.[33] Given its significant oil reserves in the United States, Standard's hydrogenation process and other technical innovations for converting coal to oil were hardly essential to its domestic market. But in Germany the process had serious potential for long-term profit, and in fact this profit was soon delivered. By early 1933, the U.S. commercial attaché in Berlin informed the State Department that in two years' time, Germany would be able to manufacture enough oil and gas out of lignite coal to fuel a long war. He added that Standard Oil was supplying millions of dollars to help.

With German industry firmly under the Nazi thumb, and Göring's four-year plan for economic self-sufficiency going into effect in 1937, the pressure for building wartime capabilities was on. A principal component of that plan was I. G. Farben, so completely identified with Hitler's government and its aims that as Senator Homer Bone later put it bluntly: "Farben was Hitler, and Hitler was Farben."[34]

The U.S. War Department had informed the Ethyl Gasoline Corporation, owned jointly by Standard Oil and General Motors, of its concern regarding their intention to form a company to produce ethyl lead in Germany in late 1934. Ethyl lead, a critical additive to raise the octane level of aviation fuel, "would doubtless be a valuable aid to military aeroplanes," and under no circumstances was the company to reveal any technical know-how for the purpose of tetraethyl lead production in Germany.[35] Yet joint production between U.S. Ethyl and I.G.'s Ethyl G.m.b.H. was soon underway in Germany, and it was a significant help in keeping Göring's Luftwaffe aloft.[36] The American business world was pursuing its own interests, and continued to do so in spite of the War Department. Darkening war clouds did not diminish these activities; if anything, a war economy—whether on one side of the Atlantic or the other—was good for profits.

Business and its relationships also contributed mightily to the effectiveness of the Abwehr. This goes back to an earlier era, when in 1871 the economy of a newly united Germany grew exponentially under Bismarck. This growth, and colonies in regions as distant and diverse as Tsingtao in China, various Pacific Islands, such as German Samoa, and Cameroon in Africa, established trade missions all over the globe to support an economy that was increasingly dependent on global trade. The same scenario—minus the colonies—played out again after World War I and even World War II: German businesses around the world were a major source of revenue. Even now, many German towns still have active *Kolonialwarenhändler*, shops dealing in foreign wares that are a reminder of colonial days, when rare and exotic products first became available in Germany.

The result was a significant core of businessmen with a solid knowledge of foreign countries and excellent language skills. Not only were they a reliable source of recruits for the Abwehr, but German businesses did not hesitate to share their knowledge or secrets with the government, and so they were also a continuing source of information. Each businessman, each foreign office, was a source of intelligence—whether for counterintelligence, the collection of industrial secrets or political intelligence, and these reports were shared with the government.

Trade created a pool of people with business and industrial contacts and also eased the tasks of the Abwehr and the German Foreign Office considerably, for it had established a route along which intelligence traveled between Germany and the United States and many of their businesses. It may have been unofficial intelligence, but it was real and it was substantive, and as war loomed larger and darker, more of Germany's energies were focused on precisely this kind of intelligence. Canaris and his Abwehr were masters at pulling together bits of the dinner conversation of magnates and dignitaries, shoeshine boys and newspaper vendors, until the confluence provided a significant portrait of the enemy.

Had the lesson learned from the enameled silver spoons given the visiting German dignitaries in been forgotten in the years between 1902 and 1940? Hardly. Nearly three hundred years of massive emigration gave almost every German family some kind of connection to the United States in the form of letters from a family member in Wisconsin or reports of a poor weaver from Silesia who had made good in Pennsylvania. Germany's broad population knew and knew well. By the 1930s, when Hitler was putting his plans for world conquest into action and mobilization, there were ample German intelligence reports on the U.S. economy and what it might mean militarily. By 1937 Germany could hardly have viewed the United States as an unknown quantity.

THE MOTORIZATION AND MOBILIZATION OF GERMANY

When Europe, still battle scarred from World War I, began to think about reviving its indigenous automobile industry, American carmakers joined in with enthusiasm. Ford and General Motors had been in Germany since the 1920s, and had even set up assembly lines for car production there to evade the prohibitive tariffs on imported cars. Just days after seizing power in late January 1933, Hitler took the occasion of a visit to a motor show to announce a massive program of road building. Intended to provide jobs, this program eventually built the formidable autobahn. The following year, to make proper use of this great new arterial highway system, Hitler announced production of the Volkswagen—a car for Everyman. Coupled with the lifting of the tax on new automobile purchases, the Volkswagen would not only provide jobs, but reinvigorate a flagging economy and further encourage the motorization of Germany. A new day seemed to be dawning for Germany's automobile industry, and Ford and GM were on hand to share the benefits—large benefits. Between 1932 and 1938, overall car production in Germany increased nearly 600 percent.[37]

HENRY FORD, THAT KNOTTY ICON OF AMERICAN INDUSTRY, HAD FOUNDED HIS AMERICAN operation in 1903. His Model T revolutionized the American dream and the American landscape along with it. No drink, no tobacco, just plain hard work brought Ford inestimable wealth. He was a model of Franklinesque probity in everything but his personal opinions, which took an extremist turn early on, and which he was not shy about airing. While Hitler was still an obscure fanatic ranting on the streets of Munich, Ford was already venting his wrath about the international Jewish threat in his personal news organ, the *Dearborn Independent*.[38] In 1928, *The New York Times* called him an "industrial fascist—the Mussolini of Detroit."[39] He ran his company in accordance with his views and the company, not the man, is at issue here.

Ford-Werke in Germany, established first in Berlin in 1925, then in Cologne, benefited greatly from Hitler's "motorization" of Germany, the burgeoning automobile market and then the mobilization. After the Nazi takeover, Ford/U.S. increased its stake in Ford-Werke Cologne. Dearborn stepped in to supply raw materials and parts not readily available in Germany and enjoyed the results when business began booming. The years 1935 and 1936 were banner years. Between 1934 and 1938, when war production was in high gear, revenues increased 400 percent. Production jumped every year, and a delighted Nazi regime honored the company by officially designating it a German company.

This sign of official goodwill was critical to Ford. Without it, the company was not eligible for government contracts, and since government contracts constituted an ever larger part of German sales, lack of certification would cause a subsidiary acute financial pain.[40] It was in Ford's best interest to maintain this state of grace. Company leaders assured the Nazis that their sympathies were well aligned. Soon business with the Reich was so profitable that the only way to meet demand was to import prebuilt components secretly from Dearborn for rapid assembly—during special night shifts—of the 3,150 trucks required for the intended march into Czechoslovakia in 1938. The War Department would certainly have frowned, but Dearborn continued to fuel the Reich with parts and machinery for war production as late as 1941.[41] For this special effort, Henry Ford was awarded the Order of Merit of the German Eagle. Ford-Werke continued to produce and maintain trucks for the Wehrmacht, handle replacement parts, and also engage in the production of half-tracks, boat and barge motors, and gears for Junkers airplanes.

FORD WASN'T ALONE. ADAM OPEL AG, ORIGINALLY A MAKER OF BICYCLES AND SEWING machines, had begun producing automobiles in 1899, and having once begun, it lost no time. By the 1920s, Opel was the largest car manufacturer in Europe.[42] Small wonder then that General Motors showed an interest in the technologically advanced, if organizationally challenged company, striving eagerly toward what German industry then called "Fordismus," or Fordism—the paradigm of assembly-line efficiency and productiveness. GM had become a business giant in the motorcar industry by acquisition, swallowing up other companies. In the depressed German market of April 1929, it bought 80 percent of Opel shares. The remaining shares were bought in 1931, as the depression deepened. Soon Opel headquarters in Rüsselsheim in Hesse was bustling with GM executives, engineers, and managers, sent over to bring production up to snuff.

By 1935 Opel/GM's Rüsselsheim was producing 50 percent of Germany's new trucks. Tanks and airplane engines were also on the production lines, all an essential part of Germany's astonishing September 1939 blitzkrieg against Poland, in which the gallant Polish cavalry was simply no match for this lightning assault. Opel was also being converted to Junkers production at this time. Because of the steady reinvestment of earnings in technological improvements, the factories, the heavy trucks, and motors vital to war production were being constantly improved and modernized.[43] Most Americans, of course, had no idea that the company producing these efficient war machines was American-owned.

ENTER CANARIS

At 8:00 A.M. on January 2, 1935, when Captain Wilhelm Canaris arrived at his new office at 72–76 Tirpitzufer. Gallmüller, the old fellow who had been gatekeeper there for as long as anyone could remember, pulled himself to a semblance of attention.[44] Canaris knew the way; he could predict almost every creak of the ancient elevator as it labored toward the third floor. He had served here from 1924 to 1928 in naval administration when this dim rabbit warren of rooms and corridors had been the naval headquarters. Its offices had witnessed several stages of the failed naval career from which he had been suddenly been fortuitously rescued.

He knew exactly what he was up against, and he wanted an early start. The SD's two main sections, foreign affairs under Walter Schellenberg and internal affairs under Otto Ohlendorf, consisted of several active police forces, including the *Sicherheitspolizei* (Sipo, Security Police) and the *Kriminalpolizei* (Kripo, Criminal Police). The resourceful and ambitious Schellenberg was one of Heydrich's principal idea men. His lofty dreams left no room for an autonomous Abwehr and little doubt about who he hoped would eventually rule over the single German intelligence service he envisioned. Early on, Canaris recognized that he would have to treat this opponent carefully and that sorting out competencies would be a challenge.

Despite his confidence, he knew he would face the problems of which Patzig had warned him, and the biggest of those problems was Reinhard Heydrich. Calculating and ambitious, Heydrich and his boss Himmler, had made the Nazi intelligence and police services their fiefdom, a vast network of spy and control mechanisms designed to ensure the fealty of the German population and to deal with dissenters, and, for that matter, with any potential dissenters. Heydrich was head of the SD, the *Sicherheitsdienst*, formed in March 1934 as the intelligence branch of the SS. It was intended to be the only security service of the NSDAP, responsible for the security of Hitler, the Nazi party, and the Third Reich, and was directed against so-called enemies of the state. Hitler wanted to establish a first-class intelligence service, and the SD and Heydrich seemed to be his prime candidate. Whatever else Canaris may have thought of Heydrich, he recognized in him a worthy adversary.

During the transition from the Weimar Republic to the Third Reich, the Abwehr had run into trouble with other intelligence operations; within the Wehrmacht, several coexisted in a state of uneasy competition. The army and the air force each had their own intelligence units. The Abwehr provided military intelligence to the general staff and reported to the Oberkommando der Wehrmacht—OKW—the central high command coordinating army, navy, and air force affairs. Skirmishes between the high commands of the three military branches and the OKW were constant. The real problem however, was working with Heinrich Himmler, who became

Reichsführer SS in June 1936, and his right-hand man, the former naval cadet and Canaris shipmate, Reinhard Heydrich, head of the SD.

The Thousand-Year Reich was not yet two years old but tensions between the old army elite and the intelligence branches of Hitler's regime were already running high. As was so often the case, much of the difficulty stemmed from a collision of social strata—the Wehrmacht leadership represented essentially by the conservative upper classes, while the origins of the Nazi Party and the SS lay among the cooks and barkeeps of the lower-middle and working classes.[45] While Hitler set about dismantling what remained of a constitutional state and individual rights, Reichsführer Himmler and his minions muscled forward, expanding and claiming ever greater powers.

The old-school army generals saw themselves as the guardians of an honorable tradition, yet when Himmler established his SS regiments for "police actions," they fretted, but did little. They resented the incursions of these paramilitary organizations on army turf, but they had even had a hand in arming the SS for the murder of their SA rivals in June 1934. Only one prophetic voice had been raised to warn the generals that if they looked on in silence, they would eventually share the same fate.[46]

Having dispensed with his SA rivals, Himmler now wheeled in his Trojan horse without protest and began his push on the other side of the social and political spectrum—the old elites. Soon he had microphones planted in the offices of the Reichswehr and the Abwehr, to listen in on conversations, ostensibly to uncover "enemies of the Reich" within it ranks.

The day that Canaris reported for his new position, Hitler decided to head off a confrontation and calm the roiling waters of his new Reich by staging a coup de théâtre. He invited everyone who was anyone in the power structure to a gala evening at the Staatsoper. Canaris's invitation arrived within hours of his taking over as Abwehr chief, and he duly presented himself on January 3, 1935, to hear the Führer's speech of gratitude for the loyalty and faith of Germany's great Wehrmacht. The two pillars of the new Germany, said Hitler—Party and Wehrmacht—would surely bring the nation renewed esteem and power in the world. By the time the opening chords of the Führer's favorite opera, *Tannhäuser,* wafted through the great opera house, the generals and their opposites in the Party were, to all appearances, mollified and reconciled—at least temporarily. It was the first of several gatherings—a cozy beer evening with a presentation by Himmler followed—intended to blend the SS and Reichswehr into an amicable, cohesive community. It was not to be. There were too many ideological differences to overcome.

SHAPING A NEW ABWEHR

Like so much about the man, Canaris's own political convictions remain blurred and contradictory. Patzig thought him an "enthusiastic National

Socialist."[47] An article in a 1938 anthology entitled "Politics and Wehr-macht" by "Vice Admiral Canaris" supports his assessment.[48] It reads like a fervent avowal of Nazism, and closes: "We will reach our goal and fulfill our professional duty if we believe in our National Socialist and soldierly mission as unconditionally as the Führer, our Supreme Commander, has believed in victory." Yet there were many who perceived a very different Canaris.

Deciphering the man's complex personality provides work suitable for the sharpest of intelligence services. "Of extraordinary sensitivity to different psychologies and mentalities," reads a senior officer's report dated 1926. It goes on: ". . . unusual linguistic capabilities . . . he understands how to deal with unfamiliar personalities—from the lowliest to the most prominent—in an exemplary fashion, quickly winning their confidence. Such tasks present no obstacles for him. . . . No room is locked so securely that he cannot gain access to it, approach the relevant people, and be in complete control in an astonishingly short time—his face a picture of childlike innocence all the while."[49] His personnel files describe a young man who is discreet, modest, and reserved, but also diplomatic, reliable, serious, and professionally diligent. One evaluation recommended that young Canaris become more energetic—a modern version of this assessment might read "more proactive."

Conservative by nature, military by training, Canaris considered Versailles and its terms humiliating and insulting, and he was passionate about rebuilding the military. He had in fact supported Hitler's early reforms and rearmament policy, but gradually, as Hitler's aims and methods became clearer, he wavered. Biographers agree that his opposition to National Socialism and Hitler's risky foreign policies developed over time. Some believe that he even considered resigning from the Abwehr in 1937. The major political upheavals such as the Blomberg-Fritsch crisis of 1938, and Nazi measures against the Wehrmacht, certainly triggered his growing anger and disgust.[50] But Canaris, like many others in positions of influence, decided to stay on and work from within the regime and so perhaps lessen the total destruction he feared would be the result of Hitler's mad dreams.

To the surprise of the staff already on hand, generally unimpressed by their first glimpse of the new chief, Canaris hit the slightly derelict, slow-functioning Abwehr like a firestorm. In making the Abwehr his own, Canaris first divided the organization into two groups: people he liked, and people he did not like, according to staffer Werner von Geldern. Colonel Erwin von Lahousen, an Abwehr section head, elaborated: Canaris rarely estimated men by their accomplishments or their character. Sympathy and antipathy were what guided his view of men—along with an intense love of animals. In his opinion anyone who did not love dogs was evil.

The newly minted admiral hated lawlessness and arbitrary rule (other than his own) and forbade unnecessary violence. He tried to keep radical Nazis out of the organization in any case, and the only candidates retained for service in the Berlin headquarters were those unlikely to be Party devotees. Convinced Nazis with a talent for intelligence were assigned to field offices—a personnel policy justified by the official prohibition against political activity for members of the Wehrmacht. To keep out the zealots, he also relied on careful screening and intuition. With few exceptions, whatever their political stripe, Canaris's recruits, like their chief, welcomed the vision of a new Germany, back on its feet and again a recognized participant among nations.

AT THE BEGINNING OF THE HITLER ERA, THE ABWEHR COUNTED 150 EMPLOYEES. FROM 1935 on, an increasingly aggressive German foreign policy set a higher value on enemy intelligence, and by 1937, Abwehr staff numbered more than 900. Under Canaris's stewardship, the operation underwent enormous changes, some of them his doing, others due to political circumstances and the rehabilitation of the military. Supplementary officers—*Ergänzungsoffiziere* (E-Offiziere)—from the ranks of World War I veterans were reactivated for a new intelligence mission for which they often lacked training. These officers usually served out of a strong sense of patriotism—sometimes tinged with loyalty to the imperial tradition. Having learned soldiering under the old system, they had come to accept German national policy unquestioningly. But neither the officers with roots in the old imperial army nor those who were the products of the Reichswehr were political.[51] Many civilians with no personal or family military background also entered the Abwehr at this time. Coming from civilian jobs, they brought an independent spirit, a brisk unbureaucratic style, and some refreshing and welcome new air into mix. Of these lawyers, architects, and businessmen joining the Abwehr, few had any inherent loyalty to the military system. Many in fact detested it, and were also skeptical of National Socialism.[52] Among the subalterns and younger captains who owed their military careers to Hitler's expansion of the Wehrmacht, however, support for the Nazi regime was noticeable.

The expansion of the mid-1930s also brought a series of name changes to the Abwehr, each shift in nomenclature a kind of shorthand, signaling organizational changes and a higher status. The Abwehr's responsibilities now went well beyond the protection of German forces from sabotage and foreign spies. However, the rapid expansion had come at a price: a clash of interests; disunity among disparate personnel, and lowered quality standards. There was simply no time for proper training and Canaris's penchant for improvisation only compounded the problems. He hated administrative details and typically left the implementation of his decisions to section and station heads, yet he seemed almost pathologically incapable of truly delegating responsibility. The result was frequent confusion and occasional chaos.

The Abwehr was growing at the same hectic pace as the Wehrmacht, and a growing number of field offices in Spain, Turkey, Portugal, Japan, and Italy reflected its geographical expansion.[53] In assembling the cast of characters for what became known as the "CC"—Club Canaris—the little admiral flung his net wide. He recruited staff by tapping personal acquaintances and friends of friends. "Make sure you get into the Reserve," he would say. "Then you'll be in Wehrmacht uniform, and won't have to disguise yourself further. We're all ending up in uniform these days anyway."[54] Members were added on the basis of recommendations and Canaris's personal choice. The Abwehr was designed to serve all Wehrmacht branches without being incorporated into any of them, and even as the range of its tasks increased, Canaris was able to preserve its independent status.[55]

The cluster of Abwehr officers Canaris gathered about him were individuals whose thinking was close to his own. Traditionalists and loyal Germans, they, too, had come to find the increasingly hysterical and repressive Hitler repugnant, and were deeply disturbed by anti-Jewish legislation and persecution. On his arrival, Canaris had found a conservative spirit and a well-established team of senior officers, older men with their share of life experience. Section chiefs were often staff officers with several years on the job, who ensured continuity in departmental activities. Abwehr members moved to other offices only rarely; most spent their careers in intelligence. This made for strong bonds between them, but it also led to a certain distance and alienation from the corps of field officers.

The core leadership evolved from a nucleus inherited from Patzig, who knew one another and stuck together. This crew included Major Hans Oster, whose name is probably the best known among high Abwehr officials, and among the most controversial. Nominally, Major Oster was deputy chief of the Abwehr and the chief of its *Zentralabteilung,* or central section, in charge of organization, administration, and maintaining archives and records for the operational departments. Oster did not participate in any actual intelligence operations, but thanks to an extraordinary network of connections that almost constituted a private information service within the Abwehr, he stayed very well informed.

In an interview thirty years after the fact, Patzig recalled that one day in February 1934, Oster had presented himself at the office of the then Abwehr chief in plain clothes, looking careworn, sheepish, and slightly down-at-the-heels. "Herr Kapitän," Oster had said to Patzig, "you have to help me." He had been discharged from the Wehrmacht in 1932 *cum infamia*—with dishonor—because during carnival week he had breached the military honor code with an extramarital indiscretion. He wanted Patzig take him into the Abwehr as an E-Offizier, preferably in what was called a "black position."

"I did not think much of his character," said Patzig, "but felt I should take advantage of his abilities, so I hired him as a civilian employee. Then, as an anti-Nazi, he tried to win my support for all sorts of things. For example, he got his friend Gisevius onto me . . . and attempted to gain more and more influence over the Abwehr. He wanted to take over my outer office—to control what visitors I would or would not receive."[56]

Militarily and ideologically, Oster's roots were firmly planted in Imperial Germany and the Reichswehr. Convinced of the superiority of the monarchy even after its downfall, he felt a lifelong personal obligation to the Hohenzollern Kaiser, and wore the uniform of the Weimar Republic only reluctantly. While Oster yearned for the restoration of an authoritarian regime founded on discipline and ruled by a strong leader, it had become clear to him over the course of the early thirties and Hitler's trajectory to power that it could not be just *any* strong leader.[57] Behind Oster's intense patriotism and conservatism lay high standards of honor. He was revolted by Hitler's brutal murders of his enemies within the regime, and the June 1934 Night of the Long Knives turned him into a virulent anti-Nazi. The Nazi persecution of the Jews only strengthened his resolve to eliminate the Führer. Gregarious, sharp-witted, slender, and charming, he could also be rash and impulsive. Though some of his colleagues regarded him as a careerist dilettante and womanizer, all agreed that he "deplored Hitler and detested Nazis . . . abhorred corruption, and was contemptuous of politicians."[58] Fabian von Schlabrendorff, an officer and fellow conspirator who knew him well, described him as a "man after God's own heart."[59] It was likely under the influence of the volatile, activist Oster that Canaris moved cautiously—very cautiously—toward a more emphatic anti-Nazi stance.

Apart from Canaris's personal preferences, the Amtsgruppe Ausland/Abwehr was divided into five sections: a central section, a foreign section, and three main operational sections in charge of espionage, sabotage, and counterintelligence.[60] (See chart, page 30.) Oster's section was designated by a Z for Zentral, with an additional letter, denoting a specific function. ZI for instance, engaged in the bread and butter of active espionage: procuring enemy intelligence, recruiting informants, and establishing networks of agents. Abwehr/Ausland, the foreign section, maintained and evaluated relations with foreign powers and foreign media—especially Allied—and served as liaison with foreign military attachés and between the OKW and the German Foreign Office. ZB, probably the most important section, was responsible for foreign policy reports and was eventually headed by Hans von Dohnanyi, a highly intelligent civilian lawyer and former judge, recruited by Oster. Absent foreign support, Dohnanyi at least hoped for foreign understanding. His extensive liaison work abroad, particularly with Josef Müller and the Vatican, was to have serious repercussions.

Colonel Hans "Piki" Piekenbrock took over Abwehr I, responsible for

STRUCTURE OF THE AMT AUSLAND/ABWEHR

Amt Ausland/Abwehr

Admiral Wilhelm Canaris

Adjutant: *Lieutenant Colonel Jenke*

Foreign and counterintelligence of the High Command of the armed forces

Amtsgruppe Ausland (Foreign Branch)	**Zentralabteilung** (Central Section)	**Abteilung I** (Section I)	**Abteilung II** (Section II)	**Brandenburg Division**	**Abteilung III** (Section III)
Vice Admiral Leopold Bürkner	*Major General Hans Oster (1938–43)*	*Colonel Hans Piekenbrock (1937–43)*	*Major Helmuth Groscurth (1938–39)*	*Major General Alexander von Pfuhlstein*	*Major Randolf Bamler (1933–39)*
	Colonel Jacobsen (1943–44)	*Colonel Georg Hansen (1943–44)*	*Colonel Erwin Lahousen (1939–43)*		*Colonel Franz-Eccard von Bentivegni (1939–44)*
			Colonel Wessel von Freytag-Loringhoven (1943–44)		
Evaluation of military relations with foreign powers; liaison with Armed Forces Operations Staff, the attaché groups of the armed services, foreign military attachés in Berlin, and German Foreign Office	Organization and administration on behalf of other sections	Procurement of enemy intelligence through agents' network	Sabotage in enemy territory, countersabotage, planning of commando operations	Special formation employed in sabotage and commando operations	Armed forces security, combatting espionage and treason, infiltration of foreign intelligence

foreign military intelligence in 1937. Good-natured and outgoing, he brought high intelligence to his work, along with dry humor and a vast fund of general knowledge that Canaris appreciated deeply. Wherever Piekenbrock's agents went, they took with them the miracle weapons of intelligence—Leica cameras able to penetrate fog or reduce images to a pinpoint.[61] In his straightforward and jovial way, Piekenbrock sometimes called his boss "Excellency," a designation appropriate to officers of the Imperial Army.[62] The two men had a friendly rapport and it was to "Piki" that Canaris spoke most freely.[63]

Abwehr II was in charge of sabotage, active protection against sabotage, and the training of command units for "special duties." It was headed from 1938 to 1939 by Major Helmuth Groscurth, a man of such obvious character and moral stature that, according to Abwehr section chief Leopold Bürkner, his hatred of the Nazis was written all over him. He had Canaris's complete confidence and Canaris teased that the conscientious "Muffel" was the perfect man for the Abwehr "because you always tell the truth, and in our business, nobody believes it."[64] Groscurth was a devout Christian with close ties to the *Bekennende Kirche,* or Confessional Church. He and Oster were the Abwehr officers who worked most actively to overthrow the Nazi regime, but Groscurth suffered considerably from his sense of conflicting duties. He left the Abwehr to take over commandos in France and later in Russia.[65] It was Groscurth, according to his successor Erwin von Lahousen, who "with Oster . . . undertook concrete preparations . . . to get rid of Hitler, with Himmler and Heydrich too, if possible, by assassination. . . . It was not Groscurth's fault that those plans were not realized. It was the indecisiveness and wavering on the part of some generals . . . at the highest levels of the Wehrmacht that was to blame."[66] As the military conflict escalated, the section grew and became more active.

Colonel Lahousen was an Austrian import, what was called a "war booty officer" after the *Anschluss.* Born in Vienna, he had served as a junior infantry officer in the imperial and royal army of Emperor Franz Joseph. After graduating from the Austrian War School for the general staff in the mid-1930s, he entered the Intelligence Department of the Austrian general staff as a Czech specialist. Soon his linguistic expertise brought him recognition as an authority on the Balkans. Bald, soft-spoken, and blessed with independent means, Lahousen epitomized the charming, cosmopolitan aristocrat—a far cry from the stiff and arrogant Prussian soldier stereotype Canaris despised.[67] He combined diligence with intelligence and at more than six feet, he was affectionately nicknamed "Long L" at headquarters.[68] Canaris trusted him completely and relied on his judgment and efficiency.[69]

Abwehr III engaged in counterspionage, countersabotage, and security, and worked to infiltrate foreign intelligence services. It was also charged with protecting German armed forces against infiltration, countering treason and espionage in civilian institutions. Major Rudolf Bamler, its head from 1933 until 1939, had boundless admiration for the Nazi regime and worked hard to establish close, friendly relations with the SD.[70] This caused many colleagues to regard him as the black sheep of the Abwehr. Canaris in fact tried to remove him from office, but when war began, Bamler removed himself, asking for a command on the eastern front.[71]

Canaris had known naval officer Leopold Bürkner since his days in Wilhelmshaven.[72] Despite major character differences they enjoyed good personal relations. Canaris found Bürkner personable and loyal, if inefficient. Beginning in 1938 Bürkner headed the Ausland branch, which put him in close contact with Karl Ritter of the Foreign Office and General Alfred Jodl at the Wehrmacht Operations Staff. Canaris disliked Ritter intensely, and regarded Jodl as a shameless Führer worshipper, but at least he could let Bürkner deal with them. Canaris described Bürkner as a "true-blue seaman and a rose-red optimist" who believed in the ultimate triumph of Germany and seemed blind to the threat Himmler and Heydrich posed to the Abwehr.[73]

CANARIS'S NAME IS SURROUNDED BY ALLEGATIONS OF COWARDLY TREASON AS WELL AS legends of brave opposition to the Nazi regime, with little room for agreement. Under his leadership the Abwehr became not only an instrument of the German war effort but also, surprisingly, something of an umbrella for forces fighting to bring down the Third Reich. Early in his tenure at the Abwehr, he set about feeding the Nazi machine only selected information, hoping this might tug the Führer's wildly risky foreign policy into a more acceptable shape. Some of Hitler's policies and all of his thugs appalled him.

Several conditions made such resistance within the Abwehr possible: The head of the Abwehr had relative autonomy in hiring decisions and policies. Military leaders of the old school often regarded secret intelligence services with either indifference or the disdain that Hindenburg had demonstrated. Furthermore, in the chain of command, the Abwehr was relatively independent of the OKW, which saw itself as politically neutral in any case, and was significantly less ardent about the regime than were the Party organizations. The Abwehr's decentralized organizational structure, and the fact that its individual sections and stations operated with a high degree of autonomy, also allowed pockets of dissent to form.

Allen W. Dulles, the station chief of the OSS in Bern, evaluated German intelligence after the war and found that only a few leading officers of the Abwehr belonged to the inner circle of the opposition to Hitler. "I don't want to give the impression that the entire Abwehr spent its time only conspiring against Hitler. Nothing would be further from the truth. Maybe 95 percent of the Abwehr gathered information and conspired against the Allies; about 5 percent of the staff, including some of the men at the top, were anti-Nazi and formed a loose network that supported the plotters."[74]

To this day the former offices of the Abwehr can be seen in central Berlin in the Bendlerblock, the heart of the old German military headquarters on what used to be known as the Tirpitzufer, overlooking the Landwehr Canal, and located not far from Berlin's biggest park, the Tiergarten.[75] Canaris's third-floor office was sometimes referred to as the Fox's Den, for its principal inhabitant, "the Old Fox"—Canaris himself. Not particularly old, but with hair gone prematurely white, he liked to sit in the dark, wood-paneled room, only a few scattered lamps casting pools of light across his papers.[76] A small cot served Canaris on many late nights. "It was a comfortable office and very much a refuge for many," recalled Captain Axel von dem Bussche-Streithorst, who spent time there in the company of others who shared Canaris's views.[77]

THE INTELLIGENCE WARS

Canaris had first met Heydrich in 1922, when he was first officer on the cruiser *Berlin* and Heydrich a raw cadet, an unpopular loner whose surprisingly high, bleating voice caused his shipmates to call him Ziege—"goat." The son of an opera singer and an actress, Heydrich was later cashiered from the navy for "conduct unbecoming," and was left with a vengeful, abiding hatred of the military. Disaffected, and one of many millions of Germany's unemployed, he had connected with Himmler in the summer of 1931 and mapped out for the later Reichsführer SS a security service after the Führer's own heart, with himself in charge.

Over time, Canaris and Heydrich developed a relationship as puzzling as the men themselves. As longtime neighbors, they played croquet in Heydrich's garden or dined chez Canaris, with a dinner prepared by Canaris himself, an excellent cook, complete with his chef's toque. They also enjoyed music making, for, surprisingly, the bloodless and arrogant Heydrich was a gifted violinist, a fact that endeared him to Canaris's wife, Erica, another music lover. When they played together, Mrs. Canaris observed that Heydrich "became soft and mild, had beautiful manners and marked musical sensitivity."[78]

The Canaris-Heydrich relationship endured, and was surely at least partly responsible for the relative lack of scrutiny to which the Abwehr might otherwise have been subjected. A number of the Abwehr's V-men— *Vertrauensleute*, or confidential informants—for instance, did not meet the requirements of the Nuremberg Laws on racial purity, and would almost certainly have been dismissed under other circumstances.[79] Predictably, the coexistence of military and civilian intelligence services resulted in constant competition and collisions on the division of responsibilities between the SD and the Abwehr. Canaris knew that the Abwehr would reap the benefits of Hitler's massive rearmament program only if he could keep it out of the crossfire. He also understood that his resources were stretched thin relative to the other great powers, and there was need for reform. He would continue Patzig's efforts to decentralize the bureaucratic behemoth; he would give individual officers more autonomy. The Abwehr would be more nimble, quicker to respond. It would become a power to be reckoned with.[80] Himmler, meanwhile, envisioned a central Reich police, free of administrative and legal constraints. Canaris was well aware that to keep the Abwehr out of their reach, he would have to reach some accommodation with Himmler, more particularly with his able and ambitious underling, Heydrich.

In 1935, SS microphones tapped into the Abwehr and Wehrmacht offices and the Nazi intelligence and police apparatus continued to press forward. By mid-1936, it was ready for the next move. Himmler became chief of German police and, as Reichsführer SS, was given ministerial rank on a par with Wehrmacht commanders in chief. Heydrich assumed control of the security police, including the Gestapo and criminal police, and now held in his hand the perfect tool for tyranny. Early in 1937, legal considerations were dispensed with, and orders went out to take "criminals or dangerous offenders against morality" and "anti-social malefactors" into what was termed "preventive custody," in concentration camps run by the SS.[81] The Nazi intelligence operation had acceded to unprecedented power over the ideological life of the nation. It was up to Canaris to rein it in and preserve the Abwehr's independence.

CANARIS KNEW WHAT HE WANTED, AND ARMED WITH PATZIG'S WARNING, HE KNEW HOW to go about getting it.[82] By December 21, 1936, he had in hand a document that became known as the Ten Commandments. Crafted by Canaris and SS lawyer Werner Best, it spelled out the respective responsibilities of the Abwehr and the SD. The Abwehr was to handle military espionage abroad and all proceedings with the Wehrmacht. Civil intelligence outside the scope of the Wehrmacht, such as treason and follow-up police action, were SD territory. Theoretically at least, the two forces had defined their borders. Heydrich called his underlings to Berlin: Full and frictionless cooperation with their Abwehr counterparts was the order of the day. In joint appearances with Canaris across Germany, total cooperation and the leadership role of the Abwehr were consistently emphasized.[83] Some Abwehr colleagues thought Canaris had ceded too much political influence to Heydrich, but it seemed he had won the first round in the intelligence wars.

CHAPTER 2

1933–1939

THE OTHER GERMANY

During the darkest years of her history, the "other Germany," the Germany of ordinary decent people, of thinkers, poets, farmers and shopkeepers and musicians, was a country that disappeared from the world's consciousness. Germany came to be seen only as a terrifying totalitarian monolith inhabited by monsters. In fact, Hitler's monolith was deeply divided, and within its confines the "other Germany," the better Germany, was trying to survive. Much of the opposition was concentrated in centers of power—the army, the diplomatic service, the Foreign Office. In a regime bereft of decency they struggled to become standard-bearers of decency and hoped for a return to universal, humanitarian principles. In this struggle, oddly enough, they faced enemies and a lack of understanding not only within, but also outside the Reich.

THE GREAT PRISON

In the early years of the Third Reich, some who later resisted the regime hoped that Hitler's takeover might bring renascence and stability to Germany after years of poverty and turmoil. Others felt from the first that a disaster had befallen their country. They sensed war in the offing and feared the worst. Some chose a life of exile and emigrated to Switzerland, France, or the United States, forming a kind of satellite opposition whose location outside the confines of the regime and its inescapable surveillance helped those who stayed to fight from within to make and maintain critical contacts with the outside world.

Just eight months after Hitler's takeover, a memorandum from Theodor Steltzer on conditions in Germany addressed to Kurt von Schuschnigg, later Austria's chancellor, voiced concern that the "deification of ideology" would lead to a cult of power and race; Steltzer appealed to Schuschnigg to take a stand.[1] By the mid-1930s Reinhold Schairer was living as an "exile" in London, where he was in contact with Robert Vansittart in the British Foreign Office. Schairer urged another prominent exile, Joseph Wirth, living in Switzerland, to write to Neville Chamberlain on behalf of what he called the *bürgerlich*—the middle-class—opposition and ask the British for support against Hitler to help "free the people who are victims of aggression."[2] Like messages in a bottle, word was already going out beyond Germany's borders in search of contacts and support in fighting off the Nazi menace.

During these years Hitler's terror stamped out any hope of a broad domestic resistance. The political resistance of the communists and socialists was wiped out and any remnants were driven deep underground. As an OSS report later pointed out, "Totalitarianism and a widespread underground are a contradiction in terms."[3] But this period also marked the beginnings of another kind of resistance, largely individual, unorganized, and in fact sometimes barely recognizable as resistance even by those involved. The repression and terror used to create the much-trumpeted Nazi *Volksgemeinschaft*—folk community—rather than bringing people together, had instead brought about a kind of social atomization among the opponents of the regime.

OPPOSITION TO A TOTALITARIAN REGIME IS A DOUBLE-EDGED SWORD; THERE IS NO COMfortable way to grasp it. If it takes the form of channeling information to the enemy, it is seen as collaboration and conjures up images of shaven heads heaped with popular scorn. If it takes the form of active resistance, the plotting and execution of a coup, for example, it is seen as treason. The German opposition to Hitler was trapped between a patriotic love of their country and hatred of a regime. For them, treason ultimately became an act of great courage for which most of them were rewarded with death.

The Nazi climate was not conducive to the rise of a popular resistance, but gradually, in the churches, within the military, in political and social groups, opposition took shape. Often it only took the form of a kind of mental distancing that became known as "inner emigration," but as the 1930s ground on, like-minded individuals found each other and dared to put their thoughts into words and gradually to plan and undertake action. Even before Hitler came to power, there were those who thought that he spelled catastrophe for Germany. By 1935, Helmuth von Moltke told his English friend Lionel Curtis that life had become profoundly isolating, but that even if his life were to be spent entirely in a small cell, he would try to maintain connections to the "greater world."[4]

Moltke, one of the many resisters condemned for having fought on what the SS referred to as the "internal battlefield," saw an extraordinary irony in his sentence: "In other countries suppressed by Hitler's tyranny even the ordinary criminal has a chance of being classified a martyr. With us it is different: Even the martyr is certain to be classed as an ordinary criminal."[5] Stauffenberg, the principal actor in the final, failed putsch of July 1944, understood perfectly that anyone who dared to take action would enter German history as a traitor. If he did not dare, however, he would be a traitor to his conscience.[6]

A bald recitation of figures—the number of nameless political prisoners included in a Gestapo tally of 1939—demonstrates that there was resistance in spite of the terror. By April of that year, 162,734 people were in preventive custody for political reasons; 27,369 were awaiting trial for political crimes; and 112,432 were under sentence. Over a six-year period, in the regular courts alone, 225,000 people were sentenced to an aggregate of 600,000 years in prison, and between 1933 and 1945, roughly three million Germans had spent time in a concentration camp or prison for political reasons, some briefly, some for the entire twelve years of the Thousand-Year Reich. About 800,000 of these had been involved in active resistance. Of the even more numerous cases—those held without trial or murdered outright—there is no accounting.[7]

The "great prison" was how one opposition member, Social Democrat Wilhelm Leuschner, described the Germany of the Hitler years. Operating within that great prison was not easy. Moltke enumerated some of the difficulties the opposition faced as "lack of unity, lack of communication, and lack of men." Accounting in part for Moltke's "lack of unity" was the fact that there was not one resistance but many.

Thus it is not the story of a movement, but of individuals who felt a moral imperative to step beyond garden-variety patriotism in the name of humanity, decency, and a higher code of justice. In searching for support, these people collected gradually in improvised groups, in circles that touched or overlapped occasionally. There were ideological differences, different expectations for Germany's future, and further splits along generational lines. Often they had little in common beyond strong religious beliefs and the conviction that things could not be allowed to go on as they were. Typically, the older, more conservative, and more hesitant generation was the product of the Wilhelmine age, accustomed to order, honor, impeccable manners. The younger generation was more activist, less averse to a violent solution, and pressed harder for a quick coup.

• • •

COMMUNICATION TOO, WAS A PERNICIOUS PROBLEM. THOSE WHO REFUSED EXILE AND stayed, but resisted imprisonment, found themselves in a quandary. The best way to fight the system was from within, and that meant leading a double life. Ernst von Weizsäcker, state secretary at the Foreign Office, was only one of many who labored under the strain of this schizophrenic existence. Tried at Nuremberg for working within the Nazi framework while trying to bring down the rafters, he told the court: "The story of what the Germans did for peace at that time will always be full of gaps insofar as the documents go."[8] A simple reading of the documents could never communicate the reality of what was happening. Nazispeak made it incomprehensible to anyone except the initiate, and even then it was important to consider how the sender would have tailored his message to the addressee—the verbal subterfuges involved in communicating without actually saying what you were saying. A dash at the end of a sentence for example, might indicate that the opposite was meant. Weizsäcker recalled using code even with his family, and Hassell used code names for virtually everyone mentioned in his diaries.

The army, the diplomatic corps, the intelligence service were the main sources of the opposition, and here issues of class, education, foreign connections, marriages, and family relationships played a significant part. Many opposition members had British or American wives and relatives. These were the people with access to information and in the best position to effect change. There were others, too, of course—socialists, industrialists, church leaders, communists, and the occasional loner. Given the oppressive rigidity of the regime, the possibilities for "resistance" were nearly endless, but breaking out of the "great prison" entailed huge risks. Almost invariably, fighting the sense of powerlessness that Hitler's terror had bestowed on any opposition involved a search for allies outside the walls.

THE SEARCH FOR ALLIES ABROAD

Hitler had been in power for only three months when Sir Horace Rumbold, then British ambassador to Germany, recognized the need for extraordinary vigilance among Germany's neighbors. Rumbold's alarms were echoed by another member of the Whitehall establishment, Sir Robert Vansittart, head of the Foreign Office since 1930. The concerns of these two Englishmen also preoccupied a significant number of well-placed Germans who had no illusions about Hitler's territorial ambitions, his lust for Lebensraum, and his willingness to make war to acquire it. In 1933, the Nazi march to totalitarianism was marked by, among other things, the dissolution of the Reichstag, the granting of police powers to the paramilitary SS and SA, the

Reichstag fire, the banning of demonstrations and of all political parties and trade unions, the Enabling Act, the boycott of Jewish shops, book burning, and Germany's withdrawal from the League of Nations. The parliamentary system was dismantled. Hitler's second year saw the disappearance of civil liberties and the Night of the Long Knives. A personal oath of loyalty to Hitler was demanded of members of the armed forces. Then came waves of arrests and the introduction of the Nuremberg Laws. One by one, Hitler abrogated the terms imposed by the Versailles Treaty. He rearmed and soldiers marched baldfaced into the Rhineland with no real protest from the Allies.

With each daring and successful move, the Führer's prestige climbed, and not only at home. A stream of distinguished visitors from France, England, and the United States came to pay their respects to the new Germany and its leaders. Lord Lothian, later British ambassador to the United States, came away from his visit in early 1935 very favorably inclined toward the regime. Moltke, then studying for the English bar, met with the recently returned Lothian briefly in England and found him cheerfully confident that Hitler was "sincerely anxious for peace."[9] In time, Lothian told the dubious Moltke, the Nazi regime would become respectable; making concessions now would help bring that respectability about. Besides, no regime change was feasible at the moment. Lord Halifax, a power at Whitehall and an avid hunter, had shown such obvious delight over his elaborate hunting expeditions with Göring that the Nazi newspapers hailed him as Hallali-fax.[10] The 1936 Olympics made a deep and lasting impression on visitors awed by the Nazi talent for choreographed spectacle; their letters and diaries bubbled with delighted descriptions of the extraordinary scene. Charles Lindbergh visited and went home outspokenly pro-Nazi, as was Henry Ford. The Duke and Duchess of Windsor, extravagantly entertained by the Nazi bigwigs, were commensurately impressed and not at all shy about expressing their admiration.

THE GERMAN OPPOSITION THAT WAS IN A POSITION TO DO SO LOOKED TO ENGLAND. They hoped to stiffen spines in Whitehall and nudge Britain into a stance firm enough to give Hitler pause. Moltke was often in England and had, he said, "driven some very important points into some equally important heads." Still, he worried that British appeasement would mislead Hitler into counting on British neutrality.[11] An emphatic no from England to Hitler's aggressive foreign policy would undermine Hitler's prestige, precipitate a crisis in the regime, and provide an opportunity to bring down from within a dictatorship that spelled disaster not only for Germany, but also for Europe and beyond.

By the time the crisis years of British-German diplomacy arrived in the later 1930s, the perspicacity and prophetic vision of Rumbold, then must needed, had been replaced by shortsightedness of Sir Nevile Henderson, who, as British ambassador to Germany, was apparently blinded to Hitler's true aims by the lights, the parades, the panoply of Nazi power. By then, Whitehall had changed, too.

Sir Robert Vansittart, head of the Foreign Office, was an unpopular figure at Whitehall. His labored memoranda on his pet topic—the Hitler threat—were not welcome among his colleagues. Both he and his antiappeasement message were received with a proverbial rolling of the eyes and his warnings went unheard He was thoroughly alienated, a situation of which Vansittart himself was painfully aware: "It seems that nobody will listen to me or believe me. I will never know why."[12] He had an enemy in Anthony Eden, then foreign secretary, and in late 1937, Chamberlain removed Vansittart from the direction of Foreign Office policy by shuffling him off to a previously nonexistent position—chief diplomatic advisor. "Van," with his many long-term German contacts, had recognized the opposition as a priceless source of impeccable intelligence that cost England nothing, and that might serve as an effective weapon against the bellicose Führer. But his words fell on deaf ears.[13]

He was replaced by Alexander Cadogan, whose conspicuous antagonism to the German opposition was exacerbated by the fact that Vansittart, now odd man out at the Foreign Office, continued to be their contact man. The first-rate intelligence from these sources was now routinely buried. Chamberlain was delighted to have sidelined Vansittart, and expected "that in Rome and Berlin rejoicings will be loud and deep."[14] Hitler may well have rejoiced, but among the opposition there was unease. They no longer had a "receptive ear" in the Foreign Office, which did not bode well for their cause.[15] Hitler, meanwhile, was taking every opportunity to consolidate his power.

CONSOLIDATING POWER, CRYSTALLIZING OPPOSITION

For a few hectic weeks in January 1938, Fräulein Erna Gruhn became a cause célèbre and something of a history maker when she became the bride of Hitler-anointed Field Marshal von Blomberg. Soon after the small wedding, graced by the presence of the Führer and Göring, it became known that not only was Fräulein Gruhn not of the appropriate class, but the new *Frau Feldmarschall* had a past. Highly placed officers in the Bendlerstrasse— the site of military headquarters—were receiving telephone calls from Berlin's ladies of the night offering congratulations on their former colleague's new status.[16] The officer corps was outraged; the Führer had been drawn unwittingly into a social catastrophe: Blomberg must go. The Himmler and Heydrich team, ever inventive, laid before Hitler fabricated evidence detailing the homosexual practices of Blomberg's logical successor, Colonel

General Werner von Fritsch. Hitler demanded Fritsch's resignation, which the nearly apoplectic Fritsch refused, demanding a court-martial. Bendler-strasse was again in an uproar. There was gnashing of teeth, and the hope that Fritsch would strike back. The next day was the Kaiser's birthday—a suitable occasion for a military coup—but instead, Fritsch docilely wrote out the requested resignation.

Hitler was always alert to any weakness in the enemy camp that might be used to enhance his own position, and Himmler and Heydrich had provided him perfect ammunition. He used the confusion and the Wehrmacht's lack of leadership and resolve to declare himself not only the new minister of war (replacing Blomberg), but also supreme commander of the Wehrmacht on February 4, 1938. The army was not only humiliated, but broken. In one stroke, the Fuhrer had rid himself of a large thorn in his side; the army was now simply another tool for furthering his aims. Levering himself into position as commander in chief of the Wehrmacht, Hitler was working to strip any potential challengers of their authority. There would be no one to stand in the way of his plans, military or political; he intended to do exactly as he pleased.

Again Hitler had triumphed, but this triumph would have unintended consequences. For the first time, the isolated and disparate oppositional elements within his Reich—generals, government ministers, young officers, businessmen, lawyers, churchmen, and police officials—began to coalesce into the outlines of what would become resistance. Hitler marched into Austria and orchestrated the Anschluss, then immediately turned his attention to Czechoslovakia, where he intended to take over the Sudetenland, populated largely by ethnic Germans. When the Czechs mobilized in response to his demands and saber rattling, Hitler was quick to take offense. France, Britain, and Russia were all committed in varying degrees to defending Czech neutrality, and in May they issued a concerted diplomatic warning.

It was a serious blow, not only to Hitler's amour propre, but to his popular support. His mood caromed from volcanic rage to inscrutable, brooding silences, and ten days later he announced Operation Green to his generals: It was his unalterable decision to crush Czechoslovakia by force, and soon; preparations were to be in place by October 1. The crystallizing civilian and military opposition had recognized the unmistakable value to their cause of the firm international rebuff in May. Hitler's setback brought them new focus and impetus. They set about enlisting the "greater world" to help bring an end to the hated regime.

DIALOGUES WITH THE DEAF

In the spring and summer of 1938, the trouble simmering over the Sudetenland had pushed General Ludwig Beck, chief of staff of the German army, to make his concerns known.[17] He felt duty-bound to warn Hitler of the dangers inherent in his aggressive plan. Beck was widely acknowledged as the "sovereign" of the military opposition and, to some extent, of the opposition as a whole.[18] A man of unshakable integrity, he was unquestionably a military man, but hardly the militaristic Prussian officer who stalked the British imagination. Deliberate and thoughtful, a gifted violinist with a strong philosophical bent, his reexamination of traditional loyalties in the raking light of Hitler's policies had led him to conclude that a soldier's duty to obey ended when his conscience forbade it.[19] In fact, this notion was entirely in keeping with the lessons of Carl von Clausewitz, Helmuth von Moltke, and other German military theoreticians. War, according to Clausewitz, entails innumerable unforeseeable situations that can be handled only by an officer trained and able to think and take decisions on his own.

For soldiers on all fronts of the opposition, the summer of 1938 was a season of almost frantic activity. The civilian and diplomatic opposition dispatched a parade of highly placed Germans with English connections to London to try to persuade the British political establishment that Hitler was an aggressive expansionist, set on war. Nothing would stop him; no appeasement or compromise would ever satisfy him. He was set on more, and a sharp reprimand was the only way to avoid an otherwise inevitable conflict.

The emissaries were repeatedly frustrated by Whitehall's refusal to hear them, or to believe that Hitler could not be trusted. The Foreign Office files bulge with examples of its unwillingness to extend a hand to these Germans hoping for support. Willem Visser't Hooft, the Dutch clergyman serving as head of the World Council of Churches, called these conversations between the German emissaries streaming to England in the late 1930s and the British politicians to whom they addressed their pleas "dialogues of the deaf." He knew the players on both sides and understood the tragedy that was unfolding.

Archconservative, aristocrat, and monarchist, Ewald von Kleist-Schmenzin was also a confirmed anti-Nazi. He had been scheduled for elimination in the wave of murders of June 30, 1934, but he had been warned by a fellow anti-Nazi—a communist. In August 1938—with an assist from Canaris, Beck's blessing, and a special request from Hans Oster—Kleist undertook a risky trip to England "with a rope around his neck," he said. His mission included discussions with Vansittart, Lord Lloyd, and Churchill, and his message was clear: Unless the British exhibited an unwavering and consistent unwillingness to compromise with Hitler, war was a certainty. The top German generals, Kleist reported, were anti-Hitler and dead set against war, nor was there much popular enthusiasm for either Hitler or for war. A well-timed diplomatic slap would set him back sharply, focus antiwar sentiment within Germany, and mark the beginning of his end. With the promise of a firm commitment from England and France, Beck and Oster would set the Führer's undoing in motion.

Kleist's message was relayed, but at the Foreign Office the feeling was that "there is something suspicious about anti-Nazis coming [to Britain] in fear for their lives, especially if they get away with it."[20] The implication was clear: If anti-Nazis were arrested and perhaps executed on their return to Germany, they might be considered more trustworthy. Chamberlain was reminded of the British supporters of James II going to France for help in overthrowing William of Orange. He felt that much of what Kleist said should obviously be discounted. British foreign policy circles were of the opinion that Czechoslovakia was not worth a war in any case, a consensus that played neatly into Chamberlain's policy of appeasement.[21]

In fairness, England was not ready for war; World War I had left a lasting mark, and the nation was not physically or psychologically prepared for another conflict. Chamberlain knew the military was woefully unprepared, and to him, as to many outsiders, it seemed that Hitler had restored order in Germany. In any case, he felt that German domestic issues should remain in Germany. He was confident that he could bring Herr Hitler around to "peace in our time," and neither the Führer's belligerence nor his ever-increasing demands could persuade him to stray from that path. Some "imaginative statesmanship" might well have saved the day, but this was not in Chamberlain's repertoire, so politics as usual was its familiar stand-in.[22] In Chamberlain's view, the best way to handle the situation would be to pressure the Czechs to knuckle under.

Churchill, then still a backbencher in the House of Commons, realized that there would be no official initiative, but gave a report of his meeting with Kleist to the Foreign Office and wrote a letter offering the words Kleist had hoped would come officially and publicly—from higher up.[23] With Cadogan golfing in France for the month of August and the prime minister in Scotland, shooting grouse, the German Foreign Office descended into despair. How could they jolt the vacationing British into action?

In Berlin, State Secretary Weizsäcker buttonholed Carl Burckhardt, the high commissioner of the League of Nations in Danzig who was en route to his home in Switzerland, pleading with him to go to the British representatives there. They must persuade London to scare Hitler out of his aggressive plans in plain, unequivocal language. They should send someone "not too high in rank. No Prime Minister, not some oh-so-polite Englishman of the old school . . . [but] perhaps some energetic General . . . with a riding crop." Hitler would understand someone who could shout and pound on the table. If Chamberlain came, Weizsäcker insisted, "the louts will triumph."[24] In Burckhardt's words, Weizsäcker "was conspiring with a potential enemy [to] preserve the peace—a double game of the utmost peril."[25]

During the 1930s, the Auswärtiges Amt, or AA, the German Foreign Office, always a bastion of the establishment, had resisted Hitler's relentless nazification and reorganization. State Secretary Weizsäcker and those who worked with him shared an anti-Nazi stance, but also the daily tightrope walk demanded of those working against the regime from within. Weizsäcker, with a crew of like-minded men, many of them younger and calling themselves the "circle of friends," managed to establish the Foreign Office as a conduit of up-to-date information to Whitehall on the where and when of Hitler's plans. Their story was always the same: If Whitehall would deal Hitler a stinging diplomatic defeat, this would provide the opportunity for a successful coup; otherwise Hitler would start a war for which Germany was unprepared, to which much of his military was opposed, for which a war-weary German people had no enthusiasm, and which no sensible person wanted.

As secretary to Joachim von Ribbentrop, then Hitler's ambassador to London, Erich Kordt had formed a close relationship with Vansittart. When Ribbentrop was appointed foreign minister in 1938, he took Kordt back with him to Berlin, and Erich's place in London was taken by his brother Theo. The brothers, both staunch anti-Nazis, had been recruited for the resistance by Canaris in the mid-1930s. In their respective roles, Erich as the head of Ribbentrop's secretariat, and Theo as counselor in London, they formed a direct communications link from the innards of one government to the innards of another. Under Weizsäcker's guardianship, they were essential to the opposition's efforts. The family connection made it somewhat easier for them to meet and communicate without arousing undue suspicion, but personal visits were not always feasible. Ever mindful of the Gestapo, they sometimes asked their cousin Susanne Simonis, to memorize long, detailed messages and serve as their courier. Then, decked out to look as hopelessly German as possible to British eyes, she traveled to London to report to her cousin.

But it was not only the German diplomatic community that was struggling for a hearing from the British Foreign Office. Carl Goerdeler had served under Chancellor Heinrich Brüning, and later under Hitler as Reich price commissioner. From 1930 to 1937 he was mayor of Leipzig, but resigned in protest over Nazi policies against Jews and the Christian church. An activist, and one of the major motivators of the anti-Hitler opposition, he worked tirelessly to establish contacts with the British. His early contacts with Vansittart had been agreeable and promising, but much of the Foreign Office questioned his integrity. Goerdeler was rooted in the German imperial tradition, and they suspected that while the means differed, he was essentially pursuing the same ends as Hitler.

In 1936, Goerdeler had prepared a report in cooperation with the so-called Langnamverein on the state of German industry, particularly in regard to military capacity, detailing the lack of military preparedness. In July 1937, this Langnam Report had found its way to Vansittart, in whose hand a terse "Suppressed by Eden" is written across the top of the file.[26] Vansittart was also hearing from Captain Malcolm Christie, whose unparalleled contacts in German industry, finance, and the military were telling him that, barring a strong deterrent statement from France and Britain, Hitler intended to take Czechoslovakia in the fall. Christie's reports were corroborated by Philip Conwell-Evans, whose ties to Ribbentrop put him close to the center of Nazi power. Through Erich Kordt, he was aware of the truth behind the Nazi façade, which he relayed regularly to Vansittart, but by this time, the Foreign Office routinely discounted any information that came from "Van." Ambassador Henderson, called to London to discuss Hitler's intentions, told the ministers that information on Hitler's posture was coming from members of the opposition who were probably not privy to the facts.[27]

From August to December 1937, Goerdeler traveled extensively in the United States. His trip had been arranged by a "conservative democratic" organization associated with the Episcopal Church that stood close to Roosevelt and had ties to both General Motors and U.S. Steel. Most important, it meshed neatly with Goerdeler's own views.[28] He relied on private contacts, British historian John Wheeler-Bennett among them, and former German chancellor Heinrich Brüning, then living in the States, also tried to smooth his path. Goerdeler had no political mandate on his visit, but his itinerary included much politics and many speeches. While he made no secret of his disdain for the Nazis, he was greeted with suspicion. George Messersmith, of the State Department, suspected that he was traveling on behalf of Hjalmar Schacht and conservative leaders.[29] Goerdeler warned against underestimating a "state of anarchy, lawlessness, moral corruption, economic fantasy, and financial carelessness" in Germany, but he was not heard.[30]

It was clear that Chamberlain intended to preserve the peace, whatever the cost, and Czechoslovakia was not too big a price to pay. He had a plan up his sleeve: The Sudeten crisis would be resolved by "Plan Z," a man-to-man meeting with the fractious Herr Hitler. He would rely on his personal diplomatic charm, and if that entailed flying back and forth at Hitler's whim, so be it. "If at first you don't succeed," quipped one wag, "fly, fly again."

THE GENERALS' PLOT: "EXTRAORDINARY TIMES, EXTRAORDINARY MEASURES"

Relatively early in Hitler's reign, on August 2, 1934, the army had been required to take a sacred oath of unconditional obedience, not to the nation, its constitution, or its people, but "to the Führer of the German Reich and

People, Adolph Hitler."[31] Every soldier was to be prepared to lay down his life for this oath. Beck described that day as the blackest day of his life. The modern, more cynical reader may find it difficult to understand how great an obstacle this oath was to the military opposition, but many of them held firm religious principles, and an oath sworn before God was not to be broken lightly—if at all. Its significance cannot be overstressed.

Beck still hoped to deter Hitler by reason. He warned that a thrust into Czechoslovakia would precipitate a broader war that Germany could not sustain. He labored over carefully considered memoranda to persuade Hitler and General Walther von Brauchitsch, who had succeeded Fritsch as commander in chief of the army, of the folly of aggression by force of reason. Brauchitsch was also critical of Hitler's aggressive policies, but he was to become the eternal vacillator of the opposition, hesitating on the threshold of action, willing perhaps, but also weak-willed.

As Beck lost faith in reasoning with Hitler, he began sounding out the generals. A mass resignation among the general staff might bring the Führer to his senses. If it did not, there would have to be a concerted, meticulously planned, military effort to effect a coup. Instigating an impetuous revolt was not Beck's way, but he had concluded that "extraordinary times demand extraordinary measures."[32] If the Führer gave the order to invade Czechoslovakia, he would be seized. Were he to cave in to Allied pressure, he would no longer be seen as invincible, which would create an opportune moment for a coup. Goerdeler and Colonel Oster offered emphatic support.

At this juncture, assassination was not being considered. Beck and many others were opposed to murder on religious grounds; not only was it a poor foundation for a new government, but it also ran the risk of enshrining the Führer as a martyr. This was anathema to them. Hitler should be brought to justice and made to atone for his crimes. Some controversy on this issue persisted, but meanwhile Beck and Oster put their heads together to prepare a speech for Brauchitsch, urging the generals to stand behind the protest. Brauchitsch would be pressed hard.

By early August, the generals of the Bendlerstrasse were agreed, and most senior officers supported Beck's assessment: It was time to act. But Brauchitsch wavered, and Beck, confronted first by Hitler's hysteria, then by his calm refusal to consider any arguments, decided that he had no choice but to resign. Hitler was well aware of Beck's enormous prestige and reputation. If his resignation were made known, the repercussions might erode morale on the eve of his Czech move. Hitler refused to allow the resignation to be made public until after the Sudetenland takeover, and this tactic seriously blunted the effect of Beck's dramatic gesture. Beck was without illusions; war would be with the world always, but he would now devote his energies to fighting Hitler and preserving peace.

His successor as army chief of staff was General Franz Halder, next in line for the appointment, a dedicated officer of deep religious principles and with ties to Oster and Weizsäcker. If Hitler had any reservations about Halder, there would have been few options. Not only were qualified officers in very short supply, but he was in no mood for more controversy with his general staff. It would only interfere with the speedy execution of his plans. In any event, the notion of resistance within his officer corps was inconceivable. Halder would do.

Halder was no Beck, but as a firm opponent of Hitler he was thoroughly engaged in the plans percolating through the various circles of resistance. In planning for the coup, Beck and Oster knew that General Erwin von Witzleben, commander of the army in the Berlin area, could be counted on. So could Wolf Heinrich von Helldorf, the chief of Berlin police. Walter von Brockdroff-Ahlefeldt, commander of the famous Potsdam division, was also in. Hjalmar Schacht, president of the Reichsbank, and Hans Bernd Gisevius of the Abwehr were working out details, with help from Arthur Nebe of the SS criminal division.

The plan was to occupy major communications centers—the post office, telegraph, telephone and radio. The SS had to be dealt with and the Reich Chancellery and critical ministries would have to be brought under control, all of which demanded the cooperation of numerous generals and military units. What precisely would happen after the Chancellery had been isolated and stormed and the Führer seized was not entirely clear. Halder preferred the idea of Hitler's meeting with an "accident" to outright assassination, as a safeguard against civil unrest. Dohnanyi, who had been collecting documentation of Nazi crimes for years, was already preparing for a trial. Goerdeler weighed in on elections, a new government, a new constitution. Plans were moving forward; tension was high. The excitement at the prospect of a successful coup that would save Germany from Hitler was barely controllable.

On September 7, 1938, Theo Kordt crept through the garden gate to 10 Downing Street for a secret meeting with Halifax. His cousin Simone had relayed an anxious message from his brother Erich and Weizsäcker: Time was short. The British must make it clear to the German nation that Hitler's aggression would bring war. In cooperation with England, they hoped to "prevent the greatest crime . . . ever committed."[33] If Hitler persisted, Kordt said that the circles he represented would—and here he quoted Hamlet— "take arms against a sea of troubles, and by opposing end them."

In mid-September the pillars of the British Foreign Office were back in London and the Führer's heady rush after the Party rally of the fourteenth and fifteenth was beginning to subside. Hitler was due to return to Berlin, and, in Oster's words, "the bird would be back in the cage." Everything was ready. When Hitler gave the order to march against Czechoslovakia, Halder, as chief of staff, would be the first to know and would give the signal to launch the coup. Then came word that Hitler, rather than returning to Berlin, was going to Berchtesgaden. Chamberlain was to meet him there.

After the frenetic pace and tensions of the covert preparations, the conspirators were brought up short. Doubt alternated with despair. Beck, the calm voice of reason, insisted that little had changed, and, indeed, Paul Otto Schmidt, Hitler's interpreter, informed them that Hitler's demands were sure to be unreasonable and unacceptable to Chamberlain.[34] The hope that had flagged, revived. But apparently the only spine that had been stiffened over that summer of repeated efforts was Hitler's. Chamberlain acceded to his demand; Hitler could have the Sudetenland.

When the British prime minister flew back to Germany on September 22 to formalize the agreement, he found that Hitler had upped the ante; the Sudetenland would not be his "last territorial demand" after all.[35] Furthermore, there were questions of borders and a plebiscite; failing an agreement by September 28, at 2:00 P.M., the Wehrmacht would march into Czechoslovakia. He would go to war on October 1.

On the twenty-sixth, the firm ultimatum the opposition had been urging for so long was delivered at last. If Hitler marched into Czechoslovakia, France, England, and Russia would fight. Next day, Hitler delivered a rabid speech. Panzers rolled past the Reich Chancellery at dusk, ostensibly to rouse excited throngs to war fever. But one observer, William L. Shirer, in Berlin as a correspondent for CBS, noted in his diary that the rush-hour crowd was sullen and "refused to look on, and the handful that did stood . . . in utter silence. . . . It has been the most striking demonstration against war I've ever seen. . . . They were dead set against war."[36]

Hitler was livid but determined, and war seemed inevitable after all. The Czechs were unwilling to compromise, the French were mustering divisions, the Maginot Line was being manned, and the British fleet was being mobilized. The conspirators were on high alert, even Brauchitsch. The moment was at hand, the tension nearly unbearable. Late on the morning of the twenty-eighth Mussolini dispatched his ambassador, Bernardo Attolico, to Hitler; Britain had asked the Italian dictator to intervene in the crisis. Faced with an unequivocal Allied response, Hitler hesitated, then decided to postpone his own mobilization for a day. As Witzleben arrived at Halder's office to receive orders to begin the putsch, word came that Chamberlain and French premier Edouard Daladier were flying to Munich to talk with Hitler the next day.

Hitler no longer had to back off; Chamberlain was doing it for him. The sense of anticlimax was staggering. Halder collapsed at his desk in tears of frustration. He testified later at Nuremberg that he had rescinded the order for the putsch because "now came Mr. Chamberlain, and with one stroke the danger of war was averted . . . the critical hour for force was avoided."[37]

On the eve of Munich, Goerdeler telephoned the British Foreign Office, imploring intransigence: "Don't give away another foot. Hitler is in a most uncomfortable position . . . keep the responsibility for any use of force on his shoulders. The [mood] against Hitler and his henchmen has risen remarkably during the last few days."[38]

Within Germany, anti-Nazi groups listened tensely to the 1938 radio broadcasts on the negotiations over Czechoslovakia with alternating relief, disbelief, and despair. Helmuth von Moltke, wrote to his wife from England that though he was only "an onlooker . . . that is nerve-wracking enough because the principles which are at stake are the ones which make life in Europe tolerable. If they get thrown overboard, one will have to get out as quickly as possible. . . . I cannot believe that Chamberlain is seriously considering a partition of Czechoslovakia."[39]

At Munich Hitler was granted the immediate occupation of the Sudetenland, the plebiscite he had demanded—which never took place—and a rearrangement of Czech borders in favor of Poland and Hungary. The firm ultimatum had been neither firm, nor lasting. The moment for a coup had passed. From across the Atlantic President Roosevelt cabled Chamberlain: "Good Man!"[40] A few days later, Ulrich von Hassell noted in his diary that Chamberlain had told the British: "It's all right this time." Then Hassell added that "the world—though in Germany only those who have heard news other than the official German news reports—would be left with a very bitter taste in their mouth, and the hatred of Hitler's methods must cut deep."[41]

Many Germans felt that the country had not had much of a breather since 1914. There had been widespread resentment of Hitler's rush to new hostilities and of the deprivation that would surely follow. The people realized that they had Chamberlain to thank for their rescue, and they saw him as a savior.[42] Patricia Meehan details reports from British consuls all over Germany attesting to the antiwar sentiment among the people, and resentment of Hitler and the Party for having so recklessly brought them to the brink. People rushed out in the morning to buy British newspapers and openly declared that Hitler was mad. At one British consulate, two poorly dressed Germans had arrived early one morning to present an expensive bouquet of flowers as a token of gratitude.[43]

But the opposition knew that this latest appeasement would not stop Hitler any more than the others had. His reckless ultimatum had provided a perfect opportunity to bring him down with minimal domestic unrest, and such an opportunity was unlikely to present itself again. Quite literally at the last minute, a stroke of the pen had robbed them of a singular chance to rescue Germany from Hitler. They were stunned, disbelieving, paralyzed. "The impossible had happened," wrote Hans Bernd Gisevius of the Abwehr; "our revolt was done for." A few days after the putsch-that-was-not, he, Schacht, and Oster gathered gloomily, "sat around Witzleben's fireplace, and tossed our lovely plans and projects into the fire. We spent the rest of the evening meditating, not on Hitler's triumph, but on the calamity that had befallen Europe."[44]

"WE HAVE SAVED HITLER AND HIS REGIME"

Munich had inadvertently foiled the military plot under Beck and Oster, but Hitler took a critical lesson from it: The Allies would not stand in his way. When he wanted the Sudetenland, it had been delivered to him, and though Munich had deprived him of a glorious triumphal march into Prague, he planned to remedy that soon by taking what he called the "rump" of Czechoslovakia by force. From Munich, Chamberlain brought back his famous piece of paper with its empty promises. Ambassador Henderson had no sympathy whatsoever for the Czechs and saw Munich as a highly desirable solution to the recent tensions. In early October he wrote Foreign Secretary Lord Halifax from Berlin with evident satisfaction that "by keeping the peace, we have saved Hitler and his regime."[45]

The long-simmering crisis over Czechoslovakia was settled at last. There would be no war, or so it appeared to the British. To the German opposition things looked quite different. Everything seemed to be conspiring to fuel the notion of Hitler's infallibility, particularly in his own mind, but also among others. Goerdeler summed up the opposition's sense of desperate disappointment and fear for the future: Had the warnings been heeded, Germany would have been free of her dictator, able to begin shaping a lasting peace and to look forward to a government of decent men and economic and social cooperation. "By refusing to take a small risk, Chamberlain has made war inevitable. Both the British and the French nations will now have to defend their freedom with arms."[46]

Chamberlain's appeasement also had its critics in the later British parliamentary debate on the Munich Pact. Munich, said Churchill, was just "the first foretaste of a bitter cup."[47] He was shouted down. Lord Lloyd, a leading Conservative and formerly a government minister, had met with Kleist in August and had reported Kleist's warning that Hitler planned to take Czechoslovakia one way or another in September. He later commented: "When the pre-war records are opened on the origins of the war, it will be found that the intelligence given was accurate and ample, the opinions sound, and the warnings—though given—were by no means always followed. Why could we not gather our courage in our hands?"[48] Meanwhile, on the other side of the water, the opposition forces regrouped.

A MIGHTY FORTRESS

Hitler's assault on the churches had begun almost immediately after he seized power. He required a church that was subservient to the state, and

very quickly the churches had found themselves engaged in border skirmishes. When the skirmishes turned into territorial warfare, the so-called
Kirchenkampf—Church Dispute—it was not the institutions that protested;
the churches preferred to limit themselves to the spiritual realm, leaving
political debate to others. But individual churchmen began to speak out
against the Nazis.

One such individual was a young, engaging submarine veteran of World
War I, Pastor Martin Niemöller, who had arrived to preach at St. Anne's in
Berlin's posh Dahlem district in 1931. His flock included several members
of the later opposition—General Kurt von Hammerstein–Equord, Oster, Canaris, and others—and by mid-1933, he was protesting Hitler's nazification
of the church. Initially Hitler was wary of alienating the power of the international church, but he soon began to move against the dissenters.

Niemöller and Bishop Theophil Wurm of Württemberg called together a
synod at Barmen in 1934 that brought into being the so-called Confessing
Church, uniting oppositional elements of the Evangelical Church.[49] As the
regime's oppression of both Jews and the church shifted into a high gear in
1935, a planned protest from all pulpits of the Confessing Church brought
mass arrests. More than seven hundred pastors were arrested in Prussia
alone, and when the criticism of the regime and state-sanctioned anti-
Semitism did not stop, concentration camp populations began to swell
with men of the cloth of all denominations, Niemöller among them.[50]

Young Dietrich Bonhoeffer had defined his position on the Nazis even
before they came to power, and while still in his twenties became an early
and articulate leader of the younger members of the Confessing Church. As
one of many children in a remarkable family of thinkers and—as it turned
out—resisters, he was made of stern intellectual stuff.[51] He had traveled
widely in the late 1920s and early 1930s, and on his return to Germany he
found a situation that depressed him enormously. The founder and guiding
light of a seminary that was closed by the Nazis in 1937, Bonhoeffer concluded that his duty as a responsible Christian lay in engaging in the
worldly sphere to fight evil, and by force if necessary. He reasoned that in
the Nazi state, "treason" had become true patriotism, and ordinary "patriotism" was treason.[52] Bonhoeffer joined his brother and his brother-in-law,
Hans von Dohnanyi in resistance work.

The Concordat between Hitler and the Vatican, signed in July 1933, ostensibly guaranteed no Nazi interference with the Catholic Church or its
organizations, and for a time, effectively blocked resistance within the
Catholic Church in Germany. But almost immediately, Hitler began to
push: He forbade all except strictly liturgical Catholic organizations and
functions; parochial schools were shut down; the Catholic press was silenced or went underground, and Josef Goebbels turned his propaganda
machine against the Catholic community.

Now individual voices spoke out: Munich's Cardinal Michael von Faul-haber, Bishop Konrad von Preysing of Berlin, who also worked with the later opposition, and Bishop Clemens von Galen, whose blistering ser-mons, particularly against the Nazi euthanasia program earned him the sobriquet "the Lion of Münster." There were other lone voices, such as lay-man Erich Klausner, who mustered large Catholic rallies and paid for his opposition with his life.

In March 1937, Pius XI issued his encyclical *Mit Brennender Sorge*, With Burning Anxiety—expressing his worry over Hitler's heedless breaking of the terms of the Concordat, his abuse of Catholics, and his utter disregard for Christian values and human rights. Smuggled into Germany, the en-cyclical's text was printed and distributed secretly. Hitler went on a ram-page. The hidden presses were hunted down and many hundreds of people were shipped off to camps. In spite of the repression, the German Catholic community cohered and held massive rallies. Swiss theologian Karl Barth concluded, however, that in the end, the Protestant "trumpet" had sounded a "clearer tune" and done more to fight the Hitler menace than had the Vatican.[53]

Of necessity, the Protestant fight gradually moved beyond German borders and its trumpet sounded in Switzerland, England, Norway, and Sweden. Willem Visser't Hooft recognized that there had arisen in Eu-rope "what might be called the theology of Resistance." His ecumenical organization in Geneva, the World Council of Churches, became a kind of clearinghouse for the resistance, the struggle he later characterized as "the war behind the war."[54] George Bell, bishop of Chichester, had come to know Bonhoeffer when the young man spent time in England, and he became a vocal champion of the German resistance. Bell met with Carl Goerdeler, and with Bonhoeffer in Sweden; he learned details about plots and leaders, which he duly forwarded to Eden. Was it right, he asked, to ignore or discourage "men in Germany also ready to wage war against the monstrous tyranny of the Nazis."[55] But his cause was not popular. Eden found Bell a constant irritant and referred to him as "this pestilent priest."[56] The archbishops of Canterbury and York, Archbishop Erling Ei-dem of Sweden, Bishop Eivind Berggrav of Oslo, all became involved with the resistance and provided a hearing for resistance members with a need to bear witness, to find support and nurture in what for them had became a desperate spiritual struggle. In other venues they were not heard, but within the ecumenical circle they could still engage in a dia-logue. When England became inaccessible, the stream of emissaries who had previously sought contact there traveled to Sweden to try to main-tain contact with the outside world and find hope and help for their cause.

CIRCLES OF RESISTANCE

Through the Wednesday Club, a small gathering of thinkers, academics, and politicians, General Beck was in contact with resisters outside the military and the Abwehr. Chief among them was Ulrich von Hassell, a distinguished old-school diplomat who had served as ambassador to several countries, most recently in Rome. When Ribbentrop was named foreign minister, Hassell had been withdrawn, but he was a political heavyweight and his diaries of the Hitler years remain an invaluable insider's view of conditions in Germany and within the resistance. In a deeply discouraged diary entry of October 1937, he wondered whether there was any way to preserve the truly sound and hopeful for the future, and shield from the pervasive evil, asking: "Can one still get one's head out through the unyielding wire mesh that has been flung over the entire nation?"[57]

Another moving force in the opposition was Carl Goerdeler, whose leadership role was the civilian equivalent to Beck's military leadership, Goerdeler had made his position clear early on. When the Nazis removed a statue of Felix Mendelssohn from a town square during his tenure as mayor of Leipzig, he had resigned in protest. Now, through Robert Bosch, a South German industrialist, Goerdeler was being provided with the financing and cover that allowed him to travel freely, proselytizing and enlisting contacts for his anti-Nazi cause. A devout Christian with unassailable faith in the power of reason and goodwill, Goerdeler was not encapsulated within any particular circle, but moved about as a free agent, pulling together wholly disparate oppositional elements and personalities, trying to get them all to march to the same drummer. He refused to take notice of divisions and difficulties among the opposition. After all, they were working toward a common end. As a conservative product of Germany's east, he was unable to distance himself from certain territorial goals. He was committed to the return to Germany of Danzig and the Polish Corridor, for instance. These goals invariably aroused Allied suspicions and almost certainly impeded the "ties to the whole world" he worked so ardently to establish.[58] But he was an indefatigable optimist, writing and traveling tirelessly, and bending every available ear to marshal support for his aim: ridding the world of Hitler.

The Abwehr's Canaris's reputation as a master spy was legendary. Besides his native German, he spoke French, English, Spanish, Portuguese, and Russian. His extensive, almost continuous travels made him extremely well informed on foreign policy and gave him an extraordinary range of foreign contacts from which the Abwehr benefited enormously. His section heads relied on his clear, unembellished reports on the political situation. But Canaris drew the line at assassinating Hitler and interfered only rarely in domestic politics, where the Abwehr in fact had no brief. He limited his resistance to throwing sand into the works of the Nazi machine and acting as guardian angel to the active resistance within his Abwehr. He made the arrangements that allowed other opposition members to travel and cloaked his passive resistance in the appearance of extraordinary activity and busyness while actually doing as little of what the Nazis required as possible. A reluctant, even slipshod administrator, even his most sympathetic chronicler admits that, "in political matters that were not his immediate responsibility, Canaris acted rarely, hesitantly, or evasively," hoping only to avert the worst.[59] This might be interpreted as indecision or irresponsibility, but it surely reflected his trademark fatalism: "He developed a blend of ruthlessness, apathy, and fatalism: let whatever must happen, happen."[60] Under the bushy brows and a thatch of hair gone prematurely white, his eyes had a veiled weariness. An apparently imperturbable workaholic with a legendary soft spot for animals, he "lived behind the scenes."[61]

STATE SECRETARY ERNST VON WEIZSÄCKER AND OTHERS IN THE GERMAN FOREIGN Office stepped up efforts to raise external support, particularly in Britain, where, as often as not, Hitler was seen as a leader who had overcome unemployment and disorder in Germany. The British also felt that German problems ought to remain in Germany. In London the continued pleas for firmness from German emissaries were an ongoing annoyance, particularly now that time had proved them right about Hitler's aims in Czechoslovakia. But an end to appeasement was not yet in sight. In looking forward to 1939, the British Foreign Office concluded that "promoting further territorial changes in Germany's favor might be advantageous." If Germany still intended to acquire "further territory at the expense of her neighbors or of other European states," Cadogan suggested initiatives to indicate that if more Lebensraum were needed, "she could always seek it in the Ukraine."[62]

In early 1939, when Philip Conwell-Evans, Group Captain Malcolm Christie, and MI-5 all reported that Hitler was determined to take whatever he wanted of Czechoslovakia, the usual departmental rivalries impeded not only the flow but, more important, the use of critical information on Germany's financial condition and war preparedness. Cadogan complained that he now suspected anyone who "came to raise my hair with tales of Germany going into Czechoslovakia in the next forty-eight hours. . . . This can wait."[63]

It did not wait for long. At roughly six-month intervals, Hitler broke one agreement after another. The opposition knew he would not be stopped, and the Abwehr soon alerted the plotters to his plans for the rest of Czechoslovakia. Despairing or not, they did not give up but began fanning the flames again. The civilian opposition tried to persuade the generals that this time, England and France really *would* intervene. The machinery of the 1938 coup was dusted off, and even the hesitant Halder agreed that if war were declared, he would oust Hitler.

Yet Hitler's next Czech landgrab, in March 1939, elicited only muted Allied protest. No war was declared, and he remained unchecked. Hitler was jubilant; he had seen his enemies and they were "worms." His confidence in his political prowess and the successes to come was boundless, overweening. He had reason to crow; he had pulled it off again. He now had his eye on the vast agricultural plain of Poland, a vision he did not immediately share with his generals. After that, the world—but first he would take Belgium, Holland, and France, Denmark and Norway. Goerderler summed up the peculiar position in which the opposition found itself just after the Czech takeover: As a German, he argued, he ought to rejoice to see Germany's power and Lebensraum growing. But he knew that Hitler was "poison," and the world's future would be governed not by justice, reason, and decency, but by naked force.

AFTER THE SCANDAL MANUFACTURED TO OUST FRITSCH IN EARLY 1938, HITLER HAD emasculated the Wehrmacht by naming himself commander in chief and set about trying to eviscerate what remained of the army's authority. He would brook no argument; there would be only complete obedience and aggressive determination. The OKH was populated largely with the old officer elites Hitler despised. He dismissed several generals, and among those who remained, there was wavering and doubt. He had proven them wrong in their disagreement and doomsaying over his past political chicanery, and army opposition circles were at loggerheads.

Many core military units had been dispersed. The earlier drive to depose Hitler had waned among some of the military opposition. Hitler had been right again and again. His successes had caused his popularity to skyrocket, and ousting him now would be foolishness, risking serious civil unrest. No one wanted a civil war. The SS had extended its reach with serious incursions into the army. Witzleben was organizing a long-range plan, but it was far from ready. Some generals were convinced that there was leeway for a coup only if war was actually declared. For the military opposition, there were also other reasons to hesitate.

THE COMING DISASTER

"At no time . . . did individuals fight as they did that summer of 1939 to avert the coming disaster," wrote the Abwehr's Hans Bernd Gisevius of the frantic efforts in which the entire spectrum of the opposition had become engaged.[64] The major civilian forces again took the initiative. The renewed resistance diplomacy was aimed at gaining time, time to recreate conditions favorable for a coup. The British, to their dismay, were again being asked to stand firm, this time to stave off an attack on Poland. Both Britain and France were sworn to intervene on behalf of Poland, but absent a British-Soviet pact, a British force was unlikely to come to Poland's rescue via the Baltic. In June, Erich Kordt pressed the British to conclude the Anglo-Russian pact already in the works as quickly as possible since it might be a serious deterrent. If Russia joined the Allies, the German generals, already feeling that the country was unprepared for war, could argue with some conviction that a war on two fronts was truly unsustainable. But Hitler was also pursuing a pact with the Soviets, and in fact, the German-Soviet nonaggression pact, including a clause agreeing to the partition of Poland, was signed on August 23.

Lieutenant Colonel Gerhard von Schwerin, head of the military intelligence on Britain and the United States, had told the British assistant military attaché, Major Kenneth Strong, that Hitler did not understand words, only deeds. To him, the Munich agreement was merely a scrap of paper, and while the army had not been behind Hitler at Munich, they now had no choice but to support him. Britain should begin conscription, Schwerin told Strong, to deter "the small clique of primitive beings now ruling Germany."[65] On a visit to London in the spring of 1939, he made several urgent recommendations: The British should stage a demonstration of naval power; Churchill should join the Cabinet; the British Air Striking Force should be stationed in France.[66] To the Foreign Office his words smacked of "gross treasonable disloyalty," and were treated as such.[67]

In the late spring, Canaris sent Fabian von Schlabrendorff to England to warn Churchill and others of the impending invasion of Poland and to alert them to the existence of a true opposition. Schlabrendorff, a young lawyer, was only one of many in the opposition who had British connections. Another emissary was Adam von Trott zu Solz, of the German Foreign Office, descended on his mother's side from the distinguished early American statesman and jurist, John Jay. As a Rhodes scholar, Trott had spent considerable time at Oxford in the early 1930s, and his charm, brains, and personal magnetism had won him many good friends. When Trott chose to return to Germany after the Hitler takeover, some of his English friends could not understand his need to return to fight for the survival of his country. Some had abandoned him, but he still had many connections in influential circles, and he traveled constantly, trying to enlist any and all in the cause. He had strong ties to Moltke, and within the opposition he came to be regarded as "the Foreign Minister."

Trott now went to England warning that revolt within was possible only if the powers without made it absolutely clear that Hitler's next move would mean war. But he found that in the new post-Czech takeover period, many English friends and acquaintances were regarding Germans and Nazis as one and the same. Still, Viscount and Lady Nancy Astor, the parents of David Astor, his friend from Oxford days, provided the venue for a high-powered dinner. Seated between Lord Lothian and Halifax, Trott had ample opportunity to explain his hopes and fears to the political establishment. Lord Astor also arranged a meeting with Chamberlain that left the prime minister sanguine about future mediation. Trott was deeply encouraged and excited, feeling that his complex message had not gone unheard. Yet his visit left lingering questions which his association with the Foreign Office did nothing to dispel. He might, after all, be Ribbentrop's agent. Or perhaps, appearances notwithstanding, an increasingly antiappeasement Britain saw him as a possible appeaser. Whatever the case, in the end, in spite of his perfect English and blue-ribbon contacts, he achieved no more than those who came before or after him.

A time line of the movements of the various members of the opposition that summer is a complicated business. Moltke, Goerdeler, and Kordt also crossed the channel. Hjalmar Schacht met with Montagu Norman of the Bank of England several times in Switzerland to ask him to take the message home to London. Ulrich von Hassell's diary of the period is full of details, meetings, worry: Weizsäcker is exhausted; Beck has a low opinion of the army leaders; Goerdeler may be too sanguine, but it is a relief "to speak with a man who wants to act rather than grumble"; Gisevius reports that Hitler is determined to strike at Poland.

Hassell's good relationship with Nevile Henderson brought him repeatedly, if covertly, to the door of the British embassy. Would the British respond positively, and quickly enough, to the memorandum the opposition had sent over with Henderson? Both Hassell and Moltke were in touch with Alexander Kirk, American chargé d'affaires in Berlin, but Kirk wanted little to do with any of it. Ribbentrop forbade Weizsäcker any further contacts with Henderson.[68] Kleist-Schmenzin was on a mission to Sweden, and Weizsäcker sent a message to the British in Danzig through Wilhelm Ulrich von Schwerin-Schwanenfeld. Time was obviously short. The opposition was straining every nerve, determined to leave no stone unturned if it might avert war.

THE OPPOSITION WAS IN A STATE OF GLOOM. FOR A TIME, EVEN THE EVER-POSITIVE GOerdeler succumbed to the discouragement his coconspirators felt. He went so far as to consider emigrating, but not for long. His energy and undaunted optimism won out over despondency, and he soon renewed his efforts by sending a blizzard of his trademark memoranda—detailed plans for peace and the shaping of Europe after Hitler—to French, British, and American contacts. He traveled extensively, knocked on doors everywhere. He talked with Daladier, and went to England four times in 1939. Unfortunately, by this time Vansittart, too, had turned against him—indeed, against all Germans—and warned that he was an untrustworthy proponent of military expansionism, which only exacerbated British fears of German hegemony in Europe. This was not a concept that sat comfortably with Whitehall in any case. But curiously, as "Van" grew increasingly Germanophobic, the Foreign Office was undergoing a slight shift in the other direction.[73]

Hitler's Czech takeover had clarified British thinking somewhat; Halifax was having a change of heart, and even Chamberlain was beginning to rethink his position. In March, Britain offered Poland its guarantee. Roosevelt also weighed in, asking for a German guarantee of nonaggression. Yet the British still regarded the procession of German opposition—Goerdeler, Trott, Schwerin, the Kordts—as an ill-assorted bunch of malcontents. Either they were talking treason or they were German agents; either way, there was no reason to trust them. To the British Foreign Office, they lacked an apparent unifying movement, and they espoused a variety of aims and interests not necessarily aligned with British interests. Furthermore, distinguishing between their insistence on restoring Germany's 1914 boundaries or certain other conditions for peace and some of Hitler's recent aggressive territorial acquisitions was not always as straightforward as might be desired. Yet Churchill kept pressing for joint communiqués from Britain, France, and Russia, and an address from FDR to Hitler that would "give the best chance to the peaceful elements in German circles to make a stand."[74]

On August 30, two days before Hitler's invasion of Poland, Goerdeler cabled the British Foreign Office from Stockholm: "Chief manager's attitude weakening. Remain completely firm. No compromise."[75] This time, at least, he met with some success, and on September 3, England declared war. Kordt in the meantime had said his farewells in England and agreed to keep communications open through coded postcard messages. When news of the invasion reached Canaris, he muttered a terse, teary, and fatalistic prediction: *"Finis Germaniae."*[76] It would be the end of Germany.[77]

Like Goerdeler, Trott had already visited the United States in 1937 on one leg of an extended study trip. He had come away with the notion that the country would one day be the locus of power—more even than it already was. In the autumn of 1939—after the invasion of Poland but during the phony war—the official reason for his trip was a conference on problems in the Pacific, but his real interest lay much closer to home. On behalf of the Foreign Office, he wanted to feel out the American attitude to a peaceful settlement before war began in earnest. Bearing the olive branch, however, turned out to be anything but straightforward.

The linchpin to his mission was to be the former chancellor of Germany, Heinrich Brüning, who had fled the country in 1934. In exile in Switzerland, he had been contacted late in 1935 by then General Gerd von Rundstedt, asking what he could do against Hitler.[69] Now living in the United States, Brüning was in contact with the German exile community and several highly placed people. Brüning sent Trott to Assistant Secretary of State George Messersmith, who introduced a Trott memorandum into the upper reaches of the State Department. It contained the hallmark Trott warning: In the event of another brutal peace à la Versailles, there was a real danger of the bolshevization of Germany. But in spite of all their concerted efforts and Trott's charm, the questions and suspicion that had hovered over his earlier trip to Britain lingered. His ambiguous situation—was he a collaborator, a resister, or a spy?—also contributed to how he was perceived. When he went to see Felix Frankfurter, any forward momentum stopped abruptly. Trott and Frankfurter had met before, and their relationship had been cordial, but in the interim an English contact had warned Frankfurter against Trott. The suspicions solidified and settled heavily around Trott's shoulders. His mission was doomed.

Brüning had also introduced Trott to the British historian John Wheeler-Bennett, who advised and encouraged him and offered the only gleam of hope he found on his trip of a possible rapprochement with England.[70] Otherwise, Trott's mission failed utterly. He had gone to Britain—like Kleist in 1937—with a "noose around his neck." He knew he was being followed, but did not know by whom.[71] His friends in England and in the American exile community begged him not to go back to Germany, but he worried that if he did not, he would endanger not only reputations but also lives at home. As it was, he had been unable to lay even one stone of any foundation for a just and lasting peace. He realized that Americans could not conceive of the kind of totalitarianism that had befallen Germany. On leaving, feeling hounded and deeply discouraged, he wrote an English friend that, in America, "they don't really empathize with anyone's troubles."[72]

THE GERMAN BLITZKRIEG HAD CRUSHED POLAND WITHIN WEEKS, AND VERY SOON THEREafter, a heavyset Bavarian lawyer undertook the first of several missions to the Vatican on behalf of Beck and the Abwehr. Joseph Müller, a devout Catholic who had been anti-Nazi from the outset, had defended numerous heads of religious orders against the Nazis and was now about to try to do another great service. Since he was traveling for the Abwehr, he was presumed to be their man gathering intelligence on the Vatican. In fact, he hoped to use his Roman connections to enlist the pope as an intermediary in reestablishing contact with the British, from whom the opposition still hoped for assurance of an equitable peace.

In Rome, Müller's friend Monsignor Ludwig Kaas put him in touch with Pater Robert Leiber, the pope's private secretary and confidant since his days as papal nuncio in Germany. As security was a great concern, Müller never dealt with the pope directly but only through Pater Leiber. From late September 1939 into the spring of 1940, Müller shuttled back and forth, bearing proposals, queries, clarifications. In October, His Holiness agreed that the German opposition should be heard in England. Müller returned to Germany with the news of the pope's willingness to engage, but between the intent and any action lay a long period of inactivity. Most likely this was due to the pope's wariness in the wake of the so-called Venlo affair, in which British agents, expecting to meet with dissident German generals, were instead abducted in early November in a plot masterminded by Schellenberg, The incident was a blow to British morale and diminished what little trust the British might have had in the opposition.

After much back-and-forth, and no small degree of misunderstanding, D'Arcy Osborne, the British minister to the Vatican, forwarded the opposition's proposals for a fair and equitable peace with the sine qua non of any agreement: a trustworthy new government to replace Hitler. In the end, despite evident willingness on the British side, the proposals were turned down, and Müller's exertions resulted only in the "X-Report," his account of his Roman conversations. When General Brauchitsch saw the report, he fumed that it represented *Landesverrat*, treason. He felt that establishing ties to a foreign power might be permissible in times of peace, but the nation was now at war, and it was out of the question.[78]

As Hitler fidgeted and vacillated over the date for beginning his offensive in the west, the pope became increasingly uneasy about funneling ever-changing assault warnings to the Low Countries. On May 4, he again warned England and France that attack was imminent. His intelligence was absolutely impeccable, but by this time the concerned parties had been inured to warnings by the repeated changes, and did not take them seriously.

CHAPTER 3

1933–1941

A RELUCTANT ALLY, RELUCTANT GENERALS

United States policy during the 1930s was deeply ambivalent. The country was climbing out of the Depression. The broad populace remembered the losses of the Great War all too clearly and was staunchly isolationist. Roosevelt's stance shifted often to accommodate the balancing of his isolationist electorate and his sense of responsibility to the threatened British. He was making supportive gestures toward Churchill but sending emissaries abroad to fathom the Führer's requirements for a negotiated peace. Was he the enemy of dictators he claimed to be, or was he an appeaser? Was he simply looking toward reelection to a third term, or was he trying to eliminate the "invisible barrier to understanding?"[1]

U.S. POLICY IN THE 1930s

Making sense of the U.S. position in regard to Hitler's Germany in the 1930s requires mental agility. In 1933 Roosevelt had personally assured Hjalmar Schacht, then president of the Reichsbank, that Hitler was the right man for Germany. To the horror of the British ambassador, he had also broached the subject of concessions to Germany, but subsequent FDR appeals made directly to Germany were unsuccessful, When Hitler marched into the Rhineland in 1936, in spite of French pleas for an American reprimand, the president said nothing. William Dodd, U.S. ambassador to Germany at the time, had recognized Hitler for the threat he was, but when he lodged a formal protest, he was withdrawn and denied further access to the president. FDR even charged Secretary of State Cordell Hull with apologizing for Dodd's outspoken anti-Nazi sentiments.[2] Yet while the president was flirting with appeasement, he was also making speeches intended to show that he was a stern opponent of all dictators. Consulting with the French ambassador in March 1938 on the matter of Czechoslovakia, Roosevelt suggested that France acquiesce to Hitler's demands. Then, a few weeks later, while U.S. Ambassador Joseph P. Kennedy was soothing the German ambassador to London with assurances of U.S. agreement with Hitler's goals and policies, FDR struck a pugilist's pose and congratulated France for standing up to aggression.

FDR may have had moments of regret at not having scripted the Munich capitulation, but at least he was free of any taint associated with it. By shuffling players and running through a series of alternating appeasement offers and belligerent poses, he had kept himself above the fray, managing all the while to give the appearance not of an opportunistic politician, but of a staunch defender of democracy and a foe of dictators. This fluid political stance left him free to trim his sails to the prevailing wind.[3]

This freedom was important; Roosevelt was aiming at both reelection in a deeply isolationist climate and a peace with Hitler.[4] Of course, the British were also aiming at a peace with Hitler, but were deeply gratified by the support implied in an interventionist speech by U.S. ambassador to France William C. Bullitt that was authorized by FDR. But the comfort of mighty U.S. backing that the British envisioned was short-lived. Almost immediately, Under Secretary of State Sumner Welles arrived to warn France that 80 percent of the American public was opposed to any intervention in the European war.

During the 1930s, Roosevelt had sent a number of businessmen to ferret out what Hitler had in mind. In 1935 he had commissioned Samuel Fuller, an old friend with important connections, to discover what Hitler might require for a lasting peace. Fuller's meeting with Hjalmar Schacht about the return of the German colonies, a stabilized currency, and a trade agreement with the United States sent Schacht rushing off to see the British, who of course were not interested. There were more talks, official with Welles, unofficial with Fuller. In late 1937, after meetings with Göring, Constantin von Neurath, and Schacht, Welles concluded that concessions on post–World War I borders, specifically those with Poland and Czechoslovakia, and softening the humiliations and injustices of the Versailles Treaty were all a part of working toward unity in Europe. Welles crowed: "I wish to God that during the past years we had been getting this type of information from Germany!"[5]

Joining Samuel Fuller among the ranks of Roosevelt emissaries was William Rhodes Davis, a Southern huckster who had profited mightily in the 1930s from the sale of Mexican oil to an oil-starved Germany. He was not at all happy when the British embargo choked off the abundant cash flow from his business and naturally had a lively interest in reviving it. Though Roosevelt was not entirely comfortable with him, Davis, too, was sent to sound out Berlin and Rome with an eye to detaching Il Duce from the Axis. Meanwhile, the convinced anti-Nazi Dodd was on ice and incommunicado when a new presidential emissary appeared on the scene.

EVEN NOW, QUESTIONS SWIRL AROUND ONE GENERAL MOTORS EXECUTIVE WHO TRIED TO play a role in the bilateral relations between Germany and the United States. His activities, both commercial and political, are certainly a part of the complex shadow game of the intelligence agencies. At the time, he was also seen as a prime example of one of the worst nightmares of professional diplomats and spies: an amateur involved in the most sensitive issues of war and peace. James David Mooney is in many ways a perplexing character, and at the very least, he represents some of the ambivalence of a number of American business enterprises before and during the war.

Mooney, a vice president of General Motors and president of GM Overseas, was energetic, affable, and direct. He had come up in GM's export division, an area where GM had not previously met with much success, and he was said to be able to "tick off the vintage years for French wines, region by region, as easily as he listed the batting averages of the starting Detroit nine."[6] He was also able to double sales once, and then again, and by 1923, he was selling 45,000 automobiles a year abroad—more than $40 million worth, which represented a hefty 7 percent of company production. By late 1925, Mooney was responsible for numerous assembly plants—six in Europe, others as distant as New Zealand and South Africa.

As an American businessman in the 1920s and 1930s, with extensive personal and business connections all over Europe, Jim Mooney was well known to many high German officials. In early May, 1934, just after Hitler had truly consolidated his power over Germany, Mooney met with the Führer at a private reception in the company of Hitler's foreign minister, Ribbentrop, to talk about Opel's role in motorizing Germany. If Opel/GM would cooperate with the regime, it might be very worthwhile.[7]

Hitler's motorization of Germany, in fact, fueled a sharp rise in Opel/GM profits, which soon contributed mightily to what became the mobilization of Germany. By 1935, more of the Reich's funds were funneled into armaments and munitions than to anything else, and Opel was a sizable part of the plan. But profits could not be repatriated, only reinvested. The Wehrmacht suggested that Opel build a plant in Brandenburg to produce trucks for the transport of troops and materiel. Opel agreed, and in 1936 the first aptly named Opel Blitz rolled off the assembly line at the new

Brandenburg facility. Production rose from 14,000 the first year to over 24,000 in 1939.[8]

In 1937, the German government wanted to give Mooney a medal—the Order of Merit of the German Eagle—presented to foreign businessmen in appreciation for services to the Reich, and also awarded to Henry Ford. As a lieutenant commander in the U.S. Naval Reserve, he first contacted his commanding officer to ask permission to accept the award. Turning it down, he explained, would be impolitic; it might offend the German government, and this could endanger GM's $100 million investment in Germany.[9] In August 1938, the acting German consul general in New York presented him with the order and an accompanying diploma, both forwarded to the State Department until permission to accept them came through. Mooney had exercised every caution in accepting it, but this particular honor was to come back to trouble him later.

AN ADVENTURE FOR PEACE

Jim Mooney was an astute businessman with major corporate assets tied up, not just in Germany but all over Europe. The lessons learned about America by visiting German dignitaries and businessmen over the years might have gathered dust in some attics, but this was hardly true for Mooney and his understanding of Europe. He had been living and breathing the business and political air on both sides of the Atlantic for many of the intervening years. He was familiar with both sides of the equation, and his vision was sharp enough to see disaster looming—for Europe and for GM's business interests.

Though no war had been declared in March 1939, Hitler was clearly pushing in that direction when Jim Mooney embarked on what he later described as "a recurrent adventure for peace." One precipitating factor was the Gestapo's seizure of Opel/GM's engineering executives, who were accused of activity "inimical to Germany's automotive industry."[10] Mooney laid the facts before Ribbentrop, who promised a full investigation and then brought up another matter: Drastic changes were required in GM's arrangement with the German government for financing crude rubber imports.

German executives had come to New York in 1936 to ask GM for $1 million to finance Opel/Germany's rubber requirements. Now the topic was being revisited. Mooney met with the director of the Reichsbank, Dr. Emil Puhl, and Dr. Helmuth Wohlthat, ministerial director on Göring's staff, responsible for the so-called four-year plan for economic self-sufficiency. Wohlthat had spent several years in the United States, studied at Columbia University, and spoke fluent, idiomatic English.[11] He was quiet, easygoing, and in no way resembled the caricature of the shouting, table-pounding Nazi type. In Mooney's view, he was the kind of man who "wanted to put the bits and pieces together and see what could be done about it all."[12] As the discussion moved across various topics, Mooney asked whether Germany would be willing to stop subsidizing exports and alter the exchange practices that were so irritating to the United States and Britain, if a gold loan could be arranged. To his surprise, both men responded enthusiastically. If a gold loan would allow resumption of normal trade relations, they would willingly toss all those restrictions overboard.

Mooney then contacted Joseph P. Kennedy, America's ambassador to the Court of St. James's, who suggested that they all meet in Paris. A gold loan might be arranged through the Bank for International Settlements (BIS). Puhl and Wohlthat agreed, but Kennedy thought that before setting off on such a venture, he ought to get Washington's approval. Washington, in the form of Secretary of State Cordell Hull, and Under Secretary Welles, refused on the grounds that it might give an "erroneous impression" and cause "unfortunate comment."[13]

Mooney had no illusions about what war would mean for Europe, and he wanted to prevent it. On a flight to London, he sketched out the main contributions he thought Germany, England, and the United States could make to "anchor" peace in Europe. Germany was to limit armaments, heed nonaggression pacts, and alter its trade practices to conform to Western notions, i.e.: free trade, no subsidized exports, a move to most-favored nations practices, and payment of debts. In return, England and the United States would provide a gold loan of $500 million to $1 billion through the Bank for International Settlements—BIS, restore German colonies seized after Versailles, eliminate embargoes on German goods, and allow credits on raw materials. There were also to be some additional arrangements on raw materials and access to Chinese markets.

Once again, Washington refused to consider this agenda, so Mooney invited Wohlthat to London to meet with Kennedy. A discouraged Mooney recorded the result: "The subject of an Anglo-American gold loan breathed its last when Ambassador Kennedy and Dr. Wohlthat said courteous farewells to each other in the Berkeley Hotel in London on May 9. I had taken what steps I could . . . toward effecting a rational solution to one of the most aggravating problems in world economics. I had failed.[14]

"My plan made no progress but I had learned, or relearned, one very interesting thing—the amazing lack of acquaintance between Berlin and London, as well as between Berlin and Washington, and the consequent lack of acquaintance among men in corresponding positions in the respective governments with each other's ideas and processes of thought. . . . there was almost no personal acquaintanceship among these groups of men . . . no medium for the interchange of thought and almost no evidence of a desire to create such an interchange."[15]

He knew that there was little understanding between Washington and

Berlin; neither side had ever really talked over matters of contention with the other. But in recent travels between Germany and England, he was shocked to find "this same invisible barrier to understanding." Just before the war, with so many issues hanging in the balance, he saw little evidence "of a sincere attempt to learn about the other side's problems and motivating factors." Not surprisingly, things reached the breaking point "when so little effort was made to analyze, learn and reconcile opposing political and economic interests."[16] Mooney's initial motivation for seeking understanding and accommodation with Germany may have been rooted in GM's business concerns, but in looking to avert the war he saw coming, he knew he would have to move into a larger arena and engage on very high levels on both sides of the Atlantic. Even unofficial peace initiatives meant power politics.

Mooney's letters, dashed off on hotel stationery from the Adlon in Berlin, the Berkeley in London, or the Colombia in Genoa, revealed the hurried, peripatetic, and high-powered life of a level-headed, humorous, and loving man: "Dear Ida May," he wrote to his wife on September 27, 1939:

> Though I was barging off this morning to see the Pope I just received a call . . . that may demand my going back to Germany. My goodness, I'm tired of executives for the moment. Guess I'll rent me a shade tree and loll under it for a change. How about it Darling will you do a bit of lolling with me?! Sunny Italy is doing its best today—beautiful sunshine in a country still at peace. My trunks have gone to Rome. . . . Now I'll have to be old dirty shirt for a few days. Oh well, 'C'est la guerre.' . . . When I get home this time I promise not to kid about anything—the cooking, the service or anything provided of course I can sleep with the landlady.[17]

Two days after the invasion of Poland, he expressed his frustration with what he regarded as "the palace guard" around Roosevelt, who looked at everything from a political and partisan point of view, and not at all from a humanitarian worldview.[18] "The propaganda, the lies and the destructionists seem to have won!" he wrote Ida May on September 3, 1939, two days after the invasion of Poland. A few weeks later: "I'm tired of the war already. . . . I hope the politicians get tired soon too. As usual they are the only ones who want war and as usual they won't be in the trenches."[19] Yet from Rome, on October 3, he was "still optimistic that a face-saving formula can be found so that the boys all can go home for Christmas. So far as I can gather there is no enthusiasm anywhere for the war."[20]

Soon after the collapse of Poland, Dr. Otto Dietrich, Hitler's personal press chief, asked American journalist working for the Associated Press and recent Pulitzer Prize–winner Louis Lochner, to come to see him. To Lochner's surprise, Dr. Dietrich hoped for "American mediation in the conflict between Germany on the one hand and England on the other, before the shooting war between them started in earnest."[21] It is likely that this approach was based in part on Hitler's obsession with England, another "Aryan" nation that might become an ally and friend.[22]

Hitler and Stalin had just agreed to the division of Poland, and Dietrich understood Lochner's firm anti-Nazi position. Whether or not this was a legitimate request, whether Hitler was simply stalling for time or trying to put the Anglo-American contingent off the scent, Dietrich suggested that if Lochner could facilitate unofficial American mediation—perhaps through a key American industrialist—it might accomplish what had been denied legions of politicians and diplomats. Eventually, such exploratory talks could then be shifted to an official footing and, with luck, avert "the slaughter of the flower of European manhood."[23] It is important to understand that Lochner did not know that senior Abwehr officers such as Oster and others linked to the Abwehr—Kleist, Schlabrendorff, and the Foreign Office's Trott—had already been on numerous missions to Britain to seek some kind of accommodation, and had been rebuffed repeatedly.

Lochner consulted with Heinrich Richter, a Berlin lawyer for the Associated Press who had extensive connections to American industry. Richter was not a Nazi. After giving the matter some thought, he came up with a name: Jim Mooney, "the Foreign Minister" of General Motors.[24] The wheels began turning immediately, and next day, October 15, the energetic Mooney appeared in Berlin. The Germans had come to him, and while he doubted Roosevelt's willingness to initiate any negotiations, he saw no harm in gauging FDR's intentions once some basis for agreement between Germany and England had been established. The thing to do first was to sound out the Germans, something with which he had experience.

In discussions with Wohlthat, Mooney argued that the British would never negotiate with Germany's present government. Wohlthat suggested that perhaps removing Hitler to some innocuous, figurehead position—Mooney thought of it as "Valhalla"—might pave the way for future negotiations. Several days later, Mooney met with Hermann Göring, Wohlthat's boss and Hitler's designated successor. After some characteristic braggadocio and bluster—"I had, so to speak, to kick him in the shins a few times," Mooney recalled—the two men settled down to talks. Mooney was typically direct: World opinion took a dim view of Germany's racial and religious persecution, he told Göring; Poland and Czechoslovakia represented acts of inexcusable aggression; Germany's present alliances with the Soviet Union and Japan were difficult to reconcile with the Nazi stance on communism and Aryan supremacy; and finally, Germany had managed to be quite convincing in conveying her interest in stamping out the British Empire.

Göring countered blandly that there was no religious persecution in Germany. As for the Jewish question, that could be resolved at some later date. Poland and Czechoslovakia would be viewed as independent states, albeit with German-controlled foreign policy, in order to prevent Germany's "encirclement." And if a negotiated peace with Britain—that bastion of the white race—were supported by the United States and France, Germany would willingly toss out the Russian and Japanese alliances.[25] The hefty field marshal concluded by wagging a finger in Mooney's face and telling him to find out from the British whether they really wanted to fight or not; Chamberlain's speeches were not at all clear on this matter. Germany would willingly leave England alone if only she would agree not to meddle in Germany's affairs. He also indicated that he was speaking with the knowledge and approval of the Führer.[26]

Mooney came away from the meeting feeling that while nothing had actually been accomplished, he had gained insight into the mentality at work, and an understanding of Germany's exasperation, not only over the humiliations heaped on her by Versailles, but also for being treated like a pariah again under Hitler. Germany also longed for recognition as a world power on a par with others. He determined to keep the relevant American diplomatic and political powers informed of his actions, and while the American ambassador had been withdrawn from Berlin, his mission had the enthusiastic support from the chargé d'affaires, Alexander Kirk.

In London, he persuaded Joseph Kennedy that this project should be pursued, and Kennedy decided that Mooney ought to see the foreign secretary, Lord Halifax, immediately. Mooney's friendship with Halifax's brother, who also worked for GM, simplified this "unofficial" mission of mediation considerably. When they met with Halifax, the foreign secretary listened attentively, took careful notes, and then asked Mooney to memorize a very particularly worded memorandum for Berlin, verbatim. Halifax's memorandum read:

> Mr. Mooney's message was delivered and listened to with interest. He got the impression that there was complete lack of confidence in the present regime in Germany. It was left that no progress could be made until somehow or other there was a government in Germany with whom the British could deal, which at present was not the case."[27]

When Mooney erred in one detail of his memorization, Halifax upbraided him. The message was specifically "a government" not "a form of government" in Germany. Apparently, "Great Britain did not necessarily oppose a National Socialist state, but rather the men now in control of it."[28]

Returning to Germany, Mooney intended to see Wohlthat again, and after chasing him to Rome, they finally met in Madrid in early December 1939. By this time Wohlthat was feeling much less sanguine; he thought it was now too late to put Hitler on ice as he had proposed earlier, and they had failed to bring about a confidential meeting between German and British authorities.

Mooney went home; Ida May was waiting, and the president had requested a briefing on his various discussions on December 22. It was a summons of enormous importance to Mooney, a meeting he thought might make the difference between war and peace.

PRESIDENTIAL EMISSARY

It was a private engagement, off the presidential calendar; there was to be no publicity whatsoever. Mooney had been alerted by a friend to expect the president to turn on the famous Roosevelt charm and in this long meeting, things went just as his friend had predicted. The president was a good listener, and spent time talking with Mooney about matters he knew were of great interest to him, such as foreign exchange. Mooney made extensive notes, sticking as closely as possible to the president's actual words: "I'm not interested in telling the Germans what they shall do about Hitler," Roosevelt told him. "That is their own affair. . . . Hitler is only one man in the sweep of history. . . . But I wish the Germans would pipe down about dominating the world." The president remarked that "it ought to be reasonably simple to get around a table with the proper will and settle problems like Silesia, Poland, Czechoslovakia, and the general attitude toward Russia."[29] The president wanted Mooney to be his emissary. Through him he hoped to get a real understanding of other nations' war aims or peace terms, and he was willing to act as moderator in any peace talks.

About a month later they met again. FDR gave Mooney a three-line note, wishing him luck, and expecting to see him when he returned.[30] It was brief and personal, but could be used to great effect if necessary, for it marked Jim Mooney as a man on close terms with the president. Mooney was unaware that he was joining Moltke, Otto John, Trott, Goerdeler, and so many others who had beaten paths to England in search of peace, but he had some enormous advantages. He did not face the almost universal distrust that greeted the Germans. He had no need to wangle meetings and gain acceptance for his peace errand. He moved easily from the top level of one government to the top level of another. He was a free agent with no official political mandate, and he did not bear the burden of any known intelligence affiliation. British Intelligence trusted him, and his commission in the U.S. Navy bolstered faith in his information further.

Before Mooney undertook any more peace efforts and meetings however, the president agreed that he should inform Cordell Hull of his mission. Mooney too, was keen to avoid any State Department interference with his travel and communications. At State, he found that Hull was ill with a bad cold, and the general atmosphere was glacial. George Messersmith, the ranking officer on hand, urged Mooney strongly not to undertake this project. When Money returned to Washington some weeks later to see Hull before he left for Europe, Hull was still keeping to his bed. When he arrived in Europe, Mooney learned that Sumner Welles was being sent—officially— on the same errands he had been sent on unofficially.

What game was Washington playing? Britain was in a ticklish situation. Roosevelt felt an obligation, yet at home he was facing an isolationist electorate that wanted nothing to do with any European conflict. Given to hands-on management, FDR's unorthodox approach often had him pursuing a variety of links and communications through personal channels and correspondence, often without apparent official White House knowledge. He was also known to play people off against one another, and the overall effect sometimes verged on the "Byzantine."[31]

To Mooney, Roosevelt had suggested that the pope might be useful in generating a formula for peace.[32] There was also a hope of breaking Italy away from Hitler's Axis. But when Mooney arrived in Rome, he discovered that the American ambassador had not been informed that he was coming, and the State Department was guarding its turf; Welles was to cover the same ground Mooney was expected to cover. It seemed to him that what was standing in the way of peace negotiations were not critical territorial and political issues, but professional jealousies and peevishness in high places. He decided to go directly to Berlin. On February 16, 1940, he wrote Hitler to propose a meeting.

> I need hardly inform you, Mr. Reich Chancellor, that the human and economic consequences of the present war are terribly disturbing to the people of the entire world.
>
> The people in my own country feel that the war can end only end in disaster for Europe and that the war will eventually have very serious consequences in America. . . .
>
> I know . . . you Mr. Reich Chancellor, belong to the group of men in Europe and the United States who believe that the present war is a poor and disastrous way to dispose of the many international political and economic mistakes that have been made since 1914, and it is on this common ground that I should like to discuss the entire problem with you.[33]

As they waited for the bureaucratic wheels to turn, Mooney swore Lochner to secrecy and enlisted his help in crafting exact, meticulously worded talking points to bring up with the Führer. It was an exercise that had Lochner in knots; as a professional reporter, he was sitting on a huge, exclusive story, but was pledged to absolute silence.[34] Mooney also wrote to Welles, then in Rome, offering to put everything he knew at his disposal, but his letter went unanswered.

When Welles arrived in Berlin, he went almost immediately to meet with Ribbentrop. Mooney had tried to contact him again through Alexander Kirk, but Kirk's earlier enthusiasm for the Mooney mission had cooled to the same chill temperature that prevailed in the rest of the State Department, and this attempt, too, went without response. Kirk had invited virtually the entire Berlin American colony to a party honoring Welles on March 3, with the exception of Mooney. It was an official snub, a clear signal that Mooney had somehow been disavowed. Appearing before Hitler without having spoken to Welles would not do. Mooney must go to the party and meet Welles, willy-nilly.

Lochner concocted the perfect ruse: He would arrive at the party claiming that he had run into Mooney and been astounded to hear that he had not been invited. Kirk would never admit to a newsman that Mooney had been omitted intentionally, and Lochner would then volunteer to telephone Mooney immediately and rectify the situation. The scheme worked perfectly; Welles and Mooney exchanged a few idle comments, but Mooney could honestly tell Hitler that yes, he had spoken with Mr. Welles.[35]

In Mooney's opinion Welles's trip was a tragedy. "None of these people knew him and he knew them very little. You can't keep track of European politics by reading the *New York Times*. You have got to get over there and feel and sense the undercurrent . . . something Welles was unprepared for." In his opinion, Welles could not have been less suitable—a "cold, fishy, stuffed-shirt diplomat" who liked to "keep his brass hat on at all times, and hide behind his position."[36]

So it was no surprise to Mooney that Welles's meeting with Ribbentrop was absolutely pro forma. When Mooney met with Ribbentrop, they spoke English, though the foreign minister apologized for his rustiness. With Welles, on the other hand, everything had gone through a translator—in both directions. Mooney asked about this later and was told that "Mr. Ribbentrop will not speak the language of the enemy."[37] At about this time, Welles also had another conversation with former Reichsbank president Hjalmar Schacht, who told him that the leading German generals were moving to supplant the regime.[38] Hassell's diary noted that he found the fact that such a conversation had taken place at all "remarkable."[39]

WHEN HITLER RECEIVED MOONEY ON MARCH 4, MANY POINTS ON MOONEY'S AGENDA were discussed. Hitler remarked that he was sure he could reach agreement with Roosevelt in "ten minutes," thought there were some ifs involved: if Britain and France would respect Germany as a world power just as Germany respected Britain and France, and if armaments could be reduced to release labor and resources for more productive purposes through better international trade agreements.[40] Even the ever-optimistic Jim Mooney may have recognized this as disingenuous.

Further talks with Wohlthat and Göring revealed that the Germans expected London—not Berlin—to respond to Roosevelt's offer to mediate. Feeling that his mission in Berlin was accomplished, Mooney left for Rome. As there was no State Department provision for him to communicate with the president, he sent five long telegrams, laboriously encrypted by the navy.

"I have not found one person, from brass hat to taxi driver who considered the war anything but a catastrophe for Europe. The disillusionment of WWI still dominates the feelings of everyone in Europe . . . poignant memories still remain—grief for the losses of millions of husbands and brothers and memories of the four years of starvation. . . . The techniques of slaughtering and maiming . . . have been multiplied . . . in horror and effectiveness. Europe entered the war of 1914–1918 with some economic fat on its bones. Europe now has scarcely economic skin on its bones. . . . I have had a ringside seat in Europe for 22 years, starting as a doughboy . . . since that time I have gone first-hand through numerous and varied European military and economic crises. Taken all together, the picture can be summed up as a fiasco of bad politics and dumb-bell economics. . . . The world has many problems just as serious as war and more worthy of sacrifice. None of these problems will be solved by war. The death of martyrs sometimes makes for a better world . . . however nobody believes that a better world will come out of this war."[41]

IN APRIL, FDR WROTE MOONEY TO THANK HIM, SAYING THAT HIS MESSAGES HAD "BEEN of real value," and he asked Mooney to continue sending him news. Mooney began to prepare a speech for the alumni association of his alma mater, the Case School for Applied Science, summarizing his political convictions and experiences in Europe. It could serve as a trial balloon on the possibilities of negotiated peace. With his usual care, he cleared the speech with a friend at the White House, and the president invited him to visit. Presidential advisor Harry Hopkins, however, vetoed the visit and the speech: The tone was too Republican; it might hurt FDR's chances in the upcoming elections.[42]

"Harry Hopkins put thumbs down on it," Mooney told Lochner later; "it was bad politics at the time with the convention coming on, the election, the administration would be accused of appeasement."[43]

THE MYTH OF THE NAZI MONOLITH

Literature on the SS, the SD, and all its branches runs the gamut from caricatures of totalitarianism to painstaking psychological and sociological studies, from wallowing in horror and condemnation to apologia. But whatever the Nazi intelligence and police operations were really like, they were never the seamless, monolithic edifice of terror that is so often envisioned and portrayed. They were in fact riddled with rivalries and contradictions, undermined by jealousies and shifting allegiances and incessant jockeying for power that kept the shadowy empire in a perpetual state of flux. Otto Ohlendorf, head of the SD's internal affairs branch, described the system in which he worked as "pluralist anarchy," essentially a revolving power struggle. This structure swarmed with seething rivalries which Hitler promoted in order to leave himself, alone and immutable, at the center of all the courtiers squabbling and groveling at his feet. From his earliest beginnings, it had been one of the great secrets of his success.

Ulrich von Hassell, working outside the system and against Hitler, took a larger view, and put it another way: "These people have no conception of what a state is."[44] But that lack of comprehension never stood in the way of amassing all possible power. Goebbels himself actually agreed with Hassell: "At best these are average men. Not one of them has the qualities of a mediocre politician, to say nothing of the caliber of a statesman. They have all remained the beer-cellar rowdies they always were . . . this gang of spiteful children, each of whom intrigues against all the rest."[45]

As the 1930s ground on and Hitler pushed toward inevitable war, Himmler, Heydrich, Party, and Reichswehr seemed to be caught in an eternal wrestling match for supremacy. The SD's web of information gatherers grew denser until, by 1937, it numbered 3,000 full-time employees and 50,000 part-time spies.[46] Tireless surveillance of religious groups with political opinions, people likely to vote against the Party's interests in "elections," anyone suspected of lack of enthusiasm for the SS, the so-called "black corps"—anyone, anyone at all—made for mountains of paperwork to be moved methodically, painstakingly through the bowels of a vast bureaucracy. The law had now become merely a tool wielded by the state to exert power over the people.

While it may have been apparent to insiders that the monolith was a myth, to the German civilian population it was an omniscient, omnipresent terror. Its eyes and ears saw and heard everything, and the net constructed by its many interconnected branches was inescapable. Though this dark, impenetrable empire seemed to know everything about the citizenry, Heydrich gloated that to the citizenry "the Gestapo, the Kriminalpolizei and the security services are enveloped in the mysterious aura of the political detective story."[47] Like his boss, Himmler, the glacial and sinister Heydrich, whom even his colleagues in terror referred to as the "blond beast," was a giddy detective fiction addict.

In 1939, the RSHA—*Reichssicherheitshauptabteilung*, or Reich Central Security Office—was set up to combine all existing police forces (Gestapo,

Kripo, and SD) with responsibility for dealing with "enemies of the state" and turning them over to the administrator of concentration camps, under Reinhard Heydrich. The unpopular young loner had matured into a cold-blooded paragon of vengefulness and ambition who had envisioned the SD and the Gestapo as interlocking branches of his invincible terror organization. But now he was forced to establish parameters that would keep them out of each other's hair. There would be a division of labor; they must not vitiate one another's aims and achievements.

Yet this Nazi police and intelligence edifice was anything but monolithic; it was a crazy quilt of competing powers and bailiwicks. Ohlendorf ridiculed Himmler's "blood and soil" fantasies of harmonious peasant villages in the east, inhabited by cheerful Germanic folk. As Ohlendorf's reports on "spheres of life" within the Nazi state became increasingly negative, they were met with growing irritation. He finally resigned in 1939, as only one of many. There were other doubters and defectors among the former stalwarts: Arthur Nebe, chief of the Reich Criminal Police, an essential cog in the wheel of totalitarian terror, was feeding information to the conspirators even before the war began. Werner Best, the founding legal mind behind the SS and coauthor with Canaris of the 1936 "Ten Commandments" agreement on division of responsibilities of Abwehr and the SD, left his position in 1940 to rescue his remaining scruples. He preferred the front to the SD.

Still, Heydrich was anxious to provide new fodder for his growing and hungry machine. He decided to move into an arena that had always held a shimmering allure for him, terrain specifically forbidden by the "Ten Commandments": foreign espionage. Patzig's warning was borne out; the Ten Commandments had only forestalled the inevitable.

For years Heydrich and Canaris had shared an essentially congenial relationship. They had even taken to riding together in the leafy Tiergarten, joined occasionally by Heydrich's lieutenant, Schellenberg, but now they were engaged in a ferocious power struggle. Heydrich leapt into his new venture with enthusiasm for the thrill of espionage. He was poaching on sacred military turf, and for Canaris this was war. He was determined to shield the Abwehr and the military from Nazi encroachments such as the Blomberg-Fritsch crisis that had augmented Hitler's power at the expense of the military. It was another turning point in his relationship to the Nazi Party.

A TURNING POINT

After their failure to avert war, the opposition was about to discover just how hard war is to stop. Hitler's invasion of Poland was a turning point: The hoped-for Allied response came at last, but too late. War had begun, and though it was still only a phony war, postures had hardened. The deafness that had greeted German peace feelers earlier was about to turn into total silence. Poland marked a shift among elements in the German army, too, for the ultimate barbarity of the regime was now unmistakably clear.

But Hitler's generals could not dissuade him from his plans for an assault in the west, and even Oster's repeated, desperate acts of treason in the hope of aborting the assault were futile. France, like Poland, fell within weeks, and other nations followed like dominoes. All that the opposition had feared was being realized: Hitler's successes were fueling his ambitions; the pestilence would only spread. But neither continued opposition contacts nor planned assassinations brought the desired result.

EVEN AS GERMAN PANZERS SWEPT ACROSS POLAND IN SEPTEMBER 1939, NEVILE HENDERson found many positive things to say about Herr Hitler. He had restored German self-respect and orderliness, for instance, and he had instituted social reforms. The ambassador found the Nazi slogans very catchy, and he particularly admired "the organization of the labor camps . . . typical of benevolent dictatorship."[48]

Hitler's bloodless successes had puffed out his sails and the Polish campaign inflated them further. He was flush with his victory. Having divided Poland with Stalin, he immediately looked westward to the Low Countries and France. Yet even as he was planning his attack, he entertained peace offers from Belgium and Holland. Again, his generals were opposed to an assault: Germany could not support a war that was sure to become a major conflict; November was too late in the season; ground conditions and fog would be huge impediments. Hitler did not want to hear it. They were all spineless, and besides, they must understand that they were no longer a factor in his decision making.

Poland, Britain, and France had declared war on Germany, but it was still a "phony war." Hostilities were on hold, and the opposition, Oster, Hassell, and others, still hoped to avert a major debacle. Late in 1939, J. Lonsdale Bryans, a self-appointed British diplomat, had learned of the German opposition from Hassell's future son-in-law in Rome. He was convinced that the disunity within the Reich should be put to use, and decided to act as intermediary between the German opposition and the British. His mission was "saving . . . millions of lives and winning the peace, [by using] the anti-Nazi nucleus in Germany as a . . . 'secret weapon' to strike at the innermost vitals of the enemy."[49] It was a commendable goal, but Bryans labored at a disadvantage: Halifax regarded him as a lightweight. Others thought he was looking only to build up his own importance. To Hassell, keen to make use of every possible means, even grasping at straws, Bryans may also have looked like a slender straw, but still a straw, and easily graspable.

So he met with Bryans in Switzerland in early 1940, gave him a memorandum explaining that a coup was planned, and warned of the bolshevization of Europe. He also underlined his most consistent concern: the need for a strong European center, i.e., Germany. Presented with Hassell's proposal, Cadogan complained to his diary that this "was about the 100th time I had heard . . . [this] . . . ridiculous stale story of a German opposition ready to overthrow Hitler if we will guarantee 'not to take advantage.' "[50] Though he had been disavowed by Cadogan, Bryans met Hassell again in April, but without a reply to Hassell's February proposals.

Hassell's diary entry of April 25, 1940, is downbeat: "Mr. X [Bryans] intimated that his people were very skeptical . . . and freely admitted that they were slow and difficult to move. . . . I had the impression that Halifax . . . had no real faith in the possibility of attaining peace . . . through a change of regime in Germany."[51] Hassell probably realized that Britain would not respond unless the generals took decisive action—if then. Bryans continued to perambulate until the Foreign Office reeled him in and discouraged further contacts with German nationals as such contacts were "not in the national interest."[52] In the meantime, Hassell had since realized that contacts with the United States would become critical. He met with Alexander Kirk on numerous occasions in Berlin, to brief him on the prevalent thinking in opposition circles.[53]

HAD IT COME A YEAR EARLIER, THE DAY CHURCHILL SUCCEEDED CHAMBERLAIN AS PRIME minister might have been a red-letter day for the German opposition. They had longed for pugnacity and toughness from England, and Churchill would certainly have delivered. England would have been under the leadership of a man whom Hitler feared. All the assaults since the Sudeten crisis might have been averted. But circumstances in the interim had changed, and for the German opposition, the fighting spirit that came in with the new prime minister on May 10, 1940, came too late.

The Polish campaign had marked a turning point in the resistance, and added significantly to Hitler's roster of crimes. The barbarities in Poland raised basic moral questions and elicited outrage and horror that went far beyond the actual conspirators. Brauchitsch, Johannes Blaskowitz, Wilhelm Ulex, Wilhelm von Leeb, and many other generals lodged repeated protests against the bloodthirsty *Einsatzkommandos*—task forces—who were murdering thousands behind the front. Canaris also protested, but Hitler dismissed all objections as "childish." Within the resistance itself, activity now reached a new pitch. This was the last opportunity to avoid an unsustainable all-out war and oust the madman.

October turned into November. Beck urged the recalcitrant Halder to attempt another coup, and although Halder had secretly carried a pistol for weeks, longing to shoot Emil—a.k.a. Hitler—himself, he fretted about how a coup would now be received, in light of Hitler's easy victory. If it failed, there might be civil war and the Bolsheviks would take over. Beck continued to press for action, and Halder tried repeatedly to persuade Hitler that Germany was not ready for war.

He was supported, among others, by General Georg Thomas, the administrator of army supply and armaments who understood the state of preparedness only too well. The senior generals were nearly unanimous in their military objections and tried to convince Hitler to drop his plans. Brauchitsch told Hitler that the army was in no condition to win a protracted European war, but Hitler was in no mood for reason; a leader should not have to urge his reluctant generals to war. He ranted and insulted Brauchitsch until his most senior officer emerged from his interview white-faced and trembling. Addressing his general staff, the Führer fulminated and vowed to "destroy the spirit of Zossen"—military headquarters south of Berlin—and the "defeatist" mood among them.[54]

WHILE HITLER INSISTED ON A MILITARY OFFENSIVE IN THE WEST, THE OPPOSITION SCRAMbled to find ways to stop him. Beck produced more memoranda, but Canaris had little faith in the irresolute Halder and Brauchitsch. When Hitler decreed that he would attack between November 15 and 20, Oster and Erich Kordt concocted a plot to "throw a bomb and liberate our generals from their scruples."[55] As aide to both Ribbentrop and Weizsäcker, Kordt had ready access to Hitler, and volunteered; all they needed was explosives. But in spite of the Abwehr connections, these were difficult to obtain. When Hitler announced the attack for November 12, there was very little time. They would aim for November 11. The pace picked up. Insofar as possible, the 1938 plans were resurrected. Beck, Brauchitsch, Halder—everyone was suddenly reenergized, back in a pre-Munich mode. "Intense activity . . . I rushed back and forth between OKW, police headquarters, the Interior Ministry, Beck, Goerdeler, Schacht, Helldorf, Nebe and others . . . ," Gisevius later remembered.[56]

Hitler was scheduled to speak at a gathering of his old comrades in arms at Munich's Bürgerbräukeller on November 8. The annual commemoration of the 1923 Munich coup attempt was one of the few fixed points on the Führer's schedule. For weeks a slightly drab socialist by the name of Georg Elser, with a passion for music and a hatred of Hitler, had hidden at the brasserie every night after closing. Painstakingly, he was hollowing out a stone and cement column near the podium where Hitler was to speak from 8:30 to 10:00. Every morning before he left, he disguised the column's disfigurement with cleverly designed cabinetwork. He had taken a job at a quarry specifically to acquire fuses and explosives. The bomb he planted in the hollowed column went off at 9:20. The building's roof collapsed, killing eight and injuring more than sixty. Hitler had spoken from 8:00 until 9:07, and had then rushed off to catch a train rather than fly back to Berlin in the November fog.

The very next day, two British MI-6 secret service agents who had been persuaded by a German agent to meet with German opposition generals were met instead by SD agents at the Dutch border town of Venlo and abducted to Germany to spend the rest of the war in German jails. For some this coincidence signaled that the Bürgerbräu bombing was all part of a dastardly British plot. Elser was arrested and the Nazis claimed that he was clearly a tool of the British.[57] In fact, Hitler was convinced that the British were behind it and had personally ordered that the two British agents be abducted.[58] For others the mystery only deepened. In the confusion, rumors swirled. No one in the opposition—or anywhere else either—knew where Elser had come from, though the Abwehr was suspected.[59] Himmler was commonly thought to be capable of almost anything, and one German, after reading his account of Elser's plot, remarked, "Now I *know* Himmler planted the bomb."[60]

Elser had come within thirteen minutes of succeeding, but his plot had only unintended consequences: Security for Hitler was tightened; the British were more skittish than ever toward representatives of the "other" Germany, and for Oster and Kordt, the search for explosives became impossible. It was the end of their plan.

AS HITLER TEETERED ON THE BRINK OF HIS PLANNED ASSAULT IN THE WEST, HIS PRECISE plans were either unknown or constantly changing, making opposition planning more problematic than ever. An attack announced for one date in the morning would be called off a few hours later, only to be reinstated within days. In the ten days between November 12 and November 22, he changed his mind about the timing of the attack four times.

General Kurt von Hammerstein-Equord—known as the "Red General" for fraternizing with trade unions during the Weimar Republic—had tried to short-circuit Hitler's accession to power back in 1933. Now his two sons in the resistance had brought him reports of the terrible killings in Poland that reinforced his anti-Hitler resolve. When Hitler called him out of retirement to serve on the Siegfried Line, where the next military moves were being planned, Hammerstein and Beck arranged to arrest Hitler on a visit to Hammerstein's headquarters. As he did so often, Hitler changed his plans and never showed up. Hammerstein was soon pushed back into retirement.

Again and again Hitler postponed the assault. His talent for the unexpected kept everyone off guard and weakened some wills.[61] But others, particularly the younger generation, were spurred to new resolve, and that autumn of 1939 there was a renewed press to take action. Plots and conspiracies seemed to be everywhere, some circles working in complete ignorance of others, underlining again one of the great obstacles Moltke had said opposition faced: communication.

In December, Beck told Hassell that he had been badgering Brauchitsch to act before the *"drôle de guerre"* turned into the real thing, but to no avail. He would gladly do it himself, but he no longer had the authority. He needed the backing of Brauchitsch, as commander in chief of the army, and that was missing. Canaris, glum and fatalistic, doubted that the generals would act on their convictions. Watching the wavering generals from the sidelines, Hassell lamented that apparently they were waiting for Hitler himself to give the order to overthrow him.[62] As winter gave way to spring, even the feisty and direct Witzleben, usually unhesitating and game, now doubted that Hitler could be stopped.

But Hans Oster was boiling with impatience. He was not one to wait for an order from the Führer. When the Dutch military attaché in Berlin, Major Gijsbertus Sas, returned to Berlin in April 1939, Oster resumed his friendship and intensified his already close connection with Sas. He confided to Sas that he felt it was his duty to free Germany and the world of this pestilence—Hitler—and initiated Sas into Hitler's planned invasions. Oster surely expected that apprising the enemy of the planned assault would guarantee a defeat such as the conspirators had always hoped for, a defeat that would loosen Hitler's grip.[63] In this case, the defeat would be military rather than political. Oster was under no illusions about what this step meant for him: It was treason. It also turned out to be a failure.

The cause of the failure was Hitler's constant changes of plan. Oster would tell Sas of an invasion planned for November 12; no sooner had Sas relayed the information to the relevant authorities than the invasion would be called off. This happened repeatedly, and the Dutch command came to regard Sas's information about planned invasions as unreliable at best. Though Sas never lost faith in Oster, the many changes in the date of attack undermined the credibility of both men. Ultimately the attack was postponed twenty-nine times, and the Dutch commander in chief told Sas that his source was "pitiful."[64] Like the pope's warnings, Oster's went unheeded.

Oster also tried to warn the Norwegian ambassador in Berlin of the plans to attack Denmark and Norway, but the ambassador chose not to forward the information. Denmark and Norway fell to the Germans.[65] At last, on the evening before the invasion of Holland, set for May 10, Oster made one last check to be sure there had been not been yet another change of plan, and alerted Sas. Then he said good-bye to his friend, and expressed his hope that they would see each other after the war. Neither the Dutch nor the Belgians chose to heed Sas's warning.

Once the war was on in earnest, keeping up with the old problem of communication was more difficult than ever. Many military contingents engaged with the opposition were again dispersed, and they were also being kept busy. For anyone so inclined, it was easy to take refuge from qualms of conscience by simply falling back on his duty as a soldier. After Paris fell in a matter of a few weeks, Hitler was intoxicated by his success. He had scored another easy triumph. To the opposition in Germany, however, the mad bell ringing to celebrate France's capitulation was ominous. Though the tide was against them, the frustrated conspirators did not give up. There were a number of plots to eliminate Hitler, when—and if—he came to France. Fritz-Dietlof von der Schulenburg, Witzleben, Ulrich Schwerin von Schwanenfeld, Hassell, and Goerdeler were all involved. One entailed shooting Hitler as he and his victorious troops paraded down the Champs-Élysées, but after several postponements, the parade was finally canceled. Schwerin's plan to blow Hitler up with a hand grenade was foiled when Hitler, with his uncanny instinct, failed to appear at Witzleben's western headquarters. By this time, the Führer's paranoia was pathological.

Hitler had humbled France and driven the British expeditionary forces into the water at Dunkirk; for the opposition, staging a coup now would be harder than ever. Hitler soon set his generals to planning his next venture, the assault on Russia. The British Foreign Office had had relative freedom to pursue possible peace initiatives just after the fall of France; there had even been thought given to welcoming Germany—once rid of Hitler—back into the community of nations.[66] But Hitler's air assault, "the Battle of Britain," in July 1940 changed the mood among the populace and in the Cabinet.[67] On the other side of the Atlantic, however, England's American cousins remained uncommitted.

AMERICA BETWEEN PEACE AND WAR

To American eyes, the war still looked like a European war. President Roosevelt, running for reelection, faced a strong isolationist contingent, whose spokesman, Charles Lindbergh, railed against the obvious "subterfuge and propaganda" being used in the United States to rally forces for the war.[68] William Donovan's reconnaissance in Europe made the need for U.S. intervention clear and America began gearing up for war. Among the preparations was the lend-lease program to support the British, and the establishment of the first American unified intelligence organization, under Donovan. This precursor to the OSS and the CIA exposed Donovan to many of the same jealousies, rivalries, and turf wars Canaris was experiencing in Germany. As the United States began to organize its response to Hitler's war, a surprising peace initiative alerted Donovan to something all his previous information networks had not uncovered: a German resistance to Hitler. For Donovan, this was a startling, thrilling discovery.

With the turmoil in Europe, President Franklin Roosevelt's office was being bombarded daily with bits of raw, unanalyzed data from intelligence sources across the nation and around the globe. The intelligence forces in the United States had evolved slowly from the simple scouting parties of the early colonies into relatively sophisticated operations by the Office of Naval Intelligence (ONI) and the War Department's military G-2.[69] Still, in the years before the war began, U.S. intelligence gathering was relatively primitive, underfunded, and uncoordinated. The army, navy, and the State Department had each developed their own assets and methods and each sent information up their own chain of command, hoping that eventually, it would reach the top, perhaps even the president. If intelligence did reach the White House, there was no system in place for putting the bits and pieces of the intelligence mosaic together into documents sufficiently coherent to be useful to the president and other policy makers. There were also other impediments: the jealousies and turf wars among military departments, and an attitude epitomized by Henry Stimson, Coolidge's secretary of state, who sniffed: "Gentlemen do not read each other's mail."[70]

German forces had moved into Czechoslovakia, roared across Poland, and in May 1940, apparently unstoppable, crashed through the Maginot Line. Within weeks, Belgium, Holland, and France were joined by Denmark and Norway under German occupation. Could England hold out alone? Would everything the last generation had fought for be lost, or would the United States be called upon to join the fight against Hitler?

In the Oval Office, FDR was not getting any clear answers to these questions. Reports from the State Department were sometimes little more than cocktail party gossip and the War Department was split between generals who insisted that the Allied defenses would hold and those who were not nearly so sure.[71] Joseph P. Kennedy, U.S. ambassador in London, was convinced that both France and England would fall to Hitler's armies; the president, he said, should not be left "holding the bag in a war in which the Allies expect to be beaten."[72] At the highest levels of government there was confusion and discord, and nothing was in place to sort fact from fiction.

Most Americans wanted to stay out of the "European War." The carnage and sacrifices of the Great War were only a generation removed, and few were anxious to jump into the fray. The only U.S. concession to the British and French pleas for help was the cash-and-carry policy allowing them to buy materials on a cash basis and transport them across the Atlantic on their own ships. Otherwise, the country remained staunchly isolationist.

Intelligence poured into the White House continually, but it did little to clarify what U.S. policy should be. Roosevelt's leadership and day-to-day management style only complicated matters. FDR seized on information to use as a tool for power plays among his key advisors. Richard M. Helms who served in the OSS and later became director of Central Intelligence recalled that the president routinely held on to vital intelligence, only to "spring it on an unsuspecting member of his administration." According to Helms, "He did also ignore intelligence that was inconvenient. Intelligence was important to [Roosevelt] but . . . he tended to toy with it."[73] Then Britain signaled that there was no time to lose.

No sooner had King George VI appointed Winston Churchill prime minister in May 1940 than Churchill asked FDR to meet with Britain's director of naval intelligence, Admiral John H. Godfrey, and Canada's William Stephenson, who was then working for the British Secret Service (SIS).[74] Both men were emphatic: The United States must implement a fully integrated intelligence agency now, in peacetime, to be prepared for war. England could not go it alone. If England fell, Hitler might conquer the world. The pressure was on and the clock was ticking. Even as they spoke, the remnants of what had been the pride of Britain's fighting forces were straggling across the wide beaches of Dunkirk, wading toward rescue by an ad hoc fleet of private boats.

On June 22, as church bells throughout Germany pealed in celebration of the fall of France, a pall fell over the rest of the western world. Hitler's quest for world domination seemed invincible. It looked as though only more free countries dedicating more men, more money, and more materiel could stop him now. In his 1940 bid for reelection, FDR had publicly promised a resolutely isolationist nation that no American boy would die in a European war. Privately however, the president was convinced that he would not be able to keep this promise. Taking Godfrey and Stephenson's advice to heart, he began to look for someone capable of the daunting task of developing the country's first integrated intelligence agency.

Frank Knox, the recently appointed secretary of the navy, knew just the man for the job—Bill Donovan, a friend from Knox's New York City social and business circles. Donovan had attended Columbia law school with FDR, and though they had not been well acquainted, Donovan had made the president's short list of candidates for secretary of war.[75] He did not get that post, but he had the respect, the intellect, and the contacts to succeed in developing a new agency, and a significant added advantage: He had been a close friend of Stephenson's during the Great War. With hard work and a little luck, the president hoped to have a working organization in place before the country put a new generation into uniform.

William Joseph Donovan had first seen daylight on January 1, 1883, in Buffalo, New York, as the eldest of nine children born to devout, first-generation Irish Catholics. At one time, he had considered the priesthood, but instead studied law at Columbia University. By his thirtieth birthday, as a partner in Buffalo's leading law firm, he had completely transcended his immigrant grandfather's hardscrabble world, where "No Irish Need Apply" was commonly appended to Help Wanted signs. In the spring of 1912, he joined the newly formed National Guard Troop I, 1st New York Cavalry, and was soon the troop's captain.[76]

Newly married and honeymooning when war broke out in Europe in 1914, Donovan and his bride broke off their honeymoon. He believed that America would inevitably join the fighting, and he wanted Troop I to be prepared. The interrupted honeymoon was the first of many times that Ruth Donovan had to come to terms with her husband's priorities; his busy life meant that he was away from home more often than not. As it happened, Troop I was not deployed for nearly two years, and when it was, it was not sent to Europe, but to patrol the Mexican border against Pancho Villa's raids. In the gulches and ravines along the Rio Grande Donovan marked himself as a natural leader and earned the nickname "Wild Bill" for his daring, a nickname that stuck with him for life.[77] He also befriended Father Francis Duffy, the chaplain of the now famous 69th Regiment, and when the chaplain's "Fighting Irish" were called up to go to France, Father Duffy requested that Donovan be assigned to the regiment as colonel.

The Fighting Irish lived up to their name in Europe, and though the war had taken a heavy toll, on April 25, 1919, Donovan led his men up New York's Fifth Avenue in a victory parade. Then he and Ruth decided to make up for their truncated honeymoon with a monthlong trip to Japan with nothing but sightseeing and relaxation on the agenda. They had been in Tokyo only a few days when the U.S. ambassador to Japan asked Donovan to accompany him on an urgent mission to Siberia to determine whether the United States should support the regime of Alexander Kolchak, leader of a White Russian outpost there, being threatened by Bolsheviks.[78] Again, Ruth was left to her own devices while Donovan took off on the first of dozens of such trips over the next twenty years. Some trips were for his personal edification, others were for the federal government, where his firsthand evaluations of social and political conditions as both businessman and soldier provided valuable insights into world events. In this capacity he eventually became a major resource for President Roosevelt.

Over the years Donovan had developed an enormous range of friendships and contacts with ambassadors, diplomats, and businessmen in New York, Washington, and around the world. He traveled extensively throughout the 1930s, using his connections to take the temperature of world hot spots and form his own opinions on developments. In Rome, he met with German ambassador Ulrich von Hassell who would later become a source of intelligence for the OSS and play a pivotal role in the German opposition to Hitler.[79] He charmed Italian dictator Benito Mussolini into allowing him to view his troops in Africa. He toured Asmara, Adsum, and Benghazi in Libya, and even stayed in a striped silk tent at Marshal Pietro Badoglio's headquarters. A year later Donovan was in Spain observing the Civil War and noting the use of both German and Soviet weaponry.[80]

As Hitler trumpeted his triumph in France, William Stephenson, chief of British intelligence in the Americas, code-named Intrepid, met with Donovan in his suite at the St. Regis Hotel in New York.[81] One question dominated their agenda: Had the Allies already been defeated, or could they come back with support from the United States? Donovan, as FDR's unofficial eyes and ears, headed for London to evaluate the situation. He was seen as a trusted observer who could provide the president with an analysis independent of the opinions of Ambassador Kennedy.

Donovan's aura as a hero of the Great War and his letters of introduction from social, business, and military leaders opened doors previously firmly shut to Americans. British leaders, hoping that Donovan's influence would bring them much-needed American help, rolled out a very plush red carpet for him. Every courtesy was extended; he met with King George, Prime Minister Churchill, captains of industry, and military attachés. He was also given unprecedented access to SIS resources and was educated on British intelligence and counterintelligence operations.

The president meanwhile was still getting contradictory opinions on the odds of Britain's survival. Military advisors argued that England could survive with U.S. support, but Ambassador Kennedy was adamant that even with help Britain was doomed. He burned diplomatic wires advising Secretary of State Hull that England could never hold out against a German invasion without U.S. aid. The president should open negotiations with Germany.[82]

In August 1940, *The Saturday Evening Post* ran Mooney's speech, "War or Peace in America," which Roosevelt's aide Harry Hopkins had vetoed as too dangerous in the preelection environment. The war was "a stupendous tragedy" for Europe, Mooney argued, and the United States should use its immense power to twist arms and force the European belligerents to the peace table. Playing on their known fears, he wanted to warn the British that if they would not talk peace, the United States would not come to their aid. The Germans should be told that if they would not talk peace now, and reasonably, "we will arm to the teeth and make war by ourselves, if need be, against you."[83]

Whether or not Sir William Wiseman had read Mooney's "War or Peace in America," he was familiar with Mooney's thinking, and in September of that year, he, too, was "groping about for some means of initiating an effective peace move."[84] Sir William had been head of British Intelligence in the United States during World War I, and he was friendly with British ambassador Lord Lothian and with Churchill. When he met with Mooney over lunch at the private dining room of Kuhn Loeb, where he was a partner, Wiseman suggested that since the United States had already expressed great sympathy for Britain, it would never be seen as sufficiently neutral to serve as an intermediary; only the pope could prepare world opinion for a negotiated peace. Since Germany was the "irresistible force" and Britain the "immovable object," as he put it, the thing was obviously a draw, and there should be a peace without further bloodshed or ado. The approach was to come from the German side.

Mooney knew New York's Archbishop Francis Spellman quite well, and suggested him as a possible avenue to the pope. Several days later, they had what Mooney described as a "general, diplomatic and guarded" lunch with Spellman during which they made very little progress. After lunch though, at Mooney's club, he and Wiseman got down to the business of how best to arrange an exchange of peace terms. Perhaps Mooney could go to England to test the mood—inside and outside of government circles—but avoid any suggestion that peace proposals were coming from Germany. But Mooney had gone to Germany before, asking for information on peace terms for the White House, and the White House had never responded. A renewed approach might be met with skepticism and a cold shoulder.

That same September, William Rhodes Davis set off on another errand for Roosevelt, only to be detained on a routine Pan Am Clipper's Bermuda stopover by the British, who suspected his business affiliations. The U.S. State Department arranged for his release, and off he went to Germany to learn from both the military and intelligence men what Hitler's requirements for peace might be. What he heard was nothing very new: a return to the borders of 1914, eased terms on trade and raw materials, and the return of German colonies.[85] By the time Davis was given the tour of Hitler's early triumphs—occupied Poland and the German fortifications in the west—the *Westwall*—American business was poised to take part in that triumph, and in the triumphs to come.

In September, too, the British Foreign Office received a report from Switzerland that General Halder was unhappy with the regime and interested in making peace. Frank Roberts of the Foreign Office's Central Department noted, "No doubt there are military circles in Germany who would like a compromise peace, but we have no indication (1) that they are able or prepared to get rid of Hitler, etc., or (2) that they would be much better in the long run than the present gang who rule Germany."[86] The British attitude toward any peace initiatives seemed to be firmly in place.

And Roosevelt? Had he been hoodwinked by his State Department into sending Welles off on a mission identical to Mooney's, or was he simply practicing his own brand of politics—charming, manipulative, shrewd, and sphinxlike—and playing both ends against the middle? If, as some have suggested, FDR was trying to forestall a Nazi offensive in the spring of 1940, he was clearly unsuccessful. He had made a point of instructing Mooney to tell Hitler that he had spent some schooldays in Germany and had many good friends there. Yet his personal letters reveal a dislike of both Germany and Germans, and Cordell Hull summed up the administration's relations with Germany as "criminations and recriminations."[87] Roosevelt had absorbed an abundance of propaganda about the Hun during World War I and now railed routinely at Prussia as the wellspring of the Nazi evil, unaware that an unbridgeable cultural chasm separated Prussian traditions and Hitler's vulgar thuggery. Presidential prejudices were to play a part in shaping American policy.

DISAVOWED BY THE WHITE HOUSE, JIM MOONEY SAID HE REGRETTED THAT PARTISAN POLitics had triumphed over morality, ethics, and humanity. A final letter to the president expressed his disappointment at not having an opportunity to present his case for returning to the negotiations of the previous winter, but he still hoped he might win the president over in the cause of peace.[88] In an unsent letter dated February 1941, he urged Roosevelt—"to whom the nation and the entire world now looks for rescue from Armageddon"— to spell out the conditions and aims for which America would fight.

He did not hear from the White House again. He resigned as president of GMC Overseas to help convert domestic GM plants to war production. He then volunteered for service with the Production Engineering Section of the Bureau of Aeronautics and eventually worked with the chief of naval operations.[89] Historians and scholars continue to puzzle over Mooney's true motivations and to wonder what game Roosevelt was really playing— if it was a game. Jim Mooney's letters and notes for his memoirs suggest that he was motivated by a genuine concern for peace, yet there were also doubters. Under Secretary of State George Messersmith was convinced that he was "fundamentally fascist in his sympathies" and suggested that in time he would become "our Quisling."[90] Mooney had been deeply wounded by what he regarded as a scurrilous smear campaign by the New York tabloid *PM* regarding the medal presented to him by the German government. Photographs had been doctored, dates and facts fudged, to make him look like an enthusiastic Nazi sympathizer. By 1943 the president's earlier warm letters had been superseded by an FBI investigation. The puzzle remains unsolved.

GENERAL DONOVAN'S INTELLIGENCE SERVICE

When Donovan returned from his European trip, he spent a few days motoring and picnicking in New England with the vacationing FDR, briefing the president.[91] He told Roosevelt that without American help, England would fall. The United States would be going to war, and the first order of business was to beef up the British fleet. Britain was running out of money fast. Resources for the cash-and-carry scheme would soon be exhausted. Knox, Stephenson, and Donovan hatched a plan to trade American materiel for British assets. The British would receive fifty mothballed U.S. Navy ships, plus aircraft, munitions, machinery, tools, anything "useful for any defense article for the government of any country whose defense the President deems vital to the defense of the United States,"[92] and in exchange the United States would be granted ninety-nine-year leases on British naval bases around the globe. Donovan argued that legally, since it was a simple trade, the president could do an end run around Congress, but FDR still had an election to win and he was not about to jeopardize it.

The lend-lease scheme was put on the back burner while FDR campaigned hard for another term, still preaching isolationism to voters who had learned of the horrors of the Great War from their parents, and who wanted no part of a European War. Politicians, however, recognized that joining the war was inevitable. In fact, the staunchly isolationist nation was gearing up for war.[93] FDR and Kennedy clashed on the issue of U.S. involvement, and on October 22, 1940, Kennedy, according to an official statement from the embassy in London "left the post."[94] Within months the United States had a new ambassador to the Court of St. James's, John Winant.

In January 1941, with the election secure and draftees entering the military services, the Lend-Lease Act went before Congress. It was a significant commitment, if only in a moral sense, but it brought the nation closer to war. Again FDR called on Donovan to go abroad to reassess the situation. He did not want to commit the United States to another war in Europe if it was a lost cause. In a truly American tabloid moment, the newspapers caught wind of the famously Republican Donovan assisting the nation's foremost Democrat and began tracking his every move. With his name sprinkling the daily papers, Donovan was forced to travel as an official representative of the navy rather than a civilian businessperson, which only heightened his celebrity. The British were especially keen to be accommodating.

Donovan visited London, the Middle East, Bulgaria, Yugoslavia, Turkey, Iraq, Palestine, North Africa, Spain, and Portugal. In mid-March 1941, he reported his observations to FDR and top White House aides.[95] As he would do so often, he also brought back choice stamps for the president's collection— possibly one additional reason for FDR's willingness to justify his high expenses. A week after his return, at the president's request, Donovan addressed the nation in a radio broadcast carried by three major networks. He described what he had seen on his 25,000-mile trek and shared with the American public his conclusion that Hitler would settle for nothing less than world domination. If the United States wanted to remain free, he said, it had to prepare to defend that freedom "while resistance is still possible."

FDR's office was still getting disconnected bits of intelligence from numerous government agencies, and he was certain that a central clearinghouse could stitch this information together into something useful. On

June 18, 1941, the president asked Donovan to head a new organization to evaluate existing information and develop new intelligence leads. Donovan accepted.

The U.S. intelligence situation Donovan stepped into when he was named Coordinator of Information (COI) was characterized by David K. E. Bruce, an early member of Donovan's operation who later headed the London OSS unit as director of the European Theater of Operations, as a "mess."[96] The COI was meant to bring order into the intelligence chaos. Its mission was to collect, analyze, and correlate all information bearing on national security and make it available to the president or others as necessary. It was also to carry out what were called "other activities" at the president's request, to secure information vital to national security. Although the COI reported to the White House, it was a civilian office, and its operations were independent of any government departments, not unlike that of its German counterpart, the Abwehr.

The new COI was established with less than $100,000 from the president's emergency fund and allotted two small rooms for offices.[97] Donovan himself became a "dollar a year" man and drew no salary. Very quickly, COI grew to eight people squeezed into an office at the State Department building, and within three months several hundred staffers were spread out in various buildings across Washington. COI—soon to be OSS—headquarters eventually found a home at the corner of 25th and E Streets in a dismal neighborhood of tenements, warehouses, and weeds. The place was so permeated by the smell of beer that some new recruits were convinced the place was a brewery.[98] In fact, it had been the National Institute of Health.

Normally government-related expenses had to be submitted to the Bureau of the Budget. However, since many COI expenditures could have put lives in jeopardy should they be revealed to the enemy, Donovan was allowed to spend his budget as Unvouchered Funds (UFs). He would certify that the expenses were incident to collecting information relevant to U.S. security and that "it would be prejudicial to the public interest to disclose the names of the recipients, the dates and the names of places in which the expenditures were made."[99]

Donovan's travels had been fact-finding missions, but also clearly in the interest of establishing an American intelligence operation. Based on what he had seen, he had developed a clear idea of what America's next intelligence agency should be able to achieve. Among other things, he felt there should be psychological warfare and sabotage, modeled after the British Psychological Warfare Executive and Special Operations Executive (SOE). This was a marked change from the prevailing attitude that war was essentially a matter of full frontal attack.

The key criteria for inclusion in Donovan's intelligence operation were analytical minds and language skills. To meet the needs of his new organization,

Donovan raided academia, the world of journalism, the social register—even Hollywood—for talent. He recruited the country's intellectual and social elite. By doing so, he eventually put together an extraordinary organization later described by McGeorge Bundy as part cops and robbers, part faculty meeting.[100] The staff list included notables such as Dr. James Baxter of Williams College, historian William Langer and Dr. Edward Mason, both of Harvard, Princeton's Dr. Edward Meade, and writers Robert Sherwood and Thornton Wilder. FDR's son James was on the team, as was a great miscellany of polo players, stuntmen, debutantes, garage mechanics, mountain climbers, and missionaries.[101]

Lacking a blueprint, Donovan often turned to history for inspiration in planning his unorthodox agency. Richard Heppner, a junior lawyer at Donovan's firm, spent hours in bookstores and libraries finding material related to earlier intelligence efforts for his boss.[102] Donovan's five-hundred-acre country estate, Chapel Hill in Virginia, lay in the heart of an area known as Mosby's Confederacy, and also offered him clues. Donovan was fascinated by Mosby's reminiscences of his days as a Confederate partisan, detailing his anti-Union activities during the Civil War, when he deployed small forces with speed to surprise and harass the enemy, raid rail lines and depots. Donovan took Mosby's lessons to heart. Later in the war, when COI's successor organization, the OSS, infiltrated Italy, France, China, and Japan, it was often Mosby's modus operandi that was applied.[103]

In many ways COI became the stepchild of the British intelligence services. Britain had spent nearly three hundred years refining its intelligence systems and operations, and had centuries of experience and dozens of facilities in place. But the war had made her cash poor. The United States, meanwhile, was starting from scratch, with no infrastructure, training programs, facilities, or agents, but it had ample funding. In the dual role of parent and mentor, the British helped America develop a working model in about a year, coaching, encouraging, and providing training to each of the four COI branches: research and analysis (R&A), foreign information service (FIS), intelligence (SAB),[104] and sabotage (SAG).[105]

Since the country was not yet at war, Donovan was not permitted to implement SAB—intelligence—or SAG—sabotage—but their heads, David K. E. Bruce and M. P. Goodfellow, had a head start in developing training and an infrastructure based on the British model. True to its word, the British intelligence service gave COI access to one of its training schools in Canada, now known as Camp X, for training America's first agents, and the school's structure and curriculum were later used as models for OSS training.[106] Until Donovan could train his people and put them in place, Stephenson served as a conduit for intelligence reports.

The U.S. government intelligence services already in existence were marked by mutual mistrust and competition. FBI director J. Edgar Hoover's ambitions to expand his bureau's mission from counterintelligence operations to active intelligence gathering only compounded the problems. He was partly successful, however, and FDR entrusted Hoover with the operation of a foreign intelligence service in the western hemisphere, in addition to domestic counterintelligence, counterespionage, and countersabotage investigations. According to Richard Helms, this Special Intelligence Service (SIS) was in direct competition with OSS and was "causing us enormous problems."[107] Later, Hoover's constant squabbles with what was by then the OSS finally forced Roosevelt to restrict the OSS mandate to outside the western hemisphere, a regulation later applied to the CIA.

Early on, COI's work mirrored efforts of the military's and the State Department's intelligence networks, which were notoriously reluctant to share information with the COI. Donovan had no official recourse to force them to share, but his experience as corporate lawyer had taught him that quantities of revealing information about companies could be gleaned from public sources—books, newspapers, and radio broadcasts. It was a huge task—the sort of task that would now be done by computers. It demanded patience, attention to minutiae and the intellect to put the pieces together, but Donovan suspected the method could be successfully applied to gathering military intelligence. To test his theory, he formed the Research and Analysis—R&A—branch of the COI, whose primary objective was to use existing data to discover Axis strengths and weaknesses. Scattered in hundreds of file cabinets throughout government agencies were geological surveys, aerial photos, economic reports, and protocol procedures—and thousands of pages of related data that would be among their most useful sources. The Library of Congress was a treasure trove of information and became the branch's chief haunt.

By sifting through government reports and public materials housed there, a COI researcher could answer a multitude of questions and analyze the strategic importance of any town in the world. Who were the area's key social, political, and economic leaders? What were its natural resources? Were there factories, and what was the potential output? What was the condition of local roads, railways, and ports? Were there military facilities nearby, or was there a suitable location for one? Had local resistance been reported? The answers could be discovered without ever leaving Washington.

The concept of using unclassified materials to develop accurate profiles was a new one. It became America's greatest contribution to intelligence gathering and is now standard practice in intelligence agencies worldwide. To this day, CIA researchers are assigned topics, then sift through newspapers, magazines, and transcripts of radio and television news broadcasts looking for bits of information that might be related to their assignment. The miscellaneous nuggets are then set before analysts who study them for clues to what is happening in areas where the CIA does not have "human assets" in place, or to corroborate reports by third-party sources.

Nearly half of the COI staff worked in Foreign Information Services (FIS). Some were experienced newspapermen or writers for radio, others were young people with degrees in journalism. Donovan wanted a strong propaganda outfit and wisely tucked a small group conducting propaganda or "black" broadcasts into a much larger official news or "white" radio broadcast team. The United States needed straightforward, no-nonsense news reports on events in Europe, and COI was able to provide them in several fifteen-minute broadcasts daily. But laced among the news stories were bits of misinformation meant to distract and confuse the enemy. COI listening posts monitored Nazi broadcasts, then spun some of the material broadcast to turn it against Hitler to rebroadcast it through Foreign Information Services. Donovan was adopting the Axis strategy of using information as a weapon of war and turned it right back at them. Though most U.S. private broadcasting companies refused to carry the FIS material, the British Security Coordinator permitted the use of the British transmitting station to broadcast to Europe.[108]

In spite of jealousies and contentiousness among Washington's intelligence circles, Donovan's outfit was up and running, a major step toward putting the United States on a wartime footing. Neither Donovan nor the ever-suspicious Hoover, who had Donovan under almost constant surveillance at the time, suspected that eventually it would become a major source of information and contact with oppositional elements within the enemy camp.

CHAPTER 4

1939–1941

FLUID NEUTRALITIES

For more than twenty-five hundred years Istanbul had represented either gateway or barrier to conflicting imperial, cultural, and ecclesiastical ambitions. The city had been the center of a vast empire, a crossroads for centuries, a jewel fought over by emperors and prelates. When the war began, though a German invasion was expected at any moment, Turkey appeared determined to maintain a smiling neutrality, and for good reason. Both Turkey's historic enemies, Germany and the Soviet Union, were set on conquest. In late August of 1939, German foreign minister von Ribbentrop had hammered out an alliance with the Soviets to bring Stalin in line with the Axis, but there was a quid pro quo: certain eastern territories, including eastern Turkey and Iran. The Soviet Baku oil fields would continue to fuel the German war machine, and the two powers determined that they would carve up the spoils of war. At least, that was the plan. The Allies were thunderstruck, but the pact did nothing to lessen the traditional power struggle between Germany and Russia, or their desperate tug-of-war over the Balkans and Turkey. It was only a matter of time before Hitler would press for more.

Portugal shared many attributes of Turkey's neutrality: spies, refugees, and pressure from Germany to deliver raw materials; it, too, found ways of dealing with all of them. American businesses, meanwhile, continued to produce for the Reich.

THE ISTANBUL CONNECTION

The scramble for Turkey began with the invasion of Poland. The British and French urged the Turks to join the Allies, and while they did sign an agreement, Turkey remained officially neutral. With a warm-water port, control of the Black Sea, and access to the Mediterranean, Turkey had long been a target for Soviet ambitions and aggression. Germany depended on Romania's oil fields and Turkey's natural resources, like chromium ore, critical to their munitions, and its railway lines were essential for the war. Turkey began to anticipate a German invasion.

Turkey had been in this position before. In World War I, however, the already moribund Ottoman Empire had signed up in support of Germany and Austria-Hungary. In some ways, Turkish reluctance to become a German military ally now was a result of that experience. For Turkey, that first global war had meant the end of the Ottoman Empire, the loss of valuable terrain in Syria, Iraq, and Palestine, and a complete change in political structure.

The anticipated invasion never came. Turkey and its international community were mystified but relieved. Hitler's announcement in late March 1942 that he would not invade, but would do everything he could to keep Turkey neutral, only deepened the mystery. Still no attack came, and it seemed that Hitler would keep his word. What had motivated Hitler's decision, no one knew, but there was nearly universal relief, since Turkey's neutrality made it a vital intelligence base for both Allies and Axis. Turkey reopened its rail bridges to the Balkans. Only later was it discovered that Germany had cracked Turkey's diplomatic code and turned Turkey into an unwitting source of vital intelligence on the USSR. Information on the eastern front was crucial to the Nazis and a fair trade for keeping Turkey intact.[1]

Turkey's geopolitical situation continued to make it a hub for competing powers. That was "the big picture." On the ground and in real life, the big picture translated into hotel lobbies with agents behind every newspaper and potted palm, nightclubs packed with diplomats and refugees—most of them spies—power brokers, information seekers and sellers, and foreign correspondents, all living large as they hustled everyone and anyone for information. Seventeen foreign intelligence services operated in Turkey during the war. Istanbul was so crowded that office space was extremely hard to come by.

Canaris's Abwehr had been in Turkey since 1941, in active competition with Reinhard Heydrich's Sicherheitsdienst, established in Ankara in 1940.[2] Under Ludwig Moyzisch, formerly of the Waffen SS, now officially listed as an economic counselor, Turkish SD was thought to be very inefficient, "using large sums of money and accomplishing very little."[3] Consequently, the Abwehr team, under the able leadership of Captain Paul Leverkühn, was currently dominant in Turkey. A well-known lawyer, a friend and former colleague of Moltke, Leverkühn was fiftyish, a tall, somewhat stooped man, deeply religious, and known for his prodigious memory.[4] Leverkühn was widely traveled and well acquainted with many attorneys around the world, including William Donovan, head of one of the Abwehr's presumed archenemies, the OSS.

Second in command at the Abwehr was "Willi" Hamburger, a "newspaper correspondent" who used the same methods Donovan encouraged. Bright, but too lazy to chase down refugees or others having information, he simply subscribed to American magazines and newspapers, then sat back with his feet up and read. By tracking items such as military sporting events and weddings, he could extrapolate considerable data on troop movements. With the help of Paula Koch, Hamburger also organized an extensive courier system throughout the Balkans. Koch has been sensationalized as the Mata Hari of World War II, but she was actually middle-aged and gray, and her competence depended not on her physical charms but on her many languages, contacts, and extensive experience in the area. Koch understood the local mentality perfectly.[5]

Then there was Wilhelmina Vargassy, whose irresistible allure made her a frequent and popular guest on the Istanbul cocktail party circuit. Vargassy's specialty was "innocently" extracting data from well-lubricated would-be suitors. Sometimes she lured her prey into her bed. One willing victim is said to have been an American intelligence officer. Vargassy was on Turkish intelligence's list.[6]

Istanbul swarmed with spies of every stripe. Its narrow, jumbled streets teemed with international agents, double agents, triple agents, smugglers, informants, forgers, black marketers—all conniving, double-dealing, and scheming for the information, power, and money that this war seemed to offer. In this anthill, the Abwehr, the SD, British intelligence, the OSS, and a miscellany of other information networks crawled all over each other, supported by money pouring in from both the Allies and the Axis.

Money, especially a great deal of money, often breeds corruption, and the city became a sort of modern Sodom and Gomorrah, rich in the seven deadly sins. Wrath, avarice, lust, and gluttony were everywhere, most particularly at places like the Taksim Casino and Elli's Bar. Champagne and caviar were staples at parties given by and for foreigners. Alcohol and beautiful women were known to loosen lips, and did. Together with money, they, too, shifted allegiances. As the stakes got higher, the price of life got lower; agents became double, triple, and even quadruple agents. Istanbul became a magnet, attracting both high and low life hoping for a piece of the action. By the war's end Istanbul alone was said to be home to nearly two hundred forgers.[7]

Not for nothing did an OSS memorandum lay down rules for American citizens on proper behavior while in Turkey: "Indiscreet conduct . . . may constitute a serious threat to our own security, to the security of our Allies, and injure us in the eyes of neutrals." Association with enemy nationals was specifically forbidden, most especially "enemy female nationals . . . as they are in fact frequently the most dangerous of enemy agents." British and American were not be identified or pointed out on the street to "friends," as it might lead to a discussion of their work and include addresses or other potentially dangerous information. In public places "greatest care should be taken to avoid mentioning confidential information where eavesdropping may occur. Not only are restaurants and bars public places, but also hotel rooms. . . ."[8]

If the rules were not followed, there might be hell to pay.

THE SCENE OF JUST ONE EVENING CAN STAND FOR THE WHOLE. THE AIR AT THE TAKSIM Casino was so thick with smoke from American cigarettes that the silky voice drifting lazily through the crowded room seemed to emanate from the smoke rather than from the woman who was actually singing. But the beautiful Hungarian Adrian Molnár was unquestionably the focus of attention of two men on opposite sides of the room. On one side sat middle-aged George Earle III, the former American ambassador to Bulgaria, who had brought the crooner to the safety of neutral Turkey. On the other side sat her most recent admirer, "Willi" Hamburger, a twenty-five-year-old Austrian, apparently just another of the idle rich, but whose cosmopolitan exterior masked a passionate longing for an independent Austria. While the two men ought to have been enemies on every level, they had more in common than just being besotted with the same women. Both were well-educated, old-money socialites with impressive family connections, and both were spies who endangered the operations they were spying for. In fact, Hamburger later became the greatest security threat imaginable: an Abwehr agent turned double agent for the Allies.

On paper, and in retrospect, it seems the stuff of absurd farce, and while there certainly were elements of farce, it was not all flirting over drinks, dancing in smoky boîtes, and assignations in hotel rooms, tawdry or otherwise. Christopher Sykes, a British intelligence agent in Cairo with close links to Istanbul, offered another take. The spy "lived in a kaleidoscope of emotions. . . . Hope would rise, sink, rise and sink again. . . . The intelligence officer's life is . . . depressing. . . . He inevitably becomes a pessimist, feels guilty . . . is suspected of cowardice . . . suspects himself. He has a double share in the anxiety, none in the danger and heroism."[9]

The danger part was not entirely true. It was dangerous and lucrative— sometimes in equal measure—though sometimes the danger outweighed the lucre by a factor of ten. Double and triple agents engaged in a perilous

juggling act; they had to remember what to tell whom. They had to balance telling just enough to keep the payers interested and paying against
the danger of tipping their hand and betraying themselves by telling too
much. If they gave the game away, execution was the price.

THE DAPPER DIPLOMAT

Franz von Papen had been offered the German ambassadorship to Turkey
in the autumn of 1938 and he had turned it down. At the time, the ambas-
sadorial post in Ankara was at the fringes of German diplomacy, a desolate
jumping-off place to nowhere, and it became vacant. But by April 1939
things had changed: Just weeks before, Germany had marched into Czechoslovakia and also signed a trade agreement with Romania, with its rich
Ploesti oil fields; Italian forces had occupied Albania; Mussolini had signed
on with Hitler to collaborate in military actions; Turkish neutrality was beginning to waver.

Istanbul's location at the intersection of geographies had always made it
a crossroads of political interests. It was the gateway to the oil fields beyond
the Caucasus. Its railroads were invaluable for transporting goods—or
soldiers—from Europe and the Balkans to Russia and Asia and vice versa.
The Allies were aware of German dependence on critical raw materials from
Turkey and were keen to prevent further Axis encroachment into southeastern Europe and the Middle East. Turkey was suddenly a hot spot, a locus of power. Papen recognized opportunity when he saw it; he was now
exactly where he wanted to be—in the thick of things, where his efforts
might lead him to a bigger, brighter future. He accepted the ambassadorship gladly. If Ankara got to be a bore, there was always the Istanbul Express
to rush him to the exciting center of it all.

By the time he became ambassador to Turkey, Papen had already been
involved in German politics and government in one way or another for
years. He had served as military attaché in Washington, DC, during World
War I, organizing sabotage in American shipyards and munitions factories.
He also tried to send military and political intelligence home, but was
found out and deported with enough press fanfare to bring him some no-
toriety in Germany.

For a short time, Papen then served as a military attaché in Spain, where
he was reportedly in contact with the doomed alleged German spy, Mata
Hari. In light of his less than successful mission to the United States and his
lackluster services in Spain, Papen was assigned in 1918 to duty in remote
Palestine, and as a spymaster for the Turks in their war against the British,
chiefly tracking down Arab guerrillas under the command of T. E. Lawrence.
Again, he was unsuccessful.

When Weimar President Paul von Hindenburg plucked him out of the confused political scene in Germany to replace Heinrich Brüning as chancellor in 1932, Papen was still an unknown quantity. According to the astute French ambassador to Berlin, André François-Poncet, his appointment was "greeted with incredulous amazement." While Hindenburg hoped that Papen would be able to hold on to the support of both right and center power, François-Poncet recognized "something about Papen that prevents either his friends or his enemies from taking him seriously; he bears the mark of frivolity, he is not a person of the first rank."[10]

Papen's remarkable survival, first in the convoluted politics of the Weimar Republic and then in the Nazi government can probably be ascribed to precisely that quality that made him so difficult to take seriously, his political malleability. In January 1933, cobbling together a coalition cabinet as chancellor, Papen realized that he could be assured of holding on to the support of the growing Nazi power only by giving Hitler his heart's desire: the chancellorship. Then Papen, as vice chancellor, would pull this Austrian upstart's strings like a puppeteer. "We have hired him!" he crowed privately. "In two months we will have pushed Hitler so far into a corner that he will squeak!"[11]

This assessment of Hitler reveals a surprising lack of political acumen, and Papen is now regarded as the man who held the stirrup and allowed Hitler vault into the saddle of power.[12] But in fairness, with the exception of a few insightful Cassandras like François-Poncet, most foreign governments indulged in the same sort of wishful thinking vis-à-vis Germany's new chancellor. If Papen was wrong, so were they.[13] Within the two months that were to have made him squeak, Hitler had already erected the framework for his totalitarian state.[14] For the most part, history has judged Papen a dapper, top-hatted aristocrat impersonating a statesman, a political lightweight, and a boundlessly ambitious opportunist. If it took flexibility to become a player, he was happy to demonstrate extraordinary political elasticity. As Hitler's ambassador to Vienna in 1938, he had helped Hitler bring Austria under Nazi control. Now there was concern that Turkey would meet the same fate.

No sooner had Papen arrived in Turkey than he set to work. His view and the view of the German Foreign Office was that Germany and the Soviet Union must put concerted pressure on Turkey, not simply to maintain her neutrality, but to enlist her on the Axis side. However, there was no dearth of players in the power game over Turkey and its periphery. In the late 1930s the Turks kept to themselves. During the war, they struggled to maintain an imperiled neutrality. But with both Germany and the Soviet Union set on conquest, the Turks were not nearly as passive as the image they tried to project.

Turkey had not been subject to the conflicting interests of various powers for centuries without learning something about the intrigue game. After

Hitler's lightning attack on Poland on September 1, 1939, Papen's efforts to shake Turkish neutrality were preempted when Turkey signed mutual defense agreements with the French and British. As the Nazis swept through the Balkans, Turks thought they saw what lay in store, lined up support, and prepared to defend themselves. Emniyet—Turkish intelligence—collaborated with the British and the Americans; they might need all the help they could get. They also had intelligence-gathering sources at nearly every restaurant, bar, apartment building, and hotel in the country, and claimed that every foreign reporter was under twenty-four-hour surveillance.

Then, in a semblance of complete neutrality, Turkish Foreign Minister Sukru Saracoglu surreptitiously began to feed as much information as he could to the British ambassador, his friend Hughe Knatchbull-Hugessen— "Knatchy" to his pals—while appeasing the Nazis any way he could. Should either the Soviets or the Germans invade, Saracoglu hoped that the British and Americans would help defend his country.

AFTER VANQUISHING POLAND, HITLER'S ARMIES HAD SWEPT THROUGH NORWAY, DENmark, Holland, Belgium, and France. Hungary, Romania, and Bulgaria fell to the Germans like so many dominoes, and though these countries were still technically neutral, they were in effect German satellites. Hitler and Stalin between them were rearranging the map. In November 1939, Soviet Foreign Minister Vyacheslav Molotov met with Hitler in Berlin. The city was improbably festooned with the Soviet hammer and sickle to celebrate the combination of German and Soviet forces that Ribbentrop announced would bring about the "end of the British Empire." Having demonstrated his military might, Hitler now thought it might be possible to negotiate a peace with Britain, but various peace feelers by Papen through the Netherlands and the Vatican failed—at least according to Papen—because of a negative stance on the part of both Hitler and Ribbentrop.[15]

In June 1940, Hitler stood at the apex of his power. Germany controlled everything from the English Channel to the river Bug in Poland, from the North Cape to the Brenner Pass. Italy was an ally, and Russia, too, at least for the moment.[16] In Turkey, Papen basked in the reflected glow; he was the man of the hour. Everyone, particularly representatives from Eastern Europe and countries now occupied by Germany, wanted to see him, to learn what might be learned from him, to bend his ear, perhaps to wield influence or win favor. But Papen also had worries, and he was not the only one.

Refugees from Poland's elite were pouring into Istanbul and Ankara, establishing schools, supporting music and the ballet, but the mood in Turkey was grim. The Balkans were clearly next on the Nazi agenda. On February 10, 1940, England broke off relations with Romania and closed its embassy; Allied citizens were to be out of the country by 10:30 P.M. or risk arrest as spies. On March 1, Bulgaria officially joined the Axis. Hitler's only concession toward Turkey was to agree that German soldiers would maintain a distance of thirty miles from Turkey's border with Bulgaria. In late March, Yugoslavia aligned itself with Germany, but protestors surrounded government buildings, the royal palace, and police stations in Belgrade and installed an anti-Nazi government. Hitler responded at 4:30 A.M. on April 6 by declaring war on Yugoslavia and Greece and bombing Belgrade for five days. The city was devastated; approximately 20,000 civilians were killed and there were countless injured. Yugoslavia surrendered quickly. Greece had fought valiantly against Mussolini's forces, but was now too weak to fend off the Germans, and surrendered three weeks later.

One thing Allied intelligence was able to do in this crisis was to send wooden fishing boats known as "caïques" from Turkey to transport food, people, information, and military materials to the Greek and Yugoslav coasts. Much-needed food relieved some of the suffering, but despite repeated requests from Jewish refugees for transportation out of Axis-controlled areas, the caïques returned to Turkey empty.

Turkey was now ringed with countries where the needs of jostling, hungry populations displaced by the war had outpaced all available resources. The world was flooded with refugees. Archbishop Angelo Giuseppe Roncalli—the future Pope John XXIII—had come to Istanbul as the representative of ecclesiastical power. As the papal nuncio and apostolic vicar, he went quietly about his work, doing whatever was in his power to help the helpless, anyone displaced, devastated, or threatened by the war.[17] Although he was forbidden by Turkish authorities to identify himself as a man of the cloth in his dress, Roncalli stood out anyway. Small, round, recognizably of peasant stock, he lived simply in a world of sleek, well-heeled operators, like a saint among sinners. By curious happenstance, he lived only a few blocks from Papen's consular office in Istanbul and became quite close to Martha von Papen, a woman less busy and more religious than her husband.

Papen began to use this friendly relationship with Roncalli to make him a conduit to Rome. He had already met with Roncalli in August 1940 to explain that while Hitler did not want to invade or destroy England, he would if Churchill refused to capitulate. The Nazis had just rolled over France and routed the English at Dunkirk. If the Vatican interceded on behalf of Hitler's regime, Papen promised that "the Reich would grant it special privileges."[18] The fifty-nine-year old priest conveyed the message to the Vatican, but Rome declined to interfere.

PORTUGAL: THE INTERNATIONAL CLEARING GROUND

Neutrality guaranteed little during the war except an influx of legions of foreigners. For Portugal, this was nothing new. It had been a target of approaches from land and sea by Greeks, Phoenicians, Romans, Celts, Visigoths, and Moors for centuries. Now, however, long lines snaked behind the crossing points from the Spanish frontier. As the flood made its way westward—with luck to America—Lisbon and Estoril were awash with people of every nationality. Just as in Switzerland and Istanbul, the opposing ambitions of several nations clashed in Portugal. Riches, misery, and powerful warring forces met, bringing with them a ready supply of spies, agents, black marketers, and a huge underbelly of those who are always ready to exploit war and misery. Chances were that eventually they would all come together in one place.

That place was the Rossio, Lisbon's expansive central square. Three of the city's main arteries end there, and all trains arriving from the rest of Europe disgorge their passengers near its northeast corner, where there is always a line of taxis. The Rossio is also the site of Lisbon's biggest café, the Chave d'Ouro—or Golden Key—which took its name from the tool shop once located on the site. By 1940, it was an institution of long standing, a place where everyone, no matter what nationality or political stripe, spent time.

In many ways the picture was immutable; clusters of men, their black shoes interrupting the orderly arrangement of the black and white tiles—*calcada*—talked of everything, or nothing. The shadow of the square's central column moved, but always in a prescribed arc, and the fountains always plashed agreeably. Sitting in a cane chair under pale-colored awnings stirring slightly in the morning breeze, one was as likely to hear several of five other languages as to hear Portuguese. And whatever the language, the conversation usually involved the latest war news, spurious conspiracy gossip, or complaints about the big problem facing most refugees: getting out of Portugal. The look of immutability was illusory. Except for the locals, the cast of characters changed constantly, even if not quickly enough to suit them.

Most of the transients were here to escape, but there were many more people waiting for transport than was available. The waiting could seem an impossible roller coaster: elation at hope, despair at hope's evanescence. Teetering between sorrow over a past life and anticipation of a new one was numbing, paralyzing. The tedium of the daily passenger-list checks, the limbo of never knowing, the peculiar mix of boredom and anxiety, carried with it an almost insurmountable inertia The wealthy refugees survived the inertia comfortably enough, moving from hotel, to beach, to hotel, to the casino at Estoril. Many more endured constant nagging from an empty stomach, sorrow, and worry about family or funds, or both.

There simply was not enough transportation to deal with the throngs. Air travel was the safest, and Sintra was the preferred point of embarkation, with the Pan-American Clipper, and KLM flights to London. But getting a spot was difficult and involved a good deal of money. The port offered alternatives; the Portuguese *Serpa Pinto* made the trip to and from Philadelphia about once every six weeks. There were also other ships, but U-boats were a constant threat, and the waiting lists went on for pages.[19]

Of the thousands clustered along the Portuguese coast, some had ample funds; others were desperate to scrape together the money for passage to safety or to bribe the visa officials by selling whatever small treasures remained to them, or even themselves. At the Chave d'Ouro they might linger for hours over *um galdo*—coffee with lots of milk—an inexpensive way to get some food value with their morning wake-up. With it, they were sure to imbibe some of Portugal's ineffable *saudade*—a longing, or yearning, with a touch of nostalgia thrown in. It was a yearning for passage to a new life and breathing space, mingled with nostalgia for a happier past. All rolled together, it was perfectly expressed in Portugal's *fado,* those melancholy songs straight from the heart. At the end of the day, if they could afford it, they might go again to the Chave d' Ouro to numb the pain with the scorch of *aguardiente*.

In World War I Portugal had fought with the Allies; in World War II, Britain and Germany were adversaries again, but Portugal remained neutral. Unlike Spain's unabashedly pro-Nazi neutrality, however, Portugal's "collaboratively neutral" stance was fuzzier. Whatever the true sympathies of Portugal's strongman, Antonio de Oliveira Salazar, and however inclined to fascism he may have been, he also had deep historical ties to England. Balancing these ties against his need to keep his economy percolating by providing Germany with wolfram for armaments was a tricky act, requiring considerable toughness and diplomacy. The tightrope Salazar walked was wobbly and he hoped not to fall to either side without assurances of a sizable net. One of the challenges Salazar faced early in the war was the man who had been—albeit briefly—England's king.

THE UNWELCOME DUKE

Edward Albert Christian George Andrew Patrick David, Prince of Wales, briefly King Edward VIII, and more recently the Duke of Windsor, had become an embarrassment. After the death of his father in 1936, he became Edward VIII by the Grace of God, of Great Britain, Ireland, and the British Dominions beyond the Seas, King, Defender of the Faith, Emperor of India. He had retained these titles for 325 days, until he famously renounced the throne for the "woman I love," Wallis Warfield Simpson, a twice-divorced American with a strong fashion sense and fascist tendencies. Demoted to simply the Duke of Windsor, he and his bride had been entertained in Germany as the personal guests of Adolf Hitler in 1937. Having hobnobbed with Nazi higher-ups, the Windsors' ongoing cordial relations with the Nazi regime turned into a serious morale problem in England. Rumors of the duchess's close, possibly intimate, contacts with Ribbentrop only made the whole business even more appalling. There was the hope that settling them into a comfortable exile at a safe distance in France would smooth the situation, and for a time, it did.

But with the fall of Paris in 1940, the Windsors fled, first to Biarritz, then to Spain, and to Portugal soon after. There, unfortunately, they nearly collided with the Duke of Kent's state visit to Salazar on behalf of King George VI. The famous couple was the darling of the international media, but in the circumstances it seemed advisable to keep them out of the limelight, and Salazar used his essentially dictatorial powers to keep things very quiet. Tucked out of sight at a sumptuous villa above the sea at Cascais, they would be out of town but in the company of others who shared their sympathies.

For the British in June of 1940, anguished after Dunkirk, the Duke of Windsor was more than an embarrassment; his pro-Nazi pronouncements were salt in an open wound. Now he was also becoming problematic for the Portuguese. Historically, morally, they felt they owed England a debt of gratitude; but something had to be done about the ex-king and his wife. Churchill was keen to bundle him off, out of sight and hearing, where his defeatist talk could neither do tangible harm to British morale nor conspicuously benefit the Nazi cause. He felt that the Duke, as governor of the Bahamas, would be at a sufficient remove. For the Windsors, this parochial exile held no charm, but apparently there was nothing better to be hoped for from the prime minister or the royal family.

The Germans, of course, were well aware of this psychologically fraught situation. They knew that the Duke would be pressed to placate his ambitious wife, and they were as interested in keeping him close by as the British were in getting him as far away as possible. What better propaganda tool than a British royal who proclaimed that the war could be ended quickly if only the English would not be so obstinate and bellicose? The German ambassador even informed Ribbentrop that the Duke was convinced that continued heavy bombardment of England would soften her up for peace.[20]

Foreign Minister Ribbentrop sent Walter Schellenberg to Portugal with an offer intended to lure the duke within reach: rescue from an unwelcome exile, a place in the heart of Europe, and plenty of money. Schellenberg was to offer the 50 million Swiss francs for the Windsors to come to Switzerland. This was a carefully considered choice; Switzerland was neutral, but it was not beyond the reach of Nazi military and political influence. Furthermore, the offer of 50 million francs was not a ceiling—the Führer could go higher. And if the vacillating royal, code-named "Willi," was still not persuaded, Schellenberg was to kidnap him if necessary.[21]

At last Churchill dispatched a lawyer and an old friend of the duke to expedite matters and persuade him to leave. The last days of July 1940 passed in a flurry of machinations and thwarted plans on both sides. The Germans were determined to nab the duke in any way they could; the British authorities in Portugal were equally determined to keep him out of Schellenberg's clutches and safe for export. Late on the first afternoon of August, the *Excalibur* nudged out of port, bound for New York. The Windsors were the only two passengers to be dropped off in the Bahamas—an expensive detour paid for by the British Exchequer.

THE WILY PROFITEER

On another August day nearly five centuries earlier, English bowmen had helped Portugal defeat a Spanish attempt to take over the Portuguese throne. One year later, John of Gaunt, Duke of Lancaster, negotiated the Treaty of Windsor, an alliance between England and Portugal intended to be an "inviolable, eternal, solid, perpetual and true league of friendship." This treaty, just a snippet of history really, was then strengthened by all the customary reinforcements: royal marriages and more battles, as when the Duke of Wellington helped to eject Napoleon from Portugal. In the end, it had an enduring impact on the relationship of the two nations and in fact played a significant role in Anglo-Portuguese relations during World War II, though the "inviolable" bonds between Britain and Portugal were put to a hard test.

When Salazar announced his intention of keeping Portugal neutral during the war, he had made a point of adding that he intended to "adhere to an iron principle—we shall not try to exploit the conflict for pecuniary gain."[22] In the dictator's hands however, this iron principle became unusually pliable. With Germany's invasion of the Soviet Union in 1941, a British embargo soon cut off the supplies of wolfram from Asia. Wolfram ore yields tungsten—a hard metal critical to the production of munitions—and the Russian offensive increased German demand for it enormously. With Europe's largest wolfram deposits located on the Iberian Peninsula, Germany was soon pressing for increased wolfram exports. Despite Spain's neutrality, Franco's heart belonged undeniably to Hitler; his Blue Divisions were fighting with the Germans in Russia, and he was compliant. As long as Germany occupied France, the ore could be shipped directly.

But Germany was pressing Portugal for more wolfram, and while the requirements of Portugal's economy and Salazar's pro-Axis inclinations would have made him more than happy to supply Germany, he was loath to irritate the British.[23] The British held wolfram mines in Portugal and also began to buy wolfram preemptively. Once the United States entered the war, the Americans joined in this effort, bringing a much-needed infusion of funds. As competition for wolfram intensified, smuggling and hidden exports played their part. Portuguese wolfram was probably being smuggled across the Spanish border and so to Germany as early as 1940. The price, in perfect accord with the laws of the marketplace, soared from just over $1,000 a ton to nearly $20,000 by late 1941.[24]

As the price rose, it encouraged ever more independent production and smuggling. The metallic glint of gray wolfram crystals was found where schist and granite collided, as they do in the Serra da Estrela, near Portugal's border with Spain, where the richest sources lay. Mining and smuggling was brutal work. Men and mules labored to muscle the heavy bags across mountain streams and over rocky crests redolent of pine resin. But the physical exertions of the *wolframistas* were matched, maybe even surpassed, by the suave efforts of countless diplomats, plying their trade over champagne, working to extract Salazar's favors in recurrent and ongoing rounds of drawn-out negotiations.

One result of Salazar's ambiguous policy was a running competition between underground British and German antagonists, involving not only the usual agents, but a considerable number of double agents. The mastermind behind Britain's double-agent operation, named XX, or double cross, was John Masterman. An Oxford don and an avid cricketer, Masterman later wrote a book in which he put his finger on what made Portugal such an extraordinary place during the war:

> It was not possible to learn in Berlin what was happening in London, but it might well be possible to hear, or guess, or deduce in neutral Portugal what was happening in both. And further, it might be possible to spread information (and make it appear credible) of what was not happening in London or Berlin and yet have it believed in the other place. And so Lisbon became a kind of international clearing ground, a busy ant-heap of spies and agents, where political and military secrets and information—true and false, but mainly false—were bought and sold and where men's brains were pitted against each other. . . .[25]

Masterman spelled out the aims of the double-cross game with characteristic succinctness: 1, to control the enemy system as much as possible; 2, to catch fresh spies; 3, to learn the personalities and methods of the German intelligence service; 4, to learn the code and cipher work of the German service; 5, to learn of enemy plans and intentions from the questions they asked; 6, to influence enemy plans by answers sent to them; and finally, 7, to deceive the enemy about British plans and intentions.[26]

Portugal had always been a poor country, but one of the unexpected consequences of the war was a whole new industry—the spy trade. It brought an influx of funds from British intelligence, from the SD, from the Abwehr, from OSS, and a miscellany of other interests. In a report prepared for FDR toward the very end of the war, Colonel Richard Park noted that businessmen in Portugal joked that whenever there were a lot of happy faces to be seen on the streets of Lisbon, it meant that it was payday for OSS informants.[27] If that made for happy faces, then payday for double agents would make for even happier faces; they were being paid by two masters, and Lisbon was "home" to a number of them.

One man who became an important part of XX, serving both Canaris and Britain's Stewart Menzies of SIS, was Dusko Popov. A nimble, well-to-do, and well-connected Yugoslav, Popov had been educated in France and Germany. At university in Freiburg, he had met Johann Jebsen, from a wealthy Hamburg shipping family, who later joined the Abwehr. When a secretary at the German embassy in Belgrade suggested that Popov, with his connections and easy entrée to British society, could make himself very useful to Germany, Jebsen apparently seconded the idea. He claimed to have relationships with Schacht, and with the Abwehr's Oster and Canaris. Popov was soon in touch with the British in Belgrade, too, and they suggested that he maintain his German contacts. The Germans were eager for Popov to elicit information from someone at the Yugoslav legation in London, and when that information was not forthcoming, Popov explained that this was because his Yugoslav contact was reluctant to use the diplomatic pouch. Impatient for results, the Germans promptly decided that Popov should go to collect the reports himself. Before he left, however, he met with his old friend Jebsen, who told him that now they were both working for the same organization. Jebsen was an anti-Hitler Abwehr agent, and so was Popov.[28] Soon he was to be more than that.

Popov arrived in England at Christmastime, 1940. Over a country-house weekend, he talked at length with Menzies, head of SIS, about becoming a double agent. After all, he was already working for the Abwehr. At the end of their conversation Menzies sized him up: "You are honest but without scruples. Your instincts and intuitions are stronger than your intellect, which is far above average. Your conscience never bothers you and you are mentally short-sighted and long-sighted at the same time. You are ambitious and ruthless and you can even be cruel. . . . Danger is a stimulant for you. . . . You have too many devices on your banner for my taste, but for your job, that's ideal."[29]

So there they had him, the ideal double agent: smooth enough to meet with people of any stratum of society, and with sufficient business cover to allow ready access to any neutral country. Best of all, he was already an established Abwehr operative. He was given the code name Scout, but that was quickly changed to Tricycle, some say because of his alleged predilection for sexual threesomes.[30]

Whatever his code name signified, he joined a motley crew of double agents known to the XX—Twenty—Committee by a variety of colorful names. Some sounded quite workaday—the Worm, Careless, Celery, Mutt, Jeff; some suitably spylike—the Snark, Macchiavelli, Dreadnought, Zigzag;

and some—Dragonfly, Sweet William, Cobweb, and Moonbeam—verged on the poetic.

"The life of a secret agent is dangerous enough," John Masterman once wrote in a novel, "but the life of a double agent is infinitely more precarious. If anyone balances on a swinging tightrope it is he. . . ."[31] Tricycle's personal credo took this into account, but he put his own twist on it: "To survive the multiple hazards of espionage, it is important not to take oneself too seriously."[32] If Tricycle was going to move along the swinging tightrope, then in the interest of boosting his survival, he would spend a good deal of time enjoying himself. To him, the Estoril Casino represented not only "the hub of the wheel of Lisbon," meaning a nexus of spies, but also a playground.[33] Gambling there one night in 1941, he met Ian Fleming, then passing through Portugal on his way to Tangiers on behalf of British Naval Intelligence. Popov's flamboyant, womanizing style made a lasting impression on Fleming. Many years later, when he created his signature agent and put him to work in a book titled *Casino Royale,* the character of James Bond was said to be modeled on Popov. However, in classic spy tradition, Fleming codenamed his agent 007.

On early forays to Lisbon, Tricycle had contacted his Abwehr controller, Kremer von Karsthoff, whose real name was von Auenrode. He was told that he had an appreciative audience at the Tirpitzufer. Berlin had decided that Popov should establish a new spy network in the United States. But first he had to find people to take over his work in England, and two subagents, Balloon and Gelatine, were soon enlisted. After careful preparations in London, he set off, again in June 1941, for Lisbon, where Karsthoff gave him a detailed questionnaire for his American mission.

The questionnaire, couched in a new microdot format, asked many questions about naval shipments, the assembling of troops for transport, shipbuilding, docks, wharves, coastal defense, and much more. Curiously, a third of the questionnaire was devoted to Hawaii. Popov was to discover as much as possible about naval ammunition and mine depots, with sketches, if possible, the extent of naval and army aerodromes, pier installations, the exact location of airfields—it went on and on for several pages. Hawaii, and specifically Pearl Harbor, was clearly of enormous interest. He passed this along to London, and within days, MI-6 delivered the questionnaire to the XX Committee, where it was translated and reviewed.

To the XX Committee, the German questionnaire's emphasis on Hawaii was a clear indication that if the United States were to enter the war, Hawaii would be the point of first attack. Masterman realized that plans were well under way, and later commented: "Obviously it was for the Americans to make their appreciation and to draw their own conclusions from the questionnaire rather than for us to do so."[34] In retrospect, he himself recognized that this attitude may have reflected undue British reserve; perhaps they should have pointed this out to their American friends. The lesson he took from it all was that once an agent was well established as reliable, his reports should be given more weight.

The real lesson to be taken, however, is larger than that: The British, needing and pleading for intercession from the United States, may have felt some resentment of their rich American "cousins," and so were slow to come to their aid. The intelligence services had a healthy sense of competition as well, and Masterman's tone seems slightly distant; perhaps cooperation should only go so far. Clearly, good intelligence is often ignored for reasons that, with hindsight, may look inexcusable.

In August, a Clipper took Tricycle to New York. In keeping with prearranged protocol that the British not operate within the United States, he was put into the hands of Sam Foxworth, the FBI's New York bureau chief. Tricycle was not the sort of man for whom life was all work and no play, and he set about playing with his usual zeal. In New York, at the Stork Club, and in Florida, he wooed and won conspicuously. He was a one-man example of everything that J. Edgar Hoover found despicable: suave, amoral, flashy, and foreign. Everything about him offended the priggish Hoover, who was not about to let Popov set up a spy ring in the United States, or anywhere else. Tricycle was denied permission to proceed to Hawaii for the detailed information his German handlers hoped for. Perhaps Hoover's refusal was for fear that Tricycle might corrupt the wahines; he certainly did not seem to suspect anything more serious.

Hoover was intrigued by the German questionnaire's microdot system, but apparently drew no meaningful conclusions from the multitude of questions specifically about Pearl Harbor. At least none were recorded, and certainly not the conclusions noted by Masterman. Controversy about the U.S. failure to recognize what the intelligence seemed to be spelling out clearly persists. Japanese-American relations were near a snapping point, but current military thinking held that Japanese aircraft carriers were incapable of coming within bombing range of Pearl Harbor. Even if Hoover had not discounted Tricycle's report for whatever reason, the military would not have wanted to believe it in any case. So whether it was a matter of a genuine lack of trust, a lack of focus, or simply wishful thinking, this became yet another instance of an intelligence connection not seen, a warning unheeded.

FORCED LABOR FOR FORD AND GM

One of the first effects of the war in Germany had been a palpable labor shortage. As the Reich conscripted more and more men, ultimately more than a million, agriculture and manufacturing languished for lack of a workforce. Having exported huge numbers to fight on foreign fronts, Germany had begun to import millions to fill the labor void they left behind. Trains that had shuttled German men and youth to Poland and France and Russia eventually shuttled workers, POWs, civilians, men and women, in the opposite direction. Their clothes marked P for Polish, or OST for eastern, this so-called *Ausländereinsatz*—deployment of foreigners—was used to sustain agriculture and to keep the war machinery humming, churning out the necessary numbers of airplane engines, motorized vehicles, and armaments.

Before foreign laborers arrived in Germany, wages were frozen and the workweek lengthened to meet the need. By early 1940, eleven-hour shifts were common, but accompanied by grumbling and a predictable decline in enthusiasm for the regime. In June of that year workers at Opel/Rüsselsheim plant bravely gave voice to these sentiments in a restroom placard: "Hitler speaks," the sign read, "I have abolished the eight-hour day for the German worker, and have granted a twelve-hour day, lower pay, and more work in exchange."[35]

So beginning in 1941, part of Ford's great profitability was due to the use of forced labor, which eventually brought to Ford/Cologne workers like Elsa Iwanowa. Soon after the German army in Russia occupied Rostov in August 1942, she had been required to register with the occupation *Arbeitsamt*—the employment office. She was sixteen. First she worked locally, harvesting fruit, but eventually, she was put on one of ten transports of about 2,000 persons each—20,000 Russian girls—and sent as labor to the German Reich for what was originally billed as a six-month stint. For many hungry twelve-hour days, for weeks, months, and years, she drilled holes in cast machine parts for cars and tanks. With the opening of the second front in the west in 1944, she was moved to another factory to produce gas masks, until she and her friend, Inna Kulagina, managed to escape.[36]

With as much as 50 percent of its workforce represented by girls like these two, Ford-Werke managed to sustain profits. Not until late 1944 and early 1945, when the war was clearly lost, did sales begin to flag. And on the very day of German surrender, May 8, 1945, Ford-Werke Cologne played host to notables, with a documentary film crew on hand to record the resumption of truck production at its plant, which, miraculously, had suffered only minor damage in a city otherwise nearly obliterated by Allied bombings.[37]

During the war, Opel remained under the technical and business leadership of GM. Even after Germany declared war on the United States just after Pearl Harbor, the connection to Detroit was maintained through neutral Switzerland.[38] After the war, both Ford and Opel/GM took up essentially where they had left off, picking up the assets that had appreciated considerably, thanks to wartime complicity and forced labor.

More than fifty years later, in March 1998, Elsa Iwanowa—now de Meyer—filed the first of several class-action suits involving forced labor. As the first plaintiff, she held that the Ford Motor Company had been "unduly enriched" by her participation in Germany's forced-labor program and should pay restitution. The complexities of such a case made for predictable delays. As Ford and GM observed from the sidelines, the German industries involved soon split into two groups: those willing to participate in a compensation pool and those not, the hard-liners. Politics, international law, and raw emotions all played a role in the protracted legal contest that ensued. Eventually the German government set aside eight billion deutschmarks for forced and slave labor, with additional funds to settle other claims. First Opel/GM, then Ford-Werke eventually joined the fund for forced labor, but significantly, in spite of a tentative agreement to pay some compensation, neither GM nor Ford, has made any definitive move or payment.[39]

Iwanowa's case was dismissed by the U.S. District Court because the ten-year statute of limitations had run out; because claims against the subsidiary would be dismissed as postwar treaties and agreements intended individual claims to be resolved as part of reparations discussions between governments; and finally, because the claims were barred by what was termed the "political question doctrine." The plaintiffs appealed the decision, but withdrew their appeal in 2001.

CHAPTER 5

1941-1942

RESPONDING TO HITLER

As the United States began to organize its response to Hitler's war, a surprising peace initiative alerted Donovan to something all his previous information networks had not uncovered: a German resistance to Hitler. For Donovan, this startling and exciting discovery marked the beginning of the OSS's interest in making and maintaining contact with the resistance. It became the opening salvo of the relationship between "enemies" allied in the war against the Nazis.

While much of Germany, and the opposition in particular, had hoped for a quick peace after Poland, the opening of the Russian front obliterated their hopes. By December, the German army had been halted outside of Moscow. Hitler declared war on the United States four days after Pearl Harbor; with that, a fearsome ally joined Churchill and Stalin. Hitler personally took over command of the army, and soon thereafter, in deep secrecy, the Wannsee Conference settled on the Final Solution for dealing with Europe's Jews.

AN ELUSIVE PEACE

The conspicuous early Nazi military triumphs of 1939–40 had enveloped the German opposition to Hitler in gloom. The peace hoped for after those quick victories turned out to be an illusion, and it seemed inevitable that, sooner or later, the United States would join the Allies. Unless they could bring it to an end quickly, a long war lay ahead.

Now Churchill would listen to no more Germans. The German generals had failed to take advantage of the phony war to overthrow Hitler, and were engaging in campaigns of conquest instead. The Battle of Britain had only reinforced his resolve; from now on, no Germans—good or bad—would be heard. In January 1941, he decreed that any German peace feelers were to be met with "absolute silence." He did not want to distress "our friends in the United States" or alienate the new ally, Russia.[1] The earlier dialogues with the deaf were about to become dialogues with the mute.

Still, the civilian opposition persisted. According to Hassell's diaries of the period, Carl Burckhardt had told him that the British seemed to think a reasonable peace might still be concluded, though Eden would be a serious stumbling block. The British consul general in Geneva, meanwhile, felt that no peace would ever be made with Hitler.[2] In May Burckhardt was approached by an agent of Himmler's to ask whether the British might be interested in a peace with Himmler rather than Hitler.[3]

Hassell himself was in touch with an American businessman whom he had met some months earlier and found to be a man of "sober and clear judgment."[4] For some time already, a Mexican-born German-American with considerable contacts and influence on both sides of the Atlantic had been keen to meet with Hassell. As a representative of various American conglomerates—insurance, steel, and oil—Federico Stallforth had acquired not only money but entrée into significant business and social circles. He had been a member of the Dawes Commission, and he had legitimate claim to hobnobbing with Morgans and Rockefellers. German government officials regarded him as a potential peace negotiator, but one very much in their camp, who could be instrumental in keeping the United States out of the war. The German ambassador in Washington sized him up as a "typical promoter . . . adroit but unreliable," and pointed out that the State Department kept files on him.[5]

Stallforth finally met with Hassell in April 1941, and also had conversations with military people. When Stallforth went to London to report and to try to broker a peace, his feelers, like others before, were rejected. Next he decided to try to find common ground between Berlin and Washington. He had made a good initial impression on Hassell and eventually elicited a peace proposal from him. This included the withdrawal of German troops from all territories taken since 1933, except for the Saar, Austria, and Danzig, and an exchange of territory for the Polish Corridor, to guarantee Poland access to the Baltic. There were no claims on the Sudetenland, and no mention of the Rhineland.[6]

This proposition was submitted to Donovan in the autumn of 1941. Donovan was given to understand that only the army could arrange and stage an anti-Hitler revolt. The army was looking for assurance of "fair play" from Britain and the United States. Germany was sick of war. But if it were to continue, Hitler planned to move his powerful forces out across the globe in a terrifying thrust toward global dominion. A Donovan memorandum to Roosevelt summed up Stallforth's arguments: If the United States was not willing to negotiate a peace now, then it should declare war—immediately.[7]

Donovan kept Roosevelt posted on Stallforth's assessments of the climate in Germany, but by this time, Roosevelt was already in a more warlike mode. He let the matter ride until some of Stallforth's business proposals gave him serious pause as to the man's true motivations and character.[8] Still, whatever his motives and with no official brief, Stallforth persisted. Through Ribbentrop, he wanted to put Hassell in touch with the American ambassador in Rome. This failed, but Stallforth explained to Hassell that Roosevelt simply wanted to bring Hitler down; then peace would be possible.[9] In October 1941, Stallforth informed Hassell that his peace "proposition" had fallen on fertile ground in Washington. Could he go to Lisbon to meet with an "authorized person?"[10] By this time, Schacht and Weizsäcker had both expressed serious reservations about Stallforth, and Hassell's stopped all contacts with him.

For Hassell, the only tangible result of his dealings with Stallforth was some attention from the SD. Stallforth's German secretary had informed Heydrich of the meetings to arrange peace discussions, and the information had been duly passed on to Himmler. The SD paid Hassell a visit on September 20, but there were no immediate repercussions. In fact, Hassell was given to believe that Himmler's people were deeply worried and looking for an escape.[11] Yet Himmler decided to follow "the thread" discreetly, perhaps, as Schöllgen suggests, because he was always keen to maintain contacts for his own ends, and perhaps just to forge another link in the chain of evidence of Hassell's contacts that excited suspicion within the Nazi security's hierarchy.

With Donovan, the Stallforth business resonated immediately. Though neither he nor his research and analysis team had much faith in Stallforth or the German generals, the information was a bombshell.[12] There *was* an opposition, and the COI had known nothing at all about it. All contacts the State Department had had with the opposition, with Trott, with Hassell, had been laid to rest in State Department files, with no ripple effect at all regarding a German resistance to Hitler. If Stallforth had done nothing else, he had offered Donovan a tantalizing glimpse behind the Nazi curtain, a glimpse that was to have a profound effect on the relationship between the OSS and the German resistance throughout the war.

Though official Washington had no interest in the opposition or its peace initiatives, Donovan was galvanized. He began to mobilize his resources.[13] He would stretch out a hand to contact this opposition as soon as possible; they might stretch a hand back. Ultimately, the bombing of Pearl Harbor effectively erased any significance Federico Stallforth may have had, but, perhaps inadvertently, he had set in motion an intelligence effort that engaged critical players on both sides of the wartime equation. The joint efforts of OSS and the German resistance who risked their lives to reach Allied intelligence brought hope to a desperate opposition to Hitler.

OPERATION BARBAROSSA

For the opposition the attack on Russia launched on June 22, 1941—Operation Barbarossa—had been another blow to morale. There would be no quick peace; instead, a vast new front had been opened. Though the first dazzling successes in Russia seemed to portend a repetition of the triumph in Poland, autumn rains and mud soon slowed the advance. There were setbacks; the weather turned cold. As in the fight against Napoleon and in World War I, Russia's immensity and her famous "General Winter" came to her aid.

As Hitler's Russian campaign faltered, the resistance gradually regrouped. Circles of opposition formed and re-formed, plans were laid. Activist groups concentrated on an actual putsch to dispose of Hitler; those with religious or ethical qualms about murder pondered further approaches to the western Allies and planned for the foundation and structure of a new post-Nazi Germany.

A founding member of the latter group was Helmuth von Moltke. The scion of a revered military family, Moltke had been anti-Nazi since the very beginning. In May 1939, he had been one of a veritable parade of well-placed Germans to London who tried to stiffen international resolve and broker a peace; they hoped that if the British showed a strong hand toward Hitler's foreign policy ambitions, war might be averted, Hitler would be stopped, and the regime would collapse. Even in the days of Hitler's heady military triumphs in Poland and France, Moltke never conceded him anything. Hitler was evil and had to be fought.

By June 1940, Moltke was thoroughly discouraged, living, as he said, "without expectations," and only hoping to prevent worse.[14] But he had begun to gather an assortment of like-minded friends—lawyers, diplomats, civil servants, and officers—who met in various Berlin apartments and occasionally at Moltke's Silesian estate—Kreisau. In 1941, what became known as the Kreisau Circle began to grow.[15] In November of that year, Moltke wrote to his wife, Freya, in his tiny hand: "What vast problems we face and what a small chance there is of finding a giant to solve them for us!"[16] Moltke himself had the moral stature, and at six feet seven inches, he might even have been the giant who could solve the immense problems the opposition faced. Personally he worked steadily toward solving those vast problems. He interceded legally on behalf of the oppressed, sent food from Kreisau to help a pastor friend and accomplice feed his

"U-boats"—persecuted people who had gone underground—and helped Jews any way he could. He was tireless, and came to be recognized as the "engine" of the Kreisau Circle opposition, while his friend, Peter Yorck von Wartenburg, was described as its "heart."[17]

Indefatigable anti-Nazi though he was, Moltke's reserve and his abhorrence of violence would not let him consider assassination. In his view, Hitler should not be brought down by some sordid putsch, but by steadfast opposition from the other, the "real" Germany.[18] He concentrated not on the mechanics of ousting Hitler, but on articulating what the new Germany should be when the despised Nazi regime was gone. He has been criticized for what some considered utopian, ivory-tower intellectualism. American journalist Dorothy Thompson, a personal friend of Moltke's, delivered a weekly radio broadcast entitled "Dear Hans," addressed to Moltke, expressing her impatience and exhorting him to act rather than just think. She concluded one broadcast by asking plaintively, "Where are you, Hans?"[19]

Moltke felt strongly that he and his friends were ill suited to a conspiratorial role. "We've not learned how to do it . . . it would go wrong, we would make an amateur job of it."[20] But he was desperately aware of the terrible losses and suffering of both sides on the Russian front: "Each day costs 6,000 Germans and 15,000 Russians, a horrible price for inaction and procrastination."[21] He was determined not to be unprepared when Hitler and the war came to an end. Germany should have new leadership and plans in place for a sound government.

The horror of the Russian front only exacerbated Moltke's worries. His relationships intensified, and the Kreisau Circle began to take on a real life. He seemed to be in touch with everyone who might help shape the new Germany: conservatives like Hassell, Beck, Preysing, and Yorck, as well as socialists Julius Leber and Adolf Reichwein, Carlo Mierendorff and Wilhelm Leuschner. He was in touch with Canaris and Dohnanyi. There was the Jesuit Alfred Delp, the Evangelical Church's Eugen Gerstenmeier, and of course Goerdeler and Adam von Trott from the Foreign Office. He even extended feelers to see if Claus Schenk von Stauffenberg might help them. They usually met at an apartment of one member or another in Berlin, for although the Gestapo had given the group the name of Moltke's Silesian estate, Kreisau, they met there only occasionally. They included a broad spectrum of political and social affiliations, and there were deep divisions among them, but they met, talked, planned for the future, and hoped. "We can only . . . overthrow this regime of terror and horror if we are able to show a picture beyond the terrifying and hopeless immediate future," Moltke wrote his English friend, Lionel Curtis, a picture sufficiently promising "for the disillusioned people to strive for, to work [for], to start again, and to believe in."[22]

Associated Press correspondent Louis Lochner's contacts with the several members of the opposition led him to attend a gathering of politicians, churchmen, intelligence people, and others in late 1941. They asked him to carry word of the opposition, its makeup and aims, to President Roosevelt and to discover what form of post-Hitler government would be acceptable. He was given a secret radio code to help them establish direct contact with the president.

When Lochner was finally able to get back to the United States in mid-1942, he was given the presidential cold shoulder and asked not to seek further contact. The White House knew about the opposition, but would do nothing to threaten the Grand Alliance. Later that year, Lochner published his book *What About Germany?* and tried to make the plight of the opposition known. Millions of Germans, he said, were eager to be delivered from the Nazi yoke and to clear Germany of the shame Hitler had brought its people.

The invasion of Russia brought a communist group known as the *Rote Kapelle*—the Red Orchestra—into the oppositional action. Originally established as a Soviet wartime intelligence operation, it eventually had numerous cells across Europe. The Berlin *apparat,* under Harro Schulze-Boysen in the Air Ministry and Arvid Harnack in the Ministry of Economics and his American wife, was not without important contacts in other resistance circles. Schulze-Boysen was a flamboyant, well-connected character, built along the lines of the Nordic Nazi dream specimen, but he was also an early anti-Nazi, a committed communist who had spent time in a concentration camp as early as 1933. Just four days after the launch of the Russian invasion, the Red Orchestra began sending intelligence to Moscow via radio transmitters, but not for long. A severe breach of Soviet security helped the Gestapo close in on them, and on August 30, 1942, Boysen was arrested. More than fifty members of the group were executed; others committed suicide.

THE UNITED STATES JOINS THE WAR

The blood and horror of Pearl Harbor had one surprising and unexpected benefit: It drove home with devastating clarity the need for more effective intelligence gathering, and as a result, the COI gained credibility. Clues to an attack on Pearl Harbor had not penetrated the U.S. military establishment, nor had Hoover picked up any hints from Popov's questionnaire. Pearl Harbor had received word of the threat only when the offensive was already under way.[23] The United States was still reeling when Hitler declared war on December 11. America was now suddenly, irrevocably committed to war, and the focus was on a swift response.

Roosevelt formed the United States Joint Chiefs of Staff (JCS) to work directly with their British counterparts, who already had an intelligence service prepared to provide them with strategic information. American intelligence was too new and still nearly empty-handed. The COI became an instrument of the JCS, not only to provide them with information, but also to help keep the somewhat unruly "Wild Bill" Donovan under control.

As for Donovan, he agreed to serve under the JCS for two reasons: First, he, too, wanted to see information shared and properly utilized. Working with the JCS would give him the opportunity to educate them on the value of having the military carry out tactical intelligence, while his groups carried out strategic intelligence. Second, it would allow him to reach into Congress's deep pockets for funding.[24] Rumor in Washington had it that Donovan wanted to raise his own army and fight the Nazis single-handed. In fact, he had wanted a field commission, but he had reinjured an old leg wound badly and realized that he would never survive the rigors of combat; he could serve his country better behind a desk.

FDR typically used the occasion to do some housekeeping. Both Donovan and his head of the Foreign Information Service—or FIS—Robert Sherwood, had the president's sympathetic ear, but there was a growing philosophical rift between the two regarding the use of "black" news.[25] For Donovan, the combat-hardened soldier, in war, any weapon—including words—was fair. For Sherwood, the liberal intellectual, ends did not justify means; his country should not stoop to Nazi tactics. Rather than see the disagreement escalate and lose either man over this issue, FDR effectively sent each man to his own corner. Executive Order 9182 split the "white" team of Foreign Information Service from the COI and folded it into the new Office of War Information. The "black" team would stick with Donovan, and there would be a clear departmental distinction between the sources of legitimate news broadcasts and propaganda.

On June 13 1942, by military order, the COI was renamed the Office of Strategic Services (OSS). Tactical and strategic intelligence were separated, and clandestine intelligence branch staffs were transferred to Donovan, who combined them and added staff. The OSS recruited both military personnel for overseas duties and civilians, primarily for work in the United States. The ideal candidate had superior analytical skills, spoke several languages, and had traveled extensively. At first, recruitment was done by word of mouth and face-to-face. Donovan or one of his branch heads would hear from a friend or fellow OSSer of someone with a particular talent that was needed, and the person would be approached for service. Again, there is a similarity with recruiting for Canaris's Abwehr, where personal connections and inclinations played a major role. Typically, potential OSSers were approached by recruiters who did not identify themselves as OSS, but used some vague cover story to persuade the candidate to contact the agency. Details were supplied only after the recruit had been accepted.

Not surprisingly, Donovan's criteria and recruitment techniques led

Washington pundits to joke that the initials OSS really stood for "Oh So Social," "Oh So Special," "Oh So Secret," "Oh So Sexy," and the like. But the reality was that those with the broadest language skills and knowledge of foreign cultures and locales were those who had the funds to travel or study abroad, and were likely to come from somewhat rarefied venues.

Julia Cuniberti's experience was fairly typical. A young Vassar graduate, Cuniberti had spent summers at La Palazzina, her family's beautiful villa in Italy. Her fluency in English, German, French, and Italian, her in-depth knowledge of Italian geography and personal contacts in Italy, made her a perfect candidate for the OSS. She was first contacted by a fellow debutante and pal from the Washington social scene. "I had kind of been sniffing around for a war job when I was recruited by Jean Wallace Douglas, the daughter of the vice president," Cuniberti recalls. "I did not know it then, but Jean was already with OSS. She called me and said that with my languages, I really needed to be 'down here.' I asked her what she meant by 'down here' but she wouldn't say. She arranged for me to have an interview with the OSS. They still did not say what the job was but they told me I was 'in.'"[26] After a background check, psychological assessment, and training, Cuniberti was assigned to registry in Strategic Intelligence, routing cables and filing for the Italian desk.[27]

It is hard to imagine too many organizations able to convince a Vassar graduate with a villa in Italy and fluent in four languages to work as a lowly clerk, but the OSS did. Donovan's famous charm combined with vitality and intellect became a hallmark of his group. From the very beginning of their training, all OSSers were made keenly aware that they were a part of the war effort and the fight for freedom.

THE JEWISH QUESTION

Back in 1940, when Germany marched into France, Roosevelt had denounced the German execution of French hostages. Churchill, too, had condemned Nazi barbarities; henceforth, one of the missions of the war would be the punishment of such war crimes. But in none of these condemnations were Jews ever mentioned specifically. In fact, it is difficult to pinpoint when the Allies finally publicly recognized Hitler's intention to exterminate European Jewry. The first mention of the fate of Jews in particular may be a COI report of late 1941. David Kelly, head of the British Legation in Switzerland, wrote to the Foreign Office in November that he had been told by a Pole that "1½ million Jews who were living in Eastern (recently Russian) Poland have simply disappeared altogether; nobody knows how and where."[28] More signs of impending catastrophe were not long in coming.

Within Germany, it was Hitler's treatment of the Jews that confirmed certain members of the opposition in the conviction that he must be brought down. Though many of them had not subscribed to his other rantings either, it was this particular issue that tipped the scales and brought them to the point of active resistance. But what about the Allies? What did they know? When and from what sources? Did they care or respond?

Early on, Allied awareness of the anguish of Europe's Jewish populations was limited, and restricted largely to diplomatic and intelligence channels. But gradually the media printed stories, not on the front pages, but tucked away on page two or page six, a reflection of considerable ambivalence about this news. World War I propaganda had produced exaggerated atrocity stories designed to fan anti-German sentiment, and the current reports were suspected of the same intentions. Reactions ranged from indifference to deep discomfort, from prejudice and an unwillingness to rouse anti-Semitic sentiments at home, to an inability to grasp such horrible possibilities. Even when the dimensions of the slaughter had finally registered, there was often a lack of true comprehension. It was simply beyond belief.

By 1941 numerous reports had already trickled in from individuals, from refugees, from diplomatic and other channels; terrible things were happening. Initially though, no real distinctions were drawn between the sufferings of Jews and others. All kinds of people—Catholics, communists, gypsies, any and all political opponents—were suffering in German-occupied nations, and Hitler's policies seemed to lack the obvious ethnocentric focus and intensity that eventually earned his determination to eradicate Europe's Jews the designation "Holocaust," with a capitol H. By mid-1942, however, information from a variety of sources had provided ample indication that the Nazis intended to make the elimination of Jews an end in itself, and of how that intention was being implemented.

British cryptologists had already cracked the German Military Police and SS codes.[29] In 1941 they had direct, incontrovertible intelligence on the treatment of Jews in Poland and Russia. But even within British intelligence and military circles, the information from the intercepts was kept under very tight wraps. Alerting the enemy that the codes had been broken would be self-defeating, so the information remained a deep secret. One British cryptologist issued a memorandum on the Soviet massacres, saying: "The fact that the police are killing all the Jews that fall into their hands should now be sufficiently well appreciated. It is not therefore proposed to continue reporting these butcheries unless so requested."[30] The closest the British came to doing anything with what they knew was Churchill's speech of late August 1941, in which he referred to "scores of thousands—literally scores of thousands—of executions . . . being perpetrated [in Russia]. . . . Not since the Mongol invasions . . . has there been methodical, merciless butchery . . . approaching such a scale. . . . We are in the presence of a crime without a name."[31]

Even before the United States entered the war, the COI was privy to a number of diplomatic dispatches, passed on to Donovan by British sources.[32] In August 1941, as the German army was deep in Russia, the Mexican minister to Portugal, Alvarez de Castillo, referred to a report in the Italian newspaper *Giornale d'Italia,* on Operation Barbarossa: "In the occupied countries the tragic number of victims who—on the pretext that they have carried on communist propaganda, that they belong to the Jewish race, or that they have committed acts of sabotage—are inhumanely sacrificed, grows incessantly."[33]

The Chilean consul in Prague, Gonzalo Montt Rivas, reported in June of that year on the Reich's firm intention of "Germanizing all territories within its living space." This wording left some room for interpretation, but by September 1941, he reported on Jews from the Czech Protectorate, Germany, and Luxembourg being transported to Poland, and on the establishment of the Warsaw Ghetto. By November 1, he wrote that the "impression is that the [Nazi] intention is to get rid of the Jews at all costs." The Reich intended to "drown in blood every attempt, every plot, and every act or word which threatens the security of the Great Germany." Later that month he added: "It has been decided to eradicate all the Jews and send some to Poland and others to the town of Terezin, whilst looking for a more remote place. The German triumph will leave Europe free of Semites."[34] There is no room for interpretation here; Montt Rivas's picture is drawn clearly, but it attracted little or no attention.

In October 1941, a certain Major Arthur Goldberg, later a Supreme Court justice, working for the COI in London, was given information by one of his contacts, Schmuel Zygielbojm, about Hitler's plan for the Final Solution, with supporting evidence. Might not the United States take serious action, Zygielbojm asked, and bomb either Auschwitz or the Warsaw Ghetto? Goldberg forwarded the information and the request to Donovan, and was at pains to explain the U.S. position to Zygielbojm when the request was denied. Goldberg later learned that his informant committed suicide the day after being denied U.S. support.[35]

Horrific reports were coming in from Poland, from Russia, and from Rumania about SS actions against Jews. An American attaché in Istanbul obtained copies of a German soldier's photos showing Rumanian Jews being deported to concentration camps in locked boxcars.[36] One possible escape from the terror was to flee to safety in the United States. In 1942, desperate families in Turkey turned to U.S. ambassador, Laurence Steinhardt. The State Department had authorized ambassadors in Europe to use their discretion in issuing visas to refugees, and since Steinhardt happened to be Jewish, many refugees thought he would be sympathetic to their cause. But Steinhardt, a wealthy, well-educated New Yorker, was burning to be accepted among the country club set and worried that an influx of poor and illiterate Jews might ruin his chances of ever being admitted to New York society. There might be German or Russian spies among the Jewish immigrants, he argued. Steinhardt personally could have saved thousands of lives by issuing visas, but he chose to turn his back on the refugees. Assistant Secretary Breckinridge Long, and plenty of other people at State, backed Steinhardt's decision fully. The State Department was not at all keen to have a tide of "huddled masses yearning to breathe free" or "wretched refuse [from a] teeming shore"[37] wash up at the feet of the Statue of Liberty. Homeless and tempest-tost they might be, but they might also be unwashed, uncouth, and possibly subversive. They were unwanted.

SHAPING THE OSS

Drawing on the social elite shaped both the OSS and its successor organization, the CIA. Key members of the OSS had strong personal ties to Europe and were often quite familiar with prominent political, military, and business figures in England, Germany, and Italy. The OSS's use of the elite had parallels in Germany and in the United Kingdom, where the Abwehr and SIS recruited heavily among the old upper classes—men and women having extensive travel experience and language skills. Private connections in the United States, Britain, and in Germany were an added benefit. A surprising number of senior Abwehr officers either had family in the United Kingdom or had married British women. Many senior OSS officers also had family relationships with Europe. As David Bruce put it, "We looked for people with existing connections into Germany."[38] In some ways the similar social backgrounds facilitated the high level of cooperation between the Abwehr and the OSS. Bruce himself fit the mold. Tall and patrician, he had married Andrew Mellon's daughter, Ailsa, said to be the world's wealthiest woman. After they divorced, his marriage to his OSS assistant, Evangeline Bell, lasted until his death in 1977.

Eventually, the invitation-by-recommendation process was opened up, and most later recruits came to the OSS by way of the military. The armed forces observed men during basic training, and noted any man with a special skill, such as parachuting, diving, or climbing. They also kept an eye out for men who were fluent in one or more foreign languages or educated in the social sciences.

Under the JCS, the OSS grew exponentially into a virtual alphabet soup of dozens of different departments and support organizations divided between intelligence branches and strategic services. The Intelligence branch included R&A, Secret Intelligence (SI), Counter Intelligence (X-2), Foreign Nationalities (FN), and Censorship & Documents (C&D). The Strategic Services side housed Special Operations (SO), Operational Group (OG), Morale Operations (MO), which split from SO in 1943, and Maritime Unit (MU).

BASIC ORGANIZATION OF THE OFFICE OF STRATEGIC SERVICES

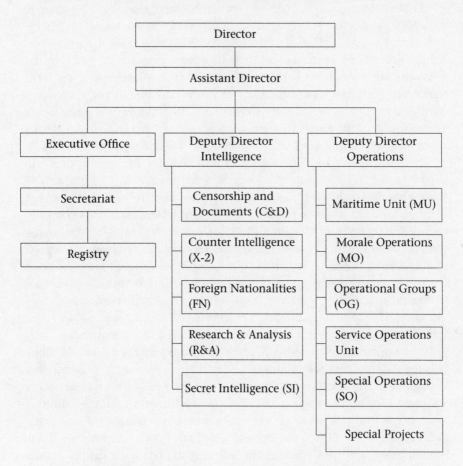

R&A was divided into four geographical regions and given some support from government agencies and the military. But in keeping with Donovan's theory that public sources could provide first-rate intelligence, R&A used newspapers, public records, and transcripts of broadcasts and speeches to piece together critical information for establishing Allied bombing objectives. Culling the lengthening German death notices for soldiers, for instance, yielded accurate estimates on dwindling German manpower. An estimated 85 percent of the data needed to plan the invasion of Sicily came from R&A scholars sifting through newspapers, magazines, academic publications, and hand-drawn maps.[39]

Undercover SI agents worked as servants, truck drivers, or tradesmen throughout Europe, Asia, and North Africa to obtain intelligence. One particularly valuable agent was planted in Paris as the valet to the Gestapo chief.[40] A job as the local greengrocer may not have seemed glamorous, but it was extremely dangerous; SI agents whose cover was blown were executed immediately. The success of Operation Torch, the Allied landings in North Africa in late 1942, hinged on information on the resources and intentions of fascist Spain and Portugal. Ensuring Franco's neutrality was essential; Spain's entry into war on the Axis side, or even its just granting the Germans safe passage to Gibraltar and Spanish Morocco, was a constant worry. To relieve the "Spanish ulcer," OSS established networks of agents in neutral countries, some as State Department oil attachés and some under "private cover." In Spain in particular, Standard Oil Company, with its many employees, and Gulf Oil provided cover for OSS agents in Madrid.

The Joint Chiefs had told Donovan initially that the interception and decoding of Axis communications would be handled solely by the State Department and the military, and OSS would not be involved. In 1943, that ban was softened to allow the British Secret Intelligence Service's crack decoding and ciphering unit, Ultra, to share Germany's greatest secrets, transmitted in the Enigma cipher. The information from Ultra was considered so secret that in June 1943 the OSS counterintelligence branch X-2 was born. X-2 became the most shrouded branch within an already highly secretive organization.[41] It was, to borrow from Churchill, a proverbial "riddle wrapped in a mystery inside an enigma."

X-2 tracked enemy intelligence agents and tried to undermine their efforts. The organization's name, X-2, was simply a play on the words "double cross." Capturing foreign agents to turn them into double agents was another goal The double-agent business involved feints within feints, with OSS agents (or double agents) trying to plant false information within the inner circles of the Third Reich to extract honest information for the Allies. In fact, it was often difficult to know whether an agent or an informant had been "turned" by the Germans, but X-2 kept the Germans just as unsure about their counterintelligence data, tying up the Reich's already strained resources.

One of X-2's tasks was to create index cards on people who might be enemy agents. At war's end, there were file cards bearing over 400,000 names of men, women, and children (members of the Hitler Youth) who might one day pose a threat to the United States. The branch shared information with other government agencies and disseminated more than 3,000 reports to the FBI, the State Department, and other agencies in the year before Germany collapsed.

The British continued to provide moral and practical support for their fledgling sister organization, but the forces were never completely combined; the Americans did not want to be perceived as puppets of a foreign service, and the British were concerned that the brash and inexperienced newcomers might endanger their established operations. The two organizations remained separate, but usually friendly entities, running both individual and combined operations, and sharing information when appropriate. The United States led no spying missions in Belgium or Holland, for example. The British, knowing that the Germans had already turned agents there, felt that putting inexperienced American agents in place would be a death sentence and could blow the covers of British assets still safely in place. On the other hand, the two countries worked hand in hand behind enemy lines in France, where their combined skills helped turn the tide.

The prime objective of the small Foreign Nationalities (FN) branch was to observe foreign nationality groups within the United States and to track dissident activities and possible fifth column. In effect, this was domestic surveillance, and Hoover was quick to respond to this perceived incursion into FBI turf by lobbying Roosevelt to suspend all domestic OSS activities. The Oral Intelligence (OI) branch interviewed tourists, businessmen, students, and immigrants arriving from abroad. Innocuous but telling details—a favorite restaurant still open, neighborhoods heavily damaged, or the name of a good tailor—were invaluable in bolstering an undercover OSSer's credibility. Censorship and Documents (C&D) was co-opted by X-2 to develop cover and documents for agents going undercover. Authentic European clothing, suitcases, and watches were collected by the truckload, both in America and in Europe. Axis uniforms with all current patches, pins, and medals were a special find. No agent's outfit would bear any traces of Allied origins.[42]

All current papers, documents, and passports were sent to C&D for faithful imitation, down to the very watermarks, typefaces, and stamps used in various regions. IDs, ration cards, sports club membership cards, travel permits—all had to be duplicated in exact detail. When matching the pigments used in German inks proved nearly impossible, the OSS did what any spy worth his salt would do: They purchased German pigments in neutral countries and were using perfect duplicates of German inks in no time.

Behind every great organization—as is said to be true of great men— there stand often unseen and unsung support services. The OSS had several Research and Development (R&D) specialists in miniaturization who designed tiny cameras, recording devices, radios, and transmitters. They created time-delayed explosives, silencers, and limpet mines and beacons—all the gadgets a secret agent might need.[43] The Special Assistants Division created drugs for field agents, such as the "K" or knockout pill, another to loosen a subject's tongue during interrogation, and the lethal "L" pill— potassium cyanide. This pill caused nearly instantaneous death and was to be used if interrogation or torture would endanger other lives. Special Funds procured more than eighty different currencies for undercover operations and worked with the Foreign Exchange Division, which transferred large sums of money abroad for salaries, to keep cover businesses running, provide funds for bribes and operational expenses without revealing the source as the U.S. government. The two groups were effective enough to send German intelligence agents scurrying to banks in neutral countries to ferret out the American money trail. They believed, quite correctly, that if they could follow the money, they could expose the agents. But OSS was laundering money through seven or eight countries before it reached its final destination, and rarely was the same means used twice. If necessary, they worked with black marketers to acquire or exchange currencies and no OSS operation was ever cancelled for lack of funds carefully screened for safe use.[44]

The taste for alphabet soup extended to the Strategic Services—SO, OG, MO, and MU—designed to serve various needs. First among these was Special Operations, whose mission was to transmit intelligence on Axis troop movements and coordinate and support local resistance groups. Given the variety of groups, their differences, and a shortage of available aircraft, this last was no simple task. Still, both Churchill and Donovan supported the idea, and despite some opposition, as the war intensified, SO air-dropped more and more supplies. Their sabotage and guerrilla activities drained enemy time, energy, and resources that would otherwise have been available for the war effort. The game was to dilute Hitler's power, forcing him to show strength everywhere, weakening him everywhere. Beyond that, conspicuous signs of enemy resistance in supposedly secure areas were deeply discouraging.

SO ranks also included the famous three-man "Jedburgh teams" involved in support and communications with the resistance. Typically Jedburghs were a multinational crew, including a British or American intelligence agent, a native of the area being infiltrated, and a radio operator. Parachuting into an area of known resistance with enough arms and ammunition for forty men, Jedburghs organized and armed the local resistance and harassed the enemy in order to tie up valuable resources. Any intelligence gathering was secondary to their paramilitary mission. The ninety-three Jedburgh teams parachuted into France in the spring and summer of 1944 were key to the success of D-Day—the June 6, 1944, invasion of Normandy.

Operational Groups (OG) responsibilities resembled those of the SO, but magnified. From the ranks of the U.S. Army, the OSS culled men who had excelled physically in basic training and had a working knowledge of a foreign language. If they were willing to volunteer for hazardous duty and immediate deployment, they underwent rigorous training and had no idea what their responsibilities would be. The washout rate for potential OG agents was high. The physical and emotional strains and the tough security screenings of the entire family meant that less than 10 percent of those who met the initial language and physical requirements became OG team members.[45] Those who did "graduate," formed an elite commando unit, to be dropped behind enemy lines in U.S. Army uniforms to support partisan activities and commit acts of sabotage. It was hoped that their clearly marked army gear would raise morale among resistance forces and also prevent them from being executed as spies immediately, if captured. Though Hitler had ordered that anyone caught behind enemy lines be shot immediately, the German high command was well aware of the Geneva Convention and hoped that when the time came, it might shield them, too, so the uniform did offer some protection.

MO—Morale Operations—became the new home of "black" propaganda—radio transmissions, brochures, newspapers, and all the psychological warfare that was designed to look as if it had been generated by German or Japanese sources unhappy with the war. Rumor was the lingua franca of MO, and a kernel of truth often served as the basis for a tale spun to demoralize the enemy. A news report on a political speech might mention, for example, that the leader looked pale. Some weeks later, it would be reported that he had taken ill and, eventually, that his illness had led to mental instability; his staff was questioning his ability to lead. If rations were short, soldiers might hear of a sumptuous banquet being prepared for officers. An operation called Soldatensender Calais, run by Britain's savvy Sefton Delmer, sent almost continuous war news, with sly tidbits slipped in to undermine morale. Inserted into one transmission was a message intended to "reassure" fathers serving in the German army that in spite of the shortage of doctors and medicine, the figure for weekly deaths of children in evacuation camps had fallen recently, from 548 to just 372.[46]

Germany's propaganda minister Josef Goebbels loathed Donovan and his "black news"—for good reason. Publicly he responded with characteristic vituperation; in private, however, he confessed to real, if grudging admiration for his adversary. The radio station "gave us something to worry about," he noted in his diary in 1943, and "does a very clever job with propaganda."[47]

Once the United States entered the war, both NBC and CBS allowed MO radio airtime on transmitters powerful enough to reach Europe and Asia. Songs—sad and romantic enough to make lonely boys far from loved ones throw down their arms and head for home—were a specialty. Not only did they catch the listener's ear for the "news" that followed, but they stirred powerful nostalgia and homesickness in the boys at the front. Marlene Dietrich volunteered her own special allure. Her breathy, heartbreaking recording of "Lili Marlene" was enough to kill any soldier's will to fight. By war's end, it was on the lips of soldiers in armies on both sides. Donovan himself could not resist; he wrote her a personal note of gratitude.[48]

THE FINAL SOLUTION

No written order from Hitler on his planned extermination of Europe's Jews has ever come to light. The Wannsee Conference, laying the organizational groundwork for the Final Solution in early 1942, made no mention of mass murders. The locutions used were vague terms like "evacuation" or "resettlement" and "special treatment." Even among themselves, the chief architects of the Holocaust apparently engaged in a sort of self-deception designed to make their proposals appear less horrifying and slightly more palatable. The dreaded Group IV of the RSHA, the realm of Adolf Eichmann, was given the special mission of implementing the so-called Final Solution of the Jewish question in 1942.

The Allies had been almost wholly silent on the issue of Hitler's policy on the Jews, and in early 1942, a distinguished German émigré living in Switzerland chastised a British official for "the embarrassed silence of the people in London on the question of the persecution of the Jews."[49] The Soviets were broadcasting reports of Nazi atrocities, he pointed out; why were the British silent?[50] The Nazis had made listening to foreign radio broadcasts a serious crime as soon as the war began, but in spite of the interdiction, the BBC had a sizable audience in Germany, hungry for real news. The BBC responded to the complaint from Switzerland with a series of broadcasts to inform their German audience of Nazi plans and the brutal steps being taken toward the Final Solution. However, the most conspicuous result of the BBC's broadcasts was a spate of Nazi propaganda to counteract them.[51] Serious German military setbacks—the Wehrmacht was hemorrhaging at Stalingrad—apparently made it more imperative than ever to keep up the fight against the universal demon, the Jew.

The British had not been the only ones maintaining radio silence on the subject of the persecution of Jews. German theologian Paul Tillich, living in the United States since the mid-1930s, had proposed a broadcast to the German people suggesting that if the Nazi persecution of the Jews continued, the German people might expect similar treatment. The Office of War Information decided that such a direct eye-for-an-eye threat might suggest that the war was a Jewish rescue mission and so lend credibility to Nazi propaganda claiming that the Jews were the bulwark of American capitalism. This would not help the war effort; there would be no broadcast.

While some voices were raised in serious protest, uncertainties and an unwillingness to believe the terrible stories remained, even as intelligence continued to come in from every conceivable source. The amount of rail traffic to a smallish town in remote Upper Silesia, for instance, had had German railway officials wondering for some time about the size and importance of formerly Polish Oswiecim, annexed by Germany in 1939 and renamed Auschwitz. The British decryption of German railroad codes might well have spurred a particularly attentive and curious analyst to wonder what the extraordinary number of trains routed there meant, but much of the information required no leap of the imagination whatsoever.

By the time the OSS became official in the summer of 1942, a Czech Jew named Joseph Goldschmied, married to an American woman, was making his escape from Prague. To his OSS interviewer, he later made a dire prediction: "If Hitler remains true to his program of destroying all European Jewry—he will have achieved that goal soon and most countries will be depleted of Jews."[52]

That summer also brought word from a source already quite familiar to western intelligence of how exactly that depletion was being accomplished. Eduard Schulte was an impressive man, big and solidly built. As the director of Giesche, one of Germany's largest mining operations, his stature in the business world was on a par with his physical presence. Schulte's position made him unusually well informed of critical details on raw materials necessary for the war. He was in touch with industrialists, bankers, and political figures, constantly picking up information on military movements and economic developments from influential friends and business associates. He was also a fervent anti-Nazi, with a deep-seated loathing for Nazi ideology, which he called the "brown poison." Since before the war, he had been feeding information of the highest quality and reliability to the Allies. He had pinpointed the invasion of Poland. The Allies had learned from him of Hitler's planned attack on Russia—ironclad nonaggression pact notwithstanding. The date was postponed several times, but he had alerted them that it was finally set for June 22.

In the 1930s, Schulte had met and befriended a Polish consul, Szczesny Chojnacki, in Breslau, Silesia, where Giesche had its headquarters. Chojnacki was later transferred to Switzerland, where he was discreetly gathering intelligence for the Polish government-in-exile in London under the alias Jacek Lubiewa. By chance the two met again in Zurich. The happy accidental encounter soon led to meetings during Schulte's frequent visits to Switzerland. Schulte shared with Chojnacki his frank views on the situation in Germany and often critical information gathered from well-placed friends and business contacts. This was transmitted via diplomatic pouch or hidden transmitter to the Polish government in London, which turned over much information to the British, who shared portions of it with the Americans.[53]

In the 1930s Schulte had repeatedly warned almost anyone who would listen about Hitler's intention, but he, like others, discovered that no matter how good the intelligence, getting it to those who could or would make use of it was not easy. Even if it reached the right people, there was no guarantee that it would be put to good use—or any use at all.

Otto Fitzner, the number-two man at Giesche came to Schulte on July 17, 1942, with some extraordinary news. In reverent tones, Fitzner, an ardent Nazi, told Schulte that Himmler was coming to visit nearby Auschwitz. This was surprising. Auschwitz was nothing, nowhere. It was a backwater. Its vitality as a medieval trading center had long since dwindled to insignificance. Over the years, it had been Austrian, then Polish. Now German, its old Austrian army barracks had been converted into a concentration camp, but there was nothing remarkable in that. Such camps had been springing up all over Germany. Reichsführer SS Himmler was famously difficult to lure away from his headquarters at all, and now he was coming to this dusty, back-of-beyond town, not just for the day, according to Fitzner, but to spend the night?

It was highly unusual, and aroused the curiosity of Schulte, who had his local sources. Fitzner was friendly with Karl Hahnke, the local gauleiter, who was given to hinting at high-level secrets over a friendly glass or two of wine. He knew that Himmler had ordered an expansion of Auschwitz in 1941, and that there were plans for a second camp and buildings for I. G. Farben as well. He was keenly interested in this, because he knew of Himmler's propensity for seizing any available property for his SS operations, and Giesche held a great deal of local property. A dinner was being given in Himmler's honor at a villa Giesche had built for visiting American directors participating in a complex financing scheme devised in the 1920s. In Schulte's view, giving another local gauleiter the villa for the duration was insurance; it might help protect Giesche interests against the huge conglomerates established to arm Hitler's forces, and possibly against Himmler's encroachments as well.[54]

Schulte's neighbor, Ewald von Kleist-Schmenzin, was well informed, and another insider, Jakob Werlin of Daimler-Benz, was also a good source. There was talk that an important decision of the Führer's was about to be realized. He himself had seen Breslau's once flourishing Jewish community dwindle. Piecing together what bits of information he could gather in the next days, Schulte discovered the reason for the extraordinary visit. Himmler was there to see the machinery of the Final Solution in action, in this instance, to witness the gassing of a trainload of Dutch Jews. Schulte had heard about Jews being deported, of course, but this part of Hitler's plan—the actual, grimly efficient extermination of Europe's Jews—the Final Solution, shocked him.

In his opinion this was far more important than mere military intelligence; it was critical. He must get the information to the Jewish community and to the Allied authorities by whatever means, immediately. It could not wait. He lost no time and traveled immediately to Switzerland to meet that rarity in Swiss banking circles, a Jewish banker. Schulte had done business with Isidor Koppelman, and he was confident that Koppelman would find a way to get word to the proper people.

Koppelman knew Schulte as a serious man, not given to exaggeration or jokes, but he found it hard to believe that what he was telling him was not some absurd rumor. Schulte insisted it was true; the information must be passed on to Roosevelt immediately. Koppelman forwarded Schulte's information to Benjamin Sagalowitz, who contacted Gerhard Riegner of the World Jewish Congress in Geneva. Riegner was energetic, but also young, and he felt it best to check his own reaction to what seemed a fantastic story with more experienced people he respected. Then he contacted the British and the American consulates, and asked them to relay secret messages to members of the World Jewish Congress: Sidney Silverman in London, and Rabbi Stephen Wise in New York.

The junior counsel in Geneva also decided to consult a higher authority, and sent the proposed Riegner telegram to be vetted by the American legation in Bern. There, the American minister Leland Harrison thought Riegner's message "a wild rumor inspired by fear," but noted that in fact, many were dying in miserable conditions of maltreatment, malnutrition, and disease. Eventually the telegram was forwarded to the OSS and the State Department, which concluded that the report represented "wild rumor based on Jewish fears."[55]

Indeed, when the shocking information reached the State Department in Washington in early August, it was regarded there, too, as a fevered fantasy. It intended to keep its distance from the issue. Before passing it on to Wise, Sumner Welles decided to try to verify its substance through Switzerland. In a triple-priority memo from the State Department, he asked Harrison to contact Riegner for substantiation and any further evidence. Harrison's assessment of the Riegner message had already been recorded: Yes, the Jews were being persecuted and subjected to terrible suffering, but the reports must be wildly exaggerated. They were unbelievable. Harrison's feeling was that, surely, the Jews were being deported for forced labor, not extermination. And Riegner's hands were tied. Schulte's identity was to be protected at all costs.[56] Welles asked Myron Taylor at the Vatican to ask the pope whether the Vatican had had any reports of "severe measures" against non-Aryans.[57] He also learned that the Warsaw Ghetto was being emptied, and its inhabitants moved to special camps.

Satisfied at last that it was true, Welles released the telegram to Rabbi Stephen Wise, who announced Hitler's proposed wholesale extermination at a press conference the same day in late November 1942. Though *The New York Times* and *The Washington Post* had both published reports on mass murders of Russian Jews by the Einsatzgruppen—SS task forces—a year earlier, Jewish leaders in Britain and the United States could now no longer discount the drastic reports about Nazi plans for the resolution of the Jewish question. The stories of deportations, the Warsaw Ghetto, and the fate of Polish Jews were also being corroborated by the vivid account of a Polish courier, Jan Karski. The Jewish leadership was alarmed; it was clearly time to go public. The U.S. State Department, however, maintained its distance, adopting an attitude more in keeping with Harrison's take on the Jewish question.

THE MEDITERRANEAN RIM

Ambassador von Papen had relished being in the thick of things in Turkey. Then one cold February morning in 1942, as he was walking with his wife on a windswept Ankara boulevard, a bomb exploded just yards away. The bomb that had clearly been intended for Papen had blown the man carrying it to pieces. Apart from Papen's distress over his mussed suit, the assassination attempt brought home the fact that his popularity was no longer what it once was. During the almost two and a half years he had been in Turkey, Germany had steamrolled over most of Europe, and Ankara was full of unhappy refugees. As the local symbol of the Nazi Party, Papen now had a list of enemies significantly longer than the list of his friends. His best suit was torn, he had a cut on his knee, and his wife's dress was bloodied, but, once again, he had survived.[58]

The botched assassination attempt loosed a flood of rumors and accusations among the international community. The British and the Russians accused the Gestapo; Ribbentrop blamed the British Security Service, but the Turkish police soon had two suspects in custody, Yugoslav Muslims who were naturalized Turks. Given their backgrounds, it would have been more than reasonable to believe that they hated Papen, but they made a shocking claim: The Soviet government had masterminded the murder attempt in the hope of pushing Germany into declaring war on Turkey. Of course the Soviets denied the assertion, but Turkish intelligence was able to verify their claim through two secret sources.

Former Czech ambassador to Turkey, Milos Hanak had as much reason as anyone to hate Papen. On his arrival in Istanbul, the German ambassador had taken over Hanak's house, his office, even his car. Since then, Hanak had been providing anti-Nazi intelligence to the Allies and had developed strong ties within the Soviet intelligence community. Leonid Naumon, the code name of Leonid Eitingon, a deputy director of Soviet military intelligence, had boasted to Hanak that he had been commissioned to kill Papen. Naumon had fully expected support from his Czech friend, but Hanak was a moral man and would not countenance murder. In shock, he threw Naumon out, but after this failed attempt, he reported the story to Turkish intelligence.

The other informant was Ismail Akhmedov, a Soviet press attaché in Istanbul and a lieutenant colonel in Soviet military intelligence. As part of the intelligence network, he knew of the mission to kill Papen. Akhmedov had discovered that the man he referred to as "Naumov" planned to make him the scapegoat and blame him for revealing the plan to the Turks, and this bit of treachery spurred him to talk to British and Yugoslav intelligence officers. Arrangements were made for Akhmedov to defect at a Turkish police station. After his debriefing by Emniyet, the Turkish security police, there was little doubt that the plot against Papen had been masterminded by the Soviets.

Ironically, the attempt on his life conferred new cachet on Papen, reviving his status. He remained exactly what he wanted to be, a key player in Turkey, a man sought out by foreign enemies and German resistance fighters alike.

BY THE TIME OTTO JOHN ARRIVED IN MADRID IN 1942 TO REORGANIZE THE SPANISH SUB-sidiary of the German airline Lufthansa there, he was already a veteran of years of anti-Hitler activity. When jobs were scarce in 1933, a schoolmate had offered to get him a staff job with his father. Fritz Göring was a nice fellow, but John declined.[59] Already he felt enormous incompatibility between what he knew was right and what the new Nazis represented. At one point, he considered emigrating, but decided against it. He refused even the "inner emigration" to which many opponents of the regime had resorted as things got worse. But in 1936, when Hitler reoccupied the Rhineland and British foreign minister Anthony Eden had remarked that there was "no reason to suppose that the present German action implies a threat of hostilities," John was stunned. His anger with the regime and his frustration with the laissez-faire attitude of Britain and France deepened.

His sense of isolation was eased only when he took a legal job at Lufthansa, where the head of his department was Klaus Bonhoeffer. Through Bonhoeffer, John met Hans von Dohnanyi and others who felt as he did. These people wanted to overthrow Hitler. There were even inklings of a conspiracy of generals. As John got to know more of them and learned of their plans, his sense of frustration lifted. He had found a path to active involvement and resistance.

During the 1938 Sudeten crisis, John had been involved in the thwarted plot headed by Oster and the generals to rid Germany of Hitler. Through Dohnanyi, he had met Beck, who was hoping to persuade the generals and officers of the OKW that resigning en masse could circumvent Hitler's push to war. Beck himself resigned, but with no effect on Hitler's plans for Czechoslovakia. At Lufthansa, John met Prince Louis-Ferdinand of Hohenzollern, a man he found remarkably straightforward and unpretentious in spite of his august title. Louis-Ferdinand was wary of political conversations with John, afraid he might be an agent provocateur. Coincidentally this was sorted out by the husband of the piano teacher to the Dohnanyi and Bonhoeffer children who often got together with the prince for musical evenings. They had become very good friends, and he soon reassured Louis-Ferdinand about John's political orientation.

Carl Goerdeler had been frustrated in his efforts to make contact with the British through the Wallenbergs in Sweden.[60] When he heard that John was to reorganize Lufthansa's Spanish subsidiary, he saw an opportunity. John's assignment provided excellent cover and enviable mobility, and Goerdeler hoped to make use of both. He met with John in a Berlin hotel room, but began to talk about his plans only after he had put a tea cozy over the telephone, then added a pillow over that to ensure the necessary privacy. Then he finally began to to lay out his hopes, explaining that Louis-Ferdinand had connections to President Roosevelt and he was eager to try to use that particular lever to establish contact with Washington. John, as Louis-Ferdinand's friend, and with his usual mobility, would be the perfect intermediary.

In Madrid, with Louis-Ferdinand's introduction, John met Juan Terrasa, a former attaché at the Spanish embassy in Washington. Terrasa then set up a meeting for John with the U.S. embassy's chargé d'affaires in Madrid, Willard Beaulac. Beaulac listened carefully as John explained the problems of the resistance and their keen interest in making contact with Washington. The American promised to put his contacts at John's disposal, and to stay in touch. "Good luck!" he said as they parted. "You need it."[61]

Beaulac put John in touch with the American military attaché Colonel William Hohenthal, a German-speaker with German roots. The two men traded stories about common acquaintances in Berlin. Both Beaulac and Hohenthal were accessible and agreeable. Both liked John and trusted him, but they did not quite know what to do with him. SIS warned Beaulac to be extremely cautious in dealing with John, and his subsequent reports on John to the State Department went unanswered. Still, in spite of the official silence, he met with John again in October 1942.

Shortly after contacting Beaulac, John met with a British intelligence officer in Lisbon, Tony Graham-Meingott. Chubby, radiating bonhomie, and, according to John, with no knowledge of German, but knowing a great deal about Germany, Graham-Meingott drove John out into rolling countryside through fields of autumnal stubble. As they walked through vineyards, far from any listening devices or unwanted company, John explained the opposition's eagerness to enlist Allied support.

Graham-Meingott looked out across the open landscape and listened. He knew of the British government's distrust of the German anti-Nazis. After a long, nerve-racking silence, he told John that if the opposition wanted to get a hearing in London, it must do something to prove itself.[62] Nothing had changed; as always, the British were determined to keep their distance from Germans, whether opposition or not.

ACCORDING TO SOME, THERE WERE ALSO BIGGER PLAYERS ON THE IBERIAN SCENE, TWO venerable spymasters who had been opponents over a considerable period: MI-5's Stewart Menzies, the famous "C" of spy literature, and Wilhelm

Canaris.[63] Canaris knew Spain well, of course, and loved it. He is thought by some to have crossed paths there with Menzies in 1916, then under orders to capture or kill him, and he had returned many, many times since.

By the autumn of 1942, Germany's second Russian offensive had disintegrated, and as Canaris contemplated what he saw as an inevitable Götterdämmerung, the admiral was even more melancholic than usual. As a firm anticommunist he had resolutely ignored potential Soviet peace overtures in spite of the urgings of his old friend Vladimir Kaulbars, a Russian émigré Baltic baron who had taught him Russian. He would never consider anything as direct, violent, and messy as throwing a bomb or wielding a dagger to end Hitler's regime and save Germany, but peace feelers toward the Allies were another matter. Kaulbars insisted that making contact with the enemy and negotiating "for the country's sake" was Canaris's patriotic duty. He predicted that in Britain his influence and connections "would be rated so highly that you could achieve something under the most adverse circumstances."[64]

In fact, some Allied quarters held Canaris in very high regard, and Menzies was one of his staunchest admirers. The two men had been aware of each other since World War I, but became official antagonists only when Menzies took over SIS in 1939. A masterspy is not easily distracted from his principal preoccupation—slipping beneath the skin of another. Reading the smile or the sneer behind the words of a report, the person behind the action, the psyche behind the spy speak is essential to the art of first-class espionage. It is an art and demands great concentration and a willingness to immerse oneself in the minutiae of another's life. It also entails a kind of clairvoyance, and a willingness to think outside one's own mind-set. Menzies had not only the preoccupation, but the requisite concentration, willingness, and clairvoyance. He had, over the years, made a meticulous study of his rival across the Channel and on the other side in the war. Not the smallest detail escaped the loupe under which he had examined Canaris's life. The men were of the same vintage and likely shared the values of a more conservative and orderly world.[65] According to Richard Deacon, who has written extensively on espionage, Menzies was aware, however subliminally, of common concerns, and more important, of a common desire to end the accursed war.[66]

There is controversy about the Menzies-Canaris dealings. Whether all or just some of it is true, it is all part of the big mystery and deserves a mention. Some historians are of the opinion that late in 1942, through Spanish or Portuguese intermediaries, the admiral proposed to meet with his British counterpart in neutral territory. Operation Torch, the Allied invasion of North Africa, was under way, so that a meeting somewhere on the Iberian Peninsula would present few obstacles.

Menzies was ready, but the Foreign Office was decidedly not ready.

Menzies was told not to meet with Canaris under any circumstances "for fear of offending the Russians." This was just another reason to chafe under the pressure of the Big Three alliance. The fellow SIS officer to whom Menzies later lamented was outraged: No, it would not have pleased Stalin, but "why we should fall over backwards to appease those who were, and are, pledged to destroy our way of life I shall never understand."[67]

There are also indications that, having failed with the British, Canaris, like others in a pattern that pertained consistently during the war, decided to try with the Americans. An initial attempt through Istanbul was turned down by FDR, but Canaris had an apparatus well suited for peace feelers. The reach of his wide network was extended through a chain of links and connections, tendrils that stretched not only horizontally across borders, but penetrated vertically, through layers. There are unsubstantiated claims that Canaris's less conspicuous emissaries began to appear in various neutral countries, probing delicately for positive responses to an early peace. While he was not exactly inconspicuous, Prince Max von Hohenlohe-Langenburg could also be very useful in this kind of venture, because the prince's Iberian connections amplified Canaris's own. Other claims credit the German ambassador to Portugal with establishing the Menzies-Canaris connection in 1943.[68]

According to author Heinz Höhne, Canaris had helped Spanish intelligence, and Spanish intelligence, wanting to repay him, set up a meeting in Santander, between the big three of World War II intelligence: Canaris, Menzies, and Donovan. It was the summer of 1943, just six months after the failed attempt with Menzies. There were surely no minutes of this rather intimate conference. Canaris understood perfectly the dangerous game he was playing. Still, historians cannot help wishing they had been the proverbial fly on the wall. The closest they can come is the recollection of Justus von Einem, who claimed to have been present and is cited by Höhne. In what he remembered as the most exciting moment of his career in the Abwehr, Einem recalled that there was general agreement based on Canaris's plan calling for the elimination of Hitler, a continuation of the war against Russia, and a cease-fire in the west.

Once again, whatever hopes may have sprung up as a result of any Santander meeting—if there was one—they were short-lived. Roosevelt ostensibly quashed Donovan's initiative immediately; there would be no flirtations with a separate peace, there would be only unconditional surrender. Menzies could easily have guessed how the Foreign Office would respond to news of such an excursion, and would have made the necessary adjustments.[69] Canaris, as always, remained a master at lying low. Any dream of a negotiated peace that these three men may have had evanesced in the face of the harsh realities.

BERN: DULLES'S "BIG WINDOW"

"Berne is the diplomatic and spy center," twenty-four-year-old Allen Welsh Dulles had written breathlessly to his mother at Christmas, 1917. Young Allen was working for the State Department's Foreign Office in Switzerland. "Also I now hobnob with all sorts of outlandish people, Czechs, Yugoslavs, Albanians, Montenegrins, Ukrainians."[70] Later he added, "We are busy with rumors . . . political projects . . . peace feelers from the Germans and Austrians. We have to sift and investigate and get at all the truths. It is a liberal education."[71] As it turned out, this time in Bern was to be a real foretaste of Dulles's future; he would spend his life hobnobbing with all sorts of people and working to get at all the truths.

Coming from a family with a history of political involvement and some secretaries of state in the family tree—grandfather John Watson Foster, briefly under Benjamin Harrison; Robert "Uncle Bert" Lansing, under Woodrow Wilson; and his older brother, John Foster Dulles, eventually became another—makes it slightly less surprising to find such a young man engaged in such critical work. Princeton, Class of '14, Dulles volunteered for National Guard duty when war broke out in Europe and Mexico, but he also sat for the Foreign Service exam. A deciding factor in his signing on with the State Department's Foreign Office, which he served during World War I in Vienna and Bern, may have been his poor eyesight.

Dulles had been attached to the American embassy in Berlin from 1916 until the United States entered the war against Germany. He had learned a great deal, and had become good friends with Dr. Gero von Schulze-Gavernitz, a political scientist, former economics professor, and member of parliament in the Weimar Republic. Gävernitz had helped to draft the Weimar Republic's constitution, and his views on reliable means of securing world peace had had a profound influence on the young Dulles. As was Dulles's way, he had come to know the entire family personally, including the children, young Gero among them. Many years later these early relationships were to prove crucial for him.

In 1919, Robert Lansing invited his nephews to the Versailles Peace Conference as part of the American delegation. Versailles left Allen Dulles somewhat disillusioned, for he believed that the harsh terms dictated to Germany represented the groundwork for trouble. He favored a more Wilsonian concept of self-determination and true multilateralism; international relations suggested to him that nations had to transcend a narrow mind-set and concentrate on working together to keep the world safe from future wars. But the conference was an invaluable experience for a young diplomat-in-the-making, and it shaped much of his thinking about foreign relations.

On returning to the United States after Versailles, Dulles was so smitten with Maryland socialite Martha Clover Todd that he later joked that he had waited three whole days before asking her to marry him only by exercising enormous restraint. Late in 1920, the newlyweds set off for his new posting in Constantinople, where he was soon made chief of the Near East Division. Dulles was twenty-nine, and his star was clearly rising. Constantinople, later Istanbul, was another city that would become important to Dulles.

Back on the Washington social circuit, Dulles's path crossed that of Bill Donovan, and not surprisingly the two men became friends. But Dulles soon discovered that living a full social life was incompatible with a government salary, so for several years he scrambled between his demanding job during the day and law school at night. In 1926, with an LLD from George Washington University in hand, he resigned from the State Department and took a lucrative job at the Wall Street law firm of Sullivan and Cromwell, where his older brother John Foster was already a partner. He also served on the elite Council on Foreign Relations and participated in high-level government conferences that brought private individuals and government officials together.

Donovan meanwhile had returned to his New York law practice, and their friendship was renewed. One month after Pearl Harbor, Donovan tapped Dulles to head the New York office of the Coordinator of Information. When he asked him later to consider going to London to help David Bruce in negotiations with the British, Dulles demurred. He had spent time in Switzerland during World War I and felt he would be far more useful on his old stomping grounds; he should head an OSS office in Bern. Donovan had been thinking of an operation in Switzerland ever since Stallforth had opened his eyes to the existence of a German opposition, and he trusted Dulles's instincts completely. It was a perfect fit.

On November 8, 1942, just as the Germans were on the point of closing the border, Dulles crossed from France into Switzerland. In fact, his timing was so close that all he had with him was what he could carry: one suitcase and about $10,000. This was a substantial sum at the time, if not the cool million that legend claims, but Dulles did describe himself as "having bags of money."[72] The American spy mission had arrived in the nick of time, and late in the game, but Dulles lost no time.

When he arrived in Bern, El Alamein was in the news, and Switzerland was already a haven for countless refugees and home to numerous intelligence operations, all operating sub rosa, in order not to violate Swiss neutrality too conspicuously. His cover as special assistant to the American minister, Leland Harrison, was tantamount to announcing that he was setting up a spy operation, but for Dulles, this obvious cover had the happy consequence of "bringing to my door purveyors of information, volunteers and adventurers of every sort, professional and amateur spies, good and bad."[73] He was entirely without staff, but mercifully the Swiss government let him get some short passes for American fliers who had made their way to Switzerland. These were trained men with military experience who understood codes and security measures. Now interned outside of Bern, they could come in to do ciphering work for him.[74]

That was a start. Clover was back in New York with the children; there were no distractions. Dulles, pushing fifty, was no newcomer to the spy business, but a seasoned professional. He was soon on his way to setting up perhaps the most effective OSS operation in Europe, which he later referred to as "the big window" on the Nazi world.[75] The Americans had been late in coming to the Swiss spy carnival, but Leland Harrison was already in touch with a considerable and diverse crew.[76] Among them was Hjalmar Schacht, former Reichsbank president and until 1937 Hitler's minister of economics, whose change of heart toward the Nazis eventually sent him to Dachau as a prisoner.

Immediately on arrival, Dulles began to develop his network, first calling socially on all the Americans in Bern. Then he fanned out throughout Switzerland to meet and greet fellow countrymen who had either taken up residence there before the war or had been trapped when the border closed. Charming, socially deft, and an extraordinarily keen judge of character, Dulles sized up everyone he met over drinks and a relaxed dinner. If they fit his requirements, they were recruited to become part of his enormous information network. If not, they often became just friends.

He renewed his acquaintance with Noel Field, the son of an old friend from the World War I era, Dr. Henry Haviland Field. Noel Field was a Quaker, communist, and an idealist who had been in Foreign Service since graduating Harvard in 1926. Dulles wasn't thrilled to be working with a communist, but on several occasions he said he would be willing to work with the Devil himself to end the war, and he invited Noel Field to work as a courier between the OSS and German communists exiled in Switzerland.[77]

At Versailles he had spent time with Wilson's "Inquiry," a collection of experts in many different fields—businessmen, historians, economists, geographers—who were intended to put their knowledge to work to cure America's ignorance of the complexities of the European continent and help forge a lasting peace. Those members who were available now became a valued resource. Many people he contacted had been established in legitimate businesses for years and aroused no suspicions. Some had relatives in German-occupied territories who might pass along tidbits from their daily lives. Though his method was seen as daring and unorthodox, in fact it resembled Donovan's. Through the chattiness of an associate's German household help with relatives in the Wehrmacht, for instance, Dulles learned—among other things—that shortly after Stalingrad Germany was unable to resupply the Wehrmacht with aluminum spoons. It was just the sort of information he found "useful," one of his favorite expressions.[78]

Allen Dulles did not look like a spy. True, he wore a trench coat, but the silhouette was all wrong, for the pockets invariably bulged with countless rumpled newspapers. With the help of a Swiss tailor, he had shed his New York lawyer wardrobe and image. His tweedy, vaguely professorial look, his pipe, his avuncular air and booming laugh were contrary to every cliché of what a spy should be. He exuded warmth, a genuine interest and concern for people, and his gift for intimacy bound people to him in enduring friendships that survived the war by decades. He had a remarkable ability to get people to tell him everything, even as he said very little. Somewhere, there was a part of him that was never exposed, always unseen and unknown, even to intimates. Perhaps that is the ingredient required of the quintessential spymaster.

When Dulles arrived, Switzerland was an island in a sea of German rule. Though the influx that had arrived before the war had slowed to a trickle, the country was awash with emigrants and refugees of many nationalities, and alive with intrigue. There were so many different intelligence outfits that the tiny nation literally swarmed with sleuths and spies. The Soviets had "Lucy," their spy ring in Lucerne. The British had operations in Bern, and Colonel Claude Dansey of Britain's SIS established the supersecret operation "Z," where else but in Zurich? The Swiss, of course, had their own operation, and through Colonel Roger Masson of the Swiss general staff, a direct line to Berlin and Walter Schellenberg.[79] To complicate matters further, there was also a full complement of spies from Eastern Europe: Czechs, Hungarians, Bulgarians, Romanians. It was a heady brew.

Confidential communication with the outside world, though, was nearly impossible. Telegraph and telephone lines ran through a commercial Swiss exchange, and Dulles was sure that the Swiss heard everything he ever said. He had a scrambling device on his telephone, but he was convinced that both the Swiss and the Germans were descrambling his calls. At one dinner party, the high Swiss functionary seated next to him smilingly repeated to him something he himself had said in a recent telephone conversation with Washington.[80] So he took to inserting things he specifically wanted the Swiss to know into his conversations, but for the rest of his almost daily communications with London and Washington, he exercised extreme caution. Assuming that the Germans were trying to decode even his truly innocent phone calls, on several occasions he even resorted to using commercial radio to send coded messages to London over the airwaves. Communication problems bedeviled Dulles until September 1944, when the liberation of France removed many complications.

Dulles set himself up in a beautiful old house at Herrengasse 23 in the old quarter of Bern, not far from where he had lived in 1917. Living near Bern's many embassies would have left him open to too much surveillance, with little ordinary foot traffic to shield his visitors and activities. It was a spacious apartment overlooking gardens and vineyards sloping down to the river and beyond, to the mountains of the Bernese Oberland. Cordelia Dodson Hood, who worked with Dulles late in the war and lived at the Herrengasse, described it as so picture postcard perfect as to be "almost kitschy."[81] But Dulles's digs had advantages beyond space and a wonderful view; a back door opened onto terraced vineyards where it was easy for a nighttime visitor to come out of—or disappear into—the leafy darkness quickly and unseen. In true spy fashion, Dulles saw to it that the streetlight opposite the house was invariably out; the more complete the darkness, the better.

By picking up such snippets as Germany's inability to replace Wehrmacht spoons because of a shortage of aluminum, Dulles began to turn Bern into a major source of valuable intelligence. From the very beginning, he deluged Washington and London with an extraordinary volume of information via cable and telephone calls, or "flashes." But the real intelligence gold from the Bern operation was to come from a source that surprised many: Germans— anti-Nazi Germans willing to go to great lengths and run huge risks in the hope of bringing down Hitler and ending the war as quickly as possible.

When a valuable "source" did come in through the back door, he or she was usually taken to Dulles's book-lined study. Here the many lines of information, a virtual spiderweb traversing Europe and running deep into Germany, came together. Over drinks, Dulles drew on his pipe and poked idly at a fire that provided a dim, cozy light. He knew perfectly well that a fire diverted attention, diffused anxiety, relaxed the visitor, and helped to engage him in hours of talk. It was part of his technique for forging intimate, trusting relationships that ultimately yielded first-class information— "product" in spy lingo—for the Allies.

This sheltered ambience was the setting for Dulles's relationship with members of the German opposition. It was a relationship that ran counter to the conventional thinking on wartime relations with the enemy, but it became one of the stronger and more meaningful connections of the period. Dulles and the German opposition to Hitler shared a common goal— an end to Hitler and a strong Germany in the midst of a stable Europe.

CHAPTER 6

1943:

A WATERSHED

The winter of 1942–43 was a watershed. At Casablanca, Roosevelt demanded unconditional surrender, a formula that proved to be divisive to Allies and Germans alike. Days later, the collapse of the German Sixth Army at Stalingrad spread a deepening sense of catastrophe in Germany. The war was turning; Allied hopes for victory were buoyed. Though intended to assure Stalin that no separate peace would be made, neither Stalin nor Churchill was pleased with the policy of unconditional surrender. FDR's generals asked that it be softened because it was toughening the German will. Only Goebbels was delighted. He committed the nation to "total war," a propaganda ploy to incite Germans to fight to the bitter end.

To the resistance, unconditional surrender felt like a death sentence. The German generals, at odds with Hitler's war plans, now focused almost exclusively on assassination and unleashed a rash of coup attempts. In intelligence operations, too, that winter was a watershed. Allen Dulles's Bern operation became an unprecendented "collaborative" effort, including many levels of the German resistance, exiles from Hitler's Reich, outsiders willing to help, and one lone, initially unprepossessing arrival who proved to be spectacular.

Though the signals had been there for some time, it was only now that the awesome reality of another dimension of Hitler's war—the Final Solution—began to take shape in the Allied consciousness.

UNCONDITIONAL SURRENDER

At a cluster of sunny villas near Casablanca, the Anglo-American Allies gathered in January 1943 to discuss how to end what was beginning to look like a war that might be won, and what should come after it. Roosevelt, about to make an announcement, introduced it with a characteristically jaunty story about the American Civil War general U. S. Grant. For a time, he said, the general had been known as "Unconditional Surrender Grant," and it had occurred to him that this formula might be just the thing—the proper way to end the war. In his view, this would placate the absent Stalin, whose armies had been staggering valiantly along a seemingly endless front for well over a year and were now engaged in a grim tooth-and-nail battle at Stalingrad. Russia was hemorrhaging, and Stalin had too many pressing worries to come to Casablanca, but allaying his suspicions and impatience about the anticipated opening of a second front by the western Allies was critical.

When FDR tossed "unconditional surrender" on the table, Churchill was stunned. He and the president had bandied about various ideas for ending the war, but as far as Churchill knew, nothing had been decided. The prime minister later confessed to Eden that he had no desire to fuse the enemy into a solid, desperate block. In his opinion, any crack in Axis unity "would be all to the good." But he choked back his reservations, and unconditional surrender became the Allied prerequisite for peace.[1]

Stalin recognized unconditional surrender as an opportunity. The war was beginning to wind down, and he was eager to expand his influence over postwar Germany. His means to this end was a group of German communists living in exile in Russia, and German prisoners of war calling themselves the Free Germany Committee. They wanted an overthrow of Hitler, the cessation of military operations, and peace negotiations, preferably with a pro-Soviet slant. An offshoot of the Free Germany Committee in the USSR was the *Bund Deutscher Offiziere*—German Officers' League, many of whom had been captured at Stalingrad.[2] Headed by General Walther von der Seydlitz-Kurzbach, they were driven by a conviction of a strong Russian and German community of interest and an enormous respect for the power and resilience of the Red Army that went back to the 1922 program of cooperation and reciprocal training agreed on at Rapallo.[3]

Within months, Roosevelt's placatory posture toward Stalin at Casablanca was reinforced. In April, German troops discovered a mass grave in the forest of Katyn near Smolensk. It held the moldering bodies of what were estimated to be 10,000 Polish officers who had surrendered to the Russians in 1940. The Germans accused the Russians; the Russians insisted it was the work of German hands. The White House took a firm stand; it had all the hallmarks of a Nazi operation and the president decried it as such.

A German investigation of 1943 predictably blamed the Russians for the massacre. The Polish government-in-exile in London tried to get the Red Cross to investigate almost immediately, but then put together a report based on documents and reports smuggled out of Poland. U.S. Colonel Henry Szymanski had worked with the Poles on the report, and felt that it contained "too much dynamite to be forwarded through regular channels," so he had it hand delivered to army intelligence in Washington. Roosevelt was sent the report on August 11, 1943.[4]

The conclusion that Katyn was Stalin's handiwork was deeply uncomfortable for the western Allies. Committed as they were to the Grand Alliance, there could be no question of severing ties with Stalin at this juncture. Everyone needed to keep Stalin pacified. Yet it appeared that they were in bed with a mass murderer, guilty of precisely the sort of thing for which the Nazis were excoriated. FDR saw both reports but opted for a policy of Rooseveltian silence. Stalin must be retained as a future ally against Japan; he would do whatever was necessary to buttress the cozy entente with the Soviets that he imagined was in the cards. The report spent the rest of the war warehoused in a file cabinet outside of Washington.[5] The British expressed considerable qualms, but also preferred to look the other way. It was one of many triumphs of political expediency over morals.[6]

Ironically, the formula of unconditional surrender was destined to become an enormous impediment to finding peace, and exacted a very heavy price. Across the spectrum of combatants it unleashed a range of responses. Within Germany, Goebbels was jubilant, claiming he could never have dreamt up a more effective strategy to persuade the doomed Germans to fight to the last breath. Canaris, fatalistic as always, could see no solution whatsoever. Kleist-Schmenzin was vitriolic: Both Hitler and Roosevelt should have their own personal vats in which to boil in hell.[7]

In the Allied ranks, too, there was concern. In time, generals George C. Marshall and Dwight D. Eisenhower figured among its critics. Eisenhower hoped to persuade both Churchill and Roosevelt to soften the policy—and German resistance on the beachheads—before D-Day, but Roosevelt was adamant. Donovan and Menzies recognized that it created difficulties for their intelligence operations and was a stumbling block to peace, but both were powerless to change it. England's Bishop Bell, long a supporter of the German opposition, questioned it. Lord Hankey, a close Churchill advisor, saw the formula as creating "icy waters."[8] The pope had his own doubts, and though General Beck knew that times had changed, he sent Joseph Müller on another Vatican mission to try again to establish contact with the British. Stalin, for whom Roosevelt had presumably custom-tailored the formula, had never equated Hitler's crew with Germany as a whole; he began to send out feelers to both Hitler and the "other Germany."

Allen Dulles was newly established in Bern when the Allied stance jelled at Casablanca. Initially he thought that the demand might benefit the Allies psychologically. But his clandestine network of anti-Nazis poured into Bern, arguing bitterly that the policy offered no encouragement to either the opposition or the general population. For Germans, unconditional surrender meant that there was nothing but total destruction and humiliation in store for them from any quarter—other than possibly the Russians. Goebbels's propaganda was shrieking that all Germany would be enslaved; there was no alternative but to fight to the bitter end. Dulles quickly changed his mind.

He came to agree with the opposition that Goebbels had been handed an extraordinary coup. Backing the nation into this cul de sac could only prolong the war. He also knew about the stab-in-the-back theory promulgated by conservatives after Versailles—namely that Germany had not really lost the war militarily, but that revolutionaries and democrats on the home front had stabbed the army in the back. Generals Hindenburg and Ludendorff had an interest in camouflaging the German defeat, and blamed it on insufficiently patriotic factions on the home front. Hitler had exploited this theory expertly, and Dulles worried that if any promises he might make to the conspirators were not honored by the Allies, this could be interpreted the same way. The Allies were extremely leery of attempts at negotiating any early settlement of the war.

THE PERFECT CONNECTION

One of the first persons Dulles encountered after his arrival in Bern was Gero von Schulze-Gävernitz, a forty-year-old German American whose father had befriended Dulles in Berlin before World War I, and from whom Dulles had learned so much. Now the son was everything Dulles could have asked for in an assistant. He had strong anti-Nazi inclinations and the desire to make himself useful in the secret war to bring down Hitler. He had family and business holdings in Switzerland. He was personable, intelligent, enterprising, and intimately connected to an international elite of politics, industry, and money.

Gävernitz was rich and handsome; all the accoutrements for playboy potential were in place, but he was also calm, even-tempered, and desperately unhappy that Germany, which he considered his country, was falling into what he described as "folly and disaster." He supplied Dulles with numerous reports on the mood in Germany in general and the opposition to Hitler in particular, noting that "members of the secret opposition in Germany state that silence on the part of the American and British governments with regard to postwar plans for the rehabilitation of Europe are apt to extend the war longer than necessary. In view of continued military setbacks opposition forces are gaining momentum . . . [but] to expand their influence . . . a clear statement of policy by American and British Governments . . . might help their task considerably."[9] His memoranda were of great help to Dulles, and reappear in many of Dulles's communications with Washington.

The younger Gävernitz presented Dulles with the perfect entrée into a Germany ruled by forces his father had hoped would never come to power. Through his American mother—from the family of financier Otto Kahn—he had taken American citizenship and then settled in Switzerland to look after business interests. He was an offshoot of "the royalty of capitalism," equally at home in Europe and the United States. His relationship with Dulles demonstrated clearly "how the circles of the elite and the like-minded strive to close, across frontiers, oceans, and the passage of time."[10] Like Dulles, he had a great capacity for making friendships, and just as the elder Gävernitz had wished, the two became friends.

It was the ideal connection. Gävernitz was in contact with both military and civilian groups of anti-Nazis hoping to rescue Germany from Hitler's grip. He was keeping Dulles informed of the public mood in Germany and the temper of the opposition. He was in touch with Eduard Schulte, the wealthy, idiosyncratic German businessman with a formidable record of delivering accurate information. Schulte became OSS #643, a man Dulles regarded as a representative of the "good Germany."

From Schulte, Gävernitz had learned back in 1940 that if American business thought it could coexist in a Europe under Hitler, it was deluding itself.[11] The United States should intervene soon. While Schulte considered it his patriotic duty to tell the outside world of the Nazi madness, but he remained personally aloof. He maintained his distance from the spy game just as he had kept himself out of the Nazi fray. Always independent, always operating on his own, Schulte never saw himself as working for anyone. He had often delivered critical and completely reliable information, usually through his channels in Switzerland. It was Schulte who had brought word of the inauguration of the gas chambers at Auschwitz, in July 1942, but little or nothing came of any of the information he passed along to the Allies.

Dulles and Gävernitz spent hours talking, pondering the intricacies of the political inclinations and the connections of anyone of influence in that turbulent time. Dulles began to use Gävernitz as a "feeler."[12] He became OSS Agent #476, Dulles's friend and right-hand man, putting him in touch with his underground networks of people who would be "useful" in the great spy game. He also had a marvelous gift for putting at ease the psychologically stressed Germans who came to Herrengasse 23 in hopes of persuading an enemy to help save their country.

In time, the close relationship between Dulles and Gävernitz led to a curious misunderstanding. Hungarian intelligence in Switzerland had been keeping an eye on Dulles, and concluded, quite correctly, that he was sleeping with one of his associates. In view of the amount of time the two men spent together, they decided that the associate must be Gävernitz. That distinction, however, was to fall to someone else.

FIFTEEN-YEAR-OLD MARY BANCROFT HAD BEEN AMONG THE CROWD JOSTLING TO WATCH wild Bill Donovan march up New York's Fifth Avenue in celebration of victory in Europe at the head of the Fighting Irish. She later remembered feeling both exhilarated and depressed on that blustery spring day in 1919, wondering whether anything exciting would ever happen to her. As a girl from a proper Boston family, she knew she was expected to become a debutante and then marry an appropriate young man, but this was not the life to which she aspired; she wanted to be a cop. She certainly could not have imagined that she would one day be working for Donovan's OSS, as a spy in another war in Europe.

By early 1943, Bancroft was approaching forty, married and living in Zurich with her second husband, a Swiss. She was lively and smart, and spoke fluent, if appallingly accented German. Dark-haired and wordly-wise, with a bright slash of lipstick, she had abundant intellectual and sexual energy and later claimed that she "used up all the oxygen" in most of the rooms she entered. She was, she said, "at the height of her sexual prowess and usually always on the prowl."[13] In the staid environs of wartime Switzerland, she was a vivid, well-connected extrovert, and she attracted considerable attention. Far from home, in a stolid, neutral country encircled by the Nazi occupation, with a husband who was often absent, she felt cloistered, restless, and bored. Once the United States entered the war, she itched to be involved and was nearly frantic with impatience to do something to help in the war effort.

Through friends at the American legation in Bern, she began to work for Gerald Mayer of the Office of War Information, writing articles for the Swiss press on America and vice versa, a mildly propagandistic venture to "further international understanding."[14] She also analyzed German newspapers and the speeches of Goebbels, Göring, and Hitler. Mayer was essentially scouting for recruits for what would soon become the OSS operation in Bern, and so it was that she met Allen Dulles, special assitant to the American minister. Bancroft felt instantly that Dulles's cover as assistant to Leland Harrison was bogus. This man, she was convinced, would not be anybody's assistant for long.[15] She also felt a powerful current of sexual attraction. Dulles decided that Bancroft, as attractive and as wired into the educated and international community in Switzerland as she was, would be useful. Besides, he, too, felt the attraction.

Allen Dulles's enthusiasm for attractive women often met with an equally enthusiastic response. His affairs were numerous and well known, not only to many colleagues but also to his wife, Clover. At a later date, Dulles's amorous past would almost certainly have barred him from the important posts he eventually held. As for Bancroft, she—like Canaris—had been fascinated by spycraft as a child, particularly the then infamous Mata Hari. As she moved appreciably closer to her childhood dreams of excitement and intrigue than she could have imagined, she, like Canaris, was also rescued from a dead end. Not only did Dulles open the door to activity and excitement, he drew her out of a marriage gone stale into a mutually agreeable, sexually rewarding affair. "It should work out very well," he told her with characteristic, cheery directness. "We can let the work cover the romance—and the romance can cover the work!"[16] Bancroft was ripe and more than ready.

Dulles was keen to "get at the truths," and Mary Bancroft, too, according to her autobiography, had always tried to discover the truth about everything. As a disciple and patient of the great psychiatrist Carl Gustav Jung, she was an enthusiastic auditor of seminars at the Psychological Club, a group of analysts, doctors, students, and intellectuals whom Bancroft later described as "Vestal Virgins, Jung of course, being the flame."[17] Sometimes she turned to the great man for his insights on people, whether they were public figures or not. Dulles was intrigued by Jung's opinions on the personalities of the Nazi higher-ups. He urged both Donovan and David Bruce not to disregard Jung's insights, into Hitler in particular. Dulles reported Jung's opinion that Hitler, in light of his psychopathic tendencies, "would take recourse in any desperate measures up to the end, but he does not exclude the possibility of suicide in a desperate moment."[18] Jung was even assigned an agent number, #488. At one point, however, Dulles told Bancroft in no uncertain terms that he had no intention of ending as a footnote to one of Jung's case histories.[19]

Mary Bancroft set to work, eagerly interviewing refugees on the situation in their countries, asking their views on the efficacy of American propaganda. She questioned journalists and businessmen and any other sources of information she and Dulles could think of about everything that seemed relevant. She became a regular at Herrengasse 23. With a cigarette dangling from her scarlet lips, she applied a Jungian slant to the speeches of Nazi bigwigs and banged out her analyses for Dulles on an old typewriter.[20] Under the gaze of Clover's photo on the mantel, she and Dulles pondered the day's reports, prepared a summary, and, once Washington had been informed, went off to bed, as often as not, for some mutually satisfactory recreation. Before long, they were joined in their pursuit of truth by another seeker after that elusive commodity.

SOURCES FROM WITHIN AND WITHOUT THE REICH

Shortly after Dulles arrived in Bern, Gävernitz put him in touch with a German friend, Hans Bernd Gisevius, serving as a vice consul at the German consulate in Zurich. Early in his career, Gisevius had been attached to what later became the Gestapo, but he was not a member of the Nazi Party. His increasingly outspoken objections to the brutality and corruption under the new Nazi leadership soon made him a focus of suspicion. Now he was in Zurich under the auspices of the Abwehr, and of his friend Hans Oster in particular. As part of the Abwehr's inner anti-Nazi circle, the so-called Black Orchestra, his mission was to maintain contacts with the Allies on behalf of the German opposition to Hitler.[21]

He had approached the British first, but claimed they were not interested in the political aspects of war. Now it was the Americans' turn.

Dulles's stint with the State Department had taught him a lesson: Wars can be won or lost on many fronts. Destroying strategic targets is vital, but sometimes destroying a regime politically is just as effective, and produces fewer casualties. If Germany became wrapped up in internal turmoil, it might not have the strength or resources to continue fighting external foes.

For once, with Gisevius, Dulles was at a loss about how exactly to handle a source. Colonel Claude Dansey of British intelligence had warned him that Gisevius might be an SD agent. In 1939, working with MI-6, Dansey had been badly burned by the ill-fated Venlo Affair, were two British secret service agents, waiting to meet with "dissident" German generals in the Dutch border town of Venlo, were met instead by Walter Schellenberg's SD agents and whisked across the border into Germany. For Dansey, the Venlo venture was an abysmal failure and a humiliation not soon forgotten. For the true anti-Nazi opposition, the incident had also had unfortunate long-term effects, for it reinforced the already common suspicion that anyone billing himself as anti-Hitler was really a Nazi agent, making this suspicion nearly insurmountable.

So was Gisevius an Abwehr plant, as the British supposed—just another suspect German—or was he to be believed? He could put Dulles in touch with the Kreisau Circle, with Hjalmar Schacht, with Pastor Martin Niemöller, even with the Old Fox, Canaris himself. Dulles decided that Gisevius's insights into opposition groups forming in Germany and the links between them were worth whatever risks were entailed. Besides, his sister Eleanor claimed that Dulles had once told her that if it would give him a clearer picture of hell, he would lift his hat to the devil himself.[22] Gävernitz had already vetted Gisevius, and Dulles decided to lift his hat, at least a little. He arranged to meet Gisevius on the steps of Bern's World Council of Churches, a rendezvous that proved portentous for later connections.

Gisevius had his own reasons to be nervous. He had been evading the tentacles of the Nazi hierarchy for more than ten years. Scuttling back and forth from Zurich to Berlin, working ostensibly for the Nazi government while actually conspiring to bring it down required constant vigilance and unwavering distrust of just about everyone. In spite of

Gisevius's fascination, even love of the game, the strain was beginning to tell. Tension between the Abwehr and Himmler's forces had been growing, and by early 1943 he had good reason to worry for his own safety and that of his friends and fellow conspirators.

Canaris was due in Switzerland momentarily, and on his visits he usually spent some time with Mme. Halina Szymanska. Highly intelligent and politically sophisticated, Symanska had come to know Canaris in Berlin when her husband, Colonel Antoni Szymanski, was serving as the last Polish military attaché there before the war. Touring Poland just after its collapse, Canaris had been horrified by the devastation, particularly in Warsaw. When he learned that Colonel Szymanksi's wife and children were in a refugee camp, he had used the resources of the Abwehr to bring them out of Poland and ultimately to safety in Switzerland.[23] Mme. Szymanska became a confidante who provided Canaris not only with stimulating company, but, according to rumor, with useful pillow talk. She was also serving as liaison between the admiral and British intelligence.

The Abwehr agent charged with shepherding Szymanska through this delicate relationship was Gisevius.[24] He could certainly offer Dulles riches, and he saw that Dulles in turn might become the golden link to the Allies the resisters had been hoping for. He also had an inkling that Dulles could be talked to on a political level, beyond mere spying—something he devoutly hoped for. But could Dulles be trusted? It was a more than reasonable question.

At six foot four inches, Gisevius could hardly rely on inconspicuousness to cover his activities; the Swiss blackout was of some help, but he cast a very long shadow even in the dimmest light. Cordelia Dodson Hood recalled that the Bern operation referred to him as "Tiny," and he depended on his official role in the Abwehr to provide cover for his early clandestine visits to the Herrengasse.[25] But one evening, sitting in Dulles's study, he announced to the startled Dulles that they might have to drop contact. Carefully, he pulled a little black book out of his pocket, and from some fragmentary notes he quickly cobbled together a more than reasonable approximation of numerous cables Dulles had recently sent in the "Burns [Dulles] to Victor [London Receiver]" code.[26]

Clearly there was a problem; Berlin had broken one of the American codes. The code was not one that Dulles used often, but such a break was a spy's nightmare.[27] Yet what alarmed Dulles on the one hand reassured him on the other, for Gisevius had informed him of the break. The incident bolstered his confidence in Gisevius's legitimacy and strengthened their relationship. Caution was still the watchword, though, so Dulles concocted a plan: He would introduce Gisevius to Mary Bancroft as "Dr. Bernhard," and she would act as translator and amanuensis for his pet project—an enormous memoir. This huge manuscript detailed his years in the Nazi hierarchy, and he desperately wanted it published after the war. Bancroft was to win his confidence, keep her eyes and ears on full alert, get him to tell her everything, and report it all to Dulles.

When Dr. Bernhard appeared with his manuscript, Bancroft was stunned, first by his height, then by the size of his manuscript: three fat volumes, 1,415 closely typed pages in excrutiatingly difficult German.[28] The table of contents read like a rundown of big moments in Nazi history to date: *The Burning of the Reichstag; The 30th of June; The Fritsch-Blomberg Crisis; Reinhard Heydrich: The Story of a Futile Terror.* There were to be four volumes in all, and Bancroft realized she would need help with the immense undertaking. On the plus side, she would be working with a real spy, a member of the Abwehr. His official position was that of Sonderführer in Abwehr section III F (counterintelligence), under cover as vice consul. Not only was that intriguing, but this "giant of a man, fair-haired, blue-eyed, with a healthy tan," had a manner "so engaging, smile so beguiling," that she did not feel at all intimidated.[29] On the contrary; once again she was feeling the electric tingle of sexual attraction.

She set to work, burning to know her author's true identity. That was not revealed until she was well into his book, when a participant in an anecdote referred to him as "Gisevius." She had seen the initials HGB on his shirt. He was Hans Bernd Gisevius, viewed by the Nazis as "politically unreliable"—Nazi code for trouble. It was all quite thrilling, but the electric tingle, delicious though it was, subsided in the face of the work ahead.

The Dulles-Gisevius-Bancroft trio enjoyed a remarkable confluence of interests: Dulles had always wanted to get at the truth, as did Mary Bancroft, and Gisevius was keen to lay the truth about the Hitler regime's horrors before the public when it was all over. Bancroft enlisted the help of her friend Mary Briner, an American woman living in Switzerland in circumstances similar to Bancroft's own. When other responsibilities forced Briner to abandon the project, Bancroft suggested the Honorable Elizabeth Scott-Montagu. From an ancient and venerable English family, she was cousin to Lord Lothian, at one time ambassador to Washington. She had been driving an ambulance in France when the German advance forced her to flee to Switzerland.

The prolific, if amateur writer Gisevius was delighted to have such ladies working on his book—and one of them with a title! The morning that Scott-Montagu was to appear for the first time, he had an immense, glorious hydrangea in full bloom delivered. Gisevius was well aware that she was a direct descendant of Mary, Queen of Scots; as such, she was surely worth the expenditure of some Abwehr funds.[30] Together or singly, the women spent many afternoons with him, charming, flattering, and teasing nuggets of gossip and information out of Gisevius that was more up-to-date and went well beyond his somewhat stiff memoir. All of it went on to Dulles.[31]

So Dulles was a busy man in early 1943. Whether or not he had time to take notice, it was at about this time that some youthful resisters, later to be among the better known of Hitler's victims, were executed. They were just a few of the many, and would scarcely have attracted much interest from the outside world, but their deaths were symptomatic of the terror ruling the Reich. Germany's tradition of youth movements, usually but not invariably church-affiliated, produced circles of resistance among the very young. Hans and Sophie Scholl, brother and sister members of a student anti-Nazi group known as the "White Rose," wrote, printed and distributed anti-Nazi leaflets, calling for the ouster of Hitler and the creation of a new, spiritual Europe. Their last defiant act, emptying leaflets from the window of a Munich university building, precipitated their arrest. They were guillotined in February 1943, and many others of the so-called Scholl clique were executed soon afterward.

Dulles had been in Bern just two months when he communicated that the lack of "encouragement or understanding was a source of deep disappointment to the opposition." He was beginning to learn about this opposition to Hitler, and it was to become a subject of the utmost importance to him. Gisevius had put him in touch with Adam von Trott, of the German Foreign Office, who communicated the desperate disappointment of the entire Kreisau Circle with the lack of Allied encouragement or support for the opposition. Trott told the English wife of his friend Peter Bielenberg that he could not "believe that they want to create a vacuum here in the center of Europe—a vacuum fills—and if this bombing goes on, it will fill from the East. Even Stalin has realized that when the Nazis are gone he will have to deal with the German people. . . . I know there are people out there who must realize that the Nazis and all they stand for are as much our enemies as theirs."[32]

In fact, Stalin tried to make contact with the opposition from mid-1943. It was a move Dulles regarded as the only positive approach to the German army and the German people on record, and he understood that it was bound to have broad appeal. In Dulles's view, OSS Morale Operations should mount a western countermove to combat Goebbels's nightmare propaganda depiction of unconditional surrender.[33] He tried to explain to U.S. policy makers that, out of a sense of community with the suffering of Russia, some of the opposition, and Germany as a whole, were turning their hopes eastward. Both Russia and Germany had "broken with the bourgeois way of living . . . are returning to Christian traditions . . . and both are looking for a radical solution to their social problems. . . . Following Hitler's fall, a completely new Europe will be based on the brotherliness and experience of the oppressed common people."[34]

Though he made the opposition no promises, Dulles began to work to influence American policy toward a more moderate stance, advocating encouragement of the resistance, and an offer of hope for Germany's future. But neither his intelligence nor his policy efforts had any tangible effect. He later said that one of the reasons there had been no truly effective opposition to Hitler was that, unlike the resistance movements in occupied countries that received large-scale assistance and funding from the Allies, the German opposition was never offered the least support.

Among Dulles's many contacts during this period was Prince Max Egon von Hohenlohe-Langenburg, a Sudeten German of great wealth and questionable character. Carlton Hayes, the U.S. ambassador to Spain, where Hohenlohe's equally wealthy wife had properties, warned Dulles that he was "utterly without scruples, lying to anyone without hesitation, including his German chiefs."[35] In fact, his claim to represent the resistance was more than counterweighted by the fact that he was Himmler's agent #144/7957.[36] Dulles, however, stayed true to form; he would talk to anyone. He agreed that caution was advisable and suggested that Himmler might be using Hohenlohe for "feelers," but that "he can be of use to us if certain kinds of information are disregarded." Besides, he argued, Hohenlohe was surely aware that his property interests would be best protected "if he plays with our side."[37] Personally, Dulles was glad of the opportunity to exploit the opportunistic prince.

The conversations between Mr. Bull—Dulles—and Herr Pauls—Hohenlohe—largely took place early in Dulles's tenure in Bern. Present at some of the conversations was Reinhard Spitzy, who had been commissioned to produce a report for Walter Schellenberg. Spitzy's report was subsequently altered several times so as to meet with the approval of Hitler and Himmler, for whom it was ultimately intended. According to Spitzy, the altered report "put words in our mouths that we would never have dared pronounce, but which were meant to be heard 'upstairs.'" Dulles ostensibly expressed deeply anti-Semitic views and emphasized that Germany should never again be forced to endure a peace as unfair as that of Versailles. The Casablanca demand for unconditional surrender, Dulles reportedly said, was merely a piece of paper, to be scrapped without further ado if Germany would sue for peace, but Hitler had to go. Spitzy declared that some of his own remarks were attributed to Hohenlohe, who was not then present, "in order to bring this older and more important person into play, and probably to enhance the standing of Schellenberg's operation."[38]

THE WAR WAS NOT GOING WELL. SOMETHING NEW WAS REQUIRED TO RAISE THE REICH out of the gloom, and Hitler promised a new "miracle weapon." As a propaganda ploy, it did not arouse signficant fear or trembling in the Allied camp, and within Germany wags had abbreviated the vaunted *Wunderwaffe* to WuWa—making it sound like something unlikely to frighten anyone over age three. The earliest hint that there really was such a thing came from a German industrialist who reported that his factory was producing a small part designed for some kind of a secret aerial weapon. It was the first in a spate of scattered reports that led Dulles to believe that the promised weapon was more than just another of the Führer's empty promises.[39]

In May and June of 1943, OSS Bern received substantive information through Gisevius on the German rocket-building project at Peenemünde. This was reported to London and Washington as a high-priority item almost immediately, and in mid-August a British bombing raid delivered a blow that set the development of Hitler's much touted miracle weapon back significantly. By September, Dulles knew that the rocket business ought to be taken seriously. Schulte reported that the August RAF bombing raid had not destroyed the facility's capacity as much as had been hoped.[40] Thereafter came a variety of reports on the V-1 and V-2 rockets, and even Hohenlohe weighed in at one point.

THE MILITARY OPPOSITION

Hitler's relationship with the army had never been a comfortable one. After he appointed himself supreme commander in December 1941, the army's fortunes had declined, and it had become increasingly corrosive, reaching a new low with Stalingrad. He had refused the advice of his top generals, and there was little doubt that the blame for this numbing defeat lay with him, but he insisted on court-martialing a number of officers. The bitterness grew. As he had gloated shamelessly over his earlier triumphs, he now met the glaring military failures of 1942–1943 with black rages. Security around the increasingly reclusive and suspicious Führer tightened; his aberrant and unpredictable behavior became even more pronounced.

Unconditional surrender, followed immediately by the collapse of Stalingrad in February, engulfed the army and the nation in an overwhelming sense of impending catastrophe. A crushing military disaster would seem an unlikely catalyst to resurrecting hope, but after the demand for unconditional surrender, when the opposition needed all the hope it could muster, the defeat at Stalingrad had a galvanizing effect. Hitler was not invincible; this catastrophic defeat proved it. Ironically, Stalingrad brought new impetus to the opposition's attempts to break the terrible silence from the Allies and end their isolation. Among the opposition at large, there was a renewed urgency, and Goerdeler, the perennial optimist, saw bright light in the darkness. A visit to the Russian front convinced him that this defeat would strengthen the anti-Hitler elements in the military. He told Dulles that a coup was in the offing.

Dulles's antennae, always fine-tuned to the mood in Germany, had picked up the signals of distress in the military and in the nation. Hitler had assumed command, and he had made a mess of it. Now he needed diversionary action, which for Hitler usually meant a bloodbath. As Dulles reported:

> Hitler will probably return the High Command to the generals. Apparently he realizes the extent to which his prestige has been affected by . . . military operations, both among officers and throughout the country . . . there is serious danger of a new and extensive purge. Many thousands of names have been included on a prepared list of "unreliables." We might publicize . . . [that a new purge would] draw attention away from [Hitler's] military reverses. . . . From a Russian source I am led to believe that the Russians are training selected German prisoners for later internal action in Germany . . . and treat German prisoners well.[41]

Always interested in playing up any psychologically advantageous angles, Dulles recommended propaganda to the effect that if Hitler retained command, tensions with the military would escalate, and the "military errors" would increase.

The Allies should suggest that Hitler would be forced to "surrender his command." Using a recent, post-Stalingrad Goebbels statement that "because we have the Führer, we believe in victory," Dulles engaged in a bit of philosophical-semantic sleight of hand: If Hitler relinquished military command at a time when military action was paramount, Germany might no longer regard him as Führer, and hence there would be no victory.[42] Dulles's assessment of the military situation was not far off the mark, but it was missing some details.

In fact, the German military on the eastern front *was* preparing to take action. The chief operations officer for Army Group Center in Russia under Field Marshal Günther von Kluge was Colonel Henning von Tresckow, whose early support for Hitler had long since soured. By 1939, it had become loathing, and that summer he told his friend and adjutant, Fabian von Schlabrendorff, that both duty and honor demanded that Hitler be brought down "to save Germany and Europe from barbarism."[43] He was outraged and vocal about the "murder squads" behind the lines on the Russian front. Hitler had removed these Einsatzgruppen from army control and had given them full authority in the occupied territories. If these murders did not stop, Tresckow said, "the German people will be burdened with a guilt the world will not forget for a hundred years. This guilt will fall not only on Hitler, Himmler, Göring and their comrades, but on you and me, your wife and mine, your children and mine. Think about it."[44] Since the beginning of the Russian campaign, he had been bringing together a team of like-minded younger officers, and tried persistently to enlist any senior officers with whom he came in contact for the resistance. Ultimately a total of nineteen anti-Hitler conspirators came out of his regiment, the Potsdam 9th Infantry.

Already in September 1941, he had sent Schlabrendorff to alert the opposition in Berlin that Army Group Center was "ready for anything."[45] Ulrich von Hassell had noted in his diary that he was gratified to hear of Tresckow's resolve, the first and very welcome initiative to come from that quarter, and tried to assuage Tresckow's anxieties regarding a benevolent attitude from England in the event of a regime change.[46]

Tresckow was not to be deterred. In early March 1943, it looked as if his wish to lure Hitler to the Smolensk headquarters, to arrest or assassinate him there, was about to come true. Philipp von Boeselager, working for Kluge at Army Group Center, was part of the conspiracy and recalled that one plan was to have Hitler shot during lunch in the officers' mess. Kluge, had been hard to pin down; his oath of loyalty to Hitler continued to give him pause, and what appeared a firm commitment to the conspiracy one day was likely to be withdrawn the next. Still, having been kept abreast of developments by Tresckow, and likely also worn down by his insistence, he at least did not object to this plan until he learned that Himmler would be tagging along and would also be shot. This was risky. It might precipitate a war between the army and Himmler's army, the SS, whose strength had increased exponentially.[47] Kluge balked, then backed out.

But Tresckow was determined. Knowing Hitler's propensity for changing his plans at the last minute, he had several plans in place to deal with different eventualities. One involved the organization of crack cavalry squadrons under Georg von Boeselager, which, Boeselager's brother claimed, "could have pulled the devil himself out of Hell."[48] Posted near Hitler's SS guards for extra "security," they were actually under orders to fire on the Führer at any opportune moment, though this proved to be impossible. On the drive back to his aircraft, Hitler changed his route from the one planned and insisted that Kluge ride with him. Any barrage of bullets aimed at the Führer might also kill Kluge, which was unacceptable.

Since the summer of 1942, Tresckow had been working with his friend Rudolf-Christoph von Gersdorff, to obtain explosives to use as opportunity arose.[49] But even for senior officers explosives were hard to come by. Finally, at an Abwehr depot, Gersdorff found what he thought would be suitable for another alternate scheme. "Operation Flash" planned to blow up the plane taking the Führer back to his Wolf's Lair after his visit to the Smolensk headquarters. Gersdorff told the Abwehr officer at the depot that he had seen remarkable demonstrations of this British "Plastic C," and that he would like to take some back to the front with him to demonstrate to Kluge. But security was rigorous and he had to sign a receipt for the explosive.

On his return to Russia, he and Tresckow agreed that Plastic C was the right choice. In the form of a small device known as "the clam," it packed a sufficient wallop to do the job. It also had an added advantage: Detonating it in an enclosed space—such as an airplane—enhanced its efficacy. So four "clams" masquerading as bottles of Cointreau were loaded into Hitler's Condor for the flight back to Rastenburg, with a detonator set for thirty minutes. The "Cointreau" was ostensibly to be delivered to Helmuth Stieff, a Tresckow recruit for the resistance, to "pay off a bet." When the plane exploded over Minsk, Hitler's death would appear to be the result of an accident so obviating the potential problems any obvious assassination would entail.

Schlabrendorff's frequent trips to Berlin had kept the army group in touch with the nerve center of the conspiracy. With the help of Beck, Oster, Canaris, Dohnanyi, Goerdeler, and General Friedrich Olbricht, they had been able to organize and establish the necessary cascade of events and takeovers that would allow them to seize control once they heard that Hitler was dead. Everything for Operation Flash was in place, and the assembled Smolensk conspirators waited anxiously. Hours later word came of Hitler's safe landing at Rastenburg.

After a day of excrutiating tension followed by numbing disappointment, Tresckow coolly called Hitler headquarters. Recovering the "Cointreau" was critical. He explained that there had been a mix-up of packages; Schlabrendorff would come to straighten it out next day. When he collected the still undelivered Cointreau and examined the explosives, Schlabrendorff found that everything had functioned as intended. Fuse and firing pin were in order and the detonator was blackened, yet there had been no explosion. Precisely what had gone wrong is unclear, but one theory suggests that a malfunctioning heater in the cargo hold had caused the temperature-sensitive explosives not to ignite properly.[50]

Tresckow wasted no time on disappointment. Within days, he snatched at a new opportunity. Heroes' Memorial Day was to have been celebrated on March 14 in Berlin, but Hitler, as he did with increasing frequency, had changed the date. It was now scheduled for a week later, and Gersdorff was to be present at an exhibition of captured war material planned for the event. All the organization for the immediate aftermath of the previous plot was still in place. Gersdorff, confident that his death would have the desired effect, volunteered to blow himself up with Hitler in a deadly, suicidal embrace, using the "clams" reclaimed from the previous attempt.

It had seemed wonderfully fortuitous, but things quickly began to unravel. In keeping with the paranoia now surrounding the Führer, the schedule of events was kept ultrasecret. Gersdorff was not listed among the attendees. Even after a reasonable approximation of Hitler's schedule was finally obtained, and Gersdorff had been added to the guest list, a serious problem remained: finding sufficiently short fuses that did not require a conspicuous pull to activate them. Oster did his best, but in the end the shortest fuses he could come up with lasted ten minutes, a very long time in such circumstances.

To Gersdorff, wearing his army greatcoat in the unheated hall, with bombs in both pockets, it looked as if the Gestapo were everywhere. With fingers stiff from the chill, an orchestra played, then Hitler spoke—very briefly. The ceremony was being broadcast, and at his distant eastern outpost, Tresckow was glued to the radio, stopwatch in hand. Hitler began to move toward the war materiel exhibit, then suddenly picked up speed and raced through it, leaving Gersdorff with the bombs intended to kill the already departed Führer ticking off the minutes, about to explode in his pockets. He hurried to a restroom to defuse them.[51] Another attempt had failed.

THE JEWISH QUESTION

By this time, Hitler's policies on Jews were fairly well known. It is safe to assume that Dulles knew a good deal about them even before he arrived in Europe. He had collected information from various sources while still in New York, and he would have received Gävernitz's report of December 1941, entitled "Germany in December 1941," describing the plight of the German Jews. It offered a twelve-point agenda for reforming Germany. Point 9 called for the repeal of the 1933 Nuremberg Laws limiting the employment of Jews in government offices; point 11 called for the cessation of the deportations of Jews; the camps were to be put under control of the International Red Cross until their dissolution, and the ghettos were to be opened.[52] The Bern American legation also had intelligence to which Dulles would have had access, and the Schulte report was almost certainly part of that material.

Dulles clearly knew whatever Gävernitz knew. He had been in Bern only a few months but was already wired into a considerable network and in touch with a wide range of combatants in the unseen war against Hitler. He was in touch with Carl Burckhardt, formerly a high commissioner of the League of Nations in Danzig. Burckhardt had been involved in peace feelers with the British for some time and represented another view of the situation.[53] Dulles was also finding his way into a new branch of resistance: the churches. The position of Willem Visser't Hooft, secretary of the World Council of Churches, and his Geneva location made him a strategic link to resistance movements throughout Europe, and he maintained contacts to the Kreisau group and others.

In early 1943, Visser't Hooft notified Washington and London that he had incontrovertible evidence of a "campaign of deliberate extermination" of Jews, and urged immediate rescue action.[54] Dulles assigned him OSS

Agent number 474, and he stayed in close touch, though the rescue he hoped for never materialized. Dulles's first mention of the treatment of Jews in his own communications from Bern, under the date of March 2, 1943, regards the situation in Hungary, where the government was practicing a political straddling technique designed to appease the Nazis without capitulating totally.

Two issues on which Hungary has been criticized, and with some justice . . . the first of these was the way in which the Jewish problem was being handled. . . . It is true that some of the measures had been adopted by Hungary under which the percentage of Jews in professional activities had been restricted, but against that there have been admitted into Hungary from Croatia, Slovakia, and Poland 70,000 Jewish refugees. Some were free and some were in camps but they were being taken care of.[55]

Then Visser't Hooft passed on information from Berlin that was even grimmer, as Dulles reported to Washington:

Fifteen thousand Jews, in which were included Jews with Aryan wives and Jewesses with Aryan husbands were arrested in homes and factories between January 26 and March 2. For this purpose all closed lorries in Berlin were requisitioned. They were brought to four centers including Bohemian Church and two of the main Gestapo prisons. There have died several hundred children who were separated from their parents and left without food. In Berlin the shooting of several hundred adults took place. Officers who are high in the SS . . . are reported to have made the decision that before the middle of March Berlin should be liberated of all Jews. Friends are sheltering about 18,000 Jews. That the above methods will be extended within the near future to other regions in Germany is definitely expected. The new policy is to kill the Jews on the spot rather than deporting them to Poland for killing there.[56]

This was a bleak picture and, as it turned out, dismally accurate.

The Joint Allied Declaration issued in December 1942, denouncing Hitler's Jewish policies, may have lifted Rabbi Wise's spirits briefly but except for some added publicity, it had had little effect. However, after the declaration, the Archbishop of Canterbury rallied public opinion, and the pressure to take substantive steps toward saving lives mounted. Government circles were hardly enthusiastic; undue publicity would only deflect attention from the war effort, but some sort of response was obviously called for. Slowly, reluctantly, the wheels of Allied diplomacy began to turn toward the organization of an Anglo-American conference on refugee matters.

The first negotiations for a conference on refugee problems involved a good deal of feinting, posturing, and diplomatic shadowboxing on both sides. The real purpose of the Bermuda Conference in April 1943 was to silence critics of the official do-nothing policies, pay lip service to humanitarian principle, and perpetuate the status quo by stalling for time. Abundant reassurances from the Roosevelt administration and His Majesty's Government notwithstanding, neither side was keen to take serious action. The American administration labored to strike a cautious balance between diplomatic proprieties and pressure, characterized by the angry and vocal Congressman Emanuel Celler as "diplomatic tight-rope walking."[57]

In the end the Americans agreed not to ruffle British feathers by insisting on anything that might offend the Arabs in Palestine. The British agreed not to press the United States on its immigration policy. It emerged that neutrals might, with the proper incentives, take some Jews, or Jewish children, and small camps for refugees could be built in North Africa. These steps, however, were seen only as interim measures, never as a long-term solution, and neither side offered any liberalized postwar resettlement options. Not surprisingly, the conference accomplished very little, and when it was over, many, like columnist Max Lerner, were left wondering: "What about the Jews, FDR?

"Neither the Americans nor the British government has a policy on the matter. Neither government recognizes that any Jewish problem exists. . . . Hitler has made out of Europe a charnel-house of the Jews. But the State Dept. and Downing St. avert their eyes from the slaughter. . . ." Lerner exhorted FDR to use his power to save millions of lives. "The problem is soluble. Not by words, but by action."[58] Action however, would have to wait.

TURKEY: THE OSS JOINS THE PARTY

The OSS had come to Istanbul as a relative latecomer, not setting up its operation until early 1943. Its purpose was to engage in a program of subversive action to infiltrate southeastern Europe through a project code-named Project Net-1. The Istanbul OSS operation lasted a only rocky sixteen months, but in that short time, it managed to acquire some very good intelligence, some very bad intelligence, more than a few double agents, and a great deal of trouble.

Neither the U.S. State Department nor British intelligence had been eager for the OSS to start operations in Turkey. The State Department thought it could do its own intelligence gathering, but the ambassador to Turkey, Laurence Steinhardt, felt in need of professional help. He agreed to provide cover jobs for operatives and to allow the OSS to use the diplomatic pouch to send messages to Washington. The experienced British network regarded its new U.S. intelligence counterpart as still wet behind the ears, so it was agreed that the British would lead operations in Turkey and share all intelligence with the Americans.

Back in the early 1920s, when Allen Dulles was working for the State Department in Istanbul, the U.S. embassy there employed a "reception clerk" by the name of Betty Carp.[59] Carp was fluent in English, French, Italian, German, Greek, and Turkish. She was smart, sensitive, resourceful, and practical. She was also well liked and well connected in Istanbul, someone who always seemed to hear and know everything worth hearing and knowing. In putting together the Turkish OSS operation, Dulles decided that she would be the perfect person to set up the Istanbul station and provide critical analysis.[60] By one of those bureaucratic ironies, her assignment meant leaving Turkey for an office in Washington, from which she would recruit OSS spies to work in Turkey and Greece.

Of course, Carp had heard the famous story of the Polish gold while she was still in Istanbul. As Poland was collapsing in 1939, the government had loaded gold reserves on trains headed for Romania en route to London, where it was to fund a government-in-exile. Romania, worried that the Nazis would attack and seize the gold, had hustled the gold to Turkey, where it was loaded onto a British tanker. The Polish ambassador worried that the tanker would sink with its precious cargo, and wanted to ship the gold to Syria by rail, but the freight charges were more than he wanted to pay. Turkey had been willing to lower the cost if it were paid in gold, but the Polish ambassador felt honor bound to deliver every last precious ounce of gold to England. He had turned to the American branch director of Socony-Vacuum Oil, Archibald Walker, for help. Walker's connections and contacts allowed him to come to Poland's rescue by lending the money. The gold arrived safely in England, the Poles were happy, and Walker was repaid promptly.

Carp knew that by the time this complicated adventure was finally wrapped up, Walker had decided it had all been quite thrilling, and what his life needed was more international intrigue. So when Carp recommended that he become the OSS's first employee in Istanbul, he accepted happily. He would take the code name "Rose."

Chicago banker Lanning "Packy" Macfarland, would head OSS Turkey. With cover as a lend-lease banker, Macfarland developed a solid working relationship with Emniyet by agreeing to share information, with American Cedric Seager acting as liaison. Seager was a tough customer. Approached by German agents claiming to be willing to sell him information about sabotage, he had turned the tables. Either they could talk, he told the agents, or they could be at Emniyet's mercy. In short order, the names, addresses, covers, and descriptions of all the German agents in their sabotage group were at Seager's disposal.

OSS's best, most reliable intelligence in Turkey came from three sources: First, the Romanian, Polish, Yugoslav, and Czech refugees who had been forced into the Germany military or to serve the Nazi war machine in civilian roles were quick to offer their services. The Czechs were especially loyal to the Allied cause. Second, sympathetic railway workers who were able not only to track supplies and troop movements and pass along information picked up from other workers and friends at different locations, but were also in a perfect position to act as smugglers. Third, Jewish refugees in Turkey, trying to make their way toward the possibility of freedom supplied reliable eyewitness accounts of recent enemy activity.

Once word got out that Turkey was a hotbed of intrigue, former U.S. ambassador to Bulgaria George Earle III made a personal request of his friend, President Roosevelt: Would FDR *please* send him to Turkey as a spy? The well-to-do Earle, a descendant of Benjamin Franklin, had already had a varied career: He had abandoned the Republican Party to follow Roosevelt. He had crossed paths with Papen as a diplomat in Vienna and been governor of Pennsylvania. He had left the ambassadorship to Bulgaria to become a navy captain chasing U-boats. Now the president agreed to Earle's request; in 1943 he was given the official title and rank of assistant naval attaché. Knowing Earle's inclination to the bottle, he was not given much solid information. In bars throughout Istanbul, Earle would drink himself silly and announce that he was a personal friend of Roosevelt. Enlarging and capitalizing on that relationship was Earle's hallmark.

Earle could be embarrassing, but he had his uses, and the OSS made good use of him. German intelligence was quickly convinced that he was either on a secret mission or heading all U.S. intelligence operations in Turkey. He was shadowed; the Germans crept through Istanbul's nightclubs and alleyways, watching his every move and hanging on his every slurred word. George Earle became the ultimate decoy, perfect for wasting German resources.

THE TEMPER OF THE OPPOSITION

Himmler's Gestapo had been eager to find incontrovertible evidence of wrongdoing at the Abwehr for some time, and in the spring of 1943 they uncovered some financial irregularities that looked promising. Hans von Dohnanyi, a highly intelligent civilian lawyer, did not meet the Nuremberg Laws' requirements for racial purity, but had been given a special dispensation to work for the Abwehr. Oster had recruited him in 1939, and he had taken over Abwehr ZB, the foreign reports section, at the beginning of the war, engaging in extensive liaison work abroad. Some of Dohnanyi's foreign exchange transactions led Gestapo investigators to a scheme designed to slip German Jews to safety in Switzerland in the guise of Abwehr agents.[61]

This venture, *Unternehmen Sieben*—Undertaking Seven, or U7—provided the perfect excuse for the desired strike against the Abwehr. Dohnanyi, Dietrich Bonhoeffer, Bonhoeffer's sister (who was Dohnanyi's wife), and Joseph Müller, the opposition's contact with the Vatican, were all arrested.[62] Oster was separated from the Abwehr and put under house arrest. The Abwehr, in shock, nearly ground to a halt. Gestapo surveillance was immeasurably tightened and also put Gisevius under increased scrutiny. Canaris surely realized that his hold on power would not last much longer. He did not, as he would have earlier, try to rescue his fellow conspirators. He sent Gisevius off to Rome to post the pope on developments, but otherwise he did little, apparently paralyzed by his fatalism.

Then Gisevius, too, was sucked into the Gestapo quicksand. On one of his trips to Germany he was pulled in for interrogation about his contacts in Switzerland. The situation became unbearably tense, but Gisevius managed to cut and run. Traveling only on byways, he made his way back to Switzerland. For Dulles, the Abwehr's troubles brought to mind his former cook at the Herrengasse—a first-class cook, but apparently also a German spy. When Dulles got wind that the Germans had information that he had had a very tall visitor with the initials HGB stamped in his hatband, he knew immediately that such news could only have come from within his own household. The cook was fired, but the incident was a reminder that in espionage, any seemingly insignificant occurrence can bring down an operation.

As an Abwehr agent, Gisevius's contacts—even with an enemy counterpart—could be cloaked in legitimacy. Canaris still held some authority and defended Gisevius as acting under his orders, but Gisevius's current troubles were serious. Safe as he might be in Switzerland, continuing his close association with Dulles would have been reckless, so the Abwehr arranged to replace him with a young lawyer attached to the German consulate.

Eduard "Eddie" Waetjen shared several characteristics with Gävernitz: an American mother, connections to the American investment banking community, and wealthy, well-placed relatives.[63] He had joined the Nazi Party in 1931, but withdrew the next year. Since 1940, he had been in close touch with his friend Moltke and the circle around him. Dulles had full confidence in him, and he became OSS # 670, a.k.a. "Gorter," the third of what were known as Dulles's "Three Musketeers"—Gävernitz, Gisevius, and Waetjen.[64] Waetjen was aided in his contacts with the "enemy" by another Abwehr man, Captain Theodor Strünck, who shuttled between Zurich and Berlin as courier, bearing all the news, good and bad, for which he later paid with his life. Waetjen, with Strünck's help, now became Dulles's link to the opposition within Germany and a major source of critical information.

After the wave of arrests at the Abwehr, Helmuth von Moltke met with Bürkner to try to pull Canaris—the "little sailor"—out of his fatalistic lethargy and into more direct action to save his friends and colleagues, even if only on purely legal grounds. Gisevius was present and later offered the following account of the meeting:

> "I can still see [Moltke's] tall thin figure . . . it must have been shortly after the blow to our office. Our conversation . . . [was on] whether one ought to put pressure on Canaris . . . so obviously threatened, and get him to use the last vestige of his influence in persuading the military chiefs to move against the rule of terror. . . . Moltke stood motionless, a thin file pressed against his chest like a parson's bible, his gaze directed into the distance as if he were a revivalist preacher. This added fascination to the restrained force with which he spoke; sharp as the words were, he did not once raise his voice and his arguments remained balanced, matter-of-fact . . . unruffled and imperturbable—he might have been pleading as a barrister in an English court."[65]

"What is happening to the opposition, the men 'of whom one hears so much and notices so little' as a headline in the paper lately said?" Moltke wrote Lionel Curtis that year.[66] He and other members of the opposition had been laboring long and hard, some of them since before 1933. After the Hitler takeover, Germany had come to feel in many ways like an occupied country—occupied by martial law Organizing resistance was a lonely, nerve-racking, and exhausting business. Since the Nazi takeover Moltke had been working steadfastly for the opposition to which the government-sanctioned newspaper—the only kind then in existence—had referred to so derisively. His letter reached Curtis in England only because it was essentially memorized by an American YMCA representative who then conveyed it orally to Bishop Bell, who in turn relayed it to Curtis. "People outside Germany do not realize," Moltke continued, "the . . . handicaps under which we labor and which distinguish the position [of the opposition] in Germany from that of the other occupied countries: lack of unity, lack of men, lack of communication."

Ulrich von Hassell's diary describes the temper of the Third Reich: "All opposition and all criticism, even those arising from the most patriotic motives, are looked upon as punishable crimes . . . [there is] trembling fear on the part of everyone."[67] Hassell dared not write his own name in his personal copy of a book published in London in 1938 by a German émigré, Kurt G. W. Ludecke, detailing the horrors of life under Hitler.[68] Instead he penciled in "C. Niderne," one of several code names he used during the Nazi period. The Nazis created a whole new language, one intended to mask what was really being said, to hide the reality and obscure the truth. Viktor Klemperer, a Jewish academic who survived the war in Berlin and Dresden, documented the astounding language of oppression and obfuscation that was Nazispeak in his now famous work *Language of the Third Reich: LTI— Lingua Tertii Imperii, A Philologist's Notebook.*[69]

In other countries under Nazi oppression, people were united. Trusting the motivations of the Norwegians, Dutch, or other nationals under Hitler's thumb was straightforward; they had one common, external enemy. Within Germany, however, there were many factions, attitudes, and expectations—political as well as social—and there was no obvious broad stratum of support. Each German had to be examined "closely as to his intentions before you can make use of him [for the opposition]: The fact that he is anti-Nazi is not enough."[70] Beyond this fragmentation, which narrowed the field of possible resistance considerably, lay, quite literally, the lack of men. With the exception of the SS, all the men of an age to make a revolution were on one front or another, in concentration camps, or under constant Gestapo surveillance. Some of those who were left were turning to Turkey to try their luck.

By mid-1943, when any hope of German victory had been quashed in all but the most fanatical Nazis, Adam von Trott went to Turkey to feel out Papen on support for the cause. Papen had held out some semblance of hope to Trott but had offered nothing substantive. Turkey also became the focus of the Kreisau Circle's reach toward peace. Establishing connections with the West was easier there, and the opposition had many friends and connections in Istanbul's German expatriate community.

From the window of the plane lumbering toward a landing that July day, the city's position at the juncture of worlds was obvious; the waters of the Golden Horn and the Bosporus glittering in the sun delineated the contours of the confluence of the Black Sea, the Sea of Marmora, and clearly defined Istanbul as the crossroads that it had always been and continued to be. Across its hills innumerable spires and minarets poked at the sky; the great domes of its many mosques humped over the clutter of narrow streets and hodgepodge of houses. It was magical, like something out of the *The 1001 Nights,* but Helmuth James von Moltke had too much on his mind to give it more than a quick, preoccupied glance. He collected his very long frame from the cramped seat; there was so much to be done.

Officially, Moltke and his colleague, Dr. Wilhelm Wengler, were here on business for the Abwehr, on the pretext of sorting out difficulties over a fleet of ships interned in the Sea of Marmora. As lawyers specializing in international law, Canaris had decided that they were the perfect team for the job. Moltke left most of this task to Wengler, however, and set off on a mission of his own, one he felt was much larger and more crucial.

This was an exploratory trip and Moltke had prepared for it meticulously. He was determined to enlist anyone willing to help Germany survive the war and become a new, socially just state. He would be in touch with Paul Leverkühn, a former law colleague who had taken over as Abwehr chief in Turkey in 1942. He had written to his journalist friend, Dorothy Thompson. He had reliable and influential friends in the German colony in Istanbul, some, like Leverkühn, working in an official capacity, some political exiles who shared his disgust with the Nazis. There was Hans Wilbrandt, whom he knew from the early 1930s, when Wilbrandt had helped him with the financing of the Kreisau estate.[71] Wilbrandt was in almost daily communication with OSS and, according to OSS files, "had spared no personal effort or risk . . . to give all solicited or unsought assistance."[72] He might even be able to arrange to see his trusted friend Alexander Kirk, now serving as ambassador in Cairo, for a real talk about Allied support for the opposition. It was a matter of exploring any and all possible collaboration between the opposition circles and the West. He would try to persuade the Allies to rescind their demand for unconditional surrender. After defeat, Germany would need protection from the Soviets; Germany should not be occupied by them, but by the western Allies. He would also pay a visit to Papen, following up on Adam von Trott's June visit to the evasive diplomat. In his *Memoirs,* Papen later identified Trott as his contact man with the resistance, though he had offered him nothing in the way of support.[73]

The opposition's assessment of Papen was that he was a weak-willed opportunist. Still, he had spoken out against Hitler in 1934 and survived numerous trials in the interim, and since he still held an official position, he might be of some use to their cause. Moltke would try again to enlist his help. If there was even a remote possibility that Papen could help them keep the Soviets off German soil and bring the war to an early end, Moltke felt he had to try.

Moltke's meeting with Papen did not accomplish his goal. Neither the bleak military outlook for Hitler's army, nor conditions in Germany—the terrible bombing and diminished rations—nor his arguments about the need to keep the Soviets out of Europe were enough for Papen. He seemed to want more evidence of which way the wind was blowing before committing himself to anything on behalf of the resistance. His response: He could not help them now; later perhaps, when he was in power, he would help them fend off the Soviets. Papen clearly dreamed of replacing Hitler as the head of state. At his trial at Nuremberg, Papen actually described himself as the spokesman for "the other Germany," but in fact he had refused to commit himself to anything. A very brief meeting with him was enough to persuade Moltke that the ambassador was indeed an "absolutely deplorable man."[74]

WHATEVER IVORY TOWER MOLTKE MAY HAVE INHABITED EARLIER, HIS TRIP TO TURKEY took him into the "eye of the hurricane."[75] Wilbrandt put him in touch with Alexander Rüstow, an economist and sociologist teaching in Istanbul, who persuaded Moltke that his expecation that the Allies would abandon their demand for unconditional surrender was "utopian" and hopeless.[76] There were lively discussions of plans and possibilities, some downright outlandish: Might it be possible, for instance, to parachute an officer of the general staff into England to present the British with military plans for the opening of an Allied western front and free passage through German lines?[77] But other plans were less fantastical. Wilbrandt and Rüstow were part of the subversive German Freedom Movement—DFB—in Istanbul. They would put Moltke in touch with the OSS. If the OSS could help him make contact with his friend Alexander Kirk to enlist Allied aid, Moltke would choke back his instinctive revulsion toward spy operations. This was how he came to be drawn—however marginally—into the OSS network.

An OSS report of September 1943 indicated that the strength of the resistance "depends at the moment upon the intelligence and character of those few who have survived, and [their plans for activating] the great amount of disaffection . . . in all classes of German society . . . which is growing enormously as the German people realize the impasses into which they have been led."[78] The fight had to be carried on by a few, working largely in isolation, a difficulty compounded by what in Moltke's view was the worst: lack of communication. "Can you imagine," he asked, "what it is like when you cannot use the telephone, cannot use the post, cannot send a messenger, cannot even speak with those with whom you are completely *d'accord* because the secret police have such methods of questioning . . . that you must limit information to those who absolutely need it."[79]

On his next visit to Istanbul, in December, Moltke, code name "Hermann," a conflation of Helmuth and German, was bitterly disappointed. OSS Istanbul had not been able to bring Kirk from Cairo for a meeting, and they now scrambled to find someone he would talk to.[80] OSS Istanbul felt great urgency in establishing these contacts with opposition members like Moltke and the Free Germany Movement, realizing that such people would be essential in the construction of a democratic post-Hitler Germany.[81]

In this regard, the OSS reflected the thinking of its top people, like Donovan and Dulles, and differed profoundly from other Allied intelligence operations and for that matter from the Washington policy makers. OSS Instanbul rushed to accommodate Moltke with a hastily arranged conversation with the military attaché, General Richard Tindall, at the apartment of an Austrian businessman. It was unsatisfactory; Tindall apparently tried to enlist Moltke as a spy. Moltke was certainly no spy. He was fighting for the resistance and he intended to contact the Allies for concrete political talks. He trusted Kirk and Kirk alone, and he revealed nothing of the so-called Hermann Plan to Tindall.[82]

The Hermann Plan was actually spelled out after Moltke's departure from Istanbul, most likely by Rüstow, Wilbrandt, and possibly some other members of the German émigré community with whom Moltke had met.[83] The top-secret OSS "Exposé" alerted the Americans to the "readiness of a powerful German group to prepare and assist Allied military operations against Nazi Germany."[84] It was meant to explain the various oppositional elements within Germany, to define the plans and concerns of the opposition, and to clarify the conditions for collaboration of the Moltke group, which hoped to establish a durable, westward-looking, democratic German state. It recognized the need for an unconditional surrender, offered military support on a large scale, and expressed the hope for an Allied, rather than a Russian occupation of Germany. The fear of Bolshevism loomed large, but the new German government would include a strong left wing, labor, and even communists, if absolutely necessary. It closed on an almost pitiful note: "It would be advisable not to subject the civilian population to indiscriminate air attack, since experience teaches that bombed-out populations are exhausted and absorbed by the effort of providing for their bare survival and subsistence that they are out of play as far as revolutionary action is concerned."[85]

Before leaving Turkey, Moltke had written Kirk very circumspectly, saying that he would return, perhaps as early as February, and would have forty-eight hours available for a conversation in Cairo or wherever Kirk might suggest. His extreme caution was understandable. Security breaches during earlier attempts at contact had resulted in numerous arrests and subsequent executions.

Blow upon blow had rained down on an exhausted and discouraged crew of conspirators, trudging from country to country, doggedly hatching plot after plot. Yet in spite of the three difficulties Moltke enumerated, and others as well, the opposition did not give up its attempts to make contact with the Allies and keep hope alive.

TURKEY: THE DOGWOOD CHAIN

When OSS Istanbul was just starting out, British intelligence officer Harold Gibson[86] had introduced them to a willing agent with "a clean bill of health," a Czech engineer and businessman named Alfred Schwarz.[87] Schwarz had an intimate knowledge of Czech, Austrian, and German heavy industry, a wide circle of friends that included papal legate Roncalli and professors from the German expatriate colony, as well as numerous contacts within the international business community. He had worked for British military intelligence, without pay, and he now wanted to devote himself entirely to political work.

Since the British apparently had no permanent assignment for him, Schwarz had signed a contract with the OSS's Macfarland in April. Then Schwarz, a.k.a. Dogwod, hired an assistant named Walter Arndt and settled into the Western Electrik Kompani in Istanbul. The company provided perfect cover for meetings with agents, since even the most highly trained observer would not be able to tell whether a visitor was a spy or a legitimate business caller.[88] Schwarz began sweet-talking Bulgarian, Romanian,

Hungarian, and Swiss couriers into violating international law by carrying American intelligence data in their diplomatic pouches. Schwarz/Dogwood's mission quickly narrowed to the penetration of Axis nations, particularly Germany, Austria, and Hungary. Anti-Nazi Central Europeans were recruited to establish communications systems and a network of people who could travel easily in the region, and they in turn established their own network. It was the beginning of the famous—and eventually infamous—Dogwood chain.

Dogwood raided the botanical lexicon for code names, and each subagent was named after a flower. Hyacinth—Moltke's friend Hans Wilbrandt—had "relations with German consular authorities." Rüstow/Magnolia was joined by Narcissus, with contacts to Junkers in Germany. Pink was in touch "with personages of the Wehrmacht and Abwehr."[89] Foxglove worked for German manufacturers and was connected with the Abwehr.[90] Stock and Cassia, Periwinkle and Gardenia, and many more made a lush, colorful bouquet. Moltke—a.k.a. Camelia—also put in an appearance, as the OSS tried desperately to help him establish contact with Kirk or someone else, but Turkish and military authorities hampered their efforts.[91] Dogwood himself never undertook direct contact with Moltke, but watched with passionate interest from a distance.[92]

The Dogwood operation seemed ideal, even charmed. Then problems began to crop up. Schwarz's exaggerated sense of his own importance meant that his idea of vetting candidates as subagents was to trust his instincts. Some of his choices were poor and others foolhardy, but he was fiercely protective, and contrary to established procedure, he refused to reveal the true identity of his subagents. He resented British and U.S. intelligence officers' attempts to check up on the data provided; after all, it was his chain.

Dogwood eventually hired sixty-seven subagents, mostly men whose work took them traveling to occupied countries. They received no formal training. If agents had trouble memorizing information, they resorted to microfilm carried, in clichéd spy fashion, in hollowed-out pencils or heels of shoes and the like.[93] OSS Cairo had to teach agents how to write critical, analytical reports rather than throwing in every bit of miscellaneous information they picked up.

As an intelligence chain grows larger, it becomes more vulnerable to infiltration, and as the Dogwood chain grew exponentially, enemy spies responded to it as they might to an engraved invitation. OSS Turkey had no X-2 counterespionage agents who specialized in keeping a chain free of double agents, but Britain's three hundred years in the spy business had taught them the value of verification. Without an identity, there was no way to be sure a Dogwood source wasn't confirming its own data. They were so wary of Dogwood intelligence that they required verification by at least two outside sources instead of the usual one for anything coming from the chain.

Macfarland claimed his office was performing security checks on the subagents, but they were perfunctory at best. He and William Coleman, who was presumably overseeing Dogwood—"running" in spy lingo—were so dazzled by Schwarz's fast footwork that they allowed him to continue to do pretty much as he pleased. The British were most likely making such niggling objections out of jealousy.

OSS CHIEF DONOVAN WAS CONVINCED THAT A SIGNIFICANT SEGMENT OF THE GERMAN population was eager to be rid of Hitler and make peace with the Allies. He now also involved himself in the seething spy scene in Istanbul. In late 1943 he dispatched Theodore Morde, a former OSSer, working as a correspondent for *The Reader's Digest,* to Istanbul to sound out Papen on the prospects of a negotiated peace. Morde told Papen that the United States would require Hitler and other leading Nazis to be turned over to the Allies and tried for war crimes.

Papen took this meeting seriously—Morde was Donovan's emissary—seeing potential for future advantage. He put forth his own terms: Austria must remain under German control and Germany must be allowed a position of economic leadership in Europe after the war. Morde returned to the States and presented the deal to presidential advisor Robert Sherwood. Sherwood was so angry about this unauthorized negotiation that he wanted to have Morde's passport revoked to prevent any further amateur diplomacy. Donovan backed Morde and saw to it that the information reached the president through his own channels, but to no known effect.

Papen had been initiated into the plans of a circle headed by former chief of the general staff Ludwig Beck and involving Berlin police chief Helldorf to overthrow Hitler.[94] Through Earle, Papen now tried to discover the Allied position vis-à-vis a post-Hitler Germany and Allied opinion on a possible withdrawal of the demand for unconditional surrender.[95] Roosevelt refused to entertain the idea.[96] If FDR would not negotiate with a man like Moltke, or what he referred to as "these east German Junkers," he would certainly not undertake dealings with Papen. There was simply too much at risk to hazard angering the Russian bear.

BERN: THE UNLIKELY CROWN JEWEL

Taking the measure of the man for the first time, Dulles and Gerry Mayer agreed: The initial impression was unprepossessing. Of middling height, maybe about five foot six or seven, almost completely bald, with wide-set blue-gray eyes and prominent ears. Fritz Kolbe came across as simple, almost

otherworldly. He seemed plain, said Dulles, a slightly naïve, romantic, ide-
alistic personality, not particularly intelligent, and certainly not crafty.[97]
On balance, neither Dulles nor Mayer would have guessed that he would
turn into what the spy trade refers to as a "crown jewel"—a source of
supremely useful and accurate information. On top of that, Kolbe came directly from the innermost chambers of the Reich.

Kolbe had turned to the British first, but with no appointment, and only
the sketchiest of introductions, he had had to cool his heels for quite some
time before the military attaché in Bern, a certain Colonel Cartwright,
made himself available—briefly. One version of what happened next runs
as follows: His visitor tells Cartwright that he is anti-Nazi and wants to end
the war and rid Germany of Hitler. Through his work at the Foreign Office
he is privy to a great deal of classified information which he is willing to
share with the Allies. He is not interested in compensation.

Cartwright is dumbfounded. This sweaty little functionary privy to
high-level documents? And willing to share them without compensation?
It is too unbelievable. He has little interest and less sympathy. Besides, orders have come down from on high: There will be no dealings with the
German opposition—if indeed there is one. If the British condone it, the
Germans will likely try it with the Russians, too. Then the Allied coalition
will come undone, and everyone will be in the soup. Cartwright dismisses
him out of hand: "I don't believe you, and if it is true, you are a cad!"[98]

That may not have been exactly how the interview went—there are several versions—but the British did make very short work of Kolbe. In any
case, the possibly apocryphal story illustrates a particular mind-set common in British intelligence and diplomatic circles at the time, a sort of old-
school revulsion at the very idea of betraying one's country. The thought
that there might be values that transcend traditional patriotism was unthinkable. How far the country had gone to betray all human values in this
particular instance seemed to make no difference whatsoever. It was this attitude that put Kolbe, and many others like him, into a virtually untenable,
no-win situation with the Allies. Damned if they betrayed their country,
they were eventually doubly damned if they did not.

Kolbe exits—crushed, devastated. His time in Switzerland was very
limited—his pass was only valid until the twentieth—and he had only
three days left. Desperate to make a real contact, he tried to think: Perhaps
Ernst Kocherthaler, his friend from the days when they were both living in
Spain in the 1930s, could help. Kocherthaler had been a Swiss resident for
some time; he was well connected and had a hefty address book. Maybe he
could put Kolbe in touch with the Americans.

Indeed. While no names and no specifics were given, Gerry Mayer was
receptive to Kocherthaler's mention of a "rare bird" with unusual access.
Both parties understood what was involved. The sheaf of papers open on

the table was clearly classified: *Geheime Reichsache,* Secret Reich Business. Each one was addressed to Ribbentrop, and signed by a diplomat. More was available from this source, Kochthaler told Mayer; he was only an emissary.

The pace picked up. Mayer rushed the documents upstairs to Dulles. The evening before, happening on Cartwright in the street, Dulles had been told that an odd duck trying to peddle suspect information might show up at his shop next. Dulles telephoned to see Cartwright immediately, and over a whiskey Cartwright warned him not to be duped.

Dulles weighed his options. The possibilities were: a German attempt to break Dulles's code by comparing his transmission of the documents to their copies; an attempt to have the Swiss expel Dulles the "diplomat" by exposing his spy activity; or the fellow might be legitimate.[99] Dulles recalled that as a young man working in Switzerland in 1917 he had been faced with a similar situation. A Russian revolutionary type passing through Switzerland had wanted to meet with him. Dulles had refused, largely because he had not wanted to break a Sunday tennis date with a charming young lady. The unknown Russian later turned out to have been Lenin. It was a lesson Dulles never forgot.[100] He would not let such a thing happen to him again. He would see this man. The fellow might be very useful; if there were even the smallest sliver of a chance that he was legitimate, he would lift his hat again—carefully.

Accounts of the August 18 meeting differ, but apparently it took place late at night, probably in Gerry Mayer's apartment. Dulles arrives later and is introduced as Mr. Douglas, Mayer's assistant. Sizing Kolbe up, he concludes that he seems more ex-boxer than diplomat. But his eyes are lively and alert, his expression open. Kolbe is dressed too warmly for the August night and he is sweating. He draws out of a pocket of his leather jacket a large manila envelope, stamped with wax seals embossed with the swastika. There is some uncomfortable small talk, drinks.

Drink eases the tension, and once the talk gets started, it goes on far into the night; Dulles listens, probes, ponders. Kolbe is the son of a Silesian saddlemaker. As a boy, he was a passionate member of the *Wandervogel*—literally, "bird of passage"—a popular movement going back to the late nineteenth century, intended to reconnect Germany's youth, trapped in a rapidly industrializing environment, with the pleasures of the outdoors. He had wanted see the world, to work on the railroad in Germany's African colonies—Cameroon and Togo—but Versailles had plucked the colonies away and put an end to that dream. Instead, over twenty years he has worked his way up in the German Foreign Office, usually the preserve of Germany's elite. He has worked in Spain, in South Africa, and is now back in Berlin, as assistant to Karl Ritter, right hand to Ribbentrop, and liaison to the Wehrmacht's high command. Kolbe sits at the nerve center of the Reich's most critical communications.

Kolbe explains that he was recalled to Berlin in late 1939. He describes how the city, the mood of the people has changed. Berliners are now living literally from one day to the next. There are noticeable signs of shortages; some shops offer to sharpen used razor blades. Families are being evacuated to escape the bombs, the trains are overcrowded, station platforms are flooded with boys in uniform—draft age had just been lowered to seventeen.[101] Abruptly, Dulles asks about Kolbe's motives.

Kolbe despises both Hitler and the Bolsheviks. His father always told him to do what he thought was right and not to be afraid. He has no faith in the success of a coup. He has access to secret Reich documents, and at a certain point, clenching one's fist in one's pocket is not enough; one must use it to strike. The only way he can think of to fight the Nazi regime is to cooperate with the Allies. He has consulted with a Catholic prelate who absolved him of his oath of loyalty to Hitler.[102] He is not a traitor to his country, he blurts out, Hitler is. He does not want any money, he says, and quotes the Bible, Mark 8:36: "For what shall it profit a man if he shall gain the whole world, and lose his own soul."[103]

He unfurls the thick bundle of papers, nearly two hundred documents, some carbon copies, some laboriously handwritten transcripts, and lays them on the table.[104] He is clammy from nerves and exhaustion; Berlin has been under almost constant bombardment recently, and the nights have allowed for only intermittent sleep. As Dulles and Mayer hunch over the intelligence gold that the British turned away, stunned by the breadth and variety of the material, Kolbe waits in silence.

Among the mass of information is a report on bomb damages to the Romanian oil fields, the plan for a meeting of German and Japanese submarines, a report from Spain that the "oranges" will be delivered. Kolbe had visited Hitler's famous East Prussian headquarters, the Wolfsschanze, several times in the course of his duties, and he has drawn a remarkably detailed map from memory. There is a onetime German cipher pad and more, much more. Dulles decides that Kolbe will become OSS 674—a.k.a. "George Wood."

For months after the Kolbe material—designated Kappa reports—began coming in, Washington and London were dubious. It seemed too good to be true; Wood must be handled with the utmost caution. Dulles should give Kolbe "tests" to determine his legitimacy. Of course, Dulles was well aware of the risks. He cabled that he appreciated the "danger of becoming so enamored with one's own sources that one falls into such traps," but argued that "Wood, while intelligent, is somewhat naïve and appears to have none of the characteristics which would qualify him to pull off double crossing game. . . . So far [the] only disturbing element has been some evidence of recklessness . . . but this is quite usual in conspirators."[105]

George Wood managed to get to Bern repeatedly, always at enormous personal risk. On each trip, he knew he was carrying something that could literally kill him. He was helped by his friendship with Fräulein Heimerdinger, the woman who arranged courier assignments in the Foreign Office, solidified by an occasional gift of Swiss chocolates, but difficulties cropped up. His absence from his Bern hotel during a late-night meeting with Dulles had been reported; an explanation was demanded. Kolbe blamed his sexual appetites, and sheepishly even produced a doctor's certificate for treatment of the evening's aftereffects. This bit of inventive forethought, combined with his fabulous material, had Dulles almost rhapsodic. Kolbe was his best intelligence source on Germany, with the kind of access intelligence officers dream about.

After his initial reports in March of 1943, Dulles had gone silent on the Jewish question until December, when a message came in to Ribbentrop's office from Rudolph Rahn, the German ambassador to Italy, on the proposed Nazi extermination of the Jews of Rome. It was part of the Wood reports originating with Fritz Kolbe.

> Obersturmbannfuehrer Kappler has been instructed from Berlin to seize the 8,000 Jews living in Rome and to take them to Northern Italy where they will be liquidated. The city commandant of Rome, General Stahel, informs me that he will permit this action only if it is consistent with the policies of the Reich Foreign Minister. I am personally of the opinion that it would be better business to use Jews as in Tunis, for work on fortifications. . . .[106]

Kolbe's days in Ritter's office were spent reading, screening, and rerouting secret Reich communications. He informed Bern that between January and September of 1943 Spain had delivered more than 700 tons of wolfram to Hitler's war machine, all in the guise of sardines, oranges, or lead. In December Dulles reported that Wood/Kolbe had seen the "entire Nazi idea of the British and American battle order for invasion . . . [of Normandy with fifty to sixty divisions ready to leave from southern England]. The Nazis think they know exactly where each division is located."[107]

The war dragged through yet another winter. Kolbe was spending more and more of his time in bomb shelters, always with the mandatory "survival suitcase" containing water, matches, zwieback, sundries. That December of 1943, Goebbels informed journalists that the word "catastrophe" was to disappear from their vocabulary.[108]

THE OSS IN LONDON

British intelligence had scoffed that Kolbe's intelligence was "chicken feed," intended to sucker the Allies into a trap. Kolbe was an obvious plant, and Dulles had fallen for it like a ton of bricks. Gradually, however, they came to rue the day they had turned Kolbe away. Kolbe discovered that a German agent in London close to Churchill was relaying information back to Germany via another spy nexus—neutral Stockholm—and he resolved to stop the flow. Proceeding very cautiously, he arranged for a contact in Alsace to alert a Parisian go-between, who then contacted the British, and the leak stopped.[109]

British agent Harold "Kim" Philby, working his way up the MI-6 ladder, was also working all the while as a double agent for the Soviets. Thinking that the Wood/Kolbe reports might do him some professional good, he decided to have a look. He knew the story behind the reports and about the professional jealousy of SIS's Claude Dansey, who had always resented Dulles's incursion into Switzerland, which he considered his own private preserve. Personally, too, Philby felt that "it was barely conceivable that anyone would have the nerve to pass through German frontier controls with a suitcase containing contraband official papers."[110] If Philby's autobiography is to be believed, Kolbe's reports made Philby a hero to the British decoders at Bletchley Park when they discovered that several of them were a precise match to messages already decoded. Others were of tremendous help in decoding variations of the complex Enigma cipher.

With this ace up his sleeve, Philby finally took on Dansey himself, though not before he had carefully smudged the evidence of the reports' provenance as Bern. Philby was well aware that Dansey regarded Switzerland as *his* intelligence turf, and leapt at every opportunity to disparage Dulles. Dansey was in fact livid, but mollified to find that Kolbe had been made to look like a British find.[111]

Over time, Kolbe's tremendous risks, his hard work, sleepless nights, nervous sweats, and anguish produced 1,600 items of "pure gold" intelligence. Ultimately, even the perpetually skeptical and skittish British intelligence decided that Wood had to be counted as an extraordinary prime intelligence source of World War II. Kolbe's reports in April—dubbed Kapril reports—aside from the "solid gold" intelligence, also provided a ringside seat to the battles among Hitler's minions, aides, and lieutenants—the infighting, plotting, and backstabbing, heightened by a growing awareness of impending disaster.

When young William Casey—future head of the CIA—arrived in London in 1943, Germany was staggering under a cascade of military defeats begun at Stalingrad. On the home front, fifteen-year-olds were manning antiaircraft batteries to defend cities being turned to rubble by massive Allied air raids. Casey, like Donovan, was of Irish immigrant stock and a parochial school product. He, too, had earned a law degree. Unlike most other high-level OSSers, however, Casey had not been recruited, but had eagerly pursued the OSS to take him on, wangling an introduction through a law partner. He had impressed Donovan's executive officer, and was assigned to help David Bruce in London. When he became chief of SI for OSS in Europe, he spearheaded a plan to turn German POWs held in Britain into OSS spies.

Colonel Bruce, the chief of OSS/Europe, was the sort of man to whom the British, particularly those in the upper echelons of intelligence and government, were naturally attracted: polished, coolheaded, and about as aristocratic as an American could get. He was also dead set against using POWs as spies. Aside from being both legally and morally questionable, Bruce instinctively felt that POWs could not be trusted. But Casey made an irrefutable argument: It was virtually impossible to insert an American agent, and using POWs would "lessen the risk and also dramatically increase the probability of a successful mission."[112]

General Eisenhower, Supreme Allied Commander in Europe from December 1943, had forbidden the active recruitment of POWs as agents, but did not specifically preclude the use of volunteers. This legal loophole did not escape the attention of OSS lawyers, and it was duly exploited. The British, by contrast, had no scruples at all about turning German nationals against their own country. Disgruntled captured soldiers were turned, trained as agents, provided with clothing, suitable identification, and transmitters and dropped behind German lines to weave their way into major cites, there to risk their lives gathering and transmitting information on industrial and military targets. If their transmitters were discovered, these agents were executed on the spot.

SI was lucky in that their OSS Seventh Army Detachment and their counterpart G-2 section worked well together to screen, train, and insert German POWs into Germany as OSS operatives. Given the huge potential for a security breach, a specific psychological profile of a trustworthy infiltrator was developed. The ideal candidate was a Catholic who had been assigned to the *Strafbattalionen*—punishment battalions—for expressing political doubts. On the basis of a soldier's *Soldbuch*—or pay book that also served as identification—SI was able to prescreen POWs before offering them an opportunity to "volunteer" for service. The POWs were trained in covert operations, and provided with a cover story and, when possible, a second identity. As genuine German soldiers, most of these men had uniforms, paperwork, and knowledge of the area they were to penetrate. They were sent out to locate motor pools, food and armament dumps, and military headquarters. On their return, they reported tactical information first, to the Army's G-2, and strategic information to the OSS. Of the thirty or so German soldiers used, only two were captured, and none turned against the Allies.

On their way behind the lines these agents faced land mines and German entrenchments. On their way back to the Allies, they faced Americans with quick trigger fingers. American writer Peter Viertel, overseeing one mission, begged for help for a POW who had been badly wounded and was in agonizing pain. Viertel found little sympathy from American medics until a Jewish doctor asked why the fellow had gone on the mission. When Viertel explained that he was an anti-Nazi working for the Americans, the POW quickly got a shot of morphine.[113]

CHAPTER 7

THE CRUCIBLE

*The cracks in the Nazi edifice had been there for some time. As the war in-
tensified, they widened. Massive Allied bombing and retreats on the Russian
front, followed by the invasion of Normandy made the end palpable, and
Hitler's minions were scrambling for the exits. As always, the neutral countries were the scene of continued efforts, but for the opposition, 1944 was
disastrous. Moltke's attemp to contact the Allies in Turkey ended with his arrest; Canaris was deposed; the Abwehr was no longer a haven for anti-
Nazis. A worn and haggard Adam von Trott was again in Sweden, hoping
against hope for contact, but the impetus was now with the military contingent, set on a coup. "Coûte que coûte"—whatever the cost—as Tresckow
put it, a coup had to be attempted, even if it was only a symbol.*

*Opposition was no longer a gesture of hope, but of desperation; success or
failure seemed less important than standing up for Germany's honor and a
personal moral code. Treason had become a moral and patriotic imperative.
The world had to know that there was another Germany.*

TROUBLES IN TURKEY

Elyesa Bazna, born in Albania and raised in Turkey, had knocked around
that part of the world quite a bit, working at the odd embassy, and always
on the lookout for a bigger opportunity. He had begun to serve as valet to
the British ambassador, Hughe Knatchbull-Hugessen, in late 1943, and

though it was not a particularly glamorous or high-paying job, it did provide opportunity, an opportunity that eventually made him one of the most famous spies of the war.

Knatchbull-Hugessen, in spite of his jovial, gregarious demeanor, was a hardworking man. Bazna noted that even after a late party, he often brought dispatch boxes of papers from the office to read at home. The ambassador tried to be security conscious and kept the papers locked in his study, but when he sent his trousers to the valet to be pressed, he often left the keys to his study in a pocket.

Bazna had once worked for Albert Jenke, Ribbentrop's son-in-law, who was now a bigwig at Turkey's German embassy, and he saw Knatchbull-Hugessen's work routine as his chance to cash in. He contacted Jenke, who passed him to SD Chief Ludwig Moyzisch, to whom he offered to sell photographs of pages from the dispatch boxes in the British ambassador's study. Moyzisch was agreeable, but thought Bazna's price—£20,000 per roll—exorbitant. Consultation with Papen and a query to Berlin brought a go-ahead signal, and Bazna set to work.

The resulting film stunned Moyzisch, who rushed it to Papen. Papen was so impressed by the richness and accuracy of the documents that he trilled to Berlin in early November that he would code-name this extraordinary source "Cicero" after the famous Roman orator. Berlin was split between believers and nonbelievers: Schellenberg was convinced and delighted; Ribbentrop resented Papen's intelligence coup, and expressed doubts. Material of extraordinary weight and importance continued to arrive—differences among the Allies about where to open the next offensive—in the Balkans or along the North Atlantic. There were details of the Big Three summit in Teheran, highlighting tensions with the Soviets, and a long-range view of British-Turkish policy.[1] A report on a planned bombing raid on Sofia proved to be 100 percent accurate, and would have saved the Germans considerable losses if they had heeded it.

By this time Fritz Kolbe had been reporting to Dulles for some months, doing essentially what Bazna was doing for the Germans: photographing sensitive documents and providing them to the enemy, in Kolbe's case, free of charge. He reported that Papen had advised that at the December 1943 Teheran Conference, Roosevelt had adopted a critical tone toward Stalin, leading German diplomatic circles to believe that a rupture between the United States and the Soviets should not be ruled out. This opened the door to a potential separate peace with the Anglo-American Allies.

Dulles, examining several Kolbe documents, immediately saw that much of the material matched English diplomatic files and realized that British security had been compromised. In December he told the British he was convinced that the leak was in their embassy. Two security men were sent from London to check it out, but though they combed through everything and interviewed all the embassy office staff, they came up with nothing. Knatchbull-Hugessen never said anything about taking files home, and there seemed to be no answer.

WHEN ABWEHR CHIEF LEVERKÜHN NEEDED ANOTHER LAWYER FOR HIS ISTANBUL OPERA-tion, he had invited young Erich Vermehren, the son of an old friend and an excellent lawyer, to join his staff in Istanbul. But on Vermehren's arrival in Turkey, he found that he had a problem: Spouses were not permitted to accompany Abwehr personnel to postings. Vermehren wanted his wife with him, and he applied for his wife, née Countess Plettenberg, to join him any-way. He had converted to her Catholic faith and both were anti-Nazi. Pre-dictably enough, Vermehren's application was refused, and he complained to his friend Adam von Trott of the Foreign Office.

A second application was also refused, but eventually, through Trott, Vermehren was able to get a passport and visa for his wife. In Turkey, she was to contact the papal legate, Monsignor Roncalli. There were some diffi-culties, and when the pair visited Roncalli without Leverkühn's permission, tension heightened. Then, on January 21, 1944, Vermehren reported sick; he would not be in the office the following Monday. He was also moving, and gave his office a new address. The following week, when he did not re-port for work, his old apartment was found to be empty, and the new ad-dress turned out to be false.

As they had intended all along, the couple had defected with bag and baggage, assisted by the British, who had staged a kidnapping. The Ver-mehrens had been "seized" from an embassy party, and flown directly to Cairo. After weeks of debriefing, they proceeded to London, where a pleasant fellow named Kim Philby was especially helpful; he even let them stay at his mother's apartment.

In the aftermath of the Vermehren affair, Leverkühn suspected that there would be more defections. Typically, defections brought serious repercus-sions for families left behind, and for anyone who might appear to have been involved, no matter how remotely.[2] Hitler was livid over these defec-tions in particular. Leverkühn was withdrawn from Istanbul and the long-standing Nazi suspicions of the Abwehr and Canaris came to a head. Hitler decided to restructure his military intelligence services.[3] On February 12, 1944, Canaris was relieved of his duties. The Abwehr was combined with the RSHA in a single unified intelligence force under Himmler.[4]

Heinrich Himmler was yet another step ahead in his push to power.[5] The Amt Ausland/Abwehr was no longer an independent organization; its chief was in disgrace, shuffled off to exile in a mountain fortress (but as a small comfort, in the company of his beloved dachshunds). Though Hey-drich had been assassinated in Czechoslovakia 1942, the Nazi intelligence machine had won after all, and the SS was triumphant. By May, the fusion of RSHA and Abwehr was completed by means of an extraordinarily complex document that spelled out exactly where and how within the bureaucracy authority for every particular function was apportioned.[6]

Canaris was eventually released and assigned a paper-shuffling job in an office for economic warfare. In June, massive Allied offensives on both the eastern and western fronts made the approaching end clear. Germany would be overrun, countless more lives lost. Canaris chose not to participate actively in any plot. He had his acute misgivings about the future, but removed himself from any action to pursue what looked like a very ordinary life, doing his useless job and taking comfort in his animals.

Allen Dulles delivered his postmortem assessment of the situation on February 24, 1944, though by this time, Canaris had already been removed:

> 659's [Canaris's] position and his whole outfit has been seriously jeopardized by . . . the V affair in Turkey. Abwehr will probably be taken over by Himmler. . . . It is likely that 659 and SD will be the recipients of an "extended leave." It is unlikely that 659 will offer a strong protest since he is somewhat of a Buddha. . . . The possibility that V may make certain disclosures concerning present relations between Turkish and Nazi intelligence is a matter of grave concern to the Nazis. This presents a possible clue to Cicero. . . . Although the liquidation of 659's group is not an accomplished fact as yet . . . contacts who were formerly optimistic, now feel that the situation is quite devoid of promise.[7]

There is no evidence that the V case ever offered any clues to Cicero/Bazna, but the increased security had made Bazna and his German paymasters nervous. Bazna did less and less work, and what work he did was no longer very valuable. All in all, he had delivered film ten times over an eight-week stretch. By March he had quit the spy game, and it was only by a peculiar happenstance when an SD secretary's dreams of a future in America led her to reveal the secret of Cicero/Bazna's identity.

How or why the chief of SD in Ankara, Ludwig Moyzisch, hired a secretary who had grown up in America and wanted to return to the States remains a mystery. Nelle Kapp had attended high school and college in the United States before the war, and she dreamed that she and her German fiancé, pilot Gustav Rengers, would marry and live there. Rengers had crash-landed in Turkey and tried to defect but had been detained. Kapp worried that since both she and Rengers were involved in fighting the Allies, they would not be allowed to go to America after the war. She decided to make a deal with the Americans: She would trade information for freedom. It was Kapp who informed them that the leak was from Knatchbull-Hugessen's home and that she suspected the manservant. Bazna quit his job and tried to make a run for it, but he was intercepted. Knatchbull-Hugessen tried to hire him back to use as a double agent, but Cicero/Bazna refused. Though Cicero has been credited with being the most important spy of the war, the truth about him is not quite as impressive as the postwar fables spread by Bazna himself, by Moyzisch, and, of course, by Hollywood.

As Dulles described the denouement of the Cicero affair:[8] "Thus our rifling of the German Embassy Office safes through an agent reporting to the Americans in Switzerland put an end to the rifling of the British ambassador's safe by a German agent in Turkey." The OSS was getting comparable information from spies in the Japanese embassies in Ankara and Sofia, and from Papen's office. In an ironic twist, Bazna, whose motives were purely mercenary, died a pauper. The impressive £300,000 he had earned for his spying turned out to be counterfeit. And Kapp? The Americans sent her to New York, where she was promptly jailed as a possible spy. She was released after the war, but her dream of married life in the USA with Rengers went unfulfilled.

IT ALL UNRAVELS

A good binding is said to be one mark of quality in a Turkish rug. A poorly bound rug will soon begin to fray and unravel. The same was true of intelligence in Turkey; once it began to fray, it came undone with alarming speed. Apparently defection was infectious, and Leverkühn worried that there might soon be an epidemic. Topping his list of potential defectors was Willi Hamburger and other members of the Austrian resistance movement. Hamburger was good at his job, and living high in Istanbul on Abwehr funds had suited him. But he was also Austrian, and vocally patriotic, and his offer to provide the Americans with information in exchange for their support of Austria's independence from Hitler did not come as a complete surprise. Hamburger and George Earle were both vying for the attentions of the beautiful singer at Taksim's, but they had also become friends, and Hamburger began to share Abwehr information with Earle.

Earle, good-natured and agreeable though he was, was not overly concerned with the details of security. He knew that he was under Axis surveillance, yet he sent one of his closest associates, a familiar figure in the Istanbul spy world, over to Hamburger's house. Hamburger lived next door to Papen's summer residence, and the man was spotted by German agents. Early one morning not long after, Hamburger heard a pounding on his door. The Germans were on to him. He quickly called a Turkish friend who contacted the British immediately. A British car arrived posthaste, to pluck Hamburger out from under the German agents' noses. During his debriefing, Hamburger exposed twenty German agents who had been working for him, and later did propaganda radio shows for the British and Americans. With handsome Willi out of the country, Earle finally got the girl.

Six German intelligence operatives defected from Istanbul in less than a year, a fact that was greeted with enthusiasm by British intelligence and the OSS, but to the German intelligence community the defections spelled trouble. With Canaris's dismissal and Leverkühn's withdrawal, there was so much anxious speculation about where it would lead and what it all meant that Propaganda Minister Goebbels thought it wise to send a deputy to boost morale on the Bosporus with ringing assurances of an imminent German victory.

THE GERMAN INTELLIGENCE OPERATIONS ON THE BOSPORUS WERE NOT THE ONLY ONES with troubles. Though OSS Istanbul had been asked to rein in the Dogwood operation, Macfarland and Coleman had essentially let things go on as before. Amateur or not, between December 1943 and February 1944, Dogwood and his many subagents had produced the bulk of Turkish intelligence. There were 157 reports, with information on top-priority areas such as oil, synthetic gasoline and rubber production, aircraft and ball bearing operations that it had made the flowery chain the darling of the OSS. Washington insisted that henceforth all reports should be routed directly there for evaluation rather than to Cairo.[9]

As usual, the British were still skeptical, and Donovan, too, had his doubts. British intelligence had developed a list of known German spies, and found that some of the reports generated by Dogwood subagents were disturbingly similar to those passed on by the Nazis on their list. Without solid information on the subsources, there was no way to rule out that their sources weren't enemy agents. Donovan, who had pushed to develop X-2, was particularly sensitive to the risks of unreliable data being used to lure Allied soldiers into an ambush.

Since OSSers could not be seen meeting officials in Budapest openly, they appointed Lieutenant Colonel Otto Hatz, code-named "Jasmine," to represent Hungary and Andre Gyorgy, "Trillium," to represent the Allies in negotiations, unaware that both men were double agents, also working for the Germans.[10] During the planning of a mission to drop three OSS men into Hungary, two reports came in that should have raised red flags among Macfarland's crew. The first was from British intelligence, expressing concern that a Dogwood report vital to this mission, "Operation Sparrow," was identical to a report from a known German agent. Clearly, Hatz was a double agent. The second, generated internally by an OSSer, complained that Dogwood's handler, Coleman, seemed to have no idea what his agent was doing and was making no effort to track down suspected enemy plants among Dogwood's subagents.

Macfarland refused to believe that Hatz was a double agent. Claiming that it was just part of Hatz's cover story, he chose to ignore the warning. The British could not decide whether Macfarland was arrogant or just stupid, but they were certain of one thing: Hatz had to be taken out of the equation. They contacted Donovan, who cabled Macfarland personally on January 9, 1944, telling him that Jasmine was unquestionably a double agent, and contact was to be terminated immediately. "Packy" Macfarland replied that the British had warned him already; he would just "be cautious" in dealing with Hatz.[11]

Donovan was furious. He shot back that he expected that his warning about Hatz had been heeded, and he wanted details. But rather than accept his boss's word, Macfarland argued that Hatz was just a courier and whatever materials OSS gave him could do no harm if they fell into enemy hands. Only Donovan's explosive reply finally convinced Macfarland to replace Hatz.

Kolbe, too, had been on to Hatz. He had informed Bern, which duly informed Washington, that several agents for the Americans were playing a double game, among them Otto Hatz in Hungary. There, unfortunately, the information was not given much weight, and red flags or no, on March 15, 1944, the three OSS agents jumped into Hungary. The Germans had been informed, and their arrival had been anticipated. The Allied agents spent the rest of war in prison; Operation Sparrow had ended in abysmal failure, and three days later, Hitler launched an offensive against Hungary.

Hatz had been handpicked by Schwarz/Dogwood, and why Macfarland turned to him for a replacement is unfathomable, but even more unfathomable was Schwarz's choice of a replacement. Luther Kovess was a vocal pro-Nazi Hungarian who at one time worked under Archibald Walker as a Socony-Vacuum tanker captain. Suspected of sabotaging his own ships, he was fired, and went to work for a company called Danube Shipping, a transparent front for the Abwehr. If anyone in Istanbul was to be suspected of being a double agent, it was Luther Kovess, but while Schwarz must have realized that Kovess was already working for both Hungarian intelligence and the Abwehr, he hired him anyway. Schwarz had personally invited Kovess to become a triple agent.

The OSS planned to drop agents into Austria to help organize and arm the resistance for guerrilla strikes and possible open warfare. Franz Joseph Messner, managing director of Semperit Company operations in Vienna and the leader of a group of about twenty calling itself the Austrian Committee of Liberation, looked like an ideal recruit. In early 1944 Messner agreed to work for the OSS and was given the code name "Cassia." OSS files described Cassia as "earnest, reliable, energetic, an Austrian patriot with strong Allied sympathies, especially for the USA."[12] Cassia and his group would identify strategic industrial and bombing targets for the Allies. In fact, Cassia very quickly reported that after the Allied bombing of Dort-mund, significant war production of carbon black, linked with buna and synthetic rubber production, was being handled at a plant in Polish Silesia, which ought to be a priority Allied bombing target.[13]

Just days after the Operation Sparrow fiasco, Messner/Cassia and his sec-retary made their way to Budapest to pick up a radio so that the resistance could maintain communication with the Allies. Again, the Gestapo had been alerted by enemy agents and was waiting for them. The two were ar-rested and, under torture, revealed the names of the Cassia group.[14] Twenty resisters, including Messner himself, were executed. Only two from the group remained alive.

Dogwood was out of control. The British Ultra decoding team provided the OSS with transcripts of German communications proving that Andre Gyorgy, a.k.a. Trillium, was a "double agent who works for the Germans, Hungarian Counterintelligence, the British and the OSS."[15] Schwarz insisted that double agents were a good source of information for anyone who could outsmart them; unfortunately, he was the one being outsmarted. By hiring Fritz Laufer (code-named "Iris") as a Budapest-Vienna courier entrusted with missions to Czechoslovakia and Switzerland, Schwarz believed that he had employed a half-Jewish Czech who hated Hitler. Instead he had brought an SD agent on board.

OSS analysts in Washington and Cairo shared with British intelligence everything they could scrape together on the identities of Dogwood's sub-agents and began backtracking through old reports. What they discovered made them sick. In going back over Dogwood reports they soon found that most of them were bogus. In May 1944, OSS headquarters radioed Macfarland: "Dogwood himself as well as the ENTIRE Dogwood chain is dangerous."[16]

As analysts reexamined the Dogwood reports, it became clear that the worst reports came from "Dahlia," Fritz Fiala, a Nazi working at the German embassy in Turkey.[17] He had defected secretly to the United States, and so he was assumed to be reliable, but OSS assessed his reports for the month of April as "ridiculous, exaggerated."[18] In early June, Macfarland instructed his office to stop disseminating any reports from Dahlia, pending an investiga-tion of his reliability.[19] Yet Fiala was still not considered a possible double agent—only unreliable. In fact, Dahlia was held in such high regard by Schwarz that he persuaded the Americans to allow Dahlia/Fiala to move to Allied territory in exchange for his meritorious service.[20]

From a recent review of Dogwood reports, including those from Dahlia, made possible by the Freedom of Information Act, it is obvious that Dahlia was suspect as early as March 17, 1944. Washington had established a sys-tem for evaluating both source and content of a report that was to be im-plemented in every instance. Sources were rated from A to F; content from

1 to 10. At one point, Dahlia's reliability had an F-2 rating: untried, probably true. But when OSS tried to verify his reports against other sources, it
was downgraded to D-3: not usually reliable, possibly true.[21]

Alfred Schwarz, a.k.a. Dogwood, had run the biggest U.S. intelligence operation in Nazi-occupied Europe, believing that the future of the world
rested on his shoulders. He remained in Istanbul for a time, but in a city
crawling with spies, he was out of the business. Years later, he maintained
that the Americans had been criminally foolish not to listen to him. Had
they responded to secret German peace offers, he argued, the war could
have ended years sooner, and millions of lives could have been saved. But as
one bruised and demoralized OSS officer in Istanbul wrote to Cairo summing up the dismal end of Dogwood: "We are pretty well reduced to the
white-flowering tree, and events have imposed a pretty severe blight on
that. Most of the blossoms fall to pieces in your hands before you can put
them in water."[22]

ISTANBUL WAS WINDING DOWN. GEORGE EARLE LEFT THE CITY THAT SPRING AND RE-
turned to Washington. He had made his own investigation into where
the responsibility for the mass graves of Katyn lay, and he was determined
to brace Roosevelt with the results. FDR, faced with Earle's collected
evidence—pages and pages of Polish testimony and grisly photographs—
dismissed it; the Russians could not possibly have done this.[23]

In the end, Earle's possibly unwitting successes in deflecting attention
from genuine OSS operations, and the information gleaned from the Abwehr's Hamburger, were not enough to make up for what became the ultimate failure of American intelligence in Turkey. They had not abided by the
ground rules of espionage, the meticulous verification of sources on which
the British were so insistent. Early warnings and some clear signs of trouble
should have persuaded station chief Macfarland to be more circumspect.
But the Dogwood chain had continued to operate with swaggering indifference. The cost was some embarrassment and many lives.

Moltke's initiatives in Turkey had also failed, but not because of any
doubts among the Allies about his courage or integrity. Why? Was it the security and logistics problems that had stood in the way of his meeting
Alexander Kirk, or did Instanbul OSS mishandle the case? Was it because of
Papen? Or was it because American policy was too entrenched in unconditional surrender, too unwilling to deal "with these Junkers," or just too
worried about offending Stalin? There were simply too many agendas at
work for anyone to step in and offer an acceptable solution.

In Germany, baseless rumors of peace negotiations with the Soviets, apparently launched from Moscow, had been circulating for some time.[24] Between the military situation in early 1944, the defections, and the general

atmosphere, Turkey's German community was nervous. Official assurances that special miracle weapons would soon snatch victory from what looked like certain and imminent defeat did little to calm widespread fears. Nor did they keep Franz von Papen from looking to his future.

Papen had a new mission: He must renew contacts with the Allies. He needed a soft place to land when this was all over, preferably a place that offered him power. Just a slight shift in political posture and he could curry favor with the United States and angle for a position in postwar Germany. Returning from a visit to Germany in May, he reported to the Americans that Germany was well prepared for an anticipated Allied invasion; a second Allied front would open both sides to negotiations, but they would have to be preceded by a change in regime. In an obvious threat to the Allies, Papen said that, barring an invasion, Hitler might take up the dropped threads of a Russian entente, and hinted that Hitler's new magic weapon was inspiring great confidence. He even suggested that the Soviet move into Hungary and Romania only gave the Germans that much more opportunity to rattle them.

The response to his request for renewed contacts noted that "the principle of unconditional surrender should be maintained," and continued: "Papen has by no means renounced his ambition to play a political role. . . . A negotiated peace is naturally in the line of Papen's personal wishes as it would leave fairly intact the Wehrmacht . . . upon whom Papen is evidently hoping to lean for support in his fancied role as a possible future spokesman of Germany."[25]

But as far as the Allies were concerned, Papen's past had stuck to him. The OSS report continued: "In circles concerned about Germany's political future nobody places any hopes in von Papen. His famous Marburg speech, which for a time made him appear as the protagonist of the German opposition has been far outweighed by his cooperation with Hitlerism before and after 1933, and by the numerous instances of his political and personal irresponsibility." However, it was not impossible "that he may play a certain limited part in the transition period."[26]

Weak-willed and politically pliable Papen may have been, but he was no fool. He realized that the Allies would look more kindly on Germans who had cooperated with them before Hitler's collapse.[27] An OSS communiqué of May 13, 1944, remarked that "any constructive and concrete proposals designed to shorten the war that may be received from a German quarter will receive consideration and aid the German cause. . . . Those elements in Germany . . . making such a contribution [that] have proved their dissociation from Nazism before the Regime and its terror was [sic] broken will naturally appear best qualified to assist in the shaping of Germany's future after her surrender."[28]

Istanbul, at the confluence of continents, with an intimate acquaintance with the struggles of superpowers over the ages, occupied a particular place in the history of this terrible war. Neutral Turkey looked to the British and the Americans to save them from being trampled in the Soviet-German power struggle. But in the end Turkey provided an important lesson to the Anglo-American allies; as the war began to come undone, it was clear that, apart from lost lives and dashed hopes, there was little to show for the fevered activity among its extraordinarily dense spy population, rife with every kind of venality, corruption, and betrayal. Meanwhile, though he seemed unable to escape his past, Franz von Papen was looking to his future.

THE JEWISH QUESTION: THE BRAND PLAN

It had been known for some time that millions of Jewish lives had been lost in Poland alone, and the exterminations continued. In Turkey the previous July, Moltke had reported in considerable if somewhat inaccurate detail on the uprising in the Warsaw Ghetto while in Turkey. He had also reported that Jews were being transported from the ghetto to extermination camps.[29] This information had gone to the OSS's Istanbul Dogwood chain, which subsequently also produced an account of the so-called Brand plan.

In the process of rounding up Jews in Hungary for deportation to Auschwitz, Adolf Eichmann had reportedly recruited two Hungarian Jews to approach the western Allies with an offer that became known as the Brand plan, or "blood for trucks." In April 1944, two Hungarian nationals, Andre Gyorgy and Joel Brand, arrived in Istanbul. According to OSS reports, Gyorgy was "an unscrupulous double agent . . . who has worked for most of the intelligence operations in Istanbul but has been faithful to none." Brand, a thirty-nine-year-old manufacturer, was an "active Zionist, and agent in the Jewish underground." Brand's avowed purpose was to save Hungarian Jews, many of whom were in concentration camps, and as many as 12,000 had already been sent off to Poland for liquidation.[30] The Brand plan, presumably under the sponsorship of Adolf Eichmann, proposed to release a million Hungarian Jews to Turkey, Portugal, and Spain in return for vast amounts of food and materiel. To this stunning offer he added a proviso: The trucks would be used only against the Soviets.

In July 1944, Donovan received a top-secret report from X-2 on the Istanbul mission that has been declassified only recently. Among the topics covered is the so-called Brand plan, "a Nazi-sponsored Jewish rescue scheme . . . laid before the Americans in Istanbul." Everything pertaining to the Brand plan was treated "on a high plane with the military authorities and the Department of State."[31] The Istanbul Mission Report goes on to describe the arrival in May, by German courier plane from Vienna, of "Andre Gross, alias Antol Gyorgy . . . with a long record as a double agent; and Joel Brand . . . by vocation a small manufacturer, but by choice an active Zionist and an agent in the Jewish underground." Despite some irregularities at entry into Turkey, these two remained at liberty in Istanbul until they were picked up by the Turkish police, Gyorgy for smuggling, Brand for not having a Turkish visa. Eventually both were released, Brand leaving behind "the Brand proposals," allegedly an official German program to free the Jews in occupied Europe.

Brand had been instructed to come to Turkey with the following proposals:

> (a.) The Germans are willing to consider the release of the Jewish population of Hungary as fast as the Jews can be admitted to Spain, Portugal and Turkey.
>
> (b.) In exchange, the Germans expect to receive the following from the Allies: (a.) 2,000,000 bars of soap (b.) 800 tons of coffee (c.) 200 tons of cocoa (d.) 800 tons of tea (e.) 10,000 trucks
>
> (c.) Of special interest is the fact . . . that Brand made clear that the Germans were willing to give a guarantee to the effect that the 10,000 trucks would be used only against the Russians, and would not under any circumstances, be sent to the Italian or "Second Front."[32]

Even as Brand and Gross were in Istanbul touting their proposition to the Allies, transports from Budapest continued to roll toward Auschwitz.[33] OSS investigators concluded:

> It was obvious from the details of Brand's trip to Turkey that his journey was actively sponsored by the Gestapo. . . . Gyorgy was a regular courier between the Jewish leaders in Istanbul and the Jewish underground in Hungary . . . and it is almost certain that Gyorgy led the Gestapo to Brand. . . . When it became essential to the German plans that these Jewish leaders should be contacted, Gyorgy and Brand became obvious choices . . . since both were under obligation to the Gestapo and known to the Jewish leaders in Istanbul."

Another report suggesting that "information lending weight to the suspicion that the 'Brand plan' was a Nazi sponsored scheme to place the Americans in an embarrassing position with regard to their Allies, particularly the U.S.S.R.," reached Washington from Bern in late June 1944. Under the heading "With Nazi Cooperation, Jewish Refugees Arrive in Lisbon from Berlin," it stated that members of the Manfred Weiss family and others had been able to buy their way out of Hungary by means of a twenty-year lease on the Manfred Weiss Works, signed under pressure. They were being sent directly to Portugal and Spain.

OSS Lisbon informed London and Washington that a group of thirty people had arrived from Berlin, prominent Jews and their families among them. Their travel arrangements had been made by the Nazis. "Deep anxiety has been expressed at our embassy, which is afraid that the Germans may be attempting a political maneuver. . . . Do you know anything about this?" There were suspicions of "malicious intent" on the part of the Nazis, and suggestions of a connection with the "Brand Plan for trading necessary supplies for freeing refugees . . . which the Germans may now use . . . to discredit us with the Russians."

Washington agreed. It was very probably all part of the

> outlandish proposition that in exchange for a supply of U.S. trucks and other staples they would deliver a group of Hungarian Jews. The . . . [motivation for] this plan is the implication that America placed more worth on saving Hungarian Jews than on the war effort . . . and is meant to cause the Allies embarrassment. Roosevelt is the chief target, for the Nazis might claim that he is impeding the war effort by his attempts to rescue Jews."[34]

The Brand plan proved to be controversial. Did it in fact offer a legitimate opportunity to "ransom" captive Jews and stop, or at least interrupt, the forward motion of the Final Solution, or was it an attempt to drive a wedge between the western Allies and the Soviets and embarrass the United States? In any case, it was not the only plan to offer to barter Jewish lives for materiel.[35] The political ramifications of such a deal would have compromised the terms of unconditional surrender and enraged the Soviets. The issue of ransom was an uncomfortable one and the proposals came to nothing.[36] The War Refugee Board was firmly opposed it on the grounds that it would help the Nazi war effort, and there was also concern about how the public would respond if it became known that the United States was exchanging money or goods for Jews. Some Jewish organizations considered rescue a holy mission that should stop at nothing; others were more ambivalent, but wavered under the impact of news like that of the proposed mass deportations of Hungarian Jews.[37]

One particularly stiff-necked British interrogator was said to have asked Brand: "Where shall we put these Jews if Eichmann keeps his word?" Where indeed? Britain had steadfastly ignored requests to accept refugees and urged other countries to block Jewish immigration as well. During the first three years of the war, when Jews were still being allowed to leave Germany, the British admitted only 10,000 into Palestine. The Zionist movement smuggled in 9,000 more, but many thousands were denied visas.[38] After the Brand plan, Britain's unofficial policy changed; any Jew who could reach Turkey would be given a visa to Palestine. But reaching Turkey was no simple task, and once there, Jews were required by Turkish law to prove that they were just "passing through." The Zionist movement responded by buying a Bucharest travel agency and arranging for boatloads of "tourists" to visit Turkey, then obtaining visas to allow them to go on to Palestine.

Roncalli, meanwhile, never faltered. He continued to try to rescue Jewish refugees and his personal appeals to friends in high places helped him save many. Humble, likable, quietly using his connections, he was also able to stop—at least temporarily—the rounding up of Italian Jews.[39] Roncalli became Pope John XXIII in 1958, and was beatified in 2000.

AUSCHWITZ: PRIORITY TARGET

The source of recently declassified OSS report no. 367, dated January 30, 1944, was Cassia/Messner of the Dogwood chain. It listed three key plants belonging to I. G. Farben as the sole suppliers of the large and small rubber processing plants in Germany and German-occupied Europe, and it included precise location and bombing coordinates. Last on the list, after Schkopau to the north and Huls, near the Dutch border, were the Oswiecim Buna Works:

> . . . operating 2 carbide furnaces, and making 20,000 tons of buna a year. OSWIECIM (German: Auschwitz) is in Polish Silesia, longitude 19°E13', latitude 50°N02'. The labor for this plant is partly drawn from a concentration camp for 62,000 forced laborers who are returned to the camp after every shift.
>
> The sub-source is of the opinion that these targets are vital to German war production and their destruction would paralyze all German and German-controlled rubber-processing and finishing plants on the Continent. All are also "easily identifiable from the air on account of the prominent carbide furnaces which cannot be camouflaged effectively"[40]

This report is followed closely by report no. 379, dated February 4, 1944, again from Cassia.

> Apart from Buna production, OSWIECIM (Auschwitz) is of great importance to Germany's war production on account of chemical production closely linked up with buna, such as carbon black and acetaldehyde. After the destruction of the I.G. carbon-black plant at Dortmund by the RAF, a large carbon-black plant was erected at Oswiecim. It is the only major factory of the kind left for the supply of German buna works. . . .
>
> Near the town there are encampments holding 62,000 prisoners, including Jews from many European countries and "aryan" non-Germans . . . a forced labor reservoir for the industrial plants. . . . Both for quantity and types of War production, Osweicim is at present among the foremost centers of German war economy and should be a priority target.[41]

OSS report no. 435, "Poison Gas Production at Oswiecim," came in from Dahlia under the date of March 17, 1944, and reads:

As one of the chief works of German buna production and the main production center for poison gas in Germany, the Upper Silesian town of . . .
Auschwitz is one of the principal targets of Eastern Germany. . . . The workers
attached to the chemical factories are kept in barracks under rigid discipline;
a large percentage of them are deportees in concentration camps."[42]

The OSS reader of this last report made a few changes and appended a
note: "Look up previous report in Poland file." He had to refresh his memory on what had come before. This glimpse into intelligence work in OSS's
Central European Division in 1944 applies anywhere, anytime. Intelligence
consists of many small fragments, and only rarely does one fragment spell
out important news. Many individual reports, scraps and pieces must be
pulled out from what might best be described as "static"—a muddle of irrelevant information about other matters and different events in which
they are embedded. These pieces must then be put together like tessera in a
mosaic and carefully set into context. Only then does their meaning and
import come together in a comprehensible picture.

These reports present Auschwitz as a priority Allied target for industrial
reasons only—clearly a military priority.[43] The mentions of forced labor,
discipline, and concentration camps are matter-of-fact and coincidental.
But Auschwitz was also proposed as a potential target for humanitarian reasons. This possibility had first been proposed in the late summer of 1943 by
the Polish government-in-exile in London, in the hope that even limited
bombing of Auschwitz-Birkenau might cripple the machinery of extermination, or at least slow the relentless progress of the Final Solution.

Literature on the subject splits into two arguments: Should Auschwitz
have been bombed? Could Auschwitz have been bombed? Operational fea-
sibility was an issue, and there were technical concerns. Was the available
intelligence sufficient, or was it, as has been argued, of "minimal utility for
military purposes."[44] The inaccuracy of high-altitude bombing, collateral
damage and casualties, the diversion of resources, potential loss of aircraft,
and the "cost . . . to no purpose" were all cited as arguments against undertaking such a mission. Those in favor of bombing considered these concerns
simply "excuses for inaction" and a moral failure.[45]

News of the Warsaw Ghetto uprising, and Polish efforts to rid themselves
of the Germans before the Soviets reached Warsaw, had spurred Churchill
and Roosevelt to send aid and weapons. Time was short, but Stalin had
turned down a joint cable asking for his help in supporting the anti-Nazis in
Warsaw. The emergence of a noncommunist Polish government was not in
his interest. He had also refused use of nearby airfields under Soviet control,
so Allied missions to drop munitions and aid were forced to fly from Foggia
in Italy. Not only did many of the drops land in German-controlled territory, but the losses among the largely volunteer RAF squadrons were fairly

high. Of the 181 planes, 31 did not return. During the same period, however, U.S. planes flying from England bombed an aircraft factory at Gdynia and two oil refineries near Auschwitz. On August 20, 127 Flying Fortresses from the 15th U.S. Air Force based at Foggia, with an escort of 100 Mustangs, dropped 1,335 bombs of 500 pounds each on an I. G. Farben factory a few miles east of Auschwitz. One bomber was lost.[46]

For those on the ground at Auschwitz and Birkenau, watching these airborne missions rumble past high overhead, left them feeling desolate. Fifteen-year-old Hugo Gryn remembered it as "the sensation of being totally abandoned."[47] There was the will and the ability to destroy nearby factories and refineries; could not at least the rail lines leading to the death factories be bombed?

When John Pehle of the Treasury broached the possibility with U.S. Assistant Secretary of War John J. McCloy, he was told that such bombing would violate War Department policy. No military resources were to be diverted from military purposes for rescue missions. There would be no bombing of the rail lines, the camp, gas chambers, or crematoria. For years afterward, McCloy was accused of chilly indifference and wrongheadedness, but eventually it emerged that the decision had not been his. Only in a 1986 interview with Morgenthau's son, almost twenty years after Morgenthau's death, did McCloy reveal that Roosevelt had utterly rejected the idea, saying that "we would [be] accused of . . . bombing these innocent people. . . . We'll be accused of participating in this horrible business."[48]

How much a bombing raid might have achieved, how many lives might have been saved, is moot. Word had come to the Allies of mass murders in Poland and Russia as early as the autumn of 1941. Schulte had reported on the Auschwitz-Birkenau death camps in the summer of 1942. If nothing else, bombing Auschwitz would have been recognized as a clear and unequivocal expression of moral outrage and condemnation; it would at least have made a statement. By late 1944 it would also have been clear that it was too little, and much too late.

THE JEWISH QUESTION: THE ALLIED STANCE

Gerhard Riegner had had a busy year. He had sent a report detailing the plight of the Jews, country by country, to the American legation in Bern. It had been duly forwarded to the State Department, which had responded with the bureaucratic equivalent of plugging its ears. Certain factions in the department did not want to hear such news. In the future, no reports of this nature were to be forwarded through diplomatic channels. But Riegner had managed to get the report to Rabbi Wise anyway. He had also conveyed the basis of what became known as the Riegner plan, by which local currency, borrowed to finance the escape, transportation, or support of Jews in

France and Romania, was guaranteed repayment through U.S. funds held in accounts in Switzerland or the United States, which were to be blocked until after the war. The only immediate effect of the plan was open warfare between factions within the State Department, which delayed any positive action, even as the work of the death factories was accelerating.

By turning the Riegner plan over to the Treasury Department, the proper venue for dealing with such matters, Sumner Welles opened the door to a new champion among Roosevelt's palace guard. Treasury Secretary Henry Morgenthau was a Hyde Park neighbor and longtime friend of the president. He was Jewish, but also a determined secularist, and he had been hesitant to involve himself with earlier appeals to intervene on behalf of Jews. His efforts to marshal Treasury resources on behalf of Jewish migration had had little success, but the picture was turning darker, and the pleas of Rabbi Wise and other Jewish leaders were now buttressed by ghastly evidence. At Wise's urging, under Morgenthau's patronage, and with presidential approval, Riegner's plan had finally been adopted, though this did not translate into any immediately visible action.

Public pressure escalated, but the protracted administrative tug-of-war between those in the government pushing for action and those pushing determinedly against it continued. A dejected Morgenthau concluded: "Roosevelt won't move on Hull, he never has; and Hull won't move on Long."[49] At last, three Treasury officials drafted a memo to Morgenthau detailing State Department underhandedness and footdragging, entitled: "On the Acquiescence of This Government in the Murder of the Jews." It was a scathing account of deliberate deception and obstructionism at the State Department, particularly on the part of Assistant Secretary Breckinridge Long, who was in charge of immigration policies. Morgenthau was incensed. Within days of its receipt, with the zeal of a convert, he took an abbreviated version of the report to the president. This action provided the final impetus for the establishment of the War Refugee Board.

Established by Executive Order 9417, the WRB became a reality on January 22, 1944, nearly eighteen months after Schulte had reported on the reason for the visit of Reichsführer SS Himmler to Auschwitz. The War Refugee Board consisted of about thirty members. According to the order, the Departments of State, Treasury, and War, as well as any others, asked to help, were to provide every assistance short of interfering with war aims. The WRB had no military muscle behind it, no airlifts or combats units would be used, but its mission was to "rescue victims of enemy oppression in imminent danger of death."

Treasury's Josiah Dubois and John Pehle were among the authors of the report on the State Department's deliberate obstructionism. Chief instigator of the creation of the WRB was Dubois. A short, sturdy spark plug of a man, he was also "brainy." He knew that if they were to tackle the problems they faced with any success, they would have to manipulate the machinery of government very deftly. The board began energetically, optimistically, and thinking big. Then, in the interminable strategy meetings on how to wiggle projects through the State Department, optimism faded. The thinking got smaller; there were complexities. The WRB was not the creation they had envisioned. One Jewish leader present at some of the meetings felt that they were "outmaneuvered by politics," and worn down by an often uncooperative bureaucracy. The elation turned to frustration, then heartache. Conceived as a broad governmental agency, the board became a charitable organization, involved in smaller-scale projects, slowing down like a train shunted onto a siding. An activist with a close relationship to Dubois witnessed the perpetual struggles with the State Department, and recalled ruefully that the WRB failed to convince the government of the United States to engage in the rescue of Jews. "We came close. We came close. We were outmaneuvered by politicians, really . . . not sinister politicians who had a master plan . . . but when we wanted the effect of a congressional bill, Roosevelt wanted to blunt it by doing without a congressional bill."[50]

Even in the slowing down though, there were some accomplishments. Camps—temporary "havens"—were established for refugees who would be repatriated after the war. The WRB was without military options, but it had publicity and psychology at its disposal. Threats, propaganda, warnings of punishment were now aimed at Hungary to stop Hitler's intended deportations of more than 700,000 Jews. In March, under pressure from the WRB, Roosevelt again spoke out against Nazi crimes, and this time he mentioned specifically "the systematic, wholesale murder of the Jews." Again he threatened punishment of the perpetrators, and promised refuge to the intended victims. To the British, the president's specific mention of the Jews smacked of shameless politicking, a courting of the Jewish vote in an election year, but whatever Roosevelt's motivation, it added to the building momentum.

The Vatican, the International Red Cross, and neutral nations were enlisted to pressure Hungary, and though it was an expressly military operation, Budapest was heavily bombed. Under the cumulative pressure, Hungarian Regent Miklós Horthy halted the deportations and offered to release Jewish children with visas and all Jews having certificates for Palestine. Britain and the United States at last pledged to find a safe haven for refugees. The WRB struggled to push the United States to set an example by opening its doors.

Samuel Grafton of the *New York Post* suggested that "a few fenced in acres of the poorest land in America" be opened up as "free ports" for refugees—Jewish or other. "They don't want to keep it. They just want to sit on it until they can go home again."[51] Grafton's idea won wide popular support, but also ran into State Department and congressional resistance. In the end, Fort

Ontario, an army camp in Oswego, New York, accepted 982 multinational refugees in August 1944.[52]

When Nazi pressure persuaded Horthy to install a pro-Nazi government rather than face a full-scale German occupation, the forward momentum stopped short.[53] Still, the WRB had begun to see results, small in light of the scale of the carnage, but results. The concerted rescue efforts saved at least a small remnant of Hungary's Jewish community; some put the overall number of Jews rescued by the WRB at 200,000, but as the WRB's John Pehle put it later, "What we did was little enough. . . . Late and little I would say."[54]

Allen Dulles weighed in with his concerns about possible repercussions of the WRB's mission in March 1944. His principal concern? Relief work would interfere with his intelligence sources and operations.

> 1. If it were publicized that I am in any way connected with refugee work I would be swamped with a multitude of applications, visitors, and irritations which would gravely handicap me in carrying out my other duties.
>
> 2. Quite aside from the attitude of the Swiss government, I am not at all convinced that it is wise to try to transport large numbers of refugees here.
>
> 3. Such action requires underground channels. . . . The Gestapo will soon uncover . . . these channels . . . and people who are trying to get across the border will be executed. . . . It is quite likely that a greater number of unfortunate persons will lose their lives if they employ these methods than if they continue in their present surroundings.
>
> 4. If an effort is made to establish underground channels for refugees, it will interfere with SO or SI lines set up for immediate military uses. . . .

Pragmatic as ever, Dulles goes on to enumerate other difficulties: Zealous but ignorant individuals, untrained for relief work, can do refugees more harm than good. He has intimate knowledge of the "hardships these people have had to endure," and his response is "as much from the standpoint of their good as from concern for the work extremely important for military operations."[55]

Those who argue insensitivity on Dulles's part vis-à-vis the refugee or Jewish problem see this as another damning example of his callousness. In fact, Dulles put his finger on the crux of the enduring argument about the Allied lack of engagement and urgency: What is the relative weight given to military versus humanitarian exigencies? This question has fueled decades of debate and produced countless harsh words. A quick glance over the Dulles communiqués at this point in the war, and the long lapses between mentions of the Jewish problem and humanitarian issues, reveals that the overriding Allied concern, right or wrong, was winning the war.

Well before Dulles arrived in Bern, he had suggested the establishment of a tribunal of Allied jurists to look into the evidence of atrocities and war crimes. As evidence accumulated and was verified, their findings would be released. It was not unreasonable to expect that the resulting publicity would put pressure on the perpetrators and deter future atrocities. Dulles's faith in psychological warfare—which this certainly was—is clear in his many communications suggesting a variety of propaganda initiatives. In spite of official skepticism, Dulles continued to press for the adoption of some version of this tactic among policy makers, but apparently Washington did not share his faith.[56] In yet another example of the failure to establish a viable communications link between intelligence and policy, policy makers, whether out of ambivalence, indecisiveness, or preoccupation with other concerns, did not respond.

THE OPPOSITION

It is infinitely easier to suffer under the orders of another than in a free act of personal responsibility. It is infinitely easier to suffer in community than in loneliness. It is infinitely easier to suffer publicly and in honor, than apart and in shame.

—DIETRICH BONHOEFFER

In early January, Moltke was back in Berlin. He warned friends, members of the so-called Solf Circle, that the telephones of several members were being tapped. This small group of anti-Nazi intellectuals was named after its founding member, Hanna Solf, the widow of a former ambassador, and worked independently to counteract the regime in humanitarian ways, helping people who had gone underground, the so-called U-boats, or anyone suffering persecution. They also had important contacts within the active resistance, such as Moltke. They had been infiltrated by a Gestapo agent in 1943 and had been under suspicion.

There was a wave of arrests. Frau Solf and her daughter, Elisabeth von Thadden, were arrested, as was Otto Kiep. Like Moltke, Kiep had studied law in England, and at the time of the Hitler takeover, he had been serving as general consul in New York. Aware that attending a banquet in honor of the physicist Albert Einstein that year might mean the end of his diplomatic career, he had accepted the invitation anyway and spoke in praise of Einstein. He even suggested that German culture and culture were currently being given short shrift. These remarks led to his withdrawal. Through Weizsäcker, he had been able to find work in other government agencies as part of the opposition network, joining the Abwehr as foreign policy officer for the OKW and liaison to the Foreign Office in 1939.

On January 19, the SD came to arrest Moltke at his office. The Kreisau Circle trembled. Moltke's hoped-for meeting with Kirk in Istanbul or in

Cairo was not to be. The defections in Turkey had enraged the Nazi hierarchy. Adam von Trott was questioned extensively by the Gestapo about his connection to the Vermehrens. Time was clearly running out. In April, an OSS communiqué noted: "Hermann has been under arrest for some time and will be unable to resume contact with us here. Talks started here in connection with the plans . . . will be continued by Hermann's associates in Switzerland."[57] The Hermann plan called for a separate German peace with the Allies, in return for which elements of the Wehrmacht with whom Moltke had established contact would withdraw from the French coast to ease invasion and occupation by the Allies.[58]

With Canaris's dismissal in February and Himmler's takeover, the Abwehr effectively ceased functioning as a center of resistance. There was chaos and disarray at the heart of the Reich; the cracks in the Nazi edifice were growing. In fact Himmler, Schellenberg, Kaltenbrunner, the whole sinister crew, had been looking to desert the severely listing Nazi ship of state for some time already. Himmler may have entertained the idea as early as the summer of 1942, possibly even before. As it gradually became clear that Germany could not win the war, Himmler nurtured a fantasy of replacing Hitler. In October 1943, his doctor-masseur, Felix Kersten, contacted OSS officer Abram Hewitt in Sweden with an eye to negotiation. Toward the very end, he negotiated quite openly with Swedish count Folke Bernadotte— trying to save himself and end the war he had helped to perpetrate with such fervor. Schellenberg had begun meeting with Colonel Roger Masson, the head of Swiss intelligence, in the fall of 1942, and Kaltenbrunner was not far behind.

HITLER'S ARMIES SEEMED TO BE CHARGING TOWARD THE ABYSS, BUT THE ONGOING EFforts of the civilian opposition were stalled. Trott and Goerdeler kept trying to reconnect with England and the United States through Switzerland and Sweden, but were met with consistent silence. They may have felt humiliated, haunted, anxious, desperate, but they did not give up. Since Casablanca, they had been on their own; not the tiniest sliver of hope was to come their way. Trying to find words for the mood, a discouraged Hassell turned to Shakespeare, as Theo Kordt had with Halifax, to utter a cry from the heart: "The world is out of joint—O cursed spite, that ever I was born to set it right!" In a more colloquial vein, he added: "Everything is going to the devil!"[59]

In the late summer and fall of 1943 the reins of the military opposition had been taken into the hands of Tresckow, Friedrich Olbricht, chief of the OKW army office in Berlin, and a relatively new player, Colonel Claus Schenk von Stauffenberg. First and foremost a soldier, Stauffenberg had been severely wounded in North Africa, but was sufficiently recovered by the fall of 1943 to take the lead as the force behind "action" against Hitler. Some saw his drive and relentless energy as obsessive, but he claimed that he had to do something to "stop this senseless slaughter."[60]

Together with Fritz von der Schulenburg, Stauffenberg set about enlisting young officers from the Potsdam 9th Regiment to orchestrate an assassination attempt. Early on, Schulenburg had supported Hitler, but like so many others, he had seen the light. Now second in command of the Berlin police, he was in a position to act. Through his close contacts with Trott and Peter Yorck, he brought the military contingent closer to the Kreisau Circle. Their first volunteer was young Axel von dem Bussche. Having witnessed mass killings at Dubno in the Ukraine in late 1942, he was determined to act against Hitler. A planned demonstration of new winter uniforms was to be his opportunity. He volunteered to blow himself up with Hitler with a bomb concealed in his overcoat. Again, everything was ready, and this time the conspirators had been able to shorten the fuse to just four and a half minutes. Then word came that the equipment to be demonstrated had been destroyed in a bombing raid. They would have to try again. Bussche returned to the front and was so badly wounded, he could no longer take an active role. The next "overcoat" attempt a few months later involved Heinrich von Kleist, whose father insisted that it was his duty to undertake this suicide mission. All parties were briefed and in readiness, literally waiting for the code word. Hitler never appeared.

Tresckow, meantime, was hoping to get himself transferred to Berlin with access to Hitler. Stauffenberg's adjutant Werner von Haeften offered to shoot Hitler with a pistol, but his brother persuaded him that such gangster methods should not be used, not even against gangsters.[61] Another attempt was foiled when the perpetrator-to-be was not permitted into the briefing room where the assassination was to take place. Hitler's paranoia was in full flower and access to him was now restricted to an innermost circle.

The focus of the conspiracy narrowed to two protagonists: Goerdeler and Stauffenberg, two men of very different natures and political convictions: Goerdeler, the civilian optimist, convinced of the power of persuasion and opposed to tyrannicide; Stauffenberg, the driven military pragmatist, bent on assassination. Additional differences complicated the relationship further. Goerdeler was conservative with a monarchist bent, Stauffenberg was willing to embrace socialists and communists if it should come to that. But as the year wore on and the situation became more desperate, these differences among the opposition lost their significance. The goal of eliminating Hitler was paramount.

The Kreisau Circle's Hans Peters later recalled that "in early 1944, all the sparrows were whistling from the rooftops that Goerderler would be the 'chancellor of the Fourth Reich.'"[62] But unless Goerdeler could induce others to bring it about, the Fourth Reich might never come into being. To his enormous frustration, he could not do it himself; he could only urge, goad, cajole, persuade, push, and wait. To that end he put his hopes in the British, imagining that they would recognize Germany's value in preventing a communist sweep across Europe, but the waiting was in vain.

The lead in the opposition was now taken by Stauffenberg, who believed that since the senior military had not acted, the younger leadership now had to step in. The war could not be won, and as Germany's military strength ebbed, the opposition would have fewer bargaining chips with which to negotiate a peace with whatever Allies might be willing. His Berlin assignment provided him with one of the key requisites for any leader of a plot: access to Hitler. Stauffenberg was direct, pragmatic, and coolheaded. He would not let the high-minded niceties that troubled many of his fellow conspirators stand in his way. When he was asked in 1942 what could be done to change Hitler's style of leadership, he had replied, "Kill him."[63]

On taking over as chief of staff to General Olbricht of the reserve army in Berlin, he had been initiated into a plan called Operation Valkyrie. Designed originally by Olbricht at Hitler's behest to quell potential "internal disturbances," specifically rebellion among the many foreign laborers in Germany, it was intended to bring all elements of the reserve army together quickly into an effective force.

Tresckow and Stauffenberg studied the Olbricht plan and concluded that there was no reason it could not be used quite effectively against Hitler. With a few revisions, the forces deployed to quash foreign laborers could just as easily be used to occupy ministries, radio, and communications and to disarm the SS.[64] The conspirators would simply add a statement that Hitler was dead, that party leaders were trying to exploit the situation, and that the Reich government had instituted martial law.

BERN: URGENT PLEAS FOR ACTION

Washington and London might have remained dubious, but Bern, at least, decided that it was time to send Kolbe a little thank-you for the enormous risks he had taken, for his late nights and his many anxious hours of hard work, and sweating through passport control so many times. In February he received a postcard of a snowy alpine panorama from the famous Davos ski resort. "I managed three ski jumps," the message read. "I'm no beginner. The weather is beautiful." Translation: Kolbe's last three messages had come through. They had deciphered his postcard, and the information was "useful."[65] Fritz Kolbe was a happy man.

Kolbe was a fount of information: Spain was continuing to deliver wolfram to Germany. "When will you people wake up?" he asked parenthetically. The Nazi satellite states were seething with unrest; it was an ongoing problem for the Reich. There was so much material that the Bern operation had a hard time keeping up with Kolbe's reports, but in Washington and London there was still deep skepticism about this mysterious Wood.

In spite of the friendly Fräulein von Heimerdinger in charge of departmental travel assignments, it had become increasingly difficult for Fritz Kolbe to arrange courier missions to Bern. His boss, arch-Nazi Ritter, had noted his frequent absences, so Kolbe had to find other ways to communicate. He began to entrust some documents to colleagues and friends who shared his views on the regime. Sometimes they would mail a postcard to him in Switzerland. One, an innocuous-looking card of pussy willows and narcissus, sent birthday greetings, with an apology for two lines of seemingly random letters typed across the card. "Apparently some beginning typist has immortalized himself here," Kolbe wrote in a large, generous hand, "but unfortunately I have no other card handy. So accept these flowers and warm greetings to you and Ernst, from Fritze."[66] The random letters, decrypted by OSS, revealed that OWI was dealing with a certain German consul Wolff in Ankara "about his defection."

Japan was a weak link in the U.S. intelligence chain, and Washington was desperate for information. Gerry Mayer had sent Kolbe a postcard asking if he might be able to locate a Japanese toy in Berlin that was no longer available in Zurich for his son's upcoming birthday. Before long, Kolbe wangled an Easter courier trip to Bern and arrived laden with microfilmed information on Japanese military, political, and economic developments.[67] In a cable dated April 12, 1944, marked "Urgent. Action: Washington," Dulles jubilantly reported the "arrival of Wood with more than 200 highly valuable Easter eggs, which will be whipped into shape and quickly forwarded."[68] The whipping-up took time, but their delivery marked a turning point. At last, Washington perked up its ears, and the material found its way to Roosevelt's desk. Washington soon cabled back: "What a bunny!"[69] Eight months had gone by since Kolbe had first appeared with his initial cache of extraordinary intelligence—all of it ignored in Washington.

Even after Kolbe's precious Kapril reports finally reached the president's desk, a frustrated Dulles complained that they were being treated "like museum pieces" rather than being put to meaningful use.[70] Dulles fumed that Kolbe's reports had been delivered, and the Germans were carrying out exactly what had been predicted, right "under our noses." While Kolbe was making his way back to a Berlin he scarcely recognized after the latest bombings, Dulles pointedly reminded Washington that he had been asked to supply material on the Far East, and had done so as a high priority, yet he still had no word on whether this material had proved to be valuable. The full operative worth of Kolbe's work was not being utilized. Dulles's deep impatience with the intelligence bureaucracy burned bright in many of his communications of this period.[71]

In mid-May, Dulles reported that Radio Paris broke off transmission of the Friday service when the "priest began a prayer for the Jews." He went on to describe the persecution of churchmen, some of whom had protested against the persecution of Jews and Gypsies. He also mentioned the Dachau concentration camp, already in use for years as a major camp for political prisoners, but only in the context of clerics interned there who had recently died of starvation.[72] Dulles also learned of a German-Hungarian agreement to deport approximately 300,000 Jews to Poland, presumably for liquidation. He urged Washington and London to make this known through radio broadcasts and to deliver a sharp warning that participation in such maneuvers would be prosecuted as a war crime.[73] Another report from this period evaluates German morale and response to the treatment of the Jews:

> No hope is felt by the people of Germany. They despair of their fate in the event of defeat, and . . . are burdened by an emotion of common guilt. Goebbels' propaganda . . . promotes this feeling [among the people]: "The people of the countries we have occupied will avenge themselves upon us for our many detestable actions and we may anticipate no mercy from the Allies. As we have annihilated Russians, Poles and Jews, etc., destruction will likewise be brought upon the people of Germany. Our only chance lies in fighting in an effort to achieve the impossible." This mental state produces a blind alley, which is encountered by activists . . . against the regime . . . when they attempt to enlarge the scope of their activities.[74]

Less than a month later, he reported on various topics—among them Hitler's state of mind—gleaned from Hans Bernd Gisevius, still working with the Abwehr in Zurich and still reporting to him regularly, if indirectly. "As he believes that they are continuing to trick him, Hitler has become infuriated with the Hungarians. Their failure to carry out anti-Jewish measures have [sic] also angered him. What action to be taken is a matter which is receiving his careful consideration."[75]

GERMANY WAS STAGGERING UNDER MAJOR ALLIED AIR ATTACKS, AND FOOD RATIONS were to be reduced again. The German submarine fleet had just been dealt heavy casualties. Increasingly isolated and at odds with his generals, Hitler was enraged by his fractious Hungarian "ally."

In June, OSS chief Donovan cabled Dulles that he had learned from a contact working with the YMCA that 4,000 French children, aged two to fourteen, were being sent via boxcars to some unknown destination, unaccompanied by adults. He wanted suggestions on how to help. Dulles's response was cool and considered; such a mission was not within the scope of his activities.

Unless our Government is willing to give consideration to a broad program whereunder in reciprocation for temporary asylum here, guarantee the issuance of visas after the war and the granting of transportation to the United States or elsewhere and possibility some assurance with respect to supplementary shipments of food in order to provide for the care of the children here, I do not see that much can be done in regard to this type of situation . . . [which] hardly comes within the scope of my activities here and since similar conditions exist in virtually all the countries which are under German domination, its ramifications are broad.[76]

A few days later, he reported again on the ongoing situation in Hungary, where Horthy continued to be a thorn in Hitler's side:

A vigorous attack was made on the [Hungarian] Regent by Hitler . . . for the way in which the Jewish question in Hungary was handled and because of his failure to follow Germany and other countries in Europe on this matter. His demand was that the Jews be completely eliminated from economic life, and that they be delivered to Germany at a monthly rate of approximately 100,000.[77]

That desperate year, two Auschwitz escapees produced a long, horrifyingly detailed, firsthand account of conditions at the camp. By his own reckoning, Rudolph Vrba had only been at Auschwitz for a few days by the time of Heinrich Himmler's to the camp in July 1942 on which Schulte had reported. At that time, Vrba and his fellow inmates had only inklings of what the future held for them. But by Himmler's return the following January, Auschwitz's system of annihilation had been streamlined into total efficiency. Vrba no longer had any illusions about his future. He and a friend decided to attempt an escape. Miraculously, they succeeded. They made their way eighty miles to the Slovakian border, where, at Zilina, they told their story to an initially incredulous Jewish Council. Countless verifiable names and details painted a ghastly picture that was topped off by the warning that a million Hungarians would die at Auschwitz,[78] and gradually the council was persuaded.

When all this was eventually circulated as the Vrba-Wetzler Report, it marked a watershed in Allied awareness of the depth and depravity of the Nazi anti-Jewish programs. In June, a representative of a British news agency gave Dulles a copy of the report in Bern and sat with him while he read it. Dulles, he recalled, "was profoundly shocked. He was as disconcerted as I was and said: 'One has to do something immediately.'"[79]

Reconciling Dulles's "profound shock" over the Vrba-Wetzler Report with his own reports to Washington from much earlier presents a puzzle. He had obviously known the starkest outlines of the truth for well over a year, and while some details may have been new to him, the essence of it must have been all too familiar. But this was an eyewitness account from survivors, and Dulles may not have looked at it through his accustomed intelligence filter. Lacking this detachment may well have been what caused the reality of the horror to penetrate. Clergyman Willem Visser't Hooft had had considerable experience, not only with news of Nazi atrocities but also with how people responded, or failed to respond, to them. He knew Dulles well over a considerable period, and his memoirs offer some insight into how such shock was possible in someone who had clearly "known" the truth for some time: "People could find no place in their consciousness for such an unimaginable horror," he wrote; "they did not have the imagination, together with the courage, to face it."[80] The enormity of it was just unfathomable.

CHAPTER 8

1944

IDEOLOGIES, ANTAGONISMS, PROFITS

The ministers of Britain, the United States, the Soviet Union, and China had met in Moscow in late 1943 to underline Allied cohesiveness in the war effort. To the resistance the conference was another indication that there would be no accommodation born of the conspicuous friction among the Allies. In Switzerland the resistance had finally found a receptive ear in Allen Dulles. That alone, even without any promises of support, was enough to make the Bern OSS operation feel like a lifeline. In response to the Moscow Conference, Goerdeler and Beck prepared an exhaustive memorandum intended to reconcile the various elements within the resistance, and to point the way to a "union of all European nation states and . . . cooperation of all peoples of the world which seek peace."[1] Proposals from them to open the western front to the Allies went to Bern and from there to Washington, where policy makers were divided.

Dulles kept pressing for propaganda and support of the resistance, but Washington could still not bring itself to act, even on the precious Kolbe intelligence. The OSS should have no impact on policy. That was the preserve of the White House, Treasury, and the Joint Chiefs of Staff.[2] OSS was requested "to inform its representative in Switzerland of the position of this government with respect to such peace feelers."[3] Dulles was being reined in.

Among the neutrals, Portugal, Switzerland, and Sweden were making hefty profits from the war. All three were trading with Germany and accepting looted gold in payment. These dealings of course spilled over both sides of the 1944 time line, but that year marked a crisis point. Even as the Allies pressed the neutrals to stop, American companies were still trading with the enemy. Spies on both sides were being pressed either to discover plans for the invasion of Europe, or to deceive the enemy on the invasion by any means possible.

DULLES AND THE OPPOSITION

There were Allied policies other than unconditional surrender with which Dulles took issue. In his view, the lack of a coherent policy in regard to postwar Germany's future was a serious mistake. The Soviets had advanced effective propaganda on schemes for rehabilitating Germany, he argued, and the Allies had remained silent. Taking the measure of German morale that spring, he observed that "the ideology of the communists finds a fertile field because Germans by the millions have lost all their material possessions. . . . An encouraging statement . . . with regard to the problem of self-government for Germany in the future" should be made. The working classes ought to be assured of Allied assistance in the reconstruction of Germany. The best effect, he suggested somewhat acerbically, would probably be achieved "by not dropping bombs and leaflets simultaneously."[4]

From his first days in Bern, Allen Dulles had to be reckoned as one of the heroes of the German resistance. His willingness to listen to anyone, his understanding of German history, his sensitivity to the problems of the opposition, and his empathy with them were unique. His status in this regard remains unchallenged. By January 1943, he had reported on the German opposition's efforts to make contact, on Adam von Trott's disappointment at the lack of encouragement from the West, and his warning of a possible German rapprochement with the Soviets. Later that year, Dulles informed Donovan that in his opinion "75 percent or more Germans opposed the Nazi regime. . . . Oppositional groups exist . . . some are known to each other, and linked . . . but Gestapo terror effectively prevented organization."[5]

Within weeks of his arrival in Bern he already had considerable detail on the subject of the opposition. "Luke's surname is John [Otto John] and [we] have been given to understand that he is one of 659's [Canaris's] men for Spain and Portugal, intended especially for Anglo-Saxon contacts . . . for the most part Breakers maintain their foreign contacts and communications through 659 [Abwehr] organization, and both our 512 [Gisevius] and Gorter [Waetjen] act as intermediaries here in Bern. . . ."[6] Dulles also asked for a check on whether Luke had been in touch with Bearcat [Beaulac], and Rocky [Meingott]. Waetjen, he noted, was dubious about the encouragement Luke received from Rocky in regard to the idea of putting the military in power and changing regime. His report to Washington noted dryly that the OSS's Thomas in Madrid had requested further information, and was "instructed to continue his contact in a cautious manner and make no commitments whatsoever."[7] John had also written to ex-Chancellor Brüning, then living in the United States, to ask his advice and support on resistance matters.

While Dulles's mission was the "passive collection" of intelligence, he was no cookie-cutter intelligence officer. His experiences in Europe before and just after World War I had shaped his political outlook. He had imbibed a certain worldly breadth of view that had stayed with him and which differentiated him sharply from many of his government colleagues, certainly from the State Department and policy makers. His outlook was less isolationist, less absolute, and decidedly less parochial. He had political interests and profound concerns for the future of Germany and Europe that transcended much of wartime thinking, and his ideas were not always welcomed by his superiors. Again and again he bumped up against objections to his advocacy of the resistance and his intrusion into the political sphere.

By mid-1943, Donovan had already reminded Dulles that his assignment was "nonpolitical," but Dulles could not stop himself.[8] He continued to promote the resistance and urged support for groups he felt could serve as a foundation for a future democratic German government. He tested the requisite passive and apolitical intelligence approach repeatedly and severely, pushing continually at the restrictive envelope, nagging for intervention and action.

His first report on what he called the Breakers was sent to Washington on January 27, 1944. They were, he said, an "opposition group composed of various intellectuals from certain military and government circles. They have a loose organization among themselves.[9] He saw three separate strands among them: the evolutionary, the revolutionary, and the military. The first believed that responsibility for the catastrophe should be borne by Hitler and his cohorts; the second two strands felt that drastic action should remove Hitler and that a newly installed government should negotiate a peace. In spite of their differing opinions, the groups were staying in touch and "are very eager to obtain political ammunition from our side. They consider this sadly lacking." He was interested in using the Breakers, but did not "know what our policy is and what offers, if any, we could give any resistance movement."[10]

Within days, he knew that there was "extreme antagonism" in the State Department toward any offers to help the German resistance that might sow dissension among the Allies.[11] He soon reported: "From a German source I am led to believe that the Russians are training selected German prisoners for later internal action in Germany and that they . . . treat German prisoners well."[12] Over several months he kept Washington posted on the leaders of the Breakers, who warned of the eastern orientation of one

Breakers faction. Washington was interested in having the zealous Bern station chief reined in, but Dulles stepped out of his passive role again to plead for an Allied initiative to inform the German people of western aims and ideas for the future. In this area, Moscow had been the only source of information and hope, whereas the Anglo-American contingent was all too silent.[13] They preferred a western orientation, but feared that events were pushing them eastward.[14]

He knew that Luke/John was back in Spain in early 1944, had spoken with William Hohenthal, the American military attaché, about Stauffenberg's plans, and was eager to learn possible dates for the planned Allied invasion. Hohenthal promised to try to make contact with Eisenhower. John was opposed to Goerderler's idea of trying to exploit possible differences among the Allies; his dispassionate, rational assessment was that the Allies would not be moved from their firm demand for setting aside "unconditional surrender." Still, he did want to approach Graham-Meingott—Dulles's Rocky—on the subject of possible British support for Stauffenberg's plans.

In Lisbon, John found that Graham-Meingott was away, but his assistant, Rita Windsor, arranged a rendezvous. She would wait in her car on a darkened side street. She could be recognized by a streak in her hair, gone gray, surprisingly and very attractively, in spite of her youth. As they negotiated Lisbon's narrow streets, bumping over cobblestones, she told him that instructions had come from London forbidding contact with any emissaries of the German opposition. Eisenhower had been appointed supreme commander of the invasion; the war would now be settled only by force of arms. She realized that she was delivering a serious blow. Perhaps he would like to have a drink at her apartment? Over a consolation whiskey, he drew a map of the Berlin environs, pinpointing Düppel, the spot not far from the Wannsee where the conspirators had been meeting.[15] Could she possibly ask the Royal Air Force not to bomb there so that they might at least work on their preparations in relative peace? She kindly promised to try.

That spring, John put together a report, pleading for cooperation between the German opposition to Hitler and the Allies "now or in the future." His Spanish friend, Juan Terrasa, who had put him in touch with Beaulac earlier, promised to deliver it to the British representative in Lisbon. This report did actually reach London, but, once there, it crossed the desk of Kim Philby of M-16, where its chances of getting any sort of hearing dropped immediately to nil. Philby's interests, and those of his Russian masters lay in subverting any such cooperation. John's report was buried.[16]

In May, John was in touch with H. Gregory Thomas, a lawyer and businessman who was OSS's man in Madrid. He was going to Germany, John told Thomas, but would be back in a week's time with a very high military authority. This person, convinced that Hitler must be disposed of as soon as possible to save Germany from total ruin, was interested in "spilling the works." He and others would welcome an invasion from the west to keep Soviet armies at bay.

PORTUGAL: A NEST OF INVENTIVE SPIES

In Lisbon Tricycle/Popov had met with his old friend Johann Jebsen again, back in the summer of 1943. Still colorfully alive and well, Jebsen was working with the Abwehr against the Nazis as "Artist," and was often to be seen shuttling between Lisbon and his Estoril villa in his Rolls-Royce. In September, it had been Artist who warned Tricycle that he ought to think about leaving London; the Germans were about to begin firing rockets at the city from launching installations on the French coast. As Schulte had warned Bern, the summer bombing of Peenemünde had not crippled the rocket program completely.

If the British had "turned" German and Abwehr agents such as Artist and his friend Tricycle to their advantage, the Germans also had agents passing on to them whatever might be useful, even if it was wholly invented. As Tricycle had been a model for Ian Fleming, others in Portugal were sufficiently beguiling to Graham Greene, working for British intelligence there, to be blended into the memorable character who became "our man in Havana."

There is a good deal about the model for certain aspects of Greene's protagonist, Wormold, that is mysterious. "After all," opines Compton Mackenzie's fictional General Westmacott, director of extraordinary intelligence, "the whole point of the Secret Service is that it should be secret."[17] And Paul Fidrmuc, a.k.a. "Ostro," still represents a true puzzle. Armed only with extraordinary linguistic ability, a few slightly out-of-date reference books, and gossip picked up in the bars and byways of Lisbon, Ostro sent a stream of reports to the Abwehr. These reports, filled with "information" fabricated out of inspired guesswork and a vivid imagination, were so well received that they provided him with a handsome living and a bonus: expenses for his network of fictitious agents.[18]

Fidrmuc, a Sudeten Czech, had arrived in Lisbon as director of an import-export company. In 1942, some suspected that it had been Fidrmuc/Ostro who informed the Abwehr that the British planned a raid at Dieppe. As a commando raid masterminded by Lord Mountbatten, the Dieppe operation was intended as a scare and, as an intelligence-gathering operation. It was to divert attention from the beleaguered Russian front, and should have been followed by a hasty departure. But the mission turned into a disaster, with more than 3,600 casualties out of a force of just under 5,000.[19] Abwehr records suggest that the warning came from Agent A3924, whose identity remains uncertain. In fact, spy literature abounds with theories about the real source of the warning, and the Dieppe-Ostro connection is an enduring pre-occupation among enthusiasts and sleuths.

To date, the consensus is that Fidrmuc and Ostro were likely one and the same, an Abwehr agent operating out of Lisbon. Beginning in early 1942, he sent reports to Berlin about twice a month, ostensibly based on reports from Tor and Mos, two fictional agents in Britain who claimed a large web of informants and access ranging from the Middle East and Africa to Canada. By late 1943, the British knew that Germany was being fed information from what appeared to be a network within Britain reporting to Ostro in Lisbon. For a time, the British saw Ostro as enough of a threat to the Allies that the Twenty Committee recommended that "C" take what was euphemistically called "direct action" against him.[20] This does not jibe entirely with another account that suggests that, toward the end of the war, the British realized that Ostro's reports were pure fantasy, the creation of what the German secret service referred to as a *Schaumschläger*, literally, a froth beater. In other words, hot air.[21]

As a piece of the German intelligence operation, Ostro became the concern of a British outfit called NID12, which was charged with checking the truth of his reports. His so-called Manche report on the invasion of Normandy attracted particular attention. The conclusion was that Ostro's reports were "not only false, but fantastically so," and his mistakes were "of a character which no agent resident in this country or traveling between this country and the continent could make." Ostro, according to author C. G. McKay, was "one of the more imaginative and enterprising paper-mills of the Second World War."[22]

There were several perceived problems with Ostro's reports: convoy reports providing names of ships either in the Far East or long since sunk, even when the sinking had been reported in the press; lengthy technical descriptions of nonexistent arms such as antisubmarine devices; and a tendency to support specific strategic plans with "thick daubs of local color" and wholly invented detail.[23] Yet occasionally he had come close enough to the truth to cause an outbreak of nerves in the War Office. His reports were fabrications, but there was always the danger that he might, by happenstance or inspired guesswork, "hit upon some 'information' which would in fact be both true and dangerous." Ultimately, however, according to Masterman, it was decided that if Ostro was feeding the Germans a diet of misinformation they found palatable, so much the better. Ostro was left to concoct his stories and send them along unmolested.[24]

So what became of Ostro? A somewhat cryptic OSS memorandum notes that "Paul Fidrmuc, who has been in Barcelona and Madrid since the beginning of June, 1944, has been charged by the Reichsstelle Chemie and the Reichsführer SS, RSHA respectively, with engaging in mysterious operations in behalf of the same interests for whom he worked in Portugal."[25] In any case, Ostro's bravura performance enjoyed a very long run. An OSS report of May 1, 1945, from Portugal noted that of the "agents operating under Abt I, source stated that Paul Fidrmuc is undoubtedly the best man . . . [believing he] has a large organization inasmuch as he received about 500,000 escudos a month. . . . [When asked] the location of military units in America and England, FIDRMUC is always able to supply the answer within three or four days."[26] For this agent at least, Ostro had apparently sustained his credibility to the very end.

THE INCOMPARABLE GARBO

John Masterman claimed that sorting out the difficulties associated with the fifty-odd volumes of files involving the Garbo case was no simple matter, and on this Masterman was a reliable source. Juan Pujol García, a Catalan, had spent a good part of the Spanish Civil War in hiding, and by 1939 he had an evenhanded loathing of both fascism and communism. When war broke out, he formed a noble, if vague plan to fight for the Allied cause and had presented himself at the British embassy in Madrid to offer himself to British intelligence as an agent. According to his own account, his reception had been haughty enough to wound his pride, so he mulled things over and then decided to turn to the Germans.[27] This time, though, he had done his homework; he would volunteer to work toward the "New Europe," but with perfidy in his heart.

He persuaded the Abwehr that with a job as a foreign correspondent in London, for example, he could provide them with ample information on whatever they wanted. With a forged Spanish diplomatic passport, he finagled an exit visa and left Spain in July 1941 with a questionnaire, secret ink, cover addresses, and money from the Germans (tucked into his toothpaste tube) and the Abwehr's best wishes ringing in his ears,

Contrary to his handlers' expectations, however, he had gone not to London but to Lisbon. There, he made some essential purchases: a large wall map of England, a Baedeker's guide to England, and a somewhat out-of-date Bradshaw's railroad timetables. Then he withdrew to Cascais to become Abwehr agent "Arabel," assisted in his work by three fictitious subagents and a fertile imagination.

He claimed that his first report, a long, detailed document, had been sent from London via courier to Portugal for posting to Spain. He claimed to have been lucky enough to engage the KLM pilot on his flight to London in friendly and animated conversation. His story had persuaded the pilot, despite an initial reluctance, to act as courier and take his mail to Portugal for posting. He had assured the pilot that his letters would not be sealed; they were only to tell his fellow Catalan patriots of his activities in England on their behalf. In invisible ink he informed his case officer that before leaving Portugal for London, he had mailed a key to a safe-deposit box at the Espirito Santo Bank to Lisbon's German embassy to be sent on to Madrid.[28] Then he embarked on a series of lengthy documents, carefully crafted, but largely, if not entirely, fabricated.

His reports to the Abwehr included fictitious newly installed defenses and camouflaged pillboxes. He had strung barbed wire along important rail lines. He was careful to remember specific queries, but answered them only after sufficient time had elapsed for his researches. Part of his genius lay in understanding what the Germans might expect to hear and dutifully reporting it, a bit of psychological astuteness that earned him the respect of his German handlers. Arabel had also calculated that as an agent for the Germans, his value to the British would likely double or even quadruple, and before long it was clear that he had been right in this as well.[29]

Under siege in early 1942, Malta had taken heavy German bombing. Arabel reported to the Abwehr that his "agent" in Liverpool had noted the departure of a convoy to relieve Malta. While the details did not coincide wholly with the realities, a British intelligence intercept discovered that there had indeed been German air reconnaissance of the Malta route, and that plans were being laid to stop the convoy. This sent the British into a nervous frenzy. Who was this German agent Arabel, and how had he managed to get into England?

Meantime, in Portugal, Arabel had also been worried: His English was rudimentary; he knew next to nothing about England, he was completely unable to come to grips with the English monetary system, and his store of English names was so minimal that his Lisbon postbox read "Mr. Smith-Jones."[30] When the Abwehr had finally begun to request specific military information, he realized how ignorant he was of even the most basic elements of the composition of fighting forces, let alone British fighting forces. He fretted that he would not be able to sustain his charade much longer. The British had turned him down once, but he tried them again, this time in Lisbon. This approach, too, was rebuffed. Perhaps he should try the Americans. As luck would have it, Arabel became part of the familiar pattern.

By this time it was February 1942. At the embassy of the newly-at-war United States, naval attaché Lieutenant Demarest listened as Arabel explained that he had wanted to work for the British and told of his contacts with the Germans, his ventures on his own, and his determination to work for the Allied cause. Demarest was intrigued and took the time to follow up and consult with his British counterparts.

Then it was the turn of the British to fret and debate the merits of Arabel's value as an agent. Was he a plant, all part of an elaborate scheme? If he was the genuine article, he would certainly enhance the XX operation, but could he be trusted? Not long after, on a café terrace overlooking the beach at Estoril, Arabel met with Gene Risso-Gil, an agent for MI-6.[31] It was the beginning of his metamorphosis from Abwehr agent Arabel to MI-5's agent "Garbo"—renamed for his acting ability, though he had made a quick stop en route as "Bovril," a thick concentrate for making beef tea, his British handler's favorite drink.

By the time he arrived in England one cold April day in 1942, the mists surrounding his identity had cleared enough for British intelligence to realize that the man who had approached their Madrid and Lisbon embassies earlier was Arabel. He had been working in Lisbon for about nine months. When they discovered that U-boats were being dispatched to Gibraltar to ambush the supposed convoy, the worry he had caused them with his report of the convoy to Malta turned to delight. It was a first-class piece of disinformation that had caused the Germans to spend time and resources to no purpose.

And it was this piece of trickery that had persuaded the British to accept him. There would be no need to "turn" him; he had turned himself some time ago. Working alone, he had created a fully formed, beautifully packaged, even gift-wrapped double agent. All they had to do was smuggle him into England, where he had presumably been working for months, and where he already had a stable of imaginary agents using their eyes and ears on the Abwehr's behalf.

The newly minted Garbo was settled in Hendon, a typically middle-class area of north London. MI-5 even brought over the wife and child he had kept carefully under wraps. Then he began the career that to Masterman made him the spy's spy, the connoisseur's double agent, and the perfect illustration of certain aspects of the double-agent game: the skill of the case officer, and the efficiency with which every conceivable advantage could be extracted from it.[32]

Upgrading Arabel's information to the Abwehr was important. The Germans must never be allowed to suspect that he was a fraud, and in this regard, MI-5 was in a position to help. Tommy Harris, the case officer for Arabel/Garbo, was fluent in Spanish; he became his friend and alter ego, supported him, and provided just the right snippets of fact and detail to be inserted in invisible ink between the lines to make his reports juicy and wholly believable.[33] Together Harris and Pujol transformed Arabel into Garbo. He told the Abwehr that he had made contact with a formidable source. This fellow was well placed in the Ministry of Information, and had not the least idea that his information was being fed to the Nazis.

When MI-5 discovered that the Madrid and Lisbon Abwehr stations had noticed a marked improvement in Arabel's reports, it was decided to speed the good word along by wireless transmission rather than the cumbersome and slow method of sending them by courier to Portugal for mailing, a process that often took a week, and could be slower if no courier was available for Lisbon. Soon Garbo had located the perfect radio operator, a Spanish

Republican with a radio license who lived on a remote farm and had even kept his (illegal) radio.[34] And just as the Abwehr felt they were benefiting from Garbo's reports, MI-5 was learning a great deal about German concerns and weaknesses from the questions they asked of him.

From here, Garbo's fanciful contacts spread ever outward, his output became ever more exciting. In 1943, according to Masterman, he "went from strength to strength. . . . The one-man band in Lisbon developed into an orchestra that played an increasingly ambitious program. Garbo himself turned out to be something of a genius. He was the master of a facile and lurid style of writing; he showed great industry and ingenuity coupled with a passionate and quixotic zeal for his task. Throughout the year he worked on an average of six to eight hours a day, drafting secret letters, enciphering, composing cover texts, and planning for the future."[35] Late that year, the Twenty Committee also asked him to make some discreet inquiries of the Germans in regard to the warning from Artist about impending rocket attacks on London. It would not do to have him subjected to the life-threatening new miracle weapon. The responses were tepid and inconclusive; it seemed that the danger would not differ greatly from earlier bombing raids.

THE GRAND DECEPTION

Operation Overlord, as D-Day was code-named, was the single biggest operation of the war, and its huge scope made the need to keep it utterly secret immensely complex. Deceiving the Germans about the when and the where of this massive and much-anticipated undertaking would require excellent disinformation, delivered discreetly and with perfect timing. Every one of Garbo's other deceptions paled by comparison. His description of the extensive Chislehurst caves—their arms and vast underground communications—had taken on exaggerated importance because of the rich and colorful detail he had fed the Abwehr about them. But several other attempts to persuade the Germans of imminent attacks had elicited little interest, and it was clear that the respective armed services would have to play carefully coordinated roles to support the fictions generated by Garbo's fertile imagination.

By early 1944, there was no disguising the fact that Allied energies were being subsumed by planning for the attack. A massive deception was needed, and MI-5's double agents were mustered for the job. The crux of the problem was to persuade the enemy of a date later than the real date of attack, to cause the enemy to concentrate defenses as far as possible from the actual site of that attack, and, finally, to leave the enemy with the powerful suggestion that the assault was merely a diversionary prelude to a larger attack still to come. Keeping tight control was critical; the enemy must have complete faith in the double agent's word. A blunder on the part of any agent could endanger the entire operation.

The double agents to be used for what became known as Operation Fortitude were carefully assessed in terms of their credibility and valuation by the enemy. The Twenty Committee decided to narrow the use of agents to the Garbo and Tricycle networks, bolstered by several additional agents. They alone would be used to disseminate disinformation to the Abwehr about troops massing on England's south coast.[36] They were to convey the sense that the invasion could not be mounted before July, that there was to be an opening attack in Norway, and that after some diversions at other points the real assault would come at the narrowest point of the Channel, the Pas de Calais, a logical choice for providing air support.

There were, however, some problems. Ostro was still operating, and there was concern that his reports might accidentally hit upon the truth and so destroy the British program. The Twenty Committee's attempts to eliminate Ostro had failed and he remained a continual worry.[37] An additional anxiety came from an entirely unexpected quarter when Canaris was removed from the Abwehr in February 1944. The Abwehr, both its pro- and anti-Nazi stances, had been a known quantity, but now Allied intelligence was faced with a new and increasingly unfamiliar Abwehr, and one that was increasingly in flux.

Then Operation Fortitude was struck what could easily have become a mortal blow. At the turn of the year, Tricycle had again spent time in Portugal and had met with Artist. On his return to London, he reported that while Jebsen/Artist was being protected by the Abwehr, he lived in fear of the Gestapo. Hoping to establish his bona fides with the Allies, he had produced a list of Abwehr agents being run from Lisbon, and the name topping the list was Juan Pujol, a.k.a. Arabel, now Garbo. Tricycle trusted Artist completely and was convinced that he knew that he—Tricycle—was working for the British. He was certain that Artist was thoroughly anti-Nazi and anti-communist, and that he considered the war a lost cause. Tricycle's assessment was supported by several other British agents who had interviewed Artist, but all this did nothing to alleviate the problem. They were faced with a conundrum.

Taking no action against any of the agents on Artist's list would serve as implicit confirmation that these agents were in fact double agents being run by the British. Evacuating Artist would also compromise all the agents on the list. Leaving Artist in place might let him continue to supply them with useful information about rockets and other weapons, but he would be extremely vulnerable, and vulnerable he proved to be.

In early May, XX learned that Artist had been abducted and taken to Germany. An OSS report from Saint BD/001, dated April 30, 1945, related that "with regard to Jepson [sic], Brandes and Deussen were very jealous of the fact that Jepson was in touch . . . with one Poppof [*sic*] who was the best German S.I. man in Portugal and who had gone to England. Jepson was receiving such good information from Poppof that Brandes and Deussen wanted to get rid of him so that they might get the credit for Poppof's work . . . [and] arranged for Jepson to be overpowered in the Abwehr offices on Rua Buenos Aires and he was drugged, put in a box and taken to France and from there presumably he was taken to a German concentration camp."[38]

Pujol and West claim that Jebsen kept a date with Graham-Meingott in Lisbon on April 28, and cite a "debriefing" of Jebsen by SIS (presumably Graham-Meingott) at which Jebsen explained that the Abwehr's Abteilung III had concluded that Tricycle was *not* controlled by the British. Earlier, he reported, "the Allies provided poor material; Artist complained to Tricycle that he was not earning his keep; Tricycle then decided to collect material himself, and the result has been his last report—so good that Abteilung III is in entire agreement with the general staff that it is inconceivable that the British should have deliberately fed it. From Artist's point of view the outcome is complete triumph. . . . To crown it all, Artist has been awarded the *Kriegsverdienstkreuz*, War Service Cross, 1st Class."[39]

So in late April Jebsen/Artist had been awarded a medal, but was under arrest days later—if indeed it was an arrest. Masterman thought there were indications that it might have been simply a matter of Jebsen's financial dealings, but if Gestapo interrogations took their normal course, there was a very real likelihood that damaging information about XX would come out. Then the house of cards would fall in on itself, and Operation Overlord would be jeopardized. The Tricycle network was shut down, though this offered no relief from concern about Artist. The only hope was that he could hold out against his interrogators long enough for XX to pull off the grand deception.

Garbo and his "network" meanwhile kept supplying enough information to add sparkle to his reputation and believability, accurate enough to make him shine, but not quite accurate enough to endanger the truth of Overlord. This meant providing an accumulated miscellany of reports to fix a firm but erroneous idea of the awaited invasion in the German military mind. Throughout May, his by now numerous "agents" sent reports of troop movements, always routed to Madrid: The British 21st Army Group under Montgomery had been spotted, as had the First Army Group under Bradley; Eisenhower would certainly assign the Americans important tasks; shipping movements were reported on the Clyde.

Occasionally Arabel/Garbo would advise that the Abwehr discount a piece of information, or he would chastise one of his agents, saying that he "had displayed the ability of a simpleton. I am very disgusted with him, though I have not let him know this." Then he himself had seen "troops with the sign of a knight with a lance at Lewes." Next, he discounted the reports of another agent. His was a work in progress; there were bound to be mistakes, but, clearly, he recognized them. His reports were well received at the Abwehr, taken on faith, enhancing his reputation.[40]

It was all a game, if a deadly serious one. As the English spring moved toward summer, the pace accelerated. June 5 was the date set, but the weather was uncooperative, and it was pushed ahead a day. A longstanding plan to transmit an early warning to Madrid just before the actual hour, but too late to allow for any meaningful changes in German plans and positions, was not to be executed until the early morning hours of June 6. Garbo, Tommy Harris, and Charles Haines, in the guise of Garbo's agent Almura, gathered at Garbo's Hendon house for the great moment. Breathlessly, Haines turned on his radio. But Abwehr Madrid gave no response to his call signal. Repeated attempts to get through at quarter-hour intervals met only with static.

D-Day dawned with no sign that anything had been extorted from Jebsen/Artist by the Gestapo. Apparently, the Germans had not yet untangled the web of XX deception. Field Marshal Rommel had been given leave to go home to Ulm for his wife's birthday; his stand-in, Colonel General Friedrich Dollman, was holding war games. In view of the rough weather being predicted, General Hans Speidel had decided to give his men a little rest and reduced the state of troop preparedness.[41] At 8:00 A.M., when Madrid at last responded to Almura, thousands of ships, men, and aircraft were well on their way to the invasion of Normandy, but it was not yet time for XX and Arabel/Garbo to heave a sigh of relief. It was critical for his reputation that Madrid understand that he had tried desperately to contact them for hours before the Allied arrival on the Normandy beaches. Furthermore, this day's massive assault must be made to look like an overture, a diversion from the real military thrust that would surely come near the Pas de Calais. Every hour, every day that the Germans did not rush reinforcements to Normandy because of an even larger assault anticipated elsewhere increased the chances of victory.

All this was accomplished. Madrid was informed that Himmler himself had expressed appreciation for Arabel's reports and asked that further information be obtained on the intended destination of the troops located in southeastern England. Five days after D-Day, on June 11, Berlin informed Madrid that "all reports received in the last week from Arabel undertaking have been confirmed without exception and are to be described as especially valuable."[42] In fact, the Germans could see for themselves that all the units that landed in France were units that had been sighted and reported by Arabel. There were further reports of training exercises with landing craft; on June 17, an Arabel transmission informed Abwehr Madrid that his operatives had spotted training exercises with landing craft. On the twenty-eighth, came word that an American division, newly arrived in England with the insignia of "a serpent which the Americans call a rattlesnake," was engaged in maneuvers on the beaches at Felixstowe.[43] For some time, the American presence in England continued to grow, and the myth of the great assault on the Pas de Calais survived.

Not long after D-Day, on June 13, Hitler's first promised *Wunderwaffe*— the V-1 "buzz bomb" arrived, striking in London's East End, and producing relatively minor damage and casualties. Its unexpected arrival outraged Arabel, who was not shy about expressing this to his Abwehr handlers. He should have been informed, he insisted, should have been saved the embarrassment of hearing word of this from the enemy. The apologetic reply informed him that, unfortunately, only the crew essential to launching the rockets had been informed of the timing. Now would he please record the exact location and time of as many V-1 hits as he could and report details? The timing of each rocket launch was meticulously recorded; an exact account of time and place of landing would allow for sharpened aim, and presumably greater damage. Garbo/Arabel was suddenly in the awkward position of calling in enemy fire.

He managed to stall for a time. He had moved out of town, which caused some delay. Not only that, but he had been asked to work from a grid on a map of London published in Berlin in 1906. Locating a copy of this particular map with the requisite grid had been very time-consuming. (In fact, the map had to be borrowed from the British Museum.)[44] Then Arabel reported that he was using an agent to cover the area of London involved, which he had enlarged considerably. Agent "Benedict" had proved ineffective, so he proposed to take over the investigations himself. Almost immediately he was told to concentrate on the location and movement of troops and other matters having to do with the anticipated assault near the Pas de Calais.

Then Abwehr Madrid received shattering news: Benedict reported that Arabel had disappeared. Over the next days, panicky messages flew from the distraught Benedict to the Abwehr. Arabel had been arrested. Gradually the story emerged. In his zeal, Arabel had gone to the scene of a V-1 attack, asked questions of the locals, and made notes. His unusual curiosity had aroused the suspicions of a detective, Arabel had been arrested and detained for days. Again Arabel was outraged, and vented his anger to the Home Secretary, who responded with a lengthy apology, which Arabel forwarded to the Abwehr with evident satisfaction in his report after his release.

The tale of Arabel's arrest was the fabrication of case officer Tommy Harris, but it achieved its goal, giving everyone time to consider what to do about Arabel vis-à-vis the V-1 situation. Duly impressed by their faithful agent, the Abwehr suggested a period of complete inactivity on his part, for the sake of security. It was a perfect opportunity for a short vacation, long overdue and much needed, for both Arabel/Garbo and Harris.

Madrid sent congratulations: The Führer had awarded Arabel the Iron Cross, normally awarded only for frontline fighters, but by sleight of hand he would receive it as part of Franco's Blue Division. Over the summer and fall of 1944, Arabel picked up his network again and continued to report. Just before Christmas, the British, not to be outdone, presented Garbo and Tommy Harris the MBE—Member of the Order of the British Empire—in recognition of their extraordinary services.

As the year wound down, there were signs that the network was unraveling. Some of Arabel's agents were restless, there was talk of breaking off, moving on. For all intents and purposes the war was over. But it was not until early May that Arabel himself contacted Madrid and asked that compromising files be destroyed, and affirmed his conviction "that our struggle will not terminate" and that a world civil war will result in the disintegration of our enemies."[45] On May 7, 1945, he and Harris—and all of "Garbo"—joined in the victory celebrations erupting all over England. The war was over.

THE LURE AND LUCRE OF NEUTRALITY

Early in the war, Germany's insatiable appetite for critical raw materials— Swedish ores, Turkish chromium, Spanish and Portuguese wolfram—had been satisfied by payment in Reichsmarks. But as Germany's military fortunes sagged, the Reichsmark lost its appeal in countries supplying these precious resources and the demands on Germany's skimpy foreign currency reserves became unsustainable. Under growing pressure from the Allies, these transactions began to be concluded on a cash-and-carry basis, preferably one that afforded the neutrals a way of distancing themselves from their Nazi trading partners, and eventually on a gold-only basis.

Salazar had brought wolfram under state control in 1942, set the price, and, in the interest of fairness, instituted allocation quotas for the purpose of equalizing deliveries to Axis and Allies. Still, moral pronouncements, ancient alliances, and Allied concerns notwithstanding, Portugal had become the beneficiary of the rising demand for wolfram. Salazar, in addition to being an economist and a realist, was also a masterful negotiator, a practiced footdragger and fence-sitter. Aiming to offend no one and gain from everyone, he adroitly pitted Allied and Axis powers against one another for Portugal's gain.

The temptations of serious pecuniary gain were too great for him to resist. He told his countrymen in a radio broadcast that, "in a word, the desire for neutrality cannot be superior to the interest of the nation."[46] He had come up with an ingenious solution to the problem of keeping both Germany and Britain placated while strengthening his economy. He would use Portugal's neutrality in an entirely new and unorthodox way. Neutrality would be her primary resource, and he would play the antagonists against one another in a carefully calibrated balancing act, enhanced by legalistic hairsplitting. His earlier ethical concerns had simply melted in the economic warmth generated by Nazi gold.

Portugal was used to being a poor country. But now, by exporting wolfram at its hugely inflated price, and by receiving Nazi gold looted from occupied countries in payment, things were changing. The German ambassador to Portugal informed Berlin that the price of Portuguese raw materials, wolfram among them, was going up.[47] With some financial prestidigitation that amounted to money laundering to satisfy legal concerns, Germany, the Banco National de Portugal, the Bank for International Settlements in Basel, and the Schweizerische Nationalbank colluded to circumvent Allied injunctions and enrich themselves at the cost of Austria, Czechoslovakia, Belgium, Holland, and Norway, whose gold reserves had been seized when they were overrun by the Nazis.[48]

The Allies, of course, were well aware not only of the gold's provenance, but also of its ultimate destination. But with an eye to the postwar future, they were loath to irritate Salazar and endanger trade relations and British holdings in Portugal. Except for the occasional protest, the gold shipments went unchallenged until early 1943. That year, the British invoked the spirit of the Treaty of Windsor and requested Portugal's permission for Allied bases on the Azores. British forces arrived in October, and the Americans soon followed.

Churchill had made every effort to be conciliatory on the wolfram issue to avoid annoying Salazar and fraying the British-Portuguese alliance. But by 1944, even he complained that Salazar was "sending raw materials to Germany to make munitions to kill our men."[49] In May the British ambassador, Sir Ronald Campbell, issued a "solemn and earnest appeal" to Portugal for a "total prohibition to the export of wolfram to the enemies of His Britannic Majesty," in the interest of shortening the war.[50] Having successfully stalled Allied demands for months, Salazar finally conceded on June 6, 1944, but the big moment was eclipsed by the excitement over D-Day.

Still, somewhat diminished and more clandestine, the wolfram trade continued. In October, OSS Lisbon noted that Schellenberg had been informed by the PVDE—the Policia de Vigilancia e Defesa do Estado—that "Salazar was finding Anglo-American pressure for rupture of Portuguese-Japanese relations rapidly mounting," and also "expected pressure for a break with Germany."[51] This he hoped to deal with on the basis of his long-standing personal relationship with the German ambassador. The Allies, the note concluded, hoped to influence Spanish policy through Portuguese diplomatic moves against Japan and Germany.[52] Another OSS report mentions a twenty-seven-ton shipment stopped by the PVDE in July, and other accounts mention submarines loaded with wolfram as late as 1945.[53]

So, in the end, Germany had paid with looted gold. The figures speak volumes. In 1939, Portugal's gold reserves totaled just over 63 tons. By late October 1945, they had swelled nearly 600 percent to a staggering 365.5 tons.[54] For Salazar this represented a foundation for putting Portugal on a solid financial footing, a feat for which he was later consistently celebrated.

The Allies, meanwhile, had paid dearly for their wolfram. In three years of wrangling with Salazar over the price, they had doled out $170,000,000 for ore that in other circumstances would have cost $155,000,000 less.[55] Portugal had definitely won the wolfram wars. Nonetheless, when those wars were over, a popular Portuguese satirical review lamented:

A vida actual manda peso
E hoja o volframio acabou-se!

Our present life weighs heavily,
And now the wolfram's gone too![56]

SWEDEN AND SKF

Sweden was Germany's most significant trading partner during the war, delivering iron and copper ores, and high-grade ball bearings from SKF, Svenske Kullagerfabriken. SKF's most important subsidiary was in Germany, and there were others in the United States and England.[57] Ball bearings played a large part in neutral Sweden's wartime economy. Without them, the machinery of war could not function; the panzers could not roll, the Luftwaffe could not fly. Thanks to an OSS agent's report on SKF deliveries to Germany, the Allies were able to pressure Sweden into an agreement whereby in return for continued "basic rations" which the Allies had been supplying since the war began, Sweden would limit further exports to hostile or occupied countries, refuse additional credit to Germany and occupied countries, reduce shipments of ores, deny sales of arms and munitions, and not reexport U.S. oil shipped to fuel Sweden to fill the tanks of German military aircraft.[58]

Had the Swedes, and others, adhered to it, this agreement might have had an impact, but profits were a powerful lure. Ore exports to Germany actually increased, and after an October 1943 bombing run inflicted heavy losses on SKF's German factory in Schweinfurt, Sweden's ball bearing shipments to Germany were increased significantly. Technically, the British Ministry of Warfare was responsible for enforcing the restrictions on Swedish shipments, but Britain's war machine was as dependent on SKF and its ball bearings as was Germany's, and enforcement had been slack.[59] There was a quid pro quo, and trying to alter it proved difficult.

There were negotiations, then unpleasantness, when Sweden threatened to embarrass the Allies by revealing the earlier agreements. American public opinion was being influenced by a deeply negative article in *PM*, charging SKF with collaboration and malfeasance.[60] It was not until April 1944 that the U.S. State Department decided to try to buy off SKF's bank, the Wallenberg family's Enskilda Bank, which also happened to be the Reichsbank's correspondent bank. In mid-1944, the Reichsbank concluded a deal to sell gold—most likely looted—to Sweden's Notenbank. After tiresome negotiations, it was at last agreed that the United States would pay Enskilda $8 million, SKF could retain its German properties, and Swedish-Nazi ties with the United States would be conveniently forgotten. But the millions were not enough to buy anyone off, and in early 1945 the ball bearings, rather than going directly to Germany, were routed through Portugal or Spain and Switzerland.[61] For the United States, voicing angry protest at this point would have been impolitic, and would only have brought unwanted publicity to a history of unsavory deals.

Dean Acheson, then serving as the assistant secretary of state, had a privileged view of the neutrals' dealings with the Nazis during that period and observed that "if the Swedes were stubborn, the Swiss were the cube of stubbornness."[62]

THE GOLD BUSINESS

"Will you keep a story on this gold business," a certain R. R. Schwarz of the American embassy in Bern wrote to a colleague in late April 1945. "I think it's going to blow up one of these days."[63] In retrospect, this laconic remark falls easily into the category of understatement. Between September 1, 1939, and June 30, 1945, German transactions in gold amounted to nearly $890 million. This is a staggering amount, particularly in view of the fact that, in 1933, German gold reserves had stood at a mere $109 million, and had been heavily drawn down to support Hitler's rearmament program intended to build the New Order.[64] The gold business certainly did blow up; where the gold came from, and how it moved through the banking and currency maze of the period, made for an extraordinary story, parts of which still have no satisfactory ending.

Germany's need for raw materials to feed the rearmament program, coupled with the inability to export machine goods because of German industry's focus on rearmament, had created a growing imbalance of trade. By the time war broke out in 1939, Germany's gold reserves dollars had shrunk to a meager $28.6 million. Reichsbank president Schacht also held nearly $83 million in currency in off-budget reserves, but when the United States halted trade in the dollar in mid-1941, gold or the Swiss franc became the only acceptable forms of payment. German reserves dwindled alarmingly.[65] The massive Russian campaign had made the German need for raw materials nearly bottomless. Few payment options existed.

Germany was in desperate need of an infusion of gold, which came when the takeover of Austria and Czechoslovakia, and the occupation of Belgium, the Netherlands, and Norway brought the Nazis an influx of resources, gold looted from the central banks of the occupied countries. The Belgian holdings alone brought the Reich 198 tons.[66] That was where the gold came from, but where did it go?

In following the money—in this case the gold—all roads lead inevitably to Switzerland, the principal gear that kept the money flowing throughout the war. Initially, Portugal shipped wolfram; the Reichsbank shipped gold. The BIS received its first delivery of gold from the Reichsbank in January 1940, with more following in later months. In late October 1941, BIS sent the first of several gold transports to Portugal, eventually totaling almost twenty tons by January 1942.[67] This arrangement, however, was perilous, and security and insurance (through Swiss insurance companies) were expensive. By early 1942, the Allies had begun to put pressure on Portugal not to accept gold from the Reichsbank and on the BIS to stop the gold traffic.

This was an occasion for creative thinking. Both the Portuguese and the Swiss pondered the possibilities for keeping the Allies pacified while still dealing in gold, never mind its origins. Then one high official at Swiss National Bank (SNB) hit on an ingenious solution. He suggested that "if the money were to pass through our hands," Portuguese nerves would be calmed, and there would be money in it for all players. "We should think about that option."[68]

The mechanism was simple and straightforward. The dirty business was eventually accomplished without anything actually moving physically. The Reichsbank sold gold to commercial Swiss banks in exchange for Swiss francs, which were then deposited in an account of the Banco de Portugal at SNB. The Banco de Portugal then used these Swiss francs to buy gold from SNB. There were transactional costs, but they benefited SNB; the thorny legal issues were circumvented, and the cost of insuring risky gold transports had been eliminated.[69]

The gold transactions between the Reichsbank and Switzerland from September 1, 1939, to June 30, 1945, came to a grand total of almost $900 million, which would translate into considerably more in today's dollars. Switzerland was without a doubt the "principal foreign market for the large quantities of foreign gold which Germany spent in financing her war. . . ."[70] At every point of the transactions; some of the gold rubbed off on the banks involved. Nearly, $388 million went to SNB, more than $56 million to the Schweizer Geschäftsbank. The rest, more than half, went to one of the main cogs in the wheel, the Bank for International Settlements.[71] As the American director of the BIS, Thomas McKittrick, later president of Chase National Bank, put it: "We keep the machine ticking because when armistice comes, the formerly hostile powers will need an efficient instrument such as the

BIS."[72] Keeping the machine ticking, by essentially laundering gold, had been very good for BIS's bottom line.

ON APRIL 13, 2005, A FEDERAL JUDGE IN BROOKLYN, N.Y., APPROVED AN AWARD OF $21.8 million to the survivors of two Austrian families who had come to Switzerland in March 1938 just before Hitler's Anschluss. The Bloch-Bauer and Pick families had no illusions about what lay ahead, and since Swiss banks had always marketed themselves as a true safe haven, they intended to tie up their ownership of Austria's biggest sugar refineries in a trust for safety's sake. Within months, the terms of the account had been violated; the business was "aryanized," and sold to a Nazi sympathizer for far less than its worth. In December 1938, the bank explained to the families that "the situation has changed."[73] Clearly, gold was not the only entity that generated profits for the Swiss. The faith of desperate depositors in the safety and integrity of Swiss banks was routinely betrayed.

The French writer and diplomat François-Auguste-Réné de Chateaubriand had been dead nearly a century by the time World War II ended, but his commentary on Switzerland still applied: "The Swiss, neutral during the great revolutions in the countries surrounding them, have enriched themselves on the destitution of others and founded a bank on the misfortune of nations."

TRADING WITH THE ENEMY

By order of the president, trading with the enemy was forbidden during the war. However, a general license was granted "licensing any transaction or act proscribed by . . . the Trading with the Enemy Act . . . provided [such transaction] is authorized by the Secretary of the Treasury."[74] And proscriptions or no, where there was money to be made, many American businesses found numerous ways to make it. By helping to fuel the beast of the Nazi war machine, they fattened not only their own coffers, but also those of their trading partners and the banks that made the transactions possible.

Recently declassified documents from the National Archives in Washington document the collaboration of U.S. companies with Hitler's Germany. They tell a complex story that may be contrary to public expectation: Large American businesses with household names did not automatically rally behind the national mission to win the war. If profits were involved, the overriding concern was to ensure business as usual with minimal wartime disruption of the existing big-money alliances. We have already looked at some of Standard Oil's activities, but there were many other companies working toward the same ends, if not quite on the same scale.

What the War Economics Board discovered in the course of its investigations was a web of corporate affiliations, patent agreements, and personal and business links that spanned the Atlantic in innumerable ways. It was an extraordinary old boys' network of industrial leaders and lawyers. Many of them had gone to school together; they sat on each others' boards, and on government advisory and investigative committees. The result was that these committees were made up of people with financial interests in the very companies and cartels from which they were presumably guarding the United States, such as I. G. Farben.

The long-term collaboration between I.G and Standard Oil resulted in a huge jump in Germany's synthetic oil and gas production. By 1944, 85 percent of Germany's synthetic fuel was created using Standard Oil's hydrogenation process, and I. G. Farben, either directly or through affiliates, had a virtual monopoly. This was not the only way in which Standard Oil helped.

An internal memorandum from an I.G. Farben official, August von Knieriem, under a date of June 1944, put into evidence at the Nuremberg trial stated:

> As a consequence of our contracts with the Americans, we received from them, above and beyond the agreement, many very valuable contributions for the synthesis and improvement of motor fuels and lubricating oils, which just now during the war are most useful to us; and we also received other advantages. . . . Without tetraethyl-lead the present method of warfare would be impossible. The fact that since the beginning of the war we could produce tetraethyl-lead is [because] . . . the Americans had presented us with the production plans, complete with their know-how. It was, moreover, the first time that the Americans decided to [license] . . . process in a foreign country . . . and this only on our urgent requests to Standard Oil. . . . Contractually we could not demand it, and we found out later that the War Department in Washington gave its permission only after long deliberation.
>
> In the field of lubricating oils Germany, through the contract with America, learned of experience which is extraordinarily important for present day warfare . . . [and] obtained not only the experience of Standard, but, through Standard, the experience of General Motors and other large American motor companies as well.
>
> As a further example of the [advantages of the contract between I.G. and Standard Oil] . . . [in] 1934–1935, our government had [a great interest] in gathering from abroad [a stock of valuable oil products to hold in reserve] to an amount of [roughly] 20 million dollars at market value. The German Government asked IG . . . on the basis of its friendly relations with Standard Oil, to buy this amount in Farben's name, [but actually] as trustee of the German Government. The fact that we . . . succeeded [after] the most difficult negotiations . . . in buying the quantity desired by our government . . . [from Standard Oil and Dutch-English Royal-Dutch-Shell] and in transporting it to Germany, was . . . possible only through the aid of the Standard Oil Co."[75]

When American GIs marched through the ruins of Frankfurt am Main in March 1945, they were met at Frankfurt's unscathed I. G. Farben plant by one of its directors, Georg von Schnitzler. "Gentlemen," Schnitzler said in welcome, "it's a pleasure to be working with you again."[76]

THERE WERE OTHER BIG CORPORATE PLAYERS IN THE FIELD, DUPONT, RCA, GAF, TEXACO, and ITT among them. ITT was the brainchild of Sosthenes Behn. Born in the Virgin Islands to a Danish father and a French-Italian mother, he became an American citizen and during World War I spent time in the U.S. Army Signal Corps. In the 1930s, ITT become a significant force in the communications business.[77] In fact, Behn, the perfectly politicized entrepreneur, became the communications czar of an entire era, with connections everywhere to the rich, the well connected, and the fascist. His multinational networks stretched across Europe, from Spain and Romania to Hungary, Germany, and Sweden—even to South America.

Through the banker Kurt von Schröder, Behn was connected to all the Nazi chieftains and so had privileged entrée to the lucrative Nazi rearmament industries. Behn helped Hitler improve his communications systems, and just before the invasion of Poland, ITT took a significant holding in Focke-Wolfe A.G. of Bremen, a major producer of military aircraft, holdings that were increased and maintained during the war. After 1933, Schröder sat on the board of directors of the Bank for International Settlements, another vital connection. Both in occupied Europe and in Germany, with Schröder's and Himmler's protection, Behn maintained his operations throughout the war. The licenses required by the Trading with the Enemy Act to permit these activities were not forthcoming from Morgenthau's Treasury Department, but that did not stand in his way. After Pearl Harbor, ITT supplied various kinds of communications equipment as well as the fuses—as many as 30,000 a month, used in artillery shells. In late February 1942, a memorandum addressed to Assistant Secretary of State Breckinridge Long from his assistant, R. T. Yingling, stated:

It seems that the International Telephone and Telegraph Corporation which has been handling traffic between Latin American countries and Axis controlled points with the encouragement of the Department desires some assurance that it will not be prosecuted for such activities. It has been suggested that the matter be discussed informally with the Attorney General and if he agrees the Corporation can be advised that no prosecution is contemplated."[78]

The villain of Edwin Black's *IBM and the Holocaust* is IBM's punch card. Since IBM had always billed itself as a "solutions" company, Black decided that he would examine their role in the Final Solution.[79] IBM's German subsidiary, Dehomag (Deutsche Hollerith Maschinen Gesellschaft), produced Hollerith machines, which produced punch cards. The Nazi drive for efficiency was surely a factor in the contract between Speer's Reich Ministry for Armaments and Munitions and IBM in August 1942, and after that date, the Hollerith machines played a bigger role in keeping tabs on the war machine's workforce and production.[80]

Oddly, though, punch cards were not used to tabulate the compulsory national registration system instituted in 1938 and still extant in Germany today. Here the authorities resorted to compiling and cross-indexing cards by hand, a task requiring many minor bureaucrats to hunch over desks for many hours. On December 11, 1941, one such functionary stood on the platform at the Düsseldorf-Derendorf station, categorizing the 1,007 Jews deported that day by age, gender, and profession, painstakingly marking sheets by hand.[81] It was not until mid-1944 that the work of such busy hands was replaced by Hollerith cards at concentration camps.[82] The Nazis had clearly been quite capable of orchestrating the Holocaust without them.

AS AN INTEGRAL PART OF AN INTERNATIONAL BUSINESS FRATERNITY IN WHICH MONEY was at least as big a common cause as the war, Gerhard Westrick acted as intermediary and facilitator in many German-American business deals during the 1930s and 1940s. A capable and apparently ubiquitous lawyer, Westrick has been characterized as the German equivalent of John Foster Dulles. He was instrumental in helping Ford, General Motors, ITT, and Standard Oil work out their arrangements with the Nazis and join in on the gainful game, and he had at least one finger in many profitable business pies. ITT was probably the biggest of them, and Westrick directed ITT operations in Germany. He was also involved with Texaco and Eastman Kodak.[83]

Kodak is a more recent addition to the list of companies trading with the enemy. While the Rochester headquarters may not have been controlling its German operations directly during the war, Spanish, Portuguese, and Swiss subsidiaries made sizable purchases from Germany, from occupied France and from Hungary, then a German ally, for transactions amounting to nearly 370,000 Swiss francs. This is hardly a major sum. It pales beside the sums other industries were involved with, but it did provide markets and currency. More important, the transactions serve to illustrate conflicting attitudes vis-à-vis trading with the enemy and the problems of trying to put the world into enemy and nonenemy compartments.

Willard Beaulac, chargé d'affaires at the American embassy in Madrid, recommended to the secretary of state that Kodak be allowed "an appropriate license" for its Spanish subsidiary to import films, chemicals, spools, and other supplies from Germany to let Kodak preserve its market position.[84] "Shutting off of German sources of supply" would serve no useful purpose, he argued; it would simply deliver business to German and other competitors and make it more difficult for Kodak to recapture market share after the war. Keeping the Kodak brand alive was crucial; Britain's Trading with the Enemy Department agreed.

Kodak transferred its German operations to several German board members in 1941, among them lawyer Gerhard Westrick. Wilhelm Keppler, Hitler's economic advisor, was considered "a Kodak Man"; he offered helpful advice on eliminating Jewish employees. Kodak used slave labor in Germany, and as the company began to manufacture triggers, detonators, and other military hardware, both the number of employees and revenues increased. "Business doing well," Rochester was informed by cable in late 1942.[85] When the war was over, the brand had been protected, and business could pick up where it had left off.

PROJECT SAFEHAVEN

By mid-May 1944, Washington saw an end to the war approaching, and a handful of policy people at the Federal Economic Administration (FEA) set to work devising a program to find and block German assets in neutral or nonbelligerent countries. Project Safehaven was designed to guarantee that such assets could not be sequestered outside the Reich to serve as seed money for future industrial power or as a springboard to renewed military might. There was not to be another war, at least not one started by Germany; these funds were to be available for rebuilding a shattered Europe. It was also intended to prevent the escape of Nazis identified as war criminals, who were to be held for trial. Safehaven turned out to be one of those good ideas that is devilishly hard to put into practice.

That summer, the FEA's Sam Klaus, one of Safehaven's architects, set off on a fact-finding mission in the company of a State Department official. To Klaus's irritation, the Department of the Treasury, bruised at being excluded, traipsed along behind. This was not the first instance of domestic departmental rivalries complicating matters, and it was far from the last. U.S. embassies had been instructed to take steps to implement the Safehaven goals, but Klaus felt that they were not devoting sufficient energies to the program. He reported his dissatisfaction with progress to date, commenting that Spain, "beyond question the country in which the most damaging Safehaven activities are going on," was the most egregious instance of obstructionism.[86] Neither State nor Treasury wanted to hear it.

They were engaged in a bureaucratic and political struggle over control of Safehaven that reflected their respective attitudes on postwar policy toward Germany. State envisioned a strong but peaceful German presence that would ensure European stability. Treasury, under Morgenthau, wanted a humbled agrarian state with no military or industrial power. Both saw Safehaven as a means for promoting these differing agendas.

Safehaven was essentially a job for intelligence. In fact OSS had already been collecting intelligence on Germany's war economy for two years, but it was late 1944 before OSS participation in Safehaven was formalized. In December 1944, Dulles, already overworked, argued:

> "Work on this project . . . might defeat direct intelligence activities and close important channels . . . Today we must fish in troubled waters. . . . To deal effectively . . . would require special staff with new cover. . . . At present we do not have adequate personnel to [be] effective in this field and meet other demands."[87]

At this point activity was limited to neutral countries and countries already under Allied control. By early 1945 an OSS X-2 operation had joined Dulles in Bern. William Casey was also eager to launch a venture from London using OSS resources for researches in Belgium, Holland, and France. Attention naturally turned to Germany's dealings in gold and so, inevitably, to Switzerland. Sweden and Spain and Portugal and their various and extensive forms of collaboration in Germany's war were also documented. Washington was being fed regular reports on Swiss gold deals, on secret Swiss bank accounts, and Reichsbank monies in Switzerland. Dulles himself was too busy with other matters.

In the spring of 1945, the State Department issued a warning to neutral governments: They were not to trade with the Nazis. The OSS stepped up its operations in response to a memo calling for a "substantial contribution" to Safehaven, and in fact created a special unit charged with collecting and analyzing all reported Safehaven activities.[88] When the war ended, funding quickly dried up. Intelligence nets were reassigned, though a small operation—Project Jetsam—remained. The focus now moved to the recovery of assets looted by the Nazis, aimed primarily at the Swiss, the principal beneficiaries of Nazi loot. Switzerland claimed dependency on Allied support and aid in rebuilding their economy. In light of this, Allied negotiations involved considerable arm-twisting, but they bumped against obstructionism, earnest assertions that consistently contradicted all available reports, and footdragging. In the end, Switzerland made only token restitution.

CHAPTER 9

ARMAGEDDON AND BEYOND

The July 20 coup attempt was the last desperate act of an ill-fated opposition to Hitler. For some, the years of opposition went back to before Hitler came to power; others had come to resistance more recently. What made this resistance different from those outside the walls of the great prison that Nazi Germany had become is that it received neither help nor encouragement from any of the Allies, and had to be carried on under nearly paralyzing conditions. The story has been told innumerable times; its sheer drama is understood by millions. But the pathos has never penetrated. It is easy to fault the plotters' plans, the lack of resolve, the individual weaknesses that contributed to its failure. What is lost is recognition of the plotters' raw courage in acting as they did, in defense of principle, knowing that they would face posterity reviled as traitors.

The Allied response was a barely concealed sneer and open gratification at the bloodbath that followed the coup's failure. Perhaps the reaction is understandable in context, but it only hardened an already unyielding policy. And the war raged on for nearly a year, at inestimable cost.

THE BREAKERS: JULY 20, 1944

As the summer days ticked by, Dulles provided detailed information gleaned from the Breakers—probably Gisevius—and other sources on the potent V-2 rockets.[1] On July 12, he reported that "a dramatic event may take place up north." Next day, he indicated that Soviet victories and the Allied invasion of Normandy had given the Breakers new vigor. The opposition generals were now concentrated in the Berlin area.[2] He also recommended suggesting that unconditional surrender apply to Nazis and the war machine, but not to the people. On the fifteenth, he noted that the Breakers were eager to keep as much of Germany and Central Europe as possible out of the Russian grasp and urged a presidential announcement to encourage the anti-Nazi groups and counter Goebbels's line about the Allied demand for complete annihilation.[3]

It would have been no great leap in mid-1944 for FDR to realize that a post-Hitler regime would want to negotiate, and that insisting on unconditional surrender to his own war-weary nation would be difficult. Churchill, too, might look favorably on a new Germany to serve as a roadblock between England and the Soviets. In fact, Roosevelt had been hearing about the resistance in Germany for some time, but he remained opposed to offering them any support.

Edwin "Ned" Putzell, a close and trusted Donovan aide, was privy to much that passed between his boss and the president. In an interview in late 2003, he suggested several possible reasons for the president's reluctance: FDR was unwilling to meddle in domestic German politics; assassination was a violation of "the rules," and might endanger both his life and Churchill's; and, finally, he did not want to support the "vons," who were so heavily represented in the opposition. American boys were fighting and dying for democracy, not aristocracy.[4] Of the three, the latter seems the most reasonable explanation. He had been unwilling to "deal with the Junkers" for some time. But whatever factors were weighed in Roosevelt's deliberations, his response was the usual silence.

On July 18, Dulles signaled that the "last opportunity . . . to prove the desire of the German people to overthrow Hitler" was at hand.[5] Since Tresckow's Operation Flash in February 1943, there had been a total of eight attempts to assassinate Hitler. Now the revised version of Operation Valkyrie was about to be launched.

What lay behind the final, fatal plot against Hitler was the awareness among the conspirators that success or failure was no longer paramount. General Beck had been fighting Hitler for years and realized that he had lost. He was no longer concerned with national aims. The decisive question was not what would become of individuals or of Germany; his concern now was on a higher plane. What had to be addressed was "the unbearable reality that for years and years crimes after crimes murders upon murders multiplied in the name of Germany . . . it is our moral duty to put an end . . . to those crimes committed in the usurped name of our nation."[6]

. . .

AS THE ONLY PLOT KNOWN TO A WIDE AUDIENCE, THE STAUFFENBERG PLOT OF JULY 20, 1944, has become standard television fare. Summoned to Führer headquarters, the Wolfsschanze at Rastenburg, Colonel Claus von Stauffenberg, the handsome if maimed veteran of the North African campaign, is on his way to the airfield by 7:00 A.M. His aide, Lieutenant Werner von Haeften, will meet him there. Stauffenberg is scheduled to brief Hitler at 1:00 P.M. on the Replacement Army, two divisions newly formed on Hitler's orders to keep the advancing Red Army at bay. At the conclusion of some earlier meetings, Stauffenberg suddenly finds that he is pressed for time. Mussolini is expected to meet with Hitler that afternoon, and Stauffenberg's briefing has been moved up.

This is not Stauffenberg's first attempt at eliminating Hitler. Ten days earlier, at Berchtesgaden, a plan to kill Hitler, Himmler, and Göring was aborted because only Hitler was present. Within the last week another attempt failed when Hitler did not appear. Even the steady Beck has expressed some doubts about the chances for success, but Stauffenberg is determined.

On his way to "freshen up" before his briefing, Stauffenberg and Haeften go into a meeting room to hurriedly, surreptitiously, rearrange the contents of two briefcases—one containing the papers for the briefing, the other containing two bombs. A young officer opens the door of the room, asks Stauffenberg to hurry, then waits by the open door. There is not enough time now to arm both bombs and get them into Stauffenberg's briefcase. Stauffenberg has lost an eye, an arm, and two fingers of his remaining hand in Africa. He manages to arm only one of the bombs and presses the fuse's acid capsule with pliers adapted to accommodate his crippled hand. The other bomb goes back into Haeften's briefcase.

The day is hot, the proceedings have been moved from the usual underground bunker to a hut with open windows, which will lessen the intensity of the explosion. Stauffenberg is late. Officers are already crowded around the massive table covered with maps and papers where the Führer is being briefed on the eastern front. Stauffenberg asks to be placed near Hitler; his hearing had been affected by his injuries in North Africa and he must hear everything for his subsequent briefing. He has a moment of worry that in the heat, the fuse might act more quickly.[7] Then he is introduced and space is cleared for him to Hitler's right. He deposits the briefcase on the floor as close to Hitler as possible without interfering with the many adjacent feet. After a few moments, he is called to the telephone, excuses himself, and steps out of the briefing room.

There is a massive explosion, fire, smoke, and confusion. Stauffenberg is confident that Hitler is dead, but he is mistaken. The open hut reduced the bomb's effect drastically, and, inadvertently, the briefcase had been moved behind a massive table support, shielding Hitler. Hitler had been spared again, as if by a miracle. Stauffenberg and Haeften rush back to the airfield, jettisoning the second, unexploded bomb en route.

In Berlin, the conspirators gathered in General Olbricht's office in the Bendlerstrasse are tense. They wait to hear from General Erich Fellgiebel in Rastenburg that Hitler is dead. At last, at about 3:30, Haeften calls to say they are back in Berlin; Hitler is dead. Berlin must now take the initiative. General Friedrich Fromm is to alert the Replacement Army to move, but he vacillates. He not convinced that Hitler is dead; there is his loyalty oath to consider. Fromm telephones Rastenburg and is told that the Führer has been wounded. Stauffenberg, now arrived at the Bendlerstrasse, insists that he himself saw Hitler's body carried out of the hut on a stretcher. Still Fromm hesitates.

What follows is muddled communications, doubts, differences of opinion, a plea for firmness from Beck. Fromm, under protest, is arrested. Orders go out to commandeer strategic points and arrest all SS, but some regional officers question the Valkyrie order. Is it legitimate, or is this a putsch? In Paris the conspiracy under General Otto von Stülpnagel and Schulenburg is in full swing. In Vienna the army moves to take over the SS and SD apparatus.

But is Hitler really dead? Some officers not privy to the conspiracy are unwilling to follow a new regime. Nerves and uncertainty set in. Communications with Rastenburg were not cut as intended, and it becomes clear that Hitler is alive. The momentum shifts. The conspirators are hopelessly compromised; Beck pleads for resolve, but there is wavering. District military leaders who were to commandeer the radio station and arrest SS do not. There is a radio announcement that Hitler is alive. Witzleben, the new commander in chief, arrives from Zossen to meet with Beck, growling: "A fine mess, this."[8]

Olbricht's plan, converted from its original intent—protecting the Reich from insurgents for use against the Reich—has been turned again. Now it is being used against the conspirators. The forces on the march to the Bendlerstrasse will not protect the new regime, but support the old one. The plot seems doomed. Only a few conspirators maintain the steady energy and courage of Stauffenberg and the group around him. There is no lack of resolve among SS troops, however. By 9:00 P.M., Berlin is under Nazi control. The forced "suicide" of Beck, the midnight march of Stauffenberg and his compatriots under guard to the courtyard to be summarily shot, the subsequent Gestapo roundups—all are amply chronicled.

All that was left was for Dulles to report that the "Breakers are breaking." And when it was clear that the plot had failed, he informed Washington that, "of course, the blood purge will be ruthless."[9] As Dulles had predicted, so it was. How many were executed in the aftermath of the failed plot is hard to determine. Numbers cited range from 200 to 5,000—a range accounted for by the fact that some scholars tally only the number of conspirators directly involved in the final plot, while others concede that Hitler's vengeance cut a much broader swath.[10]

THE REACTIONS OF THE CONSPIRATORS WERE AS VARIED AS THE CONSPIRATORS THEMselves. On July 20 Canaris took a telephone call at home. The Wolfsschanze had been bombed and Hitler was dead. Whoever placed the call was taking a huge risk; Canaris's telephone was certainly being tapped. On hearing the news the wily admiral reportedly asked, "Dead? Good God! Who did it? The Russians?"[11] He knew, of course, that if the plot had failed, he would soon be under arrest. He was, on July 23.

On the morning of July 21, Henning von Tresckow told Schlabrendorff: "Now the entire world will assail us and revile us. But I am . . . convinced that we acted properly. I consider Hitler to be not only the archenemy of Germany but . . . of the world. In a few hours when I stand before God's judgment . . . I think I will be able to stand by all I have done in the struggle against Hitler with a clear conscience. . . . No one among us can complain of his death. Whoever joined our ranks put on the poisoned shirt of Nessus. A man's moral worth is established only at the point where he is prepared to give his life for his convictions."[12] Then he walked over a low rise in the Russian landscape and blew himself up with a hand grenade.

In Berlin, Ulrich von Hassell walked openly through the streets, maintaining his familiar routines, simply waiting to be picked up. He continued his regular daily rides in the Tiergarten and received the Gestapo officers who had come to arrest him in his office. Peter Yorck von Wartenburg was arrested, but managed to communicate before he died that, as far as he knew, the Kreisau Circle had not yet been implicated. The first batch of conspirators—Yorck, Witzleben, Hoepner, Stieff, and others—were tried and executed on August 8. Adam von Trott was arrested and tortured, but was held in hopes that he would reveal more information under more torture. He was executed on January 5, 1945.

It was several weeks before Dulles learned that Gisevius was alive and hiding in Berlin. In fact, Gisevius reported that while the coup had failed, conditions in Germany were very unstable. If the Allies would only "strike hard . . . the entire German structure will collapse."[13] But months went by without further word, so Dulles concluded that Gisevius must have been caught and executed. In his later account of the German opposition, Dulles permitted himself a fairly discreet expression of frustration. "Both London and Washington were fully advised beforehand on all the conspirators were attempting to do," he wrote, "but it sometimes seemed that those who determined policy in America and England were making the military task as difficult as possible by uniting all Germans to resist to the bitter end."[14]

Schlabrendorff was arrested, tortured, and finally brought to trial in the severely overburdened People's Court on a February day in 1945 when air raid sirens again sounded over Berlin. The court took a direct hit, and Judge Roland Freisler, holding Schlabrendorff's dossier, was killed.[15] Schlabrendorff was eventually acquitted, but rearrested immediately by the Gestapo and told that the acquittal had been a mistake. He was to be shot. Awaiting execution at Flossenbürg, he was evacuated to Dachau ahead of the American advance and later liberated.

AFTER GÖTTERDÄMMERUNG

Immediate Allied reactions to the failed coup were deeply negative. In fact, there was a startling confluence between the Allied attitude toward the resistance and that of Hitler and Goebbels, who described the plotters as "a very small clique of ambitious, wicked and stupid criminal officers." The New York Herald Tribune suggested that Americans rejoice; Hitler had survived and would now save the Allies the trouble of destroying the militarists who had tried to oust him.[16] The British took essentially the same tone. On July 23 1944, The New York Times described a "German corps and . . . commanders . . . whose only hope is for a quick peace that will leave them with the nucleus to begin building for the next world conflict." By early August, a headline read: "Hitler Hangs His Generals," and went on to say that "the details of the plot suggest more the atmosphere of a gangster's lurid underworld than the normal atmosphere [of] an officers' corps and a civilized government."[17] In Walter Lippmann's opinion the "old army" and Hitler were enmeshed, and would "go down together in a bloody, envenomed death struggle. . . . The Allies have not the slightest reason to shorten or mitigate this internal German struggle."[18] He had apparently forgotten that the struggle had already engulfed millions of other lives.

The western Allies saw the failed coup as of no import, except possibly as an opportunity. On July 26, 1944 a directive from OSS Morale Operations suggested that OSS posts in Europe "give the SS names of all German officers and Nazis known to you and state that they were involved in the Putsch. This will have the effect . . . of creating confusion in the SS, and liquidating the people denounced."[19] This was entirely in accord with an earlier recommendation from Wheeler-Bennett. Since meeting with Adam von Trott of the German Foreign Office in Washington and offering him encouragement in 1939, he had decided that Trott "did not quite succeed in being an Englishman," and had chosen to abandon "the other Germany" entirely.[20] In a mid-1943 memorandum for Halifax, entitled: "On What to Do with Germany," Wheeler-Bennett offered his suggestion: The Allies should "stand outside" while the purges went on. "Total occupation . . . should not be effected until a beneficial degree of liquidation has been achieved."[21] On July 25, he rejoiced that "the Gestapo and the SS have done us an appreciable service in removing . . . those who would undoubtedly have posed as 'good' Germans after the war. . . . The killing of Germans by Germans will save us from future embarrassments of many kinds."[22]

The "beneficial liquidation" was certainly achieved. Most members of the Solf Circle were executed after the July putsch. The Edelweiss Pirates, the children of the communist and socialist working classes that had been eradicated or pushed deep underground by the Nazis, were young, disaffected, and united principally by animus toward Nazi regimentation. Their brand of resistance—singing forbidden pre-Nazi songs and defacing Nazi posters—most often looked more like boyish pranks than true opposition. Eventually, though, they had begun posting anti-Nazi fliers, pillaging supply trains, and disseminating news from illegal BBC broadcasts, activities that earned them very adult punishment. In November 1944, thirteen skinny boys were publicly hanged.

The only official exception to Wheeler-Bennett's attitude came from the Soviets. Radio Moscow was quick off the mark, with the Free Germany Committee trumpeting on July 21: "The die has been cast. Courageous men have risen against Hitler. They have given the signal for the salvation of the German people. . . . Generals, officers, and soldiers! Cease fire . . . and turn your arms against Hitler. Do not fail these courageous men." In his 1947 account of the German underground, Dulles remembered that this barrage continued; when Berlin was reached in May 1945, the city was already full of Soviet placards with Stalin's pronouncement that "Hitlers come and go, but the German people, the German state, remain."[23]

Five days after the coup, Walter C. Langer, a psychologist serving as an OSS consultant, delivered a memorandum on the plot in which he concluded, admittedly on the basis of skimpy newspaper reports, that Hitler might well have staged the coup himself.[24] Langer had done several psychological studies of Hitler for the OSS, and his memo is a fascinating portrait of Hitler's mind at work. Langer suggested that a staged coup would help the Führer eliminate the army as a threat once and for all; it would help him create a new stab-in-the-back legend, i.e., the generals sabotaged his victory; it would deflect the national disillusion and anger from himself to the generals he hated; and lastly, it would reinforce the notion of Hitler's divine protection. After several dense pages, Langer stated that his conclusion—that the plot was staged by Hitler—was "almost inescapable."[25] It was a brilliant and entirely plausible theory, but it missed one salient point that ought to have been taken into account: There had been a real opposition to Hitler.

To Washington and London the attempted coup may have seemed inconsequential, but when the news came that it had failed, Gävernitz found his friend Dulles "in utter despair." But as the conspicuous exception to Allied indifference, Dulles immediately set to work to try to remedy the failure, arguing that since the coup was being played down by the Nazis, Allied "tactics should be just the opposite."[26] He recommended lines of action, urged presidential statements and dropping leaflets to encourage internal revolt in order to end the war more quickly and to save lives. He was not entirely alone; Donovan peppered the president with a series of dense reports on the background of the coup, intimations of a possible communist orientation in Germany resulting from the fact that "Russia has throughout played a more realistic policy in dealing with the internal German situation than has either the United States or England." He forwarded Dulles's recommendations in a memorandum to the president, on 25 July 1944, about the German coup d'état.

> This attempt to overthrow Hitler was engineered largely by men who desired a western orientation of German policy. The OSS representative in Bern believes that the next attempted *putsch* against Hitler will likely come from an eastern oriented group, possibly after the Soviet occupation of East Prussia and a German Government, on the order of the Moscow Free German Committee, is set up. . . .
>
> The OSS representative also suggests . . . a statement by President Roosevelt similar to that made recently by Prime Minister Churchill suggesting to the German people that their present plight and future prospects would be improved, were they to overthrow Hitler."[27]

The Soviet bogeyman did not worry FDR, nor would he encourage any Germans. Donovan was answered with silence.

A U.S. Army Intelligence report summed up:

> On 20 July, 1944, an explosion was heard in one of the huts of Hitler's supreme headquarters. . . . For a few hours . . . many Germans believed Hitler was dead. At 1800 hours the German radio announced an attempt on the Fuehrer's life had been made but that he had miraculously escaped.
>
> The explosion had two general effects:
>
> 1. Probably the greatest single purge that even Hitler's Germany had ever seen took place. A large number of high-ranking officers were arrested immediately. Some were shot at once; some were tried and then hanged; and many others escaped a similar fate by committing suicide. Civilians too, were purged. . . . it gradually came to light that practically all the remants of the German intelligentsia, all the potential leadesrs of a non-Nazi Germany, were put in Gestapo prisons. Very few ever came out again.

2. Hitler's narrow escape from death . . . renewed his conviction that a higher destiny protected him. . . . he continued the war with increased viciousness. The last men of reason had been eliminated. . . . the Nazis reigned supreme. . . . At last, the gigantic war which the Nazis had provoked had become entirely their own.[28]

Hitler demanded the elimination—root and branch—of the conspirators' families. *Sippenhaft,* the punishment of kith and kin, derived from ancient tribal notions of revenge based on consanguinity. It meshed perfectly with the Nazi fondness for the Teutonic emphasis on bloodlines and was the ideal tool of Hitler's systematic vengeance. Property was seized; wives, children, brothers, fathers, sisters, family of any kind, were arrested, separated, kept under surveillance, imprisoned, executed. Ulrich von Hassell's family provides an example of how this barbaric system worked.

Hassell's wife, Ilse, and his elder daughter were arrested at the family home, held in various prisons, and released only after unrelenting pressure from the family's eldest son, Wolf.[29] A son serving with the general staff on the eastern front was arrested, as was the younger daughter, Fey, whose two small boys were taken from her and removed to an SS "reeducation" camp under false names. Brother and sister were held by the Gestapo and barely escaped execution in the frenzy of killings at the very end of the war. Eventually, in September 1945, with the U.S. occupation forces providing petrol as well as intelligence, the family's search for Fey's little boys succeeded.[30] Family monies were seized, and as the survivor of a traitor, Ilse von Hassell, like many others, was denied a pension until 1960. In mid-August 1948, she wrote a postcard to a friend in England whose father had been a member of the opposition of the penury in which she found herself: "Here nobody knows how to pay for postage or the telephone, not to mention electricity and taxes. One stands and gazes wistfully at the plums that have finally turned up again and cannot afford the 60 pfennigs a pound. The 'employed' are doing a little better, but so many are being laid off."

Ironically, the only family member not caught in the Gestapo net was Hassell's thirty-one-year-old son, Wolf Ulrich. As an asthmatic, he was not military material, but he had worked closely with his father. During the war his respiratory problems had provided useful cover, allowing Hassell to visit him at Arosa, Switzerland, and so to meet with OSS and British intelligence there. Wolf Ulrich was familiar with the details of the plot and its participants. In 1942, he had buried his father's diaries at the family place in Ebenhausen, safely stashed in a Ridgeway's Pure China Tea tin.[31]

On July 28, 1944, the day of his father's arrest, and repeatedly thereafter, Wolf presented himself at Gestapo headquarters in the Prinz Albrechtstrasse. Commonsense be damned: He was determined to see his father. He and his father had been in this together, he told the Gestapo; he knew everything. If they wanted his father, he insisted, they must want him as well. The Gestapo threw him out. Wolf Ulrich's mother later reasoned that most likely the Gestapo saw this as youthful bravado and decided that he knew nothing. Though he was threatened with arrest and repeatedly told unctuous lies, Wolf Ulrich had accomplished nothing. His father was tried and executed on the same day, September 8, 1944.[32] But just before the collapse of Berlin, Wolf did manage to extract his father's prison writings and a few personal items like his signet ring from the Gestapo. As the Russians advanced on the city, he managed to escape from nearby Potsdam.[33]

OTTO JOHN HAD BEEN WARNED NOT TO RETURN TO BERLIN FOR THE PUTSCH, BUT HE found it impossible to stay away. On the twentieth, a solar eclipse turned the sky murky and the atmosphere oppressive. It seemed to him an ugly omen and he suggested to his brother that it was "no weather for a revolution."[34] On that chaotic afternoon, Otto John saw Stauffenberg and others in the Bendlerstrasse, all convinced that the Führer was dead. He had gone home, confident of the coup's success, and then heard, in disbelief, Hitler's voice on the radio. He was convinced that a double was speaking. He soon learned otherwise.

As the Gestapo swarmed over the capital and arrested hundreds, John managed to fly to the relative safety of Madrid. The bar at his hotel was full of talk about the putsch. Many questions were directed his way, but he kept insisting that he knew only what was in the newspapers. Given Spain's relationship with the Hitler regime, John knew that his safety here was limited; he had to be extremely careful.

Again Juan Terrasa was invaluable. He contacted John to tell him that the British planned to evacuate him to London, and then organized his escape. John was to tell people he was going to Paris; as a senior Lufthansa employee he had the proper papers for such travel. At the train station, John headed for the Paris express. A helpful porter—Terrasa's agent—hoisted his bag. They climbed aboard the train, then scuttled immediately out the other side, where Terrasa's car was waiting to whisk him away to a safe accommodation. While he waited for the British Secret Service to get him first to Gibraltar and from there to London, he stayed with the widow of a Spanish Republican murdered by Franco. An unidentified French girl brought him newspapers every day, but they only heightened his anxiety and restlessness. Day after day he paced his tiny room, tortured by thoughts of his friends and coconspirators. Stauffenberg and Beck were already dead—four paces from bed to table. So many had been arrested, others were on the run—four paces back. The room was unbearably hot and airless, the summer heat stultifying. Days ticked by. Would the British ever come?

One day, along with the newspapers, the girl also brought a packet of black hair dye. There was concern that John's fair hair might make him too conspicuous. As messy and unpleasant as the process was, at least it felt like progress, a step ahead rather than standing still. Not long afterward, he was driven by car, not to Gibraltar, but in the opposite direction, north to Asturias. At a village on the Minho River, the border between Spain and Portugal, he was put up by a local smith-cum-smuggler who was savvy enough about the schedules kept by the border patrols to row John safely across the river at dawn. His identification consisted of a matchbox with a hundred-peseta note inside. On the other side, a clutch of peasants awaited him. They were feeding him an enormous breakfast when a car pulled up, a huge limousine with conspicuous CD—diplomatic corps—plates. It flew the Union Jack all the way to the British embassy in Lisbon.

At the embassy, the naval attaché and a Portuguese coworker, Pedro Romero, concocted Otto John's cover story: He was an RAF pilot downed over Portugal—a story that was not all that improbable at the time. In disguise, and stashed in a remote village, John passed the time struggling to read Portuguese literature. One night there was furious knocking at the door. It was the dreaded PVDE, essentially the political police, intended to maintain "order" in the regime. A powerful and multipurpose organization, it combined many functions under one umbrella: internal security, foreign intelligence and counterintelligence, criminal investigation, both foreign and counter, border patrol, immigration, and emigration.

Arrested and tossed into a miserable prison cell in the medieval fortress of Aljuba, John was convinced that this was the end. But once again, Portugal had been caught between German and British antagonists. Fortunately for John, Rita Windsor had taken a liking to him. The British had been in touch with the number-two man at PVDE, Jose Ernesto do Vale Catela. John was languishing in a primitive PVDE prison to keep him out of reach of the Gestapo. He learned only later from the British ambassador that the Gestapo had been on a determined hunt for him. When Portugal refused the Reich's request for extradition, they decided to kidnap him. Kaltenbrunner ordered that he be brought back, dead or alive, and the SD had set aside enormous sums to bribe PVDE, or whoever else might help them get their hands on John.

Major Cramer of the Lisbon SD had seen the handwriting on the wall. He deliberately failed in his mission to kidnap John, even as his boss Schellenberg was attempting to use John's contacts with what remained of the opposition.[35] With the end of the war in sight, everyone wanted to save his skin. When John was finally released, he was taken to the British embassy to be flown to Gibraltar. But the adventure was not over; his flight met with such strong winds that it was forced to turn back to Lisbon, earning John the nickname "Boomerang" at the embassy. The resourceful Windsor soon got him aboard a Clipper to London.

At Camp 001, a catchall for enemy nationals and questionable foreigners, he was interrogated. Asked repeatedly, "How long have you been a member of the Nazi Party?" John finally lost his temper. He had come to England to continue his fight against the Nazis, he protested.

"You came to England to save your skin," his interrogator replied acidly.[36] Still, one dreary November day, a chubby, vaguely bohemian fellow in command of perfect German ambled in to see him. He was Sefton Delmer, the head of an MO outfit known officially as Soldatensender Calais, but affectionately called the "Delmer circus." As Oskar Jürgens, earning £12 a week, John would be used for radio propaganda beamed at Germany, a function he fulfilled until war's end.

As a true veteran of the anti-Nazi resistance, John knew all the participants, and in spite of occasional disagreements on policy, he was good friends with many of them. He had been involved with civilian and military circles of the opposition and the Abwehr. He had been in constant contact with plotters, and had undertaken many missions on their behalf. While he did not always agree with other members—on the question of unconditional surrender, for instance—he brought his cool and reasoned assessment to bear with his friends and fellow opponents of the regime. He, like others, had hoped to restore the monarchy, but there was not to be a restoration. All the candidates for the throne were either rejected or declined and the Allies had their own ideas.

OPERATION SAUERKRAUT

There was one Allied arena, however, in which the July putsch spurred action that had a positive, if minor effect. To the small OSS Morale Ops group attached to the Fifth Army in the hills of Tuscany, the bomb that failed to kill Hitler on July 20, 1944, was a clear sign. Hitler claimed that providence alone had spared him and the little cluster of OSSers discussing it next day also sensed divine intervention. They saw the failed assassination as a God-given opportunity to undermine morale at what was surely a low point for the Wehrmacht. Within hours they had concocted an ingenious plan to spread dissension and disillusion in the German ranks.

Of their group of rather lively characters—artist Saul Steinberg was among them—only Czech-born private Barbara Lauwers, affectionately called Zuzka, and civilian Edmund "Eddie" Linder spoke German. Lauwers had joined the army wanting to put her excellent language skills (English, French, German, Flemish) to work; she was detailed to OSS, taken to Algiers, and then flown to Rome. To implement their plan, she and Linder first interviewed POWs at a camp in Aversa, north of Rome, to identify men willing to work against the Nazis, and then trained them to go undercover.[37] They named their venture Operation Sauerkraut, a humorous twist on

"Krauts" soured on the Thousand-Year Reich. Some were survivors of the Russian campaign, some had witnessed horrifying atrocities, and some were deserters. Within days, they were disseminating anti-Nazi propaganda deep behind enemy lines, locating German infantry and paratroop divisions and Tiger tanks as future bombing targets.

The speed and spontaneity of the operation were typical—very much like Confederate colonel John Mosby's method of operation—and part of its genius. "That's what the OSS was like," said Lauwers. "If you think it will work, do it!"[38] They were also lucky. The POWs were "keen to cooperate," and despite skeptics like the British, who felt POWs could not be trusted, she was sure the prisoners shared the OSS's goal: a quick end to the war.

The "spies" were outfitted with German uniforms, proper credentials, documents,[39] weapons, medals, watches, a plausible sum in Italian lire befitting their rank, and a credible miscellany to be found in their pockets. Their cover stories were that they had been injured or accidentally separated from their units and were now happy to be back. Under cover of darkness, the POWs crept through a rubble-strewn no-man's-land, each carrying roughly 15,000 propaganda leaflets. They picked their way through shellfire, mine fields, ducked under barbed wire; they posted fliers in latrines, left them in trucks and mess areas. One "spy" saw a passing German patrol stop to read the leaflets, then throw down their weapons, shouting, "The war is over!"[40] When an influx of deserters approached Allied lines with the leaflets in their pockets, the agents knew the missions were a success.

Thirteen Sauerkraut missions were completed between July 1944 and May 1945. Linder tried to get special treatment for the POWs who had participated, but they were returned to camps and repatriated. To Lauwers's regret, the Sauerkrauts never received any official recognition, but MO hatched a scheme to treat the returning "spies"—now practitioners of the world's second oldest profession—to an afternoon of fun with practitioners of the world's oldest profession. Sitting in a Jeep on a Roman street, waiting to pay the bill for her charges' R&R, Lauwers wondered how on earth the OSS disbursing officer would justify this particular expense to the American taxpayer.[41]

THE SUMMER OF 1944 SAW THE DEVELOPMENT OF THE SO-CALLED FAUST PLAN FOR INFIL-trating agents into Germany, and Operation Twilight, intended to identify virulent pockets of Nazi supporters, yet there was no effort to find or support anti-Nazis.[42] FDR told the American people that the U.S. aim was "to win the war . . . to win it overwhelmingly." And the war was won overwhelmingly—at a terrible price. More people died between July 20, 1944, and the end of the war than had died in the previous four years. William Casey recalled in his memoir that although Hitler had ordered an all-out defense of Aachen in the fall of 1944, the German commanding officer, Lieutenant General Gerhard von Schwerin-Krosigk, told the Americans that he wanted to declare Charlemagne's ancient capitol an open city to preserve it from ruin.[43] For several days, there was no response from the Americans. Then eight days of fierce fighting reduced the city to rubble, littered with corpses from both sides. In hopes of avoiding destruction and saving lives, the OSS quickly mustered five captured German generals to mediate in similar situations, but Washington rejected the idea. The United States would "not use German militarists to defeat German militarism."[44]

Rumors of a last-ditch Nazi stronghold had spread, fueled in equal parts by the myth of Nazi invincibility and Allied paranoia. The story posited that if the Nazi elite were driven out of Berlin, they would take refuge in an impregnable mountain fastness with formidable quantities of munitions safely stockpiled in caves. The concept meshed perfectly with Allied concerns about rabid partisan resistance and guerrilla bands of Hitler Youth— the so-called Werewolves—who would keep the Fascist fires burning to the last. There were plans in place to root out such fierce die-hard resistance. As it turned out the Werewolves were for the most part small groups of boys, hiding in the woods with grenades and the occasional bazooka. Hungry, frightened, and eager to go home, they usually gave up in days.

Dulles reported on this purported Nazi redoubt in September 1944, and his reports were duly forwarded. Though he himself was skeptical, the Allies remained sufficiently uneasy about it to cause Eisenhower, in March 1945, to shift the thrust of his forces away from Berlin, south toward Bavaria.[45] In fact, the Nazi redoubt, waiting somewhere in the alpine mists to receive the masters of the master race when their empire collapsed, was a phantasm, and for the Allies, it turned out to be an expensive one. With Eisenhower to the south, the Russians roared through Germany to Berlin, which went to them by right of conquest. A new world order was beginning to emerge, with the Soviets as the new antagonists.[46] Within a year Operation Twilight had shifted its focus from locating Nazis to enlisting them to help deal with a new enemy.[47]

A CHANGING POLITICAL LANDSCAPE

Wrangling among the Allies had begun long before the war ended. Imagining that the end of the war was not far off, the Big Three had convened at Teheran in late 1943 to decide on the structure of postwar Germany. It was already clear that the individual combatants, the soldiers of all armies, would leave the arena before long, and the struggle would be between more powerful, if less clearly defined, forces. What was at stake now was empire and spheres of influence—or their loss—on a global scale. What took shape at Teheran ushered in a new war—the cold war—an era that encompassed nearly fifty years and shaped millions of lives. As the opposition had warned, Germany would still be a battleground, as would huge chunks of central and eastern Europe.

Stalin set the tone at Teheran with a toast: At least 50,000 Germans—no, perhaps 100,000—should be shot. The toast alarmed Churchill, but as the talks proceeded, it became clear that the power lay with the United States and Russia. Stalin and FDR, each thinking he was outmaneuvering the other, agreed to the dismemberment of Germany and the ceding to Russia of a significant part of eastern Poland. Churchill's reservations about a balkanized Europe, with nothing to act as a buffer against the Soviets, were brushed aside. Nor did Roosevelt confide this scheme to any of his more important advisors and officials. His State Department, laboring in Washington over plans for postwar Germany, labored in complete ignorance of the president's intentions.

Less than a year after Teheran, the final coup attempt had failed. Nazi judge Roland Freisler was already haranguing the first conspirators to be "tried" in his mockery of a court when Treasury Secretary Henry Morgenthau went to England to plump for his Carthaginian plan for postwar Germany.[48] It was to be a fractured agrarian landscape of small communities of peace-loving peasants whose plowshares could never be turned into swords. Churchill, meanwhile, was pressing for continued lend-lease for a battered and impoverished Britain, whose economy needed a resuscitated Germany to buy British exports.

Morgenthau had learned only later, and by happenstance, of the planned dismemberment of Germany that was decided on at Teheran. Informed of the plan by Eden, he embraced the concept wholeheartedly. He wanted to put Germany out of business, particularly the industrial Ruhr and Saar regions, even if roughly 19 million Germans would be unemployed as a result.[49] When *The New York Times* and *The Wall Street Journal* spilled selected details of Morgenthau's vision, it created a huge stir, not only among Roosevelt's cabinet, but also among his generals.

In Germany Goebbels exploited Morgenthau's plan for propaganda instantly. He claimed that a noble fight to the death was preferable to slavery under the Allied yoke and a Jewish plot to exterminate millions of Germans. He painted the plan as the second half of a one-two punch: unconditional surrender followed by total annihilation. London newspapers were printing doggerel on mass involuntary castration of Germans, but when Morgenthau complained to Roosevelt that Churchill was soft on Germans, the president angrily endorsed castration.[50] To German soldiers, there seemed no alternative but to a fight of ferocious determination to the end. The losses continued.

General George C. Marshall complained to Morgenthau directly that his plan was only stiffening German resistance. From wintry, battle-weary Europe, Eisenhower urged the Joint Chiefs to "redouble efforts to find a solution . . . for the German will to resist." But Roosevelt would not be moved, though he did ask whether Churchill might speak to the issue.[51] Churchill replied that his war cabinet was opposed to the idea as it might "confess our errors," and added that he would remain "set in unconditional surrender, which is where you put me."[52] In December, the desperate German offensive in the Ardennes, at Bastogne, and the Battle of the Bulge resulted in horrifying casualties, perhaps as high as 750,000. It has been suggested that since that fateful day at Casablanca when unconditional surrender was decreed, 8 million—soldiers, Russian, German, and Italian civilians, and Jews—had died.[53]

PROFOUND AND POIGNANT QUESTIONS

Allen Dulles has been charged with scant coverage of the problems of Europe's Jews. He has also been accused, or at the very least suspected, of callousness and indifference. But as he himself once said, obtaining information was often easier than acting on it. It is clear from many of his long communiqués suggesting encouragement to various quarters and offering proposals for policy or propaganda in others that he was often frustrated by the lack of action in response to his intelligence. Having the information was not the same thing as getting it to people who could or would put it to good use, which in itself was no guarantee. But Dulles was a pragmatist; he recognized that while the gathering of intelligence fell within his purview, acting on it did not.

The OSS is tarred with the same brush.[54] Why did they not do something when they were confronted with such staggering information on the extermination of Europe's Jews? Tracking an OSS communiqué from Bern or Istanbul or anywhere else, through the gears and wheels of the organization and the government, is no simple matter. How it moved through the agency, whose desks it crossed, whose eyes saw it, and who signed off on it is nearly impossible to determine. Scholars have found themselves flummoxed by this continuing mystery.

Washington, and the president's office in particular, became a sort of black hole. Intelligence was certainly drawn in, but how much of it the president, nearing the end of his physical powers, was capable of dealing with is not known. Even when the path of the intelligence is clear, OSS had no power to effect policy. Donovan's and Dulles's infrequent mentions of the Holocaust reflect their perception of the official Allied stance—that of their bosses. The most that could be hoped for was that Donovan might intercede personally with the president, as he did in this instance.

OSS from Caserta, Italy, October 16, 1944:

1. Dr. Alexander Safran, Grand Rabbi of Rumania, this morning . . . expressed . . . serious fears that all Budapest Jews would be *exterminated this* week. Therefore Dr. Safran desires to appeal to President Roosevelt to issue an immediate warning to the effect that any people connected with any killings . . . will be given short shrift.

2. Dr. Filderman, head of the Rumanian Jewish Community, also declared that the only hope left to Hungarian Jews is if the highest Allied Chiefs issue a threat over the radio to all Nazis . . . connected with murders will be meted out the most dire punishment, including their families. Filderman urges us to forward this statement to Washington.[55]

"In view of the urgency of this message," Donovan wrote to the president next day, "I thought that you would like to have it brought immediately to your attention." No record exists of a presidential response to Donovan's urgent call.

No doubt much of the communication between Donovan and FDR was oral and therefore left no paper trail. Sid Schapiro, a volunteer at the National Archives, has reviewed 18,000 OSS documents from the Director's Office (M 1642). Of these, maybe 1,000 were sent from Donovan to the White House, but only a handful went the other way. The huge imbalance puzzles researchers. Shapiro suggests that the president thought of Donovan "as a cowboy" who did not belong to the inner Roosevelt circle and was not a "member of the club."[56] According to Donovan's former administrative assistant, Ned Putzell, Donovan was "not cut out of the loop," but FDR apparently shared more thoughts on policy decisions with Secretary of War Stimson and Army Chief of Staff Marshall than with the OSS director.[57] There is some speculation that FDR worried that Donovan might run against him in the next election.

An overview of only some of the specific wartime intelligence on the Final Solution raises a fundamental question: What good was all this intelligence if it brought no response? One of the great frustrations and puzzles of intelligence work is that it so rarely has any tangible impact on policy. History is littered with failures of intelligence, but far more common is the failure to use even first-rate intelligence—properly, wisely, or at all.

Hindsight offers a considerable advantage. The modern reader knows from the outset that Dulles's reports were true.[58] History has confirmed that what to Dulles were rumors, gossip, bits and pieces of unverified information that appeared over the months and years were about what would later be called the Holocaust. At the time, however, there were real questions. After the German invasions of Poland and Russia, much of the intelligence on Nazi atrocities and mass killings came from unknown and unvetted sources. Much of it was doubted or simply not believed. It was just too fantastic, and recalled the false atrocity propaganda of World War I. Meanwhile, what the British knew to be true from decrypts was kept mum.

Many Jews also disbelieved, even if somewhere in their innermost hearts, they may have "felt" that the reports were true. Friends, neighbors and relatives disappeared, maybe sent a postcard, and then were not heard from again. By the time the reality had penetrated—and had been faced head-on—it was too late for many. By that time, too, the immediate Allied concern of winning the war had taken precedence over everything else, even the larger moral and humanitarian issues.

The moral dimensions of Hitler's plan to eradicate the Jewish people and its implementation suggest that in certain instances intelligence ought to come with a moral imperative attached, that it then requires a response. But intelligence is the handmaiden of politics and war. Even when the evidence is incontrovertible, it is acted on only when it suits the actor and fits a determined political or military agenda. Otherwise, its most common fate is the file cabinet. So it was in 1943, and so it is today.

Many who gathered intelligence or passed it along were true believers; risking one's life, after all, demands a certain commitment, even passion. But those on the receiving end were another matter; information was dismissed as flawed, inaccurate, unbelievable, or unacceptable. As Dulles wrote: "The receivers of intelligence generally start out discounting a particular report as false or a plant. Then when they get over that hurdle they discard what they don't like and refuse to believe it. Finally, when they get a report they both believe and like, they don't know what to do about it."[59]

It is also important to understand that in military and government circles, the OSS was regarded as a service organization, as only one player in a field crowded with jousting rivals. Its work fell under the aegis of military and diplomatic strategy. Its task was to gather "passive" intelligence; the job of its Research and Analysis Division was to translate raw intelligence into succinct, entirely objective analyses for those who would decide tactics, strategy, and policy. Its mandate "did not include the rescue of the European Jews." William Langer, the head of R&A, had a department peopled by many German-Jewish refugees and German intellectual émigrés. He put it plainly: "There is no future in R&A as a pressure group." Pleading a special cause would mean that "we will very soon lose our entrée to all policy-makers other than those already committed to the same special cause."[60] Intelligence was most definitely not an instrument for shaping policy.

This awareness permeated the intelligence community, and could lead to frustration verging on torment. Fritz Kolbe chafed under it. He complained that long after he had communicated their strategic importance, critical factories had still not been bombed, and the Portuguese continued to sell wolfram to the Germans. Dulles, like his boss Donovan, took issue with the policy of unconditional surrender. Why wouldn't the Allies bend a bit, or support the German resistance? Frank Wisner, the OSSer sent to Istanbul after the Dogwood fiasco to salvage whatever might be salvageable, spent his hard-driving and brilliant intelligence career in situations where he was painfully aware that there was nothing he could do about what he knew. He was surely only one of the casualties of this moral anguish. When the Soviets marched into Hungary in 1956, Wisner, then chief of U.S. covert operations, with long experience in eastern Europe, realized what it meant, but was powerless; the United States was not going to do anything about it.[61]

Political expediency and prejudices also played a conspicuous part. Since the fall of 1941 the British had resolutely sat on their knowledge of the horrors in the east out of legitimate concern not to reveal that the German codes had been broken. Nor were they eager to raise troublesome Jewish refugee issues in Palestine. Roosevelt's animus toward Germany and Germans would not let him avail himself of the one group that might have been helpful in aborting Hitler's Final Solution—the German opposition. The determination that only unconditional surrender could end the war locked everyone—aggressors, combatants, and certainly victims—into ongoing destruction and bloodshed.[62] Voices of protest went unheard or unheeded.

WHAT COULD HAVE BEEN DONE, AND DONE WITHOUT DETRIMENT TO THE OBJECTIVE OF winning the war, was to bring pressure to bear on the issue—moral opprobrium, threats, warnings of dire consequences to satellite nations and to Germany. Dulles had recommended this very early on. It had had some effect in Hungary; what might have been achieved elsewhere as well, and sooner? Politics interfered. Within three different Allied contexts, a human tragedy of immense proportions lost its human face and became simply a political abstraction, secondary to other concerns: U.S. immigration policy reflected a profound conservative strain, a digging in against inundation by a disorderly, un-American tide. The British—an island nation—had their own qualms; there was even an argument that too many reports of Jewish persecution might be counterproductive, stiffening Nazi resolve and demoralizing resistance.[63] Stalin's view of Jews was not entirely out of synch with Hitler's. In addition, he was legitimately preoccupied with intense fighting along a huge front.

An avalanche of words and a spate of relatively recent literature have been devoted to the subject of the Allied stance toward Hitler's extermination policies and the lack of intervention on behalf of Europe's Jews. Essentially, it divides into two camps. One side pursues the question with a mixture of passion, moral outrage, and hurt, mingled with incomprehension. The title of David Wyman's well-known *The Abandonment of the Jews* and Monty Penkower's *The Jews Were Expendable,* are apt representatives of this side of the argument. Wyman chastises Roosevelt for indifference, foot-dragging, and lack of interest, for giving no priority to the rescue of Jews, for a response "deeply affected by political expediency," and for juggling with the relative importance of the Jewish vote.[64]

On the other side are those looking to the larger or at least a different context for explanation. They turn to the social attitudes prevalent at the time, the overall context of politics and—last but not least—the primary importance of winning the war. There are arguments aplenty on both sides. The issue has been nearly obscured in a cloud of verbiage, but both sides run head-on into the problem of reconciling realpolitik with moral leadership. In reviewing a book on a related subject, *New York Times* columnist Max Frankel wrote: "If you want to see the most profound and poignant questions raised by the Holocaust mauled and murdered in academic controversy, just try to follow the vituperations being exchanged in print. . . . The questions concern nothing less than the nature of evil. On present evidence, they should be snatched from historians and left to philosophers and poets."[65]

Leaving the question to philosophers and poets would be an easier choice, but there are at least some factors that must be considered.

Some apologists explain the skimpy record on presidential action in regard to the Jewish question by portraying FDR as trapped within a bureaucracy that prevented him from doing anything. The president had established his Advisory Committee on Political Refugees in 1938. It was headed by James G. MacDonald, a diplomat with extensive experience in Europe and Germany in particular, who had served as high commissioner of the League of Nations for refugees. MacDonald had long been aware of Hitler's planned elimination of the Jews; he had reported to Roosevelt on conditions in Germany in 1933.[66] But as a quasi-governmental agency lacking sufficient funding, and having only limited access to the president, and essentially reporting to the hidebound conservative State Department, the committee's efforts to help Jews were severely hampered. FDR's attempts to liberalize immigration policy in 1942 met with resistance from a conservative Congress that shared many of the "nativist," obstructionist views of Assistant Secretary of State Breckinridge Long.

Only after the president established the War Refugee Board in January 1944 was refugee policy finally wrested from the State Department. It had been a long fight, yet Roosevelt then installed staunchly anti-immigration Secretary of War Stimson as head of the WRB to ensure against any rash circumvention of policy and possible threats to U.S. security. By this time, however, public and political opinions had already undergone a significant shift, and the question that had nagged the Allies for so long—would the war actually be won?—seemed much closer to a positive answer.

Other apologists for Roosevelt's apparent unresponsiveness to the humanitarian catastrophe cite the specter of widespread and virulent anti-Semitism that the president faced in the United States. It was represented by such public figures as Senator William Borah of Idaho and Father Coughlin, the wildly popular "radio priest" whose excoriations of Jews found a wide audience until he was silenced by his superiors.[67] Even Sam Rosenman, one of FDR's close advisors, particularly on Jewish affairs, consistently advised him to avoid Jewish rescue missions on the grounds that this might exacerbate already potent anti-Semitic strains in American life. Politically, it was a sensitive issue.

What of Roosevelt himself? It has been pointed out that to many Jews Roosevelt was a hero, an attitude illustrated by a Jewish joke of the period. There were said to be three worlds: *die velt*—this world; *yene velt*—the world beyond—and Roose*velt*.[68] In continuing to placate Stalin, ever suspicious of a separate peace between Germany and the western Allies, FDR was probably also aiming at placating his political base—American liberals and leftists, many of whom were Jewish. Ironically enough, to a certain extent this meant abandoning Europe's Jews to the fate Hitler had in mind for them.

Meanwhile, other segments of the American populace sneered at "President Rosenfeld," who in their view was presiding over the "Jew Deal." For Roosevelt the politician, it was a balancing act. Yet no matter which side the literature on the subject comes down on, much of it is simply speculation. Roosevelt neither said nor wrote anything significant on the issue. Until 1944, very late in the game, while he clearly knew the score, he appeared to be almost completely disengaged. His secretary, Grace Tully, recalled receiving frequent intelligence reports to pass on to FDR, who liked to read them at bedtime.[69] This may well be just another instance of his political style, the sort of now-you-see-it-now-you-don't prestidigitation and ambiguity he specialized in, but it leaves the historian in a quandary. Is it possible that by ignoring an issue of such immense moral import and urgency, the famously humanitarian president apparently tacitly signed off on it by simply ignoring it?

He was, of course, also waging a global war. Churchill shared the concerns encompassed in this broader context and felt that a rapid Allied victory was the "principal hope" for the Jews. Many of the relevant British documents are still sealed, but while Churchill was more resoundingly and eloquently outspoken in denouncing Nazi policies and supporting Europe's Jewish populations than Roosevelt, in sum, Britain's immigration laws were no more welcoming than those of the United States. Until mid-1944, Britain also stood in the way of American attempts to send aid to Europe's hungry and oppressed on the grounds that it would compromise the embargo.

The grim fact is that for the Allies the war and hopes of victory preempted everything else. Unconditional surrender remained fixed as official policy. Moral obligations and humanitarian concerns were brushed aside to concentrate on the strategic, military, and tactical measures that would bring the swiftest results. The war was not seen as a rescue mission; it was a fight to quash the Nazi beast. Only when it was closer to being won did that view change somewhat.

In his *Secret War Against Hitler,* William Casey, who served with OSS London during the war, and later became director of the CIA, recalled that only when the Allies entered the concentration camps, when photos and films circulated, did the reality penetrate, even to people on the inside of intelligence. Casey wrote: "I'll never understand with all we knew . . . [how] we knew so little about the concentration camps and the magnitude of the holocaust. . . . It wasn't sufficiently real to stand out from the general brutality and slaughter which is war. Such reports as we did receive were shunted aside because the official policy in Washington and London was to concentrate exclusively on winning the war."[70]

There is no reason to doubt Casey's genuine shock and surprise. He had been concentrating all his energies on penetrating the ostensibly impenetrable Nazi empire. His attention had been elsewhere, but others knew, and had known for years.

GHOSTS

In 1944, Hitler had claimed that the perpetrators of the failed July assassination plot were a small elitist clique of corrupt aristocrats, yet the executions went on and on. Aachen had been bombed into ruins, and old men and boys were being marshaled to protect the flagging Fatherland. A sixth winter of war lay ahead. Lost though the war clearly was, there seemed to be no end to it. "Can Germany lose the war?" one underground joke asked. "No, unfortunately," came the answer. "Now that we've got it, we'll never get rid of it."

The voice crackling over the airwaves one evening in late October 1944 may not have reached many Germans; listening to foreign radio broadcasts had been a treasonous crime since 1939, and punishable by death often enough to make people hesitate before tuning in. But for those who did hear it, the voice sounded recognizable as that of Colonel General Ludwig Beck, former chief of the German general staff, and a leader of the failed putsch. It exhorted Germans to stand up against Hitler, against his gangster government, and not to squander thousands upon thousands of lives in senseless resistance to overwhelming Allied might.

Yet how could it be Beck? The Nazis claimed that he had committed suicide in the aftermath of the July plot. Still, the voice kept quoting *Mein Kampf,* in which Hitler himself had argued that when a few scoundrels subject a people to terrible oppression, obedience and duty to those scoundrels are doctrinaire madness. "At such a time, duty and responsibility to the entire nation become paramount." Furthermore: "When the government uses its power to lead people towards destruction, then rebellion is not only right, but the duty of each citizen of such a nation."[71]

How many Germans actually heard Beck's speech will never be known, but it reached the ears of the Nazis. Unwilling to welcome Beck back to this life, they quickly jammed the transmitter and continued jamming it for two weeks. The voice had actually been the voice of a German POW in England. The words, drafted by the media warriors of OSS's Morale Operations, were delivered convincingly enough in Beck's typically measured, modulated tones for the international press to speculate on the mysteriously revivified Beck's exhortation to his countrymen.

BY THIS TIME, MOLTKE HAD ALREADY BEEN IN JAIL FOR EIGHT MONTHS. BECAUSE OF THE steady Allied bombing in Berlin, he and many others from whom the Gestapo hoped to obtain information had been moved to Ravensbrück, a concentration camp north of the city. He and his wife, Freya, exchanged letters daily and she was allowed monthly visits, but he knew that sooner or later he would be drawn into the net. At their last visit, early in August, he told her that if he wrote to tell her to plow all of Kreisau's fields, there was no hope. His letters stopped in mid-August. When she came to visit, she was told she could not see him, and given a suitcase with his clothes and his diary.[72]

The mere fact that he had been in jail for so long made the case against him problematic. He had obviously not planned the July coup—any coup was profoundly against his principles. He was not tried for plotting or advocating violence, but, as he wrote Freya, "yours truly has been shown to have discussed with 2 clergymen . . . without the intention of doing anything concrete . . . matters which are the exclusive concern of the Führer." The talk had been about the practical demands of the Christian ethic. So he was to be hanged because he and some friends had thought together. At least, he said, he was being hanged for something he actually had done. Writing a farewell letter to his young sons, he told them that all his life he had fought against "the spirit of narrowness and violence, or arrogance, of intolerance, and of absolute merciless consistency." It was that spirit of merciless consistency that executed him and ten others on January 23, 1945.[73]

When the OSS learned of his death sentence, concrete plans were put forward to rescue him. They came too late.[74] George Kennan, who had met with Moltke several times when he was with the American embassy in Berlin, said of him:

> The image of this lonely, struggling man, one of the few genuine martyrs of our time, has remained for me over the intervening years as a pillar of moral conscience and an unfailing source of political and intellectual inspiration.
>
> I consider him . . . the greatest person morally, and the largest and most enlightened in his concepts that I met on either side of the battle lines in the Second World War. . . . he looked beyond the whole sordid arrogance and apparent triumphs of the Hitler regime; he had seen through to the ultimate catastrophe and had put himself to the anguish of accepting and accommodating himself to it inwardly, preparing himself—as he would have liked to prepare his people—for the necessity of starting all over again, albeit in defeat and humiliation, to erect a new national edifice on a new and better moral foundation.[75]

Were the list of those seeking to find some accommodation with the Allies to include absolutely everyone, there would be a mention of the *Freiheitsaktion Bayern*—Bavarian Freedom Action—in late April, 1945. They attempted an improbable, last-minute putsch involving the far right-wing, long-term Hitler supporter, Franz Ritter von Epp. Aside from calling attention to the shattered morale on the home front and delivering themselves up to mass murders, the insurgents accomplished little. Gävernitz had done some legwork, and the OSS knew about it. Reports had even gone to the JCS and the White House. The list could go on. There were many, and many who died, but in the end none of them had any perceptible effect on the historical dialectic.

YALTA AND THE BOND OF THE VICTORS

In February 1945, just after the brutal fighting in Belgium's ice and mud had claimed so many lives, the Big Three reconvened, this time at the Crimean resort of Yalta. They conferred in the ballroom of Livadia, once the czar summer palace, but now somewhat derelict. According to Anna Roosevelt Boettiger, who accompanied her father, there were complaints of unwelcome bedfellows. Though she had been lucky, the delousing was still going on, but there were much more serious issues to address.[76]

Roosevelt suggested that Stalin repeat his Teheran toast about shooting 50,000 German officers. The matter of war crimes was clearly an issue, and the British and the Americans were at odds about how to punish the guilty. In attempting to discover FDR's true intentions, the British encountered what Noel Annan, of British intelligence, once characterized as "the usual fog in Roosevelt's Washington." Drawing on his passion for the hunt for an apt comparison, the British ambassador, Lord Halifax, likened FDR's administration to a day's disorderly rabbit shooting: "nothing comes out where you expect . . . then suddenly something emerges at the far end of the field."[77]

Stalin had his own ideas about where and how he would find his rewards for a hard-fought war—at the expense of others. There had to be reparations and forced labor from a partitioned Germany. He wanted large stretches of Poland and of eastern and central Europe. A poll taken in the United States in late 1944 had indicated that only 44 percent of Americans trusted the Soviets, but Roosevelt was clearly indicating that he anticipated a new era of enduring cooperation with the Russians. In any case, he had his reasons for appeasing and flattering Stalin; he wanted his help in the war against Japan.

YALTA RESULTED IN EXUBERANT ROUNDS OF SELF-CONGRATULATION IN THE UNITED States, where hopes for the "dawn of a new day" ran high enough to silence the doubters on the home team, Admiral William D. Leahy and George Kennan among them. Donovan and Dulles also had their doubts. In an essay for *Time,* Whittaker Chambers brought a fanciful but significant perspective to the outcome of Yalta. His piece, "The Ghosts on the Roof," imagined the specters of the imperial family, executed in 1918, peering down from the roof of their worse-for-wear summer palace in stunned amazement at Stalin, the Georgian peasant, who was expanding their empire beyond their wildest imaginings.[78]

Around the conference table at Yalta, there were clear signs that the two superpowers were squaring off against one another. Churchill worried that nothing would stand between Stalin and the white cliffs of Dover, but he had been effectively marginalized in the proceedings. With prescience, he predicted that it would be fifty years before anyone could judge how effective the decisions being made would prove to be. On leaving Yalta, Churchill commented bitterly to Eden that "the only bond of the victors is their common hate."[79]

Among the doubters in the aftermath of Yalta was FDR's old friend George Earle. Discouraged but indefatigable, he wanted to warn the president against putting too much faith in the Soviets. He also hoped to see the president in order to finally lay to rest the ghosts of the Polish officers murdered at Katyn. FDR refused to see him and forbade him to publish "any information or opinion about an ally that you might have acquired while in the service of the United States Navy." Any such unfavorable opinion "might do irreparable harm to our war effort."[80]

Sixty years later, Yalta continues to be a subject for extended and sometimes bitter debate. While visiting Latvia in May 2005, President George W.

Bush characterized the agreement as "one of the greatest wrongs of history," and equated it with the capitulation at Munich.[81] Yalta, Bush argued, had sacrificed the freedom of many for the hope of stability but left Europe divided and fearful, and much of it under Soviet hegemony. There are historians who disagree, and in any case, Yalta has been superseded by history; whatever happened as a result of it has now been undone. Anger and sadness may remain, but the political configurations established at Yalta have disappeared, leaving only ghosts and regrets.

IN GERMANY, MEANWHILE, THE EXECUTIONS CONTINUED. THE BRITISH RESPONSE TO urgent pleas from Bishop George Bell, Eden's "pestilent priest," that it intervene on behalf of members of the resistance still either on the run, like Goerdeler, or imprisoned but not yet executed, involved sending memoranda from one member of the Foreign Office to another.[82] If enough time elapsed, the need to act would pass, which, for the most part, came true. Talk among the Allies of rescuing certain members of the resistance—capable men of high moral fiber, men like Hassell and Moltke and Eduard Schulte who could be useful in building the new Germany after the collapse of the Hitler regime—had remained just that: talk. Many of the conspirators had already been executed. There were more executions to come.

THE CANARIS DIARIES

Sooner or later, every historian eventually faces some baffling lacunae, holes that pockmark the centuries where there seems to be little or no information. The very nature of espionage guarantees that any student of its history will face even more and larger lacunae. Where testimony survives in letters, journals, even random notes scribbled in the margins of a book, it is pored over for every clue to the foggy past, but many unanswered questions remain. While it is well known that Admiral Wilhem Canaris kept diaries, historians are tormented by the realization that they are, or at least seem to be, lost.

According to Canaris's friend Lahousen, the "diary is impregnated with understanding of the impending disaster," and Canaris's notes "constitute the essential contemporary contribution to the history of this war's origins . . . valuable as an expose of its character as an aggressive war. All the chief actors and the subsidiary figures too are in this document. We meet the men who bore the responsibility, the knowing and the unknowing, the guilty, the innocent and the henchmen, those who profited by and those who were robbed by the Nazi system."[83]

Canaris had written the entries himself until the summer of 1939, when he began to dictate them to his secretary, Vera Schwarte. Only one complete copy existed, though occasionally Hans Oster and Abwehr section chiefs, particularly Lahousen, copied relevant passages for their own files. Canaris kept his diary so diligently that when he was removed from office in 1944, his notes filled six binders and six notebooks of travel reports, which were entrusted to Lieutenant Colonel Werner Schrader for safekeeping, somewhere in the country, to be destroyed if necessary.

After the failure of the July 20 attempt, Hitler was raging, and in the late summer heat, the RSHA was working feverishly to identify, expose, and hunt down the plotters and anyone even remotely connected to them. Schrader knew what lay ahead and committed suicide; his widow knew that the information the diaries contained would cost more members of the resistance their lives, and destroyed them.[84]

In late September 1944 the Gestapo discovered bundles of incriminating material in an unused safe in Maybach II, the OKH bunker section at Zossen, south of Berlin. Many of these documents were from Canaris's Abwehr, particularly the central section. Originally they had been hidden at the Prussian State Bank in Berlin, but in 1943, as Allied air raids on the capital increased, they were moved to Zossen. The Zossen material probably included notes on preparations for the 1938 coup d'état, some in Oster's handwriting. There were probably minutes of Müller's negotiations with the British government through the Vatican, also referred to as the X-Report, a status report by General Ludwig Beck after the Polish campaign, and a general study by Oster regarding the realization of a coup. There were most likely also parts of Canaris's diary, including notes on the resistance movement and on visits to the front to win over several commanders for an overthrow of the Nazi government, and correspondence on the resistance activities of Dietrich Bonhoeffer. Hans von Dohnanyi, Bonhoeffer's brother-in-law, had been compiling what was called the chronicle of scandals since 1933, and he had kept his compilation in spite of Canaris's explicit order to do away with it.[86] There would also have been many documents testifying to the atrocities and absurdities of the Nazi regime.[85]

The Canaris diaries found at Zossen covered at least the period from March 1943 to July 1944. Whether the Zossen diaries were the originals or copies made by Canaris's section chiefs is difficult to establish.[87] Some scholars suggest that these pages were not the original diaries that Schwarte had typed up, but Oster's selective copies from them. Contemporaries and researchers alike confuse two separate incidents at Zossen that turned up incriminating material.

The first took place in the fall of 1944, the second in the spring of 1945. General Walter Buhle, head of the army staff at OKW, had moved into underground shelters at Camp Zeppelin in Zossen, determined to resist the advancing Red Army. Looking around for more office space, he and his officers came across a safe containing several black cloth-covered binders holding between eighty and two hundred handwritten and dated sheets.[88] Buhle immediately informed the Gestapo and notified SS-Oberführer Hans Rattenhuber, head of the security service responsible for Hitler's personal safety. On April 5, 1945, the chief of the SD, Ernst Kaltenbrunner, reported the sensational find to Hitler at the Chancellery. Hitler read some pages Kaltenbrunner had marked for him, flew into a tirade, and gave his approval to the execution of Canaris.

At the Nuremberg trials, senior SD officials confirmed that shortly before the collapse of the Third Reich, the Gestapo brought the material to Castle Mittersill in Austria, where it was burned in early May 1945.[89] Ambiguities and uncertainties about the diaries have occasioned wild speculation. Many curious minds have been induced to search for, or—if they could not find them—to forge, the "original" diaries of the Abwehr chief. Ian Colvin had spent five years in Nazi Germany as a British foreign correspondent. When his newspaper withdrew him from Germany in 1939, he worked for the Foreign Office. After the war, with help from the British Secret Service, he looked for Canaris's diary, to no avail. Regardless, he argues in his book that Canaris might have been a British agent.[90]

Revisionist historian and Holocaust denier David Irving refers to two different men who claimed to possess the entire set of Canaris diaries. The first, Klaus Benzing, produced "documents of the postwar German Intelligence Service (BND)" and original papers "signed by Canaris" to support his claim. The second, Fabian von Schlabrendorff, argued that his set had been returned to the West German government by Francisco Franco. Forensic tests on the paper and ink of a document supplied by Benzing, conducted for Irving by the London laboratory of Hehner & Cox Ltd., proved them to be fairly inept forgeries; the admiral's signature was written in ballpoint ink. An interview with Franco's chef de bureau and brother-in-law Don Felipe Polo Valdes in Madrid disposed of the second claim.[91]

Benzing had tried to sell Irving and his publishers, Williams Collins Ltd., the forged diaries in the 1970s. His 1973 book contained several lengthy quotes from what he claimed to be Canaris's diaries and testimonials from two experts attesting to the authenticity of Benzing's sources. In a subsequent edition Benzing added a postscript with a defensive disclaimer and a half-hearted apology: "I can only say: I acted to the best of my knowledge and belief and wanted to do justice to this extraordinary man. One thing is for sure, and even the 'skeptics' agree on this: the spirit and the substance of the quotations correspond with the views and actions of Admiral Wilhelm Canaris! This, however, is what the quotations were meant to achieve—substantiate the integrity and decency of this man."[92]

Others speculate that the real Canaris diary may still exist. Though the probability is very slight, the original entries could be buried in some forgotten Russian archive. There are a host of reasons why Stalinists would not have been eager to reveal them after the war, not the least of which would be information on the cooperation of the Russian State Security Service and the SD in manufacturing forged materials for use in the trials of Marshal Mikhail Tukhachevsky. Other speculation leads to Spain, where the daughter of a General Kindelan, who was very close to both Franco and Canaris, recounted that the admiral frequently visited her childhood home. Perhaps Canaris managed to get a copy of his diary to Madrid through the Spanish diplomatic pouch.

Canaris's diaries would represent pure gold to the history of intelligence in World War II—if only they could be found. As his friend and colleague Lahousen said, they would reveal so much: the chief actors, the subsidiary figures, the men who bore the responsibility, the knowing and the unknowing, the guilty, the innocent. Still, questions would remain, for he acknowledged that "only one character is absent: Canaris himself. He presented only one half, perhaps only one third of himself—the rest remains hidden."[93] Eventually, though, Canaris's diaries had given his jailers what they needed.

In the early morning darkness of April 9, 1945, Canaris, Oster, Bonhoeffer, and other resisters were escorted, naked, to the gallows by SS men at the Flossenbürg. The Armageddon Canaris had predicted was at hand; the end of Germany that he had foreseen was just weeks away.[94]

MORE THAN HALF A CENTURY AFTER HIS DEATH, ADMIRAL WILHELM CANARIS REMAINS A man of mystery, a man who has eluded characterization by contemporaries and historians alike.[95] No one seems to have been able to take the measure of the man. Some celebrate him as the great protector of the German opposition to Hitler, some call him a traitor and double agent, some despise him as a servant of the murderous Nazi machine.[96]

There are glaring inconsistencies in Canaris's political outlook. He was an ardent nationalist. He disagreed with Nazi methods on principle, but not with Hitler's objectives of reorganizing and rearming the nation, and not with his advocating and working toward German equality. By the time he was in a position to know the extent of Nazi atrocities—not as rumor but as fact—he was Abwehr director, and knew more of Hitler's plans than anyone outside the top of the Führer's hierarchy. In his view, those plans were "suicidal," and could lead only to a catastrophic end for Germany. He used the Latin *"Finis Germaniae."*[97]

How could he serve the Reich while fighting its dictator, head an intelligence service and tolerate passing information to the enemy, motivate and shield members of the German resistance, and hunt them as conspirators? It seemed "incredible that Canaris could simultaneously create a large, successful espionage system for the purpose of augmenting German conquests, while secretly opposing the leadership that planned those conquests."[98] Yet on Canaris's watch, Unternehmen Sieben, named after the program's original seven beneficiaries, succeeded in sending Jews to safety disguised as Abwehr spies. To his inner circle, Canaris let it be known that he thought Hitler was the greatest disaster ever to have struck Germany. He once told them that they were never, ever to pass a flock of sheep without giving the Nazi salute. "After all," he warned with typical humor, "you never know."

Lahousen, one of the admiral's few real intimates, lived with this "confused, iridescent personality in every conceivable situation." "As one who shared his secret plans, I know Canaris played a double game." What the limits of that game were, Lahousen could not say, yet "in all that Canaris did, or omitted to do, it is difficult to recognize a clear and undeviating line. He hated violence . . . was repelled by the war. He hated Hitler and the Nazi system. [His] weapons were intellect, influence, cunning, and above all—the double game. The circle he gathered around himself was as colorful and heterogeneous as his own personality. Men of all classes and professions, people whose horizons were broad and narrow, idealists and political adventurers, sober rationalists and mystics. Conservative noblemen and Freemasons, half-Jews and Jews, German and non-German antifascists, men and women united only by their resistance to Hitler and his system. No secret orders, but an intellectual association, only rare active intervention."[99]

In a smoking, devastated Belgrade, filled with the stench of unburied corpses, Lahousen recalled that Canaris broke down completely. Such acts of violence and brutality strengthened his resolve to prevent a Nazi victory. "In the end, Canaris probably stumbled and fell—over Canaris. But in a time of indescribable horrors he always remained, in contrast to many around him, decent and thoroughly human."[100]

Elusive as ever, Canaris shied from extreme and radical solutions. "Time and again, his patriotism stirred up doubts within him whether an overthrow of Hitler in the middle of war might not harm the interests of the fatherland."[101] So Canaris had found himself facing a painful choice: Should he serve the state or the nation? He apparently resolved this dilemma by providing a protective umbrella for active resisters and supplying them with sensitive information behind the scenes while staying out of the actual plotting. Gradually the initiative shifted to Oster, who plotted Hitler's death with a determination verging on obsession.[102]

Hindsight poses a hypothetical question: What might have happened if Canaris had been more assertive and aggressive, if he had behaved more like Oster, his energetic deputy? Apologists stress that military intelligence had no authority or mission in domestic or foreign policy and that Canaris acted completely at his own risk. Some question just how strong the admiral's opposition to the Nazis really was, but Abwehr veterans have rejected the notion that he could actually have been a secret Nazi who helped plan the war.

Ambivalence remains, and historians are tantalized by the thought that Canaris's diaries, found at intelligence headquarters in Zossen might have resolved at least some of it, but the diaries have since disappeared. The Canaris paradox still begs for explanation.

AFTER ALL POSSIBLE VICISSITUDES: OPERATION SUNRISE

By late December 1944, in spite of the surprise German offensive in the Ardennes, the war was essentially over. Then Allen Dulles had an unexpected overture, setting in motion an intelligence coup that put the feather in the cap of his Swiss adventure. This last salvo tested his skills to the utmost, requiring diplomacy, discretion, deceit, patience, bravado. Operation Sunrise combined the most thrilling aspects of storybook spycraft with high-level politics, motives both low- and high-minded, personal and geopolitical, the lust for power and the search for salvation, with just a few absurd situations tossed in for some much-needed comic relief.[103]

Everyone knew it was only a matter of time before total collapse of the Reich. Hitler had decided that if the war was to be lost, he would take Germany down with him, so it was now a question of *sauve qui peut*.[104] The first tentative feelers had been extended to the British in late 1944 through an Italian industrialist and various Catholic officials. As usual, the British were not receptive, and as before, the next approaches were to the Americans, specifically Dulles, again through the Catholic Church. Through an intermediary and in typically nonspecific terms, Dulles was informed that highly placed Germans in northern Italy had asked the British whether the Allies would join them to fight the Russians if the Germans stopped fighting in the west. The British had shut the door firmly; might Dulles be interested?

In a top-secret report Bern informed the Joint Chiefs of Staff that Constantin von Neurath, the German consul in Lugano, was in contact with generals Albert Kesselring, Wilhelm Harster, and Karl Wolff in northern Italy; "some Gestapo in North Italy might work with Kesselring for OKW re programs re use of German Army in Italy as separate unit to help liquidate Nazis."[105]

The impulse to abandon a sinking ship was running strong. Neither Dulles nor Washington was convinced that the approach was being made in good faith. Dulles's next contact came from the secretary of a Milanese cardinal eager to broker a peace between Germany and the Allies in Italy in the interests of preserving Italian infrastructure. This plan, however, required the cooperation of the partisans. Since the partisans wanted to liberate Italy from their German oppressors themselves, this was not forthcoming. Curiously, though, the plan also stated that SS General Wolff and

Field Marshal Kesselring would sign the agreement. By late February, there was word that Kaltenbrunner, second only to Himmler in the SS hierarchy, was interested in peace. Himmler had made peace overtures earlier, but Kaltenbrunner was new, though clearly motivated by the same instinct to save himself.[106]

Somewhat earlier, Gävernitz had been alerted by the German consul in Lugano that the German military leadership in Italy was looking for contacts with the West. Then a Swiss counterintelligence agent informed Dulles that messages had been received from Wolff, the top SS officer in northern Italy. In early March, Dulles cabled the OSS in Caserta, Italy, where Allied headquarters was located, that the potentialities here were "so far-reaching that I think they justify immediate consideration [in] highest quarters. If Wolff [is] really working with Kesselring, these two might pull off unconditional surrender."[107]

This was at once tantalizing and frustrating. Roosevelt had ordered that no promises were to be made to Germans willing to cooperate with the Allies. Any such promises might be misunderstood—presumably by the Soviets—perennially brimming with mistrust. Dulles had been working with what he called "Germany's Underground" for years, encouraging where he could, even without Washington's support. Now he saw the possibility of making a real change. If nothing else, it might at least shorten the war in one theater of operations—Italy. The obstacles to such a clandestine surrender were many and complex. Dulles was walking a tightrope: He was bound by the president's order to make no promises to German peace offers, duty-bound to report his activities to headquarters, but aware that alerting too many to those activities would almost guarantee failure. He had to insulate himself from these advances somehow, and find a way to prove—or disprove—that Wolff was both in earnest and acting in good faith.

Dulles sent Paul Blum, a trusted staff member as his emissary to deal with the intermediaries. Blum was armed with two slips of paper. On one was written the name Ferrucio Parri, on the other, Antonio Usmiani. Both were Italian antifascists, one active in the resistance, the other a U.S. agent, and both were now in jail in different cities.[108] Parri was probably the highest-profile political prisoner in Italy. If Wolff had the power and the will, he would release these two from SS prisons. Freeing them would be represent a serious coup, and a true indication of Wolff's authority. Then they would see about taking the next step.

Neither Dulles nor Gävernitz expected to hear any more about it, but to everyone's surprise, things began to happen very quickly. Just four days later, on March 8, 1945, word came that the two Italian prisoners had arrived in Switzerland. Wolff, too, was en route with a small retinue, all in mufti, shuttling through the alpine passes in a closed and curtained train compartment. He was certainly wasting no time.

During the five-hour trip, Wolff's intermediary worked to prepare him for his interview with Dulles. He stressed Hitler's sins, and those of the SS in particular, among them the murder of millions of Jews. As improbable as it seems, Wolff swore on his honor that this was the first that he had ever heard of this.[109] Their long trip was unexpectedly interrupted when an avalanche thundered down the mountain near the Gotthard Pass and blocked the tracks. All passengers had to clamber out and walk several hundred yards to another train that would take them on. The delay and the exposure could easily have aborted the project. Wolff was a recognizable public figure; his picture had appeared in Swiss newspapers several times. Had he been identified, it would have caused a sensation and spelled the end of his project.

Dulles laid out his negotiations with Wolff for the surrender of troops in northern Italy. He outlined the procedure by which Wolff intended to bring about the surrender, which included among other things, enlisting Kesselring, releasing Italian partisans, and arranging the "release to Switzerland of several hundred Jews interned at Bozen (Bolzano).[110] He claims he has refused any ransom money offered in this connection and possibly already swallowed up by the intermediaries."[111] This message was relayed the next day by Donovan to President Roosevelt, who was kept abreast of developments on Operation Sunrise, not only by Donovan but also by the War Department.[112]

Dulles was taking huge risks. If these talks went nowhere, but became known, the OSS would be blackened by having dealt with the infamous Black Corps. A wedge would be driven between the western Allies and the Soviets. He would have to close as many loopholes as possible. Before seeing Wolff, he first visited the two liberated Italians to make sure they were who they were said to be and that they were in good condition. The two men had been installed as "patients" in a Zurich clinic, and they were totally confused. When they were taken from their cells by their SS jailers, they had assumed that they were about to be shot. Now they were in Switzerland, in an immaculate and safe clinic. It all seemed unfathomable. Parri was agitated, teary from a peculiar mix of relief and anxiety, relief at not having been shot, anxiety about what it all meant. What kind of deal had been made to get him out? When could he return to Italy to continue his fight? Dulles was reassuring, but vague. If Parri were spotted in Italy the house of cards he was trying to construct would collapse immediately; there might be hell to pay.

In early March Dulles and Wolff met at a Zurich apartment the OSS rented for just such delicate situations. Appropriately enough, it was accessible only by passing through three locked doors, one opened by "an ancient massive key." Through intermediaries, Wolff had submitted a sort of résumé, summing up his career and complete with character references—Rudolf Hess, the pope, and a variety of churchmen and Italian nobles among them.[113] No doubt these papers were intended to reassure Dulles, but just before their meeting he was tortured by nightmarish visions of headlines trumpeting that an envoy of FDR's had received an SS officer. He took comfort in the fact that he would at least have accomplished the release of two important political prisoners.

Then he and Gävernitz began to set the stage, complete with the psychological props Dulles habitually used for meetings as sensitive as this one. "I have always tried to have important meetings around a fireplace, Dulles wrote later. "A wood fire makes people feel at ease and less inhibited in their conversation; and if you are asked a question which you are in no hurry to answer, you can stir up the fire, study the pattern of the flames . . . until you have shaped your answer. If I needed more time, I always had my pipe handy to fill and light."[114]

Just before 10:00 P.M., Gävernitz opened the door. Wolff was a handsome man, and a nervous one. Gävernitz shook his hand and, in his gracious way, mentioned that they had a friend in common, the beautiful Countess Podewils, at whose behest Wolff had protected a Catholic philosopher beleaguered by the Gestapo. The deft touch put Wolff visibly more at ease. Then the fire and the scotch did their part. Wolff began to talk.

The talk was in German, since he spoke no English, which put him further at ease. He confessed that until 1943 he had been one of Hitler's faithful. Now, however, he saw that the war could not be won. Prolonging it was a crime against the German people—not to mention Italy. At one point Hitler had called him to his East Prussian headquarters to propose that Wolff occupy the Vatican, kidnap the pope and ship both the pope and the Vatican's treasures off to Germany. He had been aghast; this harebrained idea would cause upheaval and chaos in Italy and outrage in the rest of the world. Despite Hitler's demand for progress reports, he had stalled for time. At a recent briefing in Berlin he had been horrified to hear the Führer's scorched-earth policy for Italy.

He explained that while he controlled SS forces, he had to have the cooperation of the military, but was fairly confident that Kesselring could be persuaded to cooperate. He would consult with Kesselring immediately after this meeting. He had already removed some Italian art treasures to alpine hideouts for safekeeping, and he had a plan for ending unnecessary killing and destruction in Italy. What he needed from Dulles now was the assurance of reaching the highest level of the Allied command. If this could be accomplished, he suggested, other German generals might well follow suit and the war could be truly ended.

Dulles left Gävernitz to nail down details and returned to Bern late that night to inform Washington and the Allied command in Italy. The Allies had fought their way from Sicily slowly, steadily up the peninsula, and while German forces still held the major northern cities and industrial centers, they now had their backs against the Alps, and the partisans were harassing them constantly from the south and at their flanks. At an earlier date, Dulles had once blandly asked Field Marshal Alexander at Allied headquarters in Caserta what approach he should take if the Germans were actually serious about surrender initiatives. Alexander had replied that Kesselring should just send someone through the lines with a white flag. Dulles had realized immediately that this was not a solution; Kesselring's headquarters was sure to be infested with Gestapo informers, and the marshal was likely to be on his way to a concentration camp or worse before the bearer of the white flag ever reached Allied lines.

Now a sleepless Dulles waited in hopes of hearing a more reasonable approach, and he soon had it. Alexander was sending two senior officers to Switzerland. OSS Caserta was bustling with preparations for a complex but top-secret operation. They would call it Operation Sunrise, for the rosy glow of hope that the idea of peace was shedding on those involved.

Wolff, however, was not partaking of the glow. An intermediary reported that during his absence, his superior, Kaltenbrunner, had tried to reach him to arrange a meeting at Innsbruck. Wolff's trip to Switzerland without notifying Kaltenbrunner was likely to put anyone as pathologically and professionally suspicious as Heydrich's successor on full alert. Wolff had guessed that if he showed up, Kaltenbrunner might arrest him, so he had replied that he was too busy to meet. Furthermore, Kesselring had been called to Hitler's headquarters and was apparently being transferred to the crumbling western front. Wolff would now have to go it alone, or persuade whoever succeeded Kesselring to join him. Soon he would also have to account to Himmler.

At this point in his narrative, the sleep-deprived intermediary pulled a piece of scorched fabric out of his pocket—a tattered bit of Wolff's overcoat. His car had been attacked by American aircraft; could Dulles perhaps ask that, at least east of Milan, planes not attack single autos quite so fiercely?

Gävernitz and Dulles had been traveling almost ceaselessly from one Swiss city to another; sometimes by train, sometimes driving along icy Swiss roads in the predawn hours. They navigated "by the stars," as Dulles put it, since all road signs had been removed as a safety precaution in the event of invasion. They were exhausted, but there was no time to sleep or to stop. On March 14, they rushed off to smuggle the two Allied officers Alexander had sent from Italy across the border to participate in the talks with Wolff. At the time, this involved considerable effort.

The Swiss border guards were known sticklers, and it took time for Major General Lyman Lemnitzer of the United States and Britain's Major General Terence Airey to memorize the serial numbers on borrowed dog tags and the biographical details that went with them. Lemnitzer became Sergeant

Nicholson, with a wife and children on Long Island, and the decidedly British Airey became Sergeant McNeeley, a New York Irishman. Luckily, they were not only experienced military men, but they also had a sense of humor. In the subsequent days of cloak-and-dagger dangers and ludicrous moments, they had occasion to put both experience and humor to use.

Airey and Lemnitzer were staying with Dulles in Bern, but their presence was raising eyebrows. Who were these two keeping company with FDR's "special envoy?" Then General Airey provided the men with an unusual bit of luck: he was a bona fide dachshund aficionado, and Switzerland produced a very special breed he particularly fancied. His cover as an eccentric English gentleman on the hunt for the perfect *Dackel* would help to deflect suspicions. With help from Gävernitz's secretary, kennels were contacted, discussions held. Airey's wishes were fulfilled at last. "Fritzel," the dachshund, became General Airey's constant companion.

On March 19, Wolff, Gävernitz, and Dulles met at an idyllic villa belonging to Gävernitz's brother-in-law at Ascona, on the Swiss side of the Lago Maggiore. Airey and Lemnitzer bided their time nearby. Wolff wanted to contact Kesselring, who was now already in Germany. He recognized the need for certain detailed military preparations and for better communications between his headquarters and Bern. Arrangements were made to smuggle "Little Wally," a Czech radio man covertly rescued from Auschwitz, into Italy to help ease communication. Lemnitzer and Airey were then introduced to the discussions as military advisors, and there was more talk of technicalities and the next course of action. The Allied contingent would wait; Wolff would try to enlist Kesselring.

Days crawled by. At last Wolff sent word: At the very end of March, he had won over Kesselring and would now approach Kesselring's successor, General Heinrich von Veitinghoff, and come to Ascona with Veitinghoff and Rudolph Rahn, the German ambassador to Mussolini's puppet Salò Republic, who was also in agreement with their plan. Dulles lived in excited anticipation that a "surrender might be in our pockets in no time."

On April 2, one of Wolff's go-betweens arrived to tell the assembled crew an alarming story. Some time ago, Wolff had moved his wife and children to the part of Italy that was under his control. An Easter call from Himmler had notified Wolff that his family was "now under my protection" in Austria. To Wolff this meant one thing: His family was being held hostage. The news had brought him to a standstill. The slightest false move could doom him and his family, his plan would come to nothing, and it would all have been in vain.

Throughout March, Dulles and Gävernitz's days were consumed by unending logistical details. "It is easy to start a war," Dulles wrote sourly of those days, "but difficult to stop one."[115] On a larger scale, the Anglo-American-Soviet alliance was beginning to fray. When the Soviets heard of a possible surrender in Italy, they were ready to send an entire delegation to parley. Washington's claim that these were only preliminary talks brought an angry response: Negotiations were to be broken off—*now*. Stalin was concerned to get as far west as possible—Trieste was the goal in Italy— before the war ended to give the Soviets a big foothold on the Adriatic.

The Russians took an aggrieved tone, then a rude one, and soon a flurry of warring cables was flying between the dying Roosevelt and Stalin. Churchill warned that the Russians should not be allowed to bully the western powers. "The air was opaque with mutual suspicions of separate peace feelers," recalled Kim Philby, who would have had direct knowledge that Stalin was bristling with suspicion.[116] Just hours after sending a conciliatory note to placate the irascible Stalin, Roosevelt was dead. On April 12, 1945, a stunned American nation mourned its president.

Next day, Donovan, Dulles, Casey, and the American intelligence bigwigs convened at the Paris Ritz. When Operation Sunrise became the topic of conversation, the difficulties these negotiations were causing with the Russians were spelled out. "Dulles," Casey later recalled, "fidgeted in his chair, alternately outraged and embarrassed. . . . Bluntly put, all hell broke loose."[117] Donovan had been called on the White House carpet to make sure that he was not pursuing an independent peace. When he returned to Bern, Dulles found condolences from Wolff on Roosevelt's death waiting for him.[118]

After Wolff's visit with Kesselring, he had been summoned to Berlin, where Himmler and Kaltenbrunner awaited him. Both men were secretly angling for their own peace settlement, and Wolff knew that his powers of persuasion and diplomatic charm would be lost on these two. They confronted him about his contact with Dulles. He had not asked permission, nor had he informed Schellenberg.

Hearing these charges, Wolff's reaction was relief; his superiors were irked over what was essentially a matter of protocol. He realized that they only knew of his initial conversation with Dulles, not the later, more compromising one. Did they just want to take charge of the negotiations themselves, hoping to save their skins? Yet they seemed unwilling to mention the real issue: stopping the war. Suddenly it seemed to Wolff that it was time to stand up and propose that they lay the plan before Hitler. They were dubious; Hitler was very irritable just now. Besides, Himmler had other matters to attend to. Kaltenbrunner told Wolff to stay away from the Americans and intimated that he himself could pursue the same contacts whenever he wanted.

On his return to Italy, Wolff had received Himmler's call threatening his family. Clearly, he had reason to worry after all. The Wolff-Himmler tug-of-war continued, with Wolff's family trapped in between. On April 14, Himmler again ordered Wolff to Berlin to meet with the Führer. Worried that he might be replaced in Italy by some fanatic, he managed to stall for several days, but finally prepared to leave. Understanding the odds against his return, he sent Dulles a message, a kind of testament: In the event of his death, would Dulles make Wolff's honorable intentions known and protect his family if at all possible? He then flew to Berlin, already in ruins and surrounded by Soviet troops. It was an extremely dangerous trip, but the dangers he faced came from a different quarter.

At his meeting with Hitler, Wolff was chastised for his gross disregard of authority. But now Wolff's earlier proposal to Himmler and Kaltenbrunner to broach Hitler stood him in good stead. At no time, Wolff replied, had he ever claimed to be acting with Hitler's knowledge; he had merely tried to win Allied support for Germany against the Russians. In fact, he had come to the Führer on his own initiative; surely this could not be construed as treason. He left a haggard, tremulous, but apparently kindly disposed Hitler, staggering under the weight of the coming catastrophe, expressing his gratitude and urging Wolff to hold fast. Miraculously, Wolff had extricated himself from the snake pit. He would return to Italy. Kaltenbrunner's parting words instructed that all civilian prisoners in Italy were to be liquidated. They must not fall into Allied hands.

Bern, meanwhile, was on tenterhooks. Wolff was unreachable until a relayed message informed Dulles that he had an interview with Hitler on April 18, but would return to Italy. As the Allies renewed military offensives in Italy, Berlin warned that any wavering or defeatism would have serious consequences for higher commanders. Dulles, usually the image of unruffled calm, was stricken with an agonizing attack of gout, often a by-product of stress. Would Wolff manage to get out of Berlin alive? And at what cost?

On April 20, Dulles reported that "for the first time since Hitler's accession to power, the swastika flag was not flown today over the German legation to celebrate his birthday."[119] Then came the thunderbolt: The Joint Chiefs of Staff ordered OSS Bern to break off all negotiations at once. There was no explanation, only a mention of "complications which have arisen with the Russians."[120] Dulles felt hog-tied. Wolff was out of range, and communications problems made contact with his intermediaries nearly impossible. Two days later there was astounding news: Wolff was on his way to Switzerland with Veitinghoff's agreement in hand, and Dulles was under orders not to talk to him.

After two months of ceaseless negotiation, Dulles and Gävernitz were exhausted, desperate. Waiting in Lucerne were two German proxies, ready to surrender a million German troops on behalf of Wolff and Veitinghoff, but they were hearing only silence. Wolff had also gone suddenly, inexplicably incommunicado. Early on the morning of April 26, an intelligence source brought word that Wolff had been completely surrounded by Italian partisans and might be killed.

Dulles was under strict orders against any further contact. But Gäver-nitz, though he knew he would have to be very discreet, was galvanized by this new challenge. With the help of the remarkably effective underground and partisan communication system—a sort of jungle drums in the Alps—he set about organizing an international party for an unlikely nighttime rescue mission: pulling an SS general out of the vengeful clutches of angry Italian partisans. The first car of a three-car convoy flew white flags that fluttered conspicuously in the beams of the second car. There was shooting, some lobbed hand grenades, and many anxious moments, but at last the rescue party reached the villa where Wolff was trapped, surrounded. After he had changed out of his SS uniform, he was stashed—invisibly, they hoped—in the middle car. The return was a crawling journey through in-numerable partisan checkpoints, all involving questions, papers, flashlights in the dark.

Gävernitz and a Swiss intelligence contact meanwhile waited nervously at a grubby little railroad restaurant in the border town of Chiasso. Despite the hour, the place was brimming with the usual bit players of war: refugees, partisans, spies, even a few newsmen, hoping to sniff out a story. Slowly the numbers dwindled. The newsmen made Gävernitz anxious. There must be no whiff of any of this in the press. He would wait out of sight in a car; he must not be seen talking with Wolff. But when the convoy finally rolled up, Wolff immediately marched over to shake Gävernitz's hand in gratitude. Then there was no avoiding the rush of words—of relief, of excitement, of the possible peace now actually at hand. He also handed him a piece of pa-per: Marshal Rodolfo Graziani, still commander of Mussolini's Fascist divi-sions, had signed over to Wolff the power to surrender the troops under his command. Wolff then signed this authority over to his trusted adjutant. He would return to his command.

It was early morning of April 27, 1945. With what Dulles described as this "flip of the wrist," Operation Sunrise was ready to enter its final phase. Only one thing was missing, Washington's go-ahead. As if on cue, three highest priority signals came into the office just after Dulles arrived that morning. After all that had gone on before, it seemed almost anticlimactic. Caserta was prepared to receive German envoys, and a Russian representa-tive as well. Gävernitz would interpret and put his social graces to work in smoothing the unavoidable bumps and wrinkles that arose. In the early af-ternoon of April 29, the surrender was signed. Operation Sunrise, however, was far from over.

Arranging a simultaneous cease-fire for the May 2 deadline was critical, and German field commanders had to be notified. There should be no un-necessary casualties. Gävernitz and the two German proxies had returned from Caserta, armed with crucial documents for the German commanders in Bolzano. They had hard traveling ahead of them, over terrain that was difficult both geographically and militarily. When they were detained at the sealed Swiss border, only Dulles's fast footwork with the Swiss authorities got them through. On the Italian side, Wolff had an aging car and an alarming message waiting for them: Kaltenbrunner was determined to stop the surrender. The Gestapo was waiting for them; they would have to take a longer route.

Mussolini and his mistress had already been shot and strung up in Milan. Hitler had shot himself. As the men rattled over the alpine passes carrying the papers to Bolzano, Dulles sent Donovan a cable that Sunrise seemed to be on track again "after every possible vicissitude." He meant exactly that, but did not realize that more vicissitudes were to come.[121]

On May 1, Caserta sent an urgent query: Would Veitinghoff abide by the conditions for the cease-fire, set for 2:00 P.M. next day? In the very early morning of May 2, Wolff replied: Kesselring had relieved Veitinghoff of his command and had responded to the orders of Wolff and other generals for a cease-fire with an order for their arrest. Wolff was requesting that Allied paratroopers be deployed to protect them.

In grim silence, Gävernitz and Dulles sat in Bern as the hours ticked by. Would there be a ghastly struggle to the bitterest possible end after all? It seemed unreal and impossible in the bright May sunshine. They waited. There was no word. Then at 5:00 P.M., the radio suddenly crackled with news: The Germans had surrendered in Italy. Soon after, a familiar voice resonated on the BBC. It was Churchill, announcing the simple facts in solemn, measured tones. The war in Italy was over, and so was Operation Sunrise.

Only gradually did Bern learn the facts, and the further vicissitudes, of what had gone on among the German contingent during those days of agonizing silence. There had been meetings, frantic machinations, concerns about military protocol and the chain of command, bitter division among the commanders. Kesselring could not agree to surrender. He felt bound by his oath of loyalty to Hitler. And last if not least, there was a determined Kaltenbrunner, set on his own peace negotiation. When it looked as if the SS, favoring surrender, and the military brass opposing it would kill each other, Wolff had sent his SOS to Alexander. For much of the night of May 1–2, all of Wolff's persuasive powers had been put to the test in a tortured telephone conversation with Kesselring. Hitler was dead; his oath of loyalty to the Führer was no longer binding. The war was over; peace should be concluded. At last, at 4:30 A.M. on May 2, Kesselring agreed to capitulate.[122]

WHEN NEWS OF THE SURRENDER FINALLY BROKE, GENERAL AIREY'S DACHSHUND FRITZEL had his day of fame. The front page of a London newspaper proclaimed: "Fritzel, the Dachshund That Led to the Surrender." Within days, the war was over. Fritzel's fame proved to have little staying power, but the Bern station chief was catapulted into celebrity status. The brilliant and widely recognized intelligence successes of his two and a half years in Bern made Dulles's name legend. Applauded and acclaimed, he was hailed as the great spymaster. Yet ironically, Dulles's efforts had had little or no effect on the outcome of the war. Precious information and hard-won intelligence delivered to him at the price of repeated, staggering risks, of sweat and tears and very hard work, had gone largely unused. And unused intelligence, no matter how good, is worthless.

To Kolbe's immense frustration, the bombing targets he had recommended in 1943 were still intact in mid-1944. The "Easter eggs" from the fabulous "bunny" had gone nowhere. Richard Helms, who worked with Dulles in postwar Germany and later became CIA director, noted in regard to the Kolbe reports that "the war was almost over by the time this debate . . . about those documents was resolved."[123] Only in the Far East did Kolbe's Kappa reports, with their substantive information on military matters and the political climate in Japan, get the attention they deserved. Among the Allies, Operation Sunrise was Dulles's most ballyhooed achievement. It brought the hope of peace, but it proceeded V-E Day by less than a week. In summing up, the master spy himself made an observation that has been noted previously, but is worth repeating: "It is often harder to use the product than to get it. The receivers of intelligence generally start out discounting a particular report as false or a plant. Then when they get over that hurdle they discard what they don't like and refuse to believe it. Finally, when they get a report they both believe and like, they don't know what to do about it."[124]

MOTIVATION IS ONE QUESTION THAT CONSISTENTLY BEDEVILS THE SPY TRADE. QUEStioned by the U.S. after the war as to his motives at the time, Kolbe repeated everything he had told Dulles earlier: He hated the Nazis; he wanted to do the right thing; he did not want money. His lack of interest in money already made him odd, even suspect, because intelligence has a rigid hierarchy of believability in assessing a source's motivation. The best intelligence comes from a source over whom the interested party has some sort of power—blackmail, for example, or the providing of a service, as to someone who seeks a reduced sentence or political asylum. The second best comes from someone who is being paid for it, as in prominent spy cases like the Walker Ring that penetrated the U.S. Navy, or Aldrich Ames, who spied for the Soviets within the CIA. In these instances the spies received substantial sums for some very accurate intelligence. The least reliable intelligence, it is widely agreed, comes from someone who is providing intelligence out of personal conviction and seeks no personal benefit.

Money and blackmail make a source trustworthy, but acting on principle is likely to invite suspicion. Dulles's assessment of motivations ran entirely counter to this schema, and may well have been one reason for his success. He argued that if one had to pay for an agent, there was really no point in using him at all. Anyone who betrayed his country for money would willingly sell to both sides. To him, the best agent was motivated by hatred, revenge, and passion.[125] A full agreement and like-mindedness between the agent and his control officer was ideal. In this regard, Dulles and Kolbe were partners par excellence and produced probably the finest intelligence of World War II.

Dulles's "big window" on Hitler's Germany had been opened and kept open by many. He would have been the first to credit his principal sources, the many Germans willing to risk their lives time and again if it would help save their country and the world from Nazism. They had been willing to shoulder the burden of being labeled traitors, not only at home, but among the Allies. But Dulles's efforts to encourage support of the Breakers had hit the wall of unconditional surrender. In spite of the many who died to save Germany's honor, the failed Stauffenberg coup salvaged only small, tattered remnants. And the war, murder, and bloodshed continued for almost ten months.

When the door of Herrengasse 23 closed behind Allen Dulles for the last time in May 1945, it was the end of a significant chapter in the history of the war. He would now turn his efforts to reconstruction. It also marked the beginning, if not quite the first chapter, of the cold war.

THE "GOOD GERMANS"

Hitler had once said that if he did not succeed, he would take the nation down with him, and in this respect he had won. Certainly he had managed to eradicate much and many of the best in Germany. Dulles had thought that saving some "good Germans" to help rebuild was a good idea, but the decision to wait until the regime collapsed created a situation in which few such Germans were left. Most had met the same fate as Moltke, Hassell, Trott, Canaris, Oster, and Dohnanyi; thousands had been executed.[126] If they had managed to save a few shreds of Germany's honor, it was quite some time before that was recognized, even in Germany. Millions were dead. The Papens, however, had survived again.

For most Allies "good Germans" was a contradiction in terms, but Dulles of course, was an exception. So what became of the "good Germans" who remained—Dulles's "Musketeers" Gävernitz, Gisevius, and Waetjen, and Schulte and Kolbe and the others, after the collapse? Dulles had always been acutely aware of the need to plan for Germany's future, to have people on hand to shape and hold together a stable government. Cordelia Hood, who worked with him in Bern, remembered: "We had some very good Germans who would come in to Switzerland. Dulles was trying to build up a convoy of men to go back once the Nazis were out." She recalled that Dulles thought it was extremely important to have men capable of moving into a new government in Germany.[127] Aside from personal loyalty and gratitude to his "crown jewels," he also felt a responsibility toward those who had contributed so much to his work in Bern. Once the war was over, he made it his business to look after his frontline informants as best he could. According to one observer, Dulles wanted these people to "have a fair shake from the Allies."[128] Getting that fair shake was not without its problems, and in many cases, he met with little success. Personally, he had long-term personal and business ties with Germany, and his interest lay in establishing a viable, self-governing Germany after the collapse of the Nazi regime. However, it was not until after the war that Dulles's views were put to some use in the postwar administration of Germany.

Late in 1944, Donovan had queried the president about the consideration that might be given to "those of German nationality who work for us behind German lines . . . [and] what we are prepared to do in their behalf. . . . We shall, of course, institute appropriate controls. On this we will need authority which only you can give."[129]

His answer:

The White House, Washington

MEMORANDUM FOR GENERAL DONOVAN

I do not believe that we should offer any guarantees of protection in the post-hostilities period to Germans who are working for our organization. I think that the carrying out of any such guarantees would be difficult and probably widely misunderstood both in this country and abroad. We may expect that the number of Germans who are anxious to save their skins and property by coming over . . . at the last moment will rapidly increase. Among them may be some who should properly be tried for war crimes or at least arrested for active participation in Nazi activities. Even with the necessary controls you mention I am not prepared to authorize the giving of guarantees.

Franklin Roosevelt[130]

Dulles was back in the United States when Gävernitz wrote lamenting that, Nazi or anti-Nazi, the Americans regarded all Germans as guilty. Among the Allied authorities, this was certainly the prevailing attitude. Files were studied for any and all links to Nazis, and fairly or unfairly, many were tarred with a very broad brush. Gävernitz's sister had married into the family of Ruhr industrialist Hugo Stinnes. An early Hitler supporter, Stinnes had subsequently fallen out with the Führer, but Gävernitz's own business dealings were now being questioned, and the State Department threatened to revoke his U.S. citizenship. Waetjen was accused of having supported Hitler's expansionism in the early days, though he had abandoned the party even before Hitler came to power; Gisevius was denounced as "ruthless" and also accused, anonymously, of not having worked actively for the July 20 plot. Why that should have presented a problem is a mystery; the Allies had never trusted the conspirators anyway.

Peter Sichel, with the OSS in Germany at the time, had ample opportunity to observe the attitude of American troops close up. As soon as the war was over, he watched as many GIs who had previously subscribed to a knee-jerk "kill all Krauts" mind-set came to the realization that many Krauts were actually decent, hardworking folk. German-born Sichel had always known that Germany had its fair share of good and bad, but he now found himself having to remind American soldiers not to credit *all* Germans with an honor and uprightness that might not be their due.[131] The official postwar Allied stance toward Germans, meanwhile, had found no redeeming features and remained steadfastly and profoundly suspicious, an attitude that heaped an array of obstacles in Dulles's path to getting a "fair shake."

Schulte, the reliable bearer of excellent and early information, had always despised Hitler, but he now came under the investigators' suspicion because, unbeknown to him, the Nazis had honored him as a business leader. From Schulte, Dulles had asked for and received a long document on postwar problems and a plan to bring full democracy to Germany within twenty years.[132] Dulles informed Washington:

I have been constantly in touch with 643 . . . [he] has been engaged in drawing up plans for post-war Germany of an economic-industrial nature. I believe that he is anti-Nazi and entirely trustworthy, he is one of the few technically able and up-to-date persons who could be of service to our army of occupation following the collapse of Germany. In addition I trust his judgment on anti-Nazi groups who might be relied upon to work with us. 643 is entirely realistic about the Reich and is aware of the need for both a complete clean sweep and a long occupation. In large part he is responsible for the idea . . . about an advisory German committee to help on personnel.

Even though I am aware that this matter is a bit out of our field, I would like to be advised whether we can give some encouragement to men like 643 and whether any directives could be given by men working on occupation plans, naturally without making any commitments. There will not be many Germans of his kind that we will be able to locate and I believe that those persons responsible for planning [the U.S. occupation zone] might find it advantageous . . . to line up a carefully chosen group . . . at this end so that . . . we will have first crack at their services.[133]

Dulles's support of Schulte, whose talents he had hoped to use in rebuilding Germany, failed to influence the military denazification authorities. Never mind that Schulte had been, in Dulles's words, "exerting himself in every respect to bring the downfall of the Nazi regime."[134] Much to the frustration of both Dulles and Schulte, not only were the Allies not interested, but in Schulte's later years of exile in Switzerland he was badgered by U.S Department of Justice investigations into the international financial dealings of Geische and the Silesian-American Corporation.[135] Schulte's early warning of Hitler's intentions regarding the Jews and the Holocaust remained unknown until 1986, when his identity was finally revealed by Walter Laqueur and Richard Breitman, in their book *Breaking the Silence*. The most that Dulles had been able to do for him was to obtain some scarce penicillin for his troublesome leg, seriously injured in a long-ago accident.[136]

In spite of Lionel Curtis's entreaties, Britain was unwilling to take in Moltke's widow and small children on the grounds that Moltke had actually been only part English and his wife was wholly German, an unfortunate fact that might lead to other regrettable exceptions.[137] The British had not really wanted any Jews, and they certainly did not want any Germans. The efforts of the Kordts were either ignored or damned with faint praise by their British contacts. At Nuremberg, Chief Prosecutor Telford Taylor's opening statement in the so-called Ministries Trial, described Ernst von Weizsäcker as "on the top rung of dishonor."[138] In spite of a lack of evidence, and numerous affidavits on his behalf and support from many notables—diplomats, bishops, the pope, and his old friend Carl Burckhardt, Weizsäcker was found guilty of the planning and pursuit of aggressive war and of atrocities against civilian populations. There was protest in the British press and among prominent British citizens, but Weizsäcker went to jail.

Gisevius had gone into hiding in Berlin after the putsch, a risky proposition even without the bombing. First he stayed with Theodor Strünck and his wife, living in their cellar, since their house had been bombed out. Then with the help of his friend Hans Koch, he played hide-and-seek with the Gestapo in the rubble of Berlin. Ultimately, camped out with a girlfriend, he was elated when word came from Switzerland that help was on the way.[139] But months crawled by until at last, one evening in late January, a fat envelope was dropped off at the doorstep, from a car that then sped off into the night.

It contained an official passport with a photograph of Gisevius—now "Hoffman"—and the chunky metal badge of a high-ranking Gestapo officer. There was also an order that all Nazi party and government officials were to assist Hoffmann on his mission to Switzerland. Dulles and David Bruce in London had pulled out all the stops in the OSS repertory to fashion this rescue package. It had traveled from London to Switzerland, and was then brought to Berlin by a cooperative German publisher. Stuffed into a railway car bulging with its load of desperate travelers, Gisevius left for Switzerland on one of the last civilian passenger trains to run in Germany for some time.

When he turned up in Bern, Dulles and Mary Bancroft saw a changed man. But no matter what emotional distress his questions caused his erstwhile collaborator, Dulles wanted to know all the details. Though much of the impetus for his book now seemed lost for him, Gisevius and Bancroft went back to work. His memoir chronicling the evils of the Nazi regime and the resistance was published in 1946, dedicated to Hans Oster.

As a witness for the prosecution at the Nuremberg Trials, Gisevius was hailed by Chief Prosecutor Robert Jackson as a champion of democracy. The State Department, however, objected to letting Gisevius into the United States; he had worked for the German government, after all. Gisevius had served Dulles well, and Dulles fought for him and brought him to safety in the United States, doled out dollars to help him through, and eventually settled him in Dallas, at the Council of World Affairs. It was a venture that did not take. The hulking "Tiny" returned to Berlin in 1956. After the German government granted him a pension, he eventually retired to Switzerland.[140]

With Gisevius's help, Dulles located the few Breakers who survived. A Stauffenberg cousin had been miraculously overlooked in Hitler's fury to eradicate them all, and, of course, there were widows. He looked them up to offer help, to write letters on their behalf, to pull strings, organize visas, or at least provide some money. For some informants, Dulles managed to arrange a monthly stipend. In the case of Freya von Moltke, then living at Kreisau in miserable circumstances with Marion Yorck, Peter Yorck von Wartenbug's widow, he ensured a steady stream of army rations to help keep body and soul together.[141] He later arranged to bring Moltke's widow and young children to the American sector, and eventually to the United States.

Both Dulles and Donovan fretted for the safety of some of their old informants, and Fritz Kolbe certainly fell into that category. Dulles wrote Donovan in June 1946 that he understood "steps are being taken to extract 'Wood' [from Berlin as] certain events have caused our people over there to feel he is no longer safe."[142] Working for the Americans in Berlin entailed certain privileges but also difficulties. Kolbe had been interrogated in Wiesbaden for the forthcoming Nuremberg trials, so there was concern that he might be assassinated or perhaps kidnapped by the Russians. Kolbe himself had considered emigrating to America, but given the temper of the times, the State Department objected: Kolbe, like Gisevius, had worked for the German government.

After nearly three years of delays, Kolbe and his wife, Maria, arrived in

New York on a very hot spring day in 1949. There to meet them at the pier was Peter Sichel, whom Kolbe had known through the OSS in Berlin. With a $10,000 OSS stake to help him get established, and the names of a few contacts, it was hoped he could make a new life for himself. Sichel installed the couple at a Washington Square hotel, but from the first day Kolbe felt like a displaced person in the United States.[143] His English was poor, and in spite of Dulles's efforts, work was not forthcoming. He was put off by what he viewed as America's soulless, unabashed consumerism.[144] A chance encounter with an acquaintance from South Africa held out the promise of a business deal, but the acquaintance—along with Kolbe's $10,000 nest egg—disappeared. Bilked and disillusioned, he and Maria decided to return to Germany as soon as possible. The dream of a new life had been short-lived.

For Fritz Kolbe, modest and unassuming as he was, the lack of recognition for his efforts and his difficulty in finding work after his return to Germany were deeply disappointing. He stayed in touch with Dulles and Sichel over the years, proud of his association with his Bern accomplice and the OSS.

To his old friend Ernst Kocherthaler, Kolbe wrote in 1965:

> In Germany these days, there is more and more talk of the Resistance, honoring them once a year . . . those most revered being the dead ones. . . . My efforts were to try to shorten the war for my unhappy country and to spare the unfortunates in the concentration camps further suffering. Whether I was successful or not, I don't know. But I do know one thing: The Americans I talked to at the highest level . . . came to understand that there was an internal German resistance, a resistance that was not looking for reward . . . but who resisted the loathed regime out of conviction, simply for the principle of the thing.[145]

Shortly before his own death Dulles wrote that he hoped that the new Germany would at long last recognize Kolbe's great integrity and the significant role he had played in defeating Hitler and Nazism.[146] Dulles's wish was finally fulfilled in September 2004. "It's very late," said German foreign minister Joschka Fischer in recognizing Fritz Kolbe posthumously, "but not too late to pay tribute. He was a permanent, living reproach to those [working] on the floors above him."[147]

Talk of "good Germans" raises the question: Is it conceivable that an SS general and Himmler's trusted right-hand man was one of their number? After the war Karl Wolff was held for some time as a possible defendant and as a witness at Nuremberg. During this period he sank into depressive paranoia and had to be hospitalized. Initially he was acquitted of war crimes, but later it came to light that he had organized trains for the deportation of

300,000 to Treblinka. He claimed he had not known what the trains were for; he was sentenced to eight years in prison, and died in 1980. Was he an evil man, a willing tool of his Nazi masters, looking to save himself when the end was in sight? Was he an ordinary man who bent not only to the demands, but also to the opportunities this war presented, and then had an awakening? Was he a bit of both?

CHAPTER 10

1945

REALPOLITIK: FROM CRUSADE TO DEAL

With the war nearly over, the political landscape was taking on very different contours. The common enemy Churchill had described as the Allies' only bond morphed quickly into the new ally, a resource to be exploited for whatever conflict lay ahead. The Americans, the British, and the Soviets began combing through Germany in a sordid competition for any Germans thought to be on the cutting edge of their field. Whether scientists, technicians, or intelligence experts, they were thought to hold the key to future hegemony and riches. Again the United States was divided. In the rush to acquire and import the top men, some government factions turned a blind eye to evidence of an egregious Nazi past and a deaf ear to the arguments of those trying to bring those same men to trial for war crimes. It is a sorry story of realpolitik at its most cynical and a testament to the flexibility of morals.

CHANGING ENEMIES

Speculation about when the cold war began continues. Some argue that Dulles's Bern operations and contacts with the resistance—particularly Operation Sunrise—aroused Soviet suspicion and set the western Allies on a path of caution and placatory reassurances to soothe the wary Stalin. But the fact is that this Anglo-American kid-glove treatment of Stalin was established long before 1945, most probably even well before Katyn.

In spite of Roosevelt's earlier carefree optimism about his ability to handle "Uncle Joe," Stalin had gained the upper hand. Soon after the division of Germany, the Soviets began stringing barbed wire and removing communications links in "their" Germany. Dulles had recognized early on that the next war would be fought not by force of arms, but by "maneuver and pressure," in other words, by political push and shove.[1] Richard Helms, working with Dulles just after the war at the commandeered Henkel champagne company in Wiesbaden, recalled that until the summer of 1945, the United States had not done much in the way of intelligence about the Soviets. Then "we realized that it was going to be tough sledding, that these were not four allies . . . [but] three allies and one enemy."[2] Suddenly it was important to decipher what was going on behind the hostile Soviet silence, the guard posts, and the barbed wire marking their territory.

In his book *Fire in the Ashes,* historian Theodore H. White observed that there were two diplomatic traditions operative in the United States: the crusade and the deal.[3] When the guns finally went silent in May 1945, the crusade to win the war was definitively over; America could climb off her white horse. But the next crusade—stopping communism—began almost immediately, and to fuel that crusade, the deal was suddenly of paramount importance. In the immediate postwar period, White's crusade and deal intersected in a way that was to have far-reaching results.

DEALS WITH THE DEVIL

A new kind of war had begun. Deals were being made with Germans of whatever stripe in order to benefit from their expertise, and there were plenty of Germans on hand to benefit. A few examples of these "assets" and how and why they came to the United States are enough to tell the story.

Among those who benefited from the U.S. interest in Nazi assets was General Reinhard Gehlen, not a scientist, but the former chief of FHO, Fremde Heere Ost—Foreign Armies East—the German army's eastern intelligence arm. Small, narrow-chested, even puny, Gehlen more than made up for his lack of physical stature with his analytical capabilities. He had watched the swift early successes of Hitler's Russian campaign bog down, and in the winter of 1941–42 Army Group Center's chief of staff, Henning von Tresckow, had approached him, hoping to enlist him for the anti-Hitler conspiracy. He had begun to be increasingly anti-Hitler, but Gehlen preferred to skirt the fringes. Though he knew many of the active conspirators— Stauffenberg, Wessel von Freytag-Loringhoven, Stieff, and others—he never committed himself, so he was never caught up in the Gestapo dragnet that later rounded up the plotters.

Posted to FHO in April 1942, he had experienced a bitter personal setback when he signed off on an FHO report that included a gross underestimation of the enemy and a disastrously mistaken prediction.[4] FHO clearly needed rebuilding, and he began a rigorous restructuring, scrapped its old officers almost to a man, and recruited anyone who met his exacting standards. Gehlen developed an extensive intelligence network at FHO, and this vantage point gave him a clear and early view of an unwinnable war. He was also becoming a convinced opponent of Hitler's policy in the East, arguing that the Nazi death squads and brutal occupation were effectively eradicating what remained of the Russians' enthusiasm for their German "liberators" from Stalin's tyranny. FHO began to prepare reports warning of the drastic effects of these policies.[5]

Gehlen loathed briefings at the Wolfsschanze and finally managed to avoid them altogether by having OKW chief of staff Heinz Guderian present his material to Hitler. When the Führer raged to Guderian that the author of these increasingly gloomy reports on Soviet capabilities and intentions ought to be in a lunatic asylum, the general countered that this was the assessment of one of his best officers, and he stood by it. If this was how Hitler felt, then perhaps he ought to certify Guderian as a lunatic as well.[6] Hitler in fact relieved Guderian of his command in March 1945 and dismissed Gehlen soon after.

By that time however, Gehlen had already been preparing his exit from the obviously faltering Reich for months. He had predicted in 1944 that the alliance between the western powers and the Soviets would crumble as soon as the common enemy was conquered, and the Americans would be the first to "recapture some objectivity vis-à-vis the Germans," as he put it in his memoirs. He intended to survive, and he knew that to American intelligence, his background and his deep information on the "new" enemy—the Soviet Union—would make him a desirable asset. The microfilms he and his top associates had made of FHO's immense files on their Russian underground and intelligence operation were the key. Stashed in metal drums and buried at various sites in the Austrian Alps, the films were an enticing résumé. They would ensure his future.

So it was to the Alps that Gehlen headed in the last days of the Reich, along roads clogged with refugees, bands of straggling soldiers from various armies, and roving SS units, to find an American Counterintelligence Corps unit in Bavaria. But his reception by the U.S. military was deeply disappointing. His claim of having important information that could be divulged only to the proper high authorities was dismissed with the argument that this was what all the POWs claimed. He was also astounded by what he regarded as the hopelessly naïve U.S. view of Russian intentions and expansionism. Most Americans, he complained later, "regarded the situation exclusively through propaganda spectacles," convinced that the Soviet Union "would progress from communism to a liberal state."[7] Still, if he played his cards right, this might be to his benefit.

It was not until Gehlen met Captain John Boker, a young intelligence officer with some understanding of how things stood with Russia, that he began to feel he could put his plan into action. Boker was savvy enough to recognize Gehlen's value and look beyond the interdiction on making deals with Germans desperate to save their skin. But even when he had the support of General Edwin Sibert, the top army intelligence officer, there was still the American mood of the time—a hanging rather than a deal-making mood—to be overcome.[8] According to the terms of the agreement at Yalta, the Allies were required to turn over to the Soviets any Axis intelligence on the USSR, but the Russians' acute interest in Gehlen quickly persuaded the Americans that maybe they really had something here. By late summer, Gehlen's top people and his metal cases of microfilm had been rounded up, and Walter Bedell "Beetle" Smith, chief of staff of the Supreme Allied Command, had joined Sibert in supporting the plan to make a deal with him.[9]

When word reached Allen Dulles that a German general was ready to turn a vast intelligence archive on the Soviets and Eastern Europe over to the United States, he remembered that at the very end of the war Fritz Kolbe had mentioned an intelligence officer from the East preparing to make a deal with the West. At the time, he had paid this bit of news little attention, but now he pricked up his ears. Gehlen had in his hands significant weapons for waging that war of "maneuver and pressure" that Dulles had seen coming, and he wanted to join the battle against communism. Dulles had visions of Gehlen as a new "big window," this time with a view onto the Soviet world. He and Bill Donovan began to press for authority over Gehlen's files.[10]

In August 1945, an odd-looking bunch, wearing whatever worn and ill-fitting civilian gear had been found for them, and one carrying a violin case in lieu of a suitcase, arrived at what was known as "Box 1142"—the code address for a POW detention and interrogation center at Fort Hunt, Virginia. It was Gehlen and some of his officers, the first of the Nazi "assets" to arrive in the United States. He was soon at work on a dense report on the history of FHO and, more important, on the structure and strategy of the Russian high command. It was the beginning of a chapter in U.S. intelligence history that was to become controversial. Beyond controversial, it was sometimes the subject of acrimonious debate.

Washington was not overjoyed to receive General Sibert's protégé. One of Gehlen's associates was already working for Sibert in Germany, monitoring army radio signals and prepared to gear up for full-scale espionage against the Soviets, but the United States was holding back. They were interested in his information, but not in actually spying on the recent Soviet ally. Only gradually did American intelligence come to the conclusion that Gehlen's gloomy predictions of aggressive Soviet ambitions were not so far off the mark after all. The Soviet occupation of northern Iran in early 1946 marked a critical shift in American perception and cleared the way for

Gehlen's future efforts to establish a spy network in Germany against the U.S.'s new enemy.

OPERATION PLUNDER

The Allied race to acquire the Third Reich's expertise on poison gas, aircraft design, submarines, ultrafast torpedoes, and more by snapping up German scientists and engineers was well under way before the surrender was signed in the schoolroom at Rheims. In late March, Britain's field marshal Montgomery had wished his troops stretched along an enormous front "good hunting" on the other side of the Rhine. Operation Plunder, as it was called, employed more than 3,000 experts to find any and all remnants of the Reich's armament riches and put them into Allied hands.

With the war as good as over, American, Soviet, and British armies ransacked a war-ravaged Germany on the lookout for Nazis. It was important not only to guard against any unwelcome Nazi resurgence, but also to bring the evildoers to justice. Yet even as the rubble of Berlin and Dresden was still smoking, the purposes of the Nazi hunt underwent a perceptible shift. As it became clear that East-West tensions would define the foreseeable future, the hunt had become a race for "assets," with the spoils going to whichever victor got there first. Teams of technical experts from all sides were bouncing through the ruined landscape, hoping to locate the remnants of Hitler's weaponry and the scientific and technical brains behind it. The Soviets were scooping up war booty—machinery, hardware, hospital equipment, optical works, and much more—to be carted off and shipped east. The German scientists who, according to many estimates, had put German weaponry so far ahead of the Allies were even more important.

In the last chaotic weeks before the Reich's collapse, American, British, Russian, and French investigatory teams combed the countryside, sometimes armed with intelligence maps, poking into forest caves, looking for anything scientific or technical that could be shaken loose: scientists first and foremost, and then blueprints, aircraft designs, uranium, hydraulic presses, and industrial designs.[11] They scrambled through the rubble, on the lookout for laboratories and the scientists who worked in them. The ultimate booty was the expertise that could produce the ghastly arsenal that might well determine the outcome of the next war. So many teams were scurrying through the countryside that one British officer complained that they were creating a nuisance by "pressing too hard on the heels of the combat soldiers."[12]

British reserve combined with a "we won the war, didn't we" attitude caused the British to lag behind in the wholesale Allied search and plunder that was going on. British aircraft designer Roy Fedden lamented that England had "lost a remarkable opportunity . . . in not accumulating as much information on aeronautical, and in fact on all engineering matters, as she might have done," and as the Americans had in fact done.[13] There was so much to be had—advanced designs for torpedoes and submarines, super-speed cameras, wind tunnels, groundbreaking aircraft armament designs, and more. U.S. thinking was that if Americans did not grab Walter Dornberger, the chief architect of German rocketry, or the team of doctors who worked on aviation medicine at the Göring Aeronautical Research Institute at Volkenrode, the Russians would, and what a fine mess that would be.[14]

THE HUNT FOR RARE, CHOSEN MINDS

In early April, Major Robert Staver, young and apparently unstoppable, was following the footsteps of the U.S. First Army into Nordhausen, in the Harz Mountains. His unit had survived a serious set-to with the SS, but was now entering a postcard-pretty valley, touched by spring. In the forefront of Project Hermes, his brief was to locate leading German scientists who might be able to teach the Americans a thing or two about rocketry, an area where the Germans were thought to be years ahead of the Americans. There was the hope that Hitler's fabled wonder weapon might be used in the ongoing war with Japan, and Staver was determined to succeed.

The 1943 British bombing of Peenemünde had revealed the peninsular site on the Baltic Sea as too exposed and vulnerable. Rocket assembly operations were to be relocated some 250 miles to the south in Nordhausen, where slave labor was already digging tunnels deep into the belly of the mountain, where the rockets would be immune to even the most massive bombing. Stumbling through the dank tunnels at Nordhausen, Staver was amazed. He was no newcomer to rocketry, but he had never seen anything like this. The immense, lofty tunnels bristled with V-2 rockets in every conceivable stage of completion.[15] This area would soon lie in the Russian occupation sector; the rockets and the experts were a precious resource, and whatever the cost, they must be kept out of the hands of the Russians. It was one of the opening salvos of a new war, fired even before the old one was over.

Major Staver's research also unearthed a huge cache of technical documents that had been hidden in a mine in Goslar, soon to become part of the British sector. The original U.S. plan, organized in late 1944, called for the orderly location and interrogation of "target" scientists, but it had quickly descended into a chaotic, cutthroat competition. The competition was not only between the Americans and the Soviets, but as one observer commented, the Allies were competing to keep information and scientists "even from ourselves. The competition is fierce"—even between the British and the Americans.[16]

Staver worked frantically to get crates and crates of as yet unassembled but precious V-2 rockets and documents loaded onto a convoy of trucks. He had to get everything out and into the American sector. The scientists remaining at Nordhausen were also to be kept from the British and the Soviets, but they, at least, were easier to transport. A fleet of Liberty ships loaded with almost ten thousand tons of materiel—the disassembled V-2s and documents, a wind tunnel, submarines, even an entire I. G. Farben synthetic fuel plant—was soon steaming toward the United States.

The liberators of the concentration camp at Nordhausen, Camp Dora, were struck not by rockets, but by the sight of the camp's inmates. The pitiful survivors of those who had tunneled into the mountain and supplied the labor for rocket assembly tottered like feeble stick figures or lay dying on the ground. Unspeakable conditions at the camp had led to the deaths of an estimated 20,000 inmates, at the rate of about 100 a day.[17] Emaciated corpses were stacked like cordwood. The camp was enveloped in the suffocating stench of death.

The war-crimes investigators who arrived just after Dora was liberated found the name of Arthur Rudolph near the top of the list of Nordhausen's management. He had been among the first of Peenemünde's engineers to come to Nordhausen in 1943 to supervise tunneling and construction, carried out by brutal methods. Later he had been part of a decision intended to alleviate a tricky production bottleneck that required knowledge and delicacy; the problem was solved by "importing" skilled workers from France for slave labor. The war-crimes investigators were rushed, their investigations cursory. They were not aware of all the details, but they did append Rudolph's name to their report on the brutalities and appalling conditions at the camp.

The lead scientists and design team of Germany's rocket program's had stayed on at Peenemünde initially, but by now all the top specialists— General Walter Dornberger, Wernher von Braun, Arthur Rudolph and about 450 others—had decamped to Bavaria, knowing it was scheduled to become the American sector. A joke current at the time was that the British sector got German industry, the Russians got Germany's agriculture, and the Americans got the scenery.[18] But tucked away in that scenery, at American internment camps named Dustbin, Ashcan, and the like, the scientific intelligence teams located their booty, a significant portion of Germany's scientific minds.

Braun and his fellow rocketeers surrendered to the Americans on a rainy day in early May 1945.[19] In an alpine village of almost absurd tranquility, American counterintelligence began interrogating the top rocket crew and hundreds of others. Rudolph, they learned, had joined the Party in 1931, had been in the SA, and was a staunch supporter of both Hitler's anticommunism and his anti-Semitism. His interrogator's assessment read: "One hundred percent Nazi, dangerous type, security threat. . . . Suggest internment."[20] But if the rocket scientists were interned, who would decipher the complex technical documents and put the weapons together?

Project Overcast, established by July 1945, was intended as a temporary program for the exploitation of at most 350 scientific minds that would help America win the war against Japan. As tension with the USSR escalated, the Pentagon's Joint Intelligence Objectives Agency (JIOA) prepared a press release explaining that the government had several highly trained technicians and scientists, following "close upon the heels of our conquering armies," sifting through postwar Germany, "examining manufacturing plans and equipment, records and documents [and] interrogating German personnel."[21]

The Commerce Department would make available any information of industrial value gathered from these scientists, and the exploitation would include bringing the best scientists to work in the United States. In the spring of 1946, President Harry S. Truman approved a stepped-up program, dubbed Paperclip, and a few months later the Joint Chiefs of Staff announced a project to "exploit . . . chosen, rare minds whose continuing intellectual productivity we wish to use."[22] This program included a thousand scientists and their families, and like the pot of gold at the end of the rainbow, it held the lure of implied American citizenship.

The moral rhetoric that had flooded the airwaves in the wake of the American public's discovery of the concentration camps had all but disappeared behind a new pragmatism. The focus now was on the future, not the past. With the Soviets looming large as the new bugbear, national interest and national security were the new priorities, and the German scientists could be useful to both in varying degrees. On the other hand, some of those same scientists with a particularly vivid Nazi past might also represent a danger to the national interest and security. With this in mind, President Truman approved a program that denied entry into the United States, and government contracts to any known or suspected war criminals or active supporters of Nazism.

The terms "war criminal" and "active supporter" were, of course, open to interpretation, and soon enough they became contentious. The JIOA, charged with shepherding the scientists' dossiers past a panel made up of members of the State and Justice departments, hoped to import the maximum number of rare minds. Even as Nazis were being pursued for ideological delousing and denazification, they were being recruited by U.S. intelligence and scientific headhunters. In instances of proclaimed political passivity and ignorance of any atrocities, there was no difficulty in bringing the scientists to the United States. But where there was too much evidence to the contrary, tensions developed between the JIOA and panel members who objected to whitewashing Nazis who might be a threat to the United States.

A committee of the National Academy of Sciences looked into the matter and concluded that during Nazi rule science had offered something of a haven; much of the research of these scientists, the committee contended, had actually represented a form of resistance.[23] Science had become a handmaiden of weaponry, and the dollar value of the expertise far outweighed any moral qualms.[24] It was time to find a suitable compromise, but not everyone was willing.

The State Department's Sam Klaus had been a thorn in the JIOA's side from the beginning. For some time already, he had been at work designing a postwar interagency program, Project Safehaven, intended to locate and block German assets and plunder that had been transferred to neutral and nonbelligerent countries.[25] Safehaven, Overcast, and Paperclip all dealt with Nazi assets, whether plundered gold or scientists. The original military-JIOA plan—to import only outstanding scientists at the top of their field, vital to U.S. defense and industrial concerns, and none with a record of ardent Nazism—had undergone a shift. A press release stated that participation was limited to "those who can make a positive valuable contribution to our national welfare . . . the best pure scientists . . . comparable to Prof. Einstein."[26]

Aside from his Safehaven activities, Klaus was also on the panel overseeing JIOA's scientific "imports." Now, along with the truly top-notch, second- and third-raters who were hardly in the Einstein league were also being plucked out of the postwar detritus. They, too, were to be kept out of the hands of the Soviets—and everyone else—and held at the Dustbins and Ashcans and various other internment camps to be brought to the United States eventually. In the early days of Overcast, Klaus had lain low, but gradually he began to make his objections known. If a batch of JIOA dossiers for Klaus's approval revealed that the candidates' records did not meet the standards set by Truman, he refused to turn a blind eye to unsavory pasts. He rejected them. These decisions quickly earned him enemies.

The JIOA was furious; Klaus's obstructionism was sabotaging their efforts and delaying the speedy entry of scientists. They countered his challenges with simple and efficient revisionism: The offending dossiers were returned to Germany and rewritten; the unacceptable past was simply sanitized, filtered, or deleted.[27] JIOA then presented the panel not with raw and possibly incriminating investigation reports, but with a carefully tidied-up file. The past was erased to provide the desired scientists or intelligence agents a clean slate for entry into the United States.

Harry Rositzke, at one time the head of covert operations in the USSR, put it this way: "We knew what we were doing . . . using any bastard as long as he was anti-Communist." It was a strictly utilitarian approach that "meant you didn't look at their credentials too closely."[28] If even a cursory glance revealed something you didn't want to know, a particularly unsavory

Nazi past, for instance, anticommunism effectively erased it. And there were other alternatives. In cases of targeted scientists with an obviously fervent or brutal Nazi past, the name of the "asset" was simply deleted from lists of internees in U.S. custody kept in Germany. This way, by sleight of hand, the captive scientist or other "rare mind" either no longer existed or was still at large.[29]

The name of the targeted scientist or other asset's name could then appear on a new, clean visa application for employment in the States. Or if his past was too egregious, he could be given a new identity and smuggled into the United States along what the spy trade calls "ratlines," an underground network designed to funnel agents into or fugitives out of hot spots. Naturally enough, the pressure to keep such operations secret was considerable. Some American scientists had protested, and the citizenry, too, might be alarmed at the thought of flagrant Nazis in their midst. It was best to keep such instances very quiet. Some of that uncomfortable secrecy has persisted.[30]

Meanwhile, the tug-of-war between JIOA and Sam Klaus and the visa department at State continued. The JIOA argued that more scientists—geneticists and others who might be useful to American industry—should be brought in, lest they "be irrevocably lost to American science."[31] Klaus remained adamant. The Pentagon summed up his attitude as "stubborn, arrogant, and unreasonable."[32] By 1948, in the eerie, early days of McCarthyism, Klaus's loyalties were being questioned and he was later investigated as a possible Communist sympathizer.[33]

Under the auspices of the JIOA, several leading rocket scientists—Braun and a small team—arrived in the United States with tidied-up files in September 1945, just after Gehlen's crew. They were followed over the next few months by a hundred or more rocketeers, all of whom were soon working a forty-eight-hour week, at six dollars per day plus accommodations, cheaper labor than the military could have found otherwise. In 1947, Rudolph joined the group tinkering busily in the arid south Texas desert, piecing together disassembled rockets brought over on the Liberty ships.

Another recruit for America's future in space was Dr. Hubertus Strughold, a pioneer in aviation medicine. His groundbreaking experiments on pilot endurance, the effects of acceleration, pressure, lack of oxygen, violent temperature changes, and other aviation hazards, had been carried out on Dachau inmates.[34] He had been recruited by the U.S.'s own top man in this medical specialty, a USAF surgeon. Colonel Harry Armstrong idolized Strughold, had searched for him high and low in Germany, and brought him over in 1947 under Project Paperclip. Strughold is now enshrined at the New Mexico Museum of Space History as the Father of American Space Medicine and as an inductee into the International Space Hall of Fame. He smiles out of his portrait looking benign and avuncular, a worthy recipient of the DAR's Americanism Medal. The library of the School of Aerospace Medicine at Brooks Air Force Base in Texas bore his name until documents from the Nuremberg trials linked him to medical experiments that had had fatal results at Dachau.

For the most part, the space engineers led quiet lives centered on work and family. Gradually, their presence was accepted; they were said to have embraced American values and were absorbed into their new surroundings. The rocket team worked mostly in remote and isolated spots, and but for Tom Lehrer's satirical lyrics, they receded slightly in the American consciousness until that epic day when the Saturn V rocket lifted off to carry Neil Armstrong to the moon, cradled in all the comforts Strughold could devise.[35]

USING BEELZEBUB TO DRIVE OUT SATAN

The mere fact of the American deal with Gehlen was enough to raise U.S.-Soviet tensions; at the Potsdam Conference, the perennially suspicious Soviets lodged an angry protest.[36] In the new power struggle with the Soviets, the fervently anticommunist Gehlen was happy to make common cause with the United States. He was the ace up America's sleeve. It was a clear instance of "the enemy of my (new) enemy is my friend," and he was welcomed with open arms. Returning to Germany in July 1946, Gehlen began operating with about 350 officers, most of them former colleagues and associates culled from various camps in Germany. He would be operating under U.S. control. If there were questions about his background, they were waved aside. "I don't know if he's a rascal" Dulles is reputed to have said. "There are few archbishops in espionage. He's on our side and that is all that matters. Besides, one needn't ask Gehlen to one's club."[37] In any case, the feeling at the time was that "it was legitimate to use Beelzebub to drive out Satan," as Hugh Trevor-Roper put it.[38]

Gehlen's "deal" with the United States had included his promise that he would hire no SS or SD personnel for his organization. Such people were considered war criminals. In the end he did hire former SS and SD personnel, and the U.S. intelligence community involved with Gehlen was certainly not naïve enough to believe that he did not. Not surprisingly, as Gehlen's "Org," as it became known, grew, one old SS member would recruit an old SS comrade to become another set of eyes and ears for the West. One provided entrée for another, and before long the Org was a haven for ex-Nazis, some of them spectacular specimens of the breed.[39] Gehlen himself, as ex-Wehrmacht, might not actually have relished having so many old SS in his ranks, but he wanted and needed results, and these men were often the quickest route to results. In the eager press for intelligence on the Soviets, American intelligence built the Org into the official espionage and counterespionage operation of the West German government. With the guiding hand of the CIA heavy on the tiller, the truth disappeared behind an early equivalent of "don't ask, don't tell."

Among the more notorious Org recruits was Alois Brunner, a rabid Nazi since 1931, when he had joined the party as a teenager. Brunner was later Adolf Eichmann's trusted right hand, a punctiliously efficient deportation specialist. Sentenced to death in absentia for his crimes in France, Brunner found his way onto the CIA payroll, running the Org's post in Damascus. He also assisted his equally unrepentant fellow Austrian, Otto Skorzeny, in beefing up and training intelligence and security squads in Egypt as part of a covert CIA mission to protect American interests in Egypt in the 1950s.[40]

Fueled by the growing U.S.-Soviet divide and Gehlen's expert exploitation of it, the Org expanded rapidly. Back in Germany with headquarters in Pullach outside Munich, and operating as the South German Industrial Development Organization, it mushroomed to well over 4,000, with many undercover agents in the USSR and its satellites.[41] Gehlen's handlers were beginning to lose control, but he milked his position for every advantage. Playing to the exaggerated fears of a newly insecure United States, his inflated reports of Soviet military might and mobilizations pushed the buttons guaranteed to cause panic and fan the flames of East-West tensions. Gehlen also heightened American anxieties over the so-called missile gap by delivering to the CIA reports of superior Soviet missile capabilities, presumably the product of German scientists who had eluded the Americans in 1945 and had been snatched up by the Russians.[42]

America kept its arms open to Gehlen. Funding from American intelligence continued to flow his way until April 1956. At that point, the Org became the Bundesnachrichtendiest (BND), the intelligence service of the German Federal Republic, and provided a privileged glimpse into the new German republic that Dulles had anticipated more than a decade earlier. But to everyone's embarrassment, it soon became clear that the BND had been infiltrated by the Soviets. Double agents had been feeding Gehlen disinformation for years. He had ignored all the warning signals, and in May 1968 he resigned in disgrace after a long and extraordinary career that mirrored much of the complexity and chaos of the times. With forethought, flexibility, and guile, he had attained much of what he wanted, using the cold war to gain personal power. In the process he had also opened the door to charges of blatant political hypocrisy on the part of the United States.[43]

Yet those charges in regard to Gehlen pale in comparison with the Americans' handling of another "asset" of interest to the intelligence community: a man known as the "butcher of Lyon." As Gestapo chief in Lyon from December 1942 to mid-1944, Klaus Barbie had comported himself as a Nazi's Nazi, a true poster boy for Hitler's brutality. He deported thousands to extermination camps, including the now famous children of Izieu, and had tortured and murdered thousands more.[44] He had escaped to Germany in the postwar chaos, and British and American agents were looking for him there in early 1947 in connection with the organization of an underground Nazi cell. Barbie managed to evade the joint "swoop" to pick him up, but then surfaced among the Americans, to whom he had been recommended by Kurt Merk, a former Abwehr agent in France, then working with Robert Taylor of the U.S. Counterintelligence Corps.

Taylor gave Barbie high marks: He was "honest . . . [and] without nerves or fear." His "extensive connections with high-level German intelligence circles . . . [could furnish CIC with] extremely good material" from his files and intelligence connections in Eastern Europe and France, and within the German communist party.[45] Were he to be arrested, Taylor felt it might "damage . . . the trust and faith which informants place in this organization."[46] Barbie was recruited, put on the CIC payroll, and kept under wraps, even from other CIC operations, on the grounds that his "value as an informant infinitely outweighs any use he may have in prison."[47]

Barbie was in fact arrested by the American military in December 1947 and must have thought that the game was up. Visions of extradition and execution in France may have given him sleepless nights in his bare little cell at the European Command Interrogation Center (ECIC) just outside Frankfurt, but extradition and execution were not what CIC had in mind. They were not interested in his murderous wartime activities but in his postwar activities, and he was interrogated only about those contacts. CIC's anticommunist crusade was the impetus for a deal that made Barbie's release contingent on the completeness of his answers to their questions.

Barbie's American captors allowed the French to interrogate him several times in 1948 in regard to the trial of René Hardy. Hardy was accused of having betrayed French Resistance hero Jean Moulin to Barbie, who had subsequently murdered Moulin. (The interrogations took place in the presence of CIC witnesses.) Erhard Dabringhaus was with the CIC in Germany from 1946 to 1952, recruiting agents who would later serve the CIA. As Barbie's controller for a time, he knew of, and reported, instances of Barbie's torture and other crimes. He had been told that "if the French ever found out how many mass graves Barbie was responsible for, even Eisenhower would not be able to protect him." He was ignored.[48]

Still, word of Barbie's U.S. protection seeped into newspapers in France, where a large constituency was burning to bring him to justice. In May 1949, a Paris newspaper headline screamed: "Arrest Barbie, Our Torturer!" and the clamor grew ever louder. Barbie was shielded from repeated requests for extradition to France until his name appeared in Germany on a list of persons to be found and arrested. At this point his CIC handlers kept him on the payroll but dropped him from CIC sponsorship. The French grew more insistent, but releasing him to France would be embarrassing.

Barbie's knowledge of CIC's anticommunist operations, not to mention the fact that the United States had recruited him, would be devastating. Then they hit upon a solution.

A CIC sister organization in Austria could help. In 1951, under CIC sponsorship and in the interests of U.S. intelligence, Klaus Barbie became Klaus Altmann. In the guise of a DP (displaced person) with Catholic affiliations, he was smuggled out of Germany into Austria and via Italy to South America on a ratline run by a Yugoslav priest. During the war Monsignor Krunoslav Dragonovich had been active in "relocating" Jews and Serbians to camps. Later, at a time when the United States was still ostensibly hunting down Yugoslav war criminals, he busied himself arranging safe passage through the Vatican for countless Yugoslav fascists with nasty war records.[49] The official CIC line was: "We may be able to state, if forced, that the turning over of a DP to a welfare organization falls in line with our democratic way of thinking and that we are not engaged in illegal disposition of war criminals, defectees and the like."[50] Deniability was important.

Barbie and his family sailed from Genoa to Argentina under temporary travel permit number 0121454, issued on February 20, 1951. They later made their way to Bolivia. His trade was officially listed as mechanic, but gradually his life in South America began to return to familiar patterns. He was hobnobbing with military and government figures with dictatorial ambitions, a cause with which Barbie could identify.[51] He was dealing in arms and through an old comrade, he had a direct line to Paraguay's strongman, Alfredo Stroesser. At one point the U.S. Army was interested in "reactivating" Barbie for intelligence work in South America, but the matter was deemed too sensitive. Although there is evidence that he entered the States in 1969 and 1970, little is known about these brief visits.

When Nazi hunters Serge and Beate Klarsfeld tracked Barbie down and finally got him extradited and taken back to France in early 1983, his trial unleashed bitterness and anger that had been festering since the occupation. It also brought to light Barbie's work for, and protection by, the United States. The Justice Department asked the Office of Special Investigations (OSI) to look into the Barbie case and made the results of the enquiry public that year.[52] In presenting his report to the press, the Justice Department's Allan Ryan announced that he was persuaded that Barbie's case was unique. His investigation, admittedly limited to the Barbie case, had yielded no evidence of any other former Nazis shielded from justice by the United States. The record was now closed.[53]

At the time, the record did not include a Barbie file that had originated with the U.S. Army in Europe. This was discovered only in 1991, filed among other war crimes cases as one of its "Cases Not Tried."[54] Ryan almost certainly had no idea what kind of a bombshell he was dropping when he announced the release of the Justice Department's report on Klaus Barbie and his relationship with American intelligence after the war. When he told the reporters crowded into the briefing room that the United States had recruited Barbie in all innocence, unaware of his role in France, he was not distorting the truth; he just did not realize how wrong he was.[55] But the U.S. military and civilian recruiters who had scoured Germany in 1945 and after—they did know. Those who had sanitized the records of desirable scientists and had sprung some of them from richly deserved prison sentences did know, and they could have contributed stories that would not only have reopened the record but expanded it considerably. Barbie was not the exception that Ryan imagined; there were many others.

MORE DEALS, MORE DEVILS

The war in Korea gave the U.S. another bitter taste of their uncomfortable reliance on Germany for national security. If World War III had begun—as many were convinced it had—the United States wanted Germany and German steel as a bulwark against a Soviet invasion of Europe. The price for that was freedom for certain Nazis languishing in prison for war crimes. It was time for another deal. John J. McCloy, U.S. high commissioner for Germany at the time, concluded after study that while some Nazis had to hang, there were reasonable grounds for clemency for others. Again, principle bowed to expediency, and several hundred of those convicted at Nuremberg were released.

One of them was Otto Ambros, a high-profile chemist, a director of I. G. Farben and a target of considerable interest, whose name had appeared on many wanted lists. By the time American lieutenant colonel Paul Tarr caught up with the man behind I. G. Farben's synthetic rubber and poison gas just after the war, war crimes investigators with ample evidence of Ambros's activities at Auschwitz were also eager to nab him; the poison gas had worked on humans with deadly effect. In July 1945, Ambros was arrested and transferred to Dustbin, one of the camps that held so many captive scientists. While Tarr was rushing back and forth from one authority to another, trying to arrange for the release of Ambros and other chemical warfare experts into his custody, Ambros mysteriously disappeared. He then resurfaced in the French zone, and high-handedly played the erstwhile Allies off against one another in bidding for his services.

Eventually, Ambros was turned over to American prosecutors for trial at Nuremberg. During his trial, Ambros was also a target of U.S. recruiters for Project Paperclip.[56] Convicted on charges of slavery and mass murder, among other crimes, and sentenced to eight years in prison, his sentence was commuted by American authorities after three years. Subsequently he was aided in a bid to enter the United States by J. Peter Grace, the president of the major American chemical company W. R. Grace. Other industrialists also had a lively interest in bringing him to the United States, for it was not only the military, but American industry, too, that was keen for those "rare" minds."[57] Fritz ter Meer, one of Ambros's codefendants in the I. G. Farben case, observed that ever since they had the Korean conflict on their hands the Americans had become much friendlier.[58]

The Egyptian operation which Otto Skorzeny pulled together for Gehlen under the aegis of the CIA in the 1950s was one the CIA preferred to keep very quiet. The records are spotty at best, and whether or not the CIA was aware that Alois Brunner was playing on their team has not yet been determined. OSS veteran Miles Copeland worked with the CIA on that particular operation in Egypt and described the Germans involved as "survivalists," who were for the most part "not—or in some cases not quite—war criminals."[59] The Justice Department's Ryan had thought Barbie to be the only exception, but Brunner would have been another. Brunner, Barbie, Ambros, and the other notable "exceptions" all fell under the rubric of the new realpolitik. The Russians were recruiting whoever, however, and whenever possible, and a past as a war criminal should not stand in the way. Having Nazi agents settled quietly in various parts of the world available for use was just too good to pass up. "We simply could not bring ourselves to let valuable . . . assets . . . go to waste," said Copeland. It was the amorality required in power politics.[60]

In October 1984, the U.S. Department of Justice made a brief announcement to the effect that, several months earlier, a man named Arthur Rudolph, project manager of the Saturn V rocket program in Huntsville, Alabama, had renounced his U.S. citizenship and returned to Germany. The Department's Office of Special Investigation had discovered Rudolph's past in Nazi Germany, where he had used slave labor for the German rocketry program. He had been offered two options: He could return quietly, with a pension for his many years of work for NASA, or he could contest the department's contention that he had obtained U.S. citizenship under false pretenses. If he lost the legal battle, he would face deportation. On November 4, 1984, *The Washington Post* ran a front-page article entitled: "A Long Trail to Departure of Ex-Nazi Rocket Expert."[61]

It had been a very long trail, and the Justice Department's disingenuous 1984 announcement of its "discovery" that Rudolph had obtained American citizenship under false pretenses no doubt shocked many Americans. To those involved in the machinations of the military and intelligence operations that had whisked men like Rudolph and hundreds of others into the country right after the war, it was just another sign of the times. After all, the extensive "secret" army and JIOA files on Rudolph had been in the archives all along. But by 1984, although the cold war was not over, it was perceptibly less threatening, and the United States had the rocketry and the space program that these men—now aging, retiring, and dying off—had brought into being. Having outlived their usefulness, their dirty past could be revealed. The 1984 revelation is shocking now only for its hypocrisy.

The United States had struck Faustian bargains with a number of Hitler's SS and other known war criminals in the hope that these deals would yield benefits for the nation, usually in intelligence, in the expectation that they could be kept completely secret. In fact, the deals brought the country very little of what it had hoped to gain from them, but according to historian Timothy Naftali, they do shine a harsh light on the United States' "cynical amnesia" early in the cold war. Somewhat ruefully, Naftali adds: "Rarely can any good result when a country's guardians divorce themselves from the morality of the people they are seeking to protect."[62]

THE END OF THE OFFICE OF STRATEGIC SERVICES

On April 12, 1945, a stunned nation mourned its president. For Donovan, news of Roosevelt's death was shattering. Over the years, their shared goals had kept the two men in close and constant contact and their relationship had evolved into a true kinship. Republican though he was, Donovan worried for the future of the nation without FDR. On May 8, 1945, when the Allies celebrated victory in Europe, he took some consolation in knowing that his assessment made in the summer of 1940 had proven correct: With U.S. support, England had held. Barely three months later, when victory was declared over Japan, his only regret was that FDR had not lived to see and share in the results of their efforts.

After Roosevelt's death, clouds appeared on the OSS's horizon almost immediately. As vice president, Harry Truman had never been included in OSS business. For all intents and purposes, he had been an outsider. As president, Truman was under tremendous pressure, and he was quick to assert himself in reshaping the Roosevelt administration. He was swayed by J. Edgar Hoover, whose interest at the FBI was in having the OSS disappear, and he was far less inclined to accept Donovan's prominent role. Donovan and Truman had only one brief face-to-face meeting regarding the OSS, on May 14, 1945, and those fifteen minutes were marked by mutual dislike.[63] Truman's appointment book notes curtly that "General Donovan came in to tell me how important the Secret Service [*sic*] is and how much he could do to run the country on an even basis."[64]

One week later, a dispatch from the British embassy in Washington to the Foreign Office observed: "There is some nervousness within the Office of Strategic Services as to the future of that vast and omnivorous organization under the new regime."[65] At its peak the OSS employed nearly 13,000 staffers and more than twice that number as volunteers, liaisons, and partisan fighters. Clearly, once the war was over, most of those numbers would no longer be needed.

Donovan himself had submitted a memorandum to Roosevelt in November 1944 outlining the need for a peacetime intelligence service and a draft directive of what should be preserved in establishing a central intelligence service. He assumed that the OSS's proven successes would ensure a scaled-back version after the war. A new iteration of the organization would be ready early in 1946 to deal with what he called "the problems of peace."[66] Over the summer of 1945, Donovan began to dismantle those parts of the OSS he felt would not be needed in peacetime.

The OSS had always had its share of detractors. J. Edgar Hoover had been able to convince Roosevelt that the OSS should leave domestic operations to the FBI, and so the OSS was forbidden to operate in the western hemisphere. Douglas MacArthur had been a fan of Donovan's during and after World War I, but to most career military officers, Donovan's OSS staff looked unruly and undisciplined, more like silly youngsters off on a toot and avoiding the infantry than comrades in arms. They showed little respect for the chain of command, and their boss had never drilled discipline into them. Donovan's unorthodox leadership style, staffing choices, and even his fearlessness during the great war were now seen as the mark of a loose cannon. In fact, Donovan had insisted on joining the landings in Sicily and Salerno, missions where he could easily have been captured.[67] German expertise at torture could eventually break any man, and had he been taken, thousands of lives might have been at risk. In Normandy he again insisted on being close to the front line and was wounded in the neck.[68]

Technically, Donovan was holding a civilian office, but he had been promoted to brigadier general in April 1943 and to major general in November 1944. He was results oriented, and he applauded imagination and initiative in getting a job done, even if it defied procedures. An additional security concern had to do with the OSS's recruiting communists to their ranks. This was sometimes done out of necessity, but Donovan's argument that anyone who killed Germans was a friend was perceived as unpardonably lax. So in spite of his social connections and many supporters, in spite of the respect for him as a war hero, Donovan and his OSS were shunned by MacArthur and Admiral Chester Nimitz and kept out of most operations in the Pacific Theater.

With the victory celebrations in Washington over, the effects of war as a unifying force dissipated quickly. Whatever internecine struggles, jealousies, and turf wars had been at least partly in abeyance were now vigorously revived, and knives were out for Donovan in various quarters. His Washington connections were telegraphing that the tide was running against his heading a peacetime intelligence service. America's war debt was enormous, and Congress was clamoring to cut expenses. The push to cut fat was in full swing when the Budget Office received word from Donovan that he was reconfiguring the OSS as a peacetime organization. Hoping to save the OSS by divorcing himself from the organization, he insisted that once the conversion was complete, he wanted to return to private life.

THE END CAME SUDDENLY. WHETHER IT WAS BY CLERICAL ERROR OR A PERSONAL DIG, IT came almost without warning. On September 20, 1945, Truman signed the order terminating the OSS.[69] With less than two weeks' notice, Donovan and his right-hand man and former law partner, Ned Putzell, spent nights hurriedly microfilming papers they thought might be important one day. They were also deeply concerned that sensitive material might be handled foolishly and put lives at risk. They worked so hastily that anyone viewing the films today will occasionally see their fingers intruding into the frames, but the foresight of their last actions as official OSSers preserved those pages for the future.[70]

Several OSS departments were parceled out to eager government agencies. The State Department staked a claim on the R&A branch, which was transferred without interruption. At the time R&A employed over 1,600 of the nation's top social scientists, many of them university professors, who soon returned to their former jobs, leaving the branch at a practical peacetime size.[71] Assistant Secretary of War John J. McCloy was a friend of Donovan's who personally believed in the value of SI and X-2. X-2 had information that could threaten national security, and it was vital that this information not be lost in a bureaucratic shuffle.[72] He requested that those branches of the OSS be transferred to the War Department as a new Strategic Service Unit. Secretary of War Robert Patterson concurred, and two more branches were saved.

One day in January 1946, Ruth Donovan noticed that, for the first time since she could remember, her husband was not in uniform when he came down to dinner.[73] He had been released, and would never again be an official part of the American intelligence community.

A portrait of Donovan hangs at CIA headquarters in Washington, homage to the man recognized as the founding father of American intelligence. The portrait is standard issue: A dignified, mature soldier, his eyes fixed at some indeterminate distance, he looks disappointingly like many other honorable old soldiers who walked away into the sunset. There is none of the immediacy or candor of the young face peering out from under his tilted World War I helmet in an early photograph. The charm, the energy, and the intelligence that inspired thousands, made his name legend, and shaped his astonishing legacy are missing.

Yet he left a lasting mark. OSSers by the hundreds went on to serve in the CIA. OSS alumni William Colby, Allen Dulles, and William Casey each served as director of the organization. In the short term, even Truman soon came to realize that his office had run more smoothly when all information was filtered through a single source. In January 1946, he established the Central Intelligence Group. Donovan's dream was realized. He returned to his New York law practice but continued to lobby for a peacetime intelligence agency. His efforts left an indelible imprint not only on U.S. intelligence services but also ultimately on foreign policy—and are still felt today. Donovan's veterans are intensely loyal to the memory of the man who led them, to their mission to ensure freedom, and to the education of future generations in the art of strategic intelligence.

More than sixty years after the end of World War II, and nearly that long since the dissolution of the Office of Strategic Services, a heavy veil of secrecy is still in place. Many surviving OSS members are reluctant to talk about their experiences, invoking wartime restrictions. There is a suspicion that a substantial body of files in the U.S. National Archives remains classified. The bulk of the papers now available to historians were declassified only in 1997; even more amazing is the fact that some documents have been reclassified as secret.

Why this level of secrecy? Several issues continue to be treated with the greatest possible sensitivity. One is the very close collaboration with Germans during and after the war, and the active assistance of German officials who served in postwar West Germany. Equally sensitive is the mystery of why the OSS was shut down so quickly. It has been argued that parts of the OSS were deeply penetrated by the Soviet intelligence services, primarily the KGB. Documentation, based on relatively unfettered access to Soviet intelligence files, is cited in detail in *The Haunted Wood*, published in 1999.[74] The longstanding rivalry between the FBI's J. Edgar Hoover and OSS leaders also played a significant role.

Even in wartime Washington, the OSS had never been truly accepted; suspicions and jealousies colored the views of many. For a good portion of the war, the OSS was excluded from the critical Pacific Theater and information vital to the war there—the details on the Japanese naval order of battle supplied to the OSS by a Fritz Kolbe—were ignored. Had they been acted on, the history books might be telling a different story.

CONCLUSION

In 1947 Allen Dulles wrote to England's Bishop George Bell that, for him, the most important aspect of his mission on behalf of his "good Germans" was to make the sacrifices of the opposition understood.[1] But his efforts in this regard encountered firm resistance. Americans were wholly, blissfully ignorant of what resistance to a totalitarian regime meant, and they were unrelenting. In the fight for his "good Germans," Dulles was tilting at windmills. The official view, as Gävernitz had suggested earlier, was that there were no good Germans, only Nazis, or dangerous rebels, bankrupt generals, and, of course, traitors of questionable motivation who were not to be trusted.

Meanwhile, the history of World War II, like that of most wars, was being written—at least for a time—by the victors. It has left a bitter legacy, and a record of breathtaking hypocrisy in Allied dealings with those of the enemy who collaborated with the Allies to work toward peace, and other recent enemies who suddenly seemed desirable for other reasons. Leland Harrison, the U.S. minister under whose aegis Dulles worked in Bern, had warned in 1945 that if anything were granted to survivors of the July 20 plot, they might "exploit these liberties for goals incompatible with the goals of the United States."[2] Evidently Harrison's warning did not apply to intelligence agents, rocket scientists, engineers, chemists, or even war criminals whose résumés made them more compatible with the goals of the United States.

Also compatible with those goals, apparently, was the compensation of Ford, GM, and others for their losses because of a war they had helped to support. On December 14, 1998, *Newsweek* ran an article entitled "Dirty Business," in which readers learned that recently declassified documents revealed that roughly three hundred American companies had done business with Germany throughout the war.[3] It may have surprised the readers, but it was hardly news. Shortly after the end of the war, Eleanor Roosevelt commented on a recent news article: "I hope a great many people read the story about the Ford plants in Germany . . . with its record of the actions permitted to these foreign plants. . . . Business complications," she concluded, "do strange things to our patriotism and our ethics!"[4] Ford had been compensated by the Nazis for wartime losses, and in 1942 the Vichy government agreed to pay for damages in France.[5] Yet Ford later appealed to the United States government for an additional $8 million. GM, after prolonged negotiations, was granted a $33 million tax exemption for the difficulties and destruction of its factories in Germany and Austria during the war.[6]

In 1960, the United States and Poland signed an agreement on compensation for seized properties. Giesche, in what had in the meantime become Polish soil, was among them. The Poles were to pay $10 million a year for twenty years to compensate the Swiss, the American government, and the Silesian-American Corporation, the American consortium put together in the 1920s, for which Giesche had built the luxurious villa that had played host to Himmler in 1942.[7] By that time the contributions of Eduard Schulte, whom the Allies had refused to denazify, to the defeat of the Nazis had been long forgotten.

Writing about the German opposition, Dulles summed up what he had learned from his years of dealing with Germany's underground, whether directly or indirectly. "There *was* an anti-Nazi underground working in Germany, despite the general impression to the contrary," and their story was "incontrovertible proof that even in a totalitarian state the struggle for individual liberty does not cease."[8] It also revealed, he said,

> how the various strata of Germany reacted when a dictator set out to destroy democracy. In Germany, at least, there were no defenses in depth against totalitarian attack. When the line was broken at a vital point, the battle was lost. It should make all of us consider how adequate our own institutions are for democracy's preservation and how far its survival must depend upon the devotion to these institutions of men and women ready and willing to act *in time* to defend them.[9]

What is called for in such instances is encapsulated in one composite German word: *Zivilcourage,* meaning simply the garden-variety courage of one's convictions. Unfortunately this kind of courage is usually one of the first casualties of trying times. Yet surprisingly, in some of the most trying times of the last century, it survived, and survived in a much larger and broader resistance within the vast prison of Nazi Germany than anyone had imagined.

On the surface, supporting such resistance would seem a logical place to begin fighting the Nazi monster, but to the immense frustration of Dulles and Donovan, the Allies steadfastly refused to offer any assistance at all to the German opposition to Hitler. Was it because of Roosevelt's deep distrust and dislike of all Germans, or did the need to placate Stalin trump all else? Most likely both played their part in the mind of the ailing Roosevelt, for whom the need to keep "Uncle Joe" happy may have provided justification for his refusal to deal with the "Junkers," no matter the circumstances. But the consistent appeasement of Stalin, who was increasingly truculent about the failure to open a second front, came at enormous expense. While Russia had borne up at great cost and with terrible casualties along an immense front, the price for Stalin's promise to help fight the Japanese was morally and politically high; his fist was closing down on Poland and Eastern Europe even before the end of the war.

Hindsight offers a comfortable seat from which to consider these issues. There is little point in speculating about any changes in Hitler's agenda, which was set from the start, but the temptation to replay the tragic story in a what-if mode is almost irresistible. What if the British Foreign Office had realized in 1938–39, that what was truly in the national interest was rising *above* the national interest? In the debate in the House of Lords after Munich, Lord Lloyd noted that he had informed the foreign secretary in early August of the entire German plan—to the very day. "Why," he lamented, "did we not take our courage in our hands?"[10]

It would have taken courage to shed the legacy of anti-German prejudices, to look beyond the fears of German hegemony in Europe, to stand up early to Hitler's threat in spite of the lack of military preparedness, and such courage was lacking. So, "for want of a nail . . ." the shoe, the horse, many, many riders, and battles were lost, consumed in a catastrophic war, and all for the want of that handy item, in this case, courage and imagination.

What if Chamberlain had not flown, flown again to Munich, to capitulate to Hitler's changing demands? Conditions were certainly ripe for a coup. German generals and populace alike were opposed to Hitler's plan for war; everything was in place, and the timing was as right as it would ever be for a coup unlikely to stir up the civil unrest the opposition dreaded. Would the coup have been successful? General Halder was asked at Nuremberg whether—barring Chamberlain's flight to Munich—the coup would have been set in motion and have succeeded in deposing Hitler. "We were firmly convinced we would be successful," he replied, but "the critical hour for force was [lost] . . . I can only say that the plan would have been executed."[11]

What if, despite that November fog in 1939, Hitler had spoken for an additional thirteen minutes next to the Munich beer hall pillar that Elser had spent a month of evenings painstakingly hollowing out to house his bomb? Hitler would almost certainly have been killed even before the roof collapsed on so many of his old-time Party comrades in arms. As it was, Elser's attempt served only to sensitize Hitler to the danger of assassination attempts by "some criminal or idiot."[12] It also made explosives harder to come by, a development that consistently bedeviled the conspirators.

Suppose Roosevelt had been more forthright, and cut short his flirtation with appeasement, and replaced the on-off switch he used so adroitly until his reelection was secure with a firm stand? England might have been emboldenened by the backing of a strong ally, and dared to issue the rebuff the opposition longed for. In the end, Pearl Harbor and Hitler finally left him no alternative but war.

What if the German questionnaire Popov brought with him to the United States in the summer of 1941 had elicited any interest in Hoover beyond its microdot format? Or the British had called their American counterparts' attention to what seemed to them the questionnaire's astonishing focus on Pearl Harbor? Would the United States have entered the war in December anyway, or would there have been a wait for another viable excuse?

What if FDR had not blurted his amusing story about General Grant at Casablanca, offering his nickname as the perfect solution to this war. An immense impediment to peace could have been lifted, a prolonged war shortened, an appalling casualty count lessened. Adam von Trott lamented to Dulles that the demand for unconditional surrender would create a vast hole in Europe's center, a hole that would be filled by Stalin, whose political agenda shaped the lives of millions of people for more than fifty years. Unconditional surrender was a slap in the face of the German resistance, for it took an "all Germans are Nazis" attitude. Yet even given Casablanca's terms, what if FDR had acceded to his generals' pleas for softening the demand? Would an earlier accommodation have been reached, and many lives spared?

Though Roosevelt neglected to mention it at Casablanca, Grant had never imposed such terms on Lee at Appomattox. And Bismarck, in all the wars that reshaped the map of Europe, had had the good sense not to demand unconditional surrender or impose a a peace so harsh that it would only engender rancor and ensure future conflict. The German generals knew that the war was lost in 1942. Canaris, presented with the prospect of unconditional surrender by his friend and colleague Lahousen, could no longer see any solution, and even the feisty Witzleben, ever ready to embrace anti-Hitler action, argued that no reasonable, honorable man could lead the German people into such a cul-de-sac.

Yet the combined efforts of Stalin and Churchill at Teheran to ease the official policy were not enough to change FDR's mind. Both needed the

United States, and Roosevelt had seen what happened to Wilson and his Fourteen Points after World War I. There was a contingent at home that felt that the reason the United States had been sucked into this war was because there had been no unconditional surrender in that war.[13] No, Roosevelt was not interested. Though even the pope weighed in, reminding the president that unconditional surrender was not compatible with Christian doctrine, and peace was allied to charity, not hate and vindictiveness, Roosevelt was unmoved.[14] His hugely contentious policy would not be eased, not to satisfy the Allies, the generals, not Donovan, not Dulles, and certainly not the German resistance.

THE OSS'S RESEARCH AND ANALYSIS BRANCH, MANNED LARGELY BY ANTI-NAZI GERMANS, many of whom were Jewish, regarded the opposition to Hitler as "a tribute to human endurance and courage, and the revelation of a great hope." They argued that unconditional surrender played directly into the Nazi propagandists' hands and urged the Allies to make contact with the resistance and perhaps give some "substance to the hope."[15] Their pleas were ignored.

As soon as he arrived in Bern in November 1942, Dulles began advocating for, and then sending support in the way of funds to, the French resistance, across the full political spectrum: socialists, labor, the Maquis, even Vichy. Two million here, half a million there, then 400,000 French francs, Swiss francs somewhere else, may not have seemed like much to the Americans.[16] But it was enough to infuriate de Gaulle, of the Free French, who saw himself as the sole savior of France, and cause him to behave "cantankerously," as Dulles put it.[17] Money, men, materiel, and intelligence continued to go to France, often via parachute—a hazardous undertaking—and the French resistance benefited enormously from the Jedburgh teams. In early February 1944, Dulles informed Washington that he was restricting operations "to 4,000,000 each month for the Maquis."[18]

What if he had been able to do something—anything—for the German resistance? A short, efficient fuse or explosives slipped to one of the Abwehr couriers would have done the trick. One or another of the suicide missions to eliminate Hitler that failed for want of such items would likely have succeeded. But other than listening, and truly hearing them, Dulles was not allowed to offer a scintilla of help or hope. What if American policy makers had at least made the "clear statement of policy" on the postwar rebuilding of Europe that the Dulles-Gävernitz team asked for, to help strengthen and expand the opposition in Germany that was already gaining momentum because of military setbacks? If nothing else, it would certainly have boosted morale. Would it also have broadened the resistance, as Gävernitz predicted?

In this context, it is interesting to speculate about how things might have turned out had Dulles been given what the Bush administration decreed in late 2005 was the third top mission objective of intelligence operations: "to bolster the growth of democracy."[19] If anyone in intelligence in World War II had the will to bolster democracy, it was Dulles. He would have been delighted to support the opposition and help them establish a new government of reason, law, and justice. In fact, he had a personal list of the names of leaders capable of forming just such a government in postwar Germany. Would FDR have recognized such a possibility, or would he have simply continued refusing to "deal with these Junkers" on whatever grounds he had decided on?

WHAT IF THE HEATER IN HITLER'S CONDOR ON THAT FLIGHT FROM SMOLENSK TO HIS headquarters at Rastenburg had not malfunctioned? Or if July 20, 1944, had not been such a hot day and Hitler's briefing had been held in the usual bunker? What if Stauffenberg had had time to arm both bombs? In all instances, it is reasonably certain that Hitler would have been killed. Questions, of course, remain: Would the other elements have been pulled together sufficiently to avoid civil war? Could the conspirators have quashed the SS and won the hearts of a war-weary, hungry, and disillusioned populace?

Moltke and others of the Kreisau Circle were willing to accept Germany's utter defeat in order to make a truly fresh start. Had his Hermann Plan to open the western front to Allied forces been adopted, and the Soviet occupation avoided, far fewer states on the political map of Europe between 1945 and 1990 might have been tinted the same shade as the Soviet Union. In late June and early July 1944, a haggard and desperate Adam von Trott was in Stockholm again, pleading for contact with the Allies. By now, the pattern was very familiar: Contact with the British did not go at all well; his approach to the Americans, begging again for a moderation of unconditional surrender, met with suspicion. But this time, he tried a new tack, establishing contact with the Soviets through Mme. Alexandra Kollontai at the Soviet embassy in Sweden.[20] It all came to nothing, and on July 18, 1944, Ulrich von Hassell summarized the bitter dilemma Germany, the opposition, and Europe as a whole faced, poised between East and West: "It is a tragedy not only for Germany but also for the whole continent that the idea of [Germany, healthy and strong, as a center] has been understood so rarely. . . . The price for not having succeeded in coming to terms—one way or another in this situation—is heavy."[21]

What if Dulles and Donovan had been heard and heeded. What if Gisevius was right, and hitting the tottering Reich hard after July 20 would have caused it to crumble? What if Roosevelt had acted on Donovan's suggestion and told the German people that they could improve their "present plight and future prospects" if they were to overthrow Hitler."[22] No word came from Washington. Instead, in "the greatest single purge that even Hitler's Germany had ever seen . . . practically all remnants of the German intelligentsia, all the potential leaders of a non-Nazi Germany, were put in Gestapo prisons. Very few ever came out again."[23]

Donovan warned FDR after the final Stauffenberg attempt that the next putsch would likely come from a group with an Eastern orientation, most likely after Soviet occupation of East Prussia. But Roosevelt still envisioned a cozy entente cordiale with the Soviets. He seemed not in the least concerned about the future freedoms of Eastern Europe, the Baltics, or Poland. What if he had taken Donovan's warning to heart? Would FDR have insisted on continuing the war anyway, or might the horrific casualties between mid-1944 and May 1945—the lives lost in the death camps, the Ardennes, the Bulge, and in the 1945 bombing of Dresden—the deaths of literally millions been averted?

BITTER CONTROVERSY ABOUT THE ALLIED REFUSAL TO ENGAGE IN EVEN MODEST EFFORTS to intervene in the Holocaust continues to this day. The fact is that in spite of the appalling scale of the disaster, humanitarian claims made little headway. The British had solid evidence of atrocities and mass murders in Poland and Russia obtained from decrypts of Nazi police and SS codes in 1941. Some information had also trickled in to the United States, though it apparently went unnoticed. Eduard Schulte communicated the plans for the exterminations at Auschwitz in mid-1942, yet when this was finally made public, there was neither significant support nor moral outcry from the British and American governments. Refugees represented an embarrassment to both nations, and both hoped the problem would simply disappear. The British had Palestine and the Arab world to contend with, and the United States maintained its staunchly anti-immigration policy.

FDR faced an electorate that was ambivalent about the war in any case, and a clear moral statement on Hitler's Jewish policies would have exposed him to a politically risky mine field of American prejudices. Any statement that might allow the war to be construed as a mission to rescue European Jewry faced a potentially devastating anti-Semitic backlash, so until 1944 it was argued that such a statement might threaten overall war aims. Only a senator from Missouri wondered how a nation purporting to be fighting under the banner of the Four Freedoms could ignore the savagery. Harry Truman insisted that the United States had to help "all those who can be grasped from the hands of the Nazi butchers" to find a refuge.[24]

Postwar arrangements between the Big Three, forged preliminarily at Teheran and then at Yalta, also raise a number of questions. Among those accompanying the ailing FDR were stalwart New Dealer Harry Hopkins and Alger Hiss. Hopkins had lived in the White House for a time, and his daily contact and influence on Roosevelt should not be underestimated. He had served FDR faithfully in many capacities, at the WPA, Lend-Lease, and, perhaps most important, at Teheran and Yalta. As ardently pro-Soviet as he was anti-German, he welcomed Yalta as the dawn of a new, eagerly awaited day. Alger Hiss, a communist sympathizer, to the point of spying for the Soviets, was also at Roosevelt's elbow at Yalta.[25] Had Hopkins awakened to the Soviet threat before Yalta rather than after, his influence, properly exercised, might have altered some of the policies established there, and changed the shape of Europe.

Instead, FDR's misguided faith in the Soviets and the hopes it carried with it, outlasted him, though not by much. Hopkins's eyes were opened to the Stalin's true intentions only after the war. In Moscow on Truman's behalf, he saw Stalin's intransigence at first hand, and two old Soviet hands, Kennan and Charles Bohlen, reinforced his anxieties about future collaboration with the Russians. Reluctantly, he was forced into a more realistic assessment, and went home, a broken, dying man.[26]

THERE ARE NO HARD ANSWERS TO ANY OF THESE WHAT-IFS. YET THE MANY QUESTIONS, even though they can always be countered as unanswerable, make for discouraging contemplation. The German opposition was always at the mercy of circumstances over which they had no control, and countless imponderables remain. But history has painted a dismal picture in which national and political interests, clothed in bright and often discordant colors, are the most visible elements. Less obvious is a recognizable and repeated motif of energy and courage. England's Bishop Bell recognized the motif as the driving moral force of the opposition, pushing—come what may—to get beyond the clamor and dissonance to a Europe able to transcend traditional nationalism and move into a new era of reason and peace.

The German opposition's first brave steps out into "the landscape of treason," to make common cause in what they regarded as a struggle against terrible evil, were wholly unorthodox. The "resistance diplomacy" of Adam von Trott and other German emissaries in the later 1930s seemed unrecognizable as diplomacy, and it found no place in the conventional framework. Not surprisingly, it was met with deep suspicion by a very orthodox British political establishment that perceived these steps as most probably thinly disguised attempts at poaching on British national interests.

Once the war had begun, it ran head-on into hard wartime realities. As opposition gradually morphed, of necessity, into planned military coups, the Allied stance became increasingly rigid, moving from distrust and puzzlement to silence, and ultimately, to intransigence. In retrospect, investing, however cautiously and marginally, in an indigenous resistance seems a logical, even intelligent strategy. But no matter how many territorial claims or other demands the various opposition factions were willing to abandon, Allied policy left the "other Germany" not even the smallest toehold. There would be no negotiation. Those like Dulles, and a handful of others who heard the voices of the opposition and recognized them for what they were, were not able to move their governments to alter the official policy by so much as a millimeter. In failing to send out any signals at all, the Allies sent a strong signal that is deeply troubling.

Many years later, George Kennan, who had seen something of both the resistance and Allied policies, remarked on the great imbalance between the claimed Allied abhorrence of Hitler and '"the very low value" put "morally and politically in the willingness of other Germans to accept the enormous risks of trying to overthrow him."'[27]

In 1945 Churchill told a Belgian audience that President Roosevelt had once asked him what World War II should be called. His reply: "the unnecessary war." If the opposition's energy and moral courage had been recognized and supported, the unnecessary war might not have happened; the twentieth century might have taken a different course.

EPILOGUE

The vast body of literature on World War II contains one particularly haunting image of a train filled with documents of the Third Reich pulling out of Berlin in the last weeks of the war, moving the records of infamy to safety or into hiding. The train is hit by a bomb. Papers fly up into the smoky turbulence, flutter, and come to rest in surrounding springtime fields. Perhaps some are picked up by the soldiers of the Russian army swarming into the ruined capital. This scattering and dispersal of fact and detail is emblematic of the historian's task, so much like that of an intelligence officer: collecting the bits and pieces, trying to put them together into a semblance of "truth."

Who owns history? Certainly not those who actually—or merely—lived it. No. It belongs to those who write it down. And deep in the heart of those who write it down—historians, if you will—there lurks a moralist who, no matter how carefully camouflaged, conveys his own message. Understandably enough, in the case of WW II the moralist was very much in evidence, busily erecting a monument to the forces of good. A myth of this terrible war was spun from documents and testimony, but also from ideology, selected memory, and sentiment. Yet sixty years after its collapse, the Third Reich is anything but put to rest; willy-nilly, it continues to provide fodder for novelists, for the press, for movies, and television, and it spawns a good deal of lurid kitsch. The story is as fascinating as it is frustrating. It defies real understanding and continues to challenge the historian.

If, as Oscar Wilde suggested, the one duty we owe history is to rewrite it, it is time for the rewrite. But before the rewrite, there should some re-thinking of this particular history. The world has shrunk to decidedly non-mythical proportion and it is time to demythologize. There are lessons to be learned from the story of the German opposition to Hitler and the Al-lies. It offers parallels to more recent events in the United States on the im-portance of meaningful cooperation between intelligence agencies and on hearing and heeding warning voices. Columns of newsprint have been de-voted to the multiple, scattered intelligence reports before September 11, 2001. The individual pieces seemed too random, too inconclusive; they were never been pieced together and puzzled over, never recognized as the pattern they really were. The story also provides parallels on the relation-ship of intelligence to policy, and more newsprint continues to examine the controversy about the dangers of shaping intelligence to political and ideological advantage.[1]

One lesson of World War II that stands out for the American reader is the hesitancy on the part of British intelligence to pass on their suspicions about the import of the 1941 German questionnaire on Pearl Harbor. Was it diffidence, or a feeling that their American allies really ought to work this out for themselves? The British were very outspoken about the Dogwood chain, persevering in their efforts to persuade the Americans to vet suspect sources, even to the point of alerting Donovan. Sixty-five years later, in July 2005, in what was termed a "major breakthrough," new intelligence guide-lines were announced, intended to guarantee that, in the future, national intelligence estimates would be based on credible, rather than unsubstanti-ated claims. New, critical scrutiny would be applied and the circle of intelli-gence officers and agencies privy to information on human and other sources would be widened.[2] Doubts and reservations on the part of intelli-gence officers would have a hearing. The intention, clearly, was to avoid precisely the sort of blind acceptance of unvetted and unreliably sourced intelligence that the British had warned against sixty-plus years ago.

ALLEN DULLES WAS DEEPLY FRUSTRATED BY THE ALLIED FAILURE TO USE EVEN THE MOST basic strategic military intelligence on bombing targets provided by Kolbe and others. Both he and Donovan felt thwarted by the refusal of policy makers to consider intelligence in shaping policy. More recently, frustra-tion has focused on what is seen as the manipulation of intelligence to suit policy makers. While it might be argued that these are simply opposite sides of the same coin, understanding the difference is critical.

In the end, the story of the German resistance to Hitler is a story of wa-vering, of mishaps, of religious and patriotic qualms, of setbacks, and of the folly of putting too much faith in the response of others. What vestiges of German honor the final, symbolic plot managed to salvage went mostly unrecognized, even—perhaps particularly—in Germany for years. Ultimately it is the story of failure, but one that bears reexamination in light of the recent focus on intelligence and its relation to policy. Carl Goerdeler, when the war he had tried so hard to avert finally broke out, cast a harsh light on the relationship: 'We do not wish to diminish the responsibility which we as Germans will have to bear, but the guilt for the tragic events rests not with the Germans alone."[3]

Goerdeler lived the tragic events that were to become at least a sliver of that terrible war. In January 1945, imprisoned and awaiting execution, Goerdeler the patriot, the devout Christian, the irrepressible optimist, convinced that good, reason, and justice would ultimately triumph, was in despair. Like Job on his dung heap, he asked why: "Are there many who have been hit as hard by the hand of God?" he asked. His son had been killed on the Russian front, his family imprisoned and dispossessed, he was reviled as a traitor. "Those whom I love are in need and sorrow, but I have no sign from them. And, God knows, I have risked everything to spare the youth, the men and women of all nations further suffering. Oh Lord, what is the answer to this puzzle? The criminals triumph!"[4] His cri de coeur speaks for others who merely lived history; they deserve a part in the rewriting of it.

GLOSSARY

Amt Ausland/Abwehr Military intelligence (secret intelligence, counterintelligence, and sabotage) service of the high command of the German Armed Forces (OKW)

Anschluß Originally a movement for political union of Germany and Austria claiming a right to national self-determination; the annexation of Austria by German troops on March 12, 1938

Bank for International Settlements (BIS) International organization that functions as a bank for central banks; headquartered in Basel, Switzerland; founded in 1930 to collect, administer, and distribute Germany's reparation payments following World War I

Bekennende Kirche (Confessional Church) Countermovement by Protestant theologians who opposed Hitler's German Faith movement; included Dietrich Bonhoeffer

Bendlerblock Building complex on the Landwehr Canal in the Tiergarten district of Berlin; it housed the Imperial Navy Office before World War I, served as headquarters of OKW after 1935, and accommodated offices of the Abwehr after 1938. It was the execution site for several conspirators against Hitler, who had coordinated their attack from there

Boston Series Mimeographed intelligence reports based on the materials supplied by Fritz Kolbe, a.k.a. George Wood; raw intelligence obtained by Kolbe was called Kappa

Breakers OSS designation for the German opposition group involved in the July 20, 1944, attempt to assassinate Hitler

Bund Deutscher Offiziere (BDO) German Officers League under the leadership of General Walther von der Seydlitz-Kurzbach; it was established in September 1943 as a union of POWs in the Soviet Union who opposed the Nazis and negotiated with German communists and the Red Army political branch

Bundesnachrichtendienst (BND) Foreign intelligence agency of the Federal Republic of Germany, led from 1956 until 1968 by General Reinhard Gehlen

Coordinator of Information (COI) Precursor to the OSS

Crown Jewels Germans deemed important by OSS for American postwar purposes

Dawes Plan Report on reparations issued by a committee headed by Charles G. Dawes in April 1924; intended to balance Germany's budget and stabilize the mark

Emniyet First intelligence organization of the Republic of Turkey, established in January 1926

Enabling Act "Law to Remove the Distress of People and State," enacted on March 24, 1933, provided the constitutional foundation for Hitler's dictatorship

Foreign Information Service (FIS) From 1941 to 1942 an office within COI that executed information programs to promote understanding of the American war effort

Fremde Heere Ost Foreign Armies East Section of the OKH (12. Abt.)

Geheime Staatspolizei (Gestapo) Secret state police under the command of the SS

I. G. Farben (Interessengemeinschaft Farbenindustrie Aktiengesellschaft) Largest German cartel in the chemicals industry, with holdings and financiers in the U.S.; it included powerful firms such as BASF, Hoechst, and Bayer, supplied the Wehrmacht, provided poison gas for extermination camps, and used Auschwitz as the site of a synthetic oil and rubber plant

Joint Chiefs of Staff (JCS) Panel comprising the highest-ranking members of each major branch of the U.S. armed services

Katyn Forest Near Smolensk in western Russia. The site of a mass execution of Polish military officers by Soviet secret police upon Stalin's orders in 1940

Kreisau Circle Opposition group of officers and professional civilians formed in 1933. Led by Peter Count Yorck von Wartenburg and Helmuth James Count von Moltke, its members met at the Moltke family estate in Kreisau, Silesia (now Poland), envisioned an alternative to Nazism

Kriminalpolizei (Kripo) Criminal Police, which with the Gestapo formed Security Police (Sipo) of the SS. In 1939 it became part of the RSHA.

Lebensraum "Living Space," slogan popular before World War I alleging German overpopulation in comparison with its arable soil and need for territorial expansion; appropriated by Hitler for aggressive foreign policy

MI-5 British domestic counterintelligence service

MI-6, also **SIS** British secret intelligence service

Morale Operations (MO) OSS propaganda branch

Nationalsozialistische Deutsche Arbeiterpartei (NSDAP) National Socialist German Workers' Party, official title of the Nazi Party

Night of the Long Knives Campaign of assassination unleashed by Hitler on the night of June 30, 1934, against SA leadership to prevent a revolution in the Nazi Party

Nuremberg Trials Public war crimes trial of Nazis involved in World War II and the Holocaust; a special court held at German city of Nuremberg from 1945 to 1949 was to judge crimes against peace, humanity, and defenseless minorities

Oberkommando des Heeres (OKH) High command of the German Army

Oberkommando der Wehrmacht (OKW) High command of the German Armed Forces

Office of War Information (OWI) Propaganda agency created in 1942 by the U.S.

government, coordinated domestic release of war news, launched information campaign abroad

Operation Sunrise Secret negotiations between Allen Dulles and SS General Karl Wolff that led to the surrender of German forces in northern Italy on May 1, 1945

Operation Valkyrie Code name for two distinct operations: a Hitler-devised contingency plan that designated Replacement Army to take over the security of Berlin and industrial centers in the event of a revolt; conspirators in the July plot of 1944 appropriated the name as cover for their coup plans

Organization Gehlen German intelligence service founded in June 1946 by Reinhard Gehlen, controlled by the CIA since 1948, supplied the West with intelligence on Warsaw Pact nations; became BND in April 1956

Peenemünde Wooded island in the Baltic Sea where German scientists worked on the secret reprisal missiles V-1 and V-2

Policia de Vigilancia e Defesa do Estado (PVDE, later PIDE and DGS) Portuguese political police

Project Paperclip Government project after World War II to bring German technological secrets and scientists to the United States before the Soviets could capture specialists in aerodynamics, rocketry, chemical weapons, and medicine

Project Safehaven Program to deny safe haven for Nazi looted assets in European neutral nations; aimed at curbing German capacity to start another war; used economic intelligence gathered by OSS

Reichsführer-SS und Chef der Deutschen Polizei Reich commander of the SS and chief of the German police, Heinrich Himmler's title from June 1936

Reichssicherheitshauptamt (RSHA) Reich Security Main Office or Central State Security Bureau or Reich Central Security Office, set up in 1939 to combine all existing police forces (Gestapo, Kripo, SD); the chief was Reinhard Heydrich until his assassination in June 1942

R&A Research and Analysis Branch of the OSS

Reichswehr After 1919 the small defensive military force of the Weimar Republic

Rote Kapelle "Red Orchestra," name created by the Gestapo for supposedly pro-Soviet resistance rings, led by Harro Schulze-Boysen and Arvid Harnack; discovered by Abwehr in 1942

Schutzstaffel (SS) Literally, protection or guard detachment; the most powerful branch and elite of the Nazi Party paramilitary force, led by Heinrich Himmler

SHAEF Supreme Headquarters Allied Expeditionary Forces

Sicherheitsdienst (SD) Security service of the SS

Sicherheitspolizei (Sipo) Security police

Sturmabteilung (SA) The Storm Troopers, early private army of the Nazi Party

Treaty of Rapallo Agreement signed in April 1922 by the Weimar Republic and the Soviet Union; each country renounced all territorial and financial claims against the other and normalized diplomatic relations a secret annex allowed Germany to train its military in Soviet territory

Treaty of Versailles Peace settlement after World War I, signed in June 1919. Article 231 established Germany's guilt in causing the war, imposed high reparations, reduced the German army to 100,000 volunteer soldiers

Ultra Name used by British for intelligence resulting from the decryption of German cipher traffic often encrypted on Enigma machines

Unternehmen Sieben Cover name for the rescue of Jews by Abwehr officers in the fall 1942. Hans von Dohnanyi enabled threatened deportees to flee to Switzerland under cover of Abwehr agents

Venlo incident Gestapo-engineered capture of two British SIS agents in November 1939 in the Dutch town of Venlo. British agents met supposed German officers who pretended to belong to the anti-Hitler resistance

War Refugee Board (WRB) Agency established in January 1944 to rescue victims of the Nazis from death in German-occupied Europe

Wehrmacht Renamed German armed forces after introduction of compulsory military service in March 1935 with Hitler as commander in chief

Wolfsschanze "Wolf's Lair," Hitler's field headquarters at Rastenburg, East Prussia

Young Plan Presented by a committee headed by Owen D. Young, replaced Dawes Plan in 1930, fixed capital value of total German reparations at $8 billion payable in 58.5 annual installments

Zossen Headquarters of German army command, located about twenty miles south of Berlin

MILITARY RANK EQUIVALENCES

German Army	U.S. Army	British Army
Generalfeldmarschall	General of the Army General	Field Marshal
Generaloberst	General	General
General	Lieutenant General	Lieutenant General
Generalleutnant	Major General	Major General
Generalmajor	Brigadier General	Brigadier
Oberst	Colonel	Colonel
Oberstleutnant	Lieutenant Colonel	Lieutenant Colonel
Major	Major	Major
Hauptmann	Captain	Captain
Oberleutnant	First Lieutenant	Lieutenant
Leutnant	Second Lieutenant	Second Lieutenant

SS	Western Equivalents
Reichsführer	National Leader
Oberstgruppenführer	General
Obergruppenführer	Lieutenant General
Gruppenführer	Major General
Brigadeführer	Brigadier General
Oberführer	no equivalent
Standartenführer	Colonel
Obersturmbannführer	Lieutenant Colonel
Sturmbannführer	Major
Hauptsturmführer	Captain
Obersturmführer	First Lieutenant
Untersturmführer	Second Lieutenant
Sturmscharführer	Sergeant Major
Stabsscharführer	Sergeant Major
Hauptscharführer	Master Sergeant
Oberscharführer	Senior Sergeant
Scharführer	Staff Sergeant
Unterscharführer	Corporal
Rottenführer	Lance Corporal
Sturmmann	Private First Class
Schütze	Private
SS-Mann	no equivalent

SHORT BIOGRAPHIES

A brief introduction to some of the principal players, many of whom may be unfamiliar to readers, and their OSS code names and/or numbers.

MARY BANCROFT, 1903–1997
American socialite, student and patient of Carl Gustav Jung, friend and special assistant of Allen W. Dulles. Helped translate Hans Bernd Gisevius's manuscript.
OSS Mrs. Pestalozzi

LUDWIG BECK, 1880–1944
Colonel general, central figure in military resistance. Named chief of staff of the armed forces in 1935. Attempted in vain in summer of 1938 to persuade German generals to resign en masse in order to prevent war. Resigned thereafter for reasons of conscience and in protest against Hitler's plan to dismantle Czechoslovakia, participated in planning assassination attempts. Failed at committing suicide twice after the attempt of July 20, 1944, then succeeded with assistance of a sergeant.
OSS Tucky

DIETRICH BONHOEFFER, 1906–1945
Protestant theologian and leading representative of the Confessional Church. Pastor in charge of German Evangelical community in London between 1933 and 1935. Drafted into the Abwehr to work with his brother-in-law Hans von Dohnanyi in August 1940, seconded to Abwehr office in Munich in late October 1940. Assembled files on crimes committed by the SS. Maintained foreign contacts with Willem A. Visser't Hooft and Bishop George Bell of Chichester. Arrested April 5, 1943, for undermining the war effort, hanged April 9, 1945, in Flossenbürg concentration camp.

JOEL BRAND, 1906–1964

Active in left-wing German politics, since 1938 leader of a Hungarian Jewish relief committee. In May 1944 failed to negotiate with Adolf Eichmann a large-scale exchange of Jews destined for extermination camps for trucks needed in Germany. Arrested by the British in Syria who suspected him of being a Nazi agent; released in October 1944. Testified at Eichmann trial in Jerusalem in 1961.

DAVID K. E. BRUCE, 1898–1977

Colonel, diplomat. Joined OSS in 1941, head of OSS outpost in London, eventually director of OSS operations in the European Theater of Operations. Ambassador to France (1949–1952), to West Germany (1957–1959), to Great Britain (1961–1969), and to China (1973–1974). Divorced from his first wife was Ailsa Mellon, one of the richest women in America, in 1945, then married to a former OSS official.
OSS No. 105

HEINRICH BRÜNING, 1885–1970

Statesman of the Weimar Republic. Named chancellor in March 1930. Used Article 48 of the Weimar Constitution to rule by decree after Nazis triumphed in elections of September 14, 1930. Worked toward revision of Treaty of Versailles. Reich President Paul von Hindenburg asked him to resign in May 1932. Relinquished chairmanship of Catholic Center Party in July 1933. Emigrated to the U.S. in late summer of 1939, led solitary life as a professor at Harvard University's Lowell House.

AXEL VON DEM BUSSCHE-STREITHORST, 1919–1993

Member of the military-conservative resistance. Career officer with rank of major, member of Potsdam-based 9th Infantry Regiment, *Regiment Graf Neun,* where he befriended Richard von Weizsäcker. Witnessed mass shooting of Jews in Dubno in 1942, which strengthened his resolve to oppose the Nazi regime. In 1943, planned to kill both Hitler and himself by detonating a bomb at a public ceremony. Avoided arrest in July 1944. Studied law after 1945. Legation councilor at German embassy in Washington, D.C. from 1954 to 1958. Led prestigious German boarding school Salem from 1959 to 1961 and directed the German Development Service after its foundation in 1963.

WILHELM CANARIS, 1887–1945

Head of German military intelligence service during World War II. Career officer with rank of admiral. Sympathized with Nazis' resentment of conditions imposed by Versailles Treaty and anticommunism but after 1933 came to despise their brutality and began active opposition to the regime with Fritsch affair. Chief of the Amt Ausland/Abwehr from January 1935 to February 1944. Made military intelligence a harbor for resistance. SS monitored opposition group led by him and Hans Oster. Arrested by Gestapo after plot of July 20, 1944. Executed April 9, 1945, in Flossenbürg concentration camp.
OSS No. 659

WILLIAM J. CASEY, 1913–1987

OSS agent 1943–1945, chief of OSS Special Intelligence Branch Europe in London. Served as head of the Securities and Exchange Commission and as under secretary of state for economic affairs in the Nixon Administration. Ran Ronald Reagan's campaign in 1980. Appointed by President Reagan as CIA director in January 1981. Central figure in Iran-Contra affair. Resigned in January 1987.

HANS VON DOHNANYI, 1902–1945
Member of the Abwehr and the German resistance. Brother-in-law of Dietrich Bonhoeffer. Became personal assistant to Reich minister of justice in 1929, then head of Bureau of Ministers. Participated in attempted coup of September 1938. Transferred to federal court in Leipzig under pressure from NSDAP headquarters. Secretly gathered information on atrocities of Nazi regime, which Gestapo discovered after July 20 plot. Since September 1939 Sonderführer in central division of the Abwehr under Hans Oster. Helped Jews escape deportation in Unternehmen Sieben. Arrested April 5, 1943, for alleged currency violations. Executed April 8, 1945, in Sachsenhausen concentration camp.

WILLIAM J. ("WILD BILL") DONOVAN, 1883–1959
Lawyer, OSS Director. Catholic and Irish heritage. Law degree from Columbia University. Earned Medal of Honor as commander of the 156th Infantry Regiment in World War I. Served as assistant attorney general in Coolidge administration. Practiced antitrust law on Wall Street. Ran for governor of New York in 1932. FDR appointed him Coordinator of Information July 11, 1941. Director of OSS from June 1942 and representative of Joint Chiefs of Staff. Promoted to brigadier general in March 1943 and to major general in November 1944. Successful attorney and ambassador to Thailand (1953–1954).
OSS No. 109

ALLEN W. DULLES, 1893–1969
Lawyer, diplomat, and senior intelligence official. Brother of Secretary of State John Foster Dulles. Joined the foreign service during World War I. Served in Vienna and at the American legation in Bern. Adviser to his uncle, Secretary of State Robert Lansing, at Versailles peace negotiations. Resigned from government in 1926 to practice law. Worked for fifteen years with Wall Street law firm Sullivan & Cromwell, which had Berlin office until 1935. Ran as Republican for Congress and lost in 1938. Headed COI's New York office. Set up intelligence operations in Switzerland in November 1942, with cover as special assistant to the American minister in Bern. Became CIA director in 1953. President John F. Kennedy forced him to resign in 1961, after the U.S. invasion at the Bay of Pigs failed.
OSS No. 110

HANS BERND GISEVIUS, 1907–1974
Civil servant, private sector lawyer, agent for OSS and Abwehr. Participated in planning abortive military coup of 1938. Called up to serve in the German army at instigation of Hans Oster and Wilhelm Canaris. Served as Sonderführer in the Abwehr in 1939. From summer 1940 until 1944 installed as counterintelligence officer in the German consulate general in Zurich, where he was appointed vice consul. Maintained contacts with western Allies, especially with Allen Dulles, on behalf of the opposition. Fled from Berlin back to Switzerland after the July 20 coup attempt failed. Wrote eyewitness account *To the Bitter End* and testified before international military tribunal at Nuremberg.
OSS No. 512 or Luber

CARL FRIEDRICH GOERDELER, 1884–1945
Leader of the German civilian resistance. Close to national conservatives. Served as lord mayor of Leipzig from 1930 until his resignation in April 1937 in protest against anti-Semitic government measures. Reich Price Control Commissioner in 1931–1932 and 1934–1935. Used frequent travels abroad to make political contacts, hoped for separate peace negotiations with Western powers. Drafted outlines for new political order, designated as future chancellor. Denounced and sentenced to death by the People's Court September 8, 1944. Hanged February 2, 1945, in Plötzensee prison after lengthy interrogations and torture.
OSS Leper or Lester

HERMANN GÖRING, 1893–1946
Hitler's heir apparent, high military and economic leader of the Third Reich. Supreme commander of the SA. Took on a number of high posts after Hitler's assumption of power: Reich minister without portfolio, Reich commissioner for air, prime minister of Prussia (1933–1945), Prussian minister of the interior, president of the Reichstag, commander in chief of the air force (1935–1945). Plenipotentiary for the implementation of the four-year plan, responsible for rearmament. Supported German expansionism but foresaw dangers of attack on Poland and tried unsuccessfully to negotiate with Neville Chamberlain. Captured by U.S. Army in May 1945. Committed suicide before he was to be hanged at Nuremberg October 15, 1946.
OSS Fat Boy

FRANZ HALDER, 1884–1972
German general of infantry. Succeeded Ludwig Beck as army chief of general staff in 1938. Was dismissed in September 1942 for opposing Hitler's decision to concentrate troops in Stalingrad. Imprisoned in several concentration camps after July 20, 1944. Freed shortly before he was to be executed. Headed U.S. Army's court-martial research staff from 1946 to 1961.
OSS Ladder

EDWARD WOOD LORD HALIFAX, 1881–1959
British Conservative politician who opposed most contacts with the German resistance. Viceroy of India from 1926 to 1931. Foreign secretary 1938–1940. Ambassador in Washington, D.C., 1941–1946.

CHRISTIAN ULRICH VON HASSELL, 1881–1944
Lawyer and diplomat stationed in Genoa, Barcelona, Copenhagen, and Belgrade. Then served as German ambassador in Rome from 1932, until he was recalled because of disagreements with Joachim von Ribbentrop in 1938. Used his position as board member of the Mitteleuropäischer Wirtschaftstag in Berlin (1940–1943) as cover for conspiratorial activities and trips abroad. Criticized Nazi foreign policy as inevitably leading to war. Used international ties to arrange contacts with representatives of Great Britain and the United States. Worked with Ludwig Beck and Carl Friedrich Goerdeler on plans for Germany after a coup, designated as prospective foreign minister. Arrested by the Gestapo July 29, 1944. Condemned to death by People's Court September 8, 1944, and executed in Plötzensee prison.

REINHARD HEYDRICH, 1904–1942

Head of the Reich Security Service (RSHA), deputy Reich protector of Bohemia and Moravia, and administrator of concentration camps. Carried out the Final Solution and Nazi terror. Closest associate of Heinrich Himmler in the SS. Became chief of Security Police and the SD in June 1936. Assassinated in the streets of Prague by members of the Czech resistance June 4, 1942. Hitler retaliated one week later by eradicating the entire village of Lidice.

HEINRICH HIMMLER, 1900–1945

Leading Nazi and practitioner of violent political oppression. Appointed head of the SS in January 1929. Carried out Blood Purge of the SA, June 30, 1934. Oversaw organization of the Nazi Party's civilian security service (SD) under Heydrich. Responsible for fifth-column activities. After 1936 head of unified police system of the Third Reich as Reichsführer of the SS and leader of the Gestapo. Reich minister of the interior after August 1943, supreme commander of the People's Army (*Volkssturm*) from July 1944. Approached Allies in April 1945 through a Swedish count by offering to free Jews from camps and calling for capitulation. Suffered from psychosomatic illnesses, believed in mysticism. Committed suicide after capture by British, May 23, 1945.

MAX EGON, PRINCE ZU HOHENLOHE-LANGENBURG, 1897–1968

Sudeten German aristocrat with access to Nazi leaders and Allied intelligence. Acted as emissary of the SS. Married to an extremely rich and titled Mexican woman. Owned large estates in the Sudetenland, Spain, and Mexico.
OSS No. 515

OTTO JOHN, 1909–1997

Legal adviser to Lufthansa and Abwehr agent in Spain. Later head of West German counterintelligence service, 1950–1954. Worked with Wilhelm Canaris's successor, Georg Hansen, in the Abwehr from February 1944. Monarchist who wanted to reestablish Hohenzollern rule under Prince Louis Ferdinand. Escaped through Madrid and Lisbon to London after July 20 plot. Disappeared in East Berlin during his tenure as the first president of the Bundesamt für Verfassungsschutz in July 1954; reappeared mysteriously three weeks later to give a press conference. Interrogated by KGB and arrested for treason in West Germany. Claimed to have been drugged and abducted. Fought for rehabilitation until his death.
OSS Luke

OTTO KIEP, 1886–1944

Lawyer and diplomat. Close to the Solf Circle and Elisabeth von Thadden. Member of German delegation to Mixed Claims Commission on reparations in 1922. Appointed counselor to the German embassy in Washington in 1927 and German consul general in New York, 1931–34. Recalled in 1933 because he attended banquet for Albert Einstein. Worked for the Abwehr as foreign policy adviser in 1939. Active in opposition from 1942. Goerdeler wanted him to lead press office of the new chancellery. Arrested by Gestapo in January 1944, condemned to death for treason, executed at Plötzensee prison August 26, 1944.

ALEXANDER KIRK, 1888–1979

Diplomat. U.S. consul general in Barcelona, 1938; American chargé d' affaires in Berlin until October 1940; minister to Egypt, 1941; minister to Saudi Arabia, 1941–1943; ambassador to Greece 1943; ambassador to Italy, 1944–1946.

FRITZ KOLBE, 1900–1971

Civil servant and most valuable asset to OSS in Europe. Joined German foreign office in 1925. Until 1935 consular employee at German embassy in Madrid. During World War II was office assistant to Karl Ritter, special envoy of the foreign office to the OKW. Turned to MI-6 in 1943, which rejected him. Then offered his services to Allen Dulles. Delivered about 1,500 secret documents (Kappa) to OSS and became most important source on German underground for Americans. Fled to Bern in March 1945. Considered a traitor in postwar Germany, unable to find employment at the foreign office again.

OSS No. 674 and 805, or George Wood

ERICH KORDT, 1903–1970

Lawyer and diplomat. Specialized in administrative law. Brother of Theo. From 1936 to 1938 counselor at German embassy in London, where he established political contacts for the resistance. From 1938 to 1941 chief of Bureau of Ministers in the foreign office. Planned to attack Hitler in November 1939. German envoy in Tokyo and Nanjing between 1941 and 1945. Served in German state government after the war.

THEO KORDT, 1893–1962

Lawyer and diplomat. Specialized in administrative law. Brother of Erich. From March 1938 counselor, in 1939 German ambassador in London. Transferred to German embassy in Bern after war broke out. Made political contacts for resistance at his foreign posts. Served as ambassador to Greece for Federal Republic of Germany from 1953 to 1958.

PAUL LEVERKÜHN, 1893–1960

Lawyer, writer, and politician. Represented Germany in Mixed Claims Commission after World War I. Maintained professional legal connection with William Donovan. Drafted into the Abwehr during World War II. In early 1940 in Persia and Afghanistan for reconnaissance as captain of the reserves and secret agent under cover of consul. Exposed the same year. 1941 in Paris on behalf of the foreign office. Head of the Abwehrnebenstelle Middle East in Istanbul, 1941–1944. Counsel for the defense at Nuremberg trial against the OKW. Member of the West German parliament for the Christian conservative CDU, 1953–1960.

LANNING "PACKY" MACFARLAND

OSS representative in Turkey.

OSS No. 550 or Packy

GERALD MAYER

Chief of the Office of War Information (OWI) outpost in Switzerland and Allen Dulles's associate in Bern. Of German-Jewish descent, had spent much of his life in Europe and spoke fluent German.

OSS No. 678

SIR STEWART MENZIES, 1890–1968

Chief of British Secret Intelligence Service from 1939 to 1952. Joined MI-6 in 1915. Appointed successor of Hugh Sinclair in 1939. Lobbied to persuade his government to aid German conspirators. His appeals fell on deaf ears and were thwarted by sabotaging efforts of Kim Philby. Opposed strict Allied policy of unconditional surrender but failed to persuade British leadership to take lenient stance on peace negotiations.

HELMUTH JAMES COUNT VON MOLTKE, 1907–1945

Lawyer and center of the Kreisau Circle, which was named after his family's estate in Silesia. Had great-granduncle Moltke who was Prussian field marshal. Practiced law in England from 1935 to 1938, then worked in Paul Leverkühn's law firm in Berlin. Peace mission to London in 1939 and peace feelers to the United States in 1943. Joined the Abwehr as specialist in international law and law of war in September 1939. Sought humane treatment of prisoners of war. Wanted to include Social Democrats and church leaders in Kreisau Circle. Arrested January 19, 1944 after he had alerted members of Solf Circle of a Gestapo spy. Condemned to death by People's Court, January 11, 1945; executed at Plötzensee prison, January 23, 1945.
OSS Hermann, Camelia

JAMES D. MOONEY, 1884–1957

Engineer and corporate executive. Naval intelligence work during interwar years. Became vice president of General Motors Corporation and president of General Motors Overseas in 1922. Traveling extensively, he met with government officials and business leaders. Involved in international affairs as President Roosevelt's unofficial emissary during World War II. Disillusioned with traditional diplomacy he attempted to apply the methods of corporate negotiation to international negotiations. Tried to broker peace between Germany, the United States, and Great Britain. Joined staff of the Chief of Naval Operations during the war. Became chairman and president of Willys-Overland Motors in 1946.

JOSEF MÜLLER ("OCHSENSEPP"), 1898–1979

German politician and member of the Catholic resistance. Confidant of Michael Cardinal von Faulhaber. Representative of the Bavarian People's Party during the Weimar Republic. Worked as lawyer until called into the army at the beginning of World War II. Posted to Abwehr office in Munich. Established contact with British envoy in Rome in fall 1939. Arrested April 5, 1943, imprisoned in different concentration camps until May 1945, when liberated by American troops. Cofounded and led the Bavarian Christian conservative CSU from 1946 until 1949. Deputy prime minister of Bavaria and Bavarian minister of justice.
OSS Robot

HANS OSTER, 1888–1945

Career officer and center of resistance group within the Abwehr. Joined counterintelligence division of ministry of the Reichswehr in 1935 as reserve officer. Leading role in conspiracy to assassinate Hitler in September 1938. Chief of staff and head of the Abwehr's central section since 1938. Informed Dutch military attaché about impending German invasion in 1940. Promoted to brigadier general in December 1941. Suspended April 16, 1943, upon Hans von Dohnanyi's arrest, on charges of violating currency laws. Arrested July 21, 1944; hanged at Flossenbürg concentration camp April 9, 1945, together with Wilhelm Canaris and Dietrich Bonhoeffer.

FRANZ VON PAPEN, 1879–1969

Politician of the Catholic Center Party and German statesman. Monarchist and nationalist. Played major role in Hitler's drive to power. Served as military attaché in Mexico before World War I. Held similar post in Washington during World War II; expelled as persona non grata for clumsy secret service activities. Succeeded Heinrich

Brüning as German Reich chancellor in June 1932, dismissed by Reich president Paul von Hindenburg in December 1932. Vice chancellor under Hitler, 1933–1934. Placed himself at disposal of Nazis believing he could control and use them in his quest for political power. Worked toward the *Anschluss* as ambassador to Austria, 1936 until March 1938. German ambassador in Ankara, April 1939 until August 1944. Arrested by U.S. Army in April 1945; tried and acquitted at Nuremberg.

ALEXANDER RÜSTOW, 1885–1963
German economist, classicist by training and a socialist by calling. Emigrated to Turkey in 1933, when his efforts to form a coalition government to keep Hitler out of power failed. Taught economics, economic geography, and philosophy at the University of Istanbul between 1933 and 1949. Active in anti-Nazi movement of German refugees in Turkey and acted as liaison between the OSS and the German resistance.

EDUARD SCHULTE, 1891–1966
German industrialist. Chief executive officer and general manager of Giesche, a leading mining firm. Warned the west of extermination of European Jews. As top industrial leader, he traveled frequently and had contact with German government and military officials. Served as informant for Swiss and Polish intelligence services, which were connected with British and American intelligence. Hoped to hasten Hitler's defeat.
OSS No. 643, Ted

GERO VON SCHULZE-GÄVERNITZ, 1901–1970
German-American businessman, assistant to Allen Dulles in Bern, ghostwriter of *Germany's Underground*.
OSS No. 476

FEDERICO STALLFORTH, 1882–?
American businessman. Worked for Dawes Commission in 1920s. Representative of New York bank Harris Forbes & Co in Berlin until 1933. Traveled to Europe at beginning of World War II on special missions of State Department. Had ties with COI. Met with Ulrich von Hassell in 1941.

CLAUS SCHENK COUNT VON STAUFFENBERG, 1907–1944
Lieutenant Colonel on the German general staff and assassin in July plot of 1944. Catholic with socialist leanings. Close to the Kreisau Circle and to conspirators led by Erwin von Witzleben. Seriously wounded in April 1943 in North Africa. Slated as secretary of state in war ministry after coup. Had access to Hitler's military briefing conferences. Tried to kill the Führer on July 20, 1944, with a bomb in the Wolf's Lair in East Prussia. Executed with other conspirators at OKW headquarters on the Bendlerstrasse in Berlin the same night.

THEODOR STRÜNCK, 1895–1945
Lawyer, captain of the reserves, and Abwehr officer. Hans Oster has him drafted to work for the Abwehr in 1937. Principal courier of information and instructions between Zurich and Berlin. Turned down opportunity to escape to Switzerland after failed July 20 plot to spare his family *Sippenhaft*. Executed April 9, 1945, in Flossenbürg.

ADAM VON TROTT ZU SOLZ, 1909–1944

Lawyer and German diplomat. Studied at Oxford as Rhodes scholar in early 1930s. Established international connections on trip around the world from March 1937 to November 1938. Went to Washington in October 1939 as member of international secretariat of the Institute of Pacific Relations to participate at conference. Similar mission to London to establish political contacts for German resistance. Unable to obtain either British or American support. Became legation counselor in Foreign Office's information division in 1940. Foreign policy adviser to Kreisau Circle. Further travels abroad in 1941 and 1943 to search for allies in support of opposition. Arrested July 26, 1944, condemned by People's Court, executed at Plötzensee prison August 26, 1944.

OSS No. 800

SIR ROBERT VANSITTART, 1881–1957

British diplomat. Attended Paris Peace Conference that resulted in Versailles Treaty. Permanent undersecretary at the Foreign Office (1930–1938), chief advisor to the British government. Germanophobe calling for British rearmament to ward off looming danger of German foreign policy, which he believed inherently inclined to aggression. Wanted Germany permanently demilitarized to preserve peace in Europe. Removed by Prime Minister Neville Chamberlain on account of his antiappeasement stance. Left the diplomatic service in 1941.

WILLEM A. VISSER'T HOOFT, 1900–1985

Dutch theologian, a leader of the Protestant ecumenical movement, general secretary of the World Council of Churches, Geneva (1938–1966).

OSS No. 474

EDUARD WAETJEN, 1907–1945

Lawyer, associate of Allen Dulles, and close friend of Helmuth James von Moltke. Managing director of the German Syndikat für Außenhandel. Working for the Abwehr, attached to the German consulate general in Zurich. Took over Hans Bernd Gisevius's function as liaison between Switzerland and Germany in January 1944. Hanged in April 1945.

OSS No. 670 or Gorter

SUMNER WELLES, 1892–1961

American diplomat. Harvard alumnus, expert on Latin America at the State Department in 1920s. Appointed assistant secretary of state by President Roosevelt in 1933, also ambassador to Cuba. Recalled from Cuba in the midst of revolutionary turmoil. Under secretary of state, 1937–1942. Went on fact-finding mission to Europe in early 1940, at same time as James Mooney. Took part in the shipboard meeting between President Roosevelt and Winston Churchill that produced the Atlantic Charter. Resigned from public service in 1943.

ERNST VON WEIZSÄCKER, 1882–1951

German diplomat. Served in German návy during World War I. Entered Foreign Office in 1920, Minister to Norway (1931–1933) and to Switzerland (1933–1936). Served the Third Reich as state secretary under Foreign Minister Joachim von Ribbentrop from 1938. Claimed to have opposed Hitler's foreign policy but played ambiguous role in resistance. From 1943 to 1945 ambassador to the Holy See;

received sanctuary in Rome after the war. Arrested by Allied authorities as war criminal, sentenced to seven years at Nuremberg, where he was defended by his son and future president of the Federal Republic of Germany Richard von Weizsäcker. Released under general amnesty in 1950.

ERWIN VON WITZLEBEN, 1881–1944

General field marshal in armed forces of Third Reich and leading older member of conspiracy against Hitler. From 1939 until October 1940, commander of First Army; until March 1941 in command of Army Group D; until February 1942 commander in chief of the Army West in France. Retired from active service in 1942. Slated to become commander in chief of the armed forces after Hitler's removal. Condemned to death by People's Court and executed August 8, 1944.

HELMUTH WOHLTHAT, 1893–1952

Economist; Hermann Göring's economic expert responsible for Four-Year Plan. Educated in the United States. Member of the Thule Society. Began career as chief of the ministry of dairy products, oils, and fats. Ended career as ministerial director of special duty under the commissioner for the Four-Year Plan. Represented the Third Reich at international financial conferences with British and American bankers. Met James Mooney in this context.

KARL WOLFF, 1906–1975

General of the Waffen SS and liaison officer of Heinrich Himmler with Hitler until 1943. German military governor of north Italy and plenipotentiary to Mussolini. Visited Allen Dulles in spring 1945 to negotiate surrender of German forces in Italy (Operation Sunrise). Taken into U.S. captivity on May 13, 1945. Appeared as witness at Nuremberg. Was tried himself in 1949 by a German court but released quickly and took up work in public relations. Attracted public attention during Eichmann trial. Arrested in 1962 and charged with deportation of 300,000 Jews to the Treblinka concentration camp. Sentenced to fifteen years' imprisonment, released in 1971. OSS Critic

INTERVIEWS AND PERSONAL CORRESPONDENCE

Philipp Freiherr von Boeselager, May 30, 2003
David K. E. Bruce, January 1977
John Brunner, December 2, 2004
Axel Freiherr von dem Bussche-Streithorst, 1980s
Robert E. Carter, March 14, 2003, and March 17, 2003
William J. Casey, 1984
Julia Cuniberti, August 21, 2003, and September 15, 2003
Pat Dailey, April 7, 2003
Wanda Dailey, April 7, 2003
James R. Donavan, Sr., April 17, 2003
Helga Fritsche (née von Hentig), August 2004
Christa von Hassell (née von Studnitz), August 11, 2004
Wolf Ulrich von Hassell, 1970–1997
Cordelia Dodson Hood, October 14, 2003
Fisher Howe, March 17, 2003, and September 29, 2003
James W. Hudson, March 19, 2003, and September 13, 2003

Betty Lussier, April 5, 2003
Albert Materazzi, September 15, 2003
Armin Mruck, September 2004–January 2005
Gottfried von Nostitz, 1970
Detalmo Pirzio-Biroli, October 19, 2003
Barbara L. Podoski, August 14, 2003
Edwin J. "Ned" Putzell, March 19, 2003, March 21, 2003, and September 12, 2003
Sid Shapiro, November 24, 2004
Peter Sichel, September and October 2004
Eugen Solf, August 20, 2004
Robert Springsteen, January 10, 2004
Carol Templeton, July 7, 2003
Richard von Weizsäcker, July 14, 2003

ARCHIVES

Bundesarchiv Berlin-Lichterfelde
Bundesarchiv-Militärarchiv Freiburg
Hassell Family Papers
Institut für Zeitgeschichte München
Lippische Landesbibliothek Detmold
National Archives and Records Administration, College Park, MD
Private Archive of Agostino von Hassell
Special Collections, Lauinger Library, Georgetown University

NOTES

PREFACE

1. Jeremy Noakes, in his introduction to Hans Mommsen, *Alternatives to Hitler,* p. 2.

2. *The Von Hassell Diaries,* dated September 17, 1938.

3. *The Von Hassell Diaries,* dated October 11, 1939.

4. This notion found its way into the U.S. Marine Corps through Marine Commandant Alfred M. Gray, who had staffers study the doctrine which he called "maneuver warfare." The essential dictum: "You know the mission. Carry it out to the best of your ability, and change or adapt your orders as needed." Many of the German manuals were translated and incorporated into official USMC doctrine.

5. Madame de Staël, *De l'Allemagne,* 1813.

6. Ger van Roon, *German Resistance to Hitler,* p. 145.

7. Mark 12.

8. In July 1932 the so-called Bonus Army of ten thousand World War I veterans marched on Washington to claim the bonus of $1.25 for every day served in the war. Though it was not payable until 1945, the hungry and unemployed veterans hoped for something.

PROLOGUE

1. Willem A. Visser't Hooft, 1900–1985, Dutch clergyman, leader of the Protestant ecumenical movement, and first general secretary of the World Council of Churches, an interdenominational organization of most major Protestant, Anglican, and Eastern Orthodox Christian churches, which first took shape in 1937.

2. John M. Keynes, *Economic Consequences of the Peace,* in *The Collected Writings of John Maynard Keynes,* vol. 2, p. 146.

3. Ibid., p. 170.

4. Lindberg speech, *America and European Wars,* September 15, 1939.

5. Thomas Fleming, *The New Dealers' War,* pp. 82–83.

6. Klemens von Klemperer, *German Resistance Against Hitler,* p. 316, points out that in November 1942, Hugh Trevor-Roper prepared a position paper for MI-6 on the split between the Canaris and Himmler, suggesting exploitation of the differences between the high command and the SS. This was quashed by none other than Philby, protecting the interests of his Soviet patrons. This was at the time of Dulles's first Abwehr contacts in Switzerland.

7. Ibid., p. 84.

8. David Astor, "Why the Revolt Against Hitler Was Ignored," p. 7.

9. Walter Laqueur, *The World of Secrets,* p. 201.

10. James D. Mooney Papers, Georgetown University Library, Washington, DC, Box 1, Folder 14.

11. T. P. Conwell-Evans, *None So Blind.*

12. William J. Casey, *The Secret War Against Hitler,* p. xiv. The italics are mine.

13. Margret Boveri, *Treason in the Twentieth Century,* pp. 19ff.

14. Patricia Meehan, *The Unnecessary War,* p. 2, quoting *The* [London] *Times,* October 17, 1938.

15. Ibid., quoting *The* [London] *Times,* November 17, 1945.

CHAPTER 1

1. Among contemporary observers, John M. Keynes wrote in *The Economic Consequences of the Peace,* 1971: ". . . the economic clauses of the treaty are comprehensive, and little has been overlooked which might impoverish Germany now or obstruct her development in the future." In his view, Versailles laid the groundwork for catastrophe.

2. Name of Germany's armed forces from 1919 until the enactment of the Wehrgesetz (Defense Law) in March 1935, when it was changed to Wehrmacht.

3. Lauran Paine, *The German Military Intelligence in World War II,* p. 7.

4. In World War I, Germany had no unified military. After unification in 1871, major German states such as Bavaria and Saxony maintained separate armies, of which the largest, the Prussian army, and its general staff, assumed overall command and control of the federal armed forces. The only imperial military force was the navy.

5. Cf. Gert Buchheit, *Der deutsche Geheimdienst,* p. 30.

6. Heinz Höhne, *Canaris,* pp. 151ff.

7. On relations with the United States see Michael Wala, "Die Abteilung 'T3' und die Beziehungen der Reichswehr zur U.S. Army, 1922–1933," pp. 53–84.

8. The name derives from the compounding of *ab,* meaning "away" or "off," and *wehr,* meaning "defense."

9. F. P. Chambers, *This Age of Conflict,* p. 149, quotes from a letter of General Joachim von Stülpnagel, chief of operations, to Seekt in June 1919: "In my opinion it is absolutely essential that an officer corps with monarchical convictions and the old stamp should be preserved for the miserable creature of the new army. Counter moves are naturally on the way. I have been informed that Herr General [Seekt] has handed in his resignation. After the decree of the war minister no other step was feasible. . . . I am hoping that within the foreseeable future the resurrection of the monarchy, a struggle with Poland and perhaps with France too will be possible, and therefore consider it my duty to ask Herr General to remain in the army for these tasks and these aims."

The Stülpnagel family produced several senior officers serving roughly at the same time, creating much confusion. General Carl-Heinrich von Stülpnagel was executed for his involvement in the July 1944 plot to assassinate Hitler, and General Otto von Stülpnagel was German commander in France in 1944.

10. The German Defense Law of March 23, 1921, stipulated in article 36: "(1) Soldiers must not be politically active. Within Germany such activity is also forbidden for military officials. (2) Soldiers are prohibited from membership of political associations and participation in political gatherings. (3) The right to vote or to participate in referenda in the Reich, the states or the communes is suspended for soldiers. The regulations of the Peace Treaty of June 28, 1919 regarding the right to participate in votes designated therein remain unaffected."

11. The treaty was named after the Italian resort town of Rapallo where it was signed.

12. General von Seekt (1866–1936) was appointed *Chef des Truppenamtes* (adjutant general) of the 100,000-man Reichswehr during the Weimar Republic.

13. This training was indeed secret. Officers training in Russia were removed from the annually published *Rangliste,* thus also allowing the Reichswehr to stay within the nominal 100,000 cap. Officers killed in training were brought back surreptitiously, and not given military funerals.

14. Interview with Axel von dem Bussche, August 12, 1988; interviews with Wolf Ulrich von Hassell, 1989–1994.

15. Defense Law of May 21, 1935, on politics in the Wehrmacht stipulated that: (1) were membership in the NSDAP, any of its organizations or its affiliated associations were to be suspended while on active duty, and (2) soldiers needed the permission of their superiors to join an organization of any kind or intend to form associations within and outside the Wehrmacht.

16. Heinz Höhne, *Canaris,* pp. 161–65, has details on the Patzig-Heydrich power struggle.

17. Hindenburg was president of the Reich until his death on August 2, 1934, when Hitler combined the offices of chancellor and president. As the official head of state, Hitler also became the commander in chief of the Reichswehr—already renamed the Wehrmacht—in 1935, with the reintroduction of compulsory service.

18. The Gestapo—*Geheimstaatspolizei,* or "secret state police"—began under Göring as the Prussian State Police in 1933, then expanded and was put under the control of Heinrich Himmler, Hitler's SS Chief.

19. Sverre Hartmann, "Zwischen Staat und System: Ein Versuch zur Klärung des Problem Canaris," p. 349. Buchheit, *Der deutsche Geheimdienst,* p. 51, quotes from the communications with Patzig.

20. Playmates had dubbed Canaris "Kieker," meaning a curious person who observes and and absorbs everything, derived from a North German dialect verb for "to look." Canaris enjoyed using the Spanish form—Kika. See Höhne, *Canaris,* p. 97. See also Brissaud, *Canaris, 1887–1945,* p. 14.

21. Ulrich von Hassell, *Der Kreis Schliesst Sich,* p. 352.

22. Höhne, *Canaris,* pp. 136ff.

23. Helmut Krausnick, "Dokumentation: Aus den Personalakten von Canaris," p. 298, reports that "not only had C. nothing to do with the 'Lohmann Affair' but he worked intelligently and actively to correct matters [rendering] outstanding services on the occasion." See also Paine, *German Military Intelligence in World War II,* pp. 8–9.

24. BA-MA Freiburg, MSg 1/1948, interview with Admiral a.D. Conrad Patzig at

the MGFA about his work for the Abwehr, as head of the Department of Human Resources of the navy, etc., 1942–1957, conducted January 18 and 19, 1966.

25. Hartmann, "Zwischen Staat und System" p. 348.

26. See Höhne, *Canaris,* pp. 74–78.

27. Berthold Rassow, ed., *Amerikanische Reiseskizzen,* p. 40.

28. NA RG 263, Box 3, Preliminary Information Report based on Eberhard Ernst Momm, October 1945, pp. 16–17. Momm, a Luftwaffe major was interrogated by U.S. forces about Abwehr activities and personalities in Turkey.

29. Ibid. In Turkey, Leverkühn headed the Abwehr office. He was a former law partner of Moltke.

30. Peter Calvocoressi, Guy Wint, and John Pritchard, *The Penguin History of the Second World War,* p. 45.

31. *New York Times,* April 28, 1929.

32. Three other members of the board of governors of American I.G. were later tried and convicted at Nuremberg.

33. Nuremberg Military Trials (NMT) I. G. Farben Case, Volumes 6, 7, pp. 1304–11. A memorandum from I. G. Farben's August von Knieriem to Farben management notes that this auspicious development also freed I. G. Farben for work on the development of synthetic rubber, or buna. Charged at Nuremberg, Knieriem testified and was found not guilty. See www.mazal.org/archive/nmt/07/NMT07-T1131.htm.

34. Senate Committee on Military Affairs, June 1943.

35. United States Congress, *Scientific and Technical Mobilization.* 1st session of the 78th Congress, S. 702, Part 16, Hearings of Subcommittee on Military Affairs, p. 939.

36. Nuremberg Military Trials, op. cit., pp. 1304–11. See also Charles Higham, *Trading with the Enemy,* pp. 34–35.

37. Reinhold Billstein et al., *Working for the Enemy,* p. 23.

38. Higham, *Trading with the Enemy,* p. 155.

39. James Flink, *The Automobile Age,* p. 125.

40. Billstein et al., *Working for the Enemy,* p. 110.

41. Ibid., pp. 111–13.

42. Ibid., p. 21.

43. Earnings could not be repatriated, hence the steady investment in improvements.

44. Höhne, *Canaris,* p. 164.

45. Heinz Höhne, *The Order of the Death's Head,* p. 20.

46. Ibid., p. 128. The voice was that of Captain Erwin Planck.

47. BA-MA Freiburg, MSg 1/1948.

48. Vizeadmiral Canaris (Berlin), "Politik und Wehrmacht," in Dr. Richard Donnevert, ed., *Wehrmacht und Partei,* pp. 43–54. Copy available in BA-MA Freiburg, MSg 1/685.

49. Helmut Krausnick, ed., "Dokumentation: Aus den Personalakten von Canaris," *Vierteljahrshefte für Zeitgeschichte,* 10, no.3 (July 1962), pp. 296–97.

50. Hitler's dismissal of these leading generals after scandals allowed him to solidify his control over the army and embark upon his program of aggression. In late 1937, widower Field Marshal Werner von Blomberg, minister of defense and supreme commander of the Wehrmacht, decided to marry his secretary, Erna Gruhn, and was accused of disgracing the officers' corps by marrying a former prostitute. After a slander campaign in the press, the indignant Führer dismissed

Blomberg in February 1938; he himself would be supreme commander of the armed forces. Meanwhile, Goering and Himmler scurrilously accused Colonel General Werner Freiherr von Fritsch of homosexual activities, an offense under Section 175 of the Criminal Code. Fritsch, like Blomberg, had opposed Hitler's quest for Lebensraum and was forced to resign, to be replaced by General Walther von Brauchitsch as commander in chief of the army. An honor court later acquitted Fritsch, but could not undo his humiliation.

51. Abshagen, *Canaris: Patriot und Weltbürger,* p. 82.

52. Paine, *German Military Intelligence,* pp. 33–34, 53. For a map with Abwehrstellen, see Mader, *Hitlers Spionagegeneräle sagen aus,* pp. 96–97, and Reile, *Geheime Westfront,* pp. 469–70.

54. Höhne, *Canaris,* p. 188.

55. Canaris established the counterespionage section as a new branch in 1935. Oscar Reile, *Geheime Westfront,* p. 21. Reile 1934 in Ast Kassel; 1938 in Nst Trier; 1940 Leiter Sonderkommando der Abwehr in Frankreich und Luxemburg; 1943 Oberstleutnant und Leiter der Abwehr III F (Gegenspionage) in Abwehrleitstelle Frankreich.

56. BA-MA Freiburg MSg 1/1948.

57. Höhne, *Canaris,* p. 259.

58. Paine, *German Military Intelligence,* p. 35.

59. Joachim Fest, *Plotting Hitler's Death,* p. 99.

60. The terms section and branch are used interchangeably by different authors to translate the German *Abteilung.*

61. Höhne, *Canaris,* p. 201.

62. Paine, *German Military Intelligence,* p. 35.

63. Abshagen, *Canaris,* p. 85. For Piekenbrock's later career, see Mader and Charisius, *Nicht länger geheim,* p. 598. Piekenbrock took an army command in 1943. Captured by the Soviets and tried as a war criminal, he was released to West Germany in 1955.

64. Höhne, *Canaris,* p. 277. In Russia, Groscurth demonstrated his opposition to Nazi policies by trying to intervene—in vain—on behalf of Jewish children in Belaja Zerkow, Ukraine. Captured by the Soviets in 1943, he died of typhus at a transit camp.

65. Buchheit, *Der deutsche Geheimdienst,* p. 115.

66. BA-MA Freiburg, N 104/7, No. 2080 Eidesstattliche Erklärung Lahousens, Seefeld/Tirol. January, 27 1948.

67. Abshagen, *Canaris,* p. 88.

68. Paine, *German Military Intelligence,* p. 37.

69. Lahousen testified for the American prosecution at the Nuremberg Trials in 1945.

70. Abshagen, *Canaris,* p. 85.

71. Bamler was captured at Mogilev Soviet Union, in June 1944, joined the National Committee for a Free Germany and the Bund Deutscher Offiziere, later moving to communist ideology and working for the Stasi in East Germany. He was succeeded by Franz-Eccard von Bentivegni. Fastidious, teutonically efficient, and never close to Canaris, Bentivegni remained in office until the dissolution of the Abwehr.

72. After 1949, Bürkner served as advisor to the West German Ministry of Foreign Affairs. Julius Mader and Albrecht Charisius, *Nicht länger geheim,* p. 580.

73. Paine, *German Military Intelligence*, p. 37.

74. See Allen Dulles, *Germany's Underground*, pp. 75–76. Also quoted in Mader and Charisius, *Nicht länger geheim*, p. 117.

75. The Bendlerblock in central Berlin is now framed by the Stauffenbergstrasse and the Reichpietschufer (formerly the Tirpitzufer, but renamed after a WW I mutineer as a slap at Admiral Tirpitz). Built between 1911 and 1914, until 1935 the complex was headquarters for the imperial navy, then housed the high command of the OKW, and was the setting for the final desperate hours of the plot against Hitler on July 20, 1944. After WW II it was turned into a memorial and museum, but since German reunification in 1990, it has housed the German Federal Ministry of Defense.

76. See also André Brissaud, *Canaris, 1887–1945*, p. 179, for a description of Canaris's office.

77. Axel von dem Bussche-Streithorst, interview with the author, August 12, 1988. Bussche served in the famous 9th Infantry Regiment in Potsdam, home to many officers who plotted against Hitler; he himself attempted to assassinate Hitler in a suicide bombing. This particular regiment was sometimes jokingly referred to as the Regiment "Graf Neun"—Count Nine—or "von Neun"—von Nine—for the high proportion of titles among its numbers.

78. Höhne, *Canaris*, p. 91. Before and even during the war Heydrich and Canaris habitually rode together in Berlin's large park, the Tiergarten, to discuss issues of the day. As the diaries of Ulrich von Hassell attest, he and others who emerged as leaders of the opposition to Hitler frequently rode together. The bridle paths of the Tiergarten were the setting for many impromptu and discreet meetings. The leadership of the pre–World War II Germany was a cohesive group; most senior military officers and major figures in civil administration and diplomacy had known each other for decades and continued social contacts, even after political views diverged. This continued into the early war years.

79. Abshagen, *Canaris*, p. 101.

80. The intelligence services under the Oberkommando des Heeres (OKH, high command of the army) were active in different war zones: Fremde Heere West (Foreign Armies West) and Fremde Heere Ost (Foreign Armies East), led by Reinhard Gehlen from April 1, 1942, to 1945.

81. Höhne, *Canaris*, p. 196.

82. BA-MA Freiburg N185, 5, pp. 1168–75.

83. Höhne, *Order of the Death's Head*, p. 180.

CHAPTER 2

1. Klemens von Klemperer, *German Resistance Against Hitler*, pp. 82–83. The memorandum was written by Theodor Steltzer, an official in Schleswig-Holstein during the Weimar Republic. When it eventually found its way to the Nazi authorities, Steltzer was charged with high treason.

2. Joseph Wirth to Chamberlain, December 24, 1939. FO371/24386/C297/6/18. Quoted in Klemperer, *German Resistance*, p. 164. To his credit, Chamberlain responded with his so-called "Mansion Speech," of January 9, 1940, in which he said that the British did not seek the annihilation of the German people, but were looking for a just and Christian settlement. For details on further negotiations with Wirth, see Klemperer.

3. NA RG 59, R&A No. 992, September 27, 1943.

4. Klemperer, *German Resistance Against Hitler*, p. 84.

5. Michael Balfour and Julian Frisby, *Helmuth von Moltke,* p. 220.

6. Klemperer, *German Resistance Against Hitler,* p. 17.

7. Peter Hoffmann, *The History of the German Resistance,* pp. 15–16. One example is the fate of German journalist Carl von Ossietzky, who received the Nobel Peace Prize in 1935. Arrested in February 1933, he was in a concentration camp when the prize was awarded. He was pressured by the government to decline it and was not allowed to leave Germany. He died in a tuberculosis sanatorium in 1938.

8. Patricia Meehan, *The Unnecessary War,* p. 27.

9. T. P. Conwell-Evans, *None So Blind,* p. 37.

10. "Hallali" is the German equivalent of "tallyho." Halifax was also called "Holy-fox," for his enthusiasm for riding to hounds. A major biography immortalizes the nickname: Andrew Roberts, *The Holy Fox: a Biography of Lord Halifax* (London: Weidenfeld and Nicolson, 1991).

11. Balfour and Frisby, *Helmuth von Moltke,* pp. 70–71.

12. Meehan, *The Unnecessary War,* p. 18.

13. Vansittart's was not the only voice however. On October 17, 1938, Winston Churchill, not then in power, bemoaned the lack of "a formidable array of peace-defending powers" that would have provided "opportunity for moderate forces in Germany . . . to establish something like sane and civilized conditions in their country." See Meehan, *The Unnecessary War,* p. 2.

14. Ibid., p. 20.

15. Ibid., p. 21.

16. John W. Wheeler-Bennett, *The Nemesis of Power,* p. 366.

17. Allen Dulles, *Germany's Underground,* pp. 39–40, quotes General Beck as telling the American military attaché Truman Smith, in the critical days before the outbreak of war: "Hitler will be German's undoing. He far overestimates our military power. Sooner or later there will be a catastrophe. Can you not do something to help my poor country?"

18. Klemperer, *German Resistance Against Hitler,* p. 65n.

19. Hoffmann, *The History of the German Resistance,* p. 71–80.

20. Meehan, *The Unnecessary War,* p. 144. Kleist did "get away with it" in 1938, but was executed in 1944.

21. Cadogan's diary noted in March 1938 that the Foreign Policy Committee was unanimous: "Czechoslovakia is not worth the bones of a single Grenadier." Meehan, *The Unnecessary War,* p. 132.

22. Willem Visser't Hooft, "The View from Geneva," p. 93.

23. The letter was sent via British diplomatic pouch to Berlin for Kleist; copies went to Canaris and others. The original, found in Kleist's desk after the July 1944 plot, did in fact put the noose around his neck. See Meehan, *The Unnecessary War,* pp. 143–45.

24. Klemens von Klemperer, *Die verlassenen Verschwörer,* pp. 99–100, 410–11. Burckhardt in fact telephoned Halifax's secretary from the Bern embassy, and set in motion a process that ultimately even selected the desired "General with a riding crop"—a certain aptly named Sir William Ironside, with an imposing physique and fluent German, but there is no indication that Ironside ever fulfilled the mission.

25. Hoffmann, *The History of the German Resistance,* pp. 64 and 550n68.

26. "Langnam," or Long Name, to substitute for a very long and unwieldy official name.

27. Meehan, *The Unnecessary War,* p. 147.

28. Sabine Gillmann and Hans Mommsen, eds., *Politische Schriften und Briefe Carl Friedrich Goerdelers*. pp. 632–36.

29. Klemperer, *German Resistance Against Hitler*, pp. 88–95.

30. Gillmann and Mommsen, *Politische Schriften und Briefe Carl Friedrich Goerdelers*, p. 636.

31. Reichsgesetzblatt, Jg. 1934, Teil I, S. 785: "Ich schwöre bei Gott diesen heiligen Eid, daß ich dem Führer des Deutschen Reiches und Volkes, Adolf Hitler, dem Obersten Befehlshaber der Wehrmacht, unbedingten Gehorsam leisten und als tapferer Soldat bereit sein will, jederzeit für diesen Eid mein Leben einzusetzen."

I swear by God, this sacred oath, that I will obey Adolph Hitler, Führer of the German Reich and people and highest commander of the Wehrmacht, unconditionally, and that, as a brave soldier, I will be ready to lay down my life for this oath at any time. (Author's translation.)

32. Meehan, *The Unnecessary War*, p. 149.

33. Ibid., p. 153.

34. Dulles, *Germany's Underground*, pp. 44–45.

35. This was a hectic period for Chamberlain, who was consistently surprised by Hitler's changing demands.

36. William Shirer, *Berlin Diary*, pp. 142–43.

37. Meehan, *The Unnecessary War*, p. 180.

38. Ibid., p. 181. The record of Goerdeler's call is in Foreign Office files.

39. Balfour and Frisby, *Helmuth von Moltke*, p. 83.

40. David Clay Large, *Between Two Fires*, p. 354.

41. Ulrich von Hassell, *Die Hassell-Tagebücher, 1938–1944*, p. 54.

42. Chamberlain, Churchill, and Eden are all credited with an expression to the effect that a war postponed is a war averted, but perhaps it simply reflected the thinking operative at the time.

43. Meehan, *The Unnecessary War*, pp. 184–85.

44. Hans Bernd Gisevius, *To the Bitter End*, p. 326.

45. Gerhard Ritter, *The German Resistance*, p. 114.

46. Gisevius, *To the Bitter End*, p. 328.

47. Fest, *Plotting Hitler's Death*, p. 97.

48. Meehan, *The Unnecessary War*, p. 184.

49. "Evangelical" here is best translated as Protestant or Lutheran, and bears no relation to the present-day American evangelicals.

50. Interned at Sachsenhausen from 1938 to 1945, he was moved to Dachau and liberated by the Americans.

51. The immediate Bonhoeffer family alone accounted for seven active resisters, and more by marriage and more distant relationships. Bonhoeffer undertook his first Abwehr mission in early 1942.

52. Jo Fox, Review Article: "Resistance and the Third Reich," p. 275.

53. Klemperer, *German Resistance Against Hitler*, p. 46.

54. Ibid., p. 267.

55. Meehan, *The Unnecessary War*, p. 303.

56. Ibid., p. 11.

57. Ulrich von Hassell, diary entry, BA-MA Freiburg, no. 527, vol. 25, p. 8.

58. Klemperer, *German Resistance Against Hitler*, p. 21.

59. Buchheit, *Der deutsche Geheimdienst*, p. 66.

60. Hartmann, "Zwischen Staat und System: Ein Versuch zur Klärung des Problem Canaris," p. 351.

61. Ibid., p. 350.

62. Meehan, *The Unnecessary War,* pp. 190–91.

63. Ibid., p. 92.

64. Gisevius, *To the Bitter End,* p. 351.

65. Klemperer, *German Resistance Against Hitler,* p. 119.

66. Meehan, *The Unnecessary War,* pp. 208–9.

67. Ibid., p. 205, quoting Orme Sargent, Cadogan's deputy in the Foreign Office, who thought such behavior on the part of a senior military officer was "very significant—or is the whole thing nothing but a Machiavellian lie, and if so with what object?" To which Cadogan replied: "To test our nerves and try to find out how far Hitler can safely bluff."

68. Hassell, *Von Hassell Diaries,* pp. 56–72, August 1939.

69. See Frank Müller, "Die 'Brüning Papers': Der letzte Zentrumskanzler im Spiegel seiner Selbstzeugnisse," p. 38.

70. Wheeler-Bennett later became violently anti-German, turning on the entire resistance with a vengeance.

71. Trott was being followed by the FBI.

72. Klemperer, *German Resistance Against Hitler,* p. 188.

73. After his retirement, Vansittart gave vent to this Germanophobia in a work entitled *The Black Record* and gave his name to an especially virulent brand of anti-Germanism known as Vansittartism. While it appalled Churchill, it delighted Goebbels, who confided to his diary that for propaganda purposes it was worth its weight in gold. He proposed that Germany should erect a monument to Vansittart as the Englishman who did the most for the German cause. See Louis P. Lochner, ed., *Goebbels Tagebücher aus den Jahren 1942–1943.*

74. Meehan, *The Unnecessary War,* p. 148.

75. Klemperer, *German Resistance Against Hitler,* Plate 8, facing p. 241.

76. Gisevius, *To the Bitter End,* p. 375.

77. Rumors of peace just after the invasion of Poland brought euphoric celebrations in Germany.

78. Gisevius, *To the Bitter End,* pp. 171–80, gives an exhaustive account of Müller's dealings with the Vatican, the proposals, responses, and the X Report, which Müller asked Dohnanyi to destroy. Found by the Gestapo among Dohnanyi's files at Zossen in September 1944, it created serious difficulties for Müller.

CHAPTER 3

1. James David Mooney, Mooney Papers, Special Collections, Georgetown University Library, Box 1, Folder 4. (Cited hereafter as Mooney Papers.) Mooney, one of FDR's principal emissaries, was appalled by the lack of understanding he found between the Germany, Britain, and the United States.

2. Ibid., p. 976.

3. Frederick W. Marks, "Six Between Roosevelt and Hitler: America's Role in the Appeasement of Nazi Germany," p. 971.

4. Ulrich von Hassell, *The Von Hassel Diaries 1938–1944,* pp. 112–13. Hassell suggests that Weizsäcker regarded Welles's visit as "purely informative and influenced by domestic political considerations"—that is, the American elections.

5. Marks, "Six Between Roosevelt and Hitler," p. 973.

6. Ed Cray, *Chrome Colossus: General Motors and Its Times,* pp. 233–34.

7. Günter Neliba, *Die Opel-Werke im Konzern von General Motors (1929–1948) in Russelsheim und Brandenburg,* p. 80.

8. Billstein et al., *Working for the Enemy,* p. 39. After the annexation of the Sudetenland, these trucks were sold exclusively to the Wehrmacht and they became the backbone of the blitzkrieg against Poland.

9. Mooney Papers, Box 1, Folder 27.

10. Ibid., Box 1, Folder 14.

11. Winfried Meyer, *Unternehmen Sieben,* pp. 130–39, details Wohlthat's connections to members of the anti-Hitler conspiracy, his efforts on behalf of the Jewish population. With the help of Canaris, Wohlthat was able to satisfy an American request that he find and rescue Head Rabbi Schneerson from occupied Poland in late 1939.

12. Mooney Papers, interview with Lochner, Box 1, Folder 20, p. 14.

13. David E. Koskoff, *Joseph P. Kennedy,* p. 221.

14. Mooney Papers, Box 1, Folder 14.

15. Ibid.

16. Ibid.

17. Ibid., Box 5, Folder 13.

18. Ibid., Lochner Interviews, Mooney Papers, Box 1, Folder 20, p. 16.

19. Mooney Papers, Box 5, Folder 29.

20. Ibid.

21. Louis P. Lochner, *Always the Unexpected,* p. 262.

22. Though the truth may never come out, Hitler's obsession may also have been the reason for the bizarre flight of Rudolf Hess to Britain and his attempts to win the Duke of Windsor as an ally.

23. Ibid. *Always the Unexpected,* p. 262.

24. Ibid., p. 263.

25. Ibid., pp. 264–65.

26. Lochner worked with Mooney on a book detailing Mooney's story that was left unfinished, but gives a full accounting in his own memoir, *Always the Unexpected.* See pp. 262–72.

27. Ibid., p. 266.

28. Ibid.

29. Mooney Papers, Box 1, Folder 12.

30. See Lochner, *Always the Unexpected,* p. 268.

31. James Leutze, "The Secret of the Churchill-Roosevelt Correspondence," p. 468.

32. Notes of the December 22, 1939, meeting with FDR are in Mooney Papers, Box 1, Folder 12.

33. Ibid., Box 1, Folder 8.

34. Lochner, *Always the Unexpected,* p. 269.

35. Ibid., p. 270.

36. Mooney Papers, Box 1, Folder 20. See also interviews between Mooney and Lochner, pp. 38–39.

37. Ibid., p. 39.

38. Schacht had resigned from this position in protest against Hitler's policies.

39. Ulrich von Hassell, *Hassell-Tagebücher, 1938–1944,* March 11, 1940, p. 175.

40. Mooney Papers, Box 3, Folder 29.

41. Mooney Papers, Box 1, Folder 13, cables to FDR, March 1940.

41. Bernd Martin, "Friedens-Planungen der multinationalen Grossindustrie, 1932–40 als politische Krisenstrategie," p. 86. Martin is convinced that FDR intended both Mooney's and Welles's missions to fail.

43. Lochner Interviews, Mooney Papers, Box 1, Folder 20, p. 16.

44. Höhne, *Order of the Death's Head*, p. 10.

45. Joachim Fest, *The Face of the Third Reich*, p. 301, quoting from Wilfred von Oven, *Mit Goebbels bis zum Ende*.

46. Höhne, *Order of the Death's Head*, p. 218.

47. Ibid., p. 1.

48. Dulles, *Germany's Underground*, p. 17.

49. J. Lonsdale Bryans, *Blind Victory*, p. 22.

50. Meehan, *The Unnecessary War*, p. 273.

51. Ulrich von Hassell, *The Von Hassell Diaries: 1938–1944*, pp. 133–34.

52. Gregor Schöllgen, "'Another' Germany: The Secret Foreign Contacts of Ulrich von Hassell During the Second World War," p. 657.

53. Hassell, *Vom Andern Deutschland*, pp. 121, 122, 126, 137.

54. Zossen was the location of OKH headquarters, just south of Berlin.

55. Hoffmann, *The History of the German Resistance, 1933–1945*, p. 256.

56. Hans Bernd Gisevius, *To the Bitter End*, p. 386.

57. Elser became a cause célèbre as a propaganda tool, and was kept in jail without trial until he was killed "accidentally" in April 1945, when many enemies of the Reich met their end.

58. Walter Schellenberg, *The Schellenberg Memoirs*, p. 94.

59. Fest, *Face of the Third Reich*, p. 105, argues that it was Heydrich who was behind the Elser attempt on Hitler's life, in "some way that is still obscure."

60. William Shirer, *Berlin Diary*, p. 252.

61. Between the original date of the plan for attack, November 7, 1939, and the actual date, May 10, 1940, it was postponed twelve times, according to Dulles, in *Germany's Underground*, p. 56, and twenty-nine times according to Fest, *Face of the Third Reich*, p. 141.

62. Dulles, *Germany's Underground*, p. 57.

63. Joachim Fest, *Plotting Hitler's Death*, p. 138.

64. Harold C. Deutsch, *Conspiracy Against Hitler in the Twilight War* (Minneapolis: University of Minnesota Press, 1968), p. 100.

65. Fest, *Plotting Hitler's Death*, p. 141.

66. Klemens von Klemperer, *German Resistance Against Hitler*, p. 220, cites a letter from Lord Lothian, the British ambassador to Washington, shortly after the fall of France, urging his young friend Adam von Trott to engage himself in the cause of Anglo-German reconciliation.

67. Lothar Kettenacker, "Die Britische Haltung," in *Das 'Andere Deutschland' im Zweiten Weltkrieg*, p. 59.

68. Charles Lindbergh, speech to the America First Committee, Des Moines, Iowa, September 11, 1941. See www.charleslindbergh.com/american-first/speech.asp.

69. The G-2 designator was assigned to the Military Intelligence Division pursuant to General Order 41, War Department, August 16, 1921. Source: Federation of American Scientists, www.fas.org/irp/agency/army/odcsint/history.htm July 23, 2003.

70. Corey Ford, *Donovan of the OSS*, p. 5.

71. Edward Hymoff, *The OSS in World War II*, p. 27.

72. Ford, *Donovan of the OSS,* p. 89.

73. Interview with Richard M. Helms, May 1990.

74. Churchill, well aware of the contributions Royal Naval code breakers made in World War I, had a strong preference for the "Senior Service," the Royal Navy. Ian Fleming, creator of James Bond, served as Godfrey's assistant for a time, and it is widely believed that Godfrey served as inspiration for Bond's superior, "M." Stephenson, best known by his code name Intrepid, was knighted after the war.

75. Ford, *Donovan of the OSS,* p. 90.

76. Ibid., p. 22, quoting *Niagara Frontier* (Buffalo, NY: Buffalo and Erie County Historical Society, 1965).

77. The regiment's official designation during World War I was the 165th Infantry, but it continued to be known by its traditional name throughout the war (Ford, *Donovan of the OSS,* p. 32).

78. Ibid., p. 59.

79. Hassell, unpublished Roman diaries of the 1930s. Hassell's wife described Donovan as a "truly smart and charming gentleman."

80. Ford, *Donovan of the OSS,* pp. 82–83.

81. Anthony Cave Brown, *The Last Hero: Wild Bill Donovan,* p. 148.

82. Hymoff, *OSS in World War II,* p. 29.

83. Mooney Papers, Box 1, Folder 4.

84. Ibid., Box 1, Folder 22, is the source of all details on the Mooney-Wiseman-Spellman talks.

85. Bernd Martin, *Friedensinitiativen und Machtpolitik im Zweiten Weltkrieg,* p. 139. Martin argues that Davis presented Roosevelt as an opportunist preoccupied with his domestic agenda, who saw an opportunity to break the British monopoly in world trade. He suggested that the president might be willing to give in on the return of the colonies, agree to 1914 German borders, and offer support for German business.

86. Lothar Kettenacker, *Das "Andere Deutschland" im Zweitem Weltkrieg,* p. 57.

87. Frederick W. Marks III, "Six Between Roosevelt and Hitler," pp. 969–70.

88. Neliba, *Die Opel-Werke im Konzern von General Motors,* p. 87.

89. Mooney Papers, Box 5, Folder 32, endnotes. After the war, Mooney returned to General Motors; he left the company in 1946 and took over Willys-Overland Motors.

90. Charles Higham, *Trading with the Enemy,* p. 173.

91. Milton J. Shapiro, *Behind Enemy Lines,* p. 14. See also Joseph E. Persico, *Roosevelt's Secret War,* p. 68.

92. U.S. Congress, Defense Act, March 11, 1941.

93. Hymoff, *OSS in World War II,* p. 29.

94. Kennedy loyalists said he resigned; those favoring FDR say Kennedy was asked to leave.

95. Hymoff, *OSS in World War II,* pp. 36–38.

96. Interview with Ambassador David K. E. Bruce, April 12, 1975. Bruce headed the London office of the OSS.

97. Anthony Cave Brown, *The Secret War Report of the OSS,* p. 10.

98. Interview with OSS veteran Pat Dailey, April 7, 2003.

99. Brown, *Secret War Report,* p. 9.

100. Persico, *Roosevelt's Secret War,* p. 111.

101. Ford, *Donovan of the OSS,* pp. 134–35.

102. Elizabeth McIntosh, *Sisterhood of Spies,* pp. 8–9.

103. Ibid.

104. Since the country was not at war, formal intelligence activity was forbidden, and the branch was named for its first head, David Bruce. SAB stood for Special Activities–Bruce.

105. Sabotage was also taboo, and COI's sabotage unit was named for its first head: SAG, for "Special Activities—Goodfellow."

106. Ford, *Donovan of the OSS,* p. 111.

107. Interview with Ambassador David K. E. Bruce, April 12, 1975.

108. Ford, *Donovan of the OSS,* p. 113.

CHAPTER 4

1. Barry Rubin, *Istanbul Intrigues,* p. 52.

2. RG 263, Box 3.

3. Ibid.

4. Ibid.

5. Ibid.

6. NA RG 226, Entry 211, Box 43, Folder 3, reports on a meeting between the U.S. naval attaché and Emniyet chief, who warned that "a number of Americans were having affairs with enemy women nationals or with women who were in the pay of the Germans." This meeting occasioned the Rules of Conduct memorandum for Americans.

7. Rubin, *Istanbul Intrigues,* p. 49.

8. NA RG 226, Entry 211, Box 447, Folder 3.

9. Rubin, *Istanbul Intrigues,* p. 135.

10. Joachim Fest, *The Face of the Third Reich,* p. 153, quoting from François-Poncet's *The Fateful Years.*

11. Schwerin von Krosigk, *Es geschah in Deutschland,* p. 147.

12. Karl Heinz Roth, "Franz von Papen und der Faschismus," p. 593.

13. François-Poncet, French ambassador in Rome and Berlin, knew both Italian and German leaders, among them Hassell, German ambassador in Rome in the 1930s and active in the resistance to Hitler, while François-Poncet was ambassador in Berlin.

14. Gordon Craig, *Germany: 1866–1945,* pp. 568–70.

15. Hans Rein, *Franz von Papen im Zwielicht der Geschichte,* p. 75.

16. John W. Wheeler-Bennett, *The Nemesis of Power,* p. 498.

17. James Carroll, *Constantine's Sword,* p. 550.

18. Rubin, *Istanbul Intrigues,* p. 47.

19. NA RG 226, Entry 210, Box 420, Folder 4. OSS Report on Operation Taurus, 1943–1944.

20. Michael Bloch, *Ribbentrop,* p. 290.

21. Walter Schellenberg, *Hitler's Secret Service,* p. 68. See also Michael Bloch, *Operation Willi,* for a full account of the scheme.

22. António Oliviera Salazar, *Discursos e Notas Políticas,* p. 187.

23. Joseph Persico, *Roosevelt's Secret War,* p. 252.

24. Donald G. Stevens, "World War II Economic Warfare," p. 544.

25. Norman Holmes Pearson, foreword to *The Double-Cross System* by J. C. Masterman, p. xiii, cites Masterman's novel of 1957, entitled *The Case of Four Friends.*

26. Masterman, *Double-Cross System,* p. 56.

27. Persico, *Roosevelt's Secret War*, p. 446.

28. Masterman, *Double-Cross System*, pp. 55–56.

29. Dusko Popov, *Spy/Counterspy*, pp. 74–75.

30. See also Nigel West, *A Thread of Deceit*, p. 72. West takes a more sober view, arguing that the code name was chosen because Popov was to lead a ring of three double agents: Balloon, Gelatine, and Dreadnought.

31. Pearson, in preface to *The Double-Cross System*, p. xiii.

32. Popov, *Spy/Counterspy*, p. vii.

33. Ibid., p. 56.

34. Masterman, *Double-Cross System*, pp. 80–81.

35. Billstein et al., *Working for the Enemy*, p. 46, makes the point that given the extent of terror already established by the regime, even such harmless bathroom graffiti represented an act of courage.

36. Ibid., pp. 167–206.

37. Billstein et al., *Working for the Enemy*, p. 118.

38. Ibid., pp. 114–18.

39. Ibid., pp. 242–45.

CHAPTER 5

1. Churchill to Eden, September 10, 1941, PRO/FO371/26543, quoted in Gregor Schöllgen, *A Conservative Against Hitler*, p. 86.

2. Ulrich von Hassell, *Von Hassell Diaries*, pp. 170–71.

3. Ibid., p. 194.

4. Ibid., pp. 190, 202.

5. Christof Mauch, *The Shadow War Against Hitler*, pp. 29, 232n39.

6. Gregor Schöllgen, *A Conservative Against Hitler*, p. 87.

7. Mauch, *Shadow War Against Hitler*, pp. 30–31.

8. See ibid., p. 30, 233n45, for details on Stallforth's corporation, which intended to sell to the Allies Axis ships docked in South America.

9. Hassell, *Von Hassell Diaries*, pp. 212–13.

10. Ibid., pp. 217–18.

11. Hassell, *Tagebücher*, September 20, p. 272. See also Schöllgen, *Conservative Against Hitler*, p. 164n55, who cites an East German study of 1965, by Gerhart Haas entitled *Von München bis Pearl Harbor*. On the basis of archival material available to him, Haas claims that Stallforth was a Gestapo agent.

12. NA RG 226, Entry 146, Box 113, Folder 1565.

13. Mauch, *Shadow War*, pp. 31–32.

14. David Balfour and Julian Frisby, *Helmuth von Moltke*, p. 131.

15. H. Peters, *Erinnerungen an den Kreisauer Kreis*, IfZ Archives ZS/A-18, Bd. 6.

16. Balfour and Frisby, *Helmuth von Moltke*, p. 333.

17. Joachim Fest, *Plotting Hitler's Death*, p. 156.

18. John Wheeler-Bennett, *The Nemesis of Power*, p. 548.

19. Dorothy Thompson, *Listen Hans*, pp. 147–87.

20. Balfour and Frisby, *Helmuth von Moltke*, p. 157.

21. Ibid., p. 155.

22. Ibid., p. 185.

23. Speculation about just how much FDR knew persists, with some convincing, if unsubstantiated, claims that he knew the attack was coming.

24. Anthony Cave Brown, *Secret War Report of the OSS*, p. 11. As the war progressed,

the OSS budget expanded significantly: For fiscal year 1942–43 an initial $3 million was expanded by an additional $10 million. In 1943–44, $21 million was appropriated ($15 million in so-called unvouchered funds), and in 1944–45, $57 million went to OSS, $37 million in UFs.

25. Sherwood had been a speechwriter for FDR and remained a personal friend.

26. Interview with Julia Cuniberti, August 21, 2003.

27. For a complete overview of the psychological assessments, see Henry A. Murray, et al., Office of Strategic Services, *Assessment of Men: Selection of Personnel for the Office of Strategic Services* (Washington, D.C.: Government Printing Office, 1948).

28. Walter Laqueur, *The Terrible Secret,* p. 96.

29. The importance of the British cracking of these codes cannot be overestimated. For a full discussion of their importance, see David Kahn, *The Codebreakers.*

30. Sam Roberts, "U.S. Study Pinpoints Near Misses by Allies in Fathoming the Unfolding Holocaust," *New York Times,* July 31, 2005, p. A6, quoting from a new book *Eavesdropping in Hell,* by Robert J. Hanyo, a historian at the National Security Agency's Center for Cryptologic History.

31. Martin Gilbert, *The Holocaust,* p. 186.

32. Richard Breitman, *"OSS's Knowledge of the Holocaust."*

33. Ibid. Breitman offers details of diplomatic dispatches forwarded to the U.S. as early as March 1942, and thereafter. We are greatly indebted to Mr. Breitman for his work.

34. NA RG 226, Entry 210, Box 386, Folder 6.

35. Laqueur, *Terrible Secret,* p. 96.

36. Rubin, *Istanbul Intrigues,* p. 113.

37. Emma Lazarus, "The New Colossus," inscribed on the base of the Statue of Liberty.

38. Interview with David K. E. Bruce.

39. Ford, *Donovan of the OSS,* p. 151.

40. Interview with James Donovan, Sr. Ironically, Germany's most-wanted spy, code-named Cicero, had an identical cover. He worked as a valet to the British ambassador in Istanbul.

41. Ultra's twenty-two-year-old mathematics wizard Alan Turing had developed a decoding machine fast enough to solve the Enigma encryption. This allowed SIS to read some of Germany's most secret transmissions, a secret that had to remain closely guarded. If the Germans learned their ciphers had been solved, they would have stopped using Enigma. By 1943, they suspected that Enigma might have been compromised.

42. Minute details such as laundry marks and the way buttons were sewn on (parallel versus crosswise) could blow an agent's cover.

43. Brown, *Secret War Report of the OSS,* p. 69.

44. Ibid., p. 17.

45. Ibid., p. 111.

46. Ibid., p. 533.

47. William J. Casey, *The Secret War Against Hitler,* p. 28.

48. Elizabeth McIntosh, *Sisterhood of Spies,* pp. 733–34.

49. NA RG 208, Entry 367, Box 255, Folder E.

50. Richard Breitman, *Official Secrets,* p. 104, proposes that the distinguished German may have been Joseph Wirth, former chancellor of Germany.

51. Adam von Trott found the broadcasts "governessy" in tone, and felt that

Germans resented the suggestion that "they alone were guilty." See Klemperer, *German Resistance Against Hitler,* p. 335.

52. NA RG 226, Entry 210, Box 258. Interview of Joseph Goldschmied by Emmy Rado, August 8, 1942.

53. Walter Laqueur and Richard Breitman, *Breaking the Silence,* p. 7.

54. See ibid., pp. 110–17 and 265, for details of Schulte's sleuthing on Himmler's Auschwitz visit.

55. Ibid., p. 149. See also: Polish Ministry of Information, *The Black Book of Poland.*

56. Grose, *Gentleman Spy,* pp. 158–62. Grose notes that among spies, linking a source by name to any particular intelligence is not only dangerous but poor form, and taboo. This is why Schulte was never credited with the first substantive report of the Holocaust until 1986. Even Dulles was not informed. Ironically, Schulte was compromised by a breach of precisely this principle; an OSS communication mentioning his name was intercepted by the Gestapo. An urgent call from Switzerland pulled him out of a business meeting—and immediately out of Germany. He never returned. The warning probably came from Gisevius.

57. Ibid., p. 155.

58. Richard W. Rolfs, *The Sorcerer's Apprentice,* p. 403.

59. Otto John, *Twice Through the Lines,* pp. 19–20.

60. In his recollections, Goerdeler also mentions having met Mooney at some point, but it is unclear whether it was on his American journey or in Germany.

61. John, *Twice Through the Lines,* p. 83.

62. Ibid., p. 99.

63. "C" was the traditional designation of the chiefs of Britain's SIS, after its founder, Sir Mansfield Cumming, who signed himself "C."

64. Heinz Höhne, *Canaris,* pp. 341, 481.

65. Ibid. In regard to both Höhne's and Brown's claims (n. 15 supra), it should be noted that Klemperer, *German Resistance Against Hitler,* pp. 396–97n3 and p. 497, regards notions of any feelers from Canaris toward Menzies et al. as nonsense, and considers Höhne's sources spurious.

66. Richard Deacon, *A History of the British Secret Service,* p. 282.

67. F. W. Winterbotham, *Secret and Personal,* p. 162.

68. Anthony Cave Brown, *Bodyguard of Lies,* p. 314. Brown provides no source for his information.

69. Höhne, *Canaris,* pp. 483–86, suggests that Moltke was acting on behalf of Canaris in Istanbul in attempting to contact the Americans, and claims a 1942 and 1943 attempt to contact Menzies.

70. James Srodes, *Allen Dulles, Master of Spies,* p. 72.

71. Ibid., p. 85.

72. Ibid., pp. 227 and 232.

73. Allen Dulles, *The Secret Surrender,* p. 18.

74. Srodes, *Allen Dulles,* pp. 244–45.

75. Christof Mauch, *Shadow War Against Hitler,* p. 132.

76. Ibid., p. 109.

77. R. Harris Smith, *OSS: The Secret History,* p. 212.

78. Mary Bancroft, *Autobiography of a Spy,* p. 177.

79. Mauch, *The Shadow War Against Hitler,* p. 108.

80. Dulles, *Secret Surrender,* p. 21.

81. Srodes, *Allen Dulles,* p. 229.

CHAPTER 6

1. Before the year was out, Churchill recommended that British embassies abroad exercise some "elasticity" in the policy, to allow for "German and other feelers." See Klemens von Klemperer, *German Resistance Against Hitler,* pp. 241 and 259n163.

2. NA RG 226, Entry 180, A 3304, Roll 68.

3. Its most illustrious member was Field Marshal von Paulus, whom Seydlitz-Kurzbach had tried to persuade to surrender at Stalingrad in November 1942, but who joined only after D-Day, when he realized that the game was up. Another member was Rudolph Bamler, head of Abwehr III until 1939. Bamler was captured at Mogilev, USSR, in 1944. In captivity, he accepted Soviet ideology, eventually working for the Stasi in East Germany.

4. See Christof Mauch, *The Shadow War,* p. 242n50. The report is to be found at the FDR Library, Hyde Park.

5. Thomas Fleming, *The New Dealer's War,* p. 301.

6. The Nuremberg War Crimes Tribunal included Katyn in its indictments and, in violation of basic judicial principle, charged the Russians—themselves accused of the massacre—with the prosecution. It is worth noting that the judgment published in 1946 makes no mention of Katyn, and no guilty verdict was ever handed down.

7. Joachim Fest, *Plotting Hitler's Death,* p. 211.

8. Klemens von Klemperer, *German Resistance,* p. 241.

9. BA-MA Freiburg, N 524, p. 17.

10. Peter Grose, *Gentleman Spy,* pp. 171–72.

11. Walter Laqueur and Richard Breitman, *Breaking the Silence,* pp. 72–73.

12. Interview with Cordelia Dodson Hood, October 14, 2003.

13. Deirdre Blair, *Jung: A Biography,* p. 487;, 809n.

14. Mayer is sometimes described as running the Office of War Information, a propaganda organ, sometimes as running the COI, precursor of the OSS.

15. Mary Bancroft, *Autobiography of a Spy,* p. 129.

16. Ibid., p. 137.

17. Ibid., pp. 92–93.

18. RG 226, Entry 134, Box 171, February 3, 1943.

19. Klemperer, *German Resistance,* p. 318.

20. Grose, *Gentleman Spy,* p. 165.

21. The term "Black Orchestra" was originally an RSHA designation for "traitors" who were members of Christian churches, Joseph Müller among them; gradually some writers began to refer to anti-Nazi Abwehr officers as the Black Orchestra.

22. Klemens von Klemperer, *Die Verlassenen Verschwörer,* p. 277.

23. Winfried Meyer, *Unternehmen Sieben,* p. 134.

24. Bericht des Generalmajor v. Lahousen, BM-MA Freiburg MSG1, col. 2872. See also John H. Waller, *The Unseen War in Europe,* pp. 92–93. Szymanska later noted that she was not a "spy." Canaris never asked her for information—he did not want it thought that he was a British spy. Rather he talked about Hitler's plans—not petty military details—but high-level policy. Through Szymanska in late 1940, Canaris informed the British of Hitler's planned invasion of Russia.

25. Interview with Cordelia Dodson Hood, October. 14, 2003.

26. Grose, *Gentleman Spy*, p. 178.

27. Allen W. Dulles, *Germany's Underground*, p. 130.

28. Bancroft, *Autobiography of a Spy*, p. 164.

29. Ibid.

30. Ibid., pp. 192–95.

31. Hans Bernd Gisevius's book, *To the Bitter End*, may have been a bit self-aggrandizing, but it does offer considerable insights into the mysteries and cast of the Third Reich. It was published in the United States in 1947 and later translated into many languages.

32. Christabel Bielenberg, *The Past Is Myself*, p. 175.

33. NA RG 226, Entry 139, Box 175, Folder 2316.

34. NA RG 226, Entry 134, Doc. 1-12, Telegram 314, January 14, 1943.

35. Petersen, *From Hitler's Doorstep*, p. 586n.

36. Peter Grose, *Gentleman Spy*, p. 156.

37. NA RG 226, Entry 134, Box 341, Tel. 1108, November 21, 1943.

38. Reinhold Spitzy, *So haben wir das Reich verspielt*, p. 456. Both the authenticity and the importance of the conversations are open to question, but they did come back to haunt Dulles many years later. The Russians revived them, attempting to suggest Dulles's double-dealing and Nazi sympathies during the cold war.

39. Mauch, *The Shadow War Against Hitler*, p. 121.

40. Mauch, *The Shadow War Against Hitler*, p. 125.

41. NA RG 226, Entry 134, Box 171, March. 10, 1943.

42. NA RG 226, Entry 134, Box 307, March. 12, 1943.

43. Peter Hoffmann, *The History of German Resistance*, p. 265. Tresckow was later promoted to General.

44. Joachim Fest, *Plotting Hitler's Death*, p. 175.

45. Ibid., p. 269.

46. Ulrich von Hassell, *Von Hassell Diaries*, pp. 219–20.

47. Interview with Philipp von Boeselager, May 30, 2003. Boeselager cites SS figures of 90,000 at the beginning of the war, and 900,000 by war's end.

48. Ibid.

49. Obtaining explosives was a persistent problem for the opposition, though Gersdorff's position in Intelligence helped somewhat. On March 7, Canaris arrived in Smolensk, in the company of Dohnanyi, Oster, and Lahousen, ostensibly for an intelligence conference, also bearing a box of explosives. See Hoffmann, *History of the German Resistance*, p. 281.

50. See Peter Hoffmann, Appendices, p. 741, for diagrams of the "clam" and the British chemical time fuse.

51. We are indebted to Peter Hoffmann's account of the Gersdorff plot; see *History of the German Resistance*, pp. 283–89.

52. BA MA Freiburg, N 5334/17, Nachlass von Gero-von Schulze-Gävernitz.

53. Ulrich von Hassell, *The Von Hassell Diaries, 1938–1944*. Hassell first mentions Burckhardt in December 1938, and intermittently thereafter. See also Klemens von Klemperer, *German Resistance Against Hitler*, p. 118, 140, 121n, 221, for details on Burckhardt's career and peace initiatives.

54. James Srodes, *Allen Dulles*, p. 258–59.

55. NA RG 226, Entry 134.

56. Ibid. See also Petersen, *From Hitler's Doorstep*, p. 570n. Petersen wonders why

Dulles, with his many and varied contacts, was not more vocal about the Jewish problem, and suggests Dulles was concerned that European anti-Semitism could make outspoken denunciation of Hitler's Jewish policy counterproductive for the western Allies.

57. Wyman, *The Abandonment of the Jews*, p. 121.

58. Max Lerner, "What About the Jews, FDR?" *PM*, July 22, 1943, p. 2.

59. Srodes, *Allen Dulles*, pp. 127–29.

60. Barry Rubin, *Istanbul Intrigues*, pp. 117–19, notes that Betty Carp's analytical skills were also sharp. In March 1943, after meeting with Soviet officials in the United States, she noted that after the war, the Soviets intended to establish "a protective ring of friendly neighboring states" around their borders." Hers was one of the few voices raised on the subject, but no one paid much attention.

61. The foreign exchange transactions were intended to compensate the fugitives for their losses.

62. Interned by the Nazis, Müller was liberated by the Americans for whom he worked after the war as "Robot." See OSS Mission for Germany, X-2 Germany, NA RG 226, Entry 213, Box 2, Folder 8, August 1945.

63. See NA RG 226, Entry 210, Box 447, Folder 4, Report 454, in which Waetjen's sister is mentioned as being married to a Rockefeller.

64. Mauch, *Shadow War*, p. 8.

65. Hans Bernd Gisevius, *Wo ist Nebe?* Quoted in Balfour and Frisby, *Helmuth von Moltke*, p. 227.

66. Michael Balfour and Julian Frisby, *Helmuth von Moltke*, pp. 214–15.

67. Hassell, *Diaries*, p. 258.

68. Kurt G. W. Ludecke, *I Knew Hitler*.

69. Viktor Klemperer, *LTI, Notizbuch eines Philologen*. Klemperer's wartime diaries provide an extraordinary picture of life under the Nazis.

70. Balfour and Frisby, *Helmuth von Moltke*, pp. 214–15.

71. Klemens von Klemperer, *German Resistance Against Hitler*, p. 61.

72. NA RG 226, Entry 210, Box 217, Folder 4, identifies Wilbrandt (Hyacinth, in the Dogwood Chain) as a contact for German industrialists, bankers, and businessmen with useful embassy channels, and included him on a list of OSS collaborators who should be offered protection.

73. Franz von Papen, *Memoirs*, p. 504.

74. Balfour and Frisby, *Helmuth von Moltke*, p. 271.

75. Thomas Childers, "The Kreisau Circle and the 20th of July." April 24–25, 1988.

76. Alexander Rüstow to Ger van Roon, December 20, 1962, Institute für Zeitgeschichte Archiv ZS/A-18, Bd. 6.

77. Klemens von Klemperer, *German Resistance Against Hitler*, pp. 327–29.

78. NA RG 59, R&A, September. 27, 1943.

79. Balfour and Frisby, *Helmuth von Moltke*, p. 215.

80. NA RG 226, Entry 214, Box 6, notes that Moltke was also identified as Camelia.

81. NA RG 226, Entry 210, Box 447, Folder 10, dated November 10, 1943, and RG 226, Entry 211, Box 16, Folder 6, dated November 22, 1943.

82. Klemens von Klemperer, *German Resistance Against Hitler*, p. 331.

83. NA RG 226, Entry 180, A 3304, Roll 68.

84. Ibid.

85. Ibid.

86. Harold Gibson had headed MI-6 in Czechoslovakia, then in Istanbul. His bother Archibald headed MI-6 in Bucharest.

87. NA RG 226, Entry 211, Box 6.

88. NA RG 226, Entry 211, Box 35, p. 1.

89. NA RG 226, Entry 211, Box 6.

90. NA RG, 226, Entry 210, Box 447, Folder 10.

91. Opinions on Moltkle's code names differ. Ibid., Folder 6, states that Moltke was both Hermann and Camelia. However, Klemperer, p. 285, argues that Camelia was the code name for the OKW, whose interests Moltke was thought to represent, and Moltke never received a flower code name and was known only as Hermann.

92. Klemens von Klemperer, *Die Verlassenen Verschwörer,* p. 285nn114–15; also p. 509.

93. Barry Rubin, *Istanbul Intrigues,* p. 168.

94. Helldorf was executed for his role in the plot on August 15, 1944.

95. Hans Rein, *Franz von Papen,* p. 76.

96. Franz von Papen, *Memoirs,* p. 504: ". . . at that meeting I had then to tell him that Mr. Earle had received no answer from the American president."

97. Lucas Delattre, *Fritz Kolbe,* p. 144.

98. Grose, *Gentleman Spy,* pp. 183–85. See also Kim Philby, *My Silent War,* p. 83, who argued that "the attitude of the British officials cannot be condemned out of hand. It was barely credible that anyone would have the nerve to pass through the German frontier controls with a suitcase containing contraband official papers."

99. Grose, *Gentleman Spy,* p. 184.

100. Delattre, *Fritz Kolbe,* p. 126. The specifics of these events are in fact rather confused; this summary relies in part on Delattre's account, fleshed out with Grose, Srodes, Philby, and others. See also Greg Bradsher, "A Time to Act: The Beginning of the Fritz Kolbe Story," pp. 6–24.

101. Ibid., p. 117.

102. Mauch, *Shadow War,* p. 127.

103. IfZ Archiv, MA-1300/2, U. S. State Dept. Special Interrogation Mission to Germany, Harold C. Vedeler interview with Kolbe, Wiesbaden, September 26, 1945.

104. Grose, *Gentleman Spy,* p. 189.

105. NA RG 226, Entry 121, Box 19, Tel. 3163-65, April. 26, 1944.

106. NA RG 226, Entry 134, Box 274, December 30, 1943.

107. Ibid.

108. Viktor Klemperer, *Ich will Zeugnis ablegen bis zum Letzten,* p. 464.

109. NA RG 59, 740,0016, EW/10-15, Box 3603, Harold C. Vedeler interview with Fritz Kolbe, September 23–24, 1945, p. 2.

110. Philby, *My Silent War,* p. 83.

111. Ibid., pp. 83–86.

112. Interview with William J. Casey, March 17, 1985.

113. Joseph Persico, *Piercing the Reich,* p. 114.

CHAPTER 7

1. Dulles communication, Jan. 1, 1944, CIA, FOIA.

2. Klemens von Klemperer, *German Resistance Against Hitler,* p. 336. This particular defection also had repercussions for Adam von Trott, who was subjected to a series of interrogations by the Gestapo on the Vermehren's account.

3. Estimates on how many employees were affected by dissolution of the Ab-

wehr and its integration into the RSHA vary. Gert Bucheit, *Der deutsche Geheimdienst,* p. 463, argues for 3,000, based on reports from former members of the Army and Navy personnel departments. East German sources during the cold war claimed that more than 2,400 full-time and 20,000 part-time Nazi agents were affected. Albrecht Mader, *Nicht Länger geheim,* p. 115 claims that 5,000 employees were affected. BA-MA Freiburg, MSG 120/58-60 contains incomplete membership lists compiled by Abwehr veterans after the war.

4. NA RG 263, Box 3, is a detailed source on German intelligence in Turkey and all characters and events involved in the Vermehren affair.

5. Had he survived the Third Reich Canaris would have been a dangerous historical witness. Unfortunately, his diaries are thought to be lost. See, for example, Helmut Krausnick, "Aus den Personalaklen von Canaris, *Vierteljahrshefte,* p. 281, and Abshagen, *Canaris,* p. 11.

6. See BA-MA Freiburg, aus Bestand RH 2, OKH. Himmler felt an admiration bordering on awe for Canaris, and in 1943, directed an already deeply suspicious Gestapo to back off. As for Canaris, he countered Himmler's adulation with manipulative disdain.

7. NA RG 226, Entry 134, Box 247.

8. Allen Dulles, *The Secret Surrender,* p. 25.

9. Barry Rubin, *Istanbul Intrigues,* p. 169.

10. NA RG 226, Entry 211, Box 35, dated July 25, 1944.

11. NA RG 226, Entry 211, Box 16, Folder 6, is a report dated May 23, 1944, from Colonel J. G. O'Connor to Whitney Shephardson, detailing O'Connor's longstanding reservations about Packy Macfarland and OSS Istanbul operations, which he found to be of "very junior status, bordering on mediocre."

12. NA RG 226, Entry 210, Box 447, Folder 6.

13. NA RG 226, Entry 210, Box 447, Folder 7.

14. NA RG 226, Entry 210, Box 447, Folder 4, May 13, 1944, notes Cassia's arrest, urges intervention on his behalf and suggests a threat of severe reprisals if he is not released.

15. Rubin, *Istanbul Intrigues,* p. 192.

16. Ibid., p. 197.

17. NA RG 226, Entry 210, Box 447, Folder 10.

18. Rubin, *Istanbul Intriuges,* p. 199.

19. NA RG 226, Entry 210, Box 44, Folder 5.

20. Not until early 1945, when Fiala was being debriefed, did OSS discover that he was a Nazi passing false information. He was deported to Czechoslovakia, tried, and executed as a traitor.

21. NA RG 226, Entry 210, Box 447, Folder 10.

22. Rubin, *Istanbul Intrigues,* p. 199.

23. Allen Paul, *Katyn,* p. 314.

24. NA RG 226, Entry 210, Box 447, Folder 9, dated November 1, 1943.

25. Ibid., Folder 1.

26. Ibid., Folder 4.

27. See NA RG 226, Entry 210, Box 30, Folder 4; also RG 226, Entry 210, Box 217, Folder 4, on U.S attitude of levels of commitment to protection of members of the Dogwood chain. Both date from August 1944.

28. NA RG 226, Entry 210, Box 447, Folder 4.

29. NA RG 226, Entry 137, Box 23, Folder 160.

30. NA RG 226, Entry 211, Box 35, pp. 40–50.

31. NA RG 226, Entry 211, Box 35, pp. ii, iii.

32. Ibid., pp. 40–42.

33. See Richard Breitman, *Other Responses to the Holocaust,* pp. 54–57. Breitman provides a detailed examination of the Brand plan and its ramifications, based on latest evidence.

34. Ibid., pp. 43–45.

35. In 1944–45, special representative to the U.S. War Refugee Board in Sweden, Ivar Olsen, was approached with a similar proposition. Also ostensibly humanitarian, it was actually an attempt by Himmler to make contact with the Allies.

36. Meredith Hindley, "Negotiating the Boundary of Unconditional Surrender," pp. 52–77.

37. David Wyman, *The Abandonment of the Jews,* p. 251.

38. Rubin, *Istanbul Intrigues,* p. 208.

39. Interestingly, Rubin, ibid., p. 685n, states that according to several sources the money Roncalli used to buy freedom for Jews came from Papen.

40. NA RG 226, Entry 210. The last paragraph of the report reads: "Source points out that he has repeatedly called Allied attention to the above targets both via Switzerland and through his contacts with us (cf. our report No. 6A of Sept. 11, 1943, and once again stressed the crucial importance to the German war effort." Curiously, this paragraph has been crossed out.

41. NA RG 226, Entry 210, Box 447, Folder 7. Buna is synthetic rubber; carbon black is used as a reinforcing agent for rubber products such as tires. This text has been slightly edited and the section in brackets is circled and marked "omit."

42. NA RG 226, Entry 210, Box 447, Folder 5.

43. While the denial of Auschwitz as an extermination camp is a particular feature of many Holocaust denials, such as those of British writer David Irving, for example, it is unlikely that Irving saw these particular OSS files, declassified only in 2003. But other evidence on Auschwitz was abundant.

44. The June 1944 Vrba-Wetzler report provided sketches and information, but was considered inadequate in some quarters. See James H. Kitchens, "The Bombing of Auschwitz Reconsidered," pp. 233–66, for details of the argument against the bombing.

45. David Wyman, "Auschwitz, Bombing of," in *The Encyclopedia of the Holocaust,* edited by Israel Gutman (New York: MacMillan, 1990), pp. 119–21.

46. Ibid., pp. 305–307.

47. Martin Gilbert, *Auschwitz and the Allies,* p. 301.

48. Michael Beschloss, *The Conquerors,* pp. 65–66, 66n12. It was also thought that bombing might precipitate vindictive SS reprisals against inmates.

49. John Morton Blum, *Years of War,* vol. 3 of *From the Morgenthau Diaries,* p. 220.

50. David S. Wyman and Rafael Medoff, *A Race Against Death,* pp. 160–64. Interview with Hillel Kook, who took the name Peter Bergson while in the United States to protect relatives in Palestine.

51. Ibid., p. 263.

52. Ibid., p. 268.

53. With the Soviet invasion of Hungary in October 1944, Horthy attempted to surrender to the Soviets but was arrested by the Germans. Captured by the American army in Bavaria at the end of the war, he was held in protective custody until late 1945.

54. Ibid., pp. 285–87.

55. NA RG 226, Entry 134, Box 191, March 20, 1944.

56. NA RG 226, Entry 144, Box 8, Folder 63.

57. NA RG 226, Entry 210, Box 447, Folder 3.

58. NA RG 226, Entry 214, Box 6, p. 24.

59. Hassell, *The Von Hassell Diaries*, pp. 338–39, February 1944.

60. Peter Hoffmann, *History of the German Resistance,* p. 321.

61. Ibid., p. 330.

62. Hans Peters, *"Erinnerungen and den Kreisauer Kreis,"* IfZ Archiv ZS/A-18 Bd. 6.

63. Fest, *Plotting Hitler's Death*, p. 217.

64. Ibid., p. 219, notes that the original plan was in effect turned upside down, and officers and men were being used to overthrow the regime whose orders they were following.

65. Lucas Delattre, *Fritz Kolbe,* pp. 194–95.

66. Ibid., pp. 191–92.

67. Kolbe continued to deliver vital additional material on Japanese morale, materiel, order of battle, etc., well into 1945.

68. NA RG 226, Entry 210, Box 463, Folder 2., dated April. 11, 1944.

69. Srodes, *Allen Dulles,* p. 295.

70. Delattre, *Fritz Kolbe,* p. 252.

71. NA RG 226, Entry 138, Box 2, early February 1945, contains several communications from Dulles in regard to Kolbe material not being given due consideration, though it was only at about this time that his reports, forwarded directly by Donovan, began to reach the inner Roosevelt circle. See Neal H. Petersen, *From Hitler's Doorstep,* p. 269.

72. NA RG 226, Entry 134.

73. See Richard Breitman, *Official Secrets,* p. 232n. Breitman argues that this added pressure on the Hungarian government had some effect, but does not specify.

74. NA RG 226, Entry 134, Box 192, May 31, 1944.

75. Ibid., June 12, 1943.

76. NA RG 226, Entry 134, Box 307, July 3, 1943. See also Petersen, *From Hitler's Doorstep,* pp. 575–76n, who regards this cable as perhaps "totally realistic," but also "reflecting an astounding lack of compassion."

77. NA RG Entry 226, Box 273, July. 7, 1943.

78. Rudolf Vrba, *I Escaped from Auschwitz,* p. 266.

79. Walter Laqueur, *The Terrible Secret,* pp. 98–99. David S. Wyman, *The Abandonment of the Jews,* pp. 114–15, asserts that Dulles passed on the material saying it was "more in their line," and that OSS received a copy only a year later.

80. Willem Visser't Hooft, *Memoirs,* p. 156.

CHAPTER 8

1. Klemens von Klemperer, *German Resistance Against Hitler,* p. 348.

2. Ibid., p. 379. This request went out over the firm objections of the man who signed it, James Riddleberger, chief of the Central European Section.

3. NA RG 56, CDF 740.0019 EW 1939/2635, May 1944.

4. NA RG 226, Entry 134, Telegram 2966–69, April. 17, 1944.

5. NA RG 226, Entry 134, Telegram 1018–20, November. 8, 1943.

6. NA RG 226, Entry 146, Box 235, Folder 3296.

7. NA RG 226, Entry 146, Box 234, Folder 3294, June 1, 1944.

8. NA RG 226, Entry 134, Box 340, Folder 1820, July 26, 1943.

9. NA RG 226, Entry 134, Box 228, Folder 1368.

10. NA RG 226, Entry 138, Box 2.

11. See Neal H. Petersen, *From Hitler's Doorstep,* p. 595; note Doc. 2-134.

12. NA RG 226, Entry 134, Box 307, February 13, 1943.

13. NA RG 226, Entry 134, Box 349, Folder 1852.

14. NA RG 226, Entry 146, Box 235, Folder 3296.

15. After the war, Düppel briefly became a camp for displaced Jews.

16. Hugh Trevor-Roper, *The Philby Affair,* pp. 28–49.

17. Compton Mackenzie, *Water on the Brain.*

18. John P. Campbell, "Some Pieces of the Ostro Puzzle," p. 26n5.

19. Nigel West, *A Thread of Deceit,* p. 85.

20. Campbell, "Some Pieces of the Ostro Puzzle," p. 246.

21. Heinz Höhne, *Canaris,* p. 493.

22. C. G. McKay, "MI-5 on Ostro: A New Document from the Archives," pp. 178–84.

23. Ibid., pp. 181–82.

24. Masterman, *The Double-Cross System,* p. 151.

25. NA RG 226, Entry 210, Box 445, Folder 3.

26. NA RG 226, Entry 211, Box 45, Folder 3.

27. Juan Pujol with Nigel West, *Operation Garbo,* p. 45.

28. Ibid., p. 68.

29. Masterman, *The Double-Cross System,* p. 115.

30. Ibid., p. 116.

31. Pujol, *Operation Garbo,* p. 72.

32. Masterman, *The Double-Cross System,* p. 114.

33. Pujol, *Operation Garbo,* pp. 179–80.

34. Ibid., p. 101.

35. Masterman, *The Double-Cross System,* p. 142.

36. Dulles reported in December 1943 that Kolbe had seen detailed information on the British and American divisions massing in the south of England.

37. Masterman, *The Double-Cross System,* p. 151.

38. NA RG 226, Entry 211, Box 45, Bolder 3. See also Pujol and West, *Operation Garbo,* pp. 121–22, who maintain that Jebsen was probably executed by the Gestapo at Oranienburg some time in April 1945.

39. Pujol, *Operation Garbo,* p. 122.

40. Ibid., pp. 121–29.

41. Ibid., p. 136.

42. Masterman, *The Double-Cross System,* p. 157.

43. Pujol, *Operation Garbo,* p. 148.

44. Ibid., p. 155.

45. Ibid., p. 179.

46. Douglas L. Wheeler, "The Price of Neutrality," pp. 106–11.

47. Lucas Delattre, *Fritz Kolbe,* p. 183.

48. See Antonio Louca and Ansgar Schafer, "Portugal and Nazi Gold," pp. 107–22, for details on the machinations involved.

49. Donald G. Stevens, "World War II Economic Warfare," p. 550.

50. Wheeler, "The Price of Neutrality," p. 109n, and pp. 546–47, suggests that the war might not have been shortened, citing various assessments, apparently shared

by Churchill, that German wolfram stores were sufficient to avoid shortages crippling to the war effort.

51. NA RG 226 Entry 210, Box 9, Folder 1.

52. Ibid.

53. NA RG 226, Entry 210, Folder 1, Operation Z report. Wheeler, "The Price of Neutrality," p. 111nn39–40.

54. Louca and Schafer, "Portugal and Nazi Gold," pp. 105–22.

55. Stevens, "World War II Economic Warfare," p. 554.

56. Wheeler, "The Price of Neutrality," p. 106.

57. Curiously, while the German subsidiary produced at 93 percent of capacity, the U.S. company produced at less than 38 percent, the British even less. For fifteen months after Pearl Harbor, the critical Curtis-Wright Corporation was unable to get adequate supplies of ball bearings from SKF, with a considerable cost in efficiency and lives. See Charles Higham, *Trading with the Enemy*, pp. 117–20.

58. Paul B. Miller, "Europe's Gold," p. 11. See also Dean Acheson, *Present at the Creation*, pp. 51–52.

59. Higham, *Trading with the Enemy*, pp. 122–23.

60. Ibid., p. 126.

61. Ibid., p. 29.

62. Acheson, *Present at the Creation*, pp. 51–52.

63. NA RG II, Record Group 131, Entry NN3-131-94-001, Box 391. Records of the Office of Alien Property, Foreign Funds Control, General Correspondence 1942–1960, Safehaven Project, "Swiss Gold."

64. Ulrich Voelklein, *Geschäfte mit dem Feind*, pp. 105–16, cites several different figures in his chapter "Die Bank-Connection," but these are reasonable ballpark estimates.

65. Ibid., pp. 109–12.

66. Louca and Schafer, "Portugal and Nazi Gold," p. 109.

67. Gian Trepp, *Bankgeschäfte mit dem Feind*, pp. 59–62.

68. Werner Rings, *Raubgold aus Deutschland*, p. 52.

69. Louca and Schafer, "Portugal and Nazi Gold," p. 111.

70. NA RG 319, Records of the Army Staff.

71. Voelklein, *Geschäfte mit dem Feind*, p. 113.

72. Grose, *Gentleman Spy*, p. 169.

73. William Glaberson, "For Betrayal by Bank and Nazis, $21 Million," *New York Times*, April, 14, 2005, p. A1.

74. General License under Section 3(a) of the Trading with the Enemy Act, signed by Roosevelt, Treasury Secretary Morgenthau and Attorney General Francis Biddle on December 13, 1941.

75. Nuremberg Trials, pp. 1310–11. See www.mazal.org/archive/nmt/07/NMT07-T1131.htm.

76. Ulrich Voelklein, *Geschäfte mit dem Feind*, p. 7.

77. Higham, *Trading with the Enemy*, p. 93.

78. Ibid., pp. 99–100.

79. Edwin Black, *IBM and the Holocaust*, p. 12. While Black does mention that Otto Kiep was on the board of Dehomag, he chooses not to mention his anti-Nazi activities or the fact that he was executed in August 1944.

80. Michael Allen, "Stranger than Fiction: Edwin Black, "IBM and the Holocaust," pp. 150–54.

81. Götz Aly and Karl-Heinz Roth, *Die restlose Erfassung,* pp. 88–89.

82. Allen, "Stranger than Fiction," p. 153.

83. Anthony Sampson, *The Sovereign State of I.T.T.,* provides an excellent overview of ITT operations.

84. Beaulac, a.k.a. Bearcat, met repeatedly with Otto John in the early 1940s.

85. John S. Friedman, "Kodak's Nazi Connections." According to Friedman, the French subsidiary did remarkably well, and the Portuguese subsidiary remitted profits to the branch in the occupied Hague. No penalties or fines were imposed on the company.

86. Margaret Clarke, *The Safehaven Project,* p. 46.

87. NA RG 226, Entry 134. Also *Studies in Intelligence* no. 9 (Summer 2000).

88. This may well have been an effort on Donovan's part to shore up OSS for future peacetime operations. See Donald P. Steury, "Tracking Nazi 'Gold,'" p. 11.

CHAPTER 9

1. NA RG 226, Entry 134, Box 192, June 28, 1944.

2. NA RA 226, Entry 46, Box 235, Folder 3296.

3. NA RG 226, Entry 134, Box 273.

4. Interview with Edwin Putzell, September 12, 2003.

5. NA RG 226, Entry 21, Box 349, L39970.

6. Quoted in Theodore S. Hamerow, *On the Road to the Wolf's Lair,* p. 350.

7. Peter Hoffmann, *The History of the German Resistance,* p. 399.

8. Bernd Gisevius, *To the Bitter End,* p. 558.

9. NA RG 226, Entry 134, Box 4, Folder 63.

10. Hoffmann, *History of the German Resistance,* p. 529, states that executions registered by the Ministry of Justice for 1943 totaled 5,684; for 1944, they were 5,764, and for 1945, an estimated 800, which he argues is too low, since registration stopped in April 1945. Of these, approximately 200 were directly related to July 20. John Wheeler-Bennett, *The Nemesis of Power,* pp. 744–52, lists only 158 names, but notes that the list is far from complete as it does not include those condemned and executed for complicity in the conspiracy. A 5,000 figure derives from files captured by the British after the war.

11. Gert Buchheit, *Der Deutsche Geheimdienst,* p. 438.

12. Fabian Schlabrendorff, *The Secret War Against Hitler,* pp. 294–95. The shirt of Nessus, a reference to classical mythology, denotes a misfortune from which there can be no escape.

13. Joseph Persico, *Roosevelt's Secret War,* p. 416.

14. Allen Dulles, *Germany's Underground,* pp. 172–73. On July 26, Donovan sent Dulles the following message: "You have done no bargaining of any kind. You are aware of all these facts and there is no blemish on your record." See Armin Mruck, "Roosevelt and the Anti-Nazi Resistance." This is an obvious "cover" for Dulles to insulate him against any charges of improper deal-making with the German opposition.

15. Hoffmann, *History of the German Resistance,* p. 527.

16. Hamerow, *On the Road to the Wolf's Lair,* pp. 357–58.

17. The italics here are the author's. Hans-Bernd von Haeften had similar objections to the "gangster methods" his brother proposed to use against Hitler.

18. Walter Lippmann, "The Coming German Civil War," *Washington Post,* July 22, 1944, p. 5.

19. NA RG 226, Entry 134, Box 303.

20. Patricia Meehan, *The Unnecessary War,* p. 402.

21. Ibid.

22. John Wheeler-Bennett, Memorandum, July 25, 1944. Public Record Office, FO 371/39062, C9896, p. 1. Quoted in Hamerow, *On the Road to the Wolf's Lair,* p. 357.

23. Dulles, *Germany's Underground,* p. 171.

24. One of these studies, based on numerous interviews of people who had known Hitler, was declassified in 1972 and published under the title *The Mind of Adolf Hitler.* Unbeknown to most people, the OSS had commissioned an earlier profile of Hitler from Henry A. Murray, a Harvard psychoanalyst, whose study was later integrated with Langer's. It is available at www.lawschool.cornell.edu/donovan/hitler/.

25. NA RG 226, Entry 190, Microfilm Roll 52, Nos. 23–27.

26. Klemens von Klemperer, *German Resistance Against Hitler,* pp. 380, 386.

27. M 1642, From the Director's Office, roll 31, frame 49.

28. NA RG 165, Entry 179, Box 702, Army Intelligence Consolidated Interrogation Report, Sept. 10, 1945. Among the many who were interrogated: Ludwig von Hammerstein, Ilse von Hassell, Wolf-Ulrich von Hassell, Jakob Kaiser.

29. Ilse von Hassell, the daughter of the legendary Admiral Tirpitz, had christened the ill-fated Nazi battleship *Tirpitz* at the behest of the Nazis.

30. Fey von Hassell, *Hostage of the Third Reich.* Fey's husband, Detalmo Pirzio Biroli, had been instrumental in arranging contacts between Hassell and the British.

31. These and later diary entries were later smuggled out of Germany into Switzerland, and published there in 1946 as the first major account of the resistance. They were translated into many languages.

32. "Today the judgment of the People's Court has come down. If it is carried out as I expect, the happiness beyond all measure that was given to me through you will end. At this moment, above all else, I am filled with deep gratitude toward God and toward you. This thought drowns out the deep pain of leaving you and the children. May God let your soul and mine find each other again. Stay always as good and as kind as you are, don't become hard. God bless you and God bless Germany!" BA-MA Freiburg N524/25 Nachlaß Gero von Schulze-Gävernitz, Brief Ulrich von Hassell an seine Frau Ilse, Berlin-Plötzensee, Königsdamm 7 den 8.9.1944.

33. Wolf Ulrich von Hassell later became West German ambassador to the United Nations.

34. Otto John, *Twice through the Lines,* p. 146–168.

35. Jose Barveiros interview with Charles de Sohl of British Intelligence, October, 1996.

36. Otto John., *Twice Through the Lines,* p. 169 ff.

37. Interview with Barbara Lauwers Podoski, August 14, 2003.

38. Ibid.

39. Documents were also created by forgers at R&A's Rome office. Clayton D. Laurie, "The 'Sauerkrauts,' " p. 57.

40. Jürgen Heideking and Christof Mauch, eds., *American Intelligence and the German Resistance to Hitler,* p. 341.

41. Christof Mauch, *The Shadow War Against Hitler,* pp. 139–42, note 281n. While in Italy with MO, Lauwers also pulled off a "Lonely Hearts" scheme so believable that the story was picked up by *The Washington Post* on October 10, 1944, and produced a propaganda leaflet that prompted the desertion of 600 Czech soldiers doing dirty work for the German army, a project that won her a Bronze Star. Interview with Barbara Lauwers Podoski, August 14, 2003.

42. On Operation Twilight, see NA RG 226, Entry 92, Box 553, Folder 5; RG 226, Entry 110, Box 48, Folder 493/II; RG 226, Entry 190, Box 284, Folder 1251, on planned OSS activities after the collapse and surrender of Germany.

43. As commanding general of the 116th Panzer Division, he was not involved with the many members of the extended Schwerin family who were active resisters.

44. William Casey, *The Secret War Against Hitler,* pp. 179–80.

45. Dulles asked SS General Wolff about the redoubt in March 1945. Wolff dismissed the idea completely.

46. Anne Armstrong, *Unconditional Surrender,* p. 211.

47. Christof Mauch, *Shadow War,* p. 210.

48. Freisler, very early on in the Hitler regime, had set out to reform the judiciary to conform to Nazi concepts. He initiated the concept of the *Volksgerichsthof* and was the principal face of the totalitarian "justice" meted out by the Nazis. He trained numerous other judges, many of whom returned to office after the war. Freisler's widow received a full pension. After conquering Carthage, Rome leveled the city and spread salt on its fields.

49. Michael Beschloss, *The Conquerors,* p. 100.

50. John Morton Blum, *Years of War,* vol. 3 of *From the Morgenthau Diaries,* p. 342. "We have got to be tough with Germany and I mean the German people, not just the Nazis. You either have to castrate [them] or . . . treat them . . . so they can't just go on reproducing people who want to continue the way they have in the past."

51. Thomas Fleming, *The New Dealer's War,* p. 466.

52. David Eisenhower, *Eisenhower at War, 1943–1945,* pp. 529–30.

53. Armstrong, *Unconditional Surrender,* p. 158. Historians speculate on what effect support of the opposition and an early peace might have had in saving lives and preventing massive destruction in Germany.

54. David S. Wyman, *The Abandonment of the Jews,* p. 114, states that the early collaboration between the OSS and WRB stopped after State Department intervention.

55. NA RA 1642, From the Director's Office, Roll 87, Frames 691-5.

56. Interview with Sid Shapiro, November. 25, 2004.

57. Interview with Ned Putzell, Sepember. 12, 2003.

58. Even at the time, there was documentary evidence to support the Dulles reports. The Polish government-in-exile in London published a detailed report, also sold in the United States, including photographs, lists of names detailing Nazi persecution of Jews. See *The Black book of Poland,* Polish Ministry of Information (New York: G. P. Putnam's Sons, 1942).

59. James Srodes, *Allen Dulles,* pp. 202–93.

60. Barry Katz, "The Holocaust and American Intelligence," pp. 303–4.

61. Christopher Simpson, *Blowback,* p. 288.

62. Barry Katz, *Foreign Intelligence, Research and Analysis in the Office of Strategic Services, 1942–1945,* pp. 39–40, makes the point that OSS's R&A branch, manned largely by anti-Nazi Germans, many of them Jewish, argued that unconditional surrender played directly into the Nazi propagandists' hands, that the opposition was "a tribute to human endurance and courage, and the revelation of great hope," and urged the Allies to "give substance to the hope."

63. Walter Laqueur, *The Terrible Secret,* pp. 91–92.

64. Wyman, *Abandonment of the Jews,* pp. 311–12.

65. Max Frankel, "Willing Executioners?" Review of *A Nation on Trial: The Gold-*

hagen Thesis and Historical Truth, by Norman Finkelstein, *New York Times Book Review,* June 28, 1998, p. 7.

66. See Wyman, *Abandonment of the Jews,* p. 315, and *New York Times,* April. 22, 2004, p. A3.

67. See Leonard Dinnerstein, "Franklin D. Roosevelt and the Jews: Another Look," pp. 3–8. Coughlin continued to broadcast until well into 1942.

68. Peter Novick, *The Holocaust and American Life,* p. 42.

69. Armin Mruck, interview with Grace Tully.

70. Casey, *Secret War,* p. 218.

71. NA RG 226, Entry 139, Box 115, Folder 1599, "General Beck Speaks Again."

72. Balfour and Frisby, *Helmuth von Moltke,* p. 311.

73. Ibid., pp. 323–33.

74. Jürgen Heideking and Christof Mauch, "Das Hermann Dossier," p. 583, and 73n. See also: NA RG 226, Entry 99, Box 14, Folder 58a: Memorandum to U.S. Sec. of State on possibilities for rescue of Moltke.

75. George Kennan, *Memoirs,* pp. 120–22, also quoted in Balfour and Frisby, *Helmuth von Moltke,* p. 169.

76. Beschloss, *Conquerers,* p. 178.

77. Noel Annan, *Changing Enemies,* p. 202.

78. Fleming, *New Dealer's War,* pp. 493–94.

79. Martin Gilbert, *Winston S. Churchill,* p. 1196.

80. Anna Roosevelt Halstead Papers, Franklin D. Roosevelt Library, Hyde Park, NY.

81. Elisabeth Bumiller, "Sixty Years after the Fact, Debating Yalta All Over Again," *New York Times,* May 16, 2005, p. A18.

82. Meehan, *Unnecessary War,* pp. 336–39.

83. This and all following Lahousen comments on the Canaris diaries are quoted in Hans Bernd Gisevius, *To the Bitter End,* pp. 440–42, unless otherwise noted.

84. Karl-Heinz Abshagen, *Canaris,* p. 11. Cf. Gert Buchheit, *Deutsche Geheimdienst,* pp. 208–10.

85. www1.jur.uva.nl/junsv/Excerpts/420a007.htm, August 31, 2003.

86. Telephone interview with Philipp von Boeselager, May 30, 2003.

87. Abshagen, *Canaris,* p. 11. BA-MA Freiburg, N 104/7 Nachlaß Helmuth Groscurth, No. 2080. Sworn Statement by Lahousen, Seefeld/Tirol dated 27, January 1948: "These facts result from the so called "Zossen File Find"—a collection of documents that severely compromise the political and military leadership of the 3rd Reich (Canaris-Diary, Memoranda of General Oster und Reichgerichtsrat Dr. Dohnany), found after the failed assassination attempt of the 20th of July in 1944 in Zossen by the Gestapo and the SD. Largely because of these documents Dr. Dohnany and later in April 1945, Canaris and Oster were murdered by the Gestapo in the Concentration Camp Flossenbürg, to eliminate these unacceptable, crucial witnesses before the Allies arrived . . ."

88. Heinz Höhne, *Canaris,* pp. 590–91. None of the authors involved in this debate noticed the contradiction between the fact that the Zossen material was handwritten and that Canaris presumably dictated his diary entries to his secretary. Telford Taylor, one of the chief prosecutors at Nuremberg, states that Lahousen regularly made handwritten notes at meetings and later turned these over to Canaris "for inclusion in Canaris's dairy." Canaris hated taking notes, and these notes and those of others of Canaris's scribes may be the material found at Zossen.

89. Abshagen, *Canaris*, p. 11.

90. Ian Goodhope Colvin, *Chief of Intelligence*.

91. www.codoh.com/irving/irvhitwar.html, August 30, 2003.

92. Klaus Benzing, *Der Admiral*. Another independent expert, on the other hand, established that the diaries had to be forgeries. See BA-MA Freiburg, MSg 1/686.

93. Lahousen, quoted in Gisevius, *To the Bitter End*, pp. 440–41.

94. Wild rumors about Canaris persist as a testament to his lasting fascination. The most extreme may be that he was smuggled to the United States by a secret arm of the Knights Templar and resettled near Canaris, Oklahoma, where he died in 1973—but not before using funds from the Knights Templar treasury to finance the assassination of John F. Kennedy. Other funds from this treasury were supposedly later used to finance the crash of TWA 800 off New York's Long Island.

95. Canaris was promoted to captain of the sea in October 1931, rear admiral May 1935, vice admiral April 1938, admiral January 1940.

96. Höhne has produced the soundest Canaris biography. See also works by Abshagen, *Canaris;* Klaus Benzing, *Der Admiral;* and André Brissaud, *Canaris*. Filmmakers tried to capture Canaris on celluloid, for example, in the British production *The Eagle Has Landed* (1976) by John Sturges, with Anthony Quayle as Canaris; and in *Canaris*, directed by Alfred Weidermann for Dominant Pictures.

97. Lauran Paine, *German Military Intelligence in World War II*, p. 31. Canaris, too, considered the "diktat of Versailles" a humiliation for Germany, and he was a driving force behind the secret and forbidden rearmament of the navy.

98. Ibid., 37.

99. Gisevius, *To the Bitter End*, pp. 439ff., 442, quoting Lahousen.

100. Ibid.

101. Buchheit, *Der Deutsche Geheimdienst*, p. 367.

102. Ibid., p. 211.

103. This account of Operation Sunrise relies considerably on Dulles's own account: *The Secret Surrender*. An additional, very informative account is that found in Jochen von Lang's biography of Wolff, *Der Adjutant, Karl Wolff*, pp. 264–316.

104. Dulles, *Germany's Underground*, p. 195. Albert Speer testified at Nuremberg that in March Hitler had ordered him to destroy Germany's remaining infrastructure—bridges, railways, factories, etc., saying, "If the war is to be lost, the nation perishes. There is no need to consider what the people would require for even a primitive existence."

105. NA RG 226, Entry 90, Box 7, Tel. 2519, December 6, 26, 1944.

106. Lang, *Der Adjutant, Karl Wolff*, p. 265, notes that Kaltenbrunner sent his special spy, Wilhelm Hoettl, to Dulles with a peace initiative. Dulles did not take it seriously.

107. RG 226, Entry 90, Box 6, March 5, 1945.

108. Lang, *Der Adjutant*, p. 266.

109. Ibid., p. 267.

110. This is Dulles's last communication on Jews.

111. NA RG 226, Entry 90, Box 7, March. 9, 1945.

112. See Neal H. Petersen, *From Hitler's Doorstep*, pp. 634–35.

113. Ibid., p. 286. After the war, such testimonials and references were known as *Persilscheine* in Germany, Persil being a popular laundry detergent. The American equivalent would be a "Tide Certificate."

114. Dulles, *Secret Surrender*, p. 95.

115. Peter Grose, *Gentleman Spy,* p. 237.

116. Kim Philby, *My Silent War,* p. 102.

117. Casey, *Secret War,* p. 201.

118. Grose, *Gentleman Spy,* p. 240.

119. NA RG 226, Entry 134, Box 93, April 20, 1945.

120. NA RG 226, Entry 90, Box 7, April 20, 1945.

121. NA RG 226, Entry 90, Box 6, Telegram. 9649, May 1, 1945.

122. Dulles, *Secret Surrender,* p. 237.

123. Mauch, *Shadow War,* p. 131.

124. Srodes, *Allen Dulles,* pp. 202–93.

125. Grose, *Gentleman Spy,* p. 320.

126. Hoffmann, *History of the German Resistance,* p. 16.

127. Interview with Cordelia Dodson Hood, October 14, 2003.

128. See Mauch, *Shadow War,* p. 208, interview with Franklin Ford, of OSS's R&A, who worked with Dulles postwar at Wiesbaden.

129. M 1642, Roll 81, Frame 710-713. From the Director's Office.

130. Ibid.

131. Interview with Peter Sichel, October 20, 2004.

132. NA RG 226, Entry 216, Box 9.

133. NA RG 226, Entry 210, Box 463, folder 4. Undated from Dulles to Director.

134. Grose, *Gentleman Spy,* p. 250n.

135. Ibid., p. 251.

136. Ibid.

137. Ibid., p. 332.

138. Ibid., p. 354. Taylor succeed Jackson as chief prosecutor after 1946.

139. Both Strünck and his wife were soon arrested, and Strünck was executed. Koch also paid with his life for his anti-Hitler activities. See Gisevius, *To the Bitter End,* p. 586–87, who states that more than a dozen people were thrown into Gestapo cellars for having actually or allegedly sheltered him.

140. Archiv für Zeitgeschichte, September 24, 2003, update. See www.afz. ethz.ch/handbuch/nachl/nachlaesseGiseviusHansBernd.htm.

141. Balfour & Frisby, *Helmuth von Moltke,* Appendix.

142. Lucas Delattre, *Fritz Kolbe,* pp. 272–73.

143. Interview with Peter Sichel, October 20, 2004.

144. Delattre, *Fritz Kolbe,* p. 276.

145. Ibid., p. 293.

146. Ibid., pp. 293–94. At Kolbe's death in 1971, a wreath was laid at the grave on behalf of then CIA director, Richard Helms.

147. Erik Kirschbaum, "Germany Honours Long-Forgotten WW2 Spy Fritz Kolbe," Reuters News, September 2, 2004.

CHAPTER 10

1. Peter Grose, *Gentleman Spy,* p. 269.

2. James Srodes, *Allen Dulles,* p. 368, 580n12.

3. Theodore H. White, *Fire in the Ashes,* p. 394.

4. Heinz Höhne and Hermann Zolling, *The General Was a Spy,* p. 11. The FHO report predicted that the Russians would not attack in the south.

5. Ibid., p. 32.

6. Ibid., p. 45. See also Mary Ellen Reese, *General Reinhard Gehlen,* p. 4.

7. Höhne and Zolling, p. 55.

8. Ibid., p. 50.

9. Höhne and Zolling, p. 56–57. See also Christopher Simpson, *Blowback,* p. 42. In late 1944, Sibert had worked with Gävernitz on a plan to recruit German officers eager to surrender, gathering quite a number willing to cooperate and act as advisors to Allied headquarters, but the idea was shot down in Washington. The subsequent surprise Ardennes offensive earned Sibert heavy criticism from Washington.

10. Christopher Simpson, *Blowback,* p. 42.

11. The amount of uranium seized was estimated at 70,000 tons, located by the so-called Alsos team under Boris Pash, concentrating on nuclear scientists and materials. See Linda Hunt, *Secret Agenda,* pp. 11–21.

12. Tom Bower, *The Paperclip Conspiracy,* p. 95.

13. Ibid., p. 102. See also John Gimbel, *Science, Technology, and Reparations,* pp. 37–59.

14. See John Gimbel, "U.S. Policy and German Scientists: The Early Cold War," pp. 443–51. Gimbel details the conditions under which scientists of all kinds were "evacuated" with minimal possessions—often under duress—and promised U.S. government contracts, only to be interned for months, even years, with no work and no contract.

15. John Gimbel, *Science, Technology, and Reparations,* p. 107.

16. Clarence G. Lasby, *Project Paperclip,* pp. 29–30.

17. Ibid., p. 112.

18. Ibid., p. 49.

19. Ibid., pp. 33–37, points out that SS General Kammler, in charge at Peenemünde where the scientific team had remained, arrested von Braun in early 1945 for "defeatism" and for showing more interest in building a spaceship than rockets. He was viewed by one observer as having "lack of loyalty to any political doctrine," and perfectly willing to put his primary interests—science and technology—to work for the Americans, just not the Russians.

20. INSCOM, Dossier No. AE529655. INSCOM is the U.S. Army Intelligence and Security Command. FO14.

21. NA RG 218, JCS Central Decimal Files, Box 95, CCS 471.9, sec. 5. Dated March 11, 1946, the press release was approved, but subsequently classified, together with all related documents.

22. Lasby, *Project Paperclip,* pp. 77–79.

23. Ibid., pp. 58–59. Claiming weapons research as resistance is surely overstating the case, but certainly some of the scientists simply wanted to pursue their work. It took time for American hardliners to come to grips with the fact that Party membership was of the price of work.

24. The estimated value put on the documents Staver extracted from the Goslar mine was put at $400 to $500 million.

25. Safehaven was initiated in May 1944, under the the Foreign Economic Administration, to prevent sequestration of German war booty and assets in neutral states such as Switzerland and Sweden, and to ensure their availability for reparations and reconstruction.

26. NA RG 218 JCS, Central Decimal files, Box 95, CCS 471.9, sec. 5.

27. Simpson, *Blowback,* pp. 34–37.

28. Ibid., p. 159.

29. To his great amusement, Gehlen was still officially listed as "fugitive" as late as 1949. He, too, had been made to disappear in this way.

30. On January 30, 2005, Douglas Jehl of *The New York Times* wrote that the CIA was refusing to abide by a 1998 law requiring release of all documents related to Nazi war criminals. Though 1.2 million pages revealing a relationship between the government and suspected war criminals that included recruitment have been released, hundreds of thousands of pages remain classified. Under law, the CIA may exempt certain national security materials from the release order, but must submit a report to Congress, which it has not done. Relevant files, including the CIA's precursors OSS and COI, cover the years from 1941 to 1998. In the ensuing flurry of publicity, the CIA agreed to release to documents.

31. NA RG 330 Office of Secretary of Defense, 383.7, Navy (Misc.) JIOA General Correspondence 1946–52, March 21, 1947.

32. Bower, *Paperclip Conspiracy,* p. 200.

33. Ibid., p. 243.

34. There are some discrepancies in accounts of these experiments, and while Strughold may not have been directly involved, he certainly knew about them. See Bower, *Paperclip Conspiracy,* pp. 214–32.

35. Lehrer, interestingly enough, had apparently picked up on Braun's lack of political convictions and allegiances, suggesting—if sarcastically—that he was much more interested in putting up the rockets that in where they came down—a hierarchy of interests less hypocritical than apolitical. See also note 19, and Lasby, *Project Paperclip,* pp. 33–37.

36. Simpson, *Blowback,* p. 43.

37. Andrew Tully, in preface to Höhne and Zolling, *The General Was a Spy* (U.S. edition), p. xv.

38. Hugh Trevor-Roper, introduction to Höhne and Zolling, *The General Was a Spy* (New York: Bantam Books, 1972). See Simpson, *Blowback,* pp. 46–51, for details of the careers of several of Eichmann's henchmen, and their role in the Gehlen Org. See also Reese, *General Reinhard Gehlen,* p. 128. In March 1952, in the *London Daily Express,* Sefton Delmer produced an article titled "Hitler's General Spies for Dollars," accusing Gehlen's outfit of harboring a veritable reunion of SS and SD officers under the protection of American intelligence. Delmer had worked with Otto John late in the war and favored John in the rivalry between BND and internal German intelligence, the Bundesamt für Verfassung-schutz, sparking a Soviet-East German attack on Gehlen.

40. Simpson, *Blowback,* p. 251.

41. BND also had other covers. Former Abwehr officer Hans-Jochen Rudloff worked for the Bundesvermogensverwaltung, Abteilung Sondervermögen from 1950 until mid-1960s. For details see BA-MAN 637/10, Nachlaß Hans-Jochen Rudloff.

42. See Simpson, *Blowback,* p. 64, for details on how Dornberger fueled U.S. anxieties by speculating on potential attacks from missiles deployed from floating devices.

43. Reese, *General Reinhard Gehlen,* pp. 178–79.

44. Perhaps Barbie's most infamous achievement was the deportation of forty-one Jewish children from the orphanage Izieu, now seen as emblematic of Nazi atrocities.

45. Magnus Linklater, Isabel Hilton, and Neal Ascherson, *The Nazi Legacy,* p. 156.

46. Allan A. Ryan, *Klaus Barbie and the United States Government: A Report of the Attorney General of the U.S.*, pp. 37–43.

47. Simpson, *Blowback*, p. 188.

48. Simpson argues (pp. 187–88) that Barbie was in an automatic arrest category, and that his name appeared in all major central files and directories as a war criminal. See also www.nara.gov/iwg/papers/weitzman.html and www.archives.gov/iwg/research_papers/barbie_irr_file.html.

49. Ibid., pp. 185–86. The 1983 Ryan Report on Klaus Barbie for the U.S. attorney general, p. 137, notes that "Dragonovic is known and recorded as a Fascist war criminal . . . and his contacts with S. American diplomats of a similar class are not generally approved by the U.S. State Department officials."

50. Ibid., p. 138.

51. See Linklater et al., *The Nazi Legacy*, for details on Barbie's life in Bolivia—arms dealing, connections with Stroesser.

52. Ryan, *Klaus Barbie*, p. iv.

53. Simpson, *Blowback*, pp. xii–xiii.

54. See Robert Wolfe, IWG Historian, *Analysis of the Investigative Records Repository (IRR) File on Klaus Barbie*, September 19, 2001. www.archives.gov/iwg/research_papers/barbie_irr_file.html. Re Barbie, the Ryan Report, pp. 191–94, concluded that while U.S. collaboration with ex-SS and Gestapo was a grave misjudgment, incomprehensible, and shameful, with Germany center stage in a new theater of animosities, pragmatic considerations made the decision to use Barbie defensible.

55. Simpson, *Blowback*, p. xii.

56. See records of the Nuremberg Military Tribunal: www.mazal.org, vol. 8, pp. 268ff., 1064ff.

57. Ambros worked as a consultant for Grace from 1951 to 1990, as well as for Dow Chemical.

58. Simpson, *Blowback*, pp. 190–92.

59. Miles Copeland, *The Game of Nations*, pp. 103–5.

60. Ibid.

61. Thomas O'Toole and Mary Thornton, "A Long Trail to Departure of Ex-Nazi Rocket Expert," *Washington Post*, November 4, 1984, p. 1.

62. Timothy Naftali, *The CIA and Eichmann's Associates*.

63. Anthony Cave Brown, *The Last Hero*, p. 791.

64. Ibid., p. 775.

65. H. G. Nicholas, ed., *Washington Dispatches, 1941–1945*, p. 566.

66. Anthony Cave Brown, *The Secret War Report of the OSS*, p. 56.

67. Donovan ordinarily carried two "L" pills in his shirt, saying he would swallow one rather than allow himself to be captured. Others countered that if he were unconscious he could be captured without the possibility of ending his own life.

68. He had forgotten his "L" pill that day in Normandy. R. Harris Smith, *OSS, The Secret History*, pp. 183–84, from a speech by David Bruce at the annual dinner of OSS veterans, Washington D.C., May 26, 1971.

69. Executive Order 9621: Termination of the Office of Strategic Services and Disposition of its Functions. Signed: September 20, 1945 Federal Register page and date: 10 FR 12033, September 22, 1945. See: EO 9652, October 31, 1945; Transfer Order 40 of the Secretary of Defense dated July 22, 1949 (14 FR 4908).

70. For security reasons, Putzell decided to burn his copies. Donovan's copies are housed at the National Archives.

71. Ford, *Donovan of the OSS,* p. 111.

72. Brown, *Secret War Report of the OSS,* p. 21.

73. Brown, *The Last Hero,* p. 84.

74. Allen Weinstein and Alexander Vassiliev, *The Haunted Wood.*

CONCLUSION

1. Christof Mauch, *The Shadow War Against Hitler,* pp. 209 and 303n. Bell was organizing a program to assist surviving relatives of the opposition, inviting some to Britain. Dulles hoped to establish a similar organization in the United States.

2. Ibid., p. 209.

3. Michael Hirsch, "Dirty Business," *Newsweek,* December 14, 1998.

4. Eleanor Roosevelt, in "My Day," her popular newspaper column, quoted in Reinhold Billstein, "How the Americans Took Over Cologne," in Billstein et al., *Working for the Enemy,* p. 122.

5. Charles Higham, *Trading with the Enemy,* p. 159.

6. Ibid., p. 177.

7. Peter Grose, *Gentleman Spy,* p. 159. See also the business article "Industrial Penetration," *Time,* vol. 7, no. 24 (June 14, 1926), which notes that Giesche, impoverished by World War I and its aftermath, appealed to Anaconda Copper Co. and to William Averell Harriman, "who has spent much time in Europe since the War snapping up industrial bargains, to refinance them."

8. Allen Dulles, *Germany's Underground,* p. xiii.

9. Ibid., p. 196.

10. Patricia Meehan, *The Unnecessary War,* p. 159.

11. Office of United States Chief of Counsel for the Prosecution of Axis Criminality, *Nazi Conspiracy and Aggression* (Washington, D.C.: U.S. Government Printing Office, 1947), pp. 1557–58.

12. Albert Zoller, *Hitler privat,* p. 177.

13. In the view of Breckenridge Long, the United States was forced into fighting World War II because there had been no unconditional surrender after World War I. So, curiously, two ailing American presidents presided over the shaping of two unsuccessful postwar policies.

14. See Anne Armstrong, *Unconditional Surrender,* p. 262.

15. Barry Katz, *Foreign Intelligence, Research and Analysis in the Office of Strategic Services, 1942–1945,* pp. 39–40. See also p. 55, section 3.

16. These figures appear in various Dulles in communications, beginning in November 1942.

17. NA RG 226, Entry 134, Box 273 75, dated October 14, 1943.

18. NA RG 226, Entry 134, Box 275, dated February 8, 1944. It is not clear from the context whether the sum was in French francs or another currency.

19. Douglas Jehl, "Spy Agencies Told to Bolster 'The Growth of Democracy,'" *New York Times,* October 27, 2005, p. A10.

20. Alexandra Kollontai, a Lenin confidante, had fallen from favor under Stalin, making her a magnet for diplomatic hopefuls who thought she might influence Soviet policies in their favor. See Klemens von Klemperer, *German Resistance Against Hitler,* p. 261, 187n.

21. Ulrich von Hassell, "Deutschland zwischen West und Ost," Bundesarchiv, Koblenz. A/K, Ritter, 150.

22. M 1642, From the Director's Office, Roll 31, Frame 49.

23. NA RG 165, Entry 179, Box 702, Army Intelligence Consolidated Interrogation Report, September 10, 1945.

24. David McCullough, *Truman*, p. 286. See also Thomas Fleming, *The New Dealers' War*, p. 263.

25. It appears that Hiss may have been fact the mysterious ALE of Soviet spy reports who flew directly to Moscow after Yalta.

26. By late May, 1945, Stalin had effectively subjugated Poland, and the three former allies were engaged in a bitter struggle over Berlin and the heart of Europe. In March 1946, Churchill delivered his "iron curtain" speech in Fulton, Missouri.

27. Klemens von Klemperer, *German Resistance Against Hitler*, p. 439, quoting from a letter to Sir Ernest Llewellyn Woodward, March 1965.

EPILOGUE

1. Douglas Jehl, "Tug of War: Intelligence vs. Politics," *New York Times*, May 8, 2005, on the dangers of administration intimidation of intelligence agencies, to encourage conclusions closely aligned to preexisting policies.

2. Douglas Jehl, "Top Spy's No. 2 Tells of Changes to Avoid Error," *New York Times*, July, 29, 2005, p. 1. The italics are mine.

3. Schlabrendorff, pp. 103–4.

4. Carl Goerdeler, *An alle Menschen*, a long passionate document written in jail, quoted in Klemperer, *Die verlassenen Verschwörer*, p. 357. (Author's translation.)

BIBLIOGRAPHY

Abshagen, Karl-Heinz. *Canaris: Patriot und Weltbürger.* Stuttgart: Union, 1957.

Acheson, Dean. *Present at the Creation: My Years in the State Department.* New York: Norton, 1969.

Allen, Michael. "Stranger than Fiction: Edwin Black, IBM and the Holocaust." *Technology and Culture* 43 (January 2002): 150–54.

Alvarez, David. *Spies in the Vatican: Espionage and Intrigue from Napoleon to the Holocaust.* Lawrence: University Press of Kansas, 2002.

Aly, Götz, and Karl Heinz Roth. *Die restlose Erfassung: Volkszählen, Identifizieren, Aussondern im Nationalsozialismus.* Berlin: Rotbuch Verlag, 1984.

Annan, Noel. *Changing Enemies: The Defeat and Regeneration of Germany.* New York: Norton, 1996.

Aretin, Felicitas von. *Die Enkel des 20. Juli 1944.* Leipzig: Faber & Faber, 2004.

Armstrong, Anne. *Unconditional Surrender: The Impact of the Casablanca Policy upon World War II.* New Brunswick, NJ: Rutgers University Press, 1961.

Aronson, Shlomo. *Hitler, the Allies, and the Jews.* Cambridge: Cambridge University Press, 2004.

Astor, David. "Why the Revolt Against Hitler was Ignored." *Encounter* 32 (June 1969).

Baker, James C. *The Bank for International Settlements. Evolution and Evaluation.* Westport, CT: Quorum, 2002.

Balfour, Michael, and Julian Frisby. *Helmuth von Moltke: A Leader Against Hitler.* London: Macmillan, 1972.

Bancroft, Mary. *Autobiography of a Spy.* New York: Morrow, 1983.

Bassett, Richard. *Hitler's Spy Chief: The William Canaris Mystery.* London: Weidenfeld & Nicolson, 2005.

Bazna, Elyesa, with Hans Nogly. *I Was Cicero.* New York: Harper & Row, 1962.

Benzing, Klaus. *Der Admiral: Leben und Wirken.* Nördlingen: Self-published, 1973.

Beschloss, Michael. *The Conquerors: Roosevelt, Truman and the Destruction of Hitler's Germany, 1941–1945.* New York: Simon & Schuster, 2002.

Bielenberg, Christabel. *The Past Is Myself.* London: Chatto & Windus, 1968.

Billstein, Reinhold, et al. *Working for the Enemy: Ford, General Motors, and Forced Labor in Germany During the Second World War.* New York: Berghahn, 2000.

Bittenfeld, Hans-Heinrich Herwarth von. *Against Two Evils: Memoirs of a Diplomat-Soldier During the Third Reich.* London: Collins, 1981.

Black, Edwin. *IBM and the Holocaust.* New York: Crown Publishers, 2001.

Blair, Deirdre. *Jung: A Biography.* Boston: Little Brown, 2003.

Bloch, Michael. *Operation Willi.* New York: Weidenfeld & Nicholson, 1986.

———. *Ribbentrop.* New York: Crown Publishers, 1992.

Blum, John Morton. *Years of War, 1941–1945.* Vol. 3 of *From the Morgenthau Diaries.* Boston: Houghton Mifflin, 1967.

Boveri, Margret. *Treason in the Twentieth Century.* Translated by Jonathan Steinberg. London: MacDonald, 1961.

Bower, Tom. *The Paperclip Conspiracy: The Hunt for the Nazi Scientists.* Boston: Little Brown, 1987.

Bradsher, Greg. "A Time to Act: The Beginning of the Fritz Kolbe Story, 1900–1943." *Prologue* 34, no. 1 (2002): 6–24.

Braunschweig, Pierre-Th. *Secret Channel to Berlin. The Masson-Schellenberg Connection and Swiss Intelligence in World War II.* Philadelphia: Casemate, 2004.

Breitman, Richard. *Official Secrets: What the Nazis Planned, What the British and Americans Knew.* New York: Hill and Wang, 1998.

———. *"OSS's Knowledge of the Holocaust."* Paper delivered at the Conference on Intelligence and the Holocaust, June 2–4, 2003.

———. *"Other Responses to the Holocaust."* In *U.S. Intelligence and the Nazis,* pp. 54ff. Washington, DC: National Archives Trust Fund Board, 2004.

———, et al., eds. *US Intelligence and the Nazis.* Washington, DC: National Archives Trust Fund Board, 2004.

Brissaud, André. *Canaris, 1887–1945.* Frankfurt am Main: Societäts-Verlag, 1976.

Brown, Anthony Cave. *Bodyguard of Lies: The Extraordinary True Story Behind D-Day.* Guilford, CT: The Lyons Press, 2002.

———. *The Last Hero: Wild Bill Donovan.* New York: Times Books, 1982.

———. *The Secret War Report of the OSS.* Edited and with an introduction by Anthony Cave Brown. New York: Berkley Medallion Book, 1976.

Bruce, David K. E. *OSS Against the Reich: The World War II Diaries of Colonel David K. E. Bruce.* Kent, OH: Kent State University Press, 1991.

Brüning, Heinrich. *Briefe und Gespräche 1934–1945.* Edited by Claire Nix. Stuttgart: Deutsche Verlags-Anstalt, 1974.

Bryans, J. Lonsdale. *Blind Victory* (Secret Communications, Halifax-Hassell). London: Skeffington, 1951.

Buchheit, Gert. *Der deutsche Geheimdienst: Geschichte der militärischen Abwehr.* Munich: List, 1966.

Bumiller, Elisabeth. "Sixty Years after the Fact, Debating Yalta All Over Again." *New York Times,* May, 16, 2005.

Calvocoressi, Peter, Guy Wint, and John Pritchard. *The Penguin History of the Second World War.* London: Penguin Books, 1989.

Carroll, James. *Constantine's Sword: The Church and the Jews; A History*. Boston: Houghton Mifflin, 2001.

Campbell, John P. "Some Pieces of the Ostro Puzzle." *Intelligence and National Security* 11, no. 2 (April 1996).

Canaris, Vizeadmiral [Wilhelm] (Berlin). "Politik und Wehrmacht." In *Wehrmacht und Partei,* edited by Richard Donnevert. Leipzig: J. A. Barth Verlag, 1938.

Casey, William J. *The Secret War Against Hitler*. Washington, DC: Regnery Gateway, 1988.

Chambers, F. P. *This Age of Conflict*. New York: Harcourt, Brace and World, 1962.

Charisius, Albrecht, and Moritz Erhard. "Zur Fusion des OKW-Amtes Ausland Abwehr mit dem Sicherheitsdienst (SD), 1944." *Militärgeschichte* [East Germany] 16, no. 1 (1977): 44–57.

Childers, Thomas. "The Kreisau Circle and the 20th of July." Paper delivered at the conference "The German Resistance Movement," New York, NY, April 24, 25, 1988.

Clarke, Margaret. *The Safehaven Project*. Foreign Economic Relations Study No. 5, Washington, DC, 1945.

Clements, Bruce. *From Ice Set Free: The Story of Otto Kiep*. New York: Farrar, Straus and Giroux, 1972.

Colvin, Ian Goodhope. *Chief of Intelligence*. London: Victor Gollancz, 1951.

Conwell-Evans, T. P. *None So Blind: A Study of the Crisis Years*. London: Self-published, 1947.

Cookridge, E. H. *Gehlen, Spy of the Century*. New York: Random House, 1972.

Copeland, Miles. *The Game of Nations: The Amorality of Power Politics*. New York, Simon & Schuster, 1970.

Craig, Gordon. *Germany: 1866–1945*. Oxford: Oxford University Press, 1978.

Cray, Ed. *Chrome Colossus: General Motors and Its Times*. New York: McGraw-Hill, 1980.

Critchfield, James H. *Partners at the Creation: The Men Behind Postwar Germany's Defense and Intelligence Establishments*. Annapolis, MD: Naval Institute Press, 2003.

Cutler, Richard W. *Counterspy: Memoirs of a Counterintelligence Officer in World War II and the Cold War*. Washington, DC: Brassey's, 2004.

Deacon, Richard. *A History of the British Secret Service*. London: Frederick Müller, 1969.

Delattre, Lucas. *Fritz Kolbe: Der wichtigste Spion des Zweiten Weltkriegs*. Munich: Piper, 2004.

Deutsch, Harold C. *The Conspiracy Against Hitler in the Twilight War*. Minneapolis: University of Minnesota Press, 1968.

Dinnerstein, Leonard. "Franklin D. Roosevelt and the Jews: Another Look." *Dimensions* 10, no. 1 (1996): 3–8.

Doerries, Reinhard R., ed. *Diplomaten und Agenten: Nachrichtendienste in der Geschichte der deutsch-amerikanischen Beziehungen*. Heidelberg: C. Winter, 2001.

Donnevert, Richard, ed. *Wehrmacht und Partei*. Leipzig: Johann Ambrosius Barth Verlag, 1938.

Dulles, Allen Welsh. *Germany's Underground: The Anti-Nazi Resistance*. New York: Da Capo Press, 2000.

———. *The Secret Surrender*. New York: Harper & Row, 1966.

Dunlop, Richard. *Donovan: America's Master Spy*. Chicago: Rand McNally, 1982.

Eisenhower, David. *Eisenhower at War, 1943–1945.* New York: Random House, 1986.

Farago, Ladislas. *The Game of the Foxes: The Untold Story of German Espionage in the United States and Great Britain During World War II.* New York: David McKay, 1972.

Feingold, Henry L. *The Politics of Rescue: The Roosevelt Administration and the Holocaust, 1938–1945.* New Brunswick, NJ: Rutgers University Press, 1970.

Fest, Joachim. *The Face of the Third Reich: Portraits of the Nazi Leadership.* New York: Pantheon, 1970.

———. *Plotting Hitler's Death: The Story of the German Resistance.* New York: Henry Holt, 1996.

Fleming, Thomas. *The New Dealers' War.* New York: Basic Books, 2001.

Flink, James. *The Automobile Age.* Cambridge, MA: MIT Press, 1988.

Ford, Corey. *Donovan of the OSS.* Boston: Little Brown, 1970.

Fox, Jo. Review Article: "Resistance and the Third Reich." *Journal of Contemporary History* (London, SAGE Publications) 39, no. 2:275.

Frankel, Max. "Willing Executioners?" Review of *A Nation on Trial: The Goldhagen Thesis and Historical Truth,* by Norman Finkelstein, *New York Times Book Review,* June 28, 1998.

Frei, Norbert. *Karrieren im Zwielicht: Hitlers Eliten nach 1945.* Frankfurt and New York: Campus, 2001.

Friedman, John S. "Kodak's Nazi Connections." *Nation,* March 26, 2001.

Gallin, Mother Mary Alice. *Ethical and Religious Factors in the German Resistance to Hitler.* Washington, DC: Catholic University of America, 1955.

Gehlen, Reinhard. *The Service: The Memoirs of Reinhard Gehlen.* Translated by David Irving. New York: World Publishing, 1972.

Gilbert, Martin. *Auschwitz and the Allies.* New York: Holt, Rinehart and Winston, 1981.

———. *The Holocaust: The Jewish Tragedy.* London: Collins, 1986.

———. *Winston S. Churchill: The Road to Victory, 1941–1945.* Boston: Houghton Mifflin, 1998.

Gill, Anton. *An Honourable Defeat. A History of German Resistance to Hitler, 1933–1945.* New York: Henry Holt, 1994.

Gillmann, Sabine, and Hans Mommsen, eds. *Politische Schriften und Briefe Carl Friedrich Goerdelers.* 2 vols. Munich: K. G. Saur, 2003.

Gimbel, John. *Science, Technology, and Reparations: Exploitation and Plunder in Postwar Germany.* Stanford: Stanford University Press, 1990.

———. "U.S. Policy and German Scientists: The Early Cold War." *Political Science Quarterly* 101, no. 3 (1986): 443–451.

Gisevius, Hans Bernd. *To the Bitter End: An Insider's Account of the Plot to Kill Hitler, 1933–1944.* Translated by Richard and Clara Winston. New York: Da Capo, 1998.

Glaberson, William. "For Betrayal by Bank and Nazis, $21 Million." *New York Times,* April, 14, 2005.

Goodwin, Doris Kearns. *No Ordinary Time: Franklin and Eleanor Roosevelt; The Home Front in World War II.* New York: Simon & Schuster, 1994.

Graml, Hermann. "Der Fall Oster." *Vierteljahrsheft für Zeitgeschichte* 4 (1966): 26–27.

Grose, Peter. *Gentleman Spy: The Life of Allen Dulles.* Boston and New York: Houghton Mifflin, 1994.

Hamerow, Theodore S. *On the Road to the Wolf's Lair: German Resistance to Hitler.* Cambridge, MA: The Belknap Press of Harvard University Press, 1997.

Hartmann, Sverre. "Zwischen Staat und System: Ein Versuch zur Klärung des Problem Canaris." *Deutsche Rundschau* 81, no. 4 (1955): 348–53.

Hass, Gerhart. "Dokumente zur Haltung Hitlerdeutschlands und der USA gegenüber der Sowjetunion im Jahre 1943." *Jahrbuch für Geschichte* [East Germany] 5 (1970): 439–73.

Hassell, Ulrich von. *Die Hassell-Tagebücher, 1938–1944: Aufzeichnungen vom Andern Deutschland.* Revised and expanded edition, edited by Friedrich Freiherr Hiller von Gaertringen with Klaus Peter Reiß. Berlin: Siedler, 1988.

———. *The Von Hassell Diaries 1938–1944: The Story of the Forces Against Hitler Inside Germany.* Garden City, New York: Doubleday, 1947.

———. *Der Kreis Schliesst Sich: Aufzeichnungen in der Haft 1944.* Berlin, Propyläen Verlag, 1994.

Heideking, Jürgen. "Die 'Breakers'-Akte: Das Office of Strategic Services und der 20. Juli 1944." In *Geheimdienstkrieg gegen Deutschland: Subversion, Propaganda und politische Planungen des amerikanischen Geheimdienstes im Zweiten Weltkrieg,* edited by Jürgen Heideking and Christof Mauch, 11–50. Göttingen: Vandenhoeck & Ruprecht, 1993.

———, ed. *USA und deutscher Widerstand: Analysen und Operationen des amerikanischen Geheimdienstes im Zweiten Weltkrieg.* Tübingen: Francke, 1993.

———, and Christof Mauch, eds. *American Intelligence and the German Resistance to Hitler: A Documentary History.* Boulder, CO: Westview Press, 1996.

———, and Christof Mauch. "Das Hermann-Dossier: Helmuth Graf von Moltke, die deutsche Emigration in Istanbul und der amerikanische Geheimdienst OSS; Dokumentation." *Vierteljahrshefte für Zeitgeschichte* 40, no. 4 (1992): 567–623.

Helms, Richard, with William Hood. *A Look over My Shoulder: Memoirs.* New York: Random House, 2003.

Hersh, Burton. *The Old Boys: The American Elite and the Origins of the CIA.* St. Petersburg, FL: Tree Farm Books, 1992.

Higham, Charles. *Trading with the Enemy: An Exposé of the Nazi-American Money Plot, 1933–1949.* New York: Delacorte, 1983.

Hillgruber, Andreas, ed. *Staatsmänner und Diplomaten bei Hitler: Vertrauliche Aufzeichnungen über Unterredungen mit Vertretern des Auslandes 1939–1941.* Frankfurt am Main: Bernard und Graefe, 1967–1970.

Hindley, Meredith. "Negotiating the Boundary of Unconditional Surrender: The War Refugee Board and Nazi Proposals to Ransom Jews, 1944–1945." *Holocaust and Genocide Studies* 10, 1997.

Hirsch, Michael. "Dirty Business," *Newsweek,* December 14, 1998.

Hoettl, Wilhelm. *The Secret Front: The Story of Nazi Political Espionage.* London: Weidenfeld & Nicolson, 1954.

Hofer, Walther. "Das Attentat der Offiziere und das Ausland." In *20. Juli: Porträts des Widerstandes,* edited by Rudolf Lill and Heinrich Oberreuther, 47–62. Düsseldorf and Vienna: Econ, 1989.

Hoffmann, Peter. *The History of the German Resistance, 1933–1945.* Translated by Richard Barry. 3rd ed. Montreal & Kingston: McGill-Queen's University Press, 1996.

———. "Peace through Coup D'Etat: The Foreign Contacts of the German Resistance, 1933–1944." *Central European History* 19, no. 1 (March 1986): 3–44.

Höhne, Heinz. *Canaris: Hitler's Master Spy.* Translated by J. Maxwell Brownjohn. New York: Doubleday, 1979.

————. *Canaris: Patriot im Zwielicht.* Munich: Bertelsmann, 1976.

————. *The Order of the Death's Head.* New York: Coward McCann, 1970.

————, and Hermann Zolling. *The General Was a Spy.* Translated by Richard Barry. New York: Coward, McCann & Geoghegan, 1972.

Hunt, Linda. *Secret Agenda: The United States Government, Nazi Scientists, and Project Paperclip, 1945 to 1990.* New York: St. Martin's Press, 1991.

Hymoff, Edward. *The OSS in World War II.* New York: Richardson and Steinman, 1986.

Jehl, Douglas. "Spy Agencies Told to Bolster 'The Growth of Democracy.'" *New York Times,* October 27, 2005.

————. "Tug of War: Intelligence vs. Politics." *New York Times,* May 8, 2005.

————. "Top Spy's No. 2 Tells of Change to Avoid Error." *New York Times,* July 29, 2005.

John, Otto. *Twice Through the Lines,* with an introduction by Hugh Trevor-Roper. Translated by Richard Barry. New York: Harper & Row, 1972.

Johnson, David Alan. *Germany's Spies and Saboteurs.* Osceola, WI: MBI, 1998.

————. *Righteous Deception: German Officers Against Hitler.* Westport, CT: Praeger, 2001.

Kahn, David. *The Codebreakers.* New York: Scribners, 1996.

————. *Hitler's Spies: German Military Intelligence in World War II.* New York: Macmillan, 1978.

Katz, Barry M. *Foreign Intelligence, Research and Analysis in the Office of Strategic Services, 1942–1945.* Cambridge, MA: Harvard University Press, 1989.

————. "The Holocaust and American Intelligence." In: *The Jewish Legacy and the German Conscience: Essays in Memory of Rabbi Joseph Asher.* Edited by Moses Rischin and Raphael Asher, 297–307. Berkeley: The Judah L. Magnes Museum, 1991.

Kennan, George. *Memoirs.* Boston: Little Brown, 1972.

Kettenacker, Lothar, ed. *Das "Andere Deutschland" in Zweiten Weltkrieg: Emigration and Widerstand in internationaler Perspective.* Veröffentlichungen des Deutschen Historischen Instituts in London, vol. 2. Stuttgart: Klett, 1977.

Keynes, John M. *The Economic Consequences of the Peace.* In *The Collected Writings of John Maynard Keynes,* vol. 2. London: Macmillan; New York: St. Martin's Press: 1971.

Kirschbaum, Erik. "Germany Honours Long-Forgotten WW2 Spy Fritz Kolbe." Reuters News, Sept. 2, 2004.

Kitchens, James H. "The Bombing of Auschwitz Reconsidered" *Journal of Military History* no. 58 (April 1994): 233–66.

Klemperer, Klemens von. *Die "Verbindung zu der großen Welt": Außenbeziehungen des deutschen Widerstandes 1938–1945.* Publications of the Memorial to German Resistance, vol. 24. Berlin, 1990.

————. *Die verlassenen Verschwörer: Der deutsche Widerstand auf der Suche nach Verbündeten, 1938–1945.* Berlin: Siedler, 1994.

————. *German Resistance Against Hitler: The Search for Allies Abroad, 1938–1945.* Oxford: Clarendon Press; New York: Oxford University Press, 1994.

Klemperer, Viktor. *Ich will Zeugnis ablegen bis zum Letzten.* Berlin: Aufbau Verlag, 1995.

————. *LTI: Notizbuch eines Philologen.* Leipzig: Reclam Verlag, 1975.

Kordt, Erich. *Nicht aus den Akten . . . : Die Wilhelmstraße in Frieden und Krieg; Erlebnisse, Begegnungen und Eindrücke, 1928–1945.* Stuttgart: Union Deutsche Verlagsgesellschaft, 1950.

Koskoff, David E. *Joseph P. Kennedy: A Life and Times.* Englewood Cliffs, NJ: Prentice-Hall, 1974.

Krausnick, Helmut. "Dokumentation: Aus den Personalakten von Canaris." *Vierteljahrshefte für Zeitgeschichte* 10, no. 3 (1962): 280–310.

Krüger, Dieter, and Armin Wagner, eds. *Konspiration als Beruf: Deutsche Geheimdienstchefs im Kalten Krieg.* Berlin: Christoph Links, 2003.

Lang, Jochen von. *Der Adjutant: Karl Wolff, der Mann zwischen Hitler und Himmler.* Translated by MaryBeth Friedrich. Munich: Herbig, 1985.

Laqueur, Walter. *The Terrible Secret: An Investigation into the Suppression of Information About Hitler's "Final Solution."* London: Weidenfeld and Nicolson, 1980.

———. *The World of Secrets.* New York: Basic Books, 1985.

———, and Richard Breitman. *Breaking the Silence: The German Who Exposed the Final Solution.* New York: Simon & Schuster, 1986.

Large, David Clay. *Between Two Fires.* New York: Norton, 1991.

Lasby, Clarence G. *Project Paperclip: German Scientists and the Cold War.* New York: Atheneum, 1971.

Laurie, Clayton D. "The 'Sauerkrauts': German Prisoners of War as OSS Agents, 1944–45." *Prologue* 26, no. 1 (1994): 49–61.

Lerner, Max. "What About the Jews, FDR?" *PM,* July 22, 1943.

Leutze, James. "The Secret of the Churchill-Roosevelt Correspondence: September 1939–May 1940." *Journal of Contemporary History* 10, no. 3 (July 1975).

Leverkuehn, Paul. *German Military Intelligence.* New York: Praeger, 1954.

Lindbergh, Charles. Speech, *America and European Wars,* September 15, 1939. See http://charleslindbergh.com/americafirst/index/asp.

Linklater, Magnus, Isabel Hilton, and Neal Ascherson. *The Nazi Legacy: Klaus Barbie and the International Fascist Connection.* New York, Holt, Rinehart & Winston, 1984.

Lippmann, Walter. "The Coming German Civil War." *Washington Post,* July 22, 1944.

Lochner, Louis P. *Always the Unexpected: A Book of Reminiscences.* New York: Macmillan, 1956.

———, ed. *Goebbels Tagebücher aus den Jahren 1942–1943.* Zurich: Atlantis Verlag, 1948.

Loeff, Wolfgang. *Spionage: Aus den Papieren eines Abwehr-Offiziers.* Stuttgart: Hans Riegler, 1950.

Louca, Antonio, and Ansgar Schafer. *Portugal and the Nazi Gold: The "Lisbon Connection" in the Sales of Looted Gold by the Third Reich.* Yad Vashem Studies 27 (1999): 105–22.

Ludecke, Kurt G. W. *I Knew Hitler: The Story of a Nazi Who Escaped the Blood Purge.* London: Jarrolds Publishers, 1938.

MacDonald, Elizabeth. *Undercover Girl.* New York: Macmillan, 1947.

MacDonogh, Giles. *A Good German: Adam von Trott zu Solz.* Woodstock, NY: Overlook Press, 1992.

McKay, C. G. "MI5 on Ostro: A New Document from the Archives," *Intelligence and National Security* 12, no. 3 (July 1997).

Mackenzie, Compton. *Water on the Brain.* London: Chatto & Windus, 1954.

MacPherson, B. Nelson. "Inspired Improvisation: William Casey and the Penetration of Germany." *Intelligence and National Security* 9, no. 4 (October 1994): 695–722.

Mader, Albrecht, and Julius Charisius. *Nicht länger geheim: Entwicklung, System und Arbeitsweise des imperialistischen deutschen Geheimdienstes.* East Berlin: Deutscher Militärverlag, 1969.

Mader, Julius. *Hitlers Spionagegeneräle sagen aus: Ein Dokumentarbericht über Aufbau, Struktur und Operationen des OkW-Geheimdienstamtes Ausland/Abwehr mit einer Chronologie seiner Einsätze von 1933 bis 1944*. East Berlin: Verlag der Nation, 1970.

Manvell, Roger, and Heinrich Fraenkel. *The Canaris Conspiracy*. New York: David McKay, 1969.

Marks, Frederick W. "Six Between Roosevelt and Hitler: America's Role in the Appeasement of Nazi Germany." *Historical Journal* 28, no. 4 (1985): 969–82.

Marquardt-Bigman, Petra. *Amerikanische Geheimdienstanalysen über Deutschland, 1942–1949*. Munich: R. Oldenbourg Verlag, 1995.

———. "Behemoth Revisited: The Research and Analysis Branch of the OSS in the Debate of US Policies Towards Germany, 1943–46." *Intelligence and National Security* 12, no. 2 (1997): 91–100.

Martin, Bernd. *Friedensinitiativen und Machtpolitik im Zweiten Weltkrieg, 1939–1942*. Düsseldorf: Droste, 1974.

———. "Friedens-Planungen der multinationalen Grossindustrie, 1932–40 als politische Krisenstrategie." *Geschichte und Gesellschaft* 2, no. 1 (1976).

Masterman, J. C. *The Double-Cross System*, with a foreword by Norman Holmes Pearson. New Haven: Yale University Press, 1972.

Mauch, Christof. *The Shadow War Against Hitler: The Covert Operations of America's Wartime Secret Intelligence Service*. Translated Jeremiah Riemer. New York: Columbia University Press, 2003.

McCullough, David. *Truman*. New York: Simon & Schuster, 1992.

McDonald, Lawrence H. "The Office of Strategic Services: America's First National Intelligence Agency." *Prologue* 23, no. 1 (1991): 7–22.

McIntosh, Elizabeth P. *Sisterhood of Spies: The Women of the OSS*. Annapolis, MD: Naval Institute Press, 1998.

Meehan, Patricia. *The Unnecessary War: Whitehall and the German Resistance to Hitler*. London: Sinclair-Stevenson, 1992.

Meyer, Winfried. *Unternehmen Sieben: Eine Rettungsaktion für vom Holocaust Bedrohte aus dem Amt Ausland/Abwehr im Oberkommando der Wehrmacht*. Frankfurt am Main: Hain, 1993.

Middendorf, Stefanie. "'Verstoßenes Wissen': Emigranten als Deutschlandexperten im 'Office of Strategic Services' und im amerikanischen Außenministerium, 1943–1955." *Neue Politische Literatur* 46 (2001): 23–52.

Miller, Paul B. "Europe's Gold: Nazis, Neutrals and the Holocaust." *Dimensions* 11, no. 1 (1997): 7–14.

Miller, Russell. *Behind the Lines: The Oral History of Special Operations in World War II*. New York: St. Martin's Press, 2002.

Moltke, Freya von. *Memories of Kreisau and the German Resistance*. Translated by Julie M. Winter. Lincoln and London: University of Nebraska Press, 2003.

Moltmann, Günter. *Amerikas Deutschlandpolitik im Zweiten Weltkrieg: Kriegs-und Friedensziele, 1941–1945*. Beihefte zum Jahrbuch für Amerikastudien. Heidelberg: Carl Winter, 1958.

Mommsen, Hans. *Alternatives to Hitler: German Resistance under the Third Reich*. Translated by Angus McGeoch. Princeton and Oxford: Princeton University Press, 2003.

Mruck, Armin. "Roosevelt and the Anti-Nazi Resistance: From Pilot School

Neukuhren to the National Archives in Washington, DC." *Towson State Journal of International Affairs* 18, no. 2 (1984): 66–76.

Müller, Frank. "Die 'Brüning Papers': Der letzte Zentrumskanzler im Spiegel seiner Selbstzeugnisse." *Europäische Hochschulschriften,* series 3, vol. 577. Frankfurt am Main: Peter Lang.

Müller, Josef. *Bis zur letzten Konsequenz: Ein Leben für Frieden und Freiheit.* Munich, 1975.

Müller, Klaus-Jürgen. *Der deutsche Widerstand und das Ausland.* Beiträge zum Widerstand 1933–1945. Berlin: Gedenkstätte Deutscher Widerstand, 1986.

Murphy, David E., Sergei A. Kondrashev, and George Bailey. *Battleground Berlin: CIA vs. KGB in the Cold War.* New Haven and London: Yale University Press, 1997.

Murray, Henry A., et al., Office of Strategic Services, *Assessment of Men: Selection of Personnel for the Office of Strategic Services,* Washington, D.C., Government Printing Office, 1948.

Naftali, Timothy. *The CIA and Eichmann's Associates.* National Archives Trust Fund Board, Nazi War Crimes and Japanese Government Records Interagency Working Group, Washington, DC.

Neliba, Günter. *Die Opel-Werke im Konzern von General Motors (1929–1948) in Rüsselsheim und Brandenburg: Produktion für Aufrüstung und Krieg ab 1935 unter nationalsozialistischer Herrschaft.* Frankfurt am Main: Brandes & Apsel, 2000.

Neufeld, Michael J., and Michael Berenbaum, eds. *The Bombing of Auschwitz: Should the Allies Have Attempted It?* New York: St. Martin's Press, 2000.

Newton, Verne W., ed. *FDR and the Holocaust.* New York: St. Martin's Press, 1996.

Nicholas, H. G., ed. *Washington Dispatches, 1941–1945: Weekly Political Reports from the British Embassy,* with an introduction by Isaiah Berlin. Chicago: University of Chicago Press, 1981.

Novick, Peter. *The Holocaust in American Life.* Boston: Houghton Mifflin Company, 1999.

O'Donnell, Patrick. *Operatives, Spies and Saboteurs: The Unknown Story of the Men and Women of the OSS.* New York: Free Press, 2004.

Office of the United States Chief of Counsel for Prosecution of Axis Criminality, *Nazi Conspiracy and Aggression,* Washington, D.C., U.S. Government Printing Office, 1947.

O'Toole, Thomas, and Thornton, Mary. "A Long Trail to Departure of Ex-Nazi Rocket Expert." *Washington Post,* November 4, 1984.

Paine, Lauran. *The German Military Intelligence in World War II: The Abwehr.* Briarcliff Manor, NY: Stein and Day, 1984.

Papen, Franz von. *Memoirs.* Translated by Brian Connell. London: Andre Deutsch, 1952.

Parssinen, Terry. *The Oster Conspiracy of 1938: The Unknown Story of the Military Plot to Kill Hitler and Avert World War II.* New York: HarperCollins, 2003.

Paul, Allen. *Katyn: The Untold Story of Stalin's Polish Massacre.* New York: Charles Scribner's Sons, 1991.

Penkower, Monty N. *The Jews Were Expendable: Free World Diplomacy and the Holocaust.* Urbana: University of Illinois Press, 1983.

Persico, Joseph E. *Piercing the Reich: The Penetration of Nazi Germany by American Secret Agents During World War II.* New York: Viking Press, 1979.

———. *Roosevelt's Secret War: FDR and World War II Espionage.* New York: Random House, 2001.

Peters, Hans. *Erinnerungen und den Kreisauer Kreis.* Institute für Zeitsgeschichte München 25/A-18, vol. 6.

Petersen, Neal H. *From Hitler's Doorstep: The Wartime Intelligence Reports of Allen Dulles, 1942–1945.* University Park: Pennsylvania State University Press, 1996.

Petropoulos, Jonathan. "Co-Opting Nazi Germany: Neutrality in Europe During World War II." *Dimensions* 14, no. 1 (2000): 13–18.

Philby, Kim. *My Silent War.* New York: Modern Library, 2002.

Podewin, Norbert, ed. *Braunbuch: Kriegs-und Naziverbrecher in der Bundesrepublik und in Berlin (West).* Reprint of the 3d. ed., 1968. Berlin: Edition Ost, 2002.

Polish Cultural Foundation. *The Crime of Katyn: Facts and Documents.* London: Polish Cultural Foundation, 1965.

Polish Ministry of Information. *The Black book of Poland,* London, 1942; New York, G. P. Putnam's Sons, 1942.

Popov, Dusko. *Spy/Counterspy.* New York: Grosset and Dunlap, 1974.

Pujol, Juan, with Nigel West. *Operation Garbo.* New York: Random House, 1985.

Quibble, Anthony. "Alias George Wood." *Studies in Intelligence* 10 (Spring 1966): 71ff.

Rassow, Berthold, ed. *Amerikanische Reiseskizzen: Berichte der Teilnehmer des "Coaltar-Trip" im Herbst, 1912.* Leipzig: Spamersche Buchdruckerei, 1913.

Read, Anthony. *The Devil's Disciples: Hitler's Inner Circle.* New York: Norton, 2004.

Reese, Mary Ellen. *General Reinhard Gehlen: The CIA Connection.* Fairfax, VA: George Mason University Press, 1990.

Reile, Oskar. *Geheime Westfront: Die Abwehr 1935–1945.* Munich: Welsermühl, 1962.

Rein, Hans. *Franz von Papen im Zwielicht der Geschichte: Sein letzter Prozess.* Baden-Baden: Nomos, 1979.

Rigg, Bryan Mark. *Rescued from the Reich: How One of Hitler's Soldiers Saved the Lubavitcher Rebbe.* New Haven and London: Yale University Press, 2004.

Rings, Werner. *Raubgold aus Deutschland.* Munich and Zurich: Artemis Verlag, 1985.

Ritter, Gerhard. *The German Resistance: Carl Goerdeler's Struggle Against Tyranny.* Translated by R. T. Clark. London: Allen & Unwin, 1958.

Roberts, Sam. "U.S. Study Pinpoints Near Misses by Allies in Fathoming the Unfolding Holocaust." *New York Times,* July 31, 2005.

Roberts, Andrew, The Holy Fox: a Biography of Lord Halifax, London, Weidenfeld and Nicolson, 1991.

Roewer, Helmut, Stefan Schäfer, and Matthias Uhl, eds. *Lexikon der Geheimdienste im 20. Jahrhundert.* Munich: F. A. Herbig Verlagsbuchhandlung, 2003.

Rolfs, Richard W. *The Sorcerer's Apprentice: The Life of Franz von Papen.* Lanham, MD: University Press of America, 1996.

Roon, Ger van. "Graf Moltke als Völkerrechtler im OKW." *Vierteljahrshefte für Zeitgeschichte* 18 (1970): 12–61.

———, ed. *Helmuth James Graf von Moltke: Völkerrecht im Dienste des Menschen; Dokumente.* Berlin: Siedler, 1986.

———. *German Resistance to Hitler: Count von Moltke and the Kreisau Circle.* New York: Van Nostrand Reinhold, 1971.

Roosevelt, Kermit. *The Overseas Targets: War Report of the OSS.* 2 vols. Washington, DC: Carrollton Press, 1976.

Roth, Karl Heinz. "Franz von Papen und der Faschismus." *Zeitschrift für Geschichtswissenschaft* 51, 7 (2003): 589–625.

Rothfels, Hans. *The German Opposition to Hitler: An Assessment.* London, 1970.
———. "Dokumentation. Adam von Trott zu Solz und das State Department." *Vierteljahrshefte für Zeitgeschichte* 7, 5 (July 1959): 318–32.
———. "Dokumentation. Trott und die Außenpolitik des Widerstandes." *Vierteljahrshefte für Zeitgeschichte* 12, 3 (July 1964): 300–25.
Rubin, Barry. *Istanbul Intrigues.* New York: Pharos Books, 1992.
Ryan, Allen. *Klaus Barbie and the United States Government: A Report of the Attorney General of the U.S.* Washington, DC: U.S. Dept. of Justice, Criminal Division, August 1983.
Salazar, António Oliveira. *Discursos e Notas Políticas.* Vol. 3, 1938–1943, 2nd ed. Coimbra: Coimbra Editora.
Sampson, Anthony. *The Sovereign State of I.T.T.* New York: Stein & Day, 1973.
Schad, Martha. *Hitler's Spy Princess: The Extraordinary Life of Stephanie von Hohenlohe.* Translated by Angus McGeoch. Gloucestershire, England: Sutton, 2004.
Schellenberg, Walter. *Hitler's Secret Service.* Translated by Louis Hagen. New York: Pyramid, 1962.
———. *The Schellenberg Memoirs.* Edited and translated by Louis Hagen. London: Andre Deutsch, 1956.
Schlabrendorff, Fabian von. *The Secret War Against Hitler.* Boulder, CO: Westview, 1994.
Schlie, Ulrich. *Kein Friede mit Deutschland: Die geheimen Gespräche im Zweiten Weltkrieg 1939–1941.* Munich: Langen Müller, 1994.
Schöllgen, Gregor. *A Conservative Against Hitler.* Translated by Louise Willmot. New York: St. Martin's Press, 1991.
———. "'Another' Germany: The Secret Foreign Contacts of Ulrich von Hassell During the Second World War." *International History Review* 11, no. 4 (November 1989): 648–67.
Schröder, Hans-Jürgen. *Deutschland und die Vereinigten Staaten, 1933–1939: Wirtschaft und Politik in der Entwicklung des deutsch-amerikanischen Gegensatzes.* Wiesbaden: Franz Steiner, 1970.
Schwab, Gerald. *OSS Agents in Hitler's Heartland.* Westport, CT and London, 1996.
Schwerin von Krosigk, Lutz, Graf. *Es geschah in Deutschland: Menschenbilder unseres Jahrhunderts.* Tübingen: Rainer Wunderlich Verlag, 1951.
Shapiro, Milton J. *Behind Enemy Lines.* New York: Julian Messner, 1978.
Shirer, William. *Berlin Diary.* New York: Galahad Books, 1995.
Simms, Brendan. "Karl Wolff: Der Schlichter." In *Die SS: Elite unter dem Totenkopf: 30 Lebensläufe,* edited by Ronald Smelser and Enrico Syring, 441–56. Paderborn: Schöningh, 2000.
Simpson, Christopher. *Blowback: America's Recruitment of Nazis and Its Effects on the Cold War.* New York: Weidenfeld & Nicolson, 1988.
Smith, Bradley F. *The Shadow Warriors: OSS and the Origins of the CIA.* New York: Basic Books, 1983.
Smith, Bradley F., and Elena Agorossi. *Operation Sunrise: The Secret Surrender.* New York: Basic Books, 1979.
Smith, R. Harris. *OSS: The Secret History of America's First Central Intelligence Agency.* Berkeley: University of California Press, 1972.
Soltikow, Michael Count. *Im Zentrum der Abwehr: Meine Jahre bei Admiral Canaris.* Gütersloh: Prisma Verlag, 1986.

Spitzy, Reinhard. *So haben wir das Reich verspielt: Bekenntnisse eines Illegalen,* 2nd ed. Munich and Vienna: Langen Müller, 1987.

Srodes, James. *Allen Dulles, Master of Spies.* Washington, DC: Regnery, 1999.

Staël, Madame de. *De l'Allemagne.* London, 1813.

Steele, Richard W. "American Popular Opinion and the War against Germany: The Issue of Negotiated Peace, 1942." *Journal of American History* 65, no. 3 (December 1978): 704–23.

Stehle, Hansjakob. "Deutsche Friedensfühler bei den Westmächten im Februar/März 1945." *Vierteljahrshefte für Zeitgeschichte* 30, no. 3 (1982): 538–55.

Steinbach, Peter. *Der 20, Juli 1944: Gesichter des Widerstands.* Munich: Siedler, 2004.

Steinbach, Peter, and Johannes Tuchel, eds. *Widerstand gegen die nationalsozialistische Diktatur, 1933–1945.* Berlin: Lukas Verlag für Kunst-und Geistesgeschichte, 2004.

Steury, Donald P. "Tracking Nazi 'Gold': The OSS and Project Safehaven." *Studies in Intelligence* 9 (Summer 2000): 35–50.

Stevens, Donald G. "World War II Economic Warfare: The United States, Britain, and Portuguese Wolfram." *Historian* 61, no. 3 (1999): 539–55.

Stover, Bernd. "Der Fall Otto John: Neue Dokumente zu den Aussagen des deutschen Geheimdienstchefs gegenüber MfS und KGB." *Vierteljahrshefte für Zeitgeschichte* 47, no. 1 (1999): 103–36.

Tarrant, V. E. *The Red Orchestra: The Soviet Spy Network Inside Nazi Europe.* London: Cassell, 1995.

Thompson, Dorothy. *Listen Hans.* Boston: Houghton Mifflin, 1942.

Trepp, Gian. *Bankgeschäfte mit dem Feind: Die Bank für Internationalen Zahlungsausgleich.* Zurich: Rotpunkt Verlag, 1993.

Treue, Wilhelm. "Eduard Schulte: Ein Unternehmer in der Zeit des Nationalsozialismus." *Zeitschrift für Unternehmensgeschichte* 33, no. 2 (1988): 118–22.

Trevor-Roper, Hugh. *The Philby Affair: Espionage, Treason, and Secret Services.* London: W. Kimber, 1968.

Troy, Thomas F. "Knifing of the OSS." *International Journal of Intelligence and Counterintelligence* 1, no. 3 (1986): 95–108.

Tully, Grace G. *FDR: My Boss.* New York: Scribner, 1949.

Turner, Henry Ashby. *General Motors and the Nazis: The Struggle for Control of Opel, Europe's Biggest Carmaker.* New Haven, CT: Yale University Press, 2005.

Visser't Hooft, Willem A. *Memoirs.* London: Westminster Press, 1973.

———. "The View from Geneva." *Encounter* 33 (September. 1969): 93.

Voelklein, Ulrich. *Geschäfte mit dem Feind.* Hamburg: Europa Verlag, 2002.

Von Hassell, Fey. *Hostage of the Third Reich: The Story of My Imprisonment and Rescue from the SS.* Edited by David Forbes-Watt. New York: Scribner, 1989.

Vrba, Rudolf. *I Escaped from Auschwitz.* Fort Lee, NJ: Barricade Books, 2002.

Wala, Michael. "Die Abteilung "T-3" und die Beziehungen der Reichswehr zur U.S. Army, 1922–1933." In Reinhard R. Doerries, ed., *Diplomaten und Agenten: Nachrichtendienste in der Geschichte der deutsch-amerikanischen Beziehungen,* pp. 53–84. Heidelberg: C. Winter, 2001.

Wallace, Max. *The American Axis: Henry Ford, Charles Lindbergh, and the Rise of the Third Reich.* New York: St. Martin's Press, 2003.

Waller, John H. *The Devil's Doctor: Felix Kersten and the Secret Plot to Turn Himmler Against Hitler.* New York: John Wiley & Sons, 2002.

———. *The Unseen War in Europe: Espionage and Conspiracy in the Second World War.* New York: Random House, 1996.

Wedemeyer, Albert C. *Wedemeyer Reports!* New York: Henry Holt, 1958.

Wegener, Peter P. *The Peenemünde Wind Tunnels: A Memoir.* New Haven: Yale University Press, 1996.

Weinberg, Gerhard L. *The Foreign Policy of Hitler's Germany: A Diplomatic Revolution in Europe, 1933–1936.* Atlantic Highland, NJ: Humanities Press, 1994.

Weinstein, Allen, and Alexander Vassiliev. *The Haunted Wood: Soviet Espionage in America; The Stalin Era.* New York: Random House, 1999.

West, Nigel. *A Thread of Deceit.* New York: Random House, 1985.

Wheeler, Douglas L. "The Price of Neutrality: Portugal, the Wolfram Question, and World War II." *Luso-Brazilian Review* 23, no. 1 (1986): 106–11.

Wheeler-Bennett, John. *The Nemesis of Power: The German Army in Politics, 1918–1945.* 2nd ed. London: Macmillan, 1964.

White, Joseph Robert. "Target Auschwitz: Historical and Hypothetical German Responses to Allied Attack." *Holocaust and Genocide Studies* 16, no. 1 (2002): 54–76.

White, Theodore H. *Fire in the Ashes.* New York: William Sloane Associates, 1953.

Whiting, Charles. *Hitler's Secret War: The Nazi Espionage Campaign Against the Allies.* South Yorkshire: Leo Cooper, 2000.

———. *The Spymasters: The True Story of Anglo-American Intelligence Operations Within Nazi Germany, 1939–1945.* New York: Saturday Review, 1976.

Wighton, Charles, and Günter Peis. *Hitler's Spies and Saboteurs: Based on the German Secret Service War Diary of General Lahousen.* New York: Henry Holt, 1958.

Wildt, Michael, ed. *Nachrichtendienst, Politische Elite und Mordeinheit: Der Sicherheitsdeinst des Reichsführers SS.* Hamburg: Hamburger Edition, 2003.

Winterbotham, F. W. *Secret and Personal.* London: William Kimber, 1969.

Wires, Richard. *The Cicero Spy Affair: German Access to British Secrets in World War II.* Perspectives on Intelligence History. Westport, CT: Praeger, 1999.

Wolfe, Robert. *Analysis of the Investigative Records Repository (IRR) File on Klaus Barbie,* September 19, 2001. www.archives.gov/iwg/research_papers/barbie_irr_file.html

Wuermeling, Henric L. *"Doppelspiel": Adam von Trott zu Solz im Widerstand gegen Hitler.* Munich: Deutsche Verlags-Anstalt, 2004.

Wyman, David S. *The Abandonment of the Jews: America and the Holocaust, 1941–1945.* New York: Pantheon, 1984.

———. "Auschwitz, Bombing of." In *The Encyclopedia of the Holocaust.* New York: Macmillan, 1990.

———, and Rafael Medoff. *A Race Against Death: Peter Bergson, America, and the Holocaust.* New York: New Press, 2002.

Zoller, Albert. *Hitler privat: Erlebnisbericht einer Geheimserkretärin.* Düsseldorf: Droste Verlag, 1949.

INDEX